THE RHETORIC
OF OUR TIMES

THE RHETORIC
OF OUR TIMES

Edited by
J. JEFFERY AUER
Indiana University

APPLETON-CENTURY-CROFTS
EDUCATIONAL DIVISION
New York MEREDITH CORPORATION

Contents

IV.

CASE STUDIES IN CONTEMPORARY RHETORIC

Preface

The social and political discontents of our times and their relationships with formal and psychological aspects of listening and speaking provide the focus for this book. It is not intended to be a textbook on public speaking. Rather, it is designed to present articles, speeches, and analyses to supplement significantly the typical textbook and, perhaps more importantly, to place the study of speech within a contemporary context and thereby point up its social relevance.

Although parts of this book can be assigned piecemeal as correlatives to pertinent portions of whatever standard textbook an instructor may choose, the anthology's integrity permits the book to be read straight through, and with profit, in its own right. Credit is largely due those authors and publishers who have generously permitted me to select, order, and reprint their publications. At appropriate places throughout the text this general acknowledgment is made specific. All but four selections are complete and reproduced in the form they appear in the source cited, and the footnote form of the original publication has been followed in every case. In those four selections, each clearly identified, slight modifications in the text adapted the material to its present purpose. The pertinence of each selection is expanded by a series of questions that reveal implications and suggest applications. Topics for discussions and speeches are suggested at the end of each part of the volume.

It is a pleasure to record the contributions of John and Julie Auer to this enterprise, he as editorial assistant, she as typist.

J. J. A.

Symbols for Periodicals and
Serial Publications

The following list contains all of the periodical and serial publication symbols used in the footnotes and bibliographies in this volume.

AC	American Child	JAP	Journal of Applied Psychology
AJO	American Journal of Orthopsychiatry	JASA	Journal of the Acoustical Society of America
AJS	American Journal of Sociology	JASP	Journal of Abnormal and Social Psychology
AP	Archives of Psychology	JC	Journal of Communication
BAAUP	Bulletin of the American Association of University Professors	JEE	Journal of Experimental Education
BJS	British Journal of Sociology	JEP	Journal of Educational Psychology
CD	Child Development	JEPM	Journal of Educational Psychological Measurement
CSSJ	Central States Speech Journal		
DA	Dissertation Abstracts	JER	Journal of Education Research
EE	Elementary English		
EER	Elementary English Review	JEP	Journal of Experimental Psychology
EF	Educational Forum		
EL	Educational Leadership	JGP	Journal of General Psychology
ERB	Educational Research Bulletin		
ESJ	Elementary School Journal	JNE	Journal of Negro Education
		JQ	Journalism Quarterly
GPM	Genetic Psychological Monographs	JSHD	Journal of Speech and Hearing Disorders
JAFA	Journal of the American Forensic Association	JSP	Journal of Social Psychology
		MLR	Monthly Labor Report

NR	New Republic	*SM*	Speech Monographs
NYTM	New York Times Magazine	*SchR*	School Review
		SR	Saturday Review
PI	Psychological Issues	*SSJ*	Southern Speech Journal
PJ	Personnel Journal	*ST*	Speech Teacher
PM	Psychological Monographs		
POQ	Public Opinion Quarterly	*TS*	Today's Speech
PS	Pedagogical Seminary	*USNWR*	U.S. News and World Report
QJS	Quarterly Journal of Speech	*WS*	Western Speech

Introduction

All communication, even a two-man dialogue, takes place in some social context, and that context helps shape into relevancy both the theory and practice of rhetoric. Thus it is appropriate to deal in the same volume with both rhetorical text and context.

The historians and critics of public address have recognized this relationship between rhetoric and the *Zeitgeist* at least since the day of Aristotle. The climate for speechmaking in a democracy, to choose an easy example, is quite different than in a totalitarian state, and this difference is reflected in the freedom of selecting which topics are discussed, how issues are developed, what images and appeals are appropriate, and so on. Or, as another example of interaction, contrast the rhetorical theory and practice in a young, undeveloped but dynamic and emerging nation, with that in an older, established and more stable society. Some nations in the world today have transformed their media of communication almost directly from the tribal tom-tom to television, without the intervening and usual cultural steps based upon a recorded language and the written word.

In our own nation, in a period of exasperation and accelerated social change, we can sense shifting moods and modes of public discourse. This book is an investigation of those shifts, and the inquiry has two dimensions.

First, we are concerned with the rhetorical climate, the impact of our times upon what people talk, and what people talk about. In an earlier day we might have done this simply by describing neat little packages labelled with the *forms* of public discourse, such as speeches of welcome, eulogies, speeches of dedication, sermons, and lectures. But while these forms of polite address are not uncommon, they are surely not definitive characteristics in an age of social and political discontent. Or, by using traditional labels like speeches to inform, speeches to motivate, speeches to actuate, and so on, we could consider the *purposes* of public discourse. But in today's chaotic arenas these fine distinctions become blurred, and all speechmaking tends to be persuasive, to agitate either for progressive change or for "Law and order" in our society. If we are really concerned with the rhetoric of our times, therefore, we must follow some other system of classification, accounting for who the *speakers* are, the *issues* that compel them to speak, and the *circumstances* in which they speak. To be realistic, we must attend to the speaking of students, Negro militants, reformers, and street-corner agitators; we must explore the issues that arise from concerns with Black Power, student activism, minority goup identification, and the special problems of rural poverty pockets and urban ghettoes; and we must look at such rhetorical settings as the street-corner, the mass demonstration, the protest rally, or the march to confrontation.

These contemporary speakers, issues, and rhetorical circumstances are not the only ones of importance, but they are what is *distinctive* about the rhetoric of our times. They are in the *foreground* of our contemporary rhetorical experience. The traditional political and religious campaign speeches, classroom lectures, Sunday sermons, and popular addresses provide the familiar *background*. If we would know the most significant and compelling rhetoric of our times, that which is most socially relevant, we must attend to the "gut issues" and to those who talk about them. In Part I of this volume, therefore, we explore "Listener Attitudes and Anxieties" through a series of surveys and commentaries on the rhetorical climate. In Part IV we focus on specific instances in a series of "Case Studies of Contemporary Rhetoric." In both parts, following each selection, we present the reader with analytical and provocative questions, concerned not merely with the substance of the selection but also with its implications, and we encourage him to be a skeptical and discriminating *consumer* of the rhetoric of our times.

Second, we are concerned with the responsible and effective practice of rhetoric in our times, with the character and behavior of listeners and speakers. In an earlier day we might have done this simply by following the long-established pattern of distilling ancient wisdom into specific advice for public speakers. We might have created the very kind of handbook that Aristotle despised, one studded with axiomatic notions expressed by earlier writers, and inevitably conveying the false impression that speaking is really a knack, requiring only a careful memorization of rules, and lots of practice. Or we might have adopted the approach of Aristotle's *Rhetoric:* "When the practiced and the spontaneous speaker gain their end, it is possible to investigate the cause of their success; and such an inquiry, we shall all admit, performs the function of an art." Such a point of departure could result in a modern treatise, presenting a complete system for the art of inquiry and advocacy and based upon the resources of traditional rhetorical theory. If we are truly concerned with the rhetoric of *our* times, however, we must look not only to the concepts and theories from scholars of traditional rhetoric but also to the quantitative and experimental research by behavioral scientists.

Even the combined products of the experimental researcher, who is primarily concerned with behaviors, and the historical-critical researcher, who is primarily concerned with values, will not tell us all we need to know about speech-communication. But if we are to understand the spoken, symbolic interaction that links speakers and listeners together in our times, we must be open-minded and eclectic in our approach to conceptual systems and research methods. In Part II of this volume, therefore, we deal with "Speaker Concepts and Concerns" through a series of studies and statements in a continuum that ranges from experimental conclusions, through ethical considerations and pedagogical speculations, to value judgments. In Part III we shift from "What should the speaker *be*?" to "What should the speaker *do*?" and present "Theories and Techniques of Listening and Speaking" in a series of articles that draws not only upon traditional rhetoric and behavioral research but also upon the personal testimony of three distinguished public speakers. Following each of the selections in these two parts, we again employ the question device to guide the reader in pursuing implications and discovering applications as well as to encourage him to be a responsible and effective *producer* of the rhetoric of our times.

I

LISTENER ATTITUDES AND ANXIETIES

Introduction

Speaking is for listening. Speeches are not effective when they are in a speaker's mind, in his notes on the lectern before him, or even when they are spoken aloud in the presence of an audience. Speeches become effective only as they are perceived in the minds of listeners. The quality and impact of listener perceptions depend, more than anything else, upon how well the speaker can reduce the anxieties and touch the dominant attitudes of his listeners. Thus any inquiry into the rhetoric of our times must begin with the listeners and an inventory of how they feel and what they fear. What concerns the listener today? To whom does he listen? What is the social, political, and rhetorical climate in which he lives? How does he perceive his society, his values, himself? The eight articles in this first section explore these and related questions. Before they are introduced, however, two characteristics of the rhetoric of this decade should be identified.

First, in the 1960's, a resurgence of popular interest has occurred in issues as against personalities. To many thoughtful observers the 1960 Kennedy-Nixon debates foreshadowed a new trend toward image-building rather than issue-resolving in American public life. Samuel Lubell, experienced public opinion analyst, felt that the debates had greatly elevated the significance of personality, "particularly on its theatrical side." "The shape of the future," he wrote in 1962, "will hinge on which of the three factors—party, issues, or personality—mounts into the ascendancy. Right now the leaders in both parties seem to believe that personality and image-making are the most powerful forces in swaying the electorate."[1] Daniel J. Boorstin, distinguished American historian, said flatly that Kennedy and Nixon's "greatest opportunity in American history to educate the voters by debating the large issues of the campaign failed," and he concluded that "pseudo-events thus lead to emphasis on pseudo-qualifications. . . . If we test Presidential candidates by their talents on TV quiz performances, we will, of course, choose presidents for precisely these qualifications."[2]

Some evidence, at least at the national political level, indicates that in the "personalities vs. issues" contest, images are ahead. As Walter Cronkite said in a July 3, 1968 pre-convention broadcast, "The way CBS News sees it,

[1]"Personalities vs. Issues," in Sidney Kraus, ed., *The Great Debates: Background—Perspective—Effects* (Bloomington, Indiana University Press, 1962), pp. 152, 162.
[2]*The Image: A Guide to Pseudo-Events in America* (New York, Atheneum Publishers, 1961), pp. 43–44.

3

the way to get to know a man is to look him straight in the eye." That this view had potency was demonstrated by Sidney J. Harris' attack upon it in his syndicated newspaper column: "Why should Governor Rockefeller, or any other potential candidate, have to 'picture himself' as anything? Why should he not say what he believes, fully and frankly, and let the chips fall where they may?" Harris is clear about the alternative: "What most of the conventional candidates are looking for, of course, is a campaign that will please the Negroes and assuage the angry whites; that will delight the laboring man without offending the capitalist; that will seem all things to all men without any genuine commitment to basic moral, social or political principles."[3] An audience responds to this sort of appeal, David Riesman suggested in *The Lonely Crowd,* because its members are losing confidence in themselves as judges of technical competence, while still continuing to believe they can judge such "image" qualities as sincerity. If the audience emphasizes an emotional quality such as sincerity, he concludes, it "escapes from the need for emotional response to the performance itself."[4]

Against this seemingly strong identification with personalities in national politics a counter-trend has emerged. In a decade of discontent a handful of major issues has become focal points for intense and often virulent rhetoric. One cluster of issues embraces civil rights, open housing, and equal educational and economic opportunity for Negroes and other minority group members. Another cluster has been shaped by university students, and sometimes by professors and administrators, seeking greater participation in formulating educational policy, and rejecting the *in loco parentis* role of their institutions. A third cluster of issues has arisen from the incongruity of pockets of rural and urban poverty (Appalachia and the ghetto) in a nation with an expanding economy. A fourth issue has been created by the conflict in Vietnam, which has shaped many related concerns about pacifism, the draft, and the role of the United States as world policeman. While the prevalence of the "don't-trust-anyone-over-thirty" conviction might be doubted, much of the force behind the emergence of these issues has come from younger people, and many of them believe in a "generation gap."

A kind of "chicken-or-egg" option may always obtain in deciding whether issues generate personalities, or vice versa. But in contemporary America—with very few exceptions and almost none involving younger leaders—the issues have emerged first. Indeed, because of the urgency of the issues many established leaders lost control of movements they had long headed. Direction was taken over by relatively anonymous committees and temporary chairmen. In time, of course, leaders with some degree of charisma did emerge in the public forum, but they did so by seizing upon existing issues, and they risked their leadership if they did not seem deeply enough committed. For those

[3]Louisville *Courier-Journal,* May 19, 1968.
[4](New York, Doubleday & Co., 1953), pp. 225–226.

who would "Tell it like it is, baby," the current focus has become sharper on the issues than on personalities.

Second, in the 1960's, the rhetoric of agitation has increased sharply as against that of traditional advocacy. The history books of the future may well characterize our times as "the age of agitation," for in the arena of public discussion it is "agitative rhetoric" that has become the chief instrument of social and political discontent. Charles W. Lomas defines this style of speech as *"persistent and uncompromising statement and restatement of grievances through all available communication channels, with the aim of creating public opinion favorable to a change in some condition."* In presenting a collection of speeches from the last eighty years he reminds us that agitation is not new in American history.[5]

Some manifestations of agitation in our society have been more extreme than others. In a notable study of the American agitator during the years of the New Deal and prior to America's entry into World War II, Lowenthal and Guterman define the reformer as one who translates complaints into specific issues that presumably can be solved by collective and democratic action. But they see the agitator, as he appeared in the American Fascist and right-wing movements, as one who "converts complaints not into an issue for action against one or another symbol of authority, but into a theme eliciting the destructive impulses of his public."[6] In our own times, thus far, few agitators, no matter how activist, have deliberately inflamed their listeners to violence. This conclusion is extensively exemplified by Supreme Court Associate Justice Abe Fortas in his timely survey of dissent in America.[7]

Agitational rhetoric, which urges drastic changes in society and challenges authority when that seems necessary, of course has its counterpart in the centrist rhetoric of compromise and control, or the more extreme form described by Vermont's Governor Philip H. Hoff as "the rhetoric of reaction and retrenchment."[8] The term confrontation, so common in the daily newspapers, refers in effect to the rigid posture often assumed by each party when those using the rhetoric of agitation encounter those using the rhetoric of control.

As will become apparent in the selections that follow, the rhetoric of agitation, contrasted with the rhetoric of traditional advocacy, is usually more rigidly anchored in content and point of view, more uncompromising in approach, more violent in language, and frequently less civil. Yet in the view of those who use it, if they *feel* they can right what they are sure are wrongs in

[5]*The Agitator in American Society* (Englewood Cliffs, N. J., Prentice-Hall, Inc., 1968), pp. 2, v.

[6]Leo Lowenthal and Norbert Guterman, "Portrait of the American Agitator," *Public Opinion Quarterly,* 12 (1948), 417. See also Lowenthal and Guterman, *Prophets of Deceit: A Study of the Techniques of the American Agitator* (New York, Harper & Brothers, 1949), esp. pp. 1–10, 135–142.

[7]*Concerning Dissent and Civil Disobedience* (New York, New American Library, 1968).

[8]Associated Press dispatch, Bloomington, Ind., *Daily Herald Telephone,* July 25, 1968.

no other way, agitative rhetoric is justified, no matter how virulent or strident it may be. For such dissenters, militants, or agitators, Frederick Douglass spoke for our time as well as his own when he declared, in his West India Emancipation Speech in 1857: "Those who profess to favor freedom yet deprecate agitation, are men who want crops without plowing up the ground; they want rain without thunder and lightning. They want the ocean without the awful roar of its many waters."[9]

Thus far we have sketched in broad outline form two differentiating characteristics of public discussion in this decade: a resurgence of popular interest in issues, and an increase in agitational rhetoric. The selections that follow are intended to expand and illuminate this outline.

In the first article Mary G. McEdwards explores the nature of agitative rhetoric and illustrates and evaluates its effect on the contemporary scene. Each of the next four articles deals with the rhetoric of those who are agitated about specific clusters of issues: the political "New Left" is treated by Leland M. Griffin, the civil rights movement by Herbert W. Simons, the "Black Power" concept by Parke G. Burgess, and student protests by Terry F. Lunsford.

In their study Paul Friedman and Gerald M. Phillips are not concerned directly with agitation, but with the development of a rhetoric appropriate for the poor. Real success in this effort might, indeed, forestall agitation.

The local lyceums, seeking polite discourses on ephemeral matters, were once the chief customers for the lecture bureaus. Today both audiences and speakers are more agitated, and business is bigger than ever. It is all reported by Natalie Gittelson.

Franklyn S. Haiman's summary and analysis of some legal and ethical considerations in the rhetoric of the streets round out the section.[10]

[9]Stokely Carmichael and Charles V. Hamilton, *Black Power: The Politics of Liberation in America* (New York, Random House, 1967), p. x.

[10]His article, published in the *QJS*, 53 (1967), 36–43, received at the December, 1968, Speech Association of America convention a Golden Anniversary Prize Fund Award as an outstanding scholarly publication of the calendar year 1967.

Agitative Rhetoric: Its Nature and Effect

Mary G. McEdwards

Agitation is a dirty word in our modern world. The most well-intentioned speaker may find himself and his ideas discredited by opponents who claim his words effect agitation. For the listener and reader of today's rhetoric, this term has pejorative connotations implying an unwarranted and unethical attack on persons, institutions, and ideas.

In its root sense *agitation* means "to put in motion" and its denotative meaning is "to move with a violent motion; to stir up or excite; to perturb." Its negative connotation of today probably has developed because people object to being stirred up or excited out of their placid *status quo* existence. However, without agitation, change in a society would come, at best, so slowly that those in need of such change would be harmed by the delay. It follows that, without change, no progress toward desired goals occurs. Because the American public professes to hold certain goals as yet far from reached, the rejection—and often the suppression—of the very device required to start the journey toward these goals seems impractical. Perhaps a closer look at the rhetoric of agitation and at our society's need for it will help more of us accept it as a necessary drive wheel of a dynamic democracy.

Agitative language belongs to a particular type of rhetoric whose end is movement away from the *status quo*. Some may argue that all rhetoric has this same end. However, the rhetoric we call *agitation* evokes extreme movement away from the *status quo*—usually a complete reversal of existing conditions or situations. Agitative rhetoric in the immediate prerevolutionary period of our country had for its purpose the removal of power from the hands of a king to the hands of his former subjects; abolitionist agitative rhetoric urged that slaves become free men; labor union agitative rhetoric aimed at privileges for workers and limitations for management; anti-war agitation today has presented the Viet Cong as "the good guys" and our own country as the villain. Such rhet-

Mary G. McEdwards is Assistant Professor of Speech, San Fernando Valley State College.
Reprinted by permission from *Western Speech*, 32(1968), 36–43.

oric calls for extreme shifts in conditions; some have been achieved and found satisfactory and others have not. Either way, agitative rhetoric has been the effective method used to create the change. We have had our Sam Adams, our Wendell Phillips, our Gompers and Debs, and presently we have our Vietniks.[1]

To achieve their agitation, these speakers of the past and present have depended upon a particular rhetorical style. With extreme action as their goal, they have found they succeed only when using language that is also extreme —extreme in the sense that pejorative poetry is extreme. Concrete diction heavy with unpleasant connotation appears; tropes and schemes with high sensory appeal carry the *inventio;* unexpected vocabulary upsets the listener's expectations of the speaker and of the occasion. It is the speaker's choice of the abrasive word instead of the bland one, his deliberate selection of the derogatory metaphor rather than the complimentary, his use of jabbing, pounding simple sentences in place of complex syntax that marks his rhetoric as agitative rather than informative or gently persuasive.

Nor does his agitative language push him into the category of invective. For our purposes, we can make the following distinction. Invective is the result of a direct one-to-one relationship of the speaker to his single enemy rather than a multiple relationship of a speaker to the enemies of a particular group in a society. The agitator has not been hurt personally by an individual who has directly harmed the speaker—or so the speaker assumes. Agitative rhetoric generally lacks this bitter and spiteful tone. Its final purpose is extreme change in the *status quo* to benefit others besides the speaker rather than a narrow personal attack to benefit only the revengeful attacker. The agitator in society deliberately tries to select the diction, the imagery, the syntax that will move his audience emotionally and intellectually to call for change; the bitter speaker uses invective for catharsis of self alone. The language of invective is churlish, malicious, and surly; agitative language is jolting, combative, and passionate —in the fullest sense of the term.

But why is such agitative rhetoric necessary for the speaker who is ostensibly talking to his own followers? They already believe as he does and require no such linguistic laceration to act as he wishes. But the agitative rhetorician knows that his physical audience is not his true audience. In reality, the audience of the agitator is always the public, the members of the community or nation. They do not hold his opinion, they are indifferent, or more probably, hostile to his view because he advocates a change so extreme that they see themselves as possible losers if the change occurs. The agitator knows that his success depends upon the emotional and intellectual involvement of the full electorate. To this end he uses the meetings of his group or his friends primarily as a convenient and free soapbox from which to prod the larger audience of the general public. He welcomes reporters to his meetings to insure that his words *do* go farther than just the back of the hall, and he eagerly accepts interviews. He wants to be heard by the community, the nation—by the world, if

[1] *Time,* October 29, 1965, p. 44.

possible. For him, ridicule and attack are a small price to pay for the achievement of that necessary "stirring up" of this, his true audience.

Perhaps the best explanation of the rationale for the use of agitative rhetoric comes from Wendell Phillips, the Boston Brahmin who spent his life and wealth shaking up the minds and emotions of his fellow citizens.

> The scholar may sit in his study and take care that his language is not exaggerated, but the rude mass of men is not to be caught by balanced periods—they are caught by men whose words are half battles. From Luther down, the charge against every reformer has been that his language is too rough. Be it so. Rough instruments are used for rough work.[2]

Phillips says further:

> The great mass of people can never be made to stay and argue a long question. They must be made to feel it through the hides of their idols.[3]

Today, nearly all questions are long and complex, and man's attention span is short. Phillips' concept of making men "feel" a question by attacking their idols (be they traditions, folk heroes, popular figures of the day or national ideals) explains the need for the agitator to gain attention by using strong, passionate language—language whose connotations evoke an immediate emotional response in the listener. Like the mule in the famous story, the public must first be "hit on the head to get its attention." Only then will it respond to intellectual argument. And even the intellectual argument must be couched in agitative language or man's attention wanders and he is lost again in his own private concerns.

Let us take the very complex and long question of civil rights which finally surfaced a few years ago. Certainly, the problem has existed far longer than have our attempts to solve it. What specifically caused the American public to pay active attention to the Negro's plight?

One probable cause among the many possible was the agitative style of speakers such as the late Malcolm X of Black Muslim fame and the founder of the Black Nationalism group. He did not, like the Reverend Martin Luther King, phrase his desires for equality in soft, abstract language that touches us but does not acerbate. While Rev. King is saying that he does not agree "that there has to be violence in the future, but this will depend on events . . . the Negro could be driven to despair and violence,"[4] Malcolm X is saying, "I'm for reciprocal bleeding," and "Every Negro ought to have a weapon in his house—a rifle or a shotgun. Any Negro who is attacked should fight back."[5]

Listening to King, we understand the possibility of violence as a concept

[2]Quoted by Ralph Korngold in *Two Friends of Man* (New York, 1950), p. 182.
[3]*Ibid.*, p. 183.
[4]*Time*, January 3, 1964, p. 27.
[5]*Life*, March 20, 1964, p. 40.

but we do not really expect it to occur. Hearing Malcolm X, we find that the possibility has become probability, and a very strong probability. King tells us that, "We will win our freedom because the sacred heritage of our nation and the eternal will of God are embodied in our echoing demands,"[6] but Malcolm X savages our emotions by saying, "Negroes are tired of turning the other cheek. . . . You are going to have an explosion."[7] King's words cause us to nod our heads sagely and intone, "Yes, yes, in good time, my friend, in good time," but we look for the storm cellar when told about the inevitability of an explosion. King advises his followers to "get the weapon of nonviolence, the breastplate of righteousness, the armour of truth, and just keep marching."[8] Malcolm's followers are exhorted to "form rifle clubs that can be used to defend our lives and our property."[9] Black Nationalist Malcolm X is the true agitator.

Wendell Phillips might have been listening to Malcolm when he produced his description of the agitator, the gadfly who darts in and out stinging us into awareness of the inadequacy of present circumstances. Phillips says the agitator is one who

> puts institutions to the question. . . . He is not always right. He may often be wrong. He may say the very worst thing that can be said, but he says something that stirs the whole atmosphere. We are crystallizing constantly down into unwise rest intellectually, and he comes along and disturbs the process and sets all the elements and atoms into a general movement and they crystallize around a new center.[10]

The most important idea in this description, and the idea that our society often finds difficult to accept, is the necessity for allowing a person to say the "very worst thing that can be said." We need someone who "stirs up the whole atmosphere." The someone who can do this is the person who uses agitative language. Comments on the inequity of our government's actions in Viet Nam such as "to engage in the large-scale killing of people when it is not in the best interest of their country, but of ours, is a grossly immoral act," made by physics professor William C. Davidson of Haverford College to a *Time* reporter, do not upset anyone (except possibly the administrators of his college, and usually for reasons not related to the content of the comments).[11] Yet, when students parading in front of the White House shout in unison, "Hey, hey, L.B.J.! How many kids did you kill today?" and when this chant is reported in the newspapers and magazines,[12] the public is shocked into identifying with the physical

---

[6]*Time*, January 3, 1964, p. 14.

[7]*U.S. News and World Report*, March 30, 1964, p. 39.

[8]*Time*, January 3, 1964, p. 14.

[9]*U.S. News and World Report*, March 30, 1964, p. 38.

[10]*National Standard*, May 27, 1871, cited by Oscar Sherwin in *Prophet of Liberty* (New York, 1958), p. 291.

[11]*Time*, October 29, 1965, p. 45.

[12]*Ibid.*, p. 44.

battles in Viet Nam. The unexpected vocabulary level of "L.B.J." instead of "President Johnson," the sassy "hey, hey" directed at the highest official in the land, and the diction of "kids" in place of "young men" or "soldiers" mark this chant as agitative rhetoric. The public thinks of its own "kids" who may be in Viet Nam or on their way; "kids" become Johnny or Sam or Bill, brother or sons of the listeners. The use of "you" to refer directly to the President gives listeners the sharp image of President Johnson, with rifle smoking and bayonet fixed, shoot-Johnny down. The students may "often be wrong," they may have said the "very worst thing that can be said," but they have certainly used agitative language to disturb "all the elements and atoms" that make up the American public.

Forced by such rhetoric to a sharp personal awareness of the situation, Americans rush to the defense of the President's policy. In doing so, they need specific knowledge of conditions in Viet Nam and must learn something about the United States' foreign policy. It is this process of evaluation, of development of proof for a judgment or an opinion that is the valuable and necessary result of agitative rhetoric.

Professor Davidson's words such as "large-scale killing" and "grossly immoral" are not concrete, cause no vivid imagery, and slide through the public mind with no impediment nor result. "How many kids did you kill today?" may be a reckless attack on President Johnson, but because of its specific, extreme diction and imagery, it makes the public feel this complex question "through the hides of their idols"—in this case, through an extreme attack on a revered office and concept, the Presidency of the United States. The hero is now the villain; agitative rhetoric has replaced Uncle Sam's white hat with a dirty, black one. That black hat sits figuratively on the head of every American who is not protesting U.S. policy in Viet Nam. To remove it, the American jumps into the national argument to give his side of the case. To do so effectively, he must consider and evaluate the logic and worth of the agitator's statement. This personal involvement with the meat of a question is the result of agitative rhetoric.

In 1964, Malcolm X stated that integration equals intermarriage and that intermarriage leads only to mongrelization of the Negro race.[13] His comment may be logically and physiologically wrong, but his choice of *mongrelization* to describe what others may call a "blending of the races" hits painfully at the ego of the WASP. Malcolm's agitative diction forces us to review an often-implied assumption that the Caucasian bestows great benefits when he condescends to marry a Negro.

Another example of the shift from abstract, denotative terms to the precise pejorative diction of agitation occurred on a college campus recently. A group of professors had organized an AFT local on the campus as a result of

---

[13]*U.S. News and World Report*, March 30, 1964, p. 38.

their dissatisfaction with the *status quo* of salaries, academic prerogatives, and working conditions.

In their bulletin, distributed to the faculty of the college, the editor calls for faculty to join the union because:

> We in the AFT believe that our organization offers unique possibilities for persuasion, because behind it lies the tradition—and voting power—of millions of Californians who like ourselves have discovered that only through collective effort are salaries improved.[14]

A month later in the bulletin, the president of the local writes:

> It is the belief of AFT that the only persuasion to which the Trustees or legislature will respond is boycott. To provide an equitable salary for State College professors the legislature needs much stronger inducements than requests for salary raises. The State College Council of the AFT hopes in the coming months to provide this inducement through an organization which, with the will of the professors, may bargain directly with the Trustees to ensure that our services will not continue to be undersold.[15]

A year later the language about union membership, purpose, and benefits has shifted noticeably. It is now concrete, connotative, and extreme:

> To view the union as an ugly creature from the swamp is perhaps natural to the conservative faculty member who now has a stranglehold on the good things of the academic life and has no intention of letting go. . . . But why do young, able professors with everything to gain from the union and nothing to gain outside it "save by long and weary dances" act as if the union were a novel and needless arrival on the academic scene?[16]

The specific imagery here of the ugly swamp monster, the implied description of the conservative faculty member as old and unable, and the quoted tag line of "long and weary dances" to describe the activities related to the achievement of higher academic rank all catch the ego of the reader. Wanting to be accused neither of having strangleholds on things nor to be thought naive or stupid, the reader hastily moves on to see what the solution is. He finds the following choices given three paragraphs later:

> First, he can become a supine, conformist, self-censoring, uncreative "good boy." Second, he can become a grant-grabbing, job-hopping participant in the destructive game of academic musical chairs. Third, he can join the AFT

---

[14]*AFT on Campus* (Local #1441, San Fernando Valley State College), October, 1964, p. 2.

[15]*Ibid.*, November, 1964, p. 1.

[16]*Ibid.*, October 29, 1965, p. 1.

> and work for effective faculty participation and the profes-
> sionalization—in fact, not in name only—of his life's
> vocation.[17]

The choices given here place the reader in a logical dilemma. Although he may not want to be a union member, he certainly does not view himself as a placid follower nor as a teacher interested only in money for his particular research. The logical dilemma becomes an emotional dilemma—an active enemy —when it appears in agitative diction. No one will willingly be catalogued as a "good boy" or as a "grant-grabbing, job-hopping" participant in his pro- fession; he wants to be thought of as effective, professional, and ethical. For those readers who are hesitant about union affiliation and yet do not see them- selves as members of the "good boy" group nor of the "musical chairs" game, the alternative is to defend themselves against such cataloguing through pres- entation of their own opinions about the value of the *status quo* and of pos- sible solutions. They may find union membership is the logical solution, but they might have been longer in reaching this conclusion if the union's agitative rhetoric had not shoved them headlong into such an evaluation. Either way (membership or not) the whole academic atmosphere is stirred up and people begin to think about the situation. During the year, the union on this par- ticular campus has moved from moderate criticism of the *status quo* in abstract terms to agitation through extreme language. Its *topoi* have not changed but its *elocutio* has. The shift to agitative rhetoric has indeed stirred up the atmos- phere as the previous year's appeal for membership did not. Much discussion of the complex question of the suitability of union membership for professors is now heard in offices, hallways, and parking lots.

> Truth never stirs up any trouble—mere speculative truth.
> Plato taught—nobody cared what he taught; Socrates
> acted, and they poisoned him. It is when a man throws him-
> self against society that society is startled to persecute and
> to think.[18]

We may not agree with what Malcolm X or the student pickets or the AFT local says, nor should we, necessarily, but we must allow them to speak and we must listen. We need to be taken from our comfortable ideological pail and be poured into that intellectual centrifuge which causes the best ideas in our society to separate from the dross. To deny citizens the use of agitative rhetoric is to eliminate a vital drive wheel of the centrifuge.

Like any organism from the amoeba up, we do not enjoy being prodded, especially on a sore spot on the body politic, but that prodding is the very necessary purpose of agitative rhetoric. The agitator must use the jagged word, the snarling word, the insulting word; he cannot clothe his ideas in eu- phemistic cotton wool to spare our sensibilities. These sensibilities are precisely

---

[17]*Ibid.*
[18]Wendell Phillips, *Speeches, Lectures and Letters,* ed. Theodore C. Pease, Second Series (Boston, 1891), p. 396.

what the agitator must rake raw, for to agitate, one must irritate and infuriate. When we try to suppress the man using the caustic metaphor, the savage adjective, that agitative rhetoric, we end by suppressing our own abilities to come nearer our ideal society.

Questions for Analysis

1. Understand the denotative and connotative meanings of *agitation*. Review the significant causes that have enlisted agitative rhetoric. What characteristics have they had in common? What has the rhetoric enlisted in these causes had in common? How has the connotative meaning of *agitation* derived from the rhetoric of Adams, Phillips, Gompers, Debs, and others?

2. What conscious adjustments of style does the agitative speaker make? Do you understand how *invective* differs from *agitative language?* Formulate a model cause. Write first a moderate statement of the cause. Adjust the statement with agitative rhetoric. Adjust it again with invective.

3. What does Phillips mean when he says, "Rough instruments are used for rough work"? What makes the "work" of the agitative speaker "rough"? What distinguishes the rhetorical "instruments" of Malcolm X from those of Martin Luther King, Jr.? Take the theme "Police and the Ghetto." How might Malcolm X have introduced it? How might King have introduced it? Think of other contemporary themes lending themselves to distinctly different approaches.

4. Describe the difference in impact of the mild and agitative statements about the Vietnam war. Can you isolate the means by which the difference is achieved? Can you generalize about audiences to whom the agitative statement does or does not appeal? Look at the three statements by the AFT. How would people you know respond to each statement?

5. Have you experienced the "logical dilemma" in which agitative rhetoric places audiences? Describe how you resolved the dilemma. How did the rhetoric finally influence your resolution? What was the "mere speculative truth" involved? Would a mild statement of that truth have stirred you?

2

The Rhetorical Structure of the "New Left" Movement: Part I

Leland M. Griffin

Politics above all is drama.—Kenneth Burke

Kenneth Burke has made a distinction between positive, dialectical, and ultimate terms. "Left" would seem to be a dialectical term—one that requires an opposite for its definition. With the development of a "New American Right" during the fifties, out of opposition to the "Old Left," it became reasonable to anticipate that a "New Left" movement would eventually make its appearance. It is the suggestion of this paper that such a movement is now in its period of inception; and that the structure of its rhetoric, both *in esse* and *in posse*, merits attention in any survey of the spectrum of contemporary political discourse.

1.

As a "watershed movement," one containing shadows and foreshadows of both the Old and the "New Left," one might take the final sentence of Howard K. Smith's *The State of Europe* (1949):

> The American liberals of both parties—in alliance with the Socialists of Europe and their allies among the liberal-minded Europeans—have their job cut out for them: to apply every means of pressure to confound the backers both of the Communist Century and of the American Century; to restore American foreign policy to its people and thereby force the same restoration at last in the East—to

Leland M. Griffin is Professor of Speech, Northwestern University.
Reprinted by permission from *Quarterly Journal of Speech*, 50(1964), 113–135.

> resume the creation, interrupted these four years, of the
> Century of One World.[1]

The "four years" interruption refers, of course, to the advent of the Cold War. It need not be said, perhaps, that the Cold War itself is the overarching scene within which all acts of political utterance in our time must be understood; that it is a scene, moreover, in its very substance rhetorical—a logomachy, a waging of war not only through the use of persuasive words, but also by means of rhetorical deeds of deterrence and ingratiation. At any rate, in his call for a united effort of American liberals and European socialists to end the Cold War, it is not surprising that Smith made no mention of American socialists.

For by 1949 the strength of the non-Communist left in America had sharply declined. The following year, at its 1950 convention in Detroit, the Socialist party debated whether or not to withdraw from politics. Norman Thomas "announced that he would not run again and urged the convention not to run a national ticket in 1952."[2] The socialists did elect to run a candidate in that year; and he received a total of 20,189 votes—fewer votes than the candidate for the Prohibition party.[3] It was the poorest showing that a socialist candidate for president had ever made; and for socialists and the left generally, the time was clearly one for peripety—a time for reversal, for a "dramatic change of identity"—if the spirit of radicalism was to survive in American life.

As the specific moment of reversal, the initiating terminus of the "New Left" movement, one might point to the inauguration of the "*Dissent* project" in the fall of 1953. The editors of *Dissent*

> . . . had diverse backgrounds and interests: some had
> been committed intellectually to the idea of socialism for
> a long time, others were veterans of American radicalism
> who had come to feel that the few remaining leftist groups
> were sterile and that a new start was necessary, and still
> others were young writers and teachers—radical though
> not always socialist—who wished to attack the spirit of
> conformity that had descended on the nation during the
> post-war years. . . .[4]

The editors—among them Lewis Coser, Irving Howe, Erich Fromm, Norman Mailer, and A. J. Muste—felt that "the socialist movement in America [had] reached its nadir and could rarely intervene as a political force in our political or trade union life."[5] They felt that their "main task was to deal with socialism in the realm of ideas, to make democratic-radicalism seem relevant

---

[1]Howard K. Smith, *The State of Europe* (New York, 1949), p. 408.
[2]David A. Shannon, *The Socialist Party in America* (New York, 1955), p. 256.
[3]*Ibid.*
[4]Irving Howe, "A Few Words About Dissent," *Voices of Dissent* (New York, 1959), p. 11.
[5]*Ibid.*

to at least part of the American intellectual community."[6] They felt it "essential to project an image of a fraternal society in which men planned and controlled their political and economic affairs in terms of democratic participation and in which no small group of owners or party bosses could dominate society."[7] They were interested in providing a "sustained radical criticism" of the "claims and pretensions" of American society; and they felt that

> . . . for a radical criticism of American society to acquire
> depth and coherence, it needed as an ideal norm some
> vision of the good—or at least of a better—society. This
> vision was what we meant by socialism.[8]

On the one hand, they set themselves off from the "authoritarians of the Left" —from "Communism in all its manifestations"; on the other, from "liberalism" and the "liberals"—whom they tended to personify in the form of Hubert Humphrey, Arthur Schlesinger, Jr., and the ADA. In the judgment of C. Wright Mills, who pressed the point in the first issue of *Dissent,* and often thereafter, the "conservative mood" of America had captured the rhetoric of liberalism. Liberalism, he felt, while once a "fighting creed," had "come to a dead end and now serves as a rationale and rhetoric for upholding the irresponsible rule of the Power Elite."[9]

In sum, taking the *"Dissent* project" as an initiating terminus, one may view the peripety as composed of the following elements: (1) an attempt by agents, viewing themselves in the main as "radical intellectuals," to make a "new start"; (2) a decision to set their course in the direction of a democratic, "socialist humanism,"[10] steering between the Scylla of Communism and the Charybdis of "liberalism" (i.e., "conservative mood," status quo "capitalism"); and (3) an inclination to direct their address primarily to intellectuals; to see the intellectual, rather than the worker, as the essential maker of history, the agent of change. And viewing the early issues of *Dissent* as a set of "representative anecdotes," a source for the discovery of "key terms," one may chart the "clusters" that have continued to prevail in the vocabulary of the "New Left": "devil terms"—such as *competition, alienation, conformity, absurdity (the irrational), loneliness, passivity, fear, bondage (authoritarianism), hate, anxiety, the "warfare state," the Holocaust;* and "god terms" —such as *"cooperation, identification, commitment, sanity (the rational), community, action, hope, freedom (autonomy), love, peace, transcendence,*

6*Ibid.*
7*Ibid.,* p. 13.
8*Ibid.*
9William F. Warde, "The Marxists," *International Socialist Review* (Summer 1962), p. 67. See also C. Wright Mills, "The Conservative Mood," *Dissent,* I (Winter 1954), 22–31. Also Mills, *The Power Elite* (New York, 1956), Ch. 14, "The Conservative Mood," pp. 325–342.
     See also Harvey Swados, "Does America Deserve the New Frontier?" *New Politics* (Summer 1963), pp. 33–51, a recent "New Left" response to Arthur M. Schlesinger, Jr., "The Administration and the Left," *New Statesman* (February 8, 1963).
10Daniel Bell, *The End of Ideology* (Glencoe, Ill., 1960), p. 295.

the "good society," utopia.[11] It is, in general, the vocabulary of existentialist humanism—whether the frame be political, religious, psychological, sociological or philosophical. And it is also, to a suggestive extent, the vocabulary of the "cosmic frame"—another name for which, as Burke notes, might be "humanism." It is for this reason that the critic of contemporary left rhetoric, in his search for compatible instruments of analysis and speculation, may well look to Burke for models and modes of "humanistic contemplation."[12]

Other points in the curve of development may be charted. Nineteen fifty-three, the year of the *Dissent* project, was also the year of the death of Stalin. Nineteen fifty-four was the year of the fall of McCarthy: with his censure the grues of the "liberals" lessened, but the long night of the "hysteria"—the ordeal of the "crucible"—had fatally transformed them in the eyes of the radicals. In the scornful phrase of C. Wright Mills, many of the "liberals" had been "so busy celebrating the civil liberties that they . . . had less time to defend them," while others had been "so busy defending them that they had neither the time nor the inclination to *use* them."[13]

Nineteen fifty-six was the year that signaled the essential ambiguity of Khrushchev as a Cold War figure: whispers of hope in the "secret speech"— thunderous denial in the smashing of the Hungarian Revolution. Nineteen fifty-six was also the year in which Mills put his finger on the "power-elite"— the morally irresponsible symbols of authority (the "political directorate, the corporate rich, and the ascendant military") that controlled the history-making process in America, and that must be rejected. And 1956, finally, was the year of the founding of *Liberation* magazine. Like the founders of *Dissent*, the editors of *Liberation*—among them Dave Dellinger, Roy Finch, A. J.

---

[11]As will be apparent, the terms have been selected and ordered in rough "equations" designed to illustrate "progressive forms" ("syllogistic progressions") that seem to be implicit in "New Left" frames of rejection and acceptance. One term in the "vocabulary," not included in the equations above, might serve to epitomize the lot—*crisis*.

[12]Particularly the first editions of *Permanence and Change, Attitudes Toward History,* and *The Philosophy of Literary Form,* books written out of a period when Burke had "plumped grandly" for a word "now locally in great disgrace" and both the *Grammar* and *Rhetoric of Motives,* two books in his current project "directed 'towards the purification of war.'" The essay in which Burke attempts to "codify" his ideas on "the relation between Freudian psychology and Marxism" ("Twelve Propositions by Kenneth Burke on the Relation between Economics and Psychology," *Science & Society: A Marxian Quarterly* [Spring 1938], pp. 242–249; also *Philosophy of Literary Form* [New York, 1957] pp. 263–270) is helpful; so also is the 1935 address on "Revolutionary Symbolism in America" (see *American Writers' Congress,* ed. Henry Hart [New York, 1935], pp. 87–93, 167–171). Attention should also be given to references to Burke in the section on "Marxian Socialism" in *Socialism and American Life,* eds. Donald Egbert and Stow Persons (Princeton, N.J., 1952), I, 189; and in Daniel Aaron, *Writers on the Left* (New York, 1961), pp. 288–291.

The filters of Burke's "humanism" have, of course, changed through the years; and the critic will also give attention to the Prologue of the emended edition of *Permanence and Change,* to both the Introduction and the After-Word to the second edition of *Attitudes Toward History,* to the "Curriculum Criticum" which appears at the end of the second edition of *Counter-Statement,* and to the final section of the *Grammar* ("A Neo-Liberal Ideal"). Note should be taken of Burke's resolve (in the 1954 Prologue of *Permanence and Change*) not to attempt "to present his brand of Crisis-thinking in current Existentialist terms."

[13]Mills, *The Power Elite,* p. 334.

Muste, Bayard Rustin, Sidney Lens, Robert Pickus, and Mulford Sibley—were concerned at the "decline of independent radicalism and the gradual falling into silence of prophetic and rebellious voices. . . ." In an initial "Tract for the Times" they offered critiques of both "Liberalism" and "Marxism," and set out guide lines for a "Politics of the Future." They found it an "illuminating insight of pragmatism that means and ends condition each other reciprocally and that the ends must be built into the means"; and they declared that any "truly radical movement today . . . must commit itself to an essentially democratic and non-violent strategy." They announced that they did "not conceive the problem of revolution or the building of a better society as one of accumulating power"; it was rather "the transformation of society by human decision and action" that they sought. Toward this end, *Liberation* would endeavor

> . . . to inspire its readers not only to fresh thinking but to *action now*—refusal to run away or to conform, concrete resistance in the communities in which we live to all the ways in which human beings are regimented and corrupted, dehumanized and deprived of their freedom; experimentation in creative living by individuals, families, and groups; day to day support of movements to abolish colonialism and racism, or for the freedom of all individuals from domination, whether military, economic, political, or cultural.[14]

In 1958, in *The Causes of World War III*, Mills continued his attack on the "power elite." In the "crack pot realism" of their Cold War policies lay the causes of World War III; in the continuance of their policies lay the inevitable Holocaust. But "to reflect upon war is to reflect upon the human condition," he wrote; and war, in becoming total, had become "absurd."[15] "What the United States ought to do," he declared

> . . . is to abandon the military metaphysics and the doctrinaire idea of capitalism, and, in the reasonableness thus gained, reconsider the terms of the world encounter. We must subvert the monolithic American dogma that now constitutes the one line of elite assumption. . . .
>
> The only realistic military view is the view that war, and not Russia, is now the enemy. The only realistic political view is the view that the cold warrior, on either side, not just the Russian, is the enemy.[16]

In line with his view that the intellectual, not the worker, had become the historic agent of social change, Mills sounded his call to "intellectuals, preachers, scientists": they must "drop the liberal rhetoric and the conservative

---

14"Tract for the Times," eds. Dave Dellinger et al., *Liberation*, I (March, 1956), 3–6.
15C. Wright Mills, *The Causes of World War III* (New York, 1958), p. 16.
16*Ibid.*, p. 19.

default . . . now parts of one and the same line." They must "transcend that line."[17] In this "disgraceful cold war," the intellectuals should at once become "conscientious objectors." They must become political; they must "set forth alternatives"; they must wage the politics of peace.[18] The "conditions of the struggle" were such that

> . . . an attack on war-making is also an attack on the U.S. power elite. An attack on this power elite is also a fight for the democratic means of history-making. A fight for such means is necessary to any serious fight for peace; it is part of that fight.[19]

Nineteen fifty-eight was significant for other signs of the rise of a "New Left" spirit. The elections of that year were interpreted, at least by the socialist Michael Harrington, as marking a "turn to the Left"; and the welcome extended to former members of the Independent Socialist League by the newly-established SP-SDF (Socialist Party-Social Democratic Federation) was hailed as "a further step in making the SP-SDF the all-inclusive party of democratic socialism in the United States."[20] Harrington was also cheered by the progress the "Yipsels" were making: he saw this youth affiliate of the SP-SDF as playing "an extremely important role in organizing socialist and political clubs on campuses throughout the nation."[21]

Nineteen fifty-eight was significant, finally, as the year which saw the founding of the "Liberal Project"—an association of political intellectuals and intellectual politicians who were, as David Riesman and Michael Maccoby have written, "in general outlook far to the left of . . . [Hubert] Humphrey," although "the tag 'left' is one of those dated legacies they hope to surmount."[22] It was the hope of the members of the Liberal Project, apparently, that they might serve the national government as a kind of "unofficial Fabian Society."[23]

In March, 1960, the Committee of Correspondence, now known as the Council for Correspondence, was formed. Its general position and purpose was set forth in the so-called "Bear Mountain Statement." In this statement

---

[17]*Ibid.*, p. 16.

[18]*Ibid.*, p. 157.

[19]*Ibid.*, p. 140.

[20]Michael Harrington, "New Hope for Socialism: The American Left Unites," *Anvil and Student Partisan* (Winter, 1959), p. 4.

[21]*Ibid.*

[22]David Riesman and Michael Maccoby, "The American Crisis," *New Left Review* (September–October 1960), p. 25.

[23]*Ibid.*, p. 24. And see Harris Dienstfrey, " 'Fabianism' in Washington," *Commentary* (July 1960), pp. 22–28. For a recent attempt to establish a "Neo-Fabian Society" in New York City, see Daniel M. Friedenberg, "A Fabian Program for America," *Dissent*, X (Summer 1963), 232–248.

While members of the "Liberal Project" might be considered a "pivotal group," it is more likely that the significant pivotal groups of the movement in its present period are those associated with the *"Dissent"* project," *Liberation* magazine, the Council for Correspondence, and Turn Toward Peace. For the place of the "pivotal group" in the development of a movement, see Burke, *Counter-Statement* (Chicago, 1957), p. 71; and the discussion of "Sect" in *Attitudes Toward History* (Boston, 1959), pp. 320–321.

members of the committee observed that "purely national loyalties have become an anachronism," and that "we must create a deep loyalty to all men, a loyalty capable of supporting international institutions, and the reign of law in international life." They recognized "the many obstacles to peace in the world today and the radical changes peace would require in our society." They asked people "to consciously reject the idea that democratic values can be defended or international problems solved by military means in the world today"; and they asked people to join with them

> . . . in a continuing attempt to construct alternatives to organized violence; to see that these alternatives receive a hearing by our government and our fellow citizens in the press, in correspondence, and by the spoken word; to direct their attention steadfastly to the problem of finding other solutions in an unremitting struggle for life.[24]

In its search for alternatives, for means of ending the Cold War, the Committee hoped to establish "a very loose affiliation of groups in different university communities," and to "enlist intellectuals in realizing an inventive and radical response to the problem of war and its implications for American culture."[25] As a kind of "discussion network," it aimed to provide "national and regional forums for the presentation and discussion of ideas intended to help find alternatives to armed violence," and to encourage the formation of local groups devoted to the same end.[26] As an historical note, the Committee pointed out that after the founding of the first Committee of Correspondence by Samuel Adams, committees

> . . . arose in Virginia and in other colonies. Through their exchange a widespread area of popular discontent was discovered and a number of mutually accepted beliefs crystallized. Out of this came the idea of holding a Continental Congress, and from this in turn came the concerted movement for independence that led to the revolution and the birth of the United States.[27]

[24]Bear Mountain Statement (March 1960), pp. 2, 5, 6. See also Barbara Deming, "Courage for the New Age: The Committee of Correspondence," *Liberation*, VII (November 1963), 13–16; and A. J. Muste, "Let's Radicalize the Peace Movement," *Liberation*, VIII (June 1963), 28.

[25]Riesman and Maccoby, *op. cit.*, p. 25. The "American Crisis" essay originally appeared in *Commentary* (June 1960), pp. 461–472, and was reprinted in *The Liberal Papers*, ed. James Roosevelt (New York 1962), pp. 13–47. The paragraph mentioning the Committee of Correspondence appears only in the *New Left Review* version of the essay.

[26]Bear Mountain Statement, back cover. In the first weeks of its operation, the Committee "held seminars in Cambridge, Massachusetts, to discuss the consequences of disarmament; and American policy *vis-a-vis* Cuba at the University of Illinois. . . ." Riesman and Maccoby, *op. cit.*, p. 25. However the writer has been informed by Theodore Olson, administrative secretary of the Council for Correspondence, that "We have not sponsored as a national group any seminars, etc., though the New York committee does this regularly. . . . Other CFC people help to further the process through their own faculties, professional societies, etc." Letter dated October 30, 1962.

[27]Bear Mountain Statement, p. 1.

The original membership of the Committee (made up of "leading pacificists," "one or two labor intellectuals," "several socialists," and a "growing group of academicians") [28] included, among others, David Riesman, Michael Maccoby, William Davidon, Erich Fromm, Robert Gilmore, H. Stuart Hughes, Sidney Lens, Stewart Meacham, A. J. Muste, Clarence Pickett, Robert Pickus, Mark Raskin, Mulford Sibley, and Harold Taylor.[29]

In October, 1960, the SP-SDF launched its official newspaper, *New America*, under the editorship of Michael Harrington. In the same month, the British publication, *New Left Review*, published C. Wright Mills' "Letter to the New Left." In that "Letter" Mills once again affirmed his belief in the "intellectual" class as a "possible, immediate, radical agency of change." He called for "ideological analysis" of the "historical agencies of structural change," and for the "rhetoric with which to carry it out."[30] In addition to Mills' "Letter," the same issue of the *New Left Review* published Riesman and Maccoby's "American Crisis" paper. This essay is important not only for its discussion of the Liberal Project and for its announcement of the formation of the Committee of Correspondence, but also for its analysis of the "trail blazer" attitude that the authors saw as motivating our current Cold War rhetoric ("talking tough"), and for its discussion of means by which that attitude might be altered ("lobbying 'upward' is necessary"). They suggested that

> . . . we need energetically to influence the military, industrial, political, and educational elites into letting go of their investments in the cold war and into working not only for a safer but for a better world.

The need of America in its time of crisis, they concluded, is for "political programs which transcend the details of the present."[31]

[28]Riesman and Maccoby, *op. cit.*, p. 25.

[29]Bear Mountain Statement, back cover. Subscribers to the statement, forty-seven in number, included Kenneth Boulding, Lewis Coser, W. J. Ferry, Paul Goodman, Michael Harrington, Mark Harris, S. I. Hayakawa, Robert Heilbroner, Hallock Hoffman, Robert Maynard Hutchins, Alexander Meiklejohn, Seymour Melman, Walter Millis, Herbert Muller, Lewis Mumford, Charles Osgood, Kenneth Rexroth, I. A. Richards, and other distinguished intellectuals.

[30]C. Wright Mills, "Letter to the New Left," *New Left Review* (September–October 1960), p. 20.

[31]Riesman and Maccoby, *op. cit.*, p. 35. For an earlier discussion of possibilities for effecting change "from below" (i.e., "lobbying upward") see David Riesman, "The College Student in an Age of Organization," *Chicago Review* (Autumn 1958), pp. 63–64. Cf. Burke on "pivotal groups" and the belief that political movements "must arise 'from the grass roots,'" *Counter-Statement* (Chicago, 1957), pp. 71–72.

For discussion of Mills' thesis that the radical intellectual should *direct* his persuasion to the "power elite," see Eugene V. Schneider, "C. Wright Mills and the American Left," *Monthly Review* (February 1963), pp. 561–562. Cf. David Riesman, *The Lonely Crowd*, rev. ed. (New Haven, Conn., 1961), pp. xxxix: ". . . political activation of new ways of thought can no longer depend on capturing the leadership of an unorganized non-elite group as the basis for a political movement; with the growth of affluence, it is the malaise of the privileged . . . that becomes increasingly relevant." And see Norman Birnbaum, "David Riesman's Image of Political Process," *Culture and Social Character*, eds. Seymour Martin Lipset and Leo Loewenthal (New York, 1961), pp. 224–225.

In the summer of 1960, the *Socialist Call* published Fromm's "socialist manifesto and program," *Let Man Prevail*. Socialism, Fromm affirmed, "differs from other party programs in that it has a vision . . . it aims at a goal which transcends the given empirical social reality." In outlining the principles of his "democratic, humanist socialism," Fromm indicated what he thought should be both the short-range and the long-range goals of the SP-SDF. He was aware that "it will take considerable time until the majority of the people of the United States will be convinced of the validity of socialist principles and goals."[32] Until that time, it must be the task of the SP-SDF to "become the moral and intellectual conscience of the United States, and divulge its analyses and judgments in the widest possible manner."[33] It must "develop an extensive educational campaign among workers, students, professionals, and members of all social classes who can be expected to have a potential understanding for socialist criticism and socialist ideals."[34]

2.

By the fall of 1961, if it was apparent that a new spirit of radicalism had been gradually emerging during the preceding half-dozen years, it was equally clear that two other movements—both more highly publicized—had been developing simultaneously and at a rapid rate: the movement for "civil rights" and the movement for "peace." During the half-dozen years preceding the fall of 1961, older groups like the "legalistic" NAACP and the Congress of Racial Equality had become more active in behalf of the "civil rights" of Negroes. In 1956, CORE (since its founding in 1942 devoted to Muste's [and Gandhi's] method of *satyagraha*—that is, to a non-violent, direct-action "rhetoric" of resistance) had "hired its first field secretary, and soon thereafter began its Southern work in earnest. . . ."[35] In 1956 Martin Luther King brought the Montgomery bus boycott to a successful conclusion; and in the following year he organized his Southern Christian Leadership Conference (SCLC). In 1960, the Student Nonviolent Coordinating Committee (SNCC), and the Negro American Labor Council (designed to combat discriminatory trade-union practices within the AFL-CIO) were established. And in 1960 the college student "sit-ins" began at Greensboro—an act which constituted, in the opinion of one student of the civil rights movement, the "truly decisive break with the past":

> These sit-ins involved, for the first time, the employment
> of nonviolent direct action on a massive South-wide scale

[32]Erich Fromm, "Let Man Prevail: A Socialist Manifesto and Program," *Socialist Call* (Summer 1960), p. 21.

[33]*Ibid.*, p. 22.

[34]*Ibid.*

[35]August Meier, "New Currents in the Civil Rights Movement," *New Politics* (Summer 1963), p. 11.

that led to thousands of arrests and elicited the participation of tens of thousands of people. Moreover, a period
was inaugurated in which youth were to become the spear-
head of the civil-rights struggle. And this is still the case—
for it has been the youth who have been the chief dynamic
force in compelling the established civil-rights organizations
to revamp their strategy [i.e., to become "committed to direct action"], which they found it imperative to do to retain their leadership in the movement.[36]

As for the peace movement, during the period under consideration, groups
of long lineage had grown more active in the name of "peace"—the American
Friends Service Committee, the Fellowship of Reconciliation, the Brotherhood
of Sleeping Car Porters, Students for a Democratic Society, the War Resisters
League, and the Women's International League for Peace and Freedom. New
groups had sprung up—the Committee for Non-Violent Action, the Committee
for World Development and Disarmament, SANE, the Council for Correspondence; and various "peace research" institutes had been established often
on university campuses.[37]

Meanwhile, other "New Left" journals had been appearing. By the fall of
1961, *Studies on the Left* (sponsored by James Baldwin, Erich Fromm, Murray
Kempton, Sidney Lens, A. J. Muste, Kenneth Rexroth, Bayard Rustin, Mulford
Sibley, Norman Thomas, and others) had been devoting itself to "a revival of
radical thought among American intellectuals" for more than a year.[38] In the
fall of 1961, *New Politics: A Journal of Socialist Thought* began publication.
Its sponsors included James Baldwin, Erich Fromm, Michael Harrington, Murray Kempton, Sidney Lens, A. J. Muste, Robert Pickus, Kenneth Rexroth,
Bayard Rustin, Mulford Sibley, Harvey Swados, Norman Thomas, and others.[39] And in the fall of 1961, perhaps moved by their belief in the need for a
"new politics," Norman Thomas and Robert Pickus combined the peace groups
that have been mentioned in the preceding paragraph—along with some twenty
other groups representing labor, religious, veterans' and public affairs interests
—into a centralized framework that they called "Turn Toward Peace."[40]

The member organizations of the TTP were in general agreement as to

[36]*Ibid.*, p. 13.

[37]For recent discussions of the peace movement, see Michael Harrington, "The New
Peace Movement," *The New Leader* (August 20, 1962), pp. 6–8; Roy Finch, "The New
Peace Movement—I," *Dissent*, IX (Winter, 1962), 86–95; "The New Peace Movement—II,"
Dissent, X (Spring, 1963), 133–148; Norman Thomas et al., "American Socialism and Ther-
monuclear War," *New Politics* (Spring 1962) ; Norman Thomas et al., "Politics and Peace
Symposium," *New America* (March 12, 1963), pp. 4–5, and (April 25, 1963), pp. 4–5; rele-
vant articles in the May and June, 1963, issues of *Liberation*.

[38]*Studies on the Left*, II, No. 2 (1961), p. 94. Cf. Andrew Hacker, "The Rebelling
Young Scholars," *Commentary* (November 1961), pp. 404–412; and Richard Chase, "The
New Campus Magazines," *Harper's* (October 1961), pp. 168–172.

[39]Advertisement, *Studies on the Left*, Vol. II, No. 2 (1961), p. 58; see also title page,
New Politics, Vol. I, No. 1 (1962).

[40]Harrington, "The New Peace Movement," *op. cit.*, (above, note 37), p. 8.

their ultimate goal—a "disarmed world under law, safe for free societies and democratic values"; and, with various exceptions, in agreement on steps that must be taken in their progress toward that goal: the "reduction of international tensions"; "disarmament"; the "development of non-violent forces to defend freedom and democratic values"; "support of just demands for revolutionary change among the oppressed peoples of the world"; the development of "economic planning for a peaceful world"; the development of "a sense of world community"; and the "growth toward world law."[41] And it may be suggested that there was also agreement, if implicit and unconscious, on a general rhetorical program. It was a program that involved two phases: *Phase one*—the substitution in the public mind of "peace consciousness" for "war consciousness" (i.e., the overcoming of the "trail-blazer" attitude) by the creation of a climate of opinion that would be receptive to the *idea* of "alternatives" to prevailing Cold War policy; and *Phase two*—the undertaking of a series of unilateral *acts* (i.e., "American initiatives") that would compel the Cold War opponent to move with America, gradually, into a permanent world of peace (i.e., a "disarmed world under law, safe for free societies and democratic values").[42] It was a rhetorical program, in short, which assumed the validity of the theory that by an act which alters the quality of a scene, one moves (or persuades) one's opponent into a new act in keeping with the new scene; whereupon one initiates a new act which creates a new scene, which requires a new act from one's opponent into a new act in keeping with the new scene; whereupon one initiates a new act which creates a new scene, which requires a new act from one's opponent—and so on, until the ultimate rhetorical objective has been achieved.

That those concerned with the establishment of a "New Left" in American politics should be interested in movements for "peace" and "civil rights," in a time of Cold War, is not surprising. In Riesman's view, as Birnbaum interprets

[41]Brochure, *Turn Toward Peace*, included in the 1962 "American Initiatives Kit." Compare this program with the one advanced in the 1962 platform of the Socialist party, "To Build a Better World."

[42]Cf. the two-phase program ("Turns Toward Peace," "Turns Toward Life" discussed by Hallock Hoffman in *The Control of National Policy*, (Council for Correspondence pamphlet, June, 1962) ; and the two-phase program ("I—reversal of the tensions/arms-race spiral," "II—maintaining the peace") discussed by Charles E. Osgood in "How We Might Win the Hot War and Lose the Cold," *Midway*, No. 4 (1960). Osgood notes (p. 88) : "It is apparent that many of the conditions supporting the Communist way of life cannot be manipulated directly in our present world situation. They all require penetration of the 'iron curtains' in one way or another, and, therefore, strategies pertaining to them belong in Phase II. On the other hand, *we can manipulate the condition of external threat directly.* This variable is at least partly under our control—because we ourselves, in our words and actions, contribute to the level of threat which the Russians perceive. We can behave so as to raise this threat or lower it. . . ." Cf. the "GRIT" program discussed by Osgood in his chapter on "Reciprocal Initiatives" in *The Liberal Papers*, ed. James Roosevelt, pp. 155–228.
For a recent critique of the unilateral initiatives idea within the context of prevailing "Confederate" and "Federal styles of rhetoric," with comment on the "American forensic climate" in general, see David Riesman, "Reflections on Containment and Initiatives," Council for Correspondence *Newsletter* (February 1963), pp. 21–30.

it, Cold War "political conditions preclude the development of human autonomy." The nation "suffers from a psychological *immobilisme*"—the result "not alone of demoniacal images of Communism, but of the lack of alternatives to America's present, extremely limited, internal political goals." Those who "should be formulating these alternatives . . . are in fact mobilized for the Cold War." Thus the "current political motivation" *(act)* "is a result of the current political situation *(scene)* and not vice versa."[43] In such a *scene*, how is one who would be truly *human* (i.e., "individual," "sane," "autonomous") to *act?* Following Emerson ("whoso would be a man must be a nonconformist"), one must choose *(act)* to "transcend" the Cold War *scene* through "rejection" of it ("nonconformity," "dissociation," "civil disobedience"), through "commitment" of oneself to *mobility*—though the movements one "accepts" must be directed, of course, toward "peace," "equality," and other virtues of the "better world" of the "good society." At any rate, it seems plain that the "good society"—or at least that utopian society envisioned by democratic, socialist humanists—cannot be achieved except in a world at peace. For as Kenneth Burke has noted, "you can't get a fully socialist *act* unless you have a fully socialist scene";[44] and such a scene requires peace—for "the standards of peace" are the "proper tests for judging a socialist economy."[45]

None of which is to suggest that all "New Leftists" have been active in movements for "peace" and "civil rights"; nor, obviously, that all supporters of these movements are "New Leftists." It is not to suggest, again, that "peace" constitutes the primary strategic concern in the rhetoric of those committed to "a fundamental restructuring of society, a redistribution of property and power, along democratic lines."[46] As the scene requires, other strategies will share place with "peace" in the rhetorical corpus of the "New Left." And as may be inevitable in what is *in esse* an *anti* movement (i.e., since the "New Leftist's" "alienation" is synonymous with his need to reject the "reigning symbols of authority," the basic "attitude" from which his "strategies" arise is necessarily one of "rejection"),[47] many of the strategies most aggressively

   [43]Birnbaum, "David Riesman's Image of Political Process," *op. cit.*, (above, note 31), pp. 225–226.
   [44]*Grammar of Motives* (New York, 1945), p. 14. Burke makes this observation within the context of a discussion of "instances of the scene-act ratio in dialectical materialism."
   [45]*Attitudes Toward History* (Boston, 1961), p. 272.
   [46]Irving Howe's recent definition of "Socialism" in "A Revival of Radicalism?" *Dissent*, X (Spring 1963), 114.
   [47]Burke, *Philosophy of Literary Form* (New York, 1957), p. 264. On the inevitability of negativistic rhetoric when a potentially *pro* movement is in its incipient, *anti* stage, Will Herberg says: "Bourgeois politics, even when radical, is essentially affirmative: its aim is to reform, improve, and consolidate the existing order. Socialist politics, however, even at its most 'moderate,' is essentially negative and oppositional; its true constructive role socialism reserves for the upbuilding of the new social order that is to supersede capitalism. Both work for tomorrow, but in a very different sense: for the one, tomorrow is but today perfected through progress; for the other, it is today negated and *transcended* in a future that marks the consummation of history." See "American Marxist Political Theory," in *Socialism and American Life*, eds. Donald Egbert and Stow Persons, I, 489.

asserted must be essentially negativistic—e.g., *against* "conformity," *against* the "uncommitted," *against* the "American Celebration," *against* the concept of the "nation state," *against* "civil defense," *against* "mass culture," *against* "HUAC," *against* the "Connolly Reservation," *against* the "Liberal Establishment," the "New Conservatives," the "Ultra Right," and *against* "the political directorate, the corporate rich, the ascendant military," et cetera. The employment of negativistic (uncooperative) strategies in a movement toward the "good society" (of democratic, socialist humanism) is perhaps anomalous, since the controlling attitude of the "good society," when realized *in posse*, is to be one of affirmation (cooperation). Yet a *pro* movement (with its rhetoric of acceptance) is not likely to replace the present *anti* movement as long as "Socialism" remains "word on the Devil's tongue,"[48] and proponents of the movement must accordingly persuade "covertly." Meanwhile, assuagement for the "discomfitures of rejection," opportunities for the employment of positive strategies, may be found through participation in movements for "peace," "equality," "civil rights," et cetera.

3.

The death of C. Wright Mills in the spring of 1962 deprived the "New Left" of one of its most forceful voices, and certainly one of its most sophisticated rhetorical theorists.[49] What specific measures Mills might have advocated had he lived to complete his projected book, a "program" for the "New Left," cannot be asserted.[50] But he surely would have continued to insist on the duty of the radical, whether socialist or not, to take an activist role in the "peace race."

At the time of Mills' death, when "Phase one" of the TTP program was in the midst of its first year, the "peace race" was in active progress. Mothers were marching, women striking, Dr. Spock speaking, professors petitioning, students demonstrating—all in the name of peace; "peace centers" were springing up in the cities and suburbs; peace "workshops," seminars, symposia, posters, vigils, walks—all abounded in the land; and it was no fault of peace advocates if "peace consciousness" was not beginning to make its way into the public mind.

But the events of October and November, 1962, dealt a heavy blow to the

---

[48]Erich Fromm, *Marx's Concept of Man* (New York, 1961), p. vii. For similar recognition of "socialism" as a "bad word," see Norman Thomas's University of Colorado speech, "The Need for Socialism," *New America* (May 12, 1963), p. 3; and Staughton Lynd, "Socialism, the Forbidden Word," *Studies on the Left*, Vol. III, No. 3 (1963), pp. 14–20.

[49]For a suggestion of the influence of Burke on the rhetorical theories of Mills, see the 1940 essay "Situated Actions and Vocabularies of Motive," reprinted in I. L. Horowitz, *Power, Politics and People* (New York, 1963), pp. 439–452; and the section on "Vocabularies of Motive," in Hans Gerth and C. Wright Mills, *Character and Social Structure* (New York, 1953), pp. 114 ff.

[50]Warde, "The Marxists," *op. cit.* (above, note 9), p. 69.

peace movement. It was not merely the decisive defeat of almost all of the thirty-two "peace candidates," including Sidney Lens and H. Stuart Hughes, that discouraged; it was the whole reversal of hopes represented by the President's aggressive response in the Cuban crisis. In moments of reversal, according to Burke, some "ritual of rebirth" is required; and for such a ritual, a "scapegoat" is needed. Perhaps this was a significance, for the left, that a Burkeian critic might attach to Howard K. Smith's broadcast on "The Political Obituary of Richard Nixon."[51]

For months, throughout the fall and winter of 1962, the peace movement remained in what Professor Hughes, in a speech before the New York local of the Socialist party, called the "post-Cuba trough."[52] At length, in the spring of 1963, *New America* invited a number of "leaders and activists in the peace, civil rights and labor" movements to participate in a symposium on "Political Directions for the Peace Movement." The assessment of the movement offered by Norman Thomas was gloomy:

> It is a bitter fact that at this moment there is small chance of the building of a vigorous democratic left in a political party or movement. We Socialists exist in large part to bring such a movement into being. In the meantime we cannot act as if we had it. The peace movement is badly divided, and the best we can do at present to pull it together is along the lines of Turn Toward Peace. It cannot function as a strong, politically organized left under present conditions.
>
> All these important problems of organization, strategy and tactics in the last analysis depend on our ability to do a much better job than we have yet done in persuading people of the position in regard to peace which I think is best expressed in our own platform.[53]

"Our present question," he remarked, "is a tactical one: how best to advance this program under our crazy political system in which there is no clear-cut alignment of the major parties on either domestic or foreign issues." On the question of tactics, other members of the symposium offered various opinions. David McReynolds, of the War Resisters League, felt that "the job of the peace movement now is to join forces with Dagmar Wilson and others in fighting the Dodd subcommittee and HUAC."[54] Sanford Bottlieb, of SANE, held that "the major emphasis of the peace movement should be directed toward work within the political parties, especially in primaries where there is a chance of winning

51That is, "symbolic slaying," in the presence of Hiss, of Nixon as "consubstantial representative" (with Kennedy) of the Cold War "power elite." It is necessary to recall the tendency of the Left to equate Nixon and Kennedy ("Tweedle-dee and Tweedle-dum") during the 1960 campaign.

52See *New America* (May 31, 1963), p. 6.

53"Symposium on Politics and Peace," *New America* (April 25, 1963), p. 4.

54*Ibid.*

party nomination."[55] Stewart Meacham, of the American Friends Service Committee, held that "peace will become politically potent not because the choice has been made between emphasis on a third party or on independent candidates on the one hand and infiltrating the major parties on the other, but rather by both things happening at once."[56] Sidney Lens disagreed "firmly with those in the peace movement who propose that we burrow into the major political parties." He argued:

> Electoral activity, though important in enlarging the peace
> constituency and gaining a voice within the establishment,
> is only part of political activity. Direct action, such as
> peace walks, demonstrations, non-violent sit-ins, are also
> politics, and politics of the highest order.[57]

Bayard Rustin, executive secretary of the War Resisters League and "Former Advisor to Martin Luther King," declared that "the main problem is to get other social forces that are in movement to see that the struggle for survival is a part of their struggles." He suggested that "the dynamic and method of the civil rights movement offers great hope":

> In the civil rights movement, people are in motion and are
> at this moment affecting the social and political climate of
> the country, and, with a little more success, may open the
> way for a realignment of the Democratic Party in the South.
>   Obviously, if this energy could be brought into a broad-
> er movement for social change, including the struggle for
> peace, the movement for a "new America" would take on
> profound political significance. I point out here merely that
> there is infinitely more of an immediate response possible
> from the civil rights movement than from labor or any
> other of the elements that are required for social change in
> the U.S.[58]

Rustin's position on the question of tactics received further support in the June issue of *Liberation*. In that issue, which carried Martin Luther King's "Letter from Birmingham Jail" and Rustin's "The Meaning of Birmingham," A. J. Muste suggested that the time had come to "radicalize the peace movement." Drawing a "lesson from the integration movement," Muste pointed out that what "is plain for everyone to see now is that there was no 'communication' . . . between Negroes and whites, even liberal whites, under the old pattern":

> Communication began when the "powers that be" had to
> listen, i.e., when real and hence controversial issues were

[55] *New America* (March 12, 1963), p. 4.
[56] *Ibid.*, p. 5.
[57] *Ibid.*, p. 4.
[58] *Ibid.*, p. 5.

talked about. In the same way, whether nationally or locally, as peace advocates we have a chance actually to communicate if we are known as dissenters, not if the fact is hidden.[59]

C. V. Parkinson, in another article, scored the philosophy of "conservative, restrained communication" that had been followed by Turn Toward Peace, SANE, and the community peace groups. He saw in this "lukewarm approach, this nibbling away at the concern of the uncommitted, the dead hand of Madison Avenue"; and he felt that all concerned with peace must now face the questions: *"Should the proper attempt of the peace movement as presently constituted be to communicate with the public at the public's level, OR Should the attempt be to create a movement that the public can reach?"* He saw a "profound difference. It is the difference between an evolving image and a firm image . . . between persuasion and conviction."[60] And Dave Dellinger, in a lead editorial denouncing "Uncle Tom-ism in the Peace Movement," concluded with the question:

> Whatever the material costs may be, can we evade the "unrespectable" direct-action tactics of economic boycott, massive social disruption, and civil disobedience which have made the nonviolent movement for integration a powerful force for revolutionary change?[61]

Two thousand extra copies of the June *Liberation* were printed "in order to get copies in the hands of key field workers and demonstrators throughout the country." But even as the magazine was being prepared for the mails, significant changes in the "objective environment" (in Muste's phrase) began to occur.

On June 11, President Kennedy spoke to the nation, in an address entitled "A Moral Imperative: Equality of Treatment," on the question of civil rights; and the preceding day, at the commencement exercises of American University, he had delivered an address on "The Strategy of Peace." In that speech, the President had identified "peace . . . as the necessary rational end of rational men"; had suggested that Americans "re-examine" their "attitude toward the Soviet Union"; had confided that American diplomats had been "instructed to avoid unnecessary irritants and purely rhetorical hostility"; had stressed the necessity for a "new effort to achieve world law—a new context for world discussion"; had affirmed that "our primary long-range interest . . . is general and complete disarmament—designed to take place by stages, permitting parallel political developments to build the new institutions of peace which would take the place of arms"; and had announced, in climax, that

---

[59]Muste, "Let's Radicalize the Peace Movement," *op. cit.* (above, note 24), VIII, 29.
[60]C. V. Parkinson, "Leveling with the Public," *Liberation*, VIII (June 1963), 25.
[61][Dave Dellinger], "Uncle Tom-ism in the Peace Movement," *Liberation*, VIII (June 1963), 3.

"high level discussions" would "shortly begin in Moscow towards early agreement on a comprehensive test ban treaty."[62]

The negotiation of the partial "Nuclear Test Ban Treaty" began in Moscow in mid-July; and on August 6 the treaty was formally signed. Described by the President as "a step toward peace—a step toward reason—a step away from war," the treaty was hailed by a heartened *New America* as "a step toward peace," a "Small step toward sanity," and "a step away from war." The socialist publication went on to advise the "democratic left" to

> . . . use the opening provided by the test ban agreement to demand a Nuclear-free zone in central Europe. Demilitarization of central Europe must be begun by the disengagement of American and Russian troops from the continent.

It warned the "left" to "continue to oppose any deals between the US and Russia to maintain the status quo and their spheres of influence"; to continue to support "self-determination for the people of Eastern Europe under Communist domination as well as for the people in the world oppressed by Western colonialism"; and to continue to work for an end to "all military and economic support to the reactionary regimes in Portugal and Viet Nam." In conclusion, *New America* declared:

> The political forces which are capable of creating this new foreign policy are marching on Washington for equal rights. All those who want further steps toward peace should join with the labor, liberal and civil rights movements in this direct assault on the Republican-Dixiecrat Coalition—the bastion of domestic and foreign reaction.[63]

In the same issue of *New America*, the official call to the "March on Washington for Jobs and Freedom," signed by the directors of the March, A. Philip Randolph and Bayard Rustin, appeared. In a separate statement in *New America*, Randolph commended the "Socialist Party's program for creating full employment and ending economic discrimination to the attention of all supporters of the civil rights movement." The "revolution for Freedom Now," he added

> . . . has moved into a new stage in its development. Its demands have necessarily become not only the end of all discrimination against black Americans, but for the creation of a new society—a society without economic exploitation and deprivation.

[62]For texts of the Kennedy addresses, see *Vital Speeches of the Day* (July 1, 1963), pp. 546–547, 558–561.
[63]Editorial, "A Step Toward Peace," *New America* (August 10, 1963), p. 2.

On the eve of the March, Michael Harrington, in a lengthy article in *New America*, praised A. Philip Randolph as "the most important Negro socialist of modern times," denied that socialists were " 'outsiders' trying to manipulate the [civil rights] movement for some secret purpose," and insisted that "there must be a political realignment in America" since

> . . . there cannot be full-scale civil rights without ranging social progress; and neither will come about unless there is a new movement, a political movement for realignment and a second party, in the United States.[64]

The editor of *New America* saw the forthcoming "demonstration" as marking "a new stage in the revolution"; declared that "every step that this host of marchers takes will be toward a new kind of action on the part of outraged and oppressed citizens in the field of national politics"; rejoiced in the "towering fact that a coalition had been begun, and is strong enough that under its aegis masses of people will command the streets of the capital on the 28th to voice a number of radical economic and social demands"; called on "every Socialist, every liberal, every trade unionist" to be "among those giving his whole-hearted support to the March," and after the March to

> . . . continue to back the movement in the fight it has outlined so well in its statement of principles—"our unalterable opposition to the forces ('Reactionary Republicans and Southern Democrats') and their century long robbery of the American people."[65]

As for August 28, *Time* magazine judged it "a day that would never be forgotten." The March on Washington, it declared, "was a triumph. But after everybody agreed on that, the question was: Why?"[66] No doubt that question will be asked for some time to come. From the standpoint of rhetorical function, however, one might suggest that the March provided the "New Left" movement with a highly appropriate symbol: a symbol of solidarity—a massive symbol of people in *movement*—of people *identifying* in the name of *freedom, justice* and *equality*—of people *committed,* and *acting in cooperation, hope,* and above all, *peace,* for "a better world."

4.

In September of 1963, then, as this analysis is completed, it seems reasonable to suggest that a "New Left" movement is now in its period of inception —and developing, indeed, toward maturer stages of that period. One stage in the inception period of a movement (if it is to achieve its period of rhetorical

[64]Michael Harrington, "Socialists and Civil Rights," *New America* (August 31, 1963), p. 3.

[65]Penn Kemble and Paul Feldman, "March Marks New Stage in Revolution," *New America* (August 31, 1963), pp. 1, 12.

[66]*Time* (September 6, 1963), pp. 15, 13.

crisis), is the decision of aggressor orators ("prophets") to forsake trite and ineffective appeals, to undertake new modes of argument.[67] If even a slight "reduction of international tensions" results from the Moscow Test Ban treaty, the "New Left" may be expected to continue its appeals for further *detente* with the Communist opponent, as well as for such broader "steps" toward "a better world" as those included in the TTP program—disarmament, development of non-violent forces for defense, aid for revolutions by the oppressed, economic planning, world community, world law. But the present interest of the "New Left" in the content and method of peace "communication" indicates, at least, that current modes of appeal are being scrutinized, and new ones considered. It may be that certain "lessons" of the civil rights movement *(urgency,* "Freedom *Now";* the "use of the 'black body' against injustice . . . as a means of creating social disruption and dislocation")[68] will lead to alterations in the manner or mode of appeals for "peace"—e.g., to the widespread adoption of "direct action tactics" (i.e., a "physical rhetoric of resistance"). If so, an ethical confusion ("act" not in keeping with "essence") would seem to arise—at least for those who make a "god term" (term of "essence") of *sanity (the rational)* but whose rhetorical action is by choice *absurd* (i.e., essentially non-rational; coercive rather than persuasive; dependent on "seat of the pants" rather than "seat of the intellect"). If debate ("forensic drama," "reasoned discourse") is the creating myth of American democracy,[69] Rustin's justification of the necessity of "body" rhetoric on the ground that "the accepted democratic channels have been denied the Negro"[70] might be entertained in light of the Burkeian "scene-act ratio" (non-rational, non-democratic "acts" in a non-rational, non-democratic "scene"); but it would seem difficult for advocates of "peace" to claim lack of access to "accepted democratic channels" of persuasion.

Other stages in the inception period of maturing movements include the decision to address broader publics, and (in "Saving Remnant" movements)[71] the decision to speak openly ("overtly," unambiguously). It may be that Muste's advice to "dissenters"—that to improve "communication" they must identify themselves openly to their publics—will be increasingly heeded. Harvey Swados has done so in his *A Radical's America;*[72] and it is interesting to note that the Council for Correspondence has decided to "go public" by making its newsletter available for "general circulation." Appropriately, the July-August issue of the newsletter bears a new name ("our old title was a study in calculated ambiguity"); and the editors indicate their awareness that, in openly addressing a broader public, they

[67]Griffin, "The Rhetoric of Historical Movements," *op. cit.* (above, note 12), p. 186.

[68]See Muste, "Let's Radicalize the Peace Movement," *op. cit.,* (above, note 24), and Bayard Rustin, "Birmingham Leads to New Stage in Struggle," *New America* (June 18, 1963), p. 7.

[69]Hugh Duncan, *Communication and Social Order* (New York, 1962), p. 259.

[70]Rustin, "Birmingham Leads to New Stage in Struggle," *op. cit.,* p. 7.

[71]Griffin, "The Rhetoric of Historical Movements," *op. cit.* (above, note 12), p. 186.

[72]Harvey Swados, *A Radical's America* (New York, 1962), p. xiii.

> . . . must assume a bit less—introduce our writers more
> carefully, explain the relevance of our topics, and generally
> design for the uncertain and perhaps only half-interested
> eye.[73]

Further stages in the development of an inception period—in addition to
the abandonment of ineffective appeals, the adoption of new modes of argument, and the decisions to speak "overtly" and to address broader publics—
include the intensified use of previously employed channels of propagation, as
well as the employment and consolidation of new channels. With the effective
utilization ("flooding") of all channels, the movement begins to "flower into
public notice"—and the way is prepared for the final stages of the inception
period: the emergence of "hosts of aggressor rhetoricians" and the consequent
generation of the "moving tide of discourse" that precipitates the period of
rhetorical crisis—the period of the collective, public (i.e., "overt") rendering
of judgment.[74] Or to restate the rhetorical process of inception periods in
Burkeian terminology: as problems of "communication" are solved, increasing
numbers of individuals "identify" with the movement (that is, "reject" the
prevailing "symbols of authority" and "accept" the symbolic ends of the movement); as they undergo "change of identity," become "committed" to the
movement, they are freed from their "alienation," "repossess their world,"
"shift their co-ordinates"; in this shift they acquire new "perspective," gain a
"sense of direction," "see around the corner"—and hence, they "prophesy."[75]
Eventually, as the ranks of the "prophets" (aggressor orators) multiply, the
period of rhetorical crisis arrives: the public renders its collective judgment,
"accepts" the new "symbols of authority"—and "transcendence" ("transformation," "social change," "revolution") is achieved.

At the present writing, the "New Left" movement cannot be said to have
"flowered into public notice" (as compared, for example, with the "neo-conser-
vative" and "radical right" movements). This stage may begin to develop,
however, as the "New Left" continues to improve and extend the range of its
rhetoric. On May 31, just as the significant summer of 1963 was about to begin, David McReynolds expressed his encouragement at the many "communities of resistance" that he had found in his tours throughout the country; but
he warned that

> . . . the task to be faced is enormous. To translate the
> many local points of resistance into a powerful new Amer-
> ican Left requires some non-dogmatic rallying point, some
> forum through which we can communicate with each other
> as we build together. If we would build a new America, then
> we must build *New America*.[76]

[73]*The Correspondent: The Monthly Newsletter of the Council for Correspondence*
(July–August 1963), p. 38.

[74]Griffin, "The Rhetoric of Historical Movements," *op. cit.* (above, note 12), p. 186.

[75]Burke, *Attitudes Toward History* (Boston, 1961), pp. 268–270.

[76]David McReynolds, " 'Communities of Resistance' Work Toward a New America,"
New America (May 31, 1963), p. 6.

And so he was "forced to the conclusion that one of the most vital functions of the socialist movement—perhaps its single most important function—is that of expanding its press, specifically *New America.*"

From the standpoint of rhetorical structure, the "New Left" movement seems indeed to have reached a stage which requires the expansion of its press, the broadening of its publics, the augmentation and consolidation of its channels of propagation. These requisites might be served, in part, through the coaching of party realignment, the rallying of the various "communities of resistance," the general achievement of "solidarity" between relevant ongoing movements. The broad problem of solidarity has for some time been of concern to Riesman.[77] Paul Goodman, disturbed by the "Caliban" theme ("Let's along and do the murder first") of Baldwin's *The Fire Next Time* and David Lytton's *The Goddam White Man,* has recently insisted that the "only grounds of solidarity" lie in "working at common worthwhile tasks"; that "in such effort men lose themselves and find themselves changed"; that "new identity" is found "in the achievement of great tasks"; that

> . . . the general effort to live better, at home and world-
> wide, will be—if we survive at all—the *solution* of race
> problems. In the effort for peace, rational economy, good
> schooling, world community, etc., race prejudice is trivial
> and must wither.[78]

On the eve of the Washington March, *New America* observed that the "new coalition built around the March . . . provides a potentially enormous power base for a common political program," but it warned that "the growing participation of white liberals, religious organizations, and the more politically conscious sections of the labor movement" could "tend to slow down the pace of action"; and therefore, to

> . . . prevent any loss of momentum during the growth of
> the movement, it becomes the task of the more militant
> civil rights activists, trade unionists and liberals to educate
> and move the tens of thousands of new participants so that
> they can catch up with the revolution underway. The enor-
> mous political weight that they can add to the struggle is
> needed now.[79]

Michael Harrington, in the same issue of *New America,* declared that the time had come for "a political realignment in America" and asked that "the powerful forces for social change band together as effectively as the forces for social reaction have done."

The Washington March, as suggested earlier, both as symbol and deed was an achievement in solidarity; and the concern for solidarity was un-

[77]Birnbaum, "David Riesman's Image of Political Process," *op. cit.* (above, note 31), p. 224.

[78]Paul Goodman, "The Only Grounds of Solidarity," *Liberation,* VIII (June 1963), 22.

[79]Kemble and Feldman, "March Marks New Stage in Revolution," *op. cit.* (above, note 65), p. 12.

doubtedly a factor in the Socialist party's announcement of a "National Con-
ference on the Civil Rights Revolution," to begin in Washington on the day
following the March. Discussion was promised on such topics as "The New
Phase: A Prospectus for Civil Rights," "A Political Strategy for Civil Rights,"
"Fair Employment—Full Employment," and "Toward Full Equality in a Progressive America"; and speakers scheduled for appearance included Norman
Thomas, Bayard Rustin, A. Philip Randolph, James Farmer (of CORE),
Robert Moses (of SNCC), and other figures identified with peace, civil rights,
trade union, and socialist organizations.[80]

In the months ahead, the search for solidarity will no doubt continue to
preoccupy the "New Left"; and in addition, efforts will be made—or theoretically should be—to expand the "New Left" press, reach broader publics, intensify use of available channels of propagation, seek new channels, and (possibly) to speak more overtly. The prevailing mood, at the moment, seems to be
one of guarded optimism. Representative, perhaps, of the present mood, and
suggestive of efforts to come, is the following account of the summer, 1963,
convention of the Students for a Democratic Society:

> SDS will attempt to draw the peace and civil rights move-
> ments closer together, where appropriate, with a common
> rejection of token solutions; aid the budding full-employ-
> ment "movement"; and at the same time maintain lines of
> communication with less radical students, this last less as
> an organizational ploy than to help SDS itself avoid the
> hubris of the "New Left."
>
> A fifth of SDS's membership attended the convention,
> a remarkably high proportion, but the most significant thing
> about them was that all were *participants in local insurgen-
> cy*—university reform, peace politics and research, or civil
> rights activism. The developing SDS strategy therefore
> flowed as much from the gathering as from the analysis,
> and it was clear that in the coming year SDS members will
> be found where social change is to be found, working,
> learning and teaching at once.[81]

5.
Postscript

> I thought that as soon as I became my own master I would
> enter public life. A sudden change, however, in the politi-
> cal situation diverted me from my plan.—Plato, *Seventh
> Letter*

Little more than a week after the preceding essay was completed the na-

---

[80]*New America* (August 31, 1963), p. 12.
[81]Todd Gitlin, "A Student Convention," *The Correspondent* (July–August, 1963), pp.
56–57.

tion was shocked by news of the bombing of the Sixteenth Street Baptist Church in Birmingham. On September 22, a week after the bombing, a National Day of Mourning was held for the six children who had died in the tragic events of the previous Sunday. Tom Kahn, Bayard Rustin's assistant in the March on Washington, informed readers of *New America:*

> It was obvious that the participants in this National Day
> of Mourning felt betrayed by the Federal government. In
> New York, 10,000 gathered in Foley Square, headquarters
> of the Justice Department, and heard Norman Thomas,
> Bayard Rustin, James Farmer, and James Baldwin indict
> the Kennedy Administration for its failure to protect be-
> leaguered southern Negroes from racist terror. . . .[82]

In his speech at the Foley Square rally, Baldwin announced that "it is time that the government knew that if the government does not represent us, if it insists on representing a handful of nostalgic Southern colonels, the government will be replaced"; that "a government and a nation are not synonymous. We can change the government and we will."[83] In a separate statement for *New America,* Baldwin declared that "the crimes committed in Birmingham Sunday must be considered as one of the American answers to the March on Washington." This "shameful day" was one of the

> . . . direct and inevitable consequences of the power held
> in Washington by the Southern oligarchy. It is a day which
> utterly destroys any claim the Kennedy administration in
> general, or the Justice Department in particular, may make
> concerning its zeal or dedication in the field of civil rights.
> . . .

The "most reactionary forces" in the country were determined

> . . . to smash the patience and break the will of the Negro
> people in order to create a situation which will justify
> the use of martial law. First, the Negroes, then all other
> dissenters and/or revolutionaries will find themselves intol-
> erably coerced, and will be broken, in or out of prison or
> driven underground. . . .

It was not enough, therefore, "to mourn the dead children: what we must do is to oppose and immobilize the power that put them to death." Baldwin confessed that he had been one of those people "stampeded by the fear of Nixon into the Kennedy camp"; that he "would certainly never have dreamed of the coming [sic] of a 'Kennedy' man under any other compulsion." Certainly the time had come "to ask a sovereign people why they should continue so abjectly

[82]Tom Kahn, "March's Radical Demands Point Way for Struggle," *New America* (September 24, 1963), p. 4.

[83]James Baldwin, "We Can Change the Country," *Liberation,* VIII (October 1963), 8. Foley Square rally speeches by James Farmer (p. 9) and Theodore Bikel (p. 5) also appear in this issue.

to choose between the interchangeable mediocrities with which Washington
continually confronts us." He refused to believe that "we are unable to envision and achieve political alignments less unrealistic and less immoral." The
great apathy which reigned in the country was symptomatic of "the bewilder-
ment and despair of people who doubt that they have the power to change and
save themselves." Such despair was "indescribably dangerous"; for when
people

> . . . allow themselves to feel that they can do nothing,
> they permit all manner of crimes to be committed in their
> names. Can anyone deny that this process is already under
> way in American life? And this means that the crimes com-
> mitted Sunday in Birmingham will be as nothing compared
> to the crimes we will find ourselves committing, unless we
> take upon ourselves the responsibility of examining and
> revising our institutions, and become more exigent than we
> are concerning the calibre of our representatives.[84]

In the September 24 issue of *New America,* speeches presented at the Socialist party's post-March "Conference on the Civil Rights Revolution" were
reported (Rustin: "The civil rights revolution will succeed to the degree that
we succeed in moving this country to the left. . . . We have an alliance now
with trade union and religious leaders. Our problem is to keep that alliance
alive for this period—with all the pressures that exist"). But under the head-
ing "Political Murder," the editor of the paper devoted his entire analysis to
the Birmingham tragedy. It was an analysis that largely agreed with Baldwin's. "The response of the Kennedy administration" had been "beyond belief,
even for cynics." "The coalition of profits and racism" ("Southern Dixiecrats
and right wing Republicans") had "demonstrated its enormous political and
economic power." It had "gotten away with political murder." He warned that
"the Federal government, by avoiding its constitutional duties, and those
liberals in Congress whose hands still tremble, are forcing Southern Negroes
to resort to violence to protect the lives of their families." There was only one
alternative:

> . . . tens of thousands of black and white bodies march-
> ing in the streets and "going to jail, and jail again," while
> at the same time carrying on an unremitting political
> struggle against the coalition of profits and racism.

"The lines are becoming more finely drawn," he concluded:

> Either we march with the revolution for equality or we
> stand guilty with the Southern racists and their allies for
> the murders of the six Birmingham children and the terror
> yet to come.[85]

[84]"James Baldwin Statement—Political Murder in Birmingham," *New America* (September 24, 1963), pp. 1, 4.
[85]Paul Feldman, "Political Murder," *New America* (September 24, 1963), p. 2.

As the autumn advanced, tones of anger, despair, and foreboding colored "New Left" discourse in the North; in the South it grew dark with themes of death and blood sacrifice. Reporting late in September from Selma, Alabama, Ronnie Dugger noted:

> Death has come up many times during the mass meetings of the Negroes. When he addressed them Monday night, Lewis [John Lewis, national chairman of SNCC] told them that if it was necessary, let blood flow in the streets; but let it be Negroes' blood, he said, because it should be innocent blood. Again and again speakers said they are ready to die if they have to for this cause. Wednesday night, a Snick speaker asked the crowd of 500 if they were ready to die, and they broke into strong applause.[86]

In the issue of *The Correspondent* which printed Dugger's report, Howard Zinn proposed that the President create and send into the South a corps of special agents ("we might call them E-men, for Equality") with the power "to make arrests on the spot, the moment a move is made to violate federal law." Expressing doubt of Zinn's notion that "many demagogic Southerners do not have the courage of their apparent convictions," Riesman pointed out that

> . . . for them shooting is a traditional way to create conviction. Are the Southern *pieds noirs* less capable than those of the French Empire of conspiracy and assassination? It may possibly be that the issue will come to this as our desperations combine and intertangle with each other. Fearing where that road leads, I wonder if other courses such as non-violence have shown conclusively their impracticality?[87]

Rustin, in the October issue of *Liberation*, called again for the use of "black bodies, backed by the bodies of as many white people as will stand with us." He insisted:

> We need to go into the streets all over the country and to make a mountain of creative social confusion until the power structure is altered. We need in every community a group of loving troublemakers, who will disrupt the ability of the government to operate until it finally turns its back on the Dixiecrats and embraces progress.

He warned that

> . . . unless those who organized and led the March on Washington hold together and give the people a program based on mass action, the whole situation will deteriorate

[86]Ronnie Dugger, "Dead End in the Deep South," *The Correspondent* (November–December 1963), p. 46.

[87]Howard Zinn, "A Question of Action"; David Riesman, "A Problem of Reaction," *The Correspondent* (November–December 1963), pp. 51, 54.

and we will have violence, tragic self-defeating violence.
. . .[88]

And yet, as the autumn advanced, events more heartening to "New Left"
causes were occurring. In October the President approved the sale of wheat to
Russia; the General Assembly of the U.N. condemned South Africa's policy of
apartheid; the pacifist Linus Pauling was awarded the Nobel Peace Prize;
Marshal Tito was welcomed at the White House—where the peripatetic ladies
Nhu were officially ignored; and on November 1, with the assassinations of
Diem and General Nhu, the "reactionary regime in Viet Nam" was abruptly
brought down. Steps, however small, toward "peace," the "relaxation of ten-
sions."

But in Dallas, where he had come to deliver a United Nations Day speech
on "peace," Adlai Stevenson (*Time* reported) was "clunked" on the head with
a picket's poster, and "a young man spat on him." Dallas, *Time* noted, "was
shocked."[89]

The arrest of Professor Frederick Barghoorn by the Russians, on the day
before the Viet Nam coup, was (in the light of post-test ban "euphoria") a
retrograde act. Unnecessary. "Seemingly pointless," *Time* felt. Both abrupt
and absurd. Understandable, perhaps, only as an existential political act—an
act existential, in Norman Mailer's phrase, "precisely because its end is unknown."

On November 16, following the President's appeal, the Russians released
the professor. The following week, *Publishers' Weekly* announced the appearance of Norman Mailer's book on existential politics, *The Presidential Papers*.
A long-time "New Leftist," and long disappointed in President Kennedy's
performance ("Tin soldier, you are depriving us of the Muse"), Mailer had
written his book "to" and "for" the President. It was designed to give him an
"existential grasp of the nature of reality." Its "unspoken thesis" was that "no
President can save America from a descent into totalitarianism without shifting
the mind of the American politician to existential styles of political thought."

> If a public speaker in a small Midwestern town were to
> say, "J. Edgar Hoover has done more harm to the free-
> doms of America than Joseph Stalin," the act would be
> existential. Depending on the occasion and the town, he
> would be man-handled physically or secretly applauded.
> But he would create a new reality which would displace
> the old psychological reality that such a remark could not
> be made. . . .[90]

The President had every qualification for greatness, Mailer told him, but one

[88]Bayard Rustin, "The Meaning of the March on Washington," *Liberation*, VIII
(October 1963), 13.
[89]*Time* (November 1, 1963), p. 26.
[90]Norman Mailer, *The Presidental Papers* (New York, 1963), p. 26.

—he had no imagination. He was expert in translating political matters into arithmetic:

> Politics is arithmetic, but politics is also rhetoric, passion,
> and an occasional idea to fire the imagination of millions.
> For his arithmetic the President gets a mark of 98 per cent.
> For his imagination: zero. For his passion: 40 per cent.
> For his rhetoric: 50 per cent.

"Existential politics," Mailer affirmed, "is rooted in the concept of the hero, it would argue that the hero is the one kind of man who *never* develops by accident, that a hero is a consecutive set of brave and witty self-creations." In John Kennedy the nation had a President with "the face of a potential hero," a President who was brave

> . . . but politically neuter, adept at obtaining power and
> a miser at spending it, an intellectual with a mind like a
> newspaper's yearbook, and a blank somewhat stricken ex-
> pression about the eyes, a numbed mind seems to speak
> behind them.[91]

And so Mailer offered his assorted papers to the President—papers on "Existential Legislation," "The Existential Hero" *(Superman Comes to the Supermarket)*, "The Existential Heroine," "On Dread," on "Red Dread," on "Death." In his final paper, "On Waste," Mailer invited the President to go along with him "on an existential journey into the deeper meaning of scatology"; for it was necessary that a President

> . . . be ready to contemplate everything human and inhuman
> in the psychic life of his Republic . . . including precisely
> those ideas which encounter the rude, the obscene, and the
> unsayable.[92]

It is unlikely that time remained for the President to profit by Mailer's scatological learning or to accompany him on his journey. Shortly after the book was published, John Kennedy was off on journeys of his own, political trips into Florida, into Texas. He went to San Antonio, Houston, Forth Worth —and came at last, on November 22, to Dallas.

He had come to deliver an address at the Merchandise Mart, an address which was to feature a warning against extremist "voices" on the Right, against those "who confuse rhetoric with reality and the plausible with the possible." He was struck down, all public evidence indicates, by a self-proclaimed "Marxist"; by an extremist of the Left, grown voiceless; by "a man of our century, for whom argument seemed a fraudulent smokescreen";[93] by

[91]*Ibid.*, pp. 5, 6, 7.
[92]*Ibid.*, p. 270.
[93]Frederick D. Kershner, Jr., in "The Meaning of the Life and Death of John F. Kennedy," *Current*, No. 45 (January 1964), p. 20.

a man, it is at least certain, for whom reality was not rhetoric but a rifle. From the standpoint of categorical expectation, whether of the "New Left" or of the public at large, John Kennedy's death was as neatly and formally chiastic as any discourse in his life had been.

It was not, however, in the words of the philosopher Charles Frankel, a death that was "morally intelligible":

> . . . what happened was an act of human will that was like an act of impersonal nature—unnecessary, purposeless, abrupt. . . . It is the kind of event that the existentialists have in mind, I suspect, when they speak of "absurdity."[94]

Without question the Birmingham bombing, as well as the assassination of the President, both sickened and stunned the nation. These were acts of consummate violence; yet their impact, insofar as the developing structure of "New Left" rhetoric is concerned, is likely to be slight. Qualitatively, both acts might easily be characterized in words drawn from the "New Left" lexicon of "devil terms"—terms descriptive of scenes in the Cold War world. Neither act, in brief, constituted a change in the "objective environment" of the "New Left"; both merely served to confirm its analysis of that environment. This being so, no significant change in rhetorical strategy is required; and thus the search for solidarity, for broader publics, for additional channels of propagation should proceed. Indeed, one week after the assassination, SNCC held its "Fourth Annual Conference on Food and Jobs"—a conference at which Baldwin and Rustin spoke; at which Jack Conway, Walter Reuther's representative to the March on Washington Committee, provided a "basis for joint struggle by the civil rights and labor movement around a common political and economic program which is concrete, radical and relevant."[95] And on December 13–15, in New York, Turn Toward Peace sponsored a conference attended by some 200 representative leaders of more than 100 organizations. In his speech at the conference, Rustin

> . . . not only demanded the economics of the unusual in the struggle for peace *and* civil rights but specified that breakthrough in both areas required fundamental changes in the structure of American society. He called for the most militant kind of pressure on President Johnson.[96]

In his report on the conference, Norman Thomas has noted that if Turn Toward Peace "cannot push at this juncture such good specifics as SANE or the Socialist Party has advanced," it can nevertheless "provide mechanisms for bringing them under discussion and getting maximum possible cooperation at local, regional and the national levels."[97]

[94]Charles Frankel, in "The Meaning of the Life and Death of John F. Kennedy," *Current*, No. 45 (January 1964), p. 38.
[95]See "Conway of IUD Lays Basis for New Left," *New America* (December 27, 1963), p. 5.
[96]Jerome Grossman, "The Peace 'Crowd,' " *The Nation* (January 20, 1964), p. 67.
[97]Norman Thomas, "Turn Toward Peace," *New America* (January 10, 1964), p. 2.

Even so, the prevailing current of the broad national rhetoric (a rhetoric of "non-extremism"), accelerating in the wake of the murders in Birmingham and Dallas, may serve to retard the "New Left" in the development of one stage in the inception phase of its movement—the decision to speak more overtly. While the rhetoric of continuity prevails (the "Eternal Flame" at Arlington; President Johnson: "Let us continue"); while "hate" remains the national scapegoat; while "rhetoric" itself stands charged with guilt (Burke: "So people went on bickering and carping, trying to catch him up . . . using the standard devices of rhetoric. . . . Go, please and read Aristotle's *Rhetoric* . . .";[98] Lippmann: "In the light of this monstrous crime, we can see that in a free country . . . unrestrained speech and thought are inherently subversive"[99]), public sanctions are likely to solidify against open appeals for radical change—whether from the Right or the Left. "Socialism," in consequence, is likely to remain "a word on the Devil's tongue," and the day deferred when the "New Left" can speak in its own name. Until it does, however, it cannot truly enter public life, cannot truly be its own master. In this sense, the bombing and the assassination may be viewed as diversions in the developing rhetoric of the "New Left" movement.

Questions for Analysis

1. Griffin says the founders of the "New Left" meant to transcend "our current Cold War rhetoric ('talking tough')." What do the "devil terms" and "god terms" suggest to you of the rhetorical task of the "New Left"? How might substitution of "god terms" for "devil terms" support the "New Left" belief "that means and ends condition each other reciprocally and that the ends must be built into the means"? As you read further, be aware of evidence of the capacity of rhetoric to direct changes in our society.

2. How does Griffin's distinction between a *pro* movement (rhetoric of acceptance) and an *anti* movement (rhetoric of rejection) help to explain the interest of the "New Left" in "peace" and "civil rights" movements? What new tactics did these movements suggest to the "New Left"?

3. How did the new tactics, culminating in the March on Washington in 1963, supplement rhetoric alone in the effort to substitute in the public mind, for example, "peace consciousness" for "war consciousness"? Can you detect the development of new rhetorical "instruments" in the "New Left" movement? Explain.

[98]Kenneth Burke, in "Reflections on the Fate of the Union: Kennedy and After," *The New York Review of Books* (December 26, 1963), p. 10. Other contributors to this symposium include Irving Howe, David Riesman, Paul Goodman, and Norman Mailer.

[99]Walter Lippmann, "Today and Tomorrow," *The Washington Post* (November 26, 1963), quoted in *Current*, No. 45 (January 1964), p. 23.

4. Why is it difficult for Griffin to accept the "physical rhetoric of resistance" as a legitimate rhetorical "instrument" for the "New Left"? Does Wendell Phillips' rationale for agitative speech extend as well to agitative action? Explain.

5. How would you characterize the rhetoric of the "New Left" recounted in Griffin's "Postscript"? Did "agitative language" become "invective"? Is this rhetoric what Griffin meant by "speaking more overtly"? What inures the rhetoric of the "scene" of the "New Left" to impact by the Birmingham "acts" of bombing and assassination?

3

Patterns of Persuasion in the Civil Rights Struggle

Herbert W. Simons

Recently, *Newsweek* magazine published the results of a second comprehensive national poll by Louis Harris on racial attitudes among Americans. For those of us who were disheartened by the apparent white bigotry and Negro hopelessness reflected in the 1963 poll, the 1966 survey was not too encouraging. Among Negroes, 15 per cent say they would join a riot. For every one who believes that the Negro cause has been weakened by Watts-like rioting, two believe that it has been helped. Among whites, 64 per cent insist that Negroes "are asking for more than they are ready for," 43 per cent assert that the Negro wants to "live off the handout" and 70 per cent think that the Negro is "trying to move too fast." These figures for whites, all up from 1963, also suggest an increasing polarization of attitudes between the two races. A further indication of the racial schism is the finding that 73 per cent of the Negroes judge demonstrations to be helpful while almost as many whites (63 per cent) see them as being harmful.

Perhaps as a reflection of these statistics, the Negro leadership stands in what Bayard Rustin has called a "valley of confusion." Divided over whether to shoot, pray or litigate and over whether to remain aligned with white liberals or disaffiliate under the banner of "Black Power," the leadership at least shares the unhappy experience of having been cursed and spat upon by members of both races. They have wisely turned within to reformulate goals and techniques.

Cursory examination suggests that the Negro leadership confronts an essentially rhetorical problem. What combination of leadership style and message appeal is likely to evoke constructive self-effort by slum-dwelling Negroes? What brand of oratorical wizardry can make a weak housing discrimination bill palatable to white senators or reverse the view held by

Herbert W. Simons is Associate Professor of Speech, Temple University.
This article is based on a paper presented at the Pennsylvania Speech Association convention, October 21, 1966. Reprinted by permission from *Today's Speech*, 15(1967), 25–27.

45

three out of five low-income whites polled by Harris that Negroes "smell different?"

Rhetoricians will not find magical answers to these questions in their bag of tricks. But from their storehouse of research and theory, they may at least shed light on the problem. Whatever his personal biases on the issue of civil rights strategy, the rhetorician is obliged to examine the race relations drama professionally, if for no other reason that it may provide an important test of his speech principles. It is in the context of communication theory that an examination of Negro leadership strategies will be undertaken in this paper.

Any communication model must necessarily be abstract and thereby over-simplify. With this qualification stated let us begin our map of contemporary civil rights rhetoric by plotting the principal actors and their corresponding styles of persuasion.

The leaders of the movement have ranged, in Gilbert Cantor's words, from those who "come on sweet and strong like a saint" to those who "come on fierce and ferocious like a Mau Mau." Near the one extreme are the business-suited legalists like Whitney Young and Thurgood Marshall. Near the other extreme are the fast-talking local hipsters of the North like Cecil Moore of Philadelphia and the slow-drawling Snicksters of the South care-fully uniformed in faded overalls. Walking a tight-rope between are the disciples of non-violence such as Rustin, Randolph, and King who themselves disagree over the demonstration tactics and tone.

Alongside this scale of leadership militancy let us classify the methods of Negro influence into two broad categories: (1) peaceful persuasion and (2) coercive persuasion. The former mode of influence is best exemplified by the rhetoric of the courtroom and the conference-table; the embodiment of reason in verbal interaction. But it is also the more strident and impassioned rhetoric of at least the early sit-ins and protest marches; the dramatic appeals to conscience by conservatively attired college students and ministers. If peace-ful persuasion is addressed to the mind and the heart, coercive persuasion is the rhetoric of direct pressure, including the threat or employment of force. It ranges from the more militant exercises in non-violence as in the marches last summer in Chicago to the massive retaliations against white injustice mani-fested by economic boycotts, rent strikes, riots and Black Panther Parties.

Peaceful persuasion is the method rhetoricians understand and character-istically prescribe. Textbooks tell us that persuasion must take place on the listener's terms, that the speaker must adapt to his auditor's needs, wants and values. It is axiomatic, we are told, that effective communication requires a shared frame of reference and a common set of symbols in an atmosphere free from fear and threat. By all of our scholarly yardsticks, the effectiveness of the civil rights advocate *ought* to be a *direct function of his psychological proximity to white audiences.*

In keeping with this postulate, non-militants such as Roy Wilkins, writing in *New York Times Magazine,* argued that the "prime, continuing racial policy looking toward eradication of inequities must be one of winning friends and influencing people among the white majority." Championing the peaceful protest, Wilkins asserted that "this type of demonstration acts as a powerful persuasive upon the national conscience, especially so in race relations where the merest schoolboy knows the Negro has been grievously mistreated."

A Matter of Vulnerability

However successful the method of peaceful persuasion *ought* to be, however much it may seem theoretically that the method is the only effective alternative, the very endurance of other rhetorics is evidence that this is not so. The reasons for this anomaly may be suggested by an expansion of our model to include the audiences addressed by the civil rights leaders.

In the context of a polarized Negro minority seeking change from an equally polarized majority, white audiences can be profitably categorized into (1) "power-vulnerables" and (2) "power-invulnerables." Persons vulnerable to coercive persuasion are those in public or quasi-public positions whose effectiveness depends upon acceptable public postures and whose professional survival may be at stake. They include elected and appointed government officials who may be removed from office or given an unfavorable press, church leaders who are obliged to express socially sanctioned public attitudes, and corporation executives whose businesses are susceptible to loss of income.

"Power-invulnerables" are those who have little or nothing to lose by publicly voicing their prejudices and acting on their self-concerns. They are the mass of white Americans who are largely unaffected by rent strikes and boycotts and who have so far defended their neighborhood sanctuaries or have physically and psychologically withdrawn to the suburbs. The average American may fear riots but he can escape from them. He may or may not approve of boycotts and demonstrations but in either case he is largely unaffected by them. He is subject to legislation but in most cases until now he has been able to circumvent it. Only through communications aimed at a change in his attitudes or through carefully formulated and tightly enforced government policies can his actions be appreciably modified.

If the foregoing analysis of white audiences is accurate, it should help to explain why peaceful and coercive civil rights persuasions have both been able to endure. Each is effective with a different audience and neither is effective with both.

The dilemma facing the Negro leadership is agonizing in the extreme. Should they strike militant postures, they are likely to actuate "power-vulnerables" but at the same time magnify the backlash among those invulnerable to coercive persuasion. Should they plead reasonably and protest peacefully they are likely to win adherents among the white masses but be ineffective with those vulnerable to power.

The reason some Negro leaders have risked a backlash is that in order to wrest changes from whites in public positions they have had to build a sizeable power base among the Negro masses. And in order to secure massive Negro support they have at least had to strike militant poses. In the face of Negro impatience and hostility, a segment of the leadership is convinced that psychological proximity to whites is political suicide. They argue that the more moderate and peaceful the leader's appeals, the more likely he is to find himself a leader without a following.

Some support for this theory is reluctantly provided by opponents of coercive persuasion. Cabinet member Robert C. Weaver has lamented that "today, a publicized spokesman may be the individual who can devise the most militant cry and the leader one who can articulate the most far-out position." And Loundon Wainwright of *Life Magazine* has written:

> ". . . if the recent rioting has illuminated anything, it has illuminated the fact that desperate people, trapped without hope in their ghettos, are beyond listening to promises they've heard many times before. It is this fact which accounts for the precariousness of Negro leadership, especially in the North; on the critical questions of more job opportunity, better housing, fully integrated school systems, the established leaders have not been able to deliver, and numbers of oppressed people might prefer to listen to the 'riot-mongers' who preach hate for 'Whitey.'"

What emerges from this analysis is a pattern of persuasion which defies our communication theorists; one which mobilizes and solidifies a Negro mass with little to lose in order to cajole an entrenched white leadership with a great deal to lose. Rather than adapt to whites by speaking the language of moderacy and restraint, militants have elected to increase their psychological distance from whites by voicing the angry epithets of their followers.

The espousal of a militant position is a necessary condition for obtaining massive Negro support. But this does not mean (in 1966 at least) that the Negro people are ready to accept the more extreme militants. According to the *Newsweek* poll, "black power" advocates Floyd McKissick and Stokely Carmichael are still among the least popular competitors for rank-and-file allegiances.

King and the Vulnerables

As of now it appears that tight-rope walker Martin Luther King is most capable of drawing upon Negro support to effect changes from vulnerable whites. King has managed to be sufficiently militant in his tactics to suit Negroes while at the same time preaching a doctrine of love which has won white sympathies. The Southern Christian Leadership Conference which he heads has not been averse to coercive techniques but it has been buttressed by an ethos of dignity and religiosity which white attackers have found it difficult to combat. King's standing with Negroes was found by Louis Harris to be as high as ever, a respectable 88 per cent.

Whether King maintains his popularity will depend on the results he can achieve. As his movement has spread northward to confront the more sensitive urban issues of open housing and full employment King has found it necessary to risk losing white supporters by relying less on pleading and more on political pressure. And as his philosophy of non-violence has been challenged by "black power" advocates he has had to compete for Negro support by speaking in more strident tones.

In the last analysis the comparative effectiveness of peaceful and coercive methods of persuasion will vary with the issues involved. The former method, for example, will probably be more effective in persuading white teachers to volunteer for work in Negro slums while the latter will probably effect a breakthrough on the issue of housing discrimination. Coercive persuasion can be combatted if whites become sufficiently united in anger to impose their majority power against the Negro. Or it can be rendered unnecessary if belief differences between the two races can be bridged. Negroes are at present unwilling to rely on the good will and compassion of whites. So long as fear of going to hell remains less compelling a motive for "power-vulnerable" whites than loss of income or the threat of removal from office, advocates of coercive persuasion will find enthusiastic supporters.

Questions for Analysis

1. On what basis might Negroes conclude that "Watts-like rioting" and "demonstrations" are helpful to the cause of civil rights? Why does this confront Negro leadership with "an essentially rhetorical problem"? How does white or institutional response to the civil rights movement further complicate the problem?

2. What makes "textbook" preparation in persuasion adequate for "peaceful" purposes but inadequate for "coercive" purposes? Contrast in some detail the hypothetical failure of "peaceful persuasion" in one situation with its success in another. Do you agree that "peaceful persuasion" and "coercive persuasion" are always mutually exclusive? Explain.

3. How have "audiences addressed by the civil rights leaders" influenced the growth of rhetorics other than "peaceful persuasion"? Why are "militant poses" necessary "to build a sizeable power base among the Negro masses"? What do other reasons Simons cites for the use of "coercive persuasion" suggest to you about the impact of the mass media on the rhetorical approaches of civil rights advocates? How is "psychological proximity" important to the selection of an approach?

4. For civil rights leaders in the moderate tradition of Martin Luther King, Jr. what conflict of "ethics" and "effectiveness" was posed by militant leaders? Compare "pleading" with "more strident tones." What difficulties of ethical distinction does the comparison entail? Does the concept "ethical persuasion" need to be redefined for the civil rights movement? Explain.

5. Simons wrote this article late in 1966. Evaluate the relative effectiveness of peaceful and coercive persuasion since that time. After you read the following article by Burgess, return to this one to consider the timeliness of this proposition: "Coercive persuasion can be combatted if whites become sufficiently united in anger to impose their majority power against the Negro. Or it can be rendered unnecessary if belief differences between the two races can be bridged." Project the future of persuasive trends in the civil rights movement.

4

The Rhetoric of Black Power: A Moral Demand?

Parke G. Burgess

"Black Power" has displaced "Freedom Now" as the most significant symbol of the civil rights movement. "Freedom Now" was a challenge directed primarily at the South; "Black Power" challenges the culture at large, more particularly in the North. The rhetoric of Black Power is a response to a long history of communications between white and black in American culture—finally putting Negro citizens unmistakably on the offensive, stating their claims as citizens and human beings. This change of strategy, however, may be shocking to a large number of Americans accustomed to seeing the Negro on the defensive. The nonviolent rhetoric of Freedom Now continued this trend, while the rhetoric of Black Power clearly reverses it. Thus, many if not most Americans find this new rhetoric abhorrent. They do not like being told, especially by Negroes, that their culture is wrong. As the current retort has it: "This time, they've gone too far!"

Neither the culture at large nor its leadership takes pains to distinguish sharply between the violence of deeds and the violence of words. If the one is threatening and therefore to be discredited and ultimately suppressed, then so is the other. The growing tendency of the culture to respond in this way to the rhetoric of Black Power could spell tragedy for Negro and culture alike. For both now seem bent upon a collision course. If the collision course is to be altered or reversed, then the civic culture may have to alter its strategy so that both parties to the conflict may undertake a different level of talk and action. Essential to such a change, however, is an alternative interpretation of the rhetoric of Black Power.

The apparent necessity for the culture at large and its leadership to answer this rhetoric threat for threat and rejection for rejection, whether in word or deed, hardens responses to the rhetoric of Black Power. This necessity may,

Parke G. Burgess is Assistant Professor of Speech, Dartmouth College.
Reprinted by permission from *Quarterly Journal of Speech*, 54(1968), 122–133.

however, be only apparent. Perhaps Black Power advocates actually do intend to "burn the culture down," to employ the idiom of H. Rap Brown, or to persuade others to do so. The leadership of the culture need not respond in kind, when to do so serves to assign this extreme meaning to the rhetoric of Black Power. By the same token, the President of the United States need not have labelled extreme Black Power advocates "poisonous propagandists."[1] Norman Cousins need not have responded in kind with a harsh editorial entitled "Black Racism" in *Saturday Review* later in the same month; he took pains to call Black Power advocates "violence-prone extremists" and "dangerous fools."[2] If the culture and its leadership choose to respond as if illegitimately attacked, they thereby solidify this particular interpretation of the rhetoric of Black Power as the ground for a battle on the public stage.

The rhetoric of Black Power may be interpreted in another way, however. Perhaps these militant Negro advocates utter not a call to arms but a call for justice, a call uttered outside law and order because they see no recourse within the institutions that prescribe what law and order actually mean for many Negro citizens. The rhetoric of Black Power may be the only strategic choice they have. Nevertheless, behind all the sound and fury of this rhetoric may lie the intention merely to force upon the culture a moral decision.

When the culture does decide to respond one way rather than the other, it will choose the strategy most suitable to its character as a democratic culture. No one, least of all the opponents, will consider an alternative interpretation, however, until convinced that an undesirable collision is all but inevitable without a change of course. Nor will anyone be convinced of this grave risk unless he first understands the major forces comprising the cultural situation from which the conflict emerges, nor until he also understands how the rhetoric of Black Power necessarily causes the conflict to reach crisis proportions the moment it enters upon the public stage. Without the Black Power advocate the clear and present danger would not exist, yet the central issue of the crisis exists whether he proclaims it or not. Examination of the trends of the conflict will reveal why he apparently *must* proclaim it; this is the first task. Examination of the crisis will reveal what happens when he *does* proclaim it; this is the second task. The final task is to offer a reinterpretation of the rhetoric of Black Power as the basis for a solution that may reverse the collision course and allow the democratic culture to be true to itself.

The three forces most directly responsible for the civil rights crisis are: the issue at the heart of the crisis, the traditional strategy of the culture as applied to this particular crisis, and the strategy of the Negro advocate. All of these forces emanate from the political context which accords each its respective nature and power. Riots, demonstrations, and volatile talk occur in all countries. In the United States, however, these indicators of crisis have a special meaning because of the democratic culture. The three major forces shaping

---

[1]*Time*, XC (September 22, 1967), 23.
[2]Norman Cousins, "Black Racism," *Saturday Review* (September 27, 1967), 34.

the crisis can be understood only after a brief digression into the fundamental nature of the democratic civil culture, its traditional profession of faith, its institutional commitments, and its understandable preference for consensus rather than conflict.

In a brilliant study of comparative democratic politics, Almond and Verba point out that a democratic civil culture functions efficiently only when relatively free from divisive conflict and strife.[3] Intense and persisting dissension over substantive issues on a culture-wide scale can be mortal. Consequently, citizens of the democratic culture tend to remain uninvolved in the decision-making process during stable periods, and, although always potentially active, they tend to become actively involved only when their interests are threatened. The tension between involvement and noninvolvement underlying normal operations of the civic culture allows its institutions to work with relative efficiency in practice, while restrained from excesses by an ideal of potential activism and involvement.

When a crisis such as the present one arises, however, the balance of tension between activity and passivity is affected. Activism heightens the conflict and a breakdown of efficient operations may threaten the normal functioning of the civic culture. Under such circumstances, the leadership and the culture at large will seek to redress the balance as quickly as possible and at minimal cost to the healthy functioning of the culture. The normal balance will be restored by satisfying the demands of those most active or by compromise. When compromise is impossible, however, and demands are not satisfied, activity may become so intense and widespread that virtually no one remains passive. In this extreme, the crisis can provoke violence, even civil war, not an unknown occurrence in American experience.

While over-activity is a sign of crisis in a democratic culture, an abundant source of crisis is the necessary tension between freedom and order. The democratic civic culture professes a fundamental moral commitment to the freedom of self-determination (liberty, equality before the law, equality of opportunity) without which it is not democratic. Yet the culture is also committed to the processes, procedures, and institutions that protect this ideal and actually permit its realization in everyday life; it is committed to "business as usual." The civic culture must maintain a balance between these two commitments—freedom and order—since a marked imbalance toward one would threaten the other, as occurs in anarchy (freedom without order) and tyranny (order without freedom). Therefore, a threat to either commitment can induce a crisis, as an attempt to restore the customary balance.

A peculiar tendency apparent in American political tradition poses dangers when crises occur; for the culture may then pay a price for its enthusiasm for consensus and tranquility. The critical balance between freedom and order,

[3]Gabriel A. Almond and Sidney Verba, *The Civic Culture: Political Attitudes and Democracy in Five Countries* (Boston, 1965), Chapter XIII, especially pp. 344–356. Only the notion of balance between activity and passivity is taken directly from their study, which would consider the balance between freedom and order a function of several factors.

between activity and passivity appears weighted clearly in the direction of order and passivity even in normal, stable times. The basic freedoms at the moral foundation of the culture are themselves actually realized for most citizens within the institutions and processes by which "business as usual" is conducted; they become submerged there, and they are unconsciously identified with the system itself. As Louis Hartz indicates, a nation "born free" has little need to make an issue of freedom;[4] consequently, citizens can afford to forget about freedom during daily operations of the culture. This imbalance of tensions is preferred also because most citizens have benefitted greatly from "business as usual": "They never had it so good!" As a result, they have an understandable commitment to order over freedom, and they may easily lose sight of the dependence of the system of order itself upon the democratic commitment to freedom as well as to order.

In normal times, any threat to individual freedom and activity is usually removed by traditional processes and procedures, and no crisis arises. Even in times of war, the external threat to the civic culture as a whole is believed to be so great that only extreme libertarians worry about the limits placed upon freedom, and again crises are normally avoided. "Business as usual" functions efficiently throughout the culture when the threat to freedom is relatively localized or when it is aimed at the survival of the culture itself. However, when the threat is no longer localized and does not yet endanger the survival of the culture as a whole, the potential for internal crisis arises. The civil rights conflict is a classic, if not historic, case. A minority suffers restriction of freedom and becomes excessively active in order to counteract the complacency, or even the aggressive opposition, of those citizens who may feel that the freedom of other citizens is expendable. A crisis may be about to be born.

The movement of the culture in relation to such crisis should be clear and understandable. The strategy that is natural and traditional to the democratic civic culture emerges, by extension, when a widespread and intense crisis threatens to upset the preferred balance of tensions. The culture at large and its leadership, in particular, tend to insist upon an increased emphasis on order and passivity so as to restrict freedom and activity and consequently to return to the required state of equilibrium and tranquility. Having no other option in the face of what may be or may become a threat to its existence, the civic culture necessarily utilizes its traditional strategy to suppress the threat. Yet it may be unable to exercise this option against such a threat without also threatening its character as a democratic culture.

From the point of view of many Negro citizens, the character of the civic culture may be precisely what is at stake in the civil rights crisis. These citizens appear to seek what they have not been given, what they cannot actually take, and yet what the democratic culture, being democratic, cannot in good faith deny them: self-determination as citizens and human beings. Negroes do not

---

[4]Louis Hartz, *The Liberal Tradition in America* (New York, 1955), Chapter II, *passim*.

ask that the basic system be altered or that something new be added to it; they cannot be identified, on this issue, with the far left or the far right. Negro citizens are in dead-center. Thus, the substantive issue dividing them from the culture at large is its denial of their right to self-determination. To resolve the issue, the culture need only reverse its denial. The issue remains unresolved, however, and worse, the crisis appears to intensify despite recent progress in civil rights reform.

How can this be? There is no controversy about the inconsistency in affirming the democratic commitment while denying its full application to Negroes, nor about the necessity to reverse this denial if the culture is to be true to itself. Why, then, does the culture not do in its many public acts what it has recently and repeatedly admitted in its public rhetoric that it must do? This is a question that long perplexed traditional civil rights advocates and framed the rationale for the rhetoric of Freedom Now, with its moral and legal emphasis upon the democratic commitment.

The inescapable conclusion is that the issue actually does not lie in the *fact* of the denial but in the *reason* for the denial. Since nearly everyone admits that the denial is morally illegitimate, then the continued denial appears to suggest that the culture does not wish to be true to itself. Yet, since the denial is not generally and systematically applied to any other group as it is to Negroes, then it is not a widespread denial of the democratic commitment itself, but only a denial of its application to Negro citizens.

Why the special treatment? The reason for the denial is revealed to be racist, and the true issue of the crisis becomes the racist moral issue. Both appear to posit the uniqueness of the Negro citizen as justification for denying him the right to self-determination. Is this justification legitimate? It is sometimes legitimate for the democratic culture to affirm its commitment to freedom and yet to deny freedom to individuals when the denial is justified, for example with regard to aliens and some criminals; such individuals are not "citizens." However, since Negroes must certainly be considered "citizens," then the only ground on which the denial could be based is that these "citizens" are Negroes. The denial is racist and its justification is illegitimate.

The core of the moral issue, then, is not the substantive and legalistic issue of self-determination for Negro citizens, nor even the moral fact of the culture's denial, but rather the racist issue that divides the culture at large from its Negro citizens. The expression of the issue in terms of self-determination and civil rights correctly denotes its substantive content in relation to the democratic tradition of the civic culture and thereby suggests steps to be taken to correct the denial once the culture decides to move fully in that direction. To express the issue in racist moral terms, however, denotes that the culture may not yet have decided to move fully in that direction, on racist grounds.

No other explanation of the conflict appears to reveal why the civic culture has moved so slowly to reverse its denial to Negro citizens, nor why the crisis harbors such intensity of feeling and divisiveness of purpose. Thus, the moral issue of race may be considered the engine that drives culture and Negro advocate alike to a choice of strategy that is likely to result in a collision course.

During the earlier, civil rights stage of the conflict, the dominant leadership of the culture showed an awareness, as it still does, of the substantive moral contradiction and of the necessity to remove it. The leadership and many citizens consequently realized their responsibility to redress the imbalance of tension between order and freedom and to move in the direction of greater freedom and equality for Negroes. Seen as a civil rights crisis of relatively limited proportions, a proportionately limited application of traditional strategy appeared effectively to maintain the normal balance of tensions. It did so, however, at cost to some citizens and institutions (primarily in the South) and at the cost of limited gains for Negro citizens. These limited gains were consistent with the limited strategy and aims of traditional civil rights advocates and the limited willingness of citizens and institutions to respond to their strategy and to the strategy of the culture. One cannot deny, however, that the strategies of the Negro advocate and the civic culture worked more or less in harmony to achieve gains, however limited, under the aegis of the civil rights movement.

A shift in the issue can bring only a shift in the use and effectiveness of traditional strategy. Once Negro advocates move from the courts, the city halls, and other sanctioned centers of decision into the streets, or, with fiery words, upon the public platform, the response of the culture at large and of its leadership also shifts. The threat posed is perceived by the culture to be out of all proportion to the issue of the crisis, when the culture and its leadership are either unable or unwilling to recognize that the issue has shifted from civil rights to race. Thus, the culture may fail to realize that its traditional strategy, so recently effective, now becomes paradoxically ineffective.

The need to apply the strategy in a form less in harmony with Negro demands now increases and yet makes its application self-defeating, as more and more citizens and institutions become active. Citizens with racist inclinations who are especially threatened by the new turn of events will seek to employ the strategy to promote whatever policy or action is likely to minimize the threat to themselves. They will utilize any part of the system of order that tends, by tradition, to be racist in its structure or composition. They will press their denial of self-determination for Negro citizens on pragmatic rather than on moral grounds, unless they can find moral grounds having no obvious relationship to racism. They have nothing to lose and perhaps everything to gain by translating a personal threat to themselves into a crisis perceived by other citizens as a threat to the culture at large. The culture responds, in turn, with insistence upon order; it becomes overly acquiescent to "white backlash;" it moves forthrightly to resolve a crisis provoked by racism in the first place.

Greatly aggravated by the issue and, indirectly, by its effects upon incipiently racist citizens, the entire culture becomes more and more embroiled. Strong pressures within the culture to correct the denial of self-determination to Negro citizens give way to overriding pressure to redress the new imbalance of tensions. The national leadership in politics and other areas of decision hardens its attitude. This very result was most noticeable, for instance, after the riots of 1967. Even highly respected Negro civil rights leaders, to say nothing of nearly all other leaders, had to disown Black Power "extremists" and, of course, had to reject rioting in no uncertain terms, insisting with the rest of leadership upon a return to law and order. Such reactions are not completely unjustified under the circumstances, but they can only postpone meeting the justified moral demands of Negro citizens. More important, however, the crisis appears more intense and widespread than ever, affected more positively by changes of season than by application of traditional strategy.

The racist, moral issue also creates a strategic paradox for the Negro advocate because of his peculiar relation to the culture as he advances his claim for self-determination. He does not advance it as worker, Democrat, intellectual, baseball player, or musician, but simply as a Negro. He cannot "pass" for anything else, being substantively a marked man. To the extent he is seen by others essentially as a Negro, he cannot be seen as are other citizens within the civic culture, as citizens "without respect to race, creed, or national origin."

It is quite normal for an advocate in the midst of crisis to be identified with his cause and to suffer the consequences, for good or ill. Yet he is rarely so completely identified with his cause that he cannot rise above it or leave it behind him and "return to private life." The situation of the Negro advocate is quite different and perhaps painfully abnormal. He does not suffer the consequences by reason of his identification with his cause but by reason of the fact that his cause is himself. He cannot simply leave his cause and "return to private life," since even when he returns he remains identified as a Negro.

The paradox he faces applies also to his relation to the claim he advances. The denial of the right to self-determination applies to him no matter what he attempts to *do* (it is the "door to other doors") and *because* of what he *is*. Unable to dodge the fact that he is essentially a Negro, he can hardly avoid the conclusion that must confront him regarding his advocacy: The right he demands is the one he must be given in order to "belong" to the culture at all, and he can be given it *only as a Negro*.

When considered in the light of the issue of the crisis and of the strategy employed by the culture to resolve it, the strategic paradox of the Negro advocate becomes clear. His only available strategic alternative is to advance his claim in the way least likely to win acceptance in a culture apparently "designed" to suppress precisely the kind of conflict this crisis and his advocacy are destined to produce. Being unable to avoid the racist implications of his advocacy, he can neither withdraw nor succeed. Here may lie the tragic irony of the rhetoric of Black Power and its potential meaning to the culture at large. The unavoidable issue in the crisis demands unavoidably that the Negro advocate press that issue, even in the face of violence.

Analysis of the historical and cultural situation reveals that the stage is set for the rhetoric of Black Power to make its entrance and to tip the balance in the direction of a collision course. This rhetoric forces the issue and creates the strategic paradox for advocate and culture alike. No rhetoric could be more provocative in teasing out the inner logic of the moral crisis and the culture's strategy to resolve it. The reason is simple. The rhetoric of Black Power is framed as if it were aimed precisely at these ends; it is a direct response to the civic culture. Yet this particular way of responding is historically inconceivable without the movement that preceded it, for the rhetoric of Black Power is also an answer to the rhetoric of Freedom Now.

The civil rights movement has addressed the traditional rhetoric of the civic culture. Despite some progress before 1954 (in the armed forces, for example), and despite increasing interest and support by many white citizens since then, the culture at large has continued to say *No* to its Negro citizens in many systematic ways. The movement sought to change this response. In the early 1960's it scored some success under the banner of Freedom Now with its "non-violent" demonstrations and compelling moral tone. The culture's answer to this plea was complex and ambiguous. In the South it answered *Yes*, but perhaps only because to answer *No* to Martin Luther King would clearly have been to answer *Yes* to George Wallace and Paul Johnson. And who is to say that the violent reactions of some Southerners did not actually command stage-center? For example, President Johnson's "historic" Voting Rights Speech of 1965 came only after the tragedy of Selma. The rhetoric of Freedom Now was never persuasive in the North, where even Martin Luther King was stopped by "the white power structure," most notably in Chicago. Freedom Now appealed to the clear-cut legal issues in the South which were easily accommodated by "business as usual." Confronted by the more subtle machinations of the culture at large, this rhetoric seemed to get a response to which Negro citizens had long been accustomed: promises, delays, and piecemeal tokens could only be taken now as an actual denial.

King has said, with some pain, that the very success of the rhetoric of Freedom Now, the "positive gains" it in part produced, only made matters worse.[5] This rhetoric was most effective in raising the hopes and expectations of Negro citizens. When hopes and expectations were not realized, however, they seemed cynically to produce worse conditions, especially in Northern ghettos.

Tempers were thereby sensitized for a new level of talk that could not be dodged, talk that would demand rather than plead, that would insist that the civic culture honor its commitment to Negro citizens—or else. The ground was laid for the militant rhetoric of Black Power, a rhetoric that voiced its demand on a tonal scale somewhere between Martin Luther King and Malcolm X. It had learned its lessons from both men, in a school built by the culture itself.

The rhetoric of Black Power acknowledges what King's rhetoric did not.

[5]Andrew Kopkind, "Soul Power," *The New York Review of Books*, Vol. IX, No. 3, 3. A review of King's book, *Where Do We Go From Here: Chags* [Sic] *or Community?*

Unlike King's rhetoric, Black Power denies that a moral plea to the democratic conscience would gain a commensurate moral response. Except in the South, King was wrong. The rhetoric of Black Power reveals that King's strategy, although logically correct, was rhetorically inadequate. Logically speaking, a clearly moral issue demands a clearly moral strategy in keeping with the democratic traditions of the civic culture. Since discrimination is itself contrary to those traditions, the logical result of this strategy, its ultimate moral demand, would be integration as the true measure of equality and freedom. What Black Power advocates have realized (due in part to King's experience) are the rhetorical realities that made the strategy inadequate. King missed the gravity of the tension within the American tradition, exacerbated by his own efforts, between "business as usual" and the commitment to self-determination. By attempting to operate within that tradition, moreover, he necessarily underemphasized the uniqueness of the Negro, as a Negro, within the same tradition; he ignored the specifically racial conflict, the racist core of the moral crisis.

The rhetoric of Black Power is more perceptive and "corrects" both errors. It acknowledges, first, that America actually has no moral conscience in the face of a threat to its "traditions," which means that only power can meet entrenched power, racist or not. It acknowledges, secondly, that the culture now confronts the Negro not as a human being or citizen-minus-rights, but as a Negro who is not yet regarded by the culture as a citizen or a human being *because* he is a Negro. This rhetoric brings to the surface and loudly proclaims what heretofore had been fearfully hidden and yet silently worked its effects. It loudly confronts the racist moral conflict.

The answer to white power is Black Power—to white racism, black racism. But this usage of the term "black racism" must be clearly distinguished from its earlier usage by some American Negro citizens. The Black Power movement has its roots in a racist perception of cultural reality no less than the Black Muslim movement, for example. Yet "Black Power" is not merely a concept which reflects these realities nor a rallying symbol addressed to Negroes alone in order to unite them; if it were merely these, this movement would be indistinguishable from that of the Black Muslims. Unlike the idiom of the Black Muslims, however, the rhetoric of Black Power is significantly addressing the civic culture no less than Freedom Now did. It speaks directly to that culture, "courting" its acceptance; it does not withdraw into its own house, pulling down the blinds, absolutely refusing to communicate with the outside world, having "lost its suit." On the other hand, to continue the metaphor, it cannot in the nature of its case win acceptance by singing romantic songs and parading before the house of the beloved.

Black Power therefore signifies a rhetorical movement which seeks entrance into the hallowed and rich house of the American culture, *but on its own terms and by means which the culture understands and accepts*. It is ironic indeed that its terms are identical with those of the American promise (self-determination with no strings attached), and perhaps still more ironic that the means it employs, including the whole strategy of black racism, so precisely portray the means used against the Negro citizen, then and now. In these facts lie the tragic justice and sadness of the rhetoric of Black Power.

The powerful logic of this rhetoric originates from a white racist culture and is apparently forced upon black citizens against their deepest desires and better judgment by the naked and subtle power of that culture. Its adoption represents a last-ditch effort by these citizens to wrest final affirmation from generations of denial. The poignant irony of this rhetoric is revealed in the different ways it seems to stand the logic of the civic culture on its own head, taking its racist attitudes with deadly seriousness.

Contradicting its democratic, procedural ideal, the civic culture regards the Negro citizen not for what he can *do,* but for what he *is,* regardless of what he can do. He is regarded as substance. The rhetoric of Black Power begins from this historic fact and *responds* as substance. Regarding the Negro citizen essentially for his difference as substance, the culture segregates him on this basis, drawing procedural and organizational lines about him—lines he can seldom cross. The separatist rhetoric of Black Power accepts this language and *responds* as substance thus segregated. Having effectually prevented his access to the procedural pursuit of happiness on substantive grounds, America yet goads the Negro citizen in countless ways to get his, as everyone else gets theirs. Again taking America to mean what it says, Black Power demands for the Negro what he has been promised and threatens to get it by the only means America has left it—"by any means necessary." Especially trying to some Negroes, and clearly one of the tragedies of the ghetto riots, is this reduction of the American promise and the Negro answer to such crass, materialistic terms. It is as if Black Power advocates had once again captured and turned against itself one of the truisms of the civic culture—the democratic commitment to self-determination becomes an acquisitive and materialistic commitment to self-interest.

This is the ruthless but nevertheless valid logic of Black Power advocates. Its naked clarity and brutal honesty put the civic culture in an unenviable position. Like the honest parent caught stealing from his child's piggy bank, what does he do when the child calls him a liar and throws the bank through the nearest picture window out of disappointment and anger? The normal response is to redress the balance by resorting to "business as usual" now clearly divorced from its moral foundation.

This response means to Negro advocates the use of traditional methods of establishing order and equilibrium, including force. It means "positive gains" only when there is token resistance against them, or, contrary to the rhetoric of the culture, when Negro demands for their achievement are violent in the extreme. Traditional strategy is interpreted as an essentially white racist response to Negro demands and thus provokes an increased hardening of a black racist response on the part of Negro citizens. The rhetoric of militant racism becomes more justified than ever.

Charging that the culture is racist and that it is moved by nothing but sheer power, the culture responds accordingly. As Norman Cousins observes, "When Negroes act like Ku Klux Klanners, they must be treated like Ku Klux Klanners."[6] Racism and power become the idiom of battle on both sides. Whatever the vocabulary of the culture may be, it is likely to be pregnant with the undertones and overtones of power, of force, of violence. And the intended target will be clear enough and often justifiable. As this response to the crisis intensifies, the full effect will be for the culture to consider Black Power advocacy in all its forms as violent, reprehensible, and un-American, and for Negroes to consider responses to it as but further evidence of the racist attitudes and rhetoric of the civic culture.

Such is the collision course predetermined by the paradoxical logic of both sides. By its own terms, this logic denies alternative interpretation and response. It would appear also to have inevitable and unavoidably harmful consequences for the civic culture: Citizens who fear increased violence and even incipient revolution may have good reason for their fears. To avoid these consequences would demand a change in course derived from a new strategy having a different logic. It would demand a reinterpretation of the rhetoric of Black Power and a commensurate response on the part of the culture at large and its Negro citizens.

The dialectic of racism and power can be transcended only by refusal to respond to the rhetoric of Black Power as if it were a call to battle. The civic culture can respond instead at a level more in keeping with the moral nature of the crisis. It can respond as if this rhetoric were a call for a just moral decision. Such a response appears neither artificial nor utopian; it may be more realistic than the present one and is certainly more just. The rapier-like logic of the rhetoric of Black Power and the elementary justice that beckons from beneath it leave no doubt that the men who talk this way mean what they say and that their appeal will probably convert an increasing number of Negro citizens in the future, for the appeal is largely to Negroes of the same mind who share the tragic lack of alternative. Beneath the call to arms may be a cry for justice and community, as beneath the anger may be disappointment and disillusion. The dominant leadership and particularly the mass media of the culture can respond to what lies beneath and cease to respond to what shouts on the surface.

This new response to the rhetoric of Black Power would require two admissions on the part of the culture and its leadership. Both would admit that the immoral racist denial constitutes the core of the present crisis. Both would admit that this denial offers adequate moral justification for the rhetoric of Black Power. These admissions would require, as a result, that the civic culture return unequivocally to its moral foundation as a democratic culture and meet there, at its own roots, the source of this crisis. In this way, the

[6]Cousins, "Black Racism," p. 34.

language of racism and power would be transcended through translation into the nonracist language of the democratic commitment. Such a shift in basic interpretation would call for a marked shift in strategy, and would portend different consequences for the civic culture and for its Negro citizens.

The civic culture would then repudiate traditional strategy in response to just Negro demands. The paradoxical effect of that strategy is that its movement toward order and away from freedom, as against Negro citizens, can only further exacerbate the crisis it seeks to forestall. Moreover, the trend of that strategy is typically to encourage greater and greater separation of institutional response from the democratic base of the civil culture. A strategy of moral commitment would reverse the trend: for the function of the new strategy would be to infuse institutional responses with the moral quality appropriate to them as institutions within the democratic culture.

By adopting the strategy of moral commitment the civic culture would acknowledge that racism of any kind is clearly immoral and therefore not to be recognized as grounds for behavior or policy. It can only do this if it accepts the black racist contention regarding the presence of, and absolute lack of moral justification for, white racism in the culture itself. The refusal to tolerate a racist justification would not be a refusal to admit its existence. On the contrary, the language of democratic morality could assert its power and its relevance exactly here: Standing firmly on moral grounds, as the traditional strategy seldom can, it would be unequivocal in its demands of all citizens precisely at those points where its traditional form equivocates in the interest of "business as usual."

Further consequences would, of course, ensue. Application of the new strategy would initially intensify the crisis and not quickly resolve it. To admit and unequivocally to confront the presence of white racism within the culture would be to oppose a real force that cannot be ignored or averted. Citizens with this cultural malady will indeed have cause for alarm. They can be expected to continue to move for order and to intensify the crisis, but with a fervor magnified to meet what would be for the first time, an open assault upon them by the civic culture. Another consequence of repudiating traditional strategy in order to arrest tensions would result in the civic culture recalling that strategy, as it were, but in a significantly different way. The culture must maintain itself and it can do so only by pressing for order and passivity over freedom and activity. The significant difference of this reapplication of old strategy would be its different target. The price to be exacted as a result of the application of institutional power and consequent loss of freedom would be paid by those who truly cause the racist crisis in the first place, and not by those whose civil rights and freedom have been unjustly withheld.

Yet even white racists might then expect better treatment under a strategy of moral commitment than Negro citizens often receive at present, especially with regard to violence. Under present strategy, the leadership of the culture often appears open to the charge that it considers violent acts of Negroes to be particularly reprehensible and therefore demanding excessively punitive suppression. Insofar as spokesmen of the new strategy sense the serious democratic commitment at stake in the racial crisis, however, any citizens continuing to respond violently in word or deed are more likely to be considered as misguided citizens, whatever their race, than as mere objects of ruthless "justice." The distinction is important, for it entails a mood and a manner more suitable to the democratic tradition and certainly more conducive to minimal conflict at a time when punitive action may be required.

Fully implemented, the new strategy would unequivocally commit the culture at large to the democratic goals formerly sought by the civil rights movement and by black separatist citizens not widely represented within that movement. It would eliminate the need for the movement to advance minority claims against the balance of the civic culture. It would also eliminate the *raison d'etre* of black separatists, including Black Power advocates. But the goal imposed upon the vast majority of citizens by the strategy of democratic commitment would be neither integration nor conformity to white demands. The goal would be self-determination for Negro citizens, consistent with the cultural realities that actually confront them.

A reinterpretation of the volatile rhetoric of Black Power may offer the democratic culture a strategic alternative to violent confrontation and therefore a more desirable way to resolve the present crisis. If interpreted as calling America to its moral self, then this rhetoric forces upon America the acknowledgment that a racist moral conflict lies at the core of the crisis. The old rhetoric of "business as usual" loses its credibility. The new rhetoric of democratic commitment arises to meet the rhetoric of violence that must be repudiated and transcended so that the culture can be true to itself and to all of its citizens. From the irony of this tragedy, the culture may derive historic opportunity.

Questions for Analysis

1. What does Burgess cite as a cultural problem of interpreting the rhetoric of Black Power? How is the problem related to Simons' discussion of "power-vulnerables" and "power-invulnerables"?

2. Give evidence to defend or dismiss Burgess' suggestion that "The rhetoric of Black Power may be the only strategic choice they [militant Negro advocates] have." Do you agree that the very fact of the rhetoric of Black Power (or of any "overactive" rhetoric) means crisis in a "democratic civic culture"? Explain.

3. In the rhetoric of the civil rights movement, Burgess observes, the displacement of "Freedom Now" by "Black Power" confirms the issue of the day to be not

the *fact* of denial of Negro rights but the *reason* for denial. How does this conclusion upset the balance in a democratic culture between "self-determination" and "business as usual"? How does Burgess interpret this imbalance to mean the issue now is racist, not substantive or legalistic?

4. What changes in rhetorical strategy have been dictated by the new labelling of this issue? What has made it impossible for the Negro to "avoid the racist implications of his advocacy"? How has recognition of the racist issue rendered the "Freedom Now" appeal "logically correct" but "rhetorically inadequate"?

5. Is it fair to say that the rhetoric of Black Power has "raised the ante" for the response of the culture at large because the Negro must respond as he *is* (black), not as what he *does*, and the culture at large must choose to respond as it *is* (white)? What does Burgess suggest as an alternative cultural response? How might racist rhetoric be transcended and the morality of institutional, rather than rhetorical, responses revived?

5

Student Protests: From Dissent to Defiance?

Terry F. Lunsford

As the organizers of this session doubtless knew, there is a wide consensus on American campuses today that the tone and character of student protest has changed, subtly but dramatically, in the past several years and months. I think that the consensus is reflected in fact. Student protests have changed. They are more militant, more frequent, occur on more campuses, cover more issues, and involve more students directly than they did several years ago. There is more threatened or actual disruption of classes and administration. More incidents of property damage occur in the course of protests. More officials of colleges, of the Dow Chemical Company, and of the armed forces have been detained by crowds, and for longer periods. More public invective has been hurled. More conviction is expressed that the students' causes are just, more "moral statements" of draft refusal, and of complicity with civil disobedients, have been registered. More flashes of violence have occurred, started by student protestors, by anti-protestors, or by the police. Outside police have more frequently and more quickly been called into campuses. Arrests and indictments have increased. And the punitive use of force by police, to disperse crowds and "teach lessons" to protestors, has risen sharply.

In short, there has been escalation and sophistication of tactics by both protestors and official authorities in the student-protest scene. That scene presents a far graver tableau today than it did a few years ago, when the so-called "Berkeley riots" of the almost entirely non-violent Free Speech Movement captured the national attention.

Terry F. Lunsford is Associate Specialist, Center for Research and Development in Higher Education, University of California, Berkeley.

This is a transcript of a speech given at a sectional meeting of the Twenty-Third Annual National Conference on Higher Education, March 4, 1968. Reprinted by permission of the American Association for Higher Education, a department of the National Education Association, from a press release copy.

There is little agreement on all of the reasons why this is so. Some observers point to the world-wide prevalence of student political demonstrations, in many types of cultures and political systems, and suggest that forces still undescribed lie at their roots. What one professor calls an extensive "psyching-out literature" has grown up in this country, devoted to analyzing the social backgrounds and personality characteristics of student activists, for clues to the sources of their activism. Still other observers seek some of the causes in the issues about which the students themselves say they are protesting.

In this context, it is clear that student protest is intimately related to issues that go far beyond the college or university campus: the war, racial inequalities, poverty, a bureaucratized society. Of these, the major issue, of course, is the war. Most of the recent campus protests have been directed at the makers of napalm, at the armed forces' recruiters, and at Selective Service induction stations. As rising military manpower demands bring the draft closer to college campuses, and hundreds of young men come face to face with the prospect of fighting and dying in a war they believe to be both useless and immoral, this issue may yet become even more explosive. But fast increasing in militancy and bitterness are black students' determined attempts to force upon the white society's attention the countless inequities to which blacks still are subject in this country.

A minority of recent student demonstrations has turned on rules of campus conduct, housing regulations, and other local issues.

It is natural to wonder why: Why are protests increasing? But I should like to suggest that it may be more revealing at this point to ask the obverse question: Why should the student protest *not* increase, *not* toughen their resistance? If they should not, it is for a number of reasons that *might* be given:

—It is not because their causes are unjust, or trivial, or are problems that are rapidly being solved. Instead, I suggest that student activists in this country have the clear "moral advantage" in their opposition to the established society —and that society is forced generally to admit it. The major targets of student attack—war, racism, poverty, bureaucracy—all are widely acknowledged, by the most influential opinion-makers and by broad segments of the society, to be serious problems that require major correctives. But few such correctives are in sight, and that also is widely admitted.

—It is not because the students are personally unaffected, and so should leave these matters to others concerned. Blacks, draft-age students, relatives and friends of ghetto-dwellers, human units in bureaucratic processing: all are plentifully represented among student protestors. Indeed, if World War III results from our present foreign policy, all of us will be "affected."

—It is not because law-breaking is contrary to American traditions, or unobservable in "respectable" adult society. From the flagrant illegalities of Southern race relations and the scandal of General Electric's executive price-fixing to the legend of Prohibition and the current fraud of narcotics-law enforcement, U.S. students have many reasons for seeing the law not as a final good or a blind goddess, but as a variable and manipulable instrument of group purposes. In the tradition of Henry David Thoreau and the world-wide legend of Gandhi, these same students find powerful precedents for placing moral law higher than the law of the state, when personal conviction demands it.

—It is not because the U.S. is a non-violent culture. The unparalleled violence of Hiroshima and Nagasaki, the bombings and napalm of our Vietnam effort, the daily diet of television brutalities, the obsession with a "sixgun" version of our frontier heritage, the murders of non-violent civil-rights workers in the South, the venom of Northern urban residents and police against peaceful demonstration marches—these things and many more provide an ample American tradition of violent "settlement" for disputes, so that one wonders how so much passionate student energy has avoided more destructive expression in the present crisis.

—It is not because the leaders of nation and campus have been truthful and worthy of the "trust" for which they long. News manipulation, the "credibility gap," the exposure of secret spying in the U-2, Bay of Pigs, and numerous other CIA affairs, have all been well publicized on the national and international scene. On the campus, official double-talk, outright public untruths, and transparent fictions of impartial benevolence have marked many a student-administration conflict.

—Finally, it is not because student protests have been ineffective in bringing responses from campus officials. Indeed, it is the clear lesson from most of the student-protest incidents on American campuses that only when student activists have pushed, hard and insistently, have significant gains been won—for campus political expression, for security of student records from government investigators, for student participation in campus governance, for re-examination of racially discriminatory practices, for procedural regularity in student discipline, and for a host of other student goals.

In other words, there are few or no *positive* reasons why students should relax their activism, as an unnecessary or futile effort. Instead, a number of *negative* reasons are usually given, to advise more student quietism on political fronts. Students are told that they will encourage "anarchy" by their civil disobedience, or social chaos by moving from "disagreement" to "dissent." They are warned to be more moderate lest they invite a "backlash" from the political right, and a new era of political witch-hunting in American life. They are told that they violate all canons of polite discussion, ignore good manners, and disrupt others' rights to go their own ways, to drive freely through the streets, to attend their classes undisturbed, or to discuss employment with whatever companies they wish.

Each of these negative responses represents a reasonable, legitimate viewpoint, and suggests a danger in the present climate of confrontation and hostility. Whether some of these objections are over-drawn (such as the image of impending "anarchy") or trivial (such as the inconvenience to a motorist when a street is blocked by protestors) is part of an argument in which reasonable men can engage. At the level of the "principles" involved, I believe that subordinating freedom of expression to "higher values," as some student activists are ready to do today, poses one of the most difficult problems for our political and educational future. But that is not because expression in this country is unqualifiedly free or because this abstract right is not greatly sullied by the realities of a social process which forbids dissenters access to many avenues of expression unless they create sensational "news" events by disruption, nudity, or exaggerated threats. The danger is, rather, that dissenters' subordination of free expression will give moral credence to a further round of restrictions on expression by the less idealistic groups in society.

Short of such a punitive "backlash" supported by large segments of the society, such "negative" responses as I have described are understandable when forceful protests threaten much of the established order. But there is an overriding problem in relying exclusively on negative responses to principled civil protest: It leaves the protestor in command of the moral heights, and provides him with intellectual and emotional ammunition to continue his assault. This, I suggest, is the basic paralysis of America today: It is not dissent or disruption or law-breaking or violence *per se* that are our problem. It is moral and political and intellectual confusion within the "adult" society which knows in its own heart that the war and racism and poverty are here, and serious, and wrong—but which cannot find ways even of stemming their tide, much less eliminating them.

In precisely such a situation of moral uncertainty and frustration, I believe, those who have power and responsibility are strongly tempted to cover their uncertainty by a strong and "authoritative response" to those who intensify the frustration. Thus we are in grave danger that much of "adult" society, precisely because of its own doubts and frustrations, will use the few incidents of student violence, property damage, or personal inconvenience as a moral basis for severe repressive measures against unpopular youthful dissent generally. There is evidence that this is happening already, in the police "sweeps" of the San Francisco Haight-Ashbury district, in the use of "punitive" force by police (now being investigated on several campuses), in the "anticipation" of riots by police where others see only peaceful protest, and in more sophisticated measures—such as the selective expulsion and imprisonment of "polical leaders" among students and other dissenting groups.

Some ask "But what has this to do with the campus? The academic world is this country's stronghold of liberal and humanitarian values, of concern with ideas and ideals. We are suffering punishment from student protestors not for our own sins but for those of the larger society, in which we actually are the young idealists' greatest allies." This is perhaps the dominant response that I hear from academic people with whom I have talked recently about the major issues of protest—this, and a pervasive wish (amounting to an operational assumption) that the protest will soon stop, go away, and leave us all in peace to do our interesting and vitally important work. Unfortunately, few careful observers of the student scene believe that the protests are likely to go away soon. Certainly they will not unless severe repressions occur or until, on the other hand, they are better understood and some of the issues they address have been faced.

Such an understanding, I believe, must give greater attention to what some student activists call American "privatism." This word is used for an overwhelming orientation toward private, individual concerns such as career advancement, specialized expertise, and freedom from messy and ambiguous "political" and moral issues. This extreme orientation, it is argued, disables us in dealing with issues in a public, political context where untidy compromises, the awareness of power, and uncertain outcome are heavily involved. Thus, it is said, comparatively small proportions of eligible American voters even bother to go to the ballot box, except in major national elections. "Politician" is almost a swear-word to many citizens. In polite society, "religion and politics" were for many years routinely avoided as subjects of conversation, lest they bring passion and disagreement into the social gathering. And political scientists have for many years debated the unreality of the political bases for this country's two great "political" parties, which overlap each other dramatically on many basic and divisive issues.

These tendencies may be seen, of course, as the obverse side of some very positive attributes of Americans, such as individualism, self-reliance, concern for personal privacy, and a mistrust of demagoguery. The point of the argument is that problems arise which cannot be solved without surmounting private concerns, to make personal sacrifices—and to let it be known what is vital and precious to you—in light of the shared interests of the political community. There is no guarantee, in such a model of public participation, that conflict will be avoided or injustice to the weaker avoided. But there is hope in such a model for the revival of a meaningful public dialogue about the purposes and ideals of our nation, its communities and institutions, and the world. The alternative to be feared is a passive, privatist acceptance of what government "experts" tell us is necessary—which means also accepting government by the relatively uninformed, mass public opinion through which those "experts" are elected. For many student activitists, the specialized academic researcher and the narrowly loyal institutional bureaucrat are outstanding examples of the "trained incapacity" for meaningful political participation which "privatism" represents. Each of us must ask himself how far those epithets apply to him.

A basic message of the student activists, then, is that we cannot escape politics, messy and troublesome as it is. We may wish to do so, and in times of lesser social discord we may succeed for long periods in devoting our attention primarily to our work and our families and our cultural enjoyments. But we pay a price, if we become so accustomed to such a life that we lose all inclination and capacity to be also active political participants, anticipating and working out on concrete terms the solutions to the great problems of our society. That task, we must then re-learn in painful ways, cannot be left to government alone, or to those citizens with a short and narrow view of our law, our culture, and our history.

One other, related problem in understanding student activism today seems especially troublesome for many academic people. This is the ready willingness of students to take strong actions on the basis of group membership, and to oppose group "interests" in the rhetoric of debate. "Student power," "black power," and similar slogans are scare-words on many campuses. Some see in such ideas and actions an ominous "class conflict" theory of all social relations, with demonic Marxian origins. And, again, such an emphasis on inexorable hostilities between groups is one possible version of the argument; it is found, significantly, in the rhetoric of leaders for presently powerless minorities— especially blacks.

But a deeper insight about society is being probed: It is that Americans must come to terms with the fact of group memberships and loyalties, with the realities of sub-cultural differences, and with the collective bases of political power. Every successful politician knows these facts, and uses them in his campaigns; so do skillful trial lawyers, when choosing juries. Ethnic, economic, educational, and other groupings, while they hold always the danger of dividing us into irreconcilable armed camps, are still realities that cannot be wished away, or obliterated by pretending in our public rhetoric that they do not exist. That is the central fact of modern American public life, that gives meaning to the cries for "power" and solidarity by leaders of status-groups scattered throughout the society.

How we will deal with the inter-group conflicts that arise from these attempts, we do not yet know. We must win *deserved* loyalty for our national life from members of all disparate groups, while we try to repair social injustices. Whether we will see this before armed repression brings armed reprisal, it is not yet clear. But Pandora's box is open; the *group* character of injustices—to blacks, to students, to the poor, and so on—has now become publicly apparent. So has the usefulness of such group membership for gaining political power in our system. The choice of *whether* to deal with these things is now out of our hands.

The danger, then, is that we as academic men and women will continue to protest our non-involvement, our "bystander" status, the need to get back to our "jobs," the separateness of our "institutions" from society. That leaves the political contest to angry student activists and to the "backlash of the right" which some of us so direly predict. To the extent that we do this, I believe, we detached observers of the social scene may confidently predict that student protest will move farther toward resistance, toward "defiance," and toward that repression of dissent by authoritarians and police that few of us really want.

Questions for Analysis

1. What form do you think the recent change in "the tone and character of student protest" has taken? Describe "escalation and sophistication" of *rhetorical* "tactics by both protestors and official authorities." What has characterized public rhetoric in response to recent protests? With perspective gained from study of the New Left and of Black Power define rhetorically "dissent" and "defiance." How does the non-rhetorical instrument "disruption" compare with these terms? Review your definitions when you read Haiman's article at the conclusion of this section of the book and when you read the statements on freedom of speech that conclude Part II.

2. By McEdwards' criteria for application of the term, how "agitative" has the rhetoric of student protest become? How does Lunsford's "why not?" approach to the fact of student protest serve to temper a negative description of the dissent? Make a rhetorically positive statement in suppport of each of Lunsford's "why not?" propositions.

3. What is the rhetorical dilemma in adult responses to student protest? Illustrate the liabilities to university administrations of rhetorically negative replies to all protests. Do you think the student protest movement, as Burgess suggests of Black Power, has shifted the responsibility for a rhetorically moral response to the culture at large? Explain.

4. Support by your own examples Lunsford's assertion that "some very positive attributes of Americans" have been obverted by the rhetoric of student activists. List current rhetorical conflicts prompted by obversion of "individualism, self-reliance, concern for personal privacy, and a mistrust of demagoguery." How would you describe the optimal rhetorical responses of professors to the charge of "privatism"?

5. How have the "strong action on the basis of group membership" tactics and opposition to "group 'interests' in the rhetoric of debate" evolved in the New Left and Black Power movements? How are these tactics being employed on campuses? Cite rhetorical examples of "an emphasis on inexorable hostilities between groups" by student minority leaders. How do you envision the eventual resolution of group conflicts on campuses? How may the rhetoric of student protest affect that resolution?

6

Toward a Rhetoric for the Poverty Class

Paul Friedman
Gerald M. Phillips

America is now confronted by the phenomenon of millions of poverty-stricken families existing in shameful contrast to its affluent society. Our legislators and educators have recently acknowledged the gravity of this problem and have begun major campaigns to deal with the problems of America's poor.

Most of these campaigns are directed at training the unemployed poor in the job skills demanded by the current employment market. A cursory glance at the want-ad section of a newspaper or at lists of target jobs for most training programs reveals a preponderant demand for people with mechanical and technical skills. However, detailed literature on current employment needs suggests a less obvious, but equally important demand: "Taken together, the employment increases occurring between 1962 and 1963 continue and reinforce a major structural transformation in the demand for manpower—the shift away from goods-producing industries and toward the service sector of the economy." (34) Service occupations require interpersonal contacts. The success of companies specializing in service depends on effective communication. Many industrialists have testified that, in the final analysis, ability to communicate is as important in success as technical knowledge. (16)

Thus, person to person interaction on the job is becoming increasingly vital. Another federal report states: "The days when a worker, literate or not, could learn his job simply by watching another are gone in most sectors of the economy. Now for the would-be worker, the ability to read, write, and communicate is essential, both in learning skills and in performance on the job." (41) Communication skills are essential to vocational success on all levels:

Paul Friedman is Assistant Professor of Communication Arts and Sciences, Queens College; Gerald M. Phillips is Associate Professor of Speech, Pennsylvania State University. Reprinted by permission from *Journal of Communication*, 17(1967), 234–249.

> For an important segment of the unemployed, occupa-
> tional training is not sufficient. Many of the unemployed
> need to be taught proper dress and grooming, how to take
> and carry out instructions, promptness, and self-control. . . .
> The typist must know how to type, but she must also have
> grasp of office etiquette. The unemployed youth needs a
> skill, but he should also have some knowledge of how to
> seek a job, then how to hold it. (37)

The increased needs for communication skills in employment provide a special
challenge to those who teach them. Little systematic effort has been exerted on
any level by communication experts to define this challenge or to develop
ways to meet it.

Some basic questions must be asked before a poverty-class pedagogy can
be planned: To what extent do poverty-class students in public schools or job
retraining centers lack necessary communication skills? What are their
specific needs? How can teachers be trained to help them to meet those needs?
Are methodologies available to teach the child or adult raised in a slum or
rural wasteland to handle the communication tasks he faces in his day-to-day
life? To assume that we already have the answers is unwise, for there is a
considerable literature calling attention to failures in present approaches to
poverty-class communication instruction. (9, 28)

The first question, are the economically poor especially speech-poor, was
investigated by a team of sociologists who studied the speaking of people in
the highest and lowest socio-economic classes in several Arkansas communities.
They summarized their findings as follows:

> Differences between the lower and upper groups were strik-
> ing; and, once the nature of the difference was grasped, it
> was astonishing how quickly a characteristic organization
> of communication could be detected and described from a
> reading of even a few paragraphs of an interview. The dif-
> ference is not simply the failure or success of lower and
> upper respectively in communicating clearly and in suffi-
> cient detail for the interviewer's purposes. Nor does the
> difference merely involve correctness or elaborateness of
> grammar or use of a more precise vocabulary. The dif-
> ference is a considerable disparity in (a) the number and
> kinds of perspectives in communication, (b) the ability to
> take the listener's role, (c) the handling of classifications,
> and (d) the framework and stylistic devices which order
> and implement the communication. (40)

A gap in communication between socio-economic classes is opened by the fact
that people tend to communicate more successfully with others of a similar
personality and value set, rather than with persons showing different person-

alities and values. (27) Even programs with specifically technical job goals have acknowledged a need for communication training to bridge this gap. For example, in a program to train "one hundred men in auto mechanics, brick-laying, electronics, sheet metal work, and janitorial duties" the following criteria was stipulated:

> Officials of the Norfolk college were convinced that it would be necessary to instruct the men in many other areas besides shop courses if they were to make their way in the modern job market. The ability to read, to write, to be fairly well-spoken—and even to listen—seemed just as essential to success. . . . The trainees were given additional instruction in reading, writing, spelling, arithmetic, and just plain communication ("How to Talk to Your Supervisor"). . . . There is enough evidence . . . to vindicate this concept. (10)

The inadequacy of the poor in communication skills has individual as well as national implications. Michael Harrington summarized the issue this way:

> The real explanation of why the poor are where they are is that they made the mistake of being born to the wrong parents, in the wrong section of the country, in the wrong industry, or in the wrong racial or ethnic group. (21)

His statement helps to identify the target population for any communication training program. S. M. Miller repeatedly emphasizes, "A clearly defined 'lower class' does not exist—it is a varied, changing group." (26) For this reason, few educational programs are adapted to the distinctive life and language styles of the poor. Most attempt to disseminate middle-class curricula in middle-class language.

Knowledge of vocational needs, however, can be used as a basis for planning the education of the poverty group. Miller points out that "lower-class life is crisis-life constantly trying to make do with string where rope is needed." (26) One way to identify the poor is by their preoccupation with satisfying immediate, basic needs, and their inability to focus on the deferred goals indigenous to middle-class education. It is, consequently, unrealistic to stress abstract goals to the economically and culturally deprived student. Their rudimentary needs must be made explicit to them in terms they understand:

> . . . while literacy and basic education for adults is one of the oldest of the adult education movements, most such programs are oriented towards vaguely defined civic, social, or personal goals rather than clear-cut occupational goals. . . . Because job-oriented social training is an integral part of job success, this area of personal development cannot be neglected. Many adults will need to develop a realistic awareness of the social and human relations aspects of the

world of work; its demands in standards of conduct, physical appearance, dress, job customs, personal cleanliness,
employer expectations; and many of the other commonly
accepted mores connected with working for a living. (47)

If the target group cannot understand middle class objectives, education
suited to middle-class needs actually broadens the gap between the groups.
(14) Such an approach to teaching is not persuasive, hence language development and thought processes become so drastically different between the two
groups, that they are pushed farther apart. (31, 4) To the extent that a
member of the poverty class lives in a social and linguistic world different
from that of the middle-class, his interaction potential with the middle-class
is reduced. (13) Any effective teaching program must be developed in terms
of a rhetoric directed at the goals of the poverty-stricken, and stylized in
language they understand.

For example, an exclusively occupational orientation to communication
training would affect only one of many problems facing the poor. Careful
investigation of the job market is not enough, if teachers are not solicitous of
the sensibilities of their students, many of whom may fear to move entirely
into another social class. A severe breakdown in training can occur because
of presumptuousness of teachers who assume that their directives about how
to live will be affirmatively received. An occupationally-oriented emphasis
would strike at the most pressing problem facing the poor provided the
definition were extended to include attention to the interpersonal requirements
of the job, to encourage entry into jobs valued by the students, regardless of
how the teacher felt about them. Care should be taken not to coerce students
into learning skills for positions which demand a radical change in values or
social behavior, for learning skills alone leads to frustration and failure. Too
often, middle-class teachers and social workers (43) succeed in materializing
testimony like the following:

> What Jim says many others like him have said, or feel
> like saying. He wants money and he badly needs money.
> For his family he wants a home, a good school and medical
> care. He is not sure that he wants to talk and dress like
> others in the suburbs do, and he resents any suggestion that
> he make a change in his speech, his appearance, or his style
> of life as the price for land and cash. He does not see any
> glory in his condition, but he can also spot in a flash a new
> attempt to humiliate him. (12)

It is a fair assumption that training for a middle-class style without offering a concordant ability to consume, will create irreconcilable tension. By
the same token, those who move into vocations manned chiefly by the middle-
class must learn to interact in their new milieu. The desire for upward
mobility is not easily fulfilled. Many subtle factors work against social
fluidity. Awareness of these factors lies behind the sociological thinking

which asks: "Do the poor fail to move from their economic lot because they lack the qualifications needed to move, or do they lack the qualifications because of their economic lot." (33) Or, more specifically, "Have residential patterns and variations in life styles and statuses given rise to a segregation of the poor which shuts them off from the norms and expectations of the larger community?" (19)

Oral communication style is undoubtedly one critical element in upward mobility. Bernard Barber says, "In all societies, proper habits of speech and language, in regard to both diction and accent, become symbols of social class position." (1) Because they lack the ability to communicate with the socio-economic class which controls most of American employment, the job-seeking and social integration efforts of the lower classes often fail. The Speech Association of America's Committee on the Field of Speech offers one possible explanation:

> Speech is man's most distinctive and significant behavior.
> Speech is learned from teachers. The "teachers" include
> all members of the social groups in which the child moves,
> as well as the persons who give direct attention to speech
> instruction in formal educational settings. (39)

The poor do not emulate the temporary and alien authority figures imposed on them. Their tendency is to habituate the verbal patterns of their own class. According to the President's Committee on Youth Employment:

> Many of the unemployed youth live in congested city areas,
> surrounded by social disorganization, poverty and despair.
> Their families usually occupy most inadequate housing.
> They are surrounded by other disadvantaged people, many
> of whom are unemployed, or intermittently employed at
> low wages. Without successful examples among their elders
> to guide them, the youth of such families are unlikely to
> succeed. (35)

There is virtually no tangency between people in these categories and the middle-class. Contact with merchants is restricted to local operators; contact with the power structure is through police. *De facto* socially segregated schools rarely provide opportunities for communication with peers from the middle-class.

Studies of language development in middle-class children indicate that a main stimulus to learning comes from parents. But, the lower classes live in a less parent-dominated environment than do middle-class children. (48) Since models to emulate must be present, their tendency is to select them from the peer group. (22) There is some reason to believe that early training could change language behavior, if offered by a teacher who took care to become a "model" before directing the students into activities that seem alien in the light of their neighborhood association. (38) However, most contacts through

"Headstart" and similar projects confront a lower-socio-economic child with a middle-class teacher who tries fruitlessly, though sincerely, to compete with the strong blandishments of the more familiar environment of poverty.

All of the factors which prevent inter-class contacts create a lack of congruence in linguistic frameworks of lower-class and middle-class groups. Increasingly, authorities in linguistics, education, and sociology report that members of the poverty group do not seem to understand many basic symbols the way they are conceived by the middle-class. Even more frustrating, the middle-class does not seem to understand that the poverty-stricken do not understand. People are much quicker to assume innate inabilities in the poor than to examine the possible communication barriers that may exist.

Bernstein has laid a theoretical sociolinguistic foundation for the language variance:

> I suggest that the measurable inter-status linguistic differences between the lower working-class and the middle-class, rather than reflecting differences in innate capacity, result from entirely different modes of speech which are dominant and typical within these strata. More formally, different possibilities are inherent in language use, and once this stress is placed, then the resulting linguistic form is one of the most important means of eliciting and strengthening ways of feeling and thinking which are functionally related to the social group. (3)

In a more functional vein Segalman discussed the pragmatic semantic problems faced by social workers in their dealing with the poor. He cited many examples, of which the following are a sample:

SUBJECT	VIEWPOINT OF MIDDLE-CLASS	VIEWPOINT OF LOWER-CLASS
Authority (courts, police, city officials, school principals, etc.).	Security, something to be taken for granted, appealed to, used.	Something to be avoided and even hated.
Education and schooling.	A means of upgrading children; a vehicle to open opportunities for life work.	Something to be gotten over with by children so they can go to work. (42)

What Segalman and others imply is that, though poverty-classes use English words, they actually speak a different language. At a recent Research Conference on Education and Cultural Deprivation, educators joined linguists and sociologists in pointing out the significant language differences between social classes:

> In many middle-class homes, the child's language is extended by parents' responses to his statements and questions. In culturally deprived homes, the parent is more likely to respond to the child with a monosyllable or to nod the head without using any words. The point of this is that one major difference between culturally deprived and more advantaged homes is the extension and development of the speech of children. (5)

The federal government has suggested a possible matrix for dealing with the problem:

> It has become clear that in most cases the occupational problems of disadvantaged workers are related to a complex of personal, social, educational, family and community factors that cannot be dealt with in the "standard" manner. The experimental and demonstration program has shown that the approach to the inter-related needs of the hardcore unemployed must be comprehensive in nature and must utilize unique methods from a variety of disciplines. (35)

The generalizations are not, however, reflected by any specific implementation. The "War on Poverty" is directed toward achieving occupational and social mobility for the poor. Its hope is that the economically and culturally deprived can be trained to participate equally in a "Great Society." Yet the government has not emphasized communication training in its large-scale poverty programs.

Attention to the explicit communication needs of the poverty stricken opens a new arena of activity for speech specialists. For generations, the rhetoric of the middle-class has been disseminated in the universities to future teachers of speech and English. In the context of an automating society, a new "rhetoric" of poverty must be found. Attention must now be directed to the specific communication problems which the poor face today.

For example, in the job interview (still the most common hiring procedure used), a potential employee needs sufficient speaking skill to represent himself as a capable, responsible representative of the company. An interview is fundamentally a subjective process in which the applicant's ability to communicate is critical. In many ways, it is the intangible referred to by rhetoricians as "ethos" that determines whether a man is selected for a job. Several authorities on interviewing note simple communication variables that are critical in influencing final judgments. (46, 20) Oldfield, for example, advises the employer that, "It would appear, in fact, that generally speaking, more can be learned from the manner than from the matter of the candidates' remarks." (30)

A job candidate is involved in a persuasive situation in which he attempts to motivate the interviewer to accept him as able to do a job. If he attempts to persuade with symbols and mannerisms that are not relevant to the interviewer's world, rejection is the most logical prognosis. An interviewer perceives a candidate in relation to the present structure of the company. It is unreasonable to expect him to regard his company as an arena in which social therapy can be conducted. Its work must be done, its commerce accelerated, *regardless* of social and economic handicaps of a deprived citizen. The members of the "other America" have the burden of learning the significant symbols and major communication styles of the class they seek to enter. Middle-class students seem to be able to adapt to interviews with little or no specific training. The poverty-class student, however, needs to understand both format and technique of interviewing, and should not be expected to do so without explicit instruction, demonstration and simulation.

Cultivation of ability to communicate with the middle-class is particularly vital for members of racial minorities, for whom a negative stereotype offers an additional handicap. Negro leaders despair at the reluctance of businessmen to hire Negroes for responsible positions. Legislation now "guarantees" employment to the qualified. It is often difficult, however, to find members of racial minorities who can meet the basic requirements of jobs requiring personal contact with middle-class people. (23) It is hard to define the word "qualified," but it can be construed legitimately to mean ability to "fit in" as well as ability to do a job.

Much of the current psychiatric writing refers to the "game" of interaction. Understanding and contact between people is described as a function of communication or projection of the self. (2) Unless the essential rules of the interaction game in a particular social or occupational group are understood, entry cannot be made. Linguists also recognize the ritual nature of most social interaction. Firth has said:

> Most of the give-and-take of conversation in our everyday life is stereotyped and very narrowly conditioned by your particular type of culture. It is a sort of roughly prescribed social ritual, in which you generally say what the other fellow expects you, one way or the other, to say. (17)

There is no question that there are deep differences between the game rules and significant roles of the various sub-cultures that make up American society. Recognition of the necessity to project the self adequately was recognized by the field of speech very early. Brigance stated:

> few, if any of us, are otherwise engaged than in selling personalities, goods, or ideas. Speech is our medium of exchange. It is almost literally true that good speech has replaced the gun and ax as an instrument of survival. (7)

Donald K. Smith recently directed the speech profession toward recognizing social change and taking it into account in their theory and pedagogy:

> First, we will, because we must, seek in the next few years
> to restore at the secondary school and undergraduate col-
> lege level, to the study of speech a strong sense of the
> relationship between speech forms and events, and the
> forms and purposes of our social institutions which shape
> and are shaped by speech. (44)

This may mean abandonment of some assumptions which have directed the
field for centuries. It will be necessary to determine the speech needs of the
poverty class and compare them with normative data about the middle class.
The classical rhetorical tradition has been regarded as appropriate for the
lawyer, teacher, and minister. The traditional public speaking training format
of lecture-performance-critique seems to be suited to the student committed to
influencing human behavior through middle-class channels. However, there is
no real evidence that these approaches to social control are at all pertinent to
the child of the slums or the backwoods farm who is forced to survive in the
new cybernated society of the population explosion. For the poor, the ways
through which the self is communicated in employment situations are not dealt
with in our current literature. Most members of middle-class society learn them
through their own "radar." (36) The poverty-class student must learn about
the society he seeks to enter, and be given active training in how to talk to it.
Participation in role playing exercises and supervised excursions into middle-
class communication situations offer more promise than the traditional performance exercises which pre-suppose an inherent middle-class value set. To
obtain economic balance the poverty-class student must learn his communication as a skill, directly related to his job. For the moment, other intangibles
are irrelevant.

Besides the pressing *economic* problems of the millions of people living
in poverty, *political* problems will become more urgent. Michael Harrington
has pointedly described the political impotence of the poor:

> The poor are politically invisible. It is one of the cruelest
> ironies of social life in advanced countries that the dis-
> possessed at the bottom of society are unable to speak for
> themselves. The people of the other America do not, by
> and large, belong to unions, to fraternal organizations, or
> to political parties. They are without lobbies of their own;
> they put forward no legislative program. As a group, they
> are atomized. They have no voice. (21)

There may well be unsuspected significance in this lack of political spokesmen. An absence of socially positive reference groups such as unions, clubs
and political organizations creates a vacuum which must be filled. As an alternative, some of the poor, particularly those who are also members of racial
minority groups, have turned to radical actionist groups, which operate outside the fabric of organized society. Recent riots and the cry of "burn, baby,
burn" dramatize the frustration of people who have no voice. But for most of

the poor, life is a process of waiting for something to happen; of looking to middle-class authority for whatever may trickle down; of resenting in sullen silence their necessity to do so. They are alienated from society and cannot nurture their self-esteem in ways deemed socially acceptable by the opulent majority. Too often they put on the "brave front" and engage in socially deviant behavior. Jerome Cohen supports this view:

> Members of the lower class have little opportunity for mastery and its anxiety-reducing function. A number of theoreticians have suggested that deviant behavior though it creates problems in other ways, sometimes offers an opportunity for mastery in an area of life and as such serves the purpose of preventing a completely damaged sense of self-worth and a feeling of "nothingness." (11)

Future increase of unemployment resulting from automation will add millions more marginals to the ranks of the dissatisfied and alienated. These people not fully adjusted to poverty can provide a feeding group for radical political movements. Donald M. Michael foresees this danger:

> Today most of the unemployed are from low educational backgrounds where leisure has always been simply a respite from labor. No particular aspirations to or positive attitudes about the creative use of leisure characterize this group. It is worth speculating that one thing they might do is to participate in radical organizations through which they could vent their hostility over feeling insecure and useless. (25)

This trend toward increased political activity on the part of the poor has already begun.

> The present American poor may prove to be more politically active than is usually true of the poor. . . . The conservative orientation of gaining change and social advance through an harmonious arrangement with local power forces is being superseded by disadvantaged groups themselves actively pressuring for the kinds of changes—in housing, in schools, and the like—that they believe to be important. (26)

For this reason, "the heads of all federal agencies are required by the Economic Opportunity Act to give preference in the allocation of funds to projects that are associated with a community action program." (43)

Clearly particular efforts must be directed at improving the political decision-making and community action of the poor. Without training in social and political uses of communication, occupational training may have little or no success. The individual without a socially acceptable and influential reference group may feel alienated and resistant to his society's values. This holistic approach to communication also implies that the individual's success in any sphere is crucially affected by his communication with those closest to him. The child who is overwhelmed by problems at home is handicapped in his learning elsewhere. The home environment of the poverty groups is often disrupted. Illness or desertion of a parent frequently thrusts excess responsibility onto an ill-prepared adolescent. Breaches often arise between children and their parents, especially when the parents are immigrants, particularly "old-fashioned," or made bitter by their lot in life. Teen-agers often know only violence as a means of settling their problems. No poverty-program specialist can afford to ignore these communication breakdowns. Each problem is unique for those experiencing it, yet each has a common ground in misunderstanding. Thus, sensitivity to the viewpoints of others and a desire to find bases for compromise are needed as approaches to solution. These have been successfully fostered in group problem-solving sessions (29) and in discussions generated by oral readings from stimulating literature. (6) Most imaginative programs designed to reduce stress in the poverty-belt capitalize on realistic training in communication. What remains is to generalize instruction; to find a common synthesis of theory and method, and apply it generally in anti-poverty training.

The communication problems of the poor are indeed manifold; the solutions are scant. The training of the poor in public schools and government programs has proved to be only moderately adequate at best. Communications specialists must direct their efforts toward the intricate and sensitive interaction difficulties which occur between various classes. New types of students must be taught to adapt to audiences new to them—and new methods must be employed to do it. Robert Coles has written:

> The school they know is not like the one that my children will attend. The teachers in that school—I have visited the classrooms—were once dutiful and eager, then became tired and angry; now finally, they are indifferent. . . . Yet, such disastrous results are by no means inevitable. To a large extent what happens will depend upon the manner of meeting, the purpose of the encounter between those in need and those wanting to be of help. (12)

Research by Vera John seems to indicate that conventional language training actually seems to broaden the "skills" gap between the poor and the middle-class. (24) In work with the poor, so far, only original and carefully tailored teaching methods seem to be effective. Adaptation must be made to this group's particular developmental and environmental problems. The trainee must not only be given new words to say and ways to say them, he must be given new things to "say about," and new reference groups to which he can be loyal. (45) If we accept, as a premise, that people learn language as a way of dealing with relevant new experience, (18) we recognize a disparity between the situations on which most communication training has been based and those that are relevant in the lives of the poor. The lecture-speech-criticism format is an example, for the poverty-class member does not view himself as an effector of social control. Thus traditional training in public address can only appear inapposite and useless to the poverty student.

Situations must be sought in his environment which meet the criteria set down by Olson and Larson, (32) those which help enhance self-concept, facilitate free expression of personal values and frustrations, improve social skills, minimize cultural differences, as well as stimulate language development. Use of the small group offers one way the problem can be approached, especially for the teaching of decision-making. Social "games" behavior may be taught through the use of role-playing. Oral reading training may be used to improve articulation deficiencies and to stimulate expression of personal ideas for which the student has no words, as well as to broaden his understanding of the literature of the main culture. There is plenty of room for experimentation. All that is needed is teachers with the courage to dare.

Along with any method used to teach content material, the "affect" or the students' attitude towards communication must be considered. According to Jerome Bruner, appeals must be made to curiosity, the desire to achieve competence, the necessity to learn in the framework of a culture, and the imperative of implanting identification with competent human models and relevant tasks. (8) An effort must constantly be made to reach across the cultural gap and interpret communication in the student's terms. The teacher must be virtually "bi-lingual" in cultural context. He must know the relevant symbols of his own society as well as that of the student. All assignments must grow directly from the needs and wants of the students, and vary depending on the nature of the group identification of the students. Assignments cannot be imposed from an "alien" middle-class tradition. Above all, the poverty student must learn that the rewards of communication effectiveness are to be prized more than the "comfort" of resisting it.

Before the poor can really benefit from communication training their minds must be won from a perspective limited to their poverty culture. This is the "readiness" which must exist before any suggested pedagogy can be successful. The trainees must have a commitment both to the need for learning job skills *and* adapting to the communication expectations of those who will hire them to practice those skills and those with whom they will work. The poor, particularly those in racial minority groups, tend to view the world outside their ghettoes as foreign territory inaccessible to them. This may lead them to hostility toward learning to live in it. They must, however, be helped to see it as an arena they want to and can learn to enter. Teaching must be directed both at raising the aspiration level, and providing the means of achievement.

America's future seems to hold the promise of unprecedented luxury— but only for those who can meet the challenges that the future presents. One of the most important challenges is the ever-increasing need for speaking ability as a requirement for economic success and political effectiveness. The poor must be trained to communicate in a dynamic, pluralistic society where traditions in employment, political power, and family ties are all undergoing change. To handle the tasks which they are undertaking, the directors of the Job Corps have set a direction for themselves: "While industry has fitted the man to the training, the Job Corps must fit the training to the man." (15) Communication specialists must view their task in the same way. Our concern must be with understanding the world of our student and his role in it, so that training can be offered in a realistic context, with hope of success.

Bibliography

1. Barber, Bernard. *Social Stratification: A Comparative Analysis of Structure and Process*. New York: Harcourt, Brace, 1957, p. 151.
2. Berne, Eric. *Transactional Psychiatry*. New York: Grove, 1961.
3. Bernstein, Basil. "Aspects of Language and Learning in the Genesis of the Social Process." *Language in Culture and Society*. Ed. Dell Hymes, New York: Harper & Row, 1964, p. 51.
4. ———. "Language and Social Class." *BJS* 11(1960) : 232–44.
5. Bloom, Benjamin, Allison Davis, and Robert Hess. *Compensatory Education for Cultural Deprivation*. New York: Holt, Rinehart & Winston, 1965, p. 14.
6. Borton, Terry. "Reaching the Culturally Deprived." *SR* 49(Feb. 19, 1966) : 78.
7. Brigance, W. Norwood. *Your Everyday Speech*. New York: McGraw-Hill, 1937, p. 20.
8. Bruner, Jerome S. "The Will to Learn." *Commentary* 41(Feb., 1966) : 41–6.
9. Calitri, Charles J. "Language and the Dignity of Youth." *SR* 46(July 20, 1963) : 46–7.
10. Canan, James. "A Second Chance for Ninety Men in Norfolk." *The Reporter* 31(July 16, 1964) : 34.
11. Cohen, Jerome. "Social Work and the Culture of Poverty." *Social Work* 9(Jan., 1964) : 9.
12. Coles, Robert. "The Poor Don't Want to Be Middle-Class." *NYTM* (Dec. 19, 1965) : 58.
13. Deutsch, Martin. "Social and Psychological Perspectives on the Development of the Disadvantaged Learner." *JNE* 33(1964) : 232–44.
14. ———. "The Role of Social Class in Language Development." *AJO* 35(1965) : 78–88.
15. Eigen, Lewis D. and David Gottleib. "Pluralism in the Job Corps." *AC* 47 (March, 1965) : 22.
16. Erickson, Eugene. *Public Leaders View of Communication*. (Pullman, Washington, Agricultural Experiment Station, Washington State University, 1964.)
17. Firth, J. R. "On Sociological Linguistics." *Language in Culture and Society*. Ed. Dell Hymes, New York: Harper & Row, 1964, p. 69.

18. Frazier, Alexander. "Helping Poorly Languaged Children." *EE* 31(1964):
149–53.
19. Gibbard, Harold A. "Segregation of the Poor." From a paper delivered at the
West Virginia Conference on Poverty Amidst Affluence, Morgantown, West
Virginia (May 3–7, 1965), *MLR* 88(1965): 837.
20. Gray, Frank W. "How to Size Up People." *PJ* 42(June, 1963): 291.
21. Harrington, Michael. *The Other America*. Baltimore: Penguin, 1963, p. 21.
22. Hartup, Willard. "Patterns of Imitative Behavior in Young Children." *Child
Development* (March, 1964): 183–90.
23. Henry, Jules. "White People's Time, Colored People's Time." *Transaction* 2
(March/April, 1965): 31–4.
24. John, Vera P. "The Intellectual Development of Slum Children: Some Preliminary Findings." *AJO* 33(1963): 813–33.
25. Michael, Donald. *Cybernation: The Silent Conquest*. Santa Barbara: Center for
The Study of Democratic Institutions, 1962, p. 29.
26. Miller, S. M. "The American Lower Classes: A Typological Approach." *Social
Research* 31 (Spring, 1964): 1–22.
27. Newton, Eunice Shaed. "The Culturally Deprived Child in Our Verbal Schools."
JNE 31(1962): 184–7.
28. New York City Youth Board. *Teenage Gangs*. New York, 1957, p. 17.
29. Nooney, James B. and Norman A. Polansky. "Influence of Perceived Similarity
and Personality on Verbal Accessibility." *Merrill Palmer Quarterly of Behavior
and Development* 8(1962): 33–40.
30. Oldfield, R. C. *The Psychology of the Interview*. London: Methuen, 1937.
31. Olson, James L. "The Verbal Ability of the Culturally Different." *EE* 29(1964):
280–4.
32. —— and Richard G. Larson. "An Experimental Curriculum for Culturally
Deprived Kindergarten Children." *EL* 22(1965): 553–8.
33. "One Big Reason Why Some People Are Poor." *USNWR* 56(Feb. 24, 1964): 98.
34. President's Commission on Youth Employment. *The Challenge of Jobless Youth*.
Washington, D.C., GPO, 1963, p. 6.
35. President's Committee on Youth Employment. *Manpower Report of the President
and a Report on Manpower Requirements, Resources, Utilization and Training
by the U. S. Department of Labor Transmitted to Congress*. Washington, D.C.,
GPO, 1964, p. xii.
36. Riesman, David. *The Lonely Crowd*. New York: Doubleday, 1950.
37. Report of the Secretary of Labor to Congress, March, 1964. *Manpower Research
and Training*. Washington, D.C., GPO, 1964, p. 54.
38. Rowley, Vinton and Beth Stone. "Changes in Verbal Behavior as a Function of
Social Approval, Experimenter Difference and Child Personality." *CD* 35(1964):
423–6.
39. S. A. A. Committee on the Nature of the Field of Speech. "The Field of Speech:
Its Purpose and Scope in Education." *ST* 12(1963): 322–3.
40. Schatzman, L. and A. L. Strauss. "Social Class and Modes of Communication."
AJS 40(1955): 330.
41. Second Annual Report of the Secretary of the Department of Health, Education
and Welfare to the Congress, April 1, 1964. *Education and Training: Key to the
Development of Human Resources*. Washington, D.C., GPO, 1964, p. 27.
42. Segalman, Ralph. "The Conflict of Cultures Between Social Work and the Under-

class." *The Rocky Mountain Social Science Journal* 2(1965) : 168–9.

43. Silberman, Charles. E. "The Mixed-Up War on Poverty." *Fortune* 72(August, 1965) : 218.

44. Smith, Donald K. "What Are the Contemporary Trends in Teaching Speech?" *ST* 10(1961) : 92.

45. Spodek, Bernard. "Poverty, Education and the Young Child." *EL* 22(1965) : 593–603.

46. Torbert, Frances. *Personnel Management in Small Companies*. Los Angeles: Institute of Industrial Relations, University of California, 1959, p. 22.

47. U. S. Department of Health, Education and Welfare. *Educationally Deficient Adults: Their Education and Training Needs*. New York: Information and Training Services, McGraw-Hill, 1965, p. 5.

48. Walters, James, Ruth Connor, and Michael Zunich. "Interaction of Mothers and Children in Lower Class Families." *CD* 35(1964) : 433–40.

Questions for Analysis

1. Define each of the following terms as a problem for the teacher of communication skills to poverty-class children: a. personality and value set, b. abstract goals, c. middle-class objectives, d. peer group emulation, e. linguistic common ground.

2. Add to the example of the job interview other examples of specific communication problems facing the poor today. Devise a technique for "teaching" a job interview or another of your projected problems.

3. What questions do Friedman and Phillips raise about the true meaning of "qualified" as it applies to job applicants? Describe the value to the poverty-class student of "role playing exercises." What are some of the "middle-class communication situations" with which to confront the poor?

4. What home and neighborhood conditions make "group problem-solving sessions" necessary to poverty-programs? Describe how you might simulate a "community action" situation in the classroom.

5. How might the "lecture-speech-criticism format" of traditional communication training be altered to increase its relevance to the poverty-class member? How do the authors propose that a teacher become "virtually 'bilingual' in cultural contexts"? How might this same linguistic reorientation serve a spokesman for the "New Left" or a member of a voter registration team in contacts with the poor?

7

No Business Like Lecture Business

Natalie Gittelson

"I myself gross more than $3-million annually. At a safe, safe estimate—conservatively speaking—the lecture business in the United States now amounts to a $100-million a year. And this is a minimum figure." The conservative speaker is Robert Walker, president of Boston's American Program Bureau ("Presenting the World's Distinguished Lecturers"), a 32-year-old entrepreneur who is the youngest, newest and—by his own proclamation—the "hottest" lecture-bureau president in the land.

Robert Walker's uncle Harry, president of New York's Harry Walker, Inc. ("the World's Greatest Platform Personalities"), claims "bigger gross billings than anyone else in the industry," although he discreetly refuses to disclose the precise extent of them, "even to Dun and Bradstreet." "I don't want to make anyone else jealous," the older Walker, formerly associated in business with the younger Walker, explains.

Dan Tyler Moore, director general of the International Platform Association, the nearest thing to a trade union the every-man-for-himself lecture trade boasts, offers $65-million as "a swift . . . curbstone estimate" of the national platform pot, "in the absence of comprehensive surveys, studies and so on." Moore claims that on a recent day this spring the voices of more than 40,000 speakers resounded through auditoriums in New York City alone. "Look, I've just written a book called 'Lecturing for Profit,' " he says. "It's selling like hot cakes. Why? Because everybody wants to get into the act."

Almost everybody has already—or so it seems. Bob Walker's A.P.B. books at least 160 lecturers, from Dick Gregory and Timothy Leary to Ralph Schoenman, secretary general of the International War Crimes Tribunal. Harry Walker's glossy, eight-page, magazine-size brochure reveals 156 famous faces —among them, Supreme Court Justice Abe Fortas, Gen. Maxwell Taylor, Barry Goldwater and Sam Levenson.

Natalie Gittelson is Special-Projects Editor of *Harper's Bazaar*.
The New York Times Magazine, June 9, 1968, pp. 32–33, 132–136. © 1968 by the New York Times Company. Reprinted by permission.

Richard Fulton, president of Richard Fulton, Inc. ("America's Finest Lecture-Entertainment Bureau") reels off an unpunctuated list of his "exclusives": "Clive Barnes of The New York Times Dore Schary Jackie Robinson Mayor Lindsay Floyd McKissick Malcolm Boyd Paul Krassner Isaac Bashevis Singer Daniel Bell. . . ."

Robert Keedick, president of The Keedick Lecture Bureau ("Since 1907 Manager of the World's Most Celebrated Lecturers") claims George Plimpton, Bennett Cerf, Jimmy Breslin and at least eight dozen other luminaries of various wattages. W. Colston Leigh, Inc., ("America's Outstanding Bureau of Lectures and Entertainment") offers Art Buchwald, Lord Harlech, Vincent Price, and the Duke and Duchess of Bedford, as well as Betty Friedan, author of "The Feminine Mystique," and Nan Birmingham (wife of Stephen "Our Crowd" Birmingham) who talks on *"What* Feminine Mystique?"

Where do these speakers by the carload speak? "Where don't they?" asks Dan Tyler Moore. "Look, every town hall, every trade association, every chapter of Rotary, Kiwanis, Eagles and Elks has its handful of lecturers. But this is the big thing: Every single college in the country books at least 10 or 15 speakers a year."

There is no doubt that Americans, as never before, hunger for face-to-face confrontation with the famous and the near-famous. And students especially— perhaps because they have lived so long on the shadows of a television screen —seem starved for the snap, crackle and pop of flesh-and-blood personalities. "We go to lectures because we anticipate an opportunity for exchange," says Larry Berger, on the board of managers of the Special Events Committee at Columbia University. As a consequence of this mass anticipation, three-quarters of American Program Bureau's revenue, or about $2,500,000, comes from the college campus. It is America's new Cloud Lecture Land. As our institutions of higher learning spend "the biggest dollar on live entertainment in this country," they also pay the biggest prices to hear real live speakers.

This great, rich audience—more than seven million strong in more than 2,500 colleges and universities—openly admires kooks, cuckoos and controversy in approximately equal proportions. Anyone who pokes pins into the establishment balloon, anyone who hates the war, anyone who shakes the power structure or "upsets the trustees, because that's what it's all about," according to 19-year-old Daniel Luria of the University of Rochester, receives a particularly cordial welcome.

It's a far cry from the forties and fifties, when a leisurely, comfortable, frayed-tweed air of refinement hung over the whole lecture scene. The scene then was made up largely of plump little Helen Hokinson matrons with flower hats and bottomless appetites for intellectual improvement, courting Culture at the 11 A.M. women's-club lecture. If the man of that hour (more than likely a literary figure, discussing something sassy like "The Books That Shape Our Minds") ate a nice lunch with the ladies, collected $100 for his talk and uttered some expectable statements about literature and life, he considered his morning well spent and his speaking engagement well paid.

But in 1968, women's clubs have been largely consigned to the Outer Slobovia of the lecture world. "This business has gotten too expensive for them," Harry Walker says. "They have their little interior decoration speaker, they have their little garden speaker. But you can't expose such people on the Johnny Carson show or the Today show. Television exposure—that creates the name today and the name creates the price."

The price per campus speaker, among those who are reasonably VIP, ranges from about $500 to $2,500 per 50-minute hour (not counting the almost inevitable Q. and A. that follows). Many of the most enterprising orators, such as A.P.B. client Bill Sands, keep two dates a day during the busy season. Sands, an ex-convict who wrote "My Shadow Ran Fast" after sharing a death-house cell with Caryl Chessman, returned recently from 54 days of college lecturing during which he made 73 speeches. For this, Sands promises—and delivers—"a bitter, vitriolic attack on modern penology," which most young audiences find quite stimulating. "Penologists across the country see in me a threat to their existence," Sands says.

Some old-line lecture bureaus seem to see a threat to their existence in this radical new breed of speaker. Unlike A.P.B., they tend to look askance at the lecturers the students like most. "The Timothy Leary-Andy Warhol kind of nut has taken over the college platform," laments an agency representative who has been watching the lecture world spin for 20 years. "These kids are sensation-mad. What's worse, the university administration has abdicated. Student organizations are almost entirely autonomous in choosing the speakers they want."

Student power has indeed become one of the looming facts of life in today's lecture business. Undergraduate managers do govern "special events" in nearly every major college and university. Only a few smaller ones are now, if not forever, still under the official thumb. Recently a Dick Gregory lecture was abruptly canceled, although paid for in full, by the Board of Trustees at Florida's Stetson University. And Dr. Albert Ellis—who interprets for students the sexual mores of the swinging sixties—was prevented by the administration from appearing at East Texas University.

At M.I.T., where science-minded students have listened to Timothy Leary, Malcolm X, Ralph Schoenman, Stokely Carmichael and almost everyone else who has lately rocked square society, Jay Hammerness, dean of Special Activities, defends the right of the student body to invite any and every speaker in for a hearing—no matter how iconoclastic, revolutionary or just plain weirdo. "These people should not go unchallenged," Dean Hammerness says. "They should submit to questioning by articulate and probing members of the university community—even if nothing of substance develops from the confrontation."

Nevertheless, the understandable strain that exists between some student boards of governors and some speakers' representatives has more or less split the lecture business down the center. Many middle-aged (i.e., over 30) agents who covet the cash at the collegians' disposal not only distrust the autonomy of the young, but they make no bones about it. "We always insist on the signature of a faculty member or an administrator, no matter what kid says he's in charge," admits Beatrice Grant of W. Colston Leigh, one of the most prestigious of the old-guard bureaus. "They don't like to be asked, but if we insist, they finally produce it."

The "comparative newcomers" to the business, like Richard Fulton and Robert Walker, don't ask. They accept student power with warm approval and consequently, they claim, the college crowd adores them. In these campus-oriented offices, some say, show-biz methods and shock value have begun to crowd out Culture, and the so-called pop attraction reigns.

Robert Walker perhaps epitomizes the pop look, and outlook, in lecture-bureau presidents. Although the trade's oldliners share a clipped-tongue tendency to speak of "the Walkers" in one breath, Harry Walker takes pains to disassociate himself, on philosophical grounds, from his nephew. "My bureau is very discriminating, very selective," he explains. "We would not dream of getting involved with an H. Rap Brown, a Stokely Carmichael or a Dick Gregory. We feel they serve no purpose on campus and we would not wish to associate our people with such names."

Such names, and any more at home like them, are meat and drink to Walker, the younger, who has walked in and—according to him—taken over where other agents feared to tread. "We are, as far as I know, number one in the college field right now," says Bob Walker, of his almost entirely under-30 organization. "I'm the old man of the company. Most of my salesmen are in their late twenties. One is only 22. When we go into a campus, we merge with the kids. They want the whole gamut of intellectual smorgasbord. Why not give them what they're after?"

The smorgasbord Walker gives them includes, besides such spicy figures as Warhol, Leary et al., "our ghost catcher, Hans Holzer [whose bag is the preternatural], Sybil Leek, our seance lady and witch; our worm man, James McConnell [Editor of The Worm-Runner's Digest, he lectures on "What Makes a Worm Learn"], our yoga woman, Marcia Moore, and our tremendous fish person, Roger Conklin." Also appearing on A.P.B.'s many-splendored list: Bill Baird, who does "the birth control and abortion bit," and Robert Ettinger, a life-restoration expert. Walker, who concocts his own promotional copy and "designs everything" himself, bills Ettinger as the man who promises "the death of death. Repair. Freeze. Wait."

When it comes to collecting these clients, the whole world is Robert Walker's oyster. He dredges up talent everywhere. One of his richest sources of speaker supply is The New York Times. "Every Sunday I rip that paper apart," Walker says. "The Book Review, the theater section, the education section, the

Sunday Magazine, the News of the Week." When he stumbles on a somebody he'd like on his list, "I pick up the lovely phone and I call him." Most prospects respond quickly and affirmatively to Walker's advances. He cites, as other "great references," The Wall Street Journal, The Christian Science Monitor, and his own hometown paper, The Boston Globe. Walker also devours "every major magazine every month, including such avant-garde publications as Ramparts and The Realist." At home or in the office, he or one of his staff tries to monitor each television show on which guests appear—"Face the Nation, Meet the Press, Merv Griffith, David Susskind, Johnny Carson." Additionally, Walker receives on the average of 15 letters every week from would-be speakers soliciting *him* to represent *them*. If the letter looks intriguing and the writer seems at least potentially a "pro," one of A.P.B.'s salesmen goes off to listen to him lecture and returns with an evaluation of his profit-making power. Otherwise, Walker may invite the hopeful into his office for an exploratory talk.

Ina Mason, a Boston University graduate, is one of the two women salespeople on Walker's staff; the other is Marguerite English, previously of M.-G.-M.'s publicity department. Besides them, Walker employs a bookkeeper, secretarial and mailroom personnel, a man who does nothing but plan speakers' itineraries, and five more salesmen—"including myself, Phil Citron, an engineering graduate from the University of Texas, who is my national sales coordinator, and Tom Sanders, the head of my sports department. He's a world champion star of the Boston Celtics."

Walker trains each of these salespeople personally and vigorously. "I want them to stereotype me, to behave like me," he explains without false modesty. "They have to know how to match people and places. They have to understand the mood of the country. You can't recommend a liberal speaker to an ultra-conservative college in a Republican state. They have to keep abreast of the news and to be able to project themselves two years into the future. Two years ago you couldn't book dates for Dick Gregory. But we projected ourselves on civil rights. We projected the change in the status of the Negro in America. And we projected ourselves on drugs. We were right every time."

"Projection"—the ability to intuit and exploit the national interests and mass preoccupations in the air—is considered by Walker to be the basic skill a man needs to make it big in the lecture business. "Beyond that, it's basically public relations," he says. "Contact with people counts most."

He is understandably proud of his young, thriving, multi-million-dollar business. Walker throws out his arms, taking in A.P.B.'s cork walls and wood paneling, built-in bar, black upholstery and citrus yellow rug. "It's a Cinderella story," he says, waving a white telephone. "I can pick up any one of these and book into 50 colleges in 50 minutes. That's rapport. I have 14 people working for me here. I'm taking over this whole floor soon, and I'm only in business for myself three years."

The Cinderella story began more than a decade ago when Walker switched from the day to the night curriculum at the C.C.N.Y. School of Business. "I wanted to start at the bottom in public relations, so I went to the top agency in the country: Hill and Knowlton. I was offered a job in the mailroom. 'Any chance for advancement?' I asked. 'Absolutely not,' they said. So I took it anyhow. I delivered all the mail and on the way I read it. That was the beginning of my real education. I saw big business from the inside."

But the ladder of upward mobility at Hill and Knowlton was slippery under Walker's feet. So in June, 1960, he took his new bride, Francine, to Boston and went to work in his Uncle Harry's lecture agency—once again learning the business from the inside. "It was a pretty good thing to begin with, but I made a monstrosity out of it," the junior Walker recalls with a flair for hyperbole that may, or may not, endear him to the cool generation. "Nothing much was doing in the college market when I came in. I figured if certain no-so-great attractions could bring in $2,500 an hour in night clubs, why not on campuses? Of course student audiences should not pay $4,000 to see some dirty-looking ignoramuses twanging guitars. They should be educated, not entertained. Would I want my kid to come out with a degree in entertainment?" Walker asks, firmly implying the negative.

So thinking, he began to develop "a serious and complete creative service for the schools. No other agency—that I know of—offers my kind of deal to the college market. A.P.B. doesn't just take orders for speakers. We create ideas. We come up with themes. We organize total yearly programs." He sketches in a hypothetical yearly program. "One speaker in international politics, like Lord Caradon; one in science, like Roger Conklin; an urbanologist (new word!); a civil-rights leader, Dick Gregory; a humorist, maybe Mort Sahl." Walker sums up: "I am a consultant to campus lecture groups. I am not a flesh peddler. Who wrote 'The Flesh Peddler'? Vance Packard?"

But the young impresario attributes his present eminence only partially to his talent for communicating with the college set. Another secret of his success, he believes, is his unorthodoxy. "I do things unorthodox," Walker explains, of his business methods. "To me, a written contract, it's a piece of paper. A piece of junk. Pearl Buck is under exclusive contract to me, but I have a handshake with Pearl Buck. Pierre Salinger is under verbal contract to me—a word on the telephone. My attorney wants me to formalize, my clients want me to formalize, but I don't care about formalizing."

Some of those who make up what may be loosely called the lecture business's orthodoxy wish that Robert Walker, and others like him, would care more. The lack of contractual "formalization" that Walker likes so much leads, they say, to a practice of "pirating," or scrambling for clients among freewheeling speakers who have not signed exclusive contracts with any single Bureau.

Robert Keedick, among others, is wry and forthright in criticizing such practices. "This has become a cutthroat business," he says. "Some of us have built up a reputation for integrity, honesty and worthwhile speakers over the course of a lifetime. Then along come these fringe operators claiming, 'I've got Johnson, I've got Eugene McCarthy.' They list everyone from Napoleon to Catherine the Great. But none of these people are under their management."

Jacqueline Susann, best-selling author of "The Valley of the Dolls," is listed in the Special Bulletin of the American Program Bureau as an "additional availability." She breaks into not quite merry laughter when she hears about it. "What is the American Program Bureau? Who is Robert Walker? I never met this man," she says.

Miss Susann takes a skeptic's view of lecture bureaus generally. She was under contract to one agency for what she refers to as "a hot 10 minutes" when she was "just a girl who wrote a dog book," namely "Every Night, Josephine." Her "break-in lecture," she remembers ruefully, took place at a country club that turned out to be, in a once-current euphemism, "restricted." "It was so gentile, you can't stand it," says Miss Susann, who is herself Jewish and who points out that "the maiden name" of her husband, TV producer Irving Mansfield, "was Mandelbaum." This country-club experience, which she characterizes as "stupid planning," so unsettled her that she asked the lecture bureau to cancel the contract. "Play or pay," was the reply. After a long-drawn-out hassle, the agreement was torn up. Then came a bill in the mail from the agency. "I owe *them* $375," Miss Susann says, still smarting at the memory. The agency had designed a promotional folder and was now demanding to be reimbursed for it.

Many speakers, however, display faith, trust and gratitude toward agents with whom they have long been on the best of terms. John Ciardi, a popular poet-lecturer, says, "Harry Walker can have his pirate's cut. As far as I'm concerned, he earns every cent he gets in commissions." (The agency usually slices 20 to 50 per cent off the top, depending on whether speaker or bureau picks up the tab for traveling expenses.) "He puts together my schedule— four weeks in the spring, four weeks in the fall, at least five lectures every week. My plane tickets are handed to me. My hotel reservations are stapled to my contracts. I don't have to think about it. Speaking engagements take about one-tenth of my time, for which I am paid about one-twenty-fifth of what I am worth. But they do buy me long stretches of free time. And I want to finish 'The Paradiso.' " Ciardi's translation of "The Inferno" is a standard text in many college literature courses.

Even some rather sedate rival agencies adopt a friendly, live-and-let-live attitude toward their unconventional new competitors. Young blood, says W. Colston Leigh, has brought "new thinking, new philosophy and new concepts" into the trade. The Leigh bureau, 39 years old, represented Eleanor Roosevelt during her entire lecturing lifetime. "These boys have fought desperately to do different things," Leigh says. "Their high-pressure tactics have helped raise prices for the industry. I cheer for them madly all the time."

Their "high-pressure tactics" also sometimes help snare unsuspecting clients. Robert Walker scheduled 50 college lecture bookings for Andy Warhol before he put through his first telephone call to the pop artist turned film-maker. But silver-haired Andy possesses no silver tongue. "Andy's a visual artist. What he has to say is that he has nothing to say," Warhol's curly-headed colleague, Paul Morrissey, told Walker. Walker was undaunted. Well, why couldn't Andy screen 40 minutes' worth of his famous underground movies and just come along, as it were, with the can?

The boys bought this scheme. But when the moment of truth arrived to take off for his first engagements, the central attraction panicked. Andy, terri-fied (he says), sent out a "double" into Missouri, Montana and Oregon, arrayed in silver hair spray and some Warhol costumery. "Anyhow, that boy was more what the kids really wanted," Andy believes. "They liked him better. He smiled prettier. He was more friendlier. He was a flower child."

The ruse of the flower child finally exploded and the American Program Bureau refunded cushy fees to several irate student managements. Since then, Andy has kept his in-person dates in person, bolstered on the platform by some interesting episodes from his 25-hour film, "****!," his superstar, Viva, and Paul Morrissey. They field questions from the audience ("How can you prove he's the *real* Andy Warhol?"), while the real Andy just stands there, presum-ably still scared and still shy.

The Andy Warhol act eliminates altogether the blurry line that Robert Walker and his ilk have drawn between lecturing and the lively arts. Here speaker (or nonspeaker) merges with show business. You can't tell where one begins and the other ends. Paul Morrissey describes the Warhol troupe's col-lege experience: "On our way into Oregon, we're sitting on the plane next to LeRoi Jones and Dr. Spock—also on the bill for the weekend. On our way out, we're standing in line in the school cafeteria behind Mercedes McCambridge, who's headlining the next show. It's like a Hollywood commissary, not a campus."

Touring the college circuit, even those with reputations as profound thinkers come to regard themselves as performers. Ralph Schoenman—who reads to students from Bertrand Russell's "War Crimes in Vietnam" and warns them, in this campaign year, against the "lesser evilism of McCarthy and Ken-nedy"—confides that he hopes to team up with Dick Gregory next season "to do a buck-and-wing and soft-shoe" on campuses across the country. Working title for their political vaudeville: "A World in Revolution."

Dr. Sidney Cohen, chief of psychiatric services at U.C.L.A., comments on his frequent campus appearances with Dr. Timothy Leary. "An act, I think we really ought to call it. He clobbers me, I clobber him," in what someone has called "a sort of psychedelic Punch and Judy show."

But the analogy between actor and speaker falls apart in performance. In an admittedly random lecture sampling that took place over a span of two months, one observer found an astonishing absence of pazazz on the plat-form. The exciting rustle of money that one hears around the lecture bureaus does not often translate itself into the rustle of intellectual excitement (or any other kind) in the lecture hall.

Many of the celebrated seem to feel that merely to present the body is more than half the battle won. Style is usually beside the point. Sometimes so is content. With a few striking exceptions, speakers ramble, whisper (shouts of "louder, louder" are heard throughout the land), scratch their heads, ears, or other places, appear ill-prepared or unprepared and indifferent not only to their young audiences but even to their own material. There are no standards, perhaps because there are no critics. There is little pride of profession, perhaps because lecturing, for almost every speaker, is only a sometime thing. And, after all, why should writers, editors, doctors, civil-rights activists, fish men, yoga women and film makers possess either stage-worthy presences or the gift of gab? Since they are not by trade performers, how should they learn the secret of keeping an old act fresh? Perhaps technique is needed more urgently than anything: a Lee Strasberg of the lecture business to hold seminars in "method" speaking.

But if the students feel swindled by the lack of art, or even craft, in the run-of-the-mill college lecture, most of them don't show it. Says Leonard Schrank, a senior at M.I.T., who was formerly director of the college lecture series: "Great speakers are few and far between. So are great professors. But we want to listen to everyone—the religious nut who sits on a rug with his bells as well as Stokely Carmichael. I was against burning cities. After I heard Stokely, I understood a little more. He opened my eyes."

Students who listen to Drs. Leary and Cohen, the two sages of psychedelia, do get their money's worth of enlightenment (Cohen) and entertainment (Leary). Cohen, taking a basically establishment and therefore courageous point of view, seeks to make "tripping" unfashionable for the young. He touts the recent decrease in the use of LSD. "The old acid heads have backed away," he reports. "They've been clobbered by anxiety reactions; they've wound up in psychotic states; they're turning to non-chemical meditative techniques; sensitivity groups, marathon therapies, Synanon, even to the Maharishi." Honesty, however, compels Cohen to point out the concurrent increase in the use of marijuana and methedrine "for its euphoric, not its religious, capability."

"I don't think it's smart or healthy," he remarks, about the druggies. "They're saying, 'I'm really worthless in my sober state, I've got to get out of it.' But the schizophrenic is not in touch with any eternal verity."

Cohen's cohort, Timothy Leary—in bare feet, beard and a suit impeccably tailored of palest beige flannel—starts his speech by standing in front of the microphone and calling to the sound crew, "Am I turned on?" Thereafter much of the audience, unaccustomed to such a bold display of showmanship in the lecture hall, is eating out of his hand.

"I am not here to debate with Dr. Cohen and I am not here to talk about drugs," Leary proclaims. ("He must be breaking in a new routine," a co-ed at Newark State College whispers.) "My message is one of individual freedom. One: Love Is Where It's At. Two: Evolution Not Revolution. . . ." He relates the message of Buddha, as trans-liberated by Leary: "Keep cool, baby, it's all spinning and changing. Keep cool, baby." The rhythms of his speech grow more orgasmic as his meanings grow more murky. He punctuates every sentence with at least one passionately whispered "Wow!" ("Kill for Christ, *Wow!* Sword in one hand, cross in the other. *Wow!*")

Then Leary jumps headlong into the generation gap, the favorite destination of many campus lecturers. Unlike some of them, however, he admonishes the kids to "be kind to your parents," who are "lumbering through this decade like strange dinosaurs." "The only issue is *age*," he reveals. "Between 18 and 22, an irreversible process begins in the nervous system: the brain cells begin to degenerate. Neurological aging starts. At 25, you can't do anything in physics. At 27, you're finished in math. At 47—my age—you're a victim of real brain damage. And at 55 you run for the Senate. . . . It is genetically and biologically suicidal for anyone over 40 to hold office today."

During a coffee hour with Leary (Cohen has already fled), one young man asks, "What makes you think we could do better than our parents?" Leary holds him with a bleary eye. "Could you do worse?" he counters. Another student confesses, "I have more confidence voting for someone who's older." The high priest of psychedelia sighs and looks away.

But most of the students seem so starved for adult recognition and the self-affirmation it may bring that they clutch at anything and anyone (including Leary) who holds out the promise of some status in the over-30 world. "Like my parents, they're so narrow, so closed," said a girl from New Jersey, waving goodby to the doctor as he drove off, in his dusty car. (A book, "The Ecstatic Adventure," and some Saran-wrapped sandwiches sat on the dashboard to sustain spirit and body, no doubt, on his pilgrimage to the next campus.) "Whatever they read, look at, listen to, my mother and father come up with the same reaction. It's those bad teen-agers again. I wish they would dig Leary, just once. They might find out that I'm a human being."

If the lure of LSD no longer hooks teen-agers en masse, neither does the cult of hip. Paul Krassner, "editor and ring-leader of The Realist," a not-so-underground newspaper, appears on the platform in blue jeans, boots and uncombed hair to pan mass media, laud LSD and ask for its legalization, promote The Pill for underage girls, and condemn coffee as "an establishment drug." Krassner warns that "six cups a day can cause chromosome damage." He also tells a long story about the censorship of "duck vomit" on a television show. The moral: "Kids can see Vietnam body counts on TV, but they can't see a duck throwing up." "Who *wants* to see a duck throwing up?" a long-haired boy in the third row asks his neighbor. Krassner, from first-hand knowledge, characterizes the LSD experience as "basically, a kind of reversion to the innocence of childhood." He admires parents who take their children on "trips" with them. "The American Legion never brought their kids to their stag parties. But be-ins are family affairs."

Nevertheless, skepticism bristles in the questions the students ask Krassner. "Who's in charge?" one inquires, of the hippie revolution. "You are," Krassner says. "There are no leaders and there is no dogma. Action first,

theory later." "Aren't you a leader?" someone baits him. "A leader tells people what to do," Krassner insists. "When something's happening in hippiedom,
C.B.S. calls me because hippies aren't listed in the Yellow Pages."

"How about free stores? What's so great about taking instead of working?" another student wants to know. Krassner describes the free-store concept as "essentially theatrical. It's street theater. Our economic system is based
on exploitation and deceit. We're all predisposed to be cheated. In the free
store, money is not required. So once inside, you go through changes. The ideal
of theater is to put the audience through changes." But the audience leaves a
Krassner lecture, apparently having been put through few, if any, changes.

Although he is mild-mannered on the podium, sometimes to the point of
inaudibility, Paul Goodman's brand of dissent falls on student ears less hol-
lowly (when they can hear it) than Krassner's. He reviles "the whole middle
class. It is not only racist but much worse. It regards all those who don't shape
up as not quite human. The fact that someone wants to be different and *not*
shape up, that won't do at all." This is a warm-up for Goodman's all-out
slaughter of contemporary schooling. "Empirical evidence is overwhelming
that formal education, as it now exists, is of no value whatever. In studies of
the relationship between college grades and life achievement, there is *no* relationship, none whatever." Knowing laughter ripples through the hall.

"I would advise your middle-class parents to boycott the schools as Negro
parents have done, to change to Summerhill methods, and to stop all this nonsense." A wistful note creeps into his voice. "But middle-class parents are quite
satisfied that their children are being destroyed. Black parents, thank God, are
not." This time no one defends mummy and daddy. The audience gets the
message, but seeks the solution with some impatience. "If it's such common
knowledge that we're not learning a relevant goddam thing, why the hell
doesn't someone do something about it?" a delicate-looking blond girl asks.

Any speaker who casts a wry eye on the current political campaigns is
well received by almost any gathering. Art Buchwald's delivery is so droll and
his charm so flagrant that nobody seems to mind the mildness of his jokes. He
is one of the few speakers on the hustings who might, if he chose, make a good
living doing a single: "Gene McCarthy went to New Hampshire with four
Vassar sophomores and a book of poems. He changed the political history of
the United States. His first telegram was from Bobby Kennedy. 'Gene, we won,'
it said." Just before Rockefeller's announcement of his candidacy, Buchwald
was lamenting, "Nixon is now left with no one to oppose but himself—which
could make this one of the dirtiest campaigns in history."

Jimmy Breslin's P.Q. (performance quotient) is not quite so high as
Buchwald's, so he never tries for the big yok. But he is, if anything, even more
irreverent and more outspoken. About the Senator from New York: "Bobby
wants young fellas around him now. Adam Walinsky, Jeff Greenfield, they're
wild. Sorenson? He's an old man, they're edging him out. He doesn't fit into
Kennedy's new world." On the funeral of Martin Luther King: "It was the

worst thing I've ever seen. There were these cleaning women with these magnificent black Southern faces—hurt, wounded, helpless people. They almost had to carry Humphrey out. He couldn't take it."

By far the most popular form of anti-establishmentarianism, the big *shtick* on campus today, is Black Power. It comes in several shades of militance but a single scorching degree of intensity. The bone-deep commitment and the hot conviction that the Black Power people display diminishes, by comparison, all the other speakers who come on half-hearted and lukewarm. In the course of attending dozens of lectures this spring, I witnessed three standing ovations. They were for (1) Dr. James Farmer, the founder of the Congress of Racial Equality; (2) Floyd McKissick, the national director of CORE, and (3) Dick Gregory, candidate for President of the United States on the Peace and Freedom ticket. Each of them plugs his pitch squarely into square society.

But only Farmer (right now running for Congress in New York City) has not yet wholly abandoned the establishment. Calling for "a sense of humanity developed out of mutual suffering," he still recalls "the young white martyrs—Andrew Goodman and Michael Schwerner—who risked and gave their lives." He even dares to invoke brotherhood and love. "Black Power is group identity, pride, self-esteem. It is a prerequisite to meaningful integration. We will love ourselves and join with you in loving mankind. Whoever will fight for us and with us to the end is our brother."

Neither love nor brotherhood nor white participation in black society appears prominently on Floyd McKissick's agenda. "I am not preaching a doctrine of love, I'm preaching a doctrine of self-interest," he says. "I want to talk about American society. Have you ever seen a commode and smelled the stench? That's American society." He brings up the then-recent riots at Columbia University. "Call in a buncha cops to put down something that happened internally on that campus, you're moving toward Nazism, you're moving toward a totalitarian state."

He mocks white gradualism. "For 400 years, the white man has his foot on you. But he must take his foot off *gradually*. If he moves too fast, he might get whiplash and it might injure him." He offers a thumbnail sketch of the American black: "He doesn't own the land, he doesn't own the building. He has a few sheets to cover his bed and some dishes he buys in the dime store. Only the 10 per cent who do better than that believe in integration. But they don't live in Harlem; they live in Queens. They're in with the system. They're in with the man." He repudiates non-violence. "To hell with it. 'My dream became a nightmare,' said Martin Luther King. Morals ain't got no position in this society. Violence is the only method of appeal."

A black male student at New York University stands up. "Brother McKissick, I've been going to this white man's school for four years. I agree that time for talk has ended. Let the white man come to us and try to redress our grievances." A female sociology student applauds vigorously. "As a white middle-class relatively bourgeois person, I find that I'm very excited over Black Power. McKissick? I mean, like, he tells it like it is." She eyes an over-30 reporter coldly. "Maybe you don't like it, but that's how it is."

Dick Gregory is the darling of the college lecture circuit. If students could vote, he really might, as he says, "paint the White House black." As do Goodman, Leary and others, Gregory winds up putting down parents. "They are siding with the Federal Government against their own kids. If 18 is too young to vote, it oughta be too young to die. Any parent is sick who don't know that."

Gregory is an attractive and selfless performer, putting on a one-man show that is two hours long without even a stop for a glass of water. He welds tough humor with a plea for humanity to which the college-aged naturally respond. Is it too farfetched to suppose that, in the power of psychology of the young, the dominating parent has come to equal white society, coloring the subjugated child symbolically black?

This much is sure: No one generates more interest on campus than the speaker who descends into the generation gap and digs, digs, digs. Memo to all lecture bureau presidents: There's gold in that thar abyss.

Questions for Analysis

1. How does the concept of "projection" ("the ability to intuit and exploit the national interests and mass preoccupations in the air") relate the lecture business to campuses? What is the nature of "the pop look, and outlet, in lecture-bureau presidents"? How should this affect evaluation of the lecture business on campuses today?

2. Rate recent lecturers on your campus for message and technique and the validity of Gittelson's charge, "Many of the celebrities seem to feel that merely to present the body is more than half the battle won. Style is usually beside the point. Sometimes so is content." Cite specific examples to support or refute the charge. Rate Stokely Carmichael and Dick Gregory when you read the studies about them in Part IV.

3. What students listen to lectures on your campus? Why do they listen? Do they truly "want to listen to everyone—the religious nut who sits on a rug with his bells as well as Stokely Carmichael"? How critically do they listen? To which rhetorical appeals do they react most overtly? In "New Left" terms, is listening to a Gregory or a Goodman lecture a form of "commitment" or of "involvement"? Explain. How genuinely can these terms be applied to campus lecture audiences?

4. Determine your reaction to this: "These kids are sensation-mad. What's worse, the university administration has abdicated. Student organizers are almost entirely autonomous in choosing the speakers they want." What are the "rights" of students who listen to lectures? Do they deserve "protection" from certain lecturers for rea-

sons of message or technique? Explain. What standards might guide the consideration of possible lecturers by a student board of governors?

5. What do Gittelson's descriptions of various campus lecturers suggest about "speaker adaptation"? Which of the lecturers appear in message and technique to be "catering" to student audiences? How might any one of them perform differently on your campus than on another? Specifically compare Leary to Cohen, Krassner to Goodman, and Farmer to McKissick. Are students treated as "power-vulnerables" or as "power-invulnerables"? Illustrate.

8

The Rhetoric of the Streets: Some Legal and Ethical Considerations

Franklyn S. Haiman

One hears considerable criticism these days of the tactics employed by contemporary protest groups—by the Vietnam war dissenters, the
civil rights movement, or students demanding a greater share in campus
decision-making. Many such challenges come from those in our society, presumably in a majority, who oppose some or all of the views of these protest
groups and who might be expected to divert a portion of their hostility toward
the methods used rather than the goals sought.

But when one finds those who profess neutrality or friendship toward
the goals of the dissenters also expressing doubt about the methods they employ, it is time to attempt a serious assessment of the situation. For, indeed,
many objective observers of the contemporary "rhetoric" of the streets do
have misgivings about its propriety and even its legality. The term "rhetoric"
as used here is put in quotation marks because only by the broadest of definition do some of the activities to be discussed fall into what has traditionally
been called the province of rhetoric. If rhetoric means only verbal communication, we are clearly dealing here with matters outside that boundary. If,
however, we take Aristotle's phrase to mean literally "*all* the available means
of persuasion," then we do have here a problem in rhetorical criticism.

Regardless of terminology, our society today is confronted with a wide
range of activities unfamiliar to those accustomed to thinking of protest in
terms of a Faneuil Hall rally or a Bughouse Square soapbox orator. With
respect to the Vietnam war we have witnessed everything from vigils, sit-ins
at draft boards, and picket signs accusing the President of murder, to the
burning of draft cards and self-immolation. On campuses across the country
we have seen mass rallies doused by the hoses of firemen, sit-ins at administration buildings, and boycotts or threatened boycotts of classes.

The civil rights movement has generated perhaps the widest range of

Franklyn S. Haiman is Chairman of the Department of Public Address and Group
Communications, Northwestern University.
Reprinted by permission from *Quarterly Journal of Speech*, 53(1967), 99–114.

new forms. Invented to protest racial discrimination by restaurants, the sit-in has been extended to churches, libraries, real estate offices, and boards of education. The mass rally, an old form in itself, has been expanded to new locations and new dimensions—before the jailhouse, in the middle of the street, or through the center of the nation's capitol city. Slogans and folksongs have assumed a new importance. Picketing, another older form, has also gone to new locations—before pavilions at the World's Fair or into a Chicago residential area to protest in front of the mayor's home. Mass marches through hostile territory—like Selma, Alabama, or all-white neighborhoods of Chicago —have attracted national attention. Going limp when arrested, obstructing the flow of traffic, and lying down in front of bulldozers on school construction sites have probably been the most extreme of the new forms—short, of course, of those employed in Harlem, Rochester, Cleveland, and Watts.

In attempting to review the major lines of criticism directed at this new array of rhetorical expressions, one finds that he can group them into three broad areas. The first line of criticism asserts that insofar as the contemporary rhetoric of the streets violates the law it produces a climate of anarchy from which, in the end, no one can gain. It is argued that to engage in the obstruction of traffic or to trespass on the property of others because one believes that his cause is good is to take the law into one's own hands and to create a society in which everyone's rights are threatened. The wanton looting and shooting which have erupted in some of our cities are alleged to be evidence of the ultimate end to which all of this leads. It is said that civil disobedience, even for the highest of motives, cannot be condoned in a society where legal channels—courts, legislatures, and the public forum—are available for the expression of grievances. One cannot condone civil disobedience for the "good guys" without allowing it for the "bad guys"; for who is to distinguish good motives from evil ones? Justice must be impartial and even-handed.

A second category of criticism is directed at those aspects of the new rhetoric, admittedly legal and even appropriate under some circumstances, but alleged to violate the proposition that, in an orderly society, there must be prescribed and proscribed times, places, and manners for protest. Critics point out that two of the leading spokesmen for the libertarian view regarding freedom of speech, philosopher Alexander Meiklejohn and Supreme Court Justice Hugo Black, have themselves supported this principle,[1] and that much

[1]"When self-governing men demand freedom of speech they are not saying that every individual has an unalienable right to speak whenever, wherever, however he chooses. . . . The common sense of any reasonable society would deny the existence of that unqualified right. No one, for example, may, without consent of nurse or doctor, rise up in a sickroom to argue for his principles or his candidate." Alexander Meiklejohn, *Political Freedom* (New York, 1960), p. 25.

"Such an argument has as its major unarticulated premise the assumption that people who want to propagandize protests or views have a constitutional right to do so whenever and however and wherever they please. That concept of constitutional law was vigorously and forthrightly rejected in . . . *Cox v. Louisiana*. . . . We reject it again." Justice Hugo Black, speaking for a majority of the Supreme Court on November 14, 1966, in *Adderley v. Florida*.

of the current rhetoric of the streets exceeds the bounds of permissible time, place, and manner.

More specifically, they argue that protest is not justified if it constitutes an invasion of the privacy of others.[2] A prime example often cited is the series of marches of August, 1965, led by Negro comedian Dick Gregory to and around the home of Mayor Richard J. Daley in Chicago's Bridgeport section, an area of modest middle-class homes. Critics have condemned this and all other instances of picketing or parading in residential areas on the ground that "a man's home is his castle" and that such an intrusion was an invasion of the mayor's privacy, as well as that of his family and neighbors. Professor Alfred Kamin of Loyola University Law School in Chicago, makes an impressively documented presentation of the legal arguments for this point of view which he summarizes: "The thesis of this article is simple. . . . In the constitutional value scale, the quiet enjoyment and privacy of residential premises—even of the privately owned homes of public officials—merits a higher priority than freedom of speech."[3] Kamin draws support for his thesis primarily from court decisions in the area of labor-management disputes, which appear to carry their grievances to the doorsteps of their employers' homes, and from the substantial number of states (nine, to be exact) which have enacted statutory bans on residential picketing.

A slightly different rationale for objecting to the time, place, or manner of expressing deviant views was that used by Federal District Judge Samuel Perry in an injunction handed down in Chicago in September, 1966. Judge Perry enjoined the American Nazi Party and its leader, George Lincoln Rockwell, from demonstrating within one-half mile of any Jewish house of worship on any Jewish holy day, if clothed in Nazi garb or displaying Nazi symbols. He argued that such demonstrations would constitute an interference with the exercise of religious freedom by Jews attending their synagogues— a right which, unlike that of privacy, is explicitly recognized by the First Amendment.

Protests have also been challenged on the grounds that, under certain circumstances, they may place an undue strain upon the community's resources or may conflict with other community interests. One of the most current and significant illustrations of this rationale, found in an injunction issued by the Circuit Court of Cook County, Illinois, in August, 1966, limited the scope of marches then being conducted by the Chicago Freedom Movement under the leadership of Martin Luther King. This injunction, still in

[2]Although the "right to privacy" is nowhere mentioned in the U.S. Constitution or Bill of Rights, it has gained increasing recognition by legal scholars and the courts as a privilege worthy of some constitutional protection. This development reached its highwater mark in 1965, when the Supreme Court invalidated Connecticut's ban on the dissemination of birth control information. In the majority opinion written by Justice William O. Douglas the Court relied upon a right of privacy which it found *implied* in the First, Third, Fourth, and Ninth Amendments, as the primary basis for striking down the Connecticut law. *Griswold v. Connecticut*, 381 US 479.

[3]Alfred Kamin, "Residential Picketing and the First Amendment," *Northwestern University Law Review*, LXI (May–June 1966), 182.

force, is of the utmost interest to the development of the law regarding freedom of speech, for it is a carefully drawn and relatively qualified ban which could well stand up on appeal to higher courts. It does not enjoin the marches entirely, but provides only that there shall not be more than one such march in Chicago per day, that only one neighborhood at a time may be the target, that no more than 500 persons may march, and that marches shall be confined to daylight times other than the rush hours. The basic justification for these limitations, argued before the Court on behalf of Chicago Police Superinten- dent O. W. Wilson, was that the police department could not simultaneously discharge its obligation to protect the marchers from the activities of hostile counter-demonstrators and fulfill its responsibilities to protect the safety and welfare of the community. Wilson charged that, at the height of the marches, when hundreds of policemen were diverted to the protection of demonstrators, crime rates had risen in other areas of the city.[4] He also suggested that the morale of the police department suffered severely during this period and that the financial costs to the city were exorbitant. How much effort, critics ask, can a city government reasonably be expected to make to protect dissenters from counter-violence, especially when the majority of taxpayers and voters may share the attitudes of those counter-demonstrators?

Finally, the time, place, or manner issue is sometimes argued on the basis of an "innocent bystander" theory which says that protest is permissible only so long as it is confined so as to affect the legitimate targets of the protest but not to inconvenience others. Hence one might concede that the mayor, as a public official, is a fair target for protest even when he is at home, but that his family and neighbors, the "innocent bystanders," should not have to be subjected to the same harassment. Similarly, the man who cannot get to work on time because of the congestion caused by a march, or the student who cannot study because of the turmoil created by campus demonstrations or boycotts of classes, may assert that their rights as innocent bystanders should take precedence over the free speech claims of the protesters. An analogy is sometimes made here to the secondary boycott in labor-managment relations —an activity which is regarded as impermissible because of its harmful effects on those who are only tangentially related to the dispute.

The third major category of criticism directed at the contemporary rhet- oric of the streets concerns objections which may be the most difficult and most profound from the point of view of the rhetorical critic. At the core of these objections is the proposition that the new rhetoric exceeds the bounds of ra- tional discourse, which teachers of rhetoric value so highly and are dedicated to promote; that the new rhetoric is "persuasion" by a strategy of power and coercion rather than by reason and democratic decision-making. This line of thought has been expressed in at least two different ways.

In an article in this journal, Professor Leland Griffin coined the phrase

---

[4]Paragraph 24 of complaint in *Wilson v. King, et. al.*, Case #66 Ch 4938 in Chancery in Circuit Court of Cook County.

"body rhetoric" to express the thesis that much of the new rhetoric is not persuasion at all, at least as rhetoricians are accustomed to defining that term, but instead constitutes the "holding of a gun at the head" of those to whom the protests are directed.[5] Pickets at a mayor's home or college students sitting in at an administration building are simply throwing their weight around, says the critic, until the authorities give them what they want. If the Chicago Freedom Movement marchers are only interested in communicating a message, then why (given mass media coverage) cannot the same point be made with 500 marchers in one neighborhood as with 5,000 marchers in six neighborhoods simultaneously? To such critics the intention of the marchers seems not to be simply to *communicate* grievances, but to throw the city into such chaos that it will be *forced* to meet their demands.

Even the greatest champions of free speech have expressed doubts about such demonstrations. Justice Hugo Black has said:

> The First and Fourteenth Amendments, I think, take away from government, state and federal, all power to restrict freedom of speech, press, and assembly *where people have a right to be for such purposes.* This does not mean, however, that these amendments also grant a constitutional right to engage in the conduct of picketing or patrolling, whether on publicly owned streets or on privately owned property. . . . Were the law otherwise, people on the streets, in their homes and anywhere else could be compelled to listen against their will to speakers they did not want to hear. Picketing, though it may be utilized to communicate ideas, is not speech, and therefore is not of itself protected by the First Amendment.[6]

A majority of the United States Supreme Court, speaking through Justice Arthur Goldberg in the same case, proclaimed: "We emphatically reject the notion . . . that the First and Fourteenth Amendments afford the same kind of freedom to those who would communicate ideas by conduct such as patrolling, marching, and picketing on streets and highways as these amendments afford to those who communicate ideas by pure speech."[7]

The second line of criticism related to the general issue of rationality of discourse raises the age-old question of the new rhetoric's resort to emotional appeals. The focus here is on the popularity among contemporary protest movements of sloganeering, folksinging, draft-card burning, and other modes of communication that appear designed to elicit signal responses.[8]

---

[5]Leland Griffin, "The Rhetorical Structure of the 'New Left' Movement: Part I," *QJS*, I, (April, 1964), 127.

[6]*Cox v. Louisiana*, 379 US 536 (1965), 578.

[7]*Ibid.*, 555.

[8]Alfred Kamin also puts picketing in this category: "The picket line elicits conditioned responses . . . a primitive and unsophisticated illustration of McLuhan's dictum, 'The medium is the message.' " "Residential Picketing," 198–199.

Catchphrases such as "Black Power," picket signs reading "Hey, Hey, LBJ, How Many Kids Have You Killed Today?" the joining of hands and the singing of "We Shall Overcome," the speeches of Mario Savio, and the folksongs of Joan Baez and Pete Seeger are all cited as evidence of this tendency.

This is the outline of a rather formidable brief challenging the contemporary rhetoric of the streets. The challenge has been posed in both legal and ethical terms, and it raises, in substance, two kinds of questions about the new rhetoric: (1) Is the particular activity in question protected, or should it be, by the First Amendment? and (2) Even if legal, is the activity ethical? Let us turn now to the case for the defense.

Regarding the question of disobedience, civil or otherwise, to the law, one must concede that such activity does have an undermining effect on established authority and tends toward an anarchic social climate. Justice must be administered without discrimination either for or against the dissenter; if he breaks the law he must be punished. Yet, having recognized this, I would note some important qualifications often overlooked.

Many who currently advocate and practice civil disobedience do not expect nor ask for exemption from punishment. They are keenly aware that a lawless society cannot survive, but they are willing to pay whatever penalties the civil law may exact in order to obey what they regard as a higher law, be it the law of their religion or their conscience, which requires them to protest what they view as some injustice in their society. They seek no special privileges, but rather hope that their willingness to suffer penalties for their convictions may communicate a message to the consciences of others and thus pave the way for social change. One can admire the courage and sympathize with the goals of such persons and still recognize, as they do, that they must be punished for their actions. One might go even further to suggest that such civil disobedience merits support, though not exemption from punishment, so long as it does no physical harm to others. Sharper distinctions may need to be made, for example, between the *inconvenience* resulting from the tying up of traffic to a World's Fair and the *physical danger* of a Watts riot. Indeed, a riot is not *civil* disobedience at all, and rioters are usually an entirely different group of people from the kind who engage in conscientious disobedience.

Critics of civil disobedience also need to be reminded that some kinds of law-breaking are, paradoxically, quite legal. Again, finer distinctions are needed. So-called civil disobedience, which involves the violation of a law believed by the protesters to be unconstitutional and later found by the courts to be unconstitutional, may be exempt from punishment. One may, under such circumstances, with both legal and moral justification, disobey a local or state law in order to obey a higher civil law, *i.e.*, the United States Constitution. Granted, one cannot embark on such a course lightly; for it is the United States Supreme Court, not the individual citizen, that, in our system, must ultimately decide whether a law is or is not constitutional. But if one is willing to run the risk of losing that decision (thereby paying the penalty, of course), he is fully justified in such a violation.

Many Supreme Court decisions, particularly those involving the First Amendment, support this position. One landmark case, in 1938, reversed the conviction of a member of the Jehovah's Witnesses, who had been arrested and fined for distributing religious literature in Griffin, Georgia, under a city ordinance which the Court found to be an unconstitutional infringement on the freedom of speech and press.[9] More recently, in 1965, a Baltimore, Maryland, theatre manager who had deliberately flaunted the state's movie censorship statute because he thought it unconstitutional and was arrested and convicted in the lower courts, saw his conviction overturned by the Supreme Court, which agreed that the law violated the First Amendment.[10] Then, of course, there have been the long line of sit-in cases from the South, some of which have been decided on narrower grounds than the First Amendment, and some of which have involved refusal to obey police orders rather than laws, but all of which have been norm-breaking activities that provoked sanctions at the local level which were later reversed by the United States Supreme Court.[11]

One cautionary note must be appended here. The Supreme Court has, on occasion, taken that attitude that if a citizen believes a law or local administrative rule to be unconstitutional he must exhaust all possible administrative and judicial remedies before proceeding to its violation.[12] This position has not been sufficiently elaborated to make clear precisely how much effort a citizen must make to seek legal remedies before resorting to disobedience. This appears to depend somewhat on the particular circumstances of the law and violation in question. But, despite these qualifications, it is clear that dissenters have no obligation to conform indefinitely to statutes and ordinances that conflict with the Constitution. If this be deleterious to established authority, then established authority had better be brought into conformity with the law.

But what of *un*civil disobedience? Can anything be said in defense of Watts and of angry voices in the streets which sometimes seem to be calling for violence? Certainly not within the framework of a democratic society, where only peaceful change can be accepted. But should we not be somewhat troubled by the awareness that, despite the destruction to property, despite the loss of lives, despite the backlash of public opinion, these outbreaks have precipitated significant reforms that previously had been notably slow in coming? It would seem that even the "rhetoric of the riot," mindless and indiscriminate as it may be, has its positive function in contemporary America. What moral can be drawn from this, short of abandoning the conviction that a civilized society is preferable to the law of the jungle? Perhaps simply that if the chan-

---

[9]*Lovell v. Griffin*, 303 US 444.

[10]*Freedom v. Maryland*, 380 US 51.

[11]See *Garner v. Louisiana*, 368 US 157 (1961) ; *Shuttlesworth v. Birmingham*, 373 US 262 (1963) ; *Peterson v. Greenville*, 373 US 244 (1963) ; *Lombard v. Louisiana*, 373 US 267 (1963) ; *Barr v. City of Columbia*, 378 US 146 (1964) ; *Robinson v. Florida*, 378 US 153 (1964) ; *Griffin v. Maryland*, 378 US 130 (1964) ; *Bouie v. City of Columbia*, 378 US 347 (1964) ; *Bell v. Maryland*, 378 US 226 (1964) ; *Hamm v. City of Little Rock*, 379 US 306 (1964) ; and *Brown v. Louisiana*, 383 US 131 (1966).

[12]See *Poulos v. New Hampshire*, 345 US 395 (1953).

nels for peaceful protest and reform become so clogged that they appear to be (and, in fact, may be) inaccessible to some segments of the population, then the Jeffersonian doctrine that "the tree of liberty must be refreshed from time to time, with the blood of patriots and tyrants" may become more appropriate to the situation than more civilized rules of the game.

The problems associated with the time, place, and manner of protest must now be addressed together with the possibility that countervailing interests such as privacy, convenience, or the safety and welfare of the community may justify some curtailments of the rhetoric of the streets. One can hardly quarrel with the general thesis, supported by Meiklejohn and Black, that there is no constitutional right to protest whenever, wherever, and however one chooses. There must be, as Professor Harry Kalven has so aptly put it, a "Robert's Rules of Order for use of the public forum of the streets," for it is an "unbeatable proposition that you cannot have two parades on the same corner at the same time."[13] The real questions in this area are not questions about the correctness of the *principle*, but rather about the reasonableness and equity of its *application* to particular conflict situations. We must look beneath the pat phrases such as "innocent bystander" and "invasion of privacy," or the surface reasonableness of the Chicago Freedom Movement injunction, to do some honest weighing of the competing interests at stake.

The "innocent bystander" theory is the first which requires closer scrutiny. As was indicated earlier, an analogy is often made here to the illegality of secondary boycotts in labor-management relations. But serious questions can be raised about the validity of applying this theory to political and social protest movements. The grievances involved in labor-management disputes are essentially grievances held by one private party, or group of private parties, against the actions or policies of another private party, whereas the grievances involved in most protest movements are directed to the body politic as a whole and are redressable only by public policy or action. Thus it is arguable that on issues such as civil rights and the Vietnam war there is no such thing as an innocent bystander. Every citizen who supports the status quo, either actively or by passive acquiescence, is a legitimate target for the communications of the dissenter.

Furthermore, an examination of particular cases may reveal important shortcomings in the innocent bystander theory. The marches to Mayor Daley's home in the summer of 1965 provide a good example. Just how "innocent" were the "bystanders" in this case, the neighbors? After all, the message being communicated by the demonstrators concerned racial discrimination, and it was no accident (in view of either the motivations or effects of the march) that the mayor happened to live in an all-white neighborhood of the city, which has, over the years, been known for its resistance to the "intrusion" of

[13]Harry Kalven, Jr., "The Concept of the Public Forum: *Cox v. Louisiana,*" *The Supreme Court Review, 1965,* pp. 25–26.

Negro homeowners from adjacent areas. Although Mayor Daley was ostensibly the primary target of communication, the protesters certainly perceived his neighbors as legitimate recipients of their message. How often, in other instances where the innocent bystander theory is invoked, may the circumstances be similar?

But some would hold that even the mayor, although admittedly not an innocent bystander, should have the right to a private life, free from the harassments of political and social turmoil. What of this right to privacy as an alleged countervailing interest to freedom of speech? What of Kamin's case for the banning of protest from all residential areas? What of the fact that even Zechariah Chafee, one of the most respected proponents of freedom of speech, has been troubled over matters related to this issue?[14]

One can hardly deny that allowing for the expression of dissent in residential areas does indeed impinge on other important rights and privileges. The question, I think, is what price a society is willing to pay to insure that the messages of minority groups are not screened out of the consciences of those to whom they are addressed. For once the principle is invoked that listeners may be granted some immunity from messages they think they would rather not hear, or which cause them annoyance, a Pandora's box of circumstances is opened in which the right of free speech could be effectively nullified. Also, difficult problems arise in defining a residential area. Would not a prohibition against demonstrations in such areas turn out to mean that those who can afford to live in neighborhoods zoned exclusively for single-family dwellings would be protected, while those who live on a street with a shopping area, a gas station, a real estate office, or a public building would have no more protection than if they resided in an office building in the heart of the downtown center?

Perhaps appropriately, the United States Supreme Court, at least at this point in its development of a theory of free speech, has been unwilling to weight the scales in the manner suggested by Chafee and Kamin. On the contrary, there are cases which makes clear the Court's view that the right to privacy, emotionally appealing as it may be, must not be purchased at major cost to the First Amendment.

An early precedent in this area was provided in 1943, in a case involving a city ordinance which prohibited the door-to-door distribution of handbills. A member of the Jehovah's Witnesses was arrested, convicted, and fined for

---

[14]"Great as is the value of exposing citizens to novel views, home is one place where a man ought to be able to shut himself up in his own ideas if he desires. . . . A doorbell cannot be disregarded like a handbill. It takes several minutes to ascertain the purpose of a propagandist and at least several more to get rid of him. . . . A man's house is his castle, and what is more important his wife's castle. A housewife may fairly claim some protection from being obliged to leave off bathing the baby and rush down to the door, only to be asked to listen to a sermon or a political speech. . . . Freedom of the home is as important as freedom of speech." Zechariah Chafee, *Free Speech in the United States* (Cambridge, 1948), pp. 406–407.

circulating a leaflet announcing a religious meeting. Although the prosecution argued, in justification of the ordinance, that this was an industrial town in which many men worked a night shift and slept during the day, the Supreme Court ruled that "door to door distribution of circulars is essential to the poorly financed causes of little people."[15] The Court indicated that a house-holder may post a notice on his door that he does not wish his door-bell rung and may enforce such a wish through the laws of trespass, but it held that a blanket prohibition of door-to-door soliciting by the city is unconstitutional. This position was reaffirmed in 1951, by implication, when the Supreme Court *upheld* a municipal ordinance prohibiting door-to-door solicitation for com-mercial magazines *only* because of the commercial element involved.[16] Had the solicitation been for political or religious causes, the Court presumably would have reached a different conclusion.

To be sure, these cases have involved only single solicitors, and a differ-ent posture might be taken by the Supreme Court if a case involving large numbers of marchers in a residential area goes up on appeal. But perhaps off-setting the numbers factor will be the consideration that marchers do not ordinarily ring doorbells and seldom walk on private property. If they remain on the public sidewalks and streets, the possible issue of trespass cannot in-trude, and the Court will have to deal simply with the clash between an alleged right of residential privacy and freedom of speech.

Closely related to the right-to-privacy and innocent-bystander arguments is the assertion that the contemporary rhetoric of the streets sometimes cre-ates inconvenience for other persons. This claim need not detain us long. Dissent is always an inconvenience to those who like the status quo, some-times maddeningly so. But, again, a Jeffersonian epigram may give perspective —reminding us that it is "timid men who prefer the calm of despotism to the turbulent sea of liberty." One is tempted to be skeptical about those who complain so loudly over the congestion or annoyance generated by a civil rights march, but who do not raise similar objections to the St. Patrick's Day parade or the Saturday afternoon football crowds. Or, as Harry Kalven puts it, in suggesting that the "equal protection" clause of the Constitution may have some bearing on this problem: "Everyone at some time or other loves a parade whatever its effects on traffic and other uses of public streets. Munici-palities pressed by concern with the protest movement may be inhibited in any rush to flat non-discriminatory prohibitions by the difficulty of distin-guishing between the parades we like and others. Equal protection may, there-fore, require freedom for the parades we hate."[17]

Much more serious than the inconvenience argument is the claim set forth in the Chicago Freedom Movement case that unless protest marches are restricted in size and scope, dangerous consequences, such as a rise in the

[15]*Martin v. Struthers*, 319 US 141, 146.
[16]*Brerard v. City of Alexandria*, 341 US 622.
[17]"The Concept of the Public Forum," p. 30.

crime rate, may ensue for the city. How many police, critics query, can the government reasonably be expected to divert to the maintenance of order at locations where dissenters choose to aggravate hostile audiences? Or, put in another form, how large a hostile audience can dissenters reasonably expect the police to contain? The answer I am inclined to give is "Everything it takes including, if necessary, calling out the National Guard."

How can such an extreme position be defended? Simply on the grounds that to take any *other* course of action is to issue an invitation to hostile audiences to veto the right of dissent whenever they desire to do so. Only by the firmest display of the government's intention to use all the power at its disposal to protect the constitutional rights of dissenters will hecklers be discouraged from taking the law into their own hands. To be sure, the temporary costs may seem astronomical, but they may be nothing compared to the costs that could be suffered in the long run through any other course. This principle was clear to our national government when it posted an army on the campus of the University of Mississippi to insure that one man, James Meredith, was granted his rights to enter and to remain at that institution. Its reverse was equally clear in Little Rock, Arkansas, when Governor Orval Faubus let it be known (either out of conviction or desire) that the state's police power could not cope with those who wished to block the entry of Negro children to Central High School.

One can agree with this principle and still take the position that limitations on the time, place, and manner of protest designed to make the task of the police more manageable, are legitimate so long as they do not interfere substantially with the right of protesters to communicate their messages. This, in essence, is the rationale for the limited kind of injunction issued against the Chicago Freedom Movement marches; and, as evidence of good faith, the police superintendent could point to the rather formidable effort his department had put forth to protect the marches which had already taken place and which had aroused hundreds of hostile counter-demonstrators to potential and actual violence. But, again, one must look more closely at the specific facts of the situation to determine just how reasonable such limitations are.

Is it reasonable, for example, to confine protest marches to daylight hours? From the police department's viewpoint it is much simpler to control the behavior of crowds in daylight than in the dark. From the viewpoint of marchers who have to work for a living during the day, and who can protest only after-hours, it appears to be an effective deprivation of the right to communicate their grievances (except on Sundays!).

Is it reasonable to limit marches to no more than 500 persons? From the police department's viewpoint, yes; for the same message can be communicated by 500 as by 5,000, and at much less strain to community resources. From the viewpoint of the marchers, as well as from the theory of Marshall McLuhan, the medium of 5,000 marchers does *not* communicate the same message as 500. Furthermore, what of the constitutional rights to free speech of the potential

501st marcher? Who is to decide which 500 gets to march and which group does not?

Is it reasonable to limit marches to one neighborhood of the city per day? From the police department's viewpoint, certainly; for with little difficulty enough police can be assigned to one area to insure the maintenance of peace and order. From the viewpoint of the marchers, however, such a limit assumes a degree of coordination and unanimity among the parties enjoined that is rather presumptuous. To tell Mr. Albert Raby that he and his associates cannot march on the northwest side of the city because the Reverend Martin Luther King and his friends are marching that day on the southeast side not only presumes a conspiracy of planning between the two, but, more important, raises important constitutional issues of equal protection of the law. If the injunction against the Chicago Freedom Movement remains on the books and becomes, as it well might, a national precedent, I believe that a significant erosion of the First Amendment will have occurred.

I turn next to Judge Perry's injunction against the Nazis and its thesis that to allow Mr. Rockwell and his dozen-or-so goons to parade in Nazi garb in front of Jewish synagogues is to interfere with the right of Jews to exercise their religious freedom. The issue was *not* that Rockwell would disrupt services by throwing rocks through the synagogue windows or by broadcasting from a sound truck on the street in front; it was *not* that his pickets would obstruct the free flow of pedestrians on their way to and from their house of worship; it was *not* that they would do anything but peacefully and quietly parade with hated symbols (which might provoke *others* to violence), and *this* is what was alleged would be such an interference with the exercise of religious freedom that it justified the denial of Rockwell's freedom of speech. When making people angry or offending their sensibilities becomes a basis for shutting off communication because they happen to be on their way to pray, one can only marvel at the rationalizations a society will invent to justify suppression of the deviant.

One final issue in the time, place, and manner category asks whether certain areas within the public domain can legitimately be declared off-limits from the rest of the public forum. The most frequently proposed site for such an exception is the courthouse, on the theory that the right to a fair trial, unencumbered by the pressures on judge and jury that might accrue from demonstrators gathered on the courthouse grounds, justifies carving this exception from the free speech realm. Indeed, laws are already on the books at all levels of government providing for just such an exception. But now the question is being raised as to whether other sites should be similarly exempt. The most recent case of importance, decided by the Supreme Court on November 14 of last year, found a narrow majority taking the position that not only was a Tallahassee, Florida, jailhouse entitled to such exemption, but even suggesting that the state may declare other public property out of bounds to protest, so long as it does so on a non-discriminatory basis.[18] The facts in this case were relatively simple, as described by Justice Black in the majority opinion:

> Disturbed and upset by the arrest of their schoolmates . . .
> a large number of Florida A. & M. students . . . decided
> to march down to the county jail. . . . A group of around
> 200 marched from the school and arrived at the jail singing
> and clapping. They went directly to the jail door entrance
> where they were met by a deputy sheriff. . . . He asked them
> to move back, claiming they were blocking the entrance.
> . . . They moved back part of the way, where they stood or
> sat, singing, clapping and dancing, on the jail driveway
> and on an adjacent area upon the jail premises.

There is then some difference of opinion about what happened. The majority asserts that "even after their partial retreat, the demonstrators continued to block vehicular passage over this driveway up to the entrance of the jail." After being warned by the sheriff to leave or face arrest, and after refusing to depart, they were arrested, and later convicted for trespass. The minority opinion, written by Justice William O. Douglas, asserts:

> The evidence is uncontradicted that the petitioners' con-
> duct did not upset the jailhouse routine; things went on
> as they normally would. None of the group entered the
> jail. Indeed, they moved back from the entrance as they
> were instructed. There was no shoving, no pushing, no dis-
> order . . . the entrance to the jail was not blocked. . . . If
> there was congestion, the solution was a further request to
> move to lawns or parking areas, not complete ejection and
> arrest.

Although this disputed emphasis in the factual situation may have had some bearing on the Court's decision, the difference between majority and minority went to more fundamental matters. The majority, in effect, seemed to be returning partially to a theory of law that had been propounded in 1897, in a case involving the use of the Boston Commons as a public forum, but which appeared to have been a dead letter since the famous *Hague v. C.I.O.* decision in 1939. In 1897, the Court had taken the position that the government has the same power to regulate the use of public property as an individual owner has to regulate the use of his private property, and that the government of Boston was fully within its rights to control the use of the Commons as it saw fit.[19] But in 1939, Justice Owen Roberts, in announcing the *Hague* decision of the Court, had said in a much-quoted passage: "Wherever the title of street

---

[18] *Adderley v. Florida.*
[19] *Davis v. Massachusetts*, 167 US 43.

or parks may rest, they have immemorially been held in trust for the use of the public and time out of mind, have been used for purposes of assembly, communicating thoughts between citizens, and discussing public questions. Such use of the streets and public places has from the ancient times, been a part of the privileges, immunities, rights, and liberties of citizens."[20]

The *Hague v. C.I.O.* philosophy seemed to prevail in all cases bearing on this issue that went to the Supreme Court after 1939. As recently as 1963, reversing the conviction of 187 Negro students who had gathered for a demonstration on the state capitol grounds at Columbia, South Carolina, an eight to one majority had declared: "The circumstances in this case reflect an exercise of these basic constitutional rights in their most pristine and classic form. The petitioners felt aggrieved by laws of South Carolina. . . . They peaceably assembled at the site of the State Government and there peaceably expressed their grievances."[21]

But now, in the *Adderley* case, a majority of the Court says, as in 1897, "The State, no less than a private owner of property, has power to preserve the property under its control for the use to which it is lawfully dedicated." This statement is reconciled with the *Edwards* decision as follows: "In *Edwards*, the demonstrators went to the South Carolina Capitol grounds to protest. In this case they went to the jail. Traditionally, state capitol grounds are open to the public. Jails, built for security purposes, are not." Here the majority seems to be taking a slightly modified Boston Commons position. The state may decide which public areas are appropriate for speech and which are not, so long as the uses to which these areas are "traditionally" and "lawfully dedicated" are taken into account.

Justice Douglas, speaking for the minority, did not think the matter so simple: "The jailhouse, like an executive mansion, a legislative chamber, a courthouse, or the statehouse itself . . . is one of the seats of government whether it be the Tower of London, the Bastille, or a small county jail. And when it houses political prisoners or those whom many think are unjustly held, it is an obvious center for protest." There are other complexities as well. What of the frequent situation at small county seats, for example, or towns and villages, where the legislative chamber, executive offices, courtroom, and jail are all housed in the same building? Are the surrounding sidewalks, driveways, and lawns to be off-limits or not?

There are even difficulties, as Professor Kalven has pointed out, with laws such as the simple prohibition of courthouse picketing, which was one of the issues in *Cox v. Louisiana* in 1965. There, Justice Goldberg had said for the Supreme Court: "There can be no question that a State has a legitimate interest in protecting its judicial system from the pressures which picketing near a courthouse might create." But Kalven asks of this ruling: "Would

[20]*Hague v. C.I.O.*, 307 US 496, 515.
[21]*Edwards v. South Carolina*, 372 US 229.

this same protest have been permissible if moved a few blocks away? Could one, for example, distribute leaflets highly critical of the Court near the court-house? Is there pressure and intimidation in the protest in front of the court-house that ceases to be present when it is in front of the state house? Or is the principle that it is all right to intimidate legislatures but not courts?[22]

I must admit to sharing some of the ambivalence which has apparently plagued the Supreme Court concerning this last question. Perhaps the right to a fair trial *is* undermined by crowds on the courthouse steps, just as it may be undermined by an unfettered freedom of the press to publicize pre-trial allegations of guilt. And perhaps some carefully drawn measures are needed to protect the conduct of a trial from such distortions. But when extensions of this line of thought lead to decisions such as the one that was made in *Adderley*, I am inclined to join with Justice Douglas' dissent:

> There may be some instances in which assemblies and petitions for redress of grievances are not consistent with other necessary purposes of public property. . . . No one, for example, would suggest that the Senate gallery is the proper place for a vociferous protest rally. . . . But this is quite different than saying that all public places are off-limits to people with grievances . . . by allowing these orderly and civilized protests against injustice to be sup-pressed, we only increase the forces of frustration which the conditions of second-class citizenship are generating amongst us.

The category of criticism of contemporary protest movements which asserts that their rhetoric exceeds the bounds of rational discourse must, finally, be addressed. The first charge here was that the "body rhetoric" em-ployed is a *physically* coercive tactic which has little to do with the exercise of freedom of *speech*. To deal intelligently with this charge a distinction must be made between demonstrations which do *not* directly obstruct the function-ing of an institution or society and those which do physically interfere with a normal flow of activity. I have already dealt with the latter type of protest in discussing civil disobedience, and wish here to address the issue solely in the context of admittedly legal and peaceful uses of the protesters' bodies to "bear witness" to their cause.

The difficulty people have in focusing exclusively on that issue and keep-ing it from being blurred with the other is itself instructive; for so often the reaction that is generated by the mass physical bearing of witness creates situations that deteriorate into physical disruption. Thus a march which be-gins as a peaceful parade of 1,000 through the strets of Chicago soon turns into a potential race riot requiring the intervention of hundreds of policemen. But let us be clear, as so few people seem to be, about what has changed this

22"The Concept of the Public Forum," pp. 30–31.

peaceful parade into such a potentially dangerous activity that the mere threat to march is perceived as a coercive weapon. The change has been wrought *by the hostile audience* which, rather than contenting itself to stay at home and ignore the demonstrators, chooses to go out on the streets to confront them. There is nothing *inherently* coercive about one dissenter, or one hundred, or one thousand, walking peaceably down a street or gathering to sing in front of a building. Their activity is endowed with coercive potential only if others go forth to do battle with them, or feel too guilty and fearful to leave them alone.

The logic of this seems so compelling that it is difficult to understand why it is so seldom perceived. It was apparently not perceived in the summer of 1966 by the mayor and police superintendent of Chicago who repeatedly suggested, in their public pronouncements on television and in the press, that the marchers, although admittedly within their legal rights, were holding a gun at the head of the city and should, for the sake of the general welfare, cease and desist. To be sure, a few appeals were also made to the white residents of affected neighborhoods to stay at home and ignore the marchers, but the burden of guilt and the call for maximum restraint were placed squarely on the shoulders of the Freedom Movement. Only Roman Catholic Archbishop John P. Cody seemed to analyze the problem more clearly, but even he ended up with essentially the same appeal:

> In the past several weeks, civil rights groups have been conducting marches and demonstrations in all-white neighborhoods of our community. Their purpose has been to draw the attention of the citizenry to the plight of minority groups, many of whose members are financially capable of buying or renting better homes but impeded from so doing by what can only be called a conspiracy of fear, suspicion and bigotry.
>
> The right of such groups to march and demonstrate is in itself beyond question. . . . Those who seek to deny this right by either threats or violence are clearly in violation of the law and morally blameworthy.
>
> This being said, it now appears that a new dimension has been added to the marches and demonstrations in the Chicago area. Because of the shameful reaction of our land, representatives of government, the police, and many other responsible groups are convinced that if the marches and demonstrations continue in the manner in which they have been proceeding, the result will very likely be serious injury to many persons and perhaps even the loss of lives.
>
> In view of all this, it would seem that the leaders of the civil rights movement are themselves confronted by a serious moral obligation, namely that they prayerfully reconsider the methods now being employed to achieve their

altogether just and laudable purposes. They have not been
guilty of violence and lawlessness. Others have. But the
action of these others are now a circumstance which they
must take into account in assessing their activities.

It is truly sad, indeed, deplorable, that citizens should
ever have to be asked to suspend the exercise of their rights
because of the evil-doing of others. However, in my opinion
and in the opinion of many men of good will, such is the
situation in which we now find ourselves.[23]

The United States Supreme Court, in its latest dealings with the "body
rhetoric" issue in *Cox v. Louisiana,* has attempted, as we noted earlier, to
fashion a distinction between "pure speech" and "conduct" such as patrolling,
picketing, or marching, which may be the *vehicle* for speech but is not, according to Justice Goldberg's majority opinion, entitled to so wide a range of
constitutional protection as speech itself. This opinion may well return to
haunt the Court as having enunciated a distinction impossible to defend and
maintain. For as Justice John Harlan wrote in 1961, in a concurring opinion
in a decision to overturn the sit-in convictions of a group of Negroes at a
Southern lunchcounter: "Such a demonstration in the circumstances . . . is
as much a part of the free trade in ideas . . . as is verbal expression more
commonly thought of as speech. It, like speech, appeals to good sense and to
the power of reason as applied through public discussion . . . just as much
as, if not more than, a public oration delivered from a soapbox at a street
corner. This Court has never limited the right to speak . . . to mere verbal
expression."[24]

Harry Kalven, too, in one of his typically keen analyses, has suggested:
"The Court's neat dichotomy of 'speech pure' and 'speech plus' will not work.
For it leaves us without an intelligible rationale. For one thing the exercise
of constitutional rights in their 'most pristine and classic form' in *Edwards*
has become an exercise in 'speech plus'. . . . If it is oral, it is noise and may
interrupt someone else; if it is written, it may be litter. Indeed this is why
the leaflet cases were an appropriate model . . . the leaflets were not simply
litter, they were litter with ideas."[25]

Having said all I have in defense of "body rhetoric," let me indicate an
important qualification. One would have to be naive to believe that the leaders
of contemporary protest groups are unaware of the power potential of their
demonstrations (even if that power is conferred upon them by the fearful or
hostile audience) or that they are unwilling to exploit such situations to their
own advantages. Some have been quite frank about it. For example, Professor
Griffin calls attention to Bayard Rustin's comments:

[23]From the statement of Archbishop John P. Cody, Chicago *Daily News,* August 10,
1966.

[24]*Garner v. Louisiana,* 368 US 157, 201–202.

[25]"The Concept of the Public Forum," p. 23.

> We need to go into the streets all over the country and
> to make a mountain of creative social confusion until the
> power structure is altered. We need in every community a
> group of loving troublemakers, who will disrupt the ability
> of the government to operate until it finally turns its back
> on the Dixiecrats and embraces progress.[26]

I have little doubt that the leaders of the Chicago Freedom Movement
hoped that their marches would so distress the key people in the city's power
structure that they would be forced to the bargaining table—which, indeed,
they were—prepared to make substantial concessions. Such tactics are certainly no part of rational discourse, although they may establish the precon-
ditions for it.

Furthermore, one cannot deny that sloganeering, folksinging, and draft-
card burning fall into a category of persuasion that hardly passes muster by
the standards of rational discourse, which this author and many others who
have written on the ethics of persuasion have proposed. This is not to suggest
that these activities are *illegal*, which is quite another question. Here I would
support, for example, the position taken by the American Civil Liberties Union
that public draft-card burning is an act of symbolic communication entitled
to the protections of the First Amendment.

But on what *ethical* basis can these strategies of physical and psychological manipulation, insofar as this may be what they are, be defended? Their
only justification, in my view, is that the norms of the democratic process may
be inapplicable to the situations in which these strategies are employed. To be
more explicit:

> When one person or a few people in a group or society
> possess all the guns, muscles, or money, and the others are
> relatively weak and helpless, optimum conditions do not
> exist for discussion, mutual influence, and democracy. Dis-
> cussion in such circumstances occurs only at the sufferance
> of the powerful; and generous as these persons may some-
> times be, they are not likely voluntarily to abdicate their
> power when vital interests are at stake. . . . The most solid
> and enduring basis for democracy exists when the partici-
> pants possess relative equality of power. Discussion is as-
> sured only when those desiring discussion—usually those
> who are dissatisfied with the present state of affairs—have
> sufficient power to make those in control of the situation
> listen to them.[27]

It is not easy to determine, in any given setting, the degree to which the

[26]Bayard Rustin, "The Meaning of the March on Washington," *Liberation*, VIII (October, 1963), 13.

[27]Dean C. Barnlund and Franklyn S. Haiman, *The Dynamics of Discussion* (Boston,
1960), p. 12.

democratic process, and hence the opportunities for reasoned discourse, are indeed available; and the situation may be perceived quite differently from various vantage points. Perhaps the best one can do is to avoid the blithe presumption that the channels of rational communication are open to any and all who wish to make use of them and attempt, instead, a careful assessment of the power structure of the situation. To whatever extent one finds an imbalance of power and a concomitant unwillingness on the part of the holders of power to engage in genuine dialogue, he may be less harsh in his judgment of those who seek to redress the balance through non-rational strategies of persuasion.

What I am suggesting here is not a lowering of the standards to be espoused for the ideal conduct of public discussion and debate. On the contrary, every effort should be made to help create the conditions under which the achievement of those standards becomes a possibility. But we will not attain those conditions by closing our eyes to the realities of the world about us and condemning out of hand the contemporary rhetoric of the streets.

Questions for Analysis

1. What in the development of protest techniques has raised questions of propriety and legality even for those sympathetic to the causes of protestors? How does Aristotle's definition allow Haiman to examine the issue rhetorically?

2. Describe briefly the three main points of criticism: a) violation of law, b) violation of time, place, and manner, c) violation of bounds of rational discourse.

3. What are the terms on which Haiman asserts truly *civil* disobedience to be a legitimate rhetorical tactic? What rationale, even historical imperative, does he suggest for *uncivil* disobedience? How does Haiman answer the "innocent bystander" question and that of police (public) responsibility for protests? What ethical questions are begged by official curtailing of demonstrations? Are there parallel questions and concerns that relate specifically to campus demonstrations? Illustrate.

4. Explain Haiman's contention that "there is nothing *inherently* coercive about one dissenter, or one hundred, or one thousand. . . ." What relevance to the issue do the terms "speech pure" and "speech plus" have? Refer to Griffin's criticism of "body rhetoric."

5. Do you think now that Haiman is right to isolate fundamentally *ethical* aspects of rhetorical strategy from aspects purely *legal?* Explain. How would you characterize Haiman's pervasive concern for the response of the "culture at large" to the "rhetoric of the streets"?

Part I

Questions for Discussions

1. How far is dissent from disruption?
2. How should White Power answer Black Power?
3. Campus lecturers: whose responsibility and how?
4. Pockets of poverty: how can we eliminate them?
5. The cost of civil disobedience: who pays the piper?

Topics for Speeches

1. Civility and civil rights
2. Student power and the future of higher education
3. A consumer's guide to minority groups
4. The rhetoric of the rejected
5. Civil rights to right a wrong
6. The self-determination of nations—and of student bodies
7. Agitative rhetoric: a calculated risk
8. "But George *won't* do it!"
9. The *real* issues on the campus
10. Appalachia and the ghetto

II

SPEAKER CONCEPTS AND CONCERNS

Introduction

If, as seems clear from the selections in Part I, listener attitudes and anxieties in our times are distinctive, if a substantial number of our citizens are caught up in the critical social and political issues of the age, and if today's rhetorical climate is shaped significantly by agitation, then surely we must examine in terms of these times, our concepts and concerns about speakers and their speaking. What should a speaker be? How should he view himself? What obligations should he feel, to his own integrity, to society, to truth? How should he acquire and perfect his skills? What freedoms and responsibilities should he have?

No one of these questions about the role and function of speakers in our times is susceptible to an easy answer. But we may make a start toward an answer by remembering that the same questions have been asked in all times. Here are some of the answers and observations:

> The most beautiful thing in the world is freedom of speech. —*Diogenes*

> The character of the speaker is a cause of persuasion when the speech is so uttered as to make him worthy of belief; for as a rule we trust men of probity more, and more quickly, about things in general, while on points outside the realm of exact knowledge, where opinion is divided, we trust them absolutely.—*Aristotle*

> The orator is the good man speaking well.—*Quintilian*

> The first and most previous quality then which contributes to the success of a public speaker is an honest heart. . . . The only advice I can give you for all emergencies is, before you enter upon that profession, to lay the foundation of your conduct in a well digested system of ethics.—*John Quincy Adams*

> This nation was conceived in liberty and dedicated to the principle—among others—that honest men may honestly disagree; that if they all say what they think, a majority of the people will be able to distinguish truth from error; that in the competition of the market place of

ideas, the sounder ideas will in the long run win out.—*Elmer Davis*

In the end it is worse to suppress dissent than to run the risk of heresy.—*Learned Hand*

If any single lesson is to be learned from the ancients and reinforced by our own experience, it is that our concept of a speaker must embrace both his competence and his character. Listeners, we know, do not accept or reject ideas merely from the way they are presented. Certainly listeners are affected by the speaker's techniques, but they also accept or reject ideas because of the person who advocates them, and because of what he is. Over a hundred years ago Ralph Waldo Emerson put it this way: "The reason why anyone refuses his assent to your opinion . . . is in you . . . you must not have given him the authentic sign." To be accepted, and believed, speakers must give their listeners "the authentic sign."

What Emerson called "the authentic sign" we are likely today to call "sincerity" or "integrity." Behavioral scientists who study this matter have commonly labelled the experimental variable in communication *credibility*, or *prestige*, and the most recent term is *interpersonal trust*.[1] In all of them is imbedded the concept that Aristotle called *ethos*, or ethical proof. The section of our volume devoted to the question "What should the speaker be?" is therefore appropriately introduced by a survey and analysis of experimental research on ethos, by Kenneth Andersen and Theodore Clevenger, Jr. We believe it well to start, whenever possible, with such a broad survey, and then to move in our readings to more particularized and philosophical interpretations.

In very practical terms the problem posed for the public speaker in any specific situation is one of ethical persuasion: what standard of values, ethics, morality, and civility will govern his behavior? The introduction here of the concept of morality is deliberate; it has always been a concern of the rhetorician. Plato may not have been the first to ask whether speakers were more concerned with winning an argument than with seeking truth, even if it meant making the worse appear the better reason. It was his student, Aristotle, who answered that speech is a skill that can be used for worthy or unworthy purposes. "What makes a man a sophist," he said, "is not his skill, but his moral purpose." In our own day we are more likely to refer to "demagogues" or "propagandists" than to "sophists," but moral purpose is still the critical element. Since we cannot, in a democratic society, bar the charlatans from the public platform, we defend ourselves against them by learning to identify their techniques, like name-calling, character assassination, double-talk, anxiety arousal, and "big lie" repetition. The more positive side of practicing ethical persuasion is a perennial problem, and Arthur N. Kruger

[1]Kim Griffin, "Interpersonal Trust in Small-Group Communication," *Quarterly Journal of Speech*, 53 (1967), 224–231.

and Douglas Ehninger each look at it afresh in articles that are clearly relevant to our times.

All of the questions dealt with by Kruger and by Ehninger apply to face-to-face communication between speakers and listeners. In what is clearly the age of the television campaigner, however, some of those questions should be specifically reviewed in terms of the mass media's impact upon traditional concepts of the speaker's responsibilities. This is done in an article by Ota Thomas Reynolds.

Among the conclusions reached by Reynolds is that teachers of speech need to reexamine their treatment of the substantive aspects of the rhetorical discipline. Good instructors are of course always reviewing and revising both the content and the method of their teaching, and this may be particularly true for teachers of speech. They are sensitive to the fact that their subject matter is really how to handle, responsibly and effectively, a weapon that can be more deadly than a gun, and that both potential democrats and potential demagogues sit in their classrooms. As Robert G. Gunderson once put it, "When leading rabble-rousers pay eloquent tribute to their academic training in public speaking, we all cringe in collective embarrassment, for obviously an ethical X-factor has been neglected, even though a success-mad society is no doubt more blameworthy than the educational system which reflects it."[2] It is unfortunate that students in general have had little interest in the teaching-learning process as such, and have seldom shared with their teachers any of the latter's philosophical concerns. Happily, this situation may be changing, as are many other aspects of student involvement in their educational programs, and teachers of speech will no doubt especially welcome student concern. As one example of the speech teacher's reaction to philosophical problems, we present an article by Waldo W. Braden in which he appraises and answers the question "What shall we do about the demand for snake oil?"

The traditional close relationship between rhetoric and political philosophy is illustrated in two sequential articles by Malcolm O. Sillars and Thomas R. Nilsen, followed by a reply by Sillars. The central focus is upon the comparative implications of conservatism and liberalism for the teacher of speech and, ultimately, for the student of speech.

In departments of speech the impact of a changing *Zeitgeist* is felt more quickly than in most other academic areas. Some of the earliest assertions of discontent and dissent on a campus, for example, are made by students in public speaking classes; and programs of discussion and debate, on the campus or intercollegiate, become understandably more dynamic as they reflect the issues of the day. This was true during the depression of the late Twenties and early Thirties, and it was true again in the years just preceding America's entry into World War II. (As John W. Black half facetiously said

[2]"Davey Crockett's Tongue-Tied Admirers: Training for An Articulate Democracy," in J. Jeffery Auer, *Brigance's Speech Communication*, 3rd ed. (New York, Appleton-Century-Crofts, 1967), p. 161.

during the early Fifties, when student apathy toward public affairs seemed at a peak and forensic activity was at a low ebb, "There's nothing wrong with intercollegiate debate that a good depression wouldn't cure!") The sharp increase in student concern during the past decade about public issues, and the expanding number of students involved in political and social action, has been welcomed in most faculty quarters, though no doubt regretted in some. While individual instructors deal with many educational problems, some are resolved only at the departmental level. Among the latter is the question of what posture a department of speech ought to take in responding to the challenge of our times. Ted J. McLaughlin's article outlines one positive program.

Running through all of these materials about speaker concepts and concerns, from Diogenes to date, is an assumption about the essentiality for our society, above all else, of freedom of speech. Even though we know that what is spoken may sometimes be divisive, its long-range effect is cohesive. As long as speech and assembly are free there is hope that we can talk our problems out, not shoot them out. Unfortunately the concept of free speech is not automatically self-sustaining; we cannot simply note that it is provided for in the Constitution and let it go at that. The principle of free speech needs constant reaffirmation and reinforcement if we are to keep it viable, especially in periods of great social and political change. For example: one new hazard in current political campaigning, and largely a consequence of the same climate that encourages agitative rhetoric, is the appearance of audience members who come not to listen but to drown out the speaker with their heckling and make it impossible for other audience members to hear. When this uncivil treatment was given to one presidential candidate on July 3, 1968, President Johnson promptly issued a Fourth-of-July reaffirmation of "freedom to speak, freedom to listen." His statement appears next in our collection.

Immediately following the Johnson statement is a series of resolutions providing a "Credo for Responsible Communication in a Free Society," and adopted by the Speech Association of America in 1963 and 1967.

The college campus, ironically enough, is one of the areas of our society in which we have been slow to implement our belief in free speech by specific action. In part this has been because a dedication to "academic freedom" has long been taken for granted. But the winds of social change and political agitation are not stopped by the walls of the ivory tower, and most university faculties and administrations are, or inevitably will be, concerned with delineating and protecting freedom of speech on their campuses. As a final document in our collection of materials bearing upon speaker concepts and concerns, therefore, we include the 1968 "Joint Statement on Rights and Freedoms of Students," initiated by the American Association of University Professors.

9

A Summary of Experimental Research
in Ethos

Kenneth Andersen
Theodore Clevenger, Jr.

Although the number of quantitative studies employing the term ethos in their titles is small, related rubrics such as credibility and prestige encompass such a quantity and variety of research clearly related to this classical concept that a summary should be valuable to those undertaking further studies. The primary purpose of this paper is to provide such a summary. In this study ethos is defined as the image held of a communicator at a given time by a receiver—either one person or a group. The use of the words communicator and receiver is deliberate, for the writers have chosen to include studies of written and nonverbal communication as well as those involving a speaker-auditor relationship.

The major sections of this paper are summaries of experimental findings pertaining to (1) the influence of ethos upon the effect of the communication, (2) techniques for generating or changing ethos, and (3) measurements of one or more aspects of ethos and attempts to assess the relative levels of ethos of individuals or groups.

Influence of Ethos upon the Intended
Effect of Communication

Experiments concerning ethos have dealt with many and varied topics: with the effects of differences in prestige, credibility, likeableness, and other variables upon attitudes toward political-social issues, upon evaluations of

Kenneth Andersen is Associate Professor of Speech, and Coordinator of the Speech Communication Research Laboratory, The University of Michigan.

Theodore Clevenger, Jr., is Chairman of the Department of Speech, Florida State University.

Reprinted by permission from *Speech Monographs*, 30(1963), 59–78.

art and literature, and upon learning; with the relative effectiveness of majority and expert opinion and the relative susceptibility of the sexes, different age groups, and persons of various educational levels to prestige suggestion; and with the temporal effects and the permanency of the attitude change and the learning induced by different levels of ethos.

It is important to remember that these studies, which arise from such fields as psychology, speech, sociology, and education, are quite diverse in origin, that many of the experimenters did not use rhetorical terminology, and that many of them also did not perceive a relationship between their studies and ethos. Studies are included, however, if the independent variable is a difference in treatment which is basically related to ethos and if the dependent variable is some measurement which is basically a communication effect index.

Theoretical and methodological differences

Studies differ so much in the definition of ethos and in certain other theoretical and methodological features that an analysis of these distinctions is a necessary preliminary to reporting the experiments.

1. *Fixed ethos vs. congruity hypothesis.* In most studies the ethical element is treated as relatively fixed in value during the communication act, and persuasion is construed as the linking of a proposition with an *approved* source for a positive effect or a *disapproved* source for a negative one.[1] However, in some recent studies, especially those using semantic differential measurement ethos is regarded as flexible, because during the act of communication alterations in the image of the speaker may be caused either by the sender's propositions or by other situational factors.[2]

2. *Ethos assumed vs. ethos measured.* Early studies of ethical effects commonly followed the pattern of employing two sources (such as Franklin Roosevelt and Herbert Hoover) assumed to differ greatly in credibility, prestige, or some other ethical component and then comparing the attitude change for Group I, which received the message credited to the first source, with that for Group II, which received the same message except that it was ascribed to the second source.[3] This method assumes that for the group of subjects in question, the experimenter can determine intuitively the relative levels of ethos of the given sources. Recent studies, in contrast, have tended to measure ethos.

[1]Such as John Highlander, "Audience Analyzer Measurements and Informational Effects of Speaker Variables in Radio Talks," unpubl. diss. (Wisconsin, 1953); Franklyn Haiman, "An Experimental Study of the Effects of Ethos in Public Speaking," unpubl. diss. (Northwestern, 1948); also briefly reported in *SM*, XVI (Sept., 1949), 190–202.

[2]Such as Charles Osgood, George Suci and Percy Tannenbaum, *The Measurement of Meaning* (Urbana: University of Illinois Press, 1957); Erwin Bettinghaus, "The Operation of Congruity in an Oral Communication Situation," unpubl. diss. (Illinois, 1959).

[3]Such as Helen Lewis, "Studies in the Principles of Judgments and Attitudes: IV. The Operation of 'Prestige Suggestion,'" *Journal of Social Psychology*, XIV (1941), 229–256.

Experimenters have either selected their sources on the basis of pretests of credibility or chosen them arbitrarily and then checked for credibility differences by direct measurement after the completion of the experiment.[4] The last of these techniques, of course, is valid only if one is willing to espouse the fixed ethos model; for if the image of the speaker may change during the speech, a measurement rendered after the address may be quite deceptive concerning ethos at the outset.

3. *Topic-oriented vs. topic irrelevant ethos.* The assumption for the majority of the studies apparently is that the prestige, the credibility, or some other ethical characteristic of the speaker varies from one topic to another. Thus, in most of the studies of *expert* opinion the authorities were selected because they were reputed to be well informed on the topic of the experimental message.[5] Some studies, on the other hand, seem to be based on a concept of generalized credibility and to discount or ignore the possibility that the prestige varies from topic to topic.[6]

4. *Average vs. individual measure.* Although the assumption in most studies is that the experimental group as an entity places the communicator at a certain level of prestige,[7] in some studies ethos is regarded as differing from one subgroup to another, and data are treated separately for such variables as sex, occupation, educational status, and political affiliation.[8] A few studies even consider the prestige of the source in respect to each individual auditor.[9] Whereas in the first two types of experiment the usual statistical test is for the significance of difference between means, in studies of the individual auditor the common method is correlation.

5. *Extent of audience analysis.* Finally, the studies differ in that some examine audience characteristics, whereas others do not. Both approaches have interpretative hazards as well as distinctive advantages. In studies which

[4]Such as Muzafer Sherif, "An Experimental Study of Stereotypes," *Journal of Abnormal and Social Psychology*, XXIX (1935), 371-375; Herbert Kelman and Carl Hovland, "'Reinstatement' of the Communicator in Delayed Measurement of Opinion Change," *Journal of Abnormal and Social Psychology*, XLVIII (1953), 327-335.

[5]Such as Malcolm Moos and Bertram Koslin, "Prestige Suggestion and Political Leadership," *Public Opinion Quarterly*, XVI (1952), 77-93; Irving Lorge with Carl Curtis, "Prestige, Suggestion and Attitudes," *Journal of Social Psychology*, VII (1936), 386-402.

[6]Such as Clare Marple, "The Comparative Susceptibility of Three Age Levels to the Suggestion of Group Versus Expert Opinion," *Journal of Social Psychology*, IV (1933), 176-186.

[7]Such as Raymond Bernberg, "Prestige Suggestion in Art as Communication," *Journal of Social Psychology*, XXXVIII (1953), 23-30; William Michael, Bernard Rosenthal, and Michael DeCamp, "An Experimental Investigation of Prestige-Suggestion for Two Types of Literary Material," *Journal of Psychology*, XXVIII (1949), 303-323.

[8]Such as Helen Lewis, *loc. cit.*

[9]Such as Herbert Birch, "The Effect of Socially Disapproved Labeling upon a Well-Structured Attitude," *Journal of Abnormal and Social Psychology*, XL (1945), 301-310; David Cole, "'Rational Argument' and 'Prestige-Suggestion' as Factors Influencing Judgment," *Sociometry*, XVII (1954), 350-354.

assess the effect upon attitude change of such audience properties as sex, age, and educational level it is also possible (although infrequently done) to investigate the interaction of ethos with each of the audience variables. Thus, a study in which two levels of prestige are employed with an audience of men and women can include data on the effect of prestige level upon attitude change (ignoring sex), the differences in the relative susceptibility of the two sexes to prestige and nonprestige communication (the interactions). Careful interpretation, however, is necessary: First, the experimenter must distinguish over-all persuasibility differences between the sexes (main effect of sex) from prestige-suggestibility (the interaction). Second, where prestige is taken with reference to the entire sample of subjects, he must note the possibility of confounding prestige level with sex—that is, a source may not have the same prestige for the two sexes, and this difference may result in a spurious sex-by-prestige level interaction if prestige level is measured as a group average. Thus, some of the results seeming to show greater prestige-persuasibility for women than for men may have been products of concealed differences in the prestige level of the source for the two sexes.

Within the limits of the five methodological distinctions described above, the studies of the effects of ethos present a reasonably harmonious body of findings. In the following pages those studies employing the conception of a fixed ethos model will be presented first, and the limited number employing the congruity model will follow.

Studies assuming that ethos is fixed

A number of studies which employ the relatively common fixed ethos model indicate that certain ethical factors can produce changes in attitude toward political and social issues. Arnett, Davidson, and Lewis found that a group of graduate students shifted significantly toward agreement with graduate educators on Harper's test of liberalism.[10] The study was conducted without a control group, however, and during the lapse of four weeks between the two administrations of the test, factors other than prestige may have operated to produce the observed shifts.

Birch studied the effect of political labels of *Fascist* or *Communist* and *Reactionary* or *Liberal* on college students' judgments of two statements.[11] No significant differences in preference for the two statements were observed, but this conclusion may be misleading. The fact that ninety-nine per cent of all subjects favored one statement over the other may have masked any possible prestige effect.

While the preceding studies were concerned with the effect of referential group or class prestige upon attitude change, a number of studies have been directed toward an investigation of the prestige of individuals. Saadi and

---

[10]Claude Arnett, Helen Davidson, and Hallett Lewis, "Prestige as a Factor in Attitude Changes," *Sociology and Social Research*, XVI (1931), 49–55.
[11]*Loc. cit.*

Farnsworth found greater acceptance for dogmatic statements which were attributed to well-liked persons than to the same assertions when attributed to disliked individuals.[12] Lorge and Curtis found a significant tendency for subjects to shift opinion toward the supposed position of a prestige source, but they found no significant negative shift when the proposition was linked with a disapproved source.[13]

In apparent conflict with these findings are the results obtained by Lewis. She reported that college students remained relatively unchanged in the evaluation of statements and that they tried to explain away the "prestige source" through relationalization.[14] Unhappily, the conclusions to the study show the bias of an author who quite evidently hoped to support an hypothesis: for example, she describes rank-order correlations of a magnitude of .50 as "high." This bias renders suspect the assertion that informal interviews with the subjects and free responses revealed that suggestions, when effective, usually redefined an ambiguous situation.

A more satisfactory design for testing a similar hypothesis was that employed by Moos and Koslin, who discovered that vague quotations were those which were the most likely to be influenced by attribution to differing sources.[15]

Hastorf and Piper, using a variety of problems, studied the effects of supposed ratings of businessmen and educators on the attitudes of subjects. They found that all groups, including one which was instructed to duplicate its pretest responses and ignore the supposed ratings, shifted significantly.[16]

Smith found that printed propaganda statements when labeled as fact produced greater belief than when labeled as rumor. The success of the "fact" label, however, clearly varied with the prior attitude of the subject and with the relation of the alleged "fact" to "truth."[17]

The objective of all of the above studies was to assess the effects of prestige upon judgment of political and social issues, and the method in all instances was to link a source with a proposition but to provide no message by which the source supported the proposition. A question of more immediate interest to students of speech is whether differences in the speaker's prestige significantly influence the persuasive outcome of a speech.

Haiman presented to three groups a tape recorded speech variously attributed to Thomas Parran, Surgeon General of the United States; to Eugene Dennis, Secretary of the Communist Party in America; and to a "Northwestern University Sophomore." Not only was Parran rated significantly more competent than the other two, but also, as measured by the Woodward Shift-

[12]Mitchell Saadi and Paul Farnsworth, "The Degrees of Acceptance of Dogmatic Statements and Preferences for Their Supposed Makers," *Journal of Abnormal and Social Psychology*, XXIX (1934), 143–150.

[13]*Loc. cit.*

[14]*Loc. cit.*

[15]*Loc. cit.*

[16]A. H. Hastorf and G. W. Piper, "A Note on the Effect of Explicit Instructions on Prestige Suggestion," *Journal of Social Psychology*, XXXIII (1951), 289–293.

[17]George Smith, "Belief in Statements Labelled Fact and Rumor," *Journal of Abnormal and Social Psychology*, XLII (1947), 80–90.

of-Opinion Ballot, his speech was significantly more effective in changing attitude than was either of the other two. The "Dennis" and the "Sophomore" speeches did not differ significantly.[18]

Employing essentially the same techniques—a tape recorded speech, differing introductions, and the Woodward ballot—Strother and Paulson in separate studies obtained results similar to Haiman's. Not only did Strother find significant differences in the persuasiveness of the "Parran" and the "Dennis" speeches, but also he noted that only those who thought they had been listening to Dennis wrote unfavorable comments concerning the speech techniques employed.[19] Paulson attributed a taped speech to a political science professor and to a student. For female auditors there was no significant difference in the effects of the "two" speeches but among the male auditors the proportion of those shifting opinion was greater for the group which thought it had been addressed by the professor.[20]

The supposed differences in prestige level in the experiments cited above were assumed to be quite large, and the methods of establishing the prestige levels were straightforward and obvious. On the other hand, Hovland and Mandell, in an effort to assess subtler sources of the speaker's image, manipulated credibility through the suggestion of differing degrees of selfish interest and self-motivation. The nonsignificant difference in attitude change which the speakers produced was very small, but the audiences, apparently reacting to their presumed prejudices, rated the "unbiased source" as the significantly fairer and more honest of the two.[21] Since these evaluations were rendered after the speech, the initial ethos of the two sources, the point at which the "biases" of one began to emerge, or the ways in which the images of the two speakers changed during the speech are unknown.

A study by Kraus likewise suggests the possibility of evaluating indirect, implicative sources of ethos. Using pairs which were racially homogeneous and others which were racially heterogeneous, he compared whites with Negroes in respect to their persuasiveness in filmed discussions of segregation issues. The results indicated that arguments favorable to integration were more persuasive when advanced by the heterogeneous pairs, and Kraus explained the results in terms of differing levels of credibility.[22]

All the studies mentioned thus far have dealt with ethos as determined

[18]*Loc. cit.*

[19]Edward Strother, "An Experimental Study of Ethos as Related to the Introduction in the Persuasive Speaking Situation," unpubl. diss. (Northwestern, 1951).

[20]Stanley Paulson, "Experimental Study of Spoken Communications; The Effects of Prestige of the Speaker and Acknowledgment of Opposing Arguments on Audience Retention and Shift of Opinion," unpubl. diss. (Minnesota, 1952); also briefly reported in *SM*, XXI (1954), 267–271.

[21]Carl Hovland and Wallace Mandell, "An Experimental Comparison of Conclusion Drawing by the Communicator and the Audience," *Journal of Abnormal and Social Psychology*, XLVII (1952), 581–588.

[22]Sidney Kraus, "An Experimental Study of the Relative Effectiveness of Negroes and Whites in Achieving Racial Attitude Change Via Kinescope Recordings," unpubl. diss. (Iowa, 1959); *SM*, XXVII (1960), 87–88.

by the position or reputation of the source. Messages, if used, have been standardized so that the only variable was the introduction given the speaker.

Other studies, in contrast, have been designed so that some internal message elements have been varied systematically. Gilkinson, Paulson, and Sikkink, who incorporated or excluded authority quotations in two versions of the same speech, found that both versions engendered a significant shift in attitude with only a trend to favor the inclusion of authorities.[23] In another study Sikkink similarly employed quotations, but neither attitude shift nor ratings of convincingness showed significant differences.[24] While the use of authorities certainly has persuasive implications beyond the ethical dimension (and indeed the authors of these experiments apparently did not consider ethos the critical variable), the fact that the speaker was not evaluated as significantly more convincing when he used authorities suggests that citing reputable sources does not necessarily enhance ethos—as some theorists have suggested.

The two studies above are included within the fixed ethos model because the prestige of the authorities seemingly served directly as the basis for the shift in opinion, if any. Other experimenters varied the procedure by apparently employing authorities for the purpose of altering the image of the speaker; this altered image, in turn, was to serve as the warrant for the persuasive effect. (Possibly both effects could occur.) Studies of attitude changes dependent upon such attempts at artistic ethos are reported in a subsequent section of this paper.[25]

Historically parallel to the study of the effects of ethos upon political and social attitudes has been the study of its effect upon judgments of literature, art, and matters of personal taste. In three experiments in Turkey and at Harvard Sherif found correlations of .45 to .53 between rankings of authors and subsequent rankings of passages to which authors' names were randomly attached. Sherif asserts that the name of the author exerts an influence upon ratings of passages.[26]

Michael, Rosenthal, and DeCamp matched authors with prose and poetry passages and found little evidence of the effect noted by Sherif.[27] Although they claimed methodological improvements over Sherif's study, their rank-of-summed-ranks technique actually produced a measure of dubious statistical reliability.[28] The entire study was conducted in such a manner that results

[23]Howard Gilkinson, Stanley Paulson, and Donald Sikkink, "Effects of Order and Authority in an Argumentative Speech," *QJS*, XL (1954), 183–192.

[24]Donald Sikkink, "Experimental Study of the Effects on the Listener of Anticlimax Order and Authority in an Argumentative Speech," *Southern Speech Journal*, XXII (1956), 73–78.

[25]See p. 71. Still other implications for a theory of ethos stemming from the authority quotation problem will be discussed in a subsequent paper.

[26]*Loc. cit.*

[27]*Loc. cit.*

[28]The problems in the use of a rank-of-summed-ranks technique are discussed by Roger Nebergall, "Some Applications of Measurement Theory to the Judgment of Speech Contests," unpublished paper read at the Central States Speech Association Conference, April 8, 1960.

confirming the Sherif finding were highly unlikely. The interpretation of their inconclusive results as evidence contrary to the Sherif hypothesis seem unjustified.

More recently, in India, Das, Rath, and Das studied the effect of author prestige upon evaluations of poetry. Working with quite small and crude statistical measures, they concluded that prestige influenced judgment greatly but that this effect was weakened when the factors of understanding and merit were stressed.[29]

Judgments of art seem to be similar. Data obtained by Farnsworth and Misumi displayed a trend indicating that recognition of the artist's name had some favorable effect on the evaluations of pictures.[30] In another experiment Bernberg found that positive and negative evaluations of alleged art critics significantly affected the judgments by artistically naive students with regard to seven of ten paintings.[31]

Cole presented abstract finger paintings for discussion in small groups. In situations in which the art teacher presented judgments in opposition to those of the group, significant shifts occurred only when the teacher was present. A peer leader, to cite a second finding, secured significant shifts only when he also presented pseudo-rational arguments. [32]

Again, similar effects have been found in the area of personal taste and perceptions. Duncker presented a story to nursery school children in which a fictional hero endorses a food actually less desirable than an alternative selection. The after-effect was decidedly positive—a large percentage of the children selected the endorsed food when given a choice. Over a period of twelve days, however, the selection of the less satisfying food declined to the level of a control group. Some of the initial preference for the less desirable food was reinstated by recalling the story, but this effect degenerated very quickly.[33]

Donceel, Alimena, and Birch presented adults and high school and college students with personality descriptions of themselves. These supposedly came from tests and expert evaluations, but actually were determined by chance. Under mild suggestion a significant number of students accepted these statements as valid, and under strong suggestion all subjects yielded. They accepted as true the false descriptions of their personalities and reversed previous answers to questions in a personality test.[34]

[29]J. P. Das, R. Rath, and Rhea Stagner Das, "Understanding Versus Suggestion in the Judgment of Literary Passages," *Journal of Abnormal and Social Psychology*, LI (1955), 624–628.

[30]Paul Farnsworth and Issei Misumi, "Further Data on Suggestion in Pictures," *American Journal of Psychology*, XLIII (1931), 632.

[31]*Loc. cit.*

[32]*Loc. cit.*

[33]Karl Duncker, "Experimental Modification of Children's Food Preference Through Social Suggestion, " *Journal of Abnormal and Social Psychology*, XXXIII (1938), 489–507.

[34]Joseph Donceel, Benjamin Alimena, and Catherine Birch, "Influence of Prestige Suggestion on the Answers of a Personality Inventory," *Journal of Applied Psychology*, XXXIII (1949), 352–355.

Aveling and Hargreaves found *personal suggestion* capable of affecting performance in a variety of perceptual and psychomotor tasks, but they also secured evidence of strong negative suggestibility among some of their subjects.[35]

Although there is little reason to suppose that those elements of ethos which are designed to obtain attitude change are also capable of producing differences in learning, a small number of studies pertain to this possibility. Weiss taught responses to groups of students, one of which was told that the answers were untrue. No differences in learning occurred, but what was learned correlated with the attitude change which took place during the experiment.[36] Paulson found no significant differences in retention between high and low ethos sources, although certain audience variables did appear to be related to learning.[37] Sikkink's results were substantially the same.[38]

An experiment by Harms shows that cloze test scores are somewhat higher when the speakers are high in status than when they are low. The inferred reason for this result is that high-status speakers are more "comprehensible." A further result, secured through a differential analysis of listener groups, is that listeners respond with greater comprehension to those from their own class than to speakers from either a higher or a lower class.[39]

The above studies were concerned with the effects of the ethos of individual communicators. A smaller number of investigations have attempted to compare the effects of expert opinions with those produced by majority opinion.

Using as a criterion the frequency with which the subjects reversed their preferences so as to conform to the prestige group, Moore measured the relative influence of majority and expert opinions upon judgments of grammar, ethics and music. The two sources were about equally effective except with respect to grammar, where the majority opinion prevailed by a ratio of 10 to 7.[40] The primitive design of this experiment may have concealed other differences.

An experiment by Marple, who found that both the group and experts influenced opinions about solutions to seventy-five assorted problems, reinforced Moore's results. Majority opinion was roughly one-third more effective than expert opinion with students and roughly one-fifth more effective with adults. [41]

[35]F. Aveling and H. L. Hargreaves, "Suggestibility With and Without Prestige in Children," *British Journal of Psychology*, XII (1921-1922), 53–75.

[36]Walter Weiss, "A 'Sleeper' Effect in Opinion Change," *Journal of Abnormal and Social Psychology*, XLVIII (1953), 173–180.

[37]*Loc. cit.*

[38]*Loc. cit.*

[39]Leroy Stanley Harms, "Social Judgments of Status Cues in Language," unpubl. diss. (Ohio State, 1959) ; *SM*, XXVII (1960), 87.

[40]Henry Moore, "The Comparative Influence of Majority and Expert Opinion," *American Journal of Psychology*, XXXII (1921), 16–20.

[41]*Loc. cit.*

With respect to religious beliefs, Burtt and Falkenberg discovered that opinions of both the majority and experts influenced judgments significantly, that expert (clerical) opinions tended to have greater influence than majority views in some matters of religious belief, and that a contrary tendency existed in other areas. [42]

Incidental findings of a number of studies bear upon the question of the relative susceptibility of various audience types to prestige as a means of suggestion. Within the narrow range which an undergraduate psychology class affords, Hovland and Mandell found that personality and intelligence were not related to prestige-suggestibility.[43] Kersten reports a similar finding for intelligence;[44] but Wegrocki reports a tendency for intelligence to be negatively associated with prestige-suggestibility.[45] Strother discovered no shifts in opinion which correlated with either sex or the urban-versus-rural dimension, but he did find that members of the audience with initially neutral views on the speech topic were significantly more responsive to variations of ethos than were either the pro or the con groups.[46] Kersten,[47] Paulson,[48] and Pross[49] obtained results confirming those of Strother.

Sikkink found that women rated the persuasiveness of all speeches significantly higher than did men, but that women were neither easier nor harder to influence than men.[50] Cathcart also concluded that sex was not significantly related to persuasibility.[51] Pross reported some indication that women were the more suggestible and Wegrocki also concluded that girls, as compared with boys, tended to be more suggestible and to react more strongly to sympathetic propaganda.[52] Paulson found that women reacted more but retained less information. Freshmen, also according to Paulson, tended to shift less in response to the high ethos source than did upperclassmen, but there was no guarantee that the freshmen and the upperclassmen perceived the high ethos source in the same light.[53] Cathcart found that education, speech training, and subject matter competence had no effect on persuasibility.[54] The discovery by Aveling and Hargreaves of great differences in suggestibility on a number of

[42]Harold Burtt and Don Falkenberg, Jr., "The Influence of Majority and Expert Opinion on Religious Attitudes," *Journal of Social Psychology*, XIV (1941), 269–278.

[43]*Loc. cit.*

[44]Barbara Kersten, "An Experimental Study to Determine the Effect of a Speech of Introduction upon the Persuasive Speech that Followed," unpubl. thesis (South Dakota State College, 1958).

[45]Henry Wegrocki, "The Effect of Prestige Suggestibility on Emotional Attitudes," *Journal of Social Psychology*, V (1934), 384–394.

[46]*Loc. cit.*

[47]*Loc. cit.*

[48]*Loc. cit.*

[49]Edward Pross, "A Critical Analysis of Certain Aspects of Ethical Proof," unpubl. diss. (Iowa, 1942) ; Paulson, *loc. cit.*

[50]*Loc. cit.*

[51]Robert Cathcart, "An Experimental Study of the Relative Effectiveness of Four Methods of Presenting Evidence," *SM*, XXII (1955), 227–233.

[52]*Loc. cit.*

[53]*Loc. cit.*

[54]*Loc. cit.*

perceptual and psychomotor tasks leads to speculation that two sharply divided groups, the suggestible and the contrasuggestible, may exist. They found no tendency, however, for suggestibility to correlate with any of a number of psychometric variables.[55] Marple found that high school and college students shift more than do adults.[56]

A single study has illustrated the possibility of investigating the effects of audience size upon the relationship between ethos and attitude change. Knower compared the effect of delivering a speech in an audience situation with giving the speech to one auditor at a time. The speech in the individual situation was somewhat more effective, women were more influenced than men, and women speakers obtained greater attitude shifts than did men. In the audience situation, however, male speakers obtained greater shifts than did women.[57]

Most of the studies described above deal primarily with the immediate effects of prestige, credibility, and other ethical elements. Hovland and his associates, however, have investigated the temporal effects of the source upon persuasion. In one of these experiments Hovland and Weiss held all of the message elements constant except for factors which produced an impression of high credibility for one source and low credibility for another. The subjects exposed to the former stimulus shifted in significantly greater numbers on immediate post-tests of attitude than did those receiving the message with low credibility. Over a period of one month the favorable effect, however, decreased, and the subjects exposed to the "inferior" source moved toward agreement with the attitudes expressed in it. Hovland postulated a "sleeper effect"—that in the absence of further stimuli agreement with high credibility sources decays while agreement with low credibility sources grows. The possible explanation is that the subject forgets the source but retains the information and the essential arguments.[58] In a specific test of the sleeper hypothesis, Kelman and Hovland found that a high ethos source, who was rated significantly fairer, better qualified to speak, and of sounder judgment than a supposedly low ethos source produced significantly greater attitude shifts. Over a three-week period, however, the extent to which subjects agreed with the positive source decreased significantly, and the extent to which they agreed with the negative source increased nonsignificantly. Reinforcing the recall of the sources by playing back the introduction of the tape-recorded messages produced greater agreement with the high prestige speaker and less agreement with the one of low ethos in an experimental group than occurred in a control group which received no repetition of the stimuli.[59]

[55]*Loc. cit.*

[56]*Loc. cit.*

[57]Franklin Knower, "Experimental Studies of Changes in Attitudes: I. A Study of the Effect of Oral Argument on Changes in Attitude," *Journal of Social Psychology,* VI (1935), 315–347.

[58]Carl Hovland and Walter Weiss, "The Influence of Source Credibility on Communication Effectiveness," *Public Opinion Quarterly,* XVI (1961), 635–650.

[59]*Loc. cit.*

In a variation of the above approach Weiss determined that a group exposed to a low credibility source showed less regression toward its original attitude than did a group exposed to a high credibility source.[60]

Also supporting the sleeper effect is the finding that over a period of time those who originally disliked a communicator became slightly more positive toward him while those who had originally liked him became slightly less favorable (nonsignificantly).[61]

The results of Duncker's study of the effect of prestige suggestion upon children's food preferences also confirm the Hovland sleeper effect findings in respect to both the decline of the effect over time and the renewal of strength following reinstatement.[62]

Studies assuming that ethos is variable

Diverse as the studies discussed above appear to be, they share a common model of ethos—that is, they are all based on the assumption that the speaker's image is relatively fixed throughout the period of communication. In sharp contrast with this view is the ethical model based on a congruity principle enunciated by Osgood.[63] Intended to explain many psychological functions, the congruity principle holds that an image (or meaning) depends upon the other concepts with which it is associated and thus is subject to perpetual change. Among the factors causing these variations are the successive parts of the message.

Drawing upon this generalized congruity hypothesis, Tannenbaum formulated predictions of attitude change toward communication sources and then compared these estimates with the results obtained when college students were exposed to written messages. Since the correlation was .91, the conclusion is that attitude changes of the college students in this experiment conformed to the congruity hypothesis.[64]

A study of the same hypotheses applied to public speakers showed that the congruity model predicted changes in attitude somewhat better than chance alone.[65] This study, however, failed to produce the goodness of fit observed in the Tannenbaum experiment.[66]

Bettinghaus hypothesized that the difference between these results was caused by the presence of a greater number of elements in the cognitive structure for oral than for written messages. Extending the congruity model to four

[60]Loc. cit.

[61]Arthur Cohen, "Need for Cognition and Order of Communication as Determinants of Opinion Change" in Order of Presentation, eds. Carl I. Hovland et al. (New Haven: Yale University Press, 1957), pp. 79–97.

[62]Loc. cit.

[63]Osgood, Suci, and Tannenbaum, loc. cit.; Charles Osgood and Percy Tannenbaum, "The Principle of Congruity in the Prediction of Attitude Change," Psychological Review, LXII (1955), 42–55.

[64]Percy Tannenbaum, "Initial Attitude Toward Source and Concept as Factors in Attitude Change Through Communication," Public Opinion Quarterly, XX (1965), 10–20.

[66]Compare the results of Berlo and Gulley with those of Osgood, Suci, and Tannenbaum, p. 212.

elements—speaker, central proposition, speech composition, and delivery—he obtained results which fit his extended model significantly better than they do the two-element model (speaker and central proposition) employed in the earlier experiments.[67]

Generating or Changing Ethos

Unlike the studies discussed in the preceding section, which typically attempted to assess the utility of a presumed or measured ethos, the experiments discussed below are concerned with the means of generating or altering a receiver's image of a communicator. These efforts, in general, fall into two categories: those which tried to establish extrinsic ethos by techniques employed before the message itself began, and those which attempted to create intrinsic ethos by techniques employed by the speaker during the presentation.[68]

Extrinsic ethos

The following experiments deal with the generation or the modification of a communicator's image by stimuli which are not part of the actual presentation.

Since the ethos of the individual depends in part upon the reputation of the group to which he belongs, experiments concerning the alteration of group images are relevant to the concept of ethos. One such experiment showed that very short speeches produced immediate attitude changes in favor of either China or Japan but that over a five month period significant regression occurred toward the original attitudes.[69] In a similar experiment Roman Catholic school children were found to be quite persuasible to some but not all items in propaganda covering a wide range of topics. Other conclusions were that attitudes toward well-known individuals seemed about as subject to change as other attitudes and that reactions toward groups outside the students' immediate experience seemed especially subject to the influence of propaganda.[70]

Closely related to the question of changing attitudes toward individuals is that of building an image. Annis and Meier set out to create an image of an unknown source through planted editorials which linked the source with certain opinions and actions. The experimenters assumed that they could predict

[67]*Loc. cit.*

[68]Extrinsic ethos is the image of the speaker as it exists prior to a given speech. Intrinsic ethos, comparable to Aristotle's artistic ethos, is the image derived from elements during the presentation of the speech, consciously or unconsciously provided by the speaker. In real life speech situations, the final ethos is a product of the interaction of extrinsic and intrinsic ethos.

[69]William Chen, "The Influence of Oral Propaganda Material upon Students' Attitudes," *Archives of Psychology*, XXIII (1933) ; "Retention of the Effect of Oral Propaganda," *Journal of Social Psychology*, VII (1936), 479–483.

[70]Wegrocki, *loc. cit.*

whether the subjects of the experiment favored or opposed these opinions and actions. As few as seven planted editorials generated the desired image, and most of the effects persisted over a period of four months.[71]

Berlo and Kumata studied the effect of a dramatic allegory, "The Investigator," in modifying images. Attitudes toward Joseph McCarthy, the subject of the satire, tended to become more favorable, while attitudes toward the source (the Canadian Broadcasting Company) and toward Congressional committees became significantly less favorable. The experimenters felt that the extreme one-sidedness of the presentation may have caused these "boomerang" effects.[72]

Using a single tape-recorded speech, Kersten compared two introductions, one of which employed techniques estimated by experts to focus attention on the speaker and his subject and to build the speaker's prestige and the other of which did not. The persons hearing the speech with the favorable introduction changed opinion significantly more than did those who heard no introduction or the poor one.[73] The confounding involved in the simultaneous manipulation of prestige and attention-focusing elements makes it impossible to conclude that the enhanced prestige of the speaker was the source of the observed difference. Indeed, Pross found that an introduction stressing the character, the reputation, and the intelligence of the speaker added little to the persuasiveness of either "ethical" or "nonethical" forms of a speech.[74]

Neither Kersten nor Pross actually measured differences in ethos; they assumed that different introductions would affect the variable. The same is true of Highlander's experiment, which seems to show that variable levels of authoritativeness of the speakers do not affect either the likeableness of radio programs or the amount of information gained from them.[75] In all such studies it is possible that the experimental treatments failed to take effect in the supposed manner.

Andersen constructed three introductions designed to establish varying levels of prestige and authoritativeness for speakers dealing with the farm problem. His conclusions were these (1) Students perceived significant differences between a college student and a Professor of Agriculture or a Farm Extension Agent on two scales: (a) the evaluative and the dynamism dimensions of a semantic differential designed to measure ethos; (b) authoritativeness as estimated by a Likert-type scale. (2) The expected differences between the professor and the extension agent did not result except on the authoritativeness scale. (3) The more rhetorically sophisticated students seemed to perceive differences in ethos that the rhetorically naive students did not. (4) There was

---

[71]Albert Annis and Norman Meier, "The Induction of Opinion Through Suggestion by Means of 'Planted Context,'" *Journal of Social Psychology*, V (1934), 65–81.

[72]David Berlo and Hideya Kumata, "The Investigator: The Impact of a Satirical Radio Drama," *Journalism Quarterly*, XXXIII (1956), 287-298.

[73]*Loc. cit.*

[74]*Loc. cit.*

[75]*Loc. cit.*

no proof that the variations in ethos and authoritativeness affected persuasive-ness.[76]

A speech of introduction, one should note, creates special theoretical prob-lems; for if the audience image of the introducer is low, this attitude through transfer may affect the ethos of the speaker. For instance, at the time of this writing, a laudatory introduction of a political candidate in the United States performed by James Hoffa or Fidel Castro might prove a serious detriment to persuasiveness. Since less obvious factors may also affect the experimental situation, it is conceivable that ethos may be more sensitive to such unforeseen and uncontrolled variables than it is to the verbal content of the introductions.

Intrinsic ethos[77]

That changes in ethos result from hearing speeches seems clear from a study of the effect of a campaign speech by Thomas E. Dewey. Comparing ratings obtained before a speech with those recorded immediately afterwards, Thompson found that students raised their estimation of Dewey as a public speaker but did not change their opinions significantly concerning the sound-ness of his ideas and his acceptability as a candidate.[78]

Studies which have altered the presentational elements may be divided into those which have manipulated characteristics of the manuscript and those which have altered such nonmanuscript stimuli as the speaker's appearance or his style of delivery.

A common type of study is the comparison of the effect of presenting both sides with the effect of giving but one—a distinction which seems to the writ-ers to be ethically significant.[79] In one such investigation Hovland, Lumsdaine, and Sheffield found (1) that the "both sides" presentation was significantly more effective for subjects with a high school education when the weight of evidence clearly supported one side; and (2) that a one-sided presentation was more effective with subjects initially favoring the advocated view and with subjects who had not completed high school.[80]

Similarly, Paulson's experiment involved two speeches, one of which omit-ted opposing arguments and the other of which made the barest mention of

[76]Kenneth E. Andersen, "An Experimental Study of the Interaction of Artistic and Non-artistic Ethos in Persuasion," unpubl. diss. (Wisconsin, 1961).

[77]*Intrinsic ethos* is defined in this study as the image of the speaker which is generated during the presentation of the message.

[78]Wayne Thompson, "A Study of the Attitude of College Students Toward Thomas E. Dewey Before and After Hearing Him Speak," *SM*, XVI (1949), 125–134.

[79]The presentation of both sides of an issue is often treated as one aspect of ethical proof. The practice also has logical connotations. It is possible to consider the impact of the treatment of both sides on the image of the speaker and the impact of this image on persuasiveness as distinct from the logical value of the treatment and the resultant persua-siveness.

[80]Carl Hovland, Arthur Lumsdaine, and Fred Sheffield, *Experiments on Mass Com-munication:* Vol. III of *Studies in Social Psychology in World War II* (Princeton: Prince-ton University Press, 1949).

them. Opinion changes did not differ significantly, but the "both sides" speech was significantly superior in respect to the amount of information which was obtained.[81] Shanck and Goodman also tested reactions to propaganda which presented equal amounts of argument on both sides or one-sided pro or con arguments. That no significant difference was observed,[82] might be explained by the extreme subtlety of the propaganda.

Another rhetorical element which is sometimes held to carry ethical implications is the use of authority and citations of source. Three studies described earlier in this paper reported that the inclusion of authority did not increase persuasiveness.[83] Cathcart presented four versions of a speech with variations from form to form in respect to the amount of specific evidence and documentation. He found that the forms which supported but did not document contentions and which supported, documented, and specified that the sources cited were experts produced significantly greater shifts at the five per cent level than did the form which merely supplied generalizations. A fourth form which supported the assertions and documented fully but did not say that the cited sources were experts was not significantly more effective than the one which merely supplied generalizations.[84] That such differences as were observed were attributable to nonethical considerations is suggested by the finding that none of the speeches differed in terms of the audience's evaluations of the speaker's competence, enthusiasm, or clarity of ideas.[85]

Ludlum constructed a speech in which he incorporated several elements designed to increase the credibility of the source. His techniques include the acknowledgment of opposing arguments, "leading thoughts rather than forcing," showing alleged facts to be consistent with known facts, showing material to be recent, and manifesting a "high degree of credibility" by means of self-praising statements. Comparing the persuasiveness of this speech with that of a "straight argumentative" address, he found the latter to be more effective.[86] Since he did not measure received ethos, the effect of the variables in the non-argumentative speech is unknown. Moreover, since all of the variables were incorporated in a single speech, it is impossible to isolate the effect of any one of them. If some of the techniques produced positive effects and others acted negatively, the effects may have counterbalanced one another. Thirdly, some of the self-praising statements in the nonargumentative speech may have had an effect quite different from that intended. Finally, argumentative technique

[81]*Loc. cit.*

[82]R. C. Shanck and Charles Goodman, "Reactions to Propaganda on Both Sides of a Controversial Issue," *Public Opinion Quarterly*, III (1939), 107–112.

[83]See the studies previously cited by Sikkink, by Cole, and by Gilkinson, Paulson, and Sikkink.

[84]*Loc. cit.*

[85]The problem of separating the logical and the ethical effects of the same complex stimulus is again at issue. The writers believe that a complex stimulus may affect both logical and ethical proof and perhaps pathetic proof as well.

[86]Thomas Ludlum, "A Study of Techniques for Influencing the Credibility of a Communication," unpubl. diss. (Ohio State, 1956).

may have an ethical dimension for college students, such as those whom Ludlum employed, with the result that the arugmentative talk may well have produced a more favorable speaker image than did the speech employing an assortment of "conciliatory" techniques.

The experiment by Ludlum points up the importance of specifying carefully any differences in content between speeches intended to produce high credibility and those against which their effects are to be compared. The same consideration applies to an early experiment by Pross, who constructed four forms of a speech on a single topic. Two of these employed techniques of "ethical appeal" (as judged by speech experts) and the other two did not. Length was kept constant.[87] The interpretation of Pross' nonsignificant findings is difficult, for matching the lengths necessitated the removal of material in order to make room for the ethical elements. As a consequence the two ethical speeches had almost no logical structure.

This investigation and other studies indicate a confusion in the use of the terms *ethos* and *ethical*. On the one hand, these terms are used to refer to the audience's image of the speaker, as when it is said that Parran is more credible or higher in ethos than is Dennis; on the other hand, certain types of speech content are labeled *ethical appeals*. For example, a speech which employs many self-references and conciliatory elements is described as higher in ethos content than an address which follows a straightforward proposition-and-proof format. Usually, when rhetoricians classify a speech content element as "ethical," they seem to mean that the elements *seem to the classifier* to be calculated to gain the good will of the audience or to enhance the speaker's ethos. In our present state of knowledge concerning audience response, such a judgment is at best only an educated guess. Therefore, when the results of the Pross and the Ludlum studies are cited in support of the proposition that ethical speeches are no more effective in inducing attitude change than are logical speeches, it should be specified very carefully that the results are based upon analysis of speech content and not upon the image of the speaker which the audience holds. The present writers as rhetorical critics believe that some of the Pross and Ludlum "ethical" speech techniques probably had decidedly negative effects on the ethos of the speaker. The basis of this judgment, of course, is intuitive, not empirical.

The message which an audience receives during a speech obviously involves more than verbal (manuscript) stimuli. Several studies indicate that nonverbal factors produce audience judgments concerning the speaker. Haiman found (1) that an audience rated a graduate male speaker higher in competence than it did an undergraduate male and two females; (2) that with content held constant, graduate speakers obtained higher rates of fair-mindedness, sincerity, and likeableness than did undergraduates; (3) that in two experiments shifts of opinion with the audience were correlated positively with the speak-

[87]*Loc. cit.*

ers' competence ratings and with nothing else; and (4) that although variations in ratings of likeableness and physical attractiveness could be produced
through changes in appearance and demeanor, significant changes in attitude
did not result.[88]

Many of the variables in the Haiman study are those associated with differences in social status. Harms has shown that, regardless of their own position, listeners in general assign high credibility to speakers of high social
status and low credibility to those of low status. Such judgments occur even
though the stimulus is nothing more than a short tape-recorded sample of
speech. The Harms study further shows that listeners can discriminate class
differences with rough accuracy and that they identify the low status speakers
somewhat more readily than they do those of superior background.[89]

Consistent with these results is the experimental finding that audiences
may construct relatively complete assessments of a speaker's personality and
physical characteristics on the basis of his voice. Other conclusions to this
study were that personality, physical characteristics and occupation were likely
to be perceived correctly, that consistency of response (right or wrong!) was
a stronger tendency than accuracy of judgment, and that gross psychological
characteristics were judged more accurately than physical features.[90]

These findings suggest the plausibility of the "truth-will-out" theory regarding the action of subliminal, nonverbal stimuli upon the ethos of the
speaker. As the theory goes, an insincere speaker's sophistry will betray itself
through unconscious behaviors which act subliminally upon the auditors. An
experiment by Hildreth, however, offers no confirmation for this hypothesis.
Defining sincerity in terms of the speaker's expressed preference for one side
of a controversial issue and using a large number of speakers who filmed
speeches on both their preferred and their non-preferred sides, he discovered
that audiences were unable to distinguish the sincere from the insincere
speeches and that the ratings of the two types of speeches did not differ significantly in effectiveness. Rather, ratings of effectiveness and *estimated* sincerity
were positively correlated.[91] Unfortunately, methodological considerations
render the results of the experiment inconclusive. Since the "sincere" speech
was composed, practiced, and delivered first in all instances, the time allowed
for composition was very brief, and making of a film was presumably unfamiliar to a majority of the speakers, a number of factors were operating to enhance performance in the "insincere" presentation as contrasted with the "sincere" one.

Indeed, the role which subliminal perception may play in the establish-

---

[88]*Loc. cit.*

[89]*Loc. cit.*

[90]Gordon Allport and Hadley Cantril, "Judging Personality from Voice," *Journal of
Social Psychology,* V (1934), 37–55; also in Hadley Cantril and Gordon Allport, *The Psychology of Radio* (New York: Harper and Row, 1935).

[91]Richard Hildreth, "An Experimental Study of Audiences' Ability to Distinguish Between Sincere and Insincere Speakers," unpubl. diss. (Southern California, 1953).

ment of ethos has been little clarified by experiments. Drawing upon the "hidden persuader" approach, Steiner found that placing visually superimposed words on a screen at subliminal intensity levels did not alter either the effectiveness of a filmed speech or the judgment of the sincerity of the speaker.[92]

Combining prior and intrinsic elements, Strother attempted to study a combination of factors. The addition of ethical techniques either singly or in combination did not significantly increase the persuasiveness of a low ethos source. However, as measured by a hostility scale, the combination of elements apparently surpassed a control speech in allaying hostility toward the low ethos source. In the control presentation neither conciliatory nor special introductory techniques were employed.[93]

In another investigation of combinations of variables Andersen used two tape-recorded speeches, both of which were attributed to three sources described in tape-recorded introductions. The principal results were these: (1) Despite great manuscript variations which speech experts predicted would produce different levels of ethos, the only significant differences between the two speeches were those measured on a dynamism scale. (2) The elements of artistic and inartistic ethos did interact significantly in producing the final image of the speaker. (3) The variations in ethos did not cause a significant difference in persuasiveness.[94]

Measurements of Ethos and Attempts to Assess the Relative Degrees of Ethos

In a few instances the development of a measure of ethos has been the main goal of a research project, but more often the measurement of prestige, credibility, or some other ethical component has been ancillary to the study of such presumed results of ethos as preferences, attitude change, and information gain. The methods of measurement in both types of investigation are the same: (1) rankings, (2) sociograms, (3) "prestige indexes" obtained from attitude change data, (4) linear rating scales, (5) Thurstone-type attitude scales, and (6) devices similar to Likert scaling techniques, including the semantic differential.

Perhaps the most elementary method of determining differences among sources in respect to prestige, credibility, likeableness, etc., is to require subjects to arrange the sources in rank order. Sherif, for example, presented a list of sixteen authors to a group of undergraduates and asked them to rank the authors according to personal preferences for their writings. A month later

[92]George Edward Steiner, "An Experimental Study of the Influence of Subliminal Cue Words on an Audience's Perception of a Filmed Speaker's Sincerity, Effectiveness, and Subject Matter," unpubl. diss. (Southern California, 1959); SM, XXVII (1960), 93-94.
[93]Loc. cit.
[94]Loc. cit.

the subjects were told to rank sixteen passages in respect to literary merit. Since all of the passages had been written by a single author not included in the list and since literary experts had judged all of them to be of equal merit, the only variable was the false attachment of a different author's name to each excerpt. Correlations between the two sets of ranks were held to represent the effects of "prestige." The replication of the study with similar results in three instances indicates the usefulness of the rank-order technique for simple experiments of this type.[95] The method was to determine the rank order for individuals, to compute rank correlations for individuals, and to draw conclusions from the average correlations. While this technique seems justified, the rank-order method employed by Michael, Rosenthal, and DeCamp was not. In an effort to discredit the "constant stimulus" theory of prestige, these authors worked with mean and median ranks—[96] statistics which are generally meaningless.

Cole demonstrated the possibility of using sociometric data for the determination of certain characteristics of ethos. Using a particular personal characteristic (judgment, personal appeal, etc.) as the basis for sociometric choices, he selected one or more members of a group as "stars" and then assumed that they were more highly regarded than their colleagues. Under some conditions, these preferred members were as persuasive as authorities from outside the group.[97]

Kulp apparently made the first attempt to develop an index of prestige based upon attitude change. In a classic design which was to be repeated with variations many times during the ensuing years, he first administered Harper's test of liberalism to more than three hundred graduate students at Columbia. Later, various subgroups were told that the responses supplied them had been written by social scientists, educators, and other learned persons. The relative amounts of attitude shift toward each of these sources was used as the basis for computing a prestige index for each of the several professional groups.[98] Bowden, Caldwell, and West replicated the essential features of Kulp's study in an experiment using junior high, high school, and college students as subjects and employing a variety of different prestige levels. Sample findings with respect to the economic problems considered were these: "Prestige of the educators seems to increase as progress is made up the educational ladder" and "Ministers received the lowest rank in every case."[99]

Underlying these measuring techniques is the assumption that the prestige of a source is directly proportional to the ability to produce attitude shift. In 1938 Lurie formalized this point of view when he defined prestige as "The

[95]*Loc. cit.*
[96]*Loc. cit.*
[97]*Loc. cit.*
[98]Daniel Kulp, II, "Prestige, as Measured by Single-Experience Changes and Their Permanency," *Journal of Educational Research,* XXVII (1934), 663–672.
[99]A. O. Bowden, Floyd Caldwell, and Guy West, "A Study in Prestige," *American Journal of Sociology,* XL (1934), 193–203.

change in scale value of certain items brought about by attaching the name of the symbol to these items." He obtained scale values for prestige by administering a test of attitude without attaching prestige labels to the items, by administering the same test two weeks later with prestige labels attached, and by then subtracting the scores on the first test from those on the second. The remainder was the index of prestige.[100]

Naturally, prestige measures obtained in this manner are not pure or independent measures of the variable. Moreover, to use any of these measures to test the hypothesis that prestige induces attitude change is impossible, for the measure of prestige *is* attitude change. In an effort to develop an independent index suitable for testing this hypothesis, Saadi and Farnsworth combined gross ratings of "like," "indifferent," and "dislike" by the formula $100 \left[(L + \frac{1}{2} I) (L + I + D) \right]$ to obtain a score for likeableness based on group data.[101]

The multiple-choice aspect of the Saadi-Farnsworth measure was an early precursor of an obvious means of measuring various aspects of ethos—the rating scale. An early experimenter with this type of measurement was Lorge, whose subjects rated seventy sources on a five-interval scale ranging from "those individuals whose opinions you respect most" to "those individuals for whose opinions you have least respect."[102] More recently, Hovland and Weiss employed a five-point linear scale of "trustworthiness" to evaluate the credibility of two sources.[103]

The well-known study by Haiman used a variety of scales. In one phase of his experiment two nationally prominent public figures were evaluated on nine-point scales of reputation and competence. In other parts of the investigation student speakers were rated on similar scales for the qualities of sincerity, fair-mindedness, physical appearance, conceit, competence, and likeableness.[104]

In addition to being one of the first experimental research workers to recognize explicitly the multi-dimensionality of ethos, Walter made the earliest effort to apply recognized test construction methods to the problem of creating a measuring device. His specific project was the development of an instrument to measure a single factor, the evaluation of character. Beginning with nearly 400 character-describing statements and employing both the Thurstone sorting techniques and the Seashore rating methods, he developed two tests of twenty-two items each. When applied to such individuals as Franklin Roosevelt and "The person with the best character I have known," the two forms of the test were normally distributed, distinguished among intuitively perceived gross character levels, and correlated well (.86) with each other. Applied to two speakers in the classroom, the two forms correlated extremely well (.96).[105]

[100]Walter Lurie, "The Measurement of Prestige and Prestige-Suggestibility," *Journal of Social Psychology*, IX (1938), 219–225.

[101]*Loc. cit.*

[102]*Loc. cit.*

[103]*Loc. cit.*

[104]*Loc. cit.*

[105]Otis Walter, Jr., "The Measurement of Ethos," unpubl. diss. (Northwestern, 1948).

The Osgood and Stagner use of bipolar nouns in a set of scales to rate occupations and occupational groups was a forerunner of the semantic differential technique. They found that the prestige of jobs and workers could be determined through the use of their scales.[106]

Although Walter asserted the multi-dimensionality of ethos and although Haiman's technique actually employed a polydimensional approach, until recently no practical way of employing multivariate measures of ethos in research seemed to exist. Now the semantic differential technique makes such research possible. Berlo and Gulley,[107] Berlo and Kumata,[108] and Bettinghaus[109] used the differential to measure attitude toward the communicator, but in each instance they reported only one dimension of the semantic space, the evaluative aspect of the image. "Although it does not tap much of the *content* of an attitude in a denotative sense . . . it does seem to provide an index to the location of the attitude object along a general evaluative continuum."[110] Employed in this manner, the semantic differential is similar in many ways to a traditional Likert scale in which a number of judgments concerning the concept are rendered on a linear scale and the sum of the scale values recorded by the subjects is used as a more-or-less unidimensional measure of the single property with which the scale is concerned.

Andersen developed a semantic differential which was specifically designed to measure ethos. Employing terms garnered from theoretical and experimental literature and securing responses to famous living people from freshmen engineering and physical education students, he obtained two major dimensions (evaluative and dynamism) in the images.[111] Berlo carried out a similar study, but he used a greater number of concepts and more students than did Andersen. Berlo also employed an oblique solution, whereas Andersen's method was the orthogonal factor solution.[112] Inspection suggests that the two structures were not essentially dissimilar if allowance is made for the difference in the factor rotation methods.

Summary

Despite the great number of experimental studies relevant to ethos, the scope of this concept is such that the findings are not yet sufficiently numerous and sophisticated to permit definitive conclusions about the operation of ethical proof.

The finding is almost universal that the ethos of the source is related in

[106]Charles Osgood and Ross Stagner, "Analysis of a Prestige Frame of Reference by a Gradient Technique," *Journal of Applied Psychology*, XXV (1941), 275–290.

[107]*Loc. cit.*

[108]*Loc. cit.*

[109]*Loc. cit.*

[110]Osgood, Suci, and Tannenbaum, p. 195.

[111]*Loc. cit.*

[112]David K. Berlo, "An Empirical Test of a General Construct of Credibility," unpubl. paper presented at the SAA convention, New York City, December 29, 1961.

some way to the impact of the message. This generalization applies not only to political, social, religious, and economic issues but also to matters of aesthetic judgment and personal taste. Some evidence even shows that "prestige-suggestion" can affect the appetite for certain foods and can influence performances of perceptual and psycho-motor tasks. On the other hand, there is not enough evidence to suggest that the amount of information gained from exposure to a message is related to the ethos of the source—at least this lack of relationship seems to be true of college populations. The effect of ethos, again according to many studies, has a temporal dimension. In other words, when the stimulus is not renewed, material presented by a high ethos source loses in persuasiveness and that given by a poor source gains. Recall of the source re-establishes some of the initial effect, but the improvement which renewal produces decays more rapidly than does the original increment.

Some auditors appear to be more susceptible to ethical appeal than others; some may be contrasuggestible. However, there is no evidence to show that suggestibility to prestige correlates well with intelligence, education, speech training, subject-matter competence, age, or sex. The only variable which seems clearly related to differences in suggestibility to prestige is the initial attitude toward the topic or the purpose: consistently, those who are neutral initially shift more often than do those who are at one extreme or the other.

Research shows that expert opinion may be about as influential as majority opinion in inducing attitude change.

While most experimentation has been conducted in a fixed ethos model, recent research shows that a congruity model can be used to predict attitude change toward both a communicator and his topic. Incorporating elements concerning speech composition and delivery increased the usefulness of the model.

Printed and oral propaganda can succeed in creating and altering images of groups or of individuals, but attempts to produce unfavorable reactions to individuals may backfire. When this response occurs, the prestige of the criticized person may increase and that of the attacker may decline.

Speeches of introduction probably influence the image of a speaker, but most of the evidence on this point is indirect.

Certain characteristics of a speech affect the ethos of the speaker. No evidence, however, supports the common beliefs (1) that giving "both sides" is a superior way to present controversial material, (2) that citing the sources of evidence increases persuasiveness, and (3) that including conciliatory remarks, statements of self-praise, and other conscious, obvious attempts at ethical appeal enhances the speaker's status.

Such noncontent stimuli as dress, voice, and manner apparently affect the attitude of the audience toward the speaker, but these factors may not be related to persuasiveness on a given occasion. There is no evidence that the audience can perceive lack of sincerity; rather, audiences appear to react to their evaluations of the competence of the speaker.

Many techniques of measurement have been applied to ethos: among these are ranking, sociograms, prestige indexes, linear rating scales, Thurstone scales, and the semantic differential. Each of these has proved useful in assessing one or more of the aspects of ethos.

This preceding body of findings suggests certain possibilities for future research:

1. The dimensions of ethos should be explored through multivariate analysis in terms of different auditors, different speakers, and different speech situations. New measurement techniques, and especially the semantic differential, make this type of research possible.

2. Ethos or ethical proof should be measured in experiments designed so that this variable is not confounded with persuasiveness.

3. The effect upon ethos of the interaction of prior reputation and the artistic elements in the message should be studied. Findings in this area would be of great importance to rhetorical theory.

4. Some research suggests that differences in ethos are not established as easily with some audiences as previous experimenters often assumed. More research dealing with the methods of establishing and modifying ethos is needed.

5. The effect of variations in auditors, situations, and topics upon the function of ethical proof in persuasion should receive renewed attention. The utilization of improved designs and measuring devices can create experimental conditions that may lead to more meaningful results than those obtained in the past.

Questions for Analysis

1. Translate Andersen and Clevenger's definition of *ethos* into a working description of what *you* think, how *you* respond, alone and in groups, to speakers of different sorts. Review the distinction between *ethos* and *ethical*. Illustrate a few of your responses by examples.

2. In your experience how have the effects of a speaker on you or on others been influenced by: a. his position or reputation; b. authorities, expert or majority opinion cited or quoted in his message; c. audience composition and interaction? Compare your findings with those in the study.

3. How are you influenced by these means of creating *intrinsic* or *extrinsic* ethos? a. image-building, b. sponsorship or introduction of speaker, c. amounts of evidence and documentation, d. social status and personality connoted by voice, e. appearance, manner, and delivery. How do your findings relate to those reported in the study?

4. From your experience and observation discuss the validity of this finding: "In the absence of further stimuli agreement with high credibility sources decays

while agreement with low credibility sources grows." If the finding is valid, what are its implications for the student of public persuasion?

5. Discuss the authors' summarizing statement about giving "both sides," citing the sources of evidence, and including conscious, obvious attempts at ethical appeal. Are you surprised by these findings? Explain.

10

The Ethics of Persuasion: A Re-Examination

Arthur N. Kruger

At fairly regular intervals college debaters are criticized for their lack of *ethos*, their refusal to capitalize on *pathos*, and their insistence upon *logos*.[1] They are told to use "ethical, emotional, and psychological" appeals if they want to be effective persuaders, and debate coaches are advised to provide instruction "in persuasion as an instrument of social control." The question of the proper role of emotion in debate is a complex one. In so far as debate is conducted by human beings and involves beliefs and aspirations, emotional and psychological factors are inevitably involved. The pertinent question, however, is, can belief which is shaped by such factors be considered rational belief—the kind of belief which educators are presumably interested in? My own view is that teaching students how to inculcate belief in others is academically indefensible if the prime criterion of such instruction is the degree of success achieved by the student rather than the nature of the means employed. In the remarks which follow I shall try to prove (1) that many teachers and writers on the theory of persuasion are much more preoccupied with successful persuasion than with rational belief and (2) that this kind of emphasis is contrary to desirable educational goals.

Arthur N. Kruger is Chairman of the Department of Speech, C. W. Post College of Long Island University.

Reprinted by permission from *Speech Teacher*, 16(1967), 295–305.

[1] For a representative sample of recent articles on persuasion, see W. S. Howell, "The Role of Persuasion in Debate," *The AFA Register*, X (Fall 1962), 20–23; K. Mosier, "Quintilian's Implications Concerning Forensics," *The AFA Register*, XI (Spring 1963), 1–7; W. H. Murrish, "Training the Debater in Persuasion," *Journal of the AFA*, I (January 1964), 7–12; G. L. Cronkhite, "Logic, Emotion, and the Paradigm of Persuasion," *Quarterly Journal of Speech*, L (February 1964), 13–18; D. O. Olson and J. L. Petelle, "A New Look at Ethos and Ethical Proof," *Speaker and Gavel*, I (March 1964), 93–97; A. Hillbruner, "Psychological Creativity in Persuasion," *Today's Speech*, XII (April 1964), 19–21; J. L. Jones, "Juries, Jargon, and Justice," *Today's Speech*, XII (April 1964), 9–11; R. B. Gregg, "Some Psychological Aspects of Argument," *Western Speech*, XXVIII (Fall 1964), 222–230; and R. L. Scott, "Some Implications of Existentialism for Rhetoric," *Central States Speech Journal*, XV (November 1964), 267–275.

First of all, I should like to clarify what is meant by rational belief. The law of rationality holds that a conclusion must be justified by relevant and sufficient evidence and that one who believes rationally tempers his acceptance of a conclusion in accordance with the kind of evidence offered to support it. If there is no evidence or if the evidence conflicts, he suspends judgment. As Bertrand Russell put it, the truly rational individual cultivates "the habit of taking account of all relevant evidence in arriving at a belief. When certainty is unattainable, a rational man will give most weight to the most probable opinion, while retaining others, which have an appreciable probability, in his mind as hypotheses which subsequent evidence may show to be preferable."[2] And Santayana effectively summed up the concept of rational belief with these words: "Believe, certainly; we cannot help believing; but believe rationally, holding what seems certain for certain, what seems probable for probable, what seems false for false."[3] Whether men have the capacity to achieve such an ideal is open to question, but whether they do or not, educators in a free society must presuppose that they do and teach accordingly.

If we accept this norm for evaluating instruction on how to influence beliefs—and I do not see how as teachers we can refuse—then it follows that any instruction on how to evade or supplant this ideal is unethical and peda-gogically indefensible. Although many beliefs are disproportional to the avail-able evidence for them and although we know that people can be duped, the teacher has an obligation, it seems to me, to point out the immorality of the doctrine that only success matters. And this statement brings me to my first point: that many teachers of persuasion today seem to have lost sight of the goal of rational belief and are far more preoccupied with teaching students how to be successful persuaders regardless of the means used.

In beginning their instruction, these teachers usually define "persuasion" as discourse "designed to win belief or stimulate action by employing all the factors that determine human behavior,"[4] or they give Aristotle's definition of "rhetoric" as "the faculty of discerning in a given case what are the available means of persuasion."[5] This is usually followed by a scientific account of those factors "that determine human behavior" and beliefs—buttressed by the latest studies of communication theory, which are impressively footnoted. All of this adds up to the conclusion that not facts and reason but "desires stamp the matrix of human beliefs. They largely determine judgment."[6] Strongly moti-vated by desire—conscious, subconscious, hidden, or otherwise—man, we are told, believes what he wants to believe, what he thinks will gratify his

[2]*Sceptical Essays* (London: George Allen & Unwin, Ltd.; New York: Barnes & Noble, Inc., 1962), p. 32.

[3]*Character and Opinion in the United States* (New York: Charles Scribner's Sons, 1920), p. 87.

[4]Wayne C. Minnick, *The Art of Persuasion* (Boston: Houghton Mifflin, 1957), p. 33.

[5]*The Rhetoric of Aristotle*, translated and edited by Lane Cooper (New York: Apple-ton-Century-Crofts, Inc., 1960), 1.2 (p. 7).

[6]Minnick, p. 19.

desires. "He is not wholly rational or wholly irrational, but a mixture of both."[7] Thus, if we wish to persuade others, to shape and control their behavior and beliefs, we must remember that "logic is not enough"; we must "use other sources of persuasion, too."[8] Such "sources," as most of us know, include style, ethos, and pathos. Strangely enough, these are called "extra-logical," "psychological," or "emotional" *modes of proof,* a designation which puzzles logicians. As I will try to show in a moment, this approach to persuasion belittles rational processes, shows little faith in man's ability to govern himself, extols the techniques of the confidence man, presumes that the end justifies the means, ignores the consequences of social manipulations, but it appeals, as one writer said of his book on persuasion, "to the advertiser, the salesman, the public relations director. . . ."[9]

In examining this theory of persuasion, let us begin with the question, are "the available means of persuasion in a given case" always justified? *Argumentum ad baculum,* or the appeal to force or threats, is often available and quite persuasive. Does the definition mean that this appeal should be used? Are "all the factors that determine human behavior" rational factors? And, apart from ethics, is it prudent for anyone to base his beliefs or actions on other than rational factors—that is, relevant and sufficient evidence? Is it prudent, for example, to substitute desire for reality or to mistake suggestion for sound inference? And even if we grant that closely reasoned arguments are ineffective, is it educationally defensible to teach the doctrine that in influencing others "valid arguments, *per se,* are not enough"?[10]

If we look closely at these so-called "extra-logical" appeals, we find that none of them can be justified from the standpoint of either responsible teaching, logic, or ethics. The first of these is usually designated as "style," that is, language that is vivid, memorable, or stirring. Quoting W. H. Murrish, "It is unrealistic to assume that mere cogency of argument can suffice without the embellishments of style and delivery to impel audience acceptance."[11] Actually, it is difficult to know what is meant here by "the embellishments of style," for one does not usually conceive of language as an embellishment but rather as a medium of communication—a means for communicating ideas to and with people as clearly and as concisely as possible. One meaning of "embellishment" might be the flowery, flamboyant language of old-time oratory, filled with invective, hyperbole, and fanciful conceits, but it is doubtful that Murrish implies this meaning. For a clue as to what he probably means, we turn to another theorist on the use of persuasive language, John Bowers, who stresses

[7]*Ibid.,* p. 23.

[8]Robert B. Huber, *Influencing Through Argument* (New York: David McKay Company, Inc., 1963), p. 322.

R. L. Scott goes so far as to say "that our common maxims, heard in speech classes and seen in texts, 'Be logical!' and 'First seek the truth!' are at best insufficient and in practice may be invidious." (*Op. cit.,* p. 267).

[9]Minnick, Preface (no p.n.).

[10]Murrish, p. 8.

[11]*Ibid.,* p. 8.

the importance of adapting one's language to the attitudes of the audience. That is, he advises the speaker to use extreme, moderate, or neutral language depending upon whether the audience is extremely friendly or hostile, moderate, or neutral. The important thing, according to Bowers, is that various examples and experiments show that this technique works. Whether it is a mark of honesty or sincerity for the speaker to become a chameleon by changing his colors in this way is a question that did not occur in his discussion. Bowers goes on to illustrate "memorable phrasing" by giving an example of what he calls "argument-naming"; thus, the argument that the testing of nuclear weapons should be discontinued because many small countries will develop the bomb he labels the "Nth country" argument and comments that this

> name impresses audiences with the speaker's linguistic
> skill the first time he uses it. This kind of skill often helps
> win arguments. Furthermore, *Nth country*, because of its
> derivation, connotes mathematical objectivity. . . . Finally,
> *Nth country* denotes a finality which a name like *country X*
> does not. . . . Hence, all of the meanings overlaying the
> labeling meaning in *Nth country* favor the affirmative.[12]

From such comments it seems clear that this type of an impressive style persuades without regard to whether or not the suggestion is justified by the evidence. This technique is the same one which advertisers use when they sell shampoo by associating it with a thrilling sexual experience, and practically all other products—whether automobiles, beer, lawnmowers, or mouthwashes —by associating them with pretty girls, usually in bathing suits or partially clad.

Ethos, or speaker credibility, is the next "extra-logical" mode of proof, also known as "ethical proof." This latter term is somewhat paradoxical, for it is neither "ethical" nor "proof" in the sense that philosophers and logicians use these terms. One of the first to explain this concept was, of course, Aristotle, who wrote in his *Rhetorica*, "Persuasion is achieved by the speaker's personal character when the speech is so spoken as to make us think him credible. We believe good men more fully and more readily than others. . . ."[13] A little further on in the same work Aristotle specified the factors of a speaker's personality or character "that induce us to believe a thing apart from any proof of it" as "good sense, good moral character, and good will."[14] Modern theorists have added other traits, such as humility, sincerity, congeniality, integrity, sense of humor, and kindness; and most of them agree with Aristotle that a speaker's personality is the most potent factor in persuasion. As Hillbruner points out, a recent Michigan State University study indicates that "the most important single factor influencing the vote in a presidential cam-

[12]"Language and Argument," *Perspectives on Argumentation,* edited by G. R. Miller and T. R. Nilsen (Chicago: Scott, Foresman and Company, 1966), p. 164.
[13]Aristotle, *Rhetoric,* translated by Rhys Roberts (Oxford: Oxford University Press, 1946), 1, 2, 1356a.
[14]*Ibid.,* II, 1, 1378a.

paign is not the argument used by the speaker . . . but rather his personality or image." Hillbruner concludes that, if we wish to train successful debaters,

> it would be well for us to spend more time in developing this total speech personality so that the debater sells himself before he attempts to sell his arguments. . . . The audience is not inclined to accept the debater's argument unless the debater demonstrates that he is one that the audience can like, trust and respect.[15]

First, it should be pointed out that "selling oneself before attempting to sell one's arguments" is precisely the art of the confidence man. Second, we may ask, how is a debater supposed to inspire "trust and respect" and all the other qualities of sincerity, humility, affability, integrity during the relatively short period of time it takes to give a speech? Trust and respect are attitudes which must be built up over a period of time. Since only the unreflective person is satisfied with appearances and illusions, it would seem that if a speaker's ethos is to be a factor, the speaker must *create the illusion* that he is trustworthy and respectable, an illusion that will work with most audiences because they are gullible or, in Aristotle's words, "because of their sorry nature." And it is precisely here that the confidence man excels.

To dispel any doubt on this point, in an article written to show how successful lawyers establish their ethos, J. L. Jones cites the example of Thomas Erskine, a very successful lawyer of the late 18th century, who in opening a case "spoke at length of 'eloquence which I never possessed' and 'my embarrassment is abundantly increased.' " After such a suggestion of modesty and humility (obviously false), Jones comments, "Thus his own ethos was established. The jury would not readily accept his statements as fact."[16] A reflective man would resent this transparent attempt to play on his emotions and would undoubtedly be on his guard against the advocate. But the point is, even if the trick did succeed (as apparently it did), what should we say of Erskine's tactics and their effect on justice?

Jones also endorses the practice of Earl Rogers, "the great Pacific Coast mouthpiece" of the early 1900's, who, we are told, "often distorted or magnified minor details until the main issues of the case were obscured." But, like Erskine,

> Rogers always worked for a friendly rapport with the jury in any trial. With a sense of timing and a flair for drama of Barrymore brilliance, he made an emotional impact on his listeners which usually left at least one unsuspecting jury member feeling a deep, personal identification with Rogers' client—the key for most of his acquittals.[17]

The key words here are "emotional impact" and "unsuspecting." In other words, Rogers was an eminent example of persuasion by personality and

[15]Hillbruner, pp. 9–10.
[16]Jones, p. 9.
[17]*Ibid.*, p. 10.

dramatic flair rather than by reason, which he apparently abused. The basis for his acquittals was not truth, mind you, but the ensnarement of an "unsuspecting juror." And Jones tells us this with almost jubilant approval.

Clearly, such a theory of persuasion is concerned only with results—with how to win a case regardless of the means employed. After telling us how effectively Rogers used the *ad hominem attack,* Jones concludes:

> However questionable Rogers' ethics may have been, he knew that winning a verdict required winning at least one juror totally. And he knew that since a jury of peers is not selected on the basis of its logical abilities, victory could often reside in appeals to emotion and personality rather than reasoned arguments.[18]

Whether the innocent is thereby wronged or the guilty exonerated seems to be a matter of indifference. What Jones and others like him unwittingly present is the best possible argument for abolishing the jury system and substituting a panel of judges selected on the basis of its logical abilities so that victory could not reside in appeals to emotion and personality rather than reasoned arguments, and so that men like Erskine and Rogers could not play fast and loose with men's lives and with justice.

Let us analyze the so-called ethical appeals a little further. We are told that the speaker must be sincere and that he should be pleasant and affable, for, to quote Murrish, "it is axiomatic that the irritated speaker irritates his audience."[19] Now, if "sincerity" means honest feeling and if the speaker is irritated—as he may be, by injustice, hypocrisy, or stupidity—is he to feign affability? And if so, would he be sincere? Similarly, should a speaker always appear confident, even when he feels unsure of his conclusions? It has been noted that thoughtful persons often seem unsure of themselves and usually qualify their remarks. As H. R. Huse put it, "Scholars are seldom voluble; competent commercial travelers and politicians find speech much easier. . . . The wise have the most reservations."[20]

As for the good man being the best persuader, how good or how ethical is one who by-passes or demeans reason and who uses tricks to gain his ends, who shows contempt for the rational processes of his fellow man and exploits him? History is filled with examples which refute the theory that the good man is always the best persuader. Unfortunately, bigots, demagogues, dictators, confidence men, and unscrupulous salesmen display as much earnestness, sincerity, and affability as do men of good will. As Eric Hoffer has observed, recent history would seem to indicate that for successful mass persuasion, "Exceptional intelligence, noble character and originality seem neither indispensable nor perhaps desirable."[21] In the final analysis, how ethical is it to teach stu-

[18]*Ibid.,* p. 10.
[19]Murrish, p. 10.
[20]*The Illiteracy of the Literate* (New York: D. Appleton-Century Company, Inc., 1933), pp. 168, 172.
[21]*The True Believer* (New York: Harper & Brothers, 1951), p. 112.

dents to get others "to believe a thing apart from any proof of it" and how rational is it to believe without proof? In answer, we need only look at some of our public officials, jury decisions, the prices we pay for some goods, and the annual loss to confidence men (according to the National Better Business Bureau) of about three billion dollars.

The usual rejoinder to this phase of my argument is that I am unrealistic. Being what they are, people are going to be persuaded by emotional and psychological factors whether I like it or not. And since we cannot eliminate this type of appeal, why not use it? In answer, I would say, yes, people *are* persuaded by irrelevant factors but they *should not be.* And our teaching should be directed to explaining why and not to demonstrating how to take advantage of others. As to a speaker's personality, I would agree that every speaker should be courteous and avoid antagonizing an audience by his manner, not for the purpose of winning them over but so as not to distract them. To win them over, he should concentrate on developing sound arguments and presenting them clearly and effectively, constantly reinforcing *understanding* by means of appropriate tones, gestures, and body movements. A truly ethical speaker respects the intelligence of his listeners and tries to get them to think about what he is saying, however difficult thinking might be for some. Only in this way does he show any respect for democratic values, which presume that people can think for themselves and govern themselves intelligently.

The last mode of non-logical proof is pathos, which may be described as a form of suggestion that plays on hidden desires, frustrations, hostilities, and prejudices. Contemporary advertising men speak of it in terms of "subliminal appeals" and "motivational techniques of audience manipulation." Students of classical and modern rhetoric spell it out as appeals to basic wants, to the hate object or the love object, to prejudice. And they give rather depressing accounts in their writings on "how to render an audience suggestible" by using emotionally loaded words ("name-calling" and "glittering generalities," personal invective and vituperation), various propaganda devices ("getting on the bandwagon" appeal, the "plain folks" approach, "we-are-in-this-together" appeal, appeal to flattery, the "yes-yes" method, the "oblique or circuitous" method), and other assorted fallacies (*argumentum ad hominem, ad misericordiam, ad populum, ad baculum, ad verecundiam*). Instead of pointing out the unsurpassed opportunities for fraud which such techniques create, many writers on persuasion endorse them. The lesson being taught here can only be described as appealing to emotions with a vengeance, the epitome of anything-goes-that-can-succeed, instructions that might have come right out of Machiavelli's *The Prince.* Its underlying premise is familiar enough to psychologists: when man experiences strong feelings, he tends to short-circuit his thinking process, to jump to conclusions, to act hastily, to yield to atavistic impulses. Reflection, on the other hand, or thinking before acting, does not come naturally and must be learned. Man must be taught to reflect, to analyze and evaluate, and to this end he must learn to check and control his emotions. Propagandists and advertisers, who realize that thinking can be fatal to their case, seek to inflame the emotions and thereby to elicit an automatic, unreflective response. And for whose benefit? Obviously for their own. Thus, it is not surprising that such an art is studied and practiced with such deadly earnestness. What is hard to believe, however, is that this art is adorned with the mantle of academic respectability and made the subject of earnest books and articles by college professors.

The most common manifestations of this art are the ubiquitous advertisements that bombard us through every medium of communication. We also see these crude appeals in the oversimplifications (usually embellished by dismal rhetoric) which characterize many political speeches. Excerpts from the latter, by the way, adorn the pages of books on persuasion and are admiringly held up as models. And to illustrate the use of pathos in the courtroom, we turn to Jones again. In writing of Clarence Darrow, he says, "The most important part of any case, according to Darrow, was the picking of the jury and if this was successful the acquittal was almost assured." Though we can be grateful for the "almost," we see here a cynical disregard of the truth claims of either side. Jones goes on to explain:

> If the selection was satisfactory, the legal aspect of the case was often entirely replaced with emotional appeal. [Here the doctrine stands unadorned.] Once when defending a criminal who was a cripple, it was a juror with a crippled brother to whom Darrow addressed his summation, creating a personal identification and acquittal. Alan Hynd says, 'He was the maestro of old, playing on the emotions.'[22]

Liebowitz, too, we are told, uses similar tactics—"ascertaining personal prejudices, such as distrust of policemen, and even conforming his behavior and dress . . . to the tastes of the jurors. If no absolute proof is attainable, the establishment of reasonable doubt, primarily by emotional appeal, in the minds of the jury is enough. . . ."[23]

Though students of rhetoric may dislike this comparison, this description of pathos could as well serve as a description of the art of the confidence man. That such techniques are effective is not the issue, but whether they are relevant to the question of innocence or guilt—to the question of truth—is another matter. Again, one is prompted to ask, what is the worth of a jury system when falsehood can be made to appear as truth and truth as falsehood?

Frankly, I find it disturbing that teachers who endorse such techniques seem unaware of their consequences. Although Vance Packard exposes this type of persuasion and underscores its dangers to a democratic society, Hillbruner, for example, declares, "*The Hidden Persuaders* should be given a vote of thanks for its salient contribution to the field of speech." And why? Because "it has reemphasized the present neglect of psychology for creative insights." All this is interpreted as "a healthy sign because it reasserts an important tradition"—the tradition of sophistry. "Our first speech teachers, the sophists, . . .

[22]Jones, pp. 9–10.
[23]*Ibid.*, p. 10.

were concerned with other than logical proof of their theories." Despite Packard's amply chronicled and often hair-raising account of the unscrupulous "explorations" of the "depth probers," Hillbruner laments that "few authors make
use of the latest explorations of the depth probers" and goes on to say, "Yet
understanding and utilization of depth psychology can make a significant contribution to persuasion."[24] Like the other writers I have quoted, he apparently
see nothing wrong in probing for man's weakness and utilizing "their points
of vulnerability" for selfish ends. Indeed, he is quite explicit on this point:
"Packard suggests that if you have a product or an idea or a person to sell, 'it
is dangerous to assume that people can be trusted to behave in a rational way.'
Most students of persuasive speaking are well aware of the truth and the importance of such a statement."[25]

Although I believe this doctrine is unethical, as I have tried to show, I do
not mean that its proponents are. Personally, I think that they are well-meaning
but misguided and unaware of what their teaching implies. It is only fair to
point out that some do try to justify their theory in various ways, and in the
next few pages I should like to consider some of these justifications.

Practically all apologists for emotional appeals of the type described here
pay lip service to the rational ideal but claim that reason alone does not suffice.
Hence, these additional appeals must be used. Hillbruner, for example, writes:

> The emphasis on logical proof is in keeping with the highest
> goals of modern education. This stress has as its aim the
> making of a rational man, certainly not a negligible goal.
> As such it makes for skepticism and for a questioning atti-
> tude. . . . It means that we should be ruled more by our
> heads than by our hearts, and so we should.

But, he goes on, to emphasize mainly logical materials "suggests several unhappy conclusions," which he sums up thus: "All of us are doing ourselves a
disservice by not searching for truth through the use of the totality of logical,
emotional, and ethical appeals."[26] Such remarks are quite typical of the confusion shown by these writers. After praising the ideal of rationality, they
apparently see no inconsistency in teaching and condoning irrationality. Moreover, it seems evident that they are unaware of what "searching for the truth"
entails. Clearly, such a search is not compatible with by-passing logical processes or with being illogical. To say that it involves "emotional and ethical appeals" betrays an unfamiliarity with philosophy and scientific method. In this
regard, the argument first put forth by the Greek sophists—that rhetoric is
neither moral nor immoral but simply unmoral, for it is like a weapon which
may be used for either good or evil, depending upon the user—is based on a
false analogy. As we have seen, persuasion by ethos or pathos either eliminates,

[24]Hillbruner, p. 19.
[25]Ibid., p. 19.
[26]Ibid., p. 19.

obscures, distorts, or actually does violence to reason and hence by its very nature is incompatible with the rational ideal. If we accept rationality as a norm, we must reject that which goes contrary to it.

Another attempt to soften the Machiavellian aspects of this doctrine is usually made by citing Quintilian's version of Aristotle's effective persuader as "the good man speaking well." Thus Murrish writes, "The responsible speaker is aware of the moral and social consequences of his utterances and acts accordingly."[27] And Robert T. Oliver: "The truly persuasive individuals are those who represent in their own characters and personalities the best traits of the society in which they live."[28] Such pronouncements, however, do not come to grips with the ethical considerations of persuasion by emotion and reveal only, I believe, a certain kind of wishful thinking. The doctrine that a man must be good to be persuasive is appealing but quixotic. It was probably first formulated by good men who wanted to believe it and hence did, even though it is at variance with the facts.

Still another—and more subtle—defense of this doctrine of persuasion is that there really is no significant difference between emotional and logical appeals because (1) most people cannot differentiate between them or (2) their overlapping nature makes them indistinguishable and hence the same.

Supporting the first reason is Ruechelle's frequently cited finding that "persuasive materials presented in tests could not be dichotomized by observers as emotional or intellectual in content."[29] This simply means that the people tested could not tell the difference between the two types of appeal. Even if we grant that most people have trouble recognizing a sound argument—and I would be the first to grant it—does it follow that there is no such thing? To say yes would make about as much sense as saying that because most people cannot differentiate between mushrooms and toadstools, there is no difference between them. But important differences are still differences whether easily recognized or not. And as our logic books tell us, there are crucial differences between sound and spurious arguments, even though the latter may resemble the former up to a point. Indeed, one of the problems with fallacies is that they often do resemble sound arguments, and only careful analysis enables us to tell the difference between them. Instead of being complacent about the fact that most people cannot detect fallacies and arming students with this information to enable them to exploit others, it seems to me we should use such knowledge to fortify students against becoming victimized by such arguments.

As to the second reason—that logical and emotional appeals are indistinguishable or the same because they overlap—Cronkhite points out that during the last fifty years rhetorical theorists have seriously questioned the distinc-

[27]Murrish, p. 9.

[28]*Persuasive Speaking* (New York: Longmans, 1950), p. 3.

[29]Randall C. Ruechelle, "An Experimental Study of Audience Recognition of Emotional and Intellectual Appeals in Persuasion," *Speech Monographs*, XXV (March 1958), 49–58.

tion between appeals to reasoning and appeals to emotion because "of the wide-spread acceptance of psychological theories emphasizing the unity of man's nature and denouncing its division into the 'faculties' [of thinking and feel-ing]."[30] Also, we are told that there is no such thing as neutral language, or purely objective meaning—that all language has emotional overtones. Now this is undoubtedly true, but what does it prove? Certainly not that cognitive meaning cannot be distinguished from its emotive associations. If objective meanings were indistinguishable from subjective meanings, knowledge would be impossible, for knowledge is objective, stable, universal, repeatable, and communicable. Moreover, the very doctrine itself would have no clear meaning if the words used to express it were blurred beyond recognition by subjective factors. Indeed, such a doctrine would render any kind of discussion impossi-ble. Thus, not only is such a doctrine reduced to nonsense by its own pro-visions, but it stems from the false assumption that because no sharp distinc-tions can be made between *continua*, no meaningful distinctions at all can be made—black is the same as white, hot is the same as cold, emotional appeals are really the same as logical appeals. It seems that better reasons than these are needed before we can accept such a rationalization.

Finally, many writers try to justify emotional proof by arguing that there are times when certain worthwhile proposals should be adopted and that the best means to this end are strong emotional appeals. Getting people to register for the draft, to buy war bonds, to give to the Heart Fund are cited as ex-amples. This argument, of course, assumes that the advocate alone knows what is worthwhile and that those being appealed to cannot be depended on to reach the same conclusion by means of reason. It also assumes that the end justifies the means. Although this may be true in rare situations, as, for example, where someone's life may be lost by telling the truth, exceptional instances do not justify such a generalization. In our own culture we do not accept the philoso-phy that a "good" program always merits support regardless of how that sup-port is obtained. Unless there is what Justice Holmes called "a clear and present danger," we do not abridge the rights of individuals to achieve what may be considered desirable goals, and by the same reasoning we would all fare better in the long run if belief and action were predicated on rational grounds. To quote Franklyn S. Haiman, who wrote an excellent article on this subject:

> The hidden persuader, whether he is aware of it or not, is
> engaging in a non-democratic practice. He takes advantage
> of the fact that although men may have the latent capacity
> for making rational, conscious choices, they are also part
> animal and as such can be exploited. . . . But because they
> *can be* so moved does not mean that they *should be* so
> moved, and anyone who so moves them only intensifies their
> tendencies to respond immaturely and thwarts their growth

---

[30]Cronkhite, p. 13. In justice to Cronkhite, he himself does maintain that there is a distinction, which he characterizes as "cognition" and "activation."

toward the more dignified humanity which democracy presumes. [Italics mine.][31]

Lest I have given the impression that there is no room for emotion in
persuasion, I should like to consider briefly before closing what I believe is its
legitimate role. I would concede that an emotional response to a speaker's
personality is inevitable but that it should be discounted by the listener because it does not constitute rational grounds for belief. The so-called pathetic
appeals should also be discounted for the same reason and should not be used
in the first place if one wishes to be rational and ethical. Where emotion legitimately comes in, I believe, is in relation to the audience's values and goals, but
some clarification is needed here. If a listener had no emotional involvement
in what was being said, he would be indifferent to the message. He is attentive
and thoughtful because he would like to achieve his heart's desire and believes
that the speaker may be able to show him how to do so. But a rational demonstration by the speaker of how certain needs can be fulfilled is far different
from (1) appealing to fraudulent or base motives or to general or incidental
values and (2) suggesting rather than proving by causal reasoning that a given
proposal is the best way to achieve certain desired goals. In short, the role of
emotion in persuasion is important, but to evoke feelings by means of quest-
ion-begging epithets, suggestion by association, and subliminal appeals is not
only illogical but unethical.

In summary, I have tried to show that teaching students how to use "all
the available means of persuasion"—including probing for and exploiting the
weaknesses of others—is pedagogically indefensible. Instead, students should
be taught how to guard themselves against unscrupulous persuaders and how
to use rational processes in persuasion rather than the fraudulent emotional
appeals so commonly advocated. In our teaching I think there should be greater
emphasis on logic, modern as well as classical, on ethics, and on philosophy in
general. Concomitantly there should be far less preoccupation with rhetorical
theory, from Aristotle's on up. Some years ago the Contest Committee of the
North Central Association stated, "Successful communication depends upon
the understanding, respect, tolerance, and sympathy which speaker and hearer
have for each other."[32] To substitute emotion for reason is hardly respectful of
an audience's intelligence; nor are deliberate efforts to modify one's language,
personality, and arguments in order to manipulate an audience. Such practices
are academically indefensible and contrary to the rationale of a free society.
In discussing educational objectives, John Dewey wrote:

> The business of education is to cultivate deep-seated and
> effective habits of discriminating tested beliefs from mere
> assertions, guesses and opinions; to develop a lively, sin-

[31]"Democratic Ethics and Hidden Persuaders," *Quarterly Journal of Speech*, XLIV
(December 1958), 388.

[32]"A Program of Speech Education," *Quarterly Journal of Speech*, XXXVII (October
1951), 350.

cere and openminded preference for conclusions that are
properly grounded and to ingrain into the individual's
working habits methods of inquiry and reasoning appropriate to the various problems that present themselves. . . . The
formation of these habits is the Training of the Mind.[33]

The question we must ask, then, is, are teachers of rhetoric and persuasion
supplying those conditions that cultivate "deep-seated and effective habits of
discriminating tested beliefs from mere assertions," that help "to develop a
lively, sincere and open-minded preference for conclusions that are properly
grounded"? From the evidence which we have seen, there is considerable doubt
that they are. Personally, I think the time has come to reevaluate some of our
preconceptions and attitudes concerning the teaching of rhetoric and persuasion and to make some very much needed changes.

Questions for Analysis

1. Do the findings of Andersen and Clevenger's study of *ethos* appear to support
Kruger's claim that *logos* has been de-emphasized? Explain. Compare "successful
persuasion" with "rational belief" in public speaking on campuses today.

2. How does Kruger show that style, ethos, and pathos can become, respectively,
persuasion by association, by personality, and by suggestion? Cite examples of these
techniques in current advertising. Has Kruger caused you to revise your previous
understanding of "ethos"? Explain.

3. Answer Kruger's question: are the techniques of persuasion he describes
"relevant to the question of innocence or guilt—to the question of truth?" What
bearing do the studies of "agitative" rhetoric in the first section of the book have on
your answer? Are these techniques *ever* justifiable? Explain.

4. Examine the question of the "morality" of rhetoric. Does rhetoric, as it is
said of guns, pull the trigger, or do men pull the trigger? Must rhetorical "morality"
always be consistent with "rationality"? Do "good men" always out-persuade "bad
men"? In the rhetorical situation is the responsibility for the distinction between
emotional and logical appeals, the speaker's or the listener's? Is this a "producer-
consumer" relationship? Does the distinction between appeals exist? Explain your
answers and compare them with Kruger's.

5. How does Kruger define the "legitimate role" of emotion in persuasion? How
do you define it?

[33]*How We Think* (New York: D. C. Heath & Co., 1911), p. 27.

11

Validity as Moral Obligation

Douglas Ehninger

In controversy as a method of decision making the validity of the conflicting cases can be enforced neither by the "club" of logic nor by the "club" of fact; instead it depends on the conscience and good will of the disputants and hence is neither more nor less than a matter of moral obligation on their part.

He who maintains that commercial airlines fly from Pittsburgh to Chicago in fifty-five minutes or that water freezes at thirty-two degrees Fahrenheit may establish his claim empirically. He who argues "If p then q; p; therefore q," or affirms the Pythagorean theorem may offer a demonstration that coerces agreement. In many of the disputes that arise among men, however, these methods do not avail. Appeals to printed data are indecisive, experimental procedures are inapplicable, and the premises required for apodeictic proofs may themselves be matters of contention.

Consider the following: Is our Far Eastern policy viable? Should one always obey his impulses? Does reality transcend the limits of sense experience? When confronted with questions of this sort, how do men argue? What method do they use to support their contentions and advance their claims?

As has long been recognized, men resort to a procedure that is *sui generis* to controversy as a mode of decision making, and this is to amass on behalf of the view they espouse a cluster or "bundle" of "independent" inducements to belief or action, no one of which individually or all of which together establish this view conclusively, but which, acting in concert, gradually build up a preponderance of probability in its favor.[1] They cite precedents, report prevailing opinions, raise questions and objections, invoke values, quote authorities, and trace the consequences of admissions. Above all, they point to weak-

Douglas Ehninger is Professor of Speech, The University of Iowa.
Reprinted by permission from *Southern Speech Journal*, 33(1968), 215–222.
[1]George Campbell, *The Philosophy of Rhetoric*, ed. Lloyd Bitzer (Carbondale: Southern Illinois University Press, 1963), pp. 45–46.

nesses or "evils" in the view they oppose and outline strengths and advantages in the view they maintain.

This procedure, though seen most clearly perhaps in the arguments of the politician as he endeavors to replace the "ins" with the "outs," is equally the method of the lawyer as he poses the claim of "guilt" against the presumption of "innocence," of the school debater as he advocates the acceptance of his "plan," and of the philosopher as he argues before his peers or before an audience of all rational men the superiority of the "system" he advocates.[2] Cut off from the resources of empirical verification on the one hand, and of formal demonstration on the other, each in his role as advocate is obliged to lay out such proofs and persuasives as are available to him in the form of a *causa* or "case"—an organized body of facts, inferences, and appeals designed to remove doubts and hesitations and to make his claim appear probable.[3]

If, however, as a more or less miscellaneous collection of *ad hoc* inducements to belief or action, a case consists neither of a formal demonstration nor of a direct appeal to experience, how is its validity to be determined? Under what circumstances are we warranted in accepting the claim it supports, and when should that claim be rejected? Are we to endorse as legitimate any case toward which we are psychologically disposed, or are we to withhold our assent until certain predetermined standards or conditions have clearly been met?[4] It is with these questions that the ensuing discussion is concerned.

Unacceptable Criteria

Let us approach our problem negatively or by a process of elimination, first considering six possible standards or criteria that do not furnish acceptable measures of the validity of a disputant's case.

[2]On the philosopher as "case builder" see especially Friedrich Waisman, "How I See Philosophy," *Logical Positivism*, ed. A. J. Ayer (New York: Free Press, 1959), pp. 345, 372–377; cf. Gilbert Ryle, *Philosophical Arguments* (Oxford: Clarendon Press, 1945), p. 5 and ff. Mortimer Adler, *Dialectic* (New York: Harcourt, Brace, 1927), p. v; and Karl R. Wallace, "The Substance of Rhetoric: Good Reasons," *The Quarterly Journal of Speech*, XLIX (October, 1963), 239–249.

[3]The notion of a "case" ("cause" or "suit") as an aggregate of data, precedents, and inferences offered to an adjudicating agency on behalf of a claim is developed in Henry Campbell Black, *Black's Law Dictionary*, 4th ed. (St. Paul: West, 1951), s.v. "Case." In those relatively rare instances in which the disputants agree in advance upon a premise in terms of which the claim in contention is to be tested, a case may consist of a single line or thread of proof, moving deductively from that premise to the claim it implies. Cases of this sort, however, actually are exercises in instruction or correction rather than in persuasion; for the purpose is to demonstrate to an antagonist that, contrary to his present assumption, a certain conclusion does or does not follow from the premise he has endorsed. Moreover, because cases of this sort force or compel the conclusion to which they point, response in the form of counter-argument is irrelevant, and rational controversy dies aborning.

[4]For a liberal interpretation of the nature of proofs and hence of the legitimacy of a case, see Ch. Perelman et L. Olbrechts-Tyteca, *Traité de l'Argumentation*, 2 tomes (Paris: Presses Universitaires de France, 1951).

At the outset we must dismiss the hypothesis that internal consistency or noncontradiction among the various elements of a case constitutes an appropriate test of its validity. For while a case that contradicts itself always is suspect, the mere absence of self-contradiction is not a guaranty of the pertinence or cogency of the arguments presented. Because the inducements of which a case consists are related to its claim psychologically rather than logically—as grounds or motives for believing rather than as proofs by which one is bound—they must appeal beyond noncontradiction to the "state of the world" and the values of the persons addressed.[5] Where assumptions are incorrect or irrelevant and data are outmoded, consistency and formal correctness are at best academic matters. In short, while consistency and non-contradiction may be necessary conditions for the validity of a case, they are by no means sufficient ones.

Secondly, the ability of a case to persuade—to win acceptance of the claim it supports—is equally unsuitable as a criterion of validity. Not only may a case be persuasive for irrelevant reasons, but sometimes it may be persuasive for no reason at all, its success resting on such extrarational factors as the language in which it is couched, the prestige of its proponent, the juncture in affairs at which it is presented, or the ineptness of the opposition. Similarly, a valid case that lacks these advantages may fail. As Charles L. Stevenson remarks, and as one's daily experiences with the blandishments of Madison Avenue confirm, "It is cognitively nonsensical to speak either of 'valid' or of 'invalid' persuasion."[6]

Thirdly, we cannot measure the validity of a case by comparing it with cases that have earlier been judged valid. Because a case *does* rather than *is* —aims at securing agreement rather than at establishing a general truth—it never can be considered apart from the audience to which it is addressed and the environment in which it is embedded. If that environment is identical with a previous one, a claim is accepted without controversy and no case is needed. If the environment is not identical, a case, though it may be word-for-word the same as a preceding one, must be evaluated in its own right. No one pretends that a case that might have been made in 1920 for the dangers of air travel is still valid today.

A fourth possibility that must be discarded is that the validity of a case is to be measured by how well any plan or proposal it entails works out when put into practice. On the one hand, such a proposal may fail because of carelessness or ineptitude on the part of those charged with its administration. On the other, a proposal for which no case can be made at all may work by accident or because of forces and circumstances that lie beyond man's present store of knowledge. Validity and pragmatic success clearly fall into quite different categories and therefore are not to be confused.

[5]Cf. Richard Whately, *Elements of Rhetoric*, ed. Douglas Ehninger (Carbondale: Southern Illinois University Press, 1963), pp. 5, 35–36.

[6]Charles L. Stevenson, *Ethics and Language* (New Haven: Yale University Press, 1944), p. 152.

Fifthly, the number or kind of facts that can be adduced in support of a case is irrelevant to its validity. In some instances a single crucial fact is sufficient; in others, massive compilations of the most varied data are inadequate. Indeed, a case may be valid even if no facts at all can be entered on its behalf, for it may refer to a completely hypothetical situation or consist of guesswork and suspicions. The presence or absence of facts may, for a variety of reasons, make a case more or less persuasive; it does not, however, render that case either more or less valid.[7]

Finally, neither the prestige of a proponent nor the motives that impel him furnish an acceptable criterion of a case's validity. A man whose reputation is meager or whose motives are base may present a valid case on behalf of his claim. Prestige, like the presence or absence of supporting evidence, relates to persuasiveness rather than to validity. Motives, as such, are irrelevant.

A Valid Case

If, then, none of the foregoing hypotheses furnishes an acceptable criterion of validity, how are we to measure this property of a case?

Clearly, our standard must meet two conditions: First, it must be broad and flexible enough to cover the myriad of forms that cases assume; and, secondly, it must help to guarantee judgments that are reliable and choices that are wise and productive.[8] In line with these desiderata I propose that as an appropriate test of its validity we ask whether a case, assuming that it is competently presented, forces a fundamental readjustment in the thinking of the person to whom it is addressed—whether, to borrow a phrase from Henry W. Johnstone, Jr., it "strikes home" in such a way that this person either must abandon or revise in a radical fashion the position to which he previously adhered.[9]

As I remarked earlier, no case in support of an arguable claim can hope to survive unscathed the attacks of an earnest and informed critic. But there is a difference between minor alterations and repairs and major revisions or abandonment. The former leave the original position modified in details but unchanged in essentials; the latter call for far-reaching alterations of a thoroughgoing nature. Similarly, there is a difference between adjustments

---

[7]At times, of course, a fact may intervene in a controversy in a way that is decisive—a way that terminates it once and for all by settling the point at issue. This is another situation, however, which is to be attributed to a miscalculation or oversight on the part of the disputants; for had they known of the existence of such an issue-settling fact they would not, except in ignorance of the nature of the decision-making method they were using, have entered upon controversy in the first place.

[8]Stevenson, *Ethics and Language*, p. 154. Stevenson's entire chapter on "Validity," pp. 152–173, is pertinent.

[9]Henry W. Johnstone, Jr., "Self-Refutation and Validity," *The Monist*, XLVIII (October, 1964), 484–485.

made with a full awareness of why they are required and adjustments made
blindly as a result of suggestion or of appeals to emotion or prejudice.

Specifically, therefore, I suggest that in order to be valid a case must
meet three requirements: (1) It must cause an opponent either to abandon
his position or to alter it in some fundamental way. (2) It must cause him to
do this out of necessity rather than choice. (3) It must make him fully aware
of the adjustments he is effecting and of the reasons why these adjustments
are required. Even though the argument itself invites rather than coerces
agreement, when confronted by a valid case a disputant is therefore no longer
a free agent. Instead he is faced by a choice between mutually exclusive alternatives: that, on the one hand, of being a reasonable person and concluding
in accordance with the weight of the evidence; or, on the other, of being unreasonable and, ignoring the evidence and inference, concluding as his own
desires or prejudices may dictate.

An invalid case, by contrast, poses no such conflict of allegiances, calls
for no such crucial choice on the part of a disputant. Following its presentation, one's adherence to his earlier position not only remains unshaken but
may actually be strengthened by the failure of the attack to disturb it. For if
the definition of a valid case is that it leaves one no choice but to abandon or
revise the position it assaults, the defining characteristic of an invalid case is
that it can be exposed, explained, or discounted in a way that leaves this
original position essentially intact. An invalid case may be shown to be irrelevant to the issue at hand, to be fallaciously argued, or to suffer from a variety
of similar maladies. Exposure of one sort or another, however, always is possible. Therefore, an invalid case never forces the position of an opponent to be
abandoned or radically revised. Instead, if either of these eventualities occurs,
it is to be attributed to obtuseness or ineptitude on the part of the disputant;
for it represents an avoidable rather than an unavoidable response to the
attack.

The power that a valid case has to force the abandonment or revision of
a previously held position makes it an essential element of productive controversy. As a result of the changes and reorderings it necessitates, erroneous
assumptions and untenable beliefs are abandoned, and the dispute advances
to more tenable ground. An invalid case, by contrast, bears no such fruit.
After it has been presented and discounted, the controversy stands exactly
where it did before, the challenged position remaining essentially unaltered.
Instead of contributing in a constructive fashion to the resolution the disputants seek, an invalid case hampers and delays it.

Finally, it should be pointed out that although, for the sake of convenience, I have delineated validity only in terms of attack, the foregoing analysis
applies equally to the second of the major movements in controversy—that of
response or defense. For, just as a case that impugns a position may be thought
of as valid if it "strikes home" against the position and invalid if it fails to
do so, so a case that defends a position may be regarded as valid if it blunts

or repels an attack in such a way that the assault either must be abandoned or
radically revised.

Moral Obligation

Earlier we saw that the relation between a case and the claim it supports
is a psychological rather than a logical one—that, instead of demonstrating
the formal validity of the claim, the case merely presents "reasons" that promote its acceptance. From this it follows that the act of judging—of actively
reflecting upon the alternatives offered and of choosing between them—is an
indispensable aspect of controversy as a mode of decision making. Instead of
supplying answers ready-made, controversy supplies only the grounds on
which judgments may be based. Though his decision may not be unrelated
to prevailing standards as determined by cultural norms and social practice,
in the end each person to whom a case is addressed is obliged to decide for
himself whether the evidence and arguments advanced are sufficient to warrant
the claim.[10] Not only the juror in the box but also the citizen and voter and
even the consumer of goods and services cannot evade this responsibility

As an important aspect of the judgmental process the decision as to
whether a case does or does not "strike home" must likewise be a matter of
personal decision or conscience on the part of the person addressed. Because
the claims the protagonist advances make statements about the real world—
to use technical language, are synthetic rather than analytic—whatever the
worth of the evidence and argument amassed in their support, no logical contradiction is involved in continuing to deny them. Because they are evaluative
or predictive rather than factual, there is no empirical "club" with which he
can be beaten into submission. After a certain point has been reached, it may
be impolitic for him to continue to resist if he hopes to retain the respect and
good will of his fellows. This, however, is a decision that rests on social rather
than logical grounds and therefore is not a measure of validity as such.

Because validity can be guaranteed by neither logical nor empirical
means, in the end it always is dependent on the cooperativeness and good will
of those persons whom a controversy concerns and in this sense consists of
neither more nor less than a moral obligation on their part. When the antagonist in a dispute fully understands the reasons why his present position is untenable, he has the obligation of revising or abandoning it. This in turn places
upon the protagonist the corresponding obligation of making his case relevant
—of seeing to it that the person addressed abandons his position only for "the
right reasons" and with full awareness of why such action is required. The
disputant who fails to respond to a relevant argument lies outside the pale of

---

[10]On social practice as a criterion of proof see Arnold Levison, "The Concept of
Proof," *The Monist*, XLVIII (October, 1964), 547–566. Cf. Douglas Ehninger, "Debate as
Method: Limitations and Values," *Speech Teacher*, XV (September, 1966), 181–182.

any method for arriving at choices and decisions rationally. The disputant who abandons relevant argument for persuasion by guile or by force resorts to methods for which the very concept of validity is irrelevant. Only when the moral obligation of each party is duly recognized and discharged—only when conscience rather than stubbornness or ambition guides behavior—will an appropriate standard of validity be struck and maintained in the discussion of those problems which men settle by preparing and presenting cases.[11]

Questions for Analysis

1. Ehninger, citing Campbell, says that "inducements to belief or action" amassed by men in support of a view do not "establish this view conclusively," but "gradually build up a preponderance of probability in its favor." In specific, how does this description of persuasion influence our consideration of persuasive, and rhetorical, principles? What does "validity" mean to our consideration? How may "validity" be related to Kruger's "rational belief"?

2. Which of Ehninger's six unacceptable standards for measuring validity may derive from "ethos" or "pathos"? Which from "logos"? Explain. Demonstrate by example the unacceptability of each of the standards (consistency, persuasiveness, precedent, practicality, evidence, prestige and motivation). How do these standards suggest a distinction, in presentation if not in judgment, between "validity" and "legality"? Are court decisions never based on such "unacceptable" standards?

3. Why might we say that Ehninger's "validity" is a concept of men, not of laws? What does this suggest to you of the extent of "responsibility" in the ideal rhetorical situation? Has your reading in this book assured you that this responsibility may be safely assumed? Explain.

4. Select several examples of persuasion today and subject them to analysis by Ehninger's requirements for validity. From your analysis, how would you characterize the validity of contemporary rhetoric and the responsibility of contemporary rhetoricians?

5. How are the "legality" and "validity" of standards for persuasion met in Ehninger's concept of "judgment"? May some standards be "legal" but not "valid" and others "valid" but not "legal"? Explain. Compare Ehninger's standards for legitimate persuasion with those of Kruger. How might the standards of one or the other more readily accommodate the "agitative" rhetoric discussed in the first section of the book?

[11]Cf. Sidney Hook, "The Ethics of Controversy," *Ethics and Persuasion*, ed. Richard L. Johannsen (New York: Random House, 1967), p. 105. "In the last analysis, only self-discipline can prevent the level of public discussion from sinking below the safety line of democratic health."

12

American Public Address and the Mass Media

Ota Thomas Reynolds

C. S. Lewis in 1954 made his inaugural address as occupant of the newly created Chair of Medieval and Renaissance Literature at Cambridge University. In that address he argued that the largest shift in the culture of western man had its beginnings, not, as was long popularly held, between the Medieval and Renaissance periods, but early in the 19th century—"somewhere between us and the Waverly Novels." Lewis noted at this time changes in politics, art, religion, and the birth of the machine which were to have the profoundest influence on our culture. Speaking of the political changes marked by this divide, he observed, among other things, that "leaders" had replaced "rulers." "Of a ruler one asks justice, incorruption, diligence, perhaps clemency; of a leader, dash, initiative, and (I suppose) what people call 'magnetism' or 'personality.' "[1] Today these personable "leaders" rely heavily on a twentieth century progeny of the machines of whose birth Lewis spoke—television. It is the impact on public address resulting from this relationship which I first wish to examine.

In 1960 that veteran American pulse taker, Elmer Roper, analyzed with some despair in the *Saturday Review* his observations of the political conventions of that year, the eleventh and twelfth which he had covered as a reporter. He was unhappy because only rarely did he hear a delegate ask, "Who is the best man?" The most important question was "Who has the best chance to win?" Mr. Roper did *not* report whether the delegates were associating their estimate of "the chance to win" with the mass media. He reported the emphasis placed upon the regional, religious, social, and similar affiliation of the candidates in

Ota Thomas Reynolds is Professor of Speech, Hunter College of the City University of New York.

This article was read as a paper at the Speech Association of America convention, December 29, 1965. Reprinted by permission from *Western Speech*, 30(1968), 44–49.

[1]C. S. Lewis, *"De Descriptione Temporum"* in *They Asked for a Paper* (London, 1962), pp. 16–17.

relation to the November ballot. But the delegates might well have asked another vital question, "Who will have the most appealing and magnetic personality in speaking before the TV cameras?"

The relevance of the question was vividly illustrated in the campaign following the 1960 conventions. The Kennedy-Nixon debates were generally agreed to have been the turning point in the ultimate outcome of that contest. And, as we know, critical and scholarly studies have repeatedly emphasized the importance of *ethos* as a vital factor in the public judgment of these confrontations. I'd like to report only two interesting comments made immediately following the first debate. John Crosby, who was then the TV and radio critic for the New York *Herald Tribune* and no stranger to the strengths and weaknesses of the media, listened to the debate on radio. A few days later he watched a videotape replay, and in his column he reported amazement at the difference in impact provided by the two experiences. As he listened to the radio he felt that Nixon clearly had the better of the argument, and he was surprised at the general agreement in the press that the laurels went to Kennedy. But after viewing the tape, the visual effect was so powerful that he could clearly understand the basis for the consensus.

The second report comes from a young member of our department who was in 1960 a doctoral candidate in public address. He recalls that he and his rhetorically-minded colleagues, having evaluated the confrontation on the basis of accepted debate standards, were agreed that Nixon had outpointed Kennedy. They were struggling futilely to understand why the popular verdict had reversed their judgment, when a fellow student, working in the theater area, observed, "You fellows are making this too complicated. The reason for the decision is that Kennedy was using Max Factor pancake makeup No. 5 and Nixon No. 7." Without submitting a brief for the profundity of this observation, I wish merely to point out that competent representatives of two types of relevant critical analysis failed to assess accurately the extent of visual and photographic elements upon the judgment of a speech. Yet both would surely have endorsed intellectually the importance of these dimensions even before this encounter.

The recent contest for Mayor of New York is another case in point. Certainly the eminently photogenic Mr. Lindsay was greatly assisted by this fortuitous circumstance. And television also aided mightily in the campaign of the Conservative candidate, Mr. Buckley. Jack O'Brian, TV critic of the far from revolutionary New York *Journal American*, maintained that the newspaper strike in the city prompted the TV and radio stations to increase coverage of the campaign, and because the Federal Communications Act demands equal time for minor as well as major political parties, Bill Buckley was permitted enough TV time to build himself into the "most delightful villain of the campaign," swelling his vote far beyond what would have been possible had the newspapers been on the streets at the time.

Obviously, in a way it has been ever thus. It is inevitable that a man be judged by what he appears to be. We like to say "Beauty is only skin deep." Yet there is more than a modicum of truth in the gruesome but realistic modern corollary to the old adage: "But take away the skin and what do you have?" And on or off the TV screen, the magnetic appeal of an Eisenhower, a Kennedy or a Lindsay has derived in large part from the mannerisms and appearance of their visible beings. Mr. Lindsay, within the last month, spoke person-to-person to a group of women—not housewives, but supposedly hard-boiled reporters. Yet the account in the New York *Herald Tribune*, written by a man, observed that the assemblage proved to be a fairly soft touch for "the tall, handsome Republican."

But television provides a new dimension: the magnifying glass has been added. The close-up which permits attention to minute detail, one of the major characteristics of the medium, reveals perspiration, twitches, worry lines, and minor movements of the eyes with subtle and powerful effects on the audience beyond our present ability to measure. Only for momentary glimpses is the TV viewer seeing the speaker from the perspective of a member of the audience. The speaker, in turn, is subjected to the strain of constant, intimate scrutiny before, during, and after the speaking, for he realizes that the cameras are always focused upon him and that the unconscious or overt prejudices of the man who selects the picture for audience viewing from among those appearing on the monitors before him may mean that the *least* rather than the *most* engaging view will have the honor to be chosen as the picture of the moment.

Evidence that the importance of photographic detail is now recognized is not hard to find. Eisenhower called upon Robert Montgomery for assistance in staging his TV appearances. In 1956 ABC established, and in 1960 expanded, its "school" to teach politicians political charm. According to Marie Torres' account in the New York *Herald Tribune*, candidates were to be shown "the right and wrong ways to take cues, how to sit and stand, how to look at or away from a camera, good and bad TV mannerisms."

I have spoken thus far of the immeasurable importance which speaking on TV has placed on visual details of appearance and movement in the assessment of the personality or *ethos* of the speaker. That personality continues to be a central factor in judging current leadership, as Lewis claimed, is underlined by a New York *Times* editorial of December 9, 1965. It details the incredible problems facing the city, voices the "honest question" whether the city's problems are of such magnitude as to be virtually insoluble, yet expresses a belief that John Lindsay can start the city in a new direction, a belief rooted in the hope that he will inspire cooperation through "courage, intelligence and leadership," a "new spirit of attack on old problems," a "lively conscience," "freedom from political motivation," "indignation over bureaucratic weaknesses," a "compassionate interest in the people and the city," and by "determination to enforce the laws," all of which must be applied with "incessant and lasting enthusiasm." Please note that there was not a word in the editorial referring to the programs of action advocated by the Mayor-elect, only words dealing with the personality demanded, and the greatest of these was *enthusiasm*.

With personality attributes molding our attitudes toward leaders and TV magnifying the importance of physical characteristics of the speaker in forming these attitudes, what then has been the effect of the mass media (not only TV) on *what* the speaker says? What has been the impact on the content or substance of current public address, the ideas, arguments, evidence, and the verbal language in which they are expressed? It is a truism, an overworked and hackneyed concept, that the mass media have miniaturized the world. We are told that "all by itself the satellite (Early Bird) blanketed more than one-third the globe." You will remember the stir occasioned by President Johnson's speech to Europe immediately upon the launching of that satellite. But even without an Early Bird, standard news coverage by TV, radio, and press means that a speech having interest or implications beyond our shores is immediately examined in some fashion in all the capitals of the world and even in the hinterlands. The audience for speeches dealing with national and international policy and American presidential elections is almost literally composed of people from all the nations of the globe. The implications for the selection and utilization of lines of argument, evidence, language, and motivational appeals are staggering. Further complicating the complexity and difficulty of such public address is the pressure of time. The combination of expense involved in TV time allocations (except that part freely given in the public interest to the administration and for political campaigns) and a contemporary American audience long since weaned from its taste for two-hour speeches and currently exhibiting a strong predilection for digests further aggravates the difficulties. Complicated lines of argument addressed to the interests of the manifold segments of the audience are clearly prohibited.

Even in public political addresses which have little import abroad, the size and complexity of the interested audience is vastly enlarged. For instance, on June 1, 1965, William McChesney Martin, Jr., Chairman of the Federal Reserve Board, spoke to the Columbia University Alumni Federation at their commencement luncheon. This was no nationwide televised speech, but one to a limited and highly selected audience. Even so, the speech included what was destined to become a sentence of national importance: "We find disquieting similarities between our present prosperity and the fabulous twenties." In the days that followed, stock market prices skidded and within a month stock values were down by an astronomical thirty-four billion dollars. Whether, as was widely claimed, these twelve little words produced such a spectacular and frightening effect is surely debatable. Martin denied it, and suggested that if it were true, he certainly must have made the most expensive speech in human history. Nevertheless, Martin joined the team of administration speakers who tried to reassure the public about the economic prospects of the nation. Speaking later at the Rutgers commencement, he referred to the public's response to the Columbia address:

> Recent experience has taught me to be wary. If I should venture to compare our life and learning today with that of Greece in the fifth century B.C. or that of Rome in the first century B.C. *or* A.D., I am sure there would be *some* who—no matter what I said about differences or similarities—would interpret my remarks as a prediction that we will be overrun by barbarians. Nor will I venture comparisons with historical periods in the American past. If I should so much as mention the year 1814, for example, I daresay there would be *some* to accuse me of advocating that the city of Washington be put to the torch again.[2]

Perhaps his use of the word *wary* best describes the major consideration in the substance of speech-making to an enlarged universe—whether that universe be a local, state, national or international one. This wariness may well be a contributing factor to what both James Reston and Walter Lippmann have recently bewailed as the decline of serious public debate in this country. Most frighteningly, the decline is occurring concurrently with an increase in the number, complexities, and magnitude of the problems we face. Coupled with this lack of debate is the continued prevalence of the political philosophy obligating representatives to reflect rather than to attempt to form the opinions within their constituencies—constituencies which have never really heard the issues argued.

If, today, television magnifies the microelements of personal attractiveness, thus placing an increased importance on the visual aspects of an *ethos* of magnetism essential to a leader, and the audience for most speeches is enlarged by all the mass media, leading to wariness and lack of candid debate, we may well ask, "What will be true tomorrow?" The plain answer is, "More of the same." On the political level, the availability of convenient TV listening to all segments of the U.S. population and its increase throughout the world means that TV rather than "live" speaking will mold public opinion. *Time* magazine asserts that, "if two more Early Birds soar into orbit, for the first time in history it will be literally true that for every nation instant contact will be possible with every inhabited spot on earth." The steady decline of newspaper reading reported since 1945 and the dependence on TV news reporting characterized by playbacks of small segments of speeches judged significant by the newscaster will increasingly emphasize the visual and audible in forming public opinion.

But it is not only political public address which will be affected. The use of TV for educational purposes goes on apace with dreams of video materials available in library carrels being no longer in the realm of fantasy. It seems unlikely that the teacher, any more than the politician, will be unaffected by the intimate nature of the media, the complexity of the audience, and the pres-

[2]*Time*, July 2, 1965, p. 73.

sure of time. Nor is preaching exempt as the churches now try to reach people in their homes. Within the past month the New York *Herald Tribune* reported that the Roman Catholic Church has established a National Catholic Office for Radio and Television, not to classify programs, not even to enter educational TV or engage in the production of shows unless in the future it is "so directed by the body of bishops." Its major objective is currently seen as assisting the bishops in using the airwaves more effectively in "proclaiming the Word of God." Implicit in this statement is certainly the possibility of modifications of preaching practice to fit the demands of the media.

What then, we ask, does our current rhetorical theory and practice in the teaching of public address contribute to the effectiveness of such address in a world where decision making will be increasingly dominated by the video machines of the mass media? Does our current teaching emphasis on the substantive aspects of the discipline—ideas, evidence, organization, style, and the verbal psychological elements—provide a healthy antidote with a bright future for influencing the realities of public address today and tomorrow? The necessities of our enlarged, problem-plagued, and insecure world cry out for vigorous and serious debate about the major issues confronting us and our teaching efforts in the field are surely directed toward securing this thoughtful appraisal. But in the light of the world in which the speaker of tomorrow will live and work, the need for re-examining our teaching to reassure ourselves that current theories and procedures make the maximum contribution to enlightened and wise decisions in the public interest seems to me hardly debatable.

Questions for Analysis

1. Which "leaders" of modern times suggest the validity of Lewis' observation? Describe the probability that they have begun an irreversible trend in public exposure to leadership.

2. What makes rhetoricians reluctant to admit consideration of "visual and photographic elements" as important dimensions of current persuasion? Why does their reluctance make sense?

3. Subject yourself and others to the test of remembering *what* has been said by "magnetic" public speakers, both live and on television. Do your reflections support Reynolds' concern that the *how* endangers the *what?* How does the extent of the danger differ for live and televised performances? Can you account for the difference?

4. Describe conditions and modifications that the mass media, deliberately or not, might ultimately impose on American public address.

5. What revisions of your code for ethical persuasion does this article suggest to you? How must the responsibility for ethical persuasion be shared by speaker, listener, *and* medium? What do you add now to your suggestions for achieving general application of such a code?

13

The Available Means of Persuasion: What Shall We Do About the Demand for Snake Oil?

Waldo W. Braden

Those of you who have heard my opening lectures have probably surmised that I am an enthusiastic teacher of speech, but if you are like many persons whom I meet you perhaps have pondered what I teach. After teaching speech for over thirty years, I am no longer sensitive to some of the confusion that surrounds my subject matter. Even on my own campus, some of my colleagues believe that I teach elocution and grammar, that my main concern is the development of precise diction, beautiful voices, and polished delivery. They call me when they have a difficult word to pronounce or when they need help in preparation of a little speech of introduction. Or, the president of a local club may send out a distress signal when he runs into a sticky problem in parliamentary law. Of course, when presented with one of these crises it is a little embarrassing not to have a ready answer. Then, I may have to fall back upon, "I am not that kind of a speech teacher."

But the impression that troubles me the most is that I conduct a kind of Toastmasters Club or Dale Carnegie course, designed to solve a great variety of personal problems in six easy lessons. It is true that some persons may even associate me with the word sophist. If they think of the term in its original sense—that of "wise man"—I am greatly flattered; but, if having read one or two of Plato's dialogues, they believe that I dispense snake oil—how to make a bad cause sound like a good one—then I am much embarrassed. Just as the young men of Athens sought to learn the secrets of personal success from the Greek sophists in the fifth century, B.C., there are those today who are eager to pay well for training in sophistry—yes sophistry in its worst sense.

Waldo W. Braden is Chairman of the Department of Speech, Louisiana State University.
This speech was delivered in honor of Mrs. Gene Rudolph at Ouachita Baptist University, Arkadelphia, Arkansas, May 1, 1968. Reprinted by permission from *Vital Speeches*, 34(June 15, 1968), pp. 538–541.

Recently a real estate salesman signed up for my class in Advanced Public Speaking. During the opening assignments, I sensed that he was disappointed with my approach. He resisted preparing and delivering speeches and he definitely rebelled at reading the textbook. Finally, at the close of the fourth class period, he lingered after the other students had departed. Straightforward and unabashed, he put to me what had been bothering him. "When are we going to get around to the tricks?" he asked.

The boldness and directness of that question startled me, but I knew why he was unhappy with Advanced Public Speaking. What he had come for was snake oil, a short course in tricks—short cuts to success. In a few hours he thought that I could unfold for him, without too much strain and effort on his part, how to be a super salesman, a brilliant conversationalist, a master of human relations, and of course, a gay, witty party goer. He was looking for the short cuts to the problems of communication.

He had confused me with that aggressive, handsome fellow in the advertisement who promised *eloquence* for five dollars and ninety-eight cents. He had believed the startling claim that promised: "Now at last you can acquire all the tricks and techniques of 'going over big' with any audience on any speaking occasion. Yes, whether it's an hour-long formal address or a brief extemporaneous talk, you'll come through with flying colors every time."

Let me immediately satisfy your curiosity. I told that eager salesman that I did not know any tricks, that I could not help him acquire any short cuts, and forcefully emphasized that if he remained in my class he would have to deliver the speeches and master the textbook. In dismay and obvious disappointment he left the room—never to return. No doubt he concluded that Louisiana State University had employed an incompetent professor.

The real estate salesman is not alone in his quest for gimmicks, the means of manipulating his clients, and the mass audience. Finding short cuts to the problems of communication is a persistent theme in our society. The skilled persuader and his teacher are more in demand today than ever before. Propaganda, salesmanship, marketing, and promotion have become the province of the expert who has dignified himself with such titles as "public relations man" or the "sales engineer."

The businessman spends millions looking for short cuts to communication. He searches for a more attractive dispenser, a better layout of colors, an appealing package, a new shaped bottle, an unforgettable jingle, a sexy label. "The package is the silent salesman," said one promoter. What else can he say? He is aware that his product is really no better than that of his competitor —after all, shampoo is shampoo and cat food is cat food. He turns to a marketing expert to ask where to stack the cans and pile the boxes in order to hypnotize the unsuspecting customer. He pays the social scientist to pursue motivational research to discover deep-seated tendencies that linger in the subconscious, but influence the buying habits of the frustrated housewife. This businessman operates upon the assumption that the sizzle sells the steak.

The politician thinks that he is in need of short cuts and gimmicks in his communication. If he strives for any office beyond that of justice of the peace or city councilman, he hires a public relations firm to handle the tiresome details of campaigning. He wants a "trained practitioner" to use "scientific principles" in defeating the opposition. He seeks help in writing speeches, arranging radio and television appearances, scheduling talks before luncheon clubs, preparing catchy spot announcements, and issuing press releases. If the campaign lags, he wants someone to change his image, perhaps suggesting a new hair cut or giving him the appearance of everybody's father. And if trends are really going against him, he may need some dishonest film editing, doctored photographs, a small rumor campaign and the exploitation of a minority or hate group. If he has a good profile, a little experience in show business, satisfactory makeup, the right lens angle, and the ability to read his lines, he may go far. The tragedy comes when, after the election, he commences to believe the nonsense that his campaign manager has said about him.

I think that occasionally even religious organizations have a desire for short cuts and snake oil in their communication. We are sometimes told that the Church must compete with other types of institutions for the mass audience. The large prosperous church should have a witty preacher, a marquee and a large neon sign, and slogan-like titles for the sermons. To see high powered persuasion at work, attend the efforts of a large evangelistic organization. Days before the meeting, the advance men arrive to prepare for the coming. All the local churches are signed up; they are told that each one must guarantee a certain number of bodies in the meetings, so many ushers, and singers in the choir. The so-called team turns out great stacks of newspaper copy and pictures, using the mass media like any business promotion. The evangelist is heralded far and wide; he is welcomed by a great delegation of prominent citizens. Every meeting is a good show. Togetherness devices, band wagon, mass response, and all types of suggestions are brought into play. And before celebration is over, the mass media reports how thousands attended, were saved, and were baptized. That community has had a Crusade.

Many little people also seek short cuts in their personal affairs. Like the real estate salesman I mentioned earlier, they want to find a source of snake oil. A few years ago a public speaking teacher wrote a best seller called *How to Win Friends and Influence People,* which has been widely read and carefully studied. Thousands have taken the Dale Carnegie Course, hoping to learn to speak effectively, to overcome their fears, to develop poise and confidence. In addition, they want to learn to sell themselves and their ideas, to improve their memories, to increase their abilities to handle people, to win more friends, to improve their personalities, and last but by no means least, to prepare for leadership. Who could resist these goals? If this type of training does not produce quick results, they may turn to glamour courses or perhaps a five-day-beauty-bath, or dancing lessons. If none of these treatments bring results, perhaps they can solve their problems with whiter teeth, a tangy mouth wash, or a deodorant. And anyone can join the Metrecal for Lunch Bunch. Could it be that beauty is only skin deep, that blonds have more fun, that a firm handshake is a sure sign of personality, and that a silly millimeter longer cigarette does separate the men from the boys.

I am sure that in this setting no one believes this nonsense. No one here will argue that the package is the product, the image is the man, the flashing light is a way of life, and a handsome profile is a substitute for a statesman. The public relations men, Madison Avenue, and the super salesmen will continue to advocate the short cuts and they will continue to strive for favorable TV ratings in order to keep their puppets in control for a while. But these methods result in surface-like communication; they do not solve race riots, slum clearance, an excessive birth rate, air and water pollution, and unemployed miners. These short cuts fail to produce good will among the parties involved, fail to lessen conflict and fail to give hope to the cynical, the bitter, the distressed, the forlorn, and the forgotten. Sooner or later listeners will become tired of the falseness of these methods and will see the stereotypes and glittering generalities for what they are—meaningless prattle.

Perhaps a simple answer has occurred to you. Legislate better communication. Outlaw unwholesome persuasion. Forbid deceiving advertising. Put the con men in jail. Demand honest labels on packages. And put our affairs in the hands of a college professor or a philosopher-king. These solutions have not proved possible or even desirable. Philosopher-kings have seldom appeared. It is true that frequently individuals have come forward to offer themselves as candidates for philosopher-kings. But by their actions they soon demonstrate that they are neither philosophers nor kings; they are dictators.

You will all agree with me that many of the problems of our society depend upon communicating more effectively with those in distress and need, upon moving men to action. In many phases and aspects of our lives we find our communication inadequate. I would hope that the graduates of Ouachita Baptist University would be able to argue for a better world and to find fuller lives for those around them. But good men must communicate new attitudes and new programs. It is doubtful whether Madison Avenue and the manipulators of the mass media have the vision or the means to implement the kinds of solutions that are needed. Instead we need a generation of vigorous communicators—yes, persuaders—to put over their message.

The desire today for short cuts and gimmicks in the art of communication is by no means a new phenomenon. In every age there have been those who sought to simplify the method through which one person reaches, instructs, and influences his fellow human beings. A similar set of circumstances caused Aristotle to write the *Rhetoric* in the fourth century B.C. Stirred by Plato's charge that rhetoric (persuasion) of the day was a sham, mere flattery, a pseudo-art like cookery and makeup, Aristotle set out to describe a complete system of communication. In contrast to what he called "trifling fragments," or a "small part" of the art that appeared in the handbooks of the day, he prepared an extensive analysis of how to influence men. What that old Greek observed so long ago has real meaning today; he gave an answer to those who seek short cuts.

Aristotle observed that the means of communication are not in themselves evil; only the men who use the devices are evil. He said that rhetoric, his word for communication, involved three important elements: logos, pathos, and ethos. This first, of course, refers to what we call the logical means: premises, arguments, and evidence. At the heart of Aristotelian system is the assumption that man is rational; that is, he can make sensible decisions, can reason and infer. He can pursue what John Dewey called reflective thinking. Associated with this concept is the belief that man has personal worth, dignity, and goodness. Those thinkers of the eighteenth century who fashioned our democratic institutions and philosophy put their faith in the rational man as we do who believe in education and fight to defend our kind of decision-making.

The modern persuader in advocating short cuts denies the soundness of this premise, acting upon the assumption that if he controls the intellectual intake, stirs emotions, biases, prejudices, and sentiments that he can control the mass. He is a very cynical fellow with little respect for others. He therefore soft soaps what he calls the "slobs" with meaningless appeals and strives to soothe them with bread and circuses.

Let us think clearly about this concept of rationality. In a sense the *rational man* is an ideal toward which to strive, and toward which to educate, but which is never completely satisfied. Not to find this ideal functioning in every circumstance is no reason to become discouraged with democratic means and appeal to baser selves. In what kind of society is the *homo sapiens* likely to approach this ideal? He is most likely to emerge in a democratic state in an atmosphere of freedom and motivation. Under the influence of the high pressured salesman, or for that matter, under the dictator, the citizen becomes soft, anemic, flabby, and helpless. He loses the desire and ability to think for himself and to be creative. If man is to approach full rationality, he must have full information about alternatives and an awareness and appreciation of values by which to evaluate alternatives.

The second means of communication is pathetic appeals, or what today we call psychological forms. The old Greek was wise enough to recognize the multi-sided nature of man, to recognize that motives, attitudes, sentiments, suggestions, and stereotypes influence our lives and that the communicator does need these means to move his listeners to action.

Someone is going to ask, are these not the very short cuts that the modern persuader relies upon? The answer is yes, of course. But those interested in short cuts strive for signal response, unthinking and immediate. Convinced of the nonlogical and irrational nature of the populace, they concentrate upon base appeals which are easier to arouse, which make the "slob" drool over soap opera sentiment. They exploit weaknesses and prejudices, seeking the lowest common denominator of a mass audience.

But Aristotle argues that pathetic appeals and logical appeals operate together, that emotional appeals need not be directed toward the baser selves, that honest emotion can be noble and uplifting. Put such appeals in the hands of good men and persuasion becomes wholesome.

My point leads to this third means of communication—that of *ethos* or what many modern textbooks call ethical appeal. At the outset we must understand that this term *ethos* as I use it in this context, is not to be confused with *ethics* that implies standards of conduct and moral judgment. By the word *ethos*, I mean the personal character of the communicator. Aristotle explains that "persuasion (or communication) is achieved by a speaker's personal character when the speech is so spoken as to make us think him credible. We believe good men more fully and more readily than others . . . character may almost be called that most effective means of persuasion he possesses."

It is this concept that Abraham Lincoln cites when he says:

> When the conduct of men is designed to be influenced,
> persuasion, kind, unassuming persuasion, should ever be
> adopted. It is an old and true maxim "that a drop of honey
> catches more flies than a gallon of gall." So with men. If you
> would win a man to your cause, first convince him that you
> are his sincere friend. Therein is a drop of honey that
> catches his heart, which, say what he will, is the great high-
> road to his reason, and which, when once gained, you will
> find but little trouble in convincing his judgment of the
> justice of your cause, if indeed that cause really is a good
> one.

In further discussion of this most potent means of communication, Aristotle finds that the three elements of importance are good sense, good moral character, and good will.

Good sense suggests that the communicator is well informed, thoughtful, competent in his field. When you have a serious illness, you want a physician who knows what he is talking about—a specialist, if you please.

Good moral character suggests that the communicator possesses these virtues: honesty, integrity, sincerity, dedication to purpose. No matter how much a physician may know, you will not go to him if he has been convicted of malpractice—you suspect his character.

Good will relates to the attitude of the communicator toward his listeners, involving the communicator's sympathy, compassion, interest in you and your cause. Again returning to the example of the physician: you seek a man who takes a personal interest in your personal welfare. In truth, you respond to a bedside manner.

The whole concept of *ethos* is a familiar one to those who believe that they should be known by their good works. It is a driving principle back of such organizations as the Friends' Service Committee and the Peace Corps. Kenneth

I. Brown, a past president of the Danforth Foundation, sometime ago suggested this spirit as follows:

> No man is an island, neither can he live within an all-inclusive government of one. He needs that sensitiveness to the incipient emotions and heart-longings of others if he is to live as a responsible member of the human race. He needs a special competence in those media of communication which are more difficult than the spoken language—the troubled eye, the quivering mouth, the withheld presence. Love is not alone the giving self, even though that giving be generous and abundant. Love is the giving of self to another's need, and that need of the other can be learned not from generalizations about mankind nor from textbooks on psychology, but through the sensitive outreach of a human spirit touching gently another human spirit. . . .
>
> There is something essentially tragic about the man who is unaware of the music in the air which he is not hearing, of the pictures in the air which he is not seeing. There is something essentially tragic about the man whose armor of personality prevents the subtle delicate shafts of human understanding that come from another, from penetrating into his own mind and heart.
>
> One of the functions of education is to make us aware of the possibility of such understanding. Perhaps education is a process of building within us, according to the latest models, antennae which will allow us to move into direct contact with the spirit and the heart and the mind of another. I suppose that comes through the multiple and varied experiences of learning and living and loving. I am sure it comes in part through the human outreach that through understanding and compassion touches those around us.

The spirit of ethos is competely ignored or scoffed at by those who are eager to take short cuts. They are likely to hide from view. It is a means that cannot be transmitted via the mass media. "The sensitive outreach of a human spirit touching gently another human spirit" never comes through a billboard, skywriting, or a television tube. It functions and operates in face to face situations such as the efforts of the Peace Corps, the American Friends' Service Committee, or the Head Start program. It is the method of a friend, a helper. To establish your probity, good character, and good will, you work together, share disappointments and enjoy successes. In many ways Christ was the greatest persuader of all times because he relied almost entirely on *ethos*.

It is evident that I firmly believe with Aristotle that to be effective, to make lasting gains, to keep man moving steadily toward rationality, the communicator must possess a combination of the three Aristotelian means. As I said to the salesman: there are no short cuts, no tricks.

Questions for Analysis

1. What is Braden's evidence for the assertion, "Finding short cuts to the problems of communication is a persistent theme in our society"? Add to the evidence illustrations from campus life.

2. How do you perceive and explain the pressures on those who deal in "snake oil" or "surface-like communication"? How might the pressure be alleviated? Discuss what may be defined as a conflict between "verbal" and "active" morality in popular persuasion.

3. What assumptions about his audience are made by the persuader who ignores logical appeal? Identify and discuss modern persuaders whose audiences justified the assumptions.

4. How does Braden illustrate the positive potential of "ethos"? Does Braden's relative emphasis on "available means" invite comparisons with the discussions of Kruger and Ehninger? Explain. Do we have to consider the "ideal" and the "realistic" potentials of "ethos"? Why?

5. How would you define the current need for a code of ethical persuasion? What would the code include about message? About technique? How do you suggest we might implement in the classroom and beyond such a code of ethical persuasion?

14

The New Conservatism and the Teacher of Speech

Malcolm O. Sillars

I

Most of modern American society is a product of the liberal-democratic tradition. We disengaged ourselves from Europe so early in our development that conservative roots are all but non-existent in our culture. Thus, the development of our democracy has been a reflection of liberal thought. Most of our political heroes, with the possible exception of Lincoln and Wilson —and these two came to the Presidency almost by accident—were heroes because of their use of liberal rhetoric and their attempts to make the liberal *ethos* work in American life. Perhaps not since Calhoun has America produced a genuinely conservative practicing politician. Thomas Jefferson, Andrew Jackson, William Jennings Bryan, Theodore Roosevelt, and Franklin Roosevelt all reflect a confidence in the individual indicative of liberal thought. When conservatism has had a part to play in American political and social life it has almost invariably had to pose as liberalism.

What are the basic constituents of this liberal philosophy which has so dominated our thought processes? Liberalism assumes that man is essentially good, possessing the inherent ability to make proper decisions on the problems which beset him. The only ingredient necessary to solve these problems, says the liberal, is liberty itself. As one student expressed it, "There is no problem Americans can't solve if they put their minds to it."

Since these assumptions are, for the liberal, premises not to be debated, the controversy is over the definition of liberty. To some, liberty means complete freedom for the individual to pursue his objectives. Others feel that liberty means the right of the people to organize and control the evil forces in society—all of which are, to the liberal, small, powerful, and, in one way or

Malcolm O. Sillars is Professor of Speech, San Fernando Valley State College. Reprinted by permission from *Southern Speech Journal*, 21(1956), 237–243.

another, "unAmerican." Thus, when the good and reasonable ninety-nine per cent are matched against the evil one per cent, society will be destined—although slowly perhaps—to solve its problems, and become better and better. Racial intolerance, economic strife, ignorance, destruction through war, and carefully planned mass murder do not dissuade the true liberal. To him, these evils are distressing, but they do not represent the essential nature of man.

If, then, this is the essence of liberalism, what, by contrast, are the fundamental conservative premises? The conservative holds that man is a combination of good and evil. Perhaps he is even more evil than good. Because of this, even under the best circumstances, good does not always emerge triumphant. Power in the hands of a minority—or a majority—can off-balance all the good intentions of the prescriptive liberal. Moreover, man is often just too dense to recognize good from evil even when there is no tyrant to provide the power to force him to evil. Man is incapable, the conservative says, of knowing absolute truth; therefore, he is also unable to bring it into operation. The seeming solution of one problem only leads to the creation of another. To use the words of J. B. Bury, "The function of history is not to solve problems but to transform them." Thus the conservative maintains that it is not just liberty for which man must strive, but order as well. Through an ordered society based on the Judeo-Christian ethic, evil can be contained in its least obnoxious form. History is not always a forward progress or even a cyclical one, but rather a series of crises for the individual from birth to death and for society eternally.

In recent years there has been an increased interest in these basic assumptions of conservatism. Some disgruntled liberals have even observed that it now is the "fashionable thing" among intellectuals to be called a "new conservative." The rash of books and articles by Reinhold Niebuhr, Clinton Rossiter, Peter Viereck, Russell Kirk, and others indicates a change at least in academic thought. Like liberalism, the "new conservatism" has taken different forms. Some conservatives are dependent on Christian thought, others on European conservatism, and still others on a reinterpretation of American leadership; but essentially they have common ingredients. If one doesn't like the shotgun attack of a non-political Peter Viereck, he can turn to the ponderous style and Republican politics of Russell Kirk. If, on the contrary, he prefers religious premises and the politics of the Americans for Democratic Action, Reinhold Niebuhr should satisfy him. Regardless of what he chooses, however, he will have a refreshing experience, for all of these writers agree in challenging the major premises of our predominating liberalism.

Now the argument which it is the purpose of this paper to develop is that our liberal tradition has had a profound effect on the ideas of most American teachers of speech; an effect which has not come as an unmixed blessing, but has resulted in certain excesses which have been accepted as natural and good, almost without testing. Furthermore, I intend to suggest how elements of the conservative analysis may, under the stimulation of the "new conservatism," act as agents by means of which these excesses can be counteracted.

II

That the teacher of speech has been among those most consumed by the liberal position is obvious even from a cursory examination of our textbooks. And the reason is manifest. Freedom of speech, to which he must as a first principle be dedicated, is basic to the liberal philosophy. All liberals, regardless of the tenacity with which they cling to particular facets of their creed, make freedom of speech the lubricant of democracy. In many ways there is nothing wrong with this faith in the power of persuasion. Persuasion *is* a vital force in our society, especially since our rules are derived from liberal premises; but this conviction has also led to evils which must be carefully noted. An examination of the current practices of our profession reveals three crucial areas of weakness. (1) We tend to over-simplify the problems of man; (2) we overuse prescription in the solution of problems; and (3) we emphasize techniques far beyond their value. We are not all guilty on all counts, but we are all, in one way or another, guilty at least in part. Moreover, we are guilty of these excesses, as I say, because we are the products of liberalism, a system of thought which leads, however subtly, to them.

A primary example of our oversimplification is the emphasis we so often place on the problem-solution analysis. In the public speaking classroom and in intercollegiate forensics we tell our students that for every problem there must be a solution. Therefore, the logical order of speech is to explain the problem and then provide the solution for it. But life is not this simple. There is no one answer to a given problem. There are multiple solutions, all with advantages and disadvantages. It is impossible to select a single answer and then set a neat pattern into action to persuade an audience of its rightness. Intellectual honesty will reveal that a particular solution chosen is nearly always selected because it has fewer disadvantages than do others. Our students must, therefore, be taught that their job is to weigh competing solutions and lead the audience to think about, and choose, the one that entails the fewest hazards. If speech is to claim a position as an intellectual discipline we cannot hide behind the ad man's excuse that it is not proper to "knock" competing products. In the realm of ideas, competing products must be "knocked," and some must be driven from the persuasion market place.

Again, the student debater is, as a matter of course, usually told that the affirmative defends the change and the negative defends the status quo. The counter plan is listed in the textbooks, but not recommended by "coaches" because of "the danger of taking on a burden of evidence." But this is pre-eminently a time for careful analysis and a time for every man to accept his burden of evidence. It is not enough to say that debate is merely an educational tool, and, therefore, not "real life persuasion," for education demands that we provide realistic experiences which teach the student to take a stand on the vital ideas of the day. No matter how we structure debate we cannot avoid the truth that every position has a burden of proof.

In the same way, we oversimplify when we say that the existence of a problem always means that a change to a more desirable state of affairs is necessary. This is patently untrue. Some problems cannot be solved and, therefore, we must suffer with imperfect solutions because there is no better way to meet them. How many liberal teachers of speech agreed with Adlai Stevenson in 1952, that the sacrifice of America's sons, money, and material was the best way to face the problems of Soviet aggression? Yet, how many of these same people would encourage their students to argue in a similar manner in a beginning speech class? Most of our students come to us with idealistic views on most matters. Do we inform them of the possibility of unpleasant but realistic positions?

But most dangerous of all, perhaps, is an unrealistic oversimplification of the nature of modern communication mechanisms. Demagogues, we are prone to say, may be able to exist in small, ignorant, rural communities, or in European dictatorships, but under the bright lights of television and among educated people natural intelligence will see the oratorical criminal for what he is and will retire him from public office. But is this so? Have we had enough historical experience to know the real power of mass communication? Is it not also possible that a man with the right appeal in the right situation can move the TV viewer just as easily as the stump speaker moved his listener? It is too easy to say, "You can't fool all of the people all of the time." In this day you don't have to fool all the people, and you only have to fool them once to send the liberal dream into a downward spiral.

Linked to this problem is an unrealistic teaching of audience analysis. We stress the necessity of knowing an audience's sex, religion, politics, economic background, educational attainment, etc. But is this enough? Is there not also a mysterious ingredient involving the speaker's own knowledge of how men are? This cannot be taught. It comes from a long study on the speaker's part of the literature, history, politics, religion, and cultural mores of America and Americans. It is known from a feeling for the cultural attitudes of Americans. The only answer to this problem is a thorough study of the liberal arts by a student who wants to know. The speech teacher can only scratch the surface and should freely admit his limitations.

Besides these sins of oversimplification we are, as I have already suggested, also guilty of faults of prescriptive analysis. We find the symptoms of a problem, plug in a formula, and presto, out comes a solution. True, we encounter difficulties along the way, but, in the true liberal spirit, fair play and logic will overcome all. Although this charge can be leveled against debate, it can be made with even more force against the teachings of group discussion. Through de-emphasizing conflict, we are told, we can find a position to which all men can repair. But this is not true, and we know it. Too frequently, with a majority speaking from ignorance, the minority member is the only person who understands the problem. Under such circumstances, the possibility of reaching unanimity on any significant topic within a representative group is extremely limited.

While more and more teachers of discussion are coming to realize this, there is one group who are particularly misled by the liberal belief in the power of man to know truth. Although the group dynamics movement is now quieting down, a few years back it seemed that it would sweep the country. This view of life attempts to eliminate all conflict through self-examination, and bring out a solution acceptable to all. It assumes that conflict is a product of the psychological insecurity of the individual. That makes it particularly dangerous because, like another prescriptive oversimplification, McCarthyism, it states or implies that the dissenter has something wrong with him. The cause for disagreement is not in the stubborn man or even the stupid man, but rather in the psychologically unfit man. At this point, the liberal should become disturbed. The dissenter is not only in the minority; he is also maladjusted. Where is the liberal's love of liberty in such a construct?

The fallacy of prescription, then, lies in the belief that a particular method will reveal truth in an almost pure form. But history tells us that this is not so. There are many paths to the solution of problems. We have at times found certain methods which better suit our needs and ethics than do others, but we have not found, nor will we ever find, *the* method of truth.

To the oversimplification of problems and the attempt to find a prescribed way to solve them must be added a third excess growing out of the liberal tradition—overemphasis on technique. I do not mean here to beat again the near-dead horse of "delivery emphasis." Our field has had some wise leadership in the past thirty years, and today "delivery emphasis" is generally deplored. At the same time, there remains a subtle technique emphasis within our content emphasis which needs to be watched. Note the fractionalization of the speech programs at many schools. See how departments of Television and Radio, Speech Education, Speech Correction, Public Speaking, Drama, and many others are springing up. At this crucial moment in our history when, as never before, worthwhile speech is important, our field is breaking down into disorganized camps. Note further the increasing number of courses being taught: Persuasion, Advanced Public Speaking, Group Leadership, Discussion, Group Dynamics, Argumentation, Business Speech, Forms of Public Address, and a multitude of others. The examination of college catalogues reveals that we vie for bizarre courses, while the bewildered student is led to believe that there is some particular type of course which will provide the specialized techniques he needs to meet any situation.

But perhaps the most shocking thing that has happened to our training is our apparent assumption that in some mysterious way students can master the "content" of their speeches through the media of speech classes and speech activities. It is true that much can be learned here. It is even more true that we provide the student with the opportunity to unify his studies into worthwhile and active knowledge. But to imply that we can take the place of the historian, the political scientist, the economist, or the theologian is a sham. Paying lip service to these disciplines is little better.

III

I do not write this paper to decry the existence of our field. Far from it. I am a member of the speech profession because I believe speech offers one of the most worthwhile opportunities a student has to understand himself and his neighbors, and to relate the two. At the same time, we must be reasonable about why we exist and what we can and cannot do. The increased interest in conservatism has provided a fresh locus for criticism. What might it mean for the teacher of oral rhetoric? If the foregoing analysis is valid, it might mean a more realistic appraisal of the complex nature of problems. It might mean a less prescriptive approach to their solution. It might mean a more realistic appraisal of the speech audience and how to reach it. It might mean the analysis of problems without concern for the immediate consequences to ourselves. It might mean an academic program with all of the fat cut out and grounded in a solid liberal arts core. Only by such a realistic realignment of our practices with the reality of our existence can we end foolish optimism and place speech where it ought to be as a legitimate phase of academic life.

Questions for Analysis

1. Sillars provides rhetorical vocabularies for "the essence of liberalism" and for "fundamental conservative premises." What utility do the vocabularies have for you? Describe your initial response to the premise that political philosophies may define the attitudes and the techniques of the teacher of speech.

2. How do you regard the proposition that freedom of speech has been made "the lubricant of democracy"? Do you think "freedom of speech" and "power of persuasion" are interchangeable terms? Explain. How may the terms be reconciled for the speech teacher's use in the classroom?

3. Consider these questions in the light of Sillars' assertion that speech teachers oversimplify: Is it obligatory in the speech class to discover *solutions*, or to discover *approaches* to solutions? Is the speech class responsible for *evaluations* of burdens of proof, or *presentations* of burdens of proof? Is the speech class to consider the *ideological* effectiveness of public speakers, or the *rhetorical* effectiveness of public speakers? In short, is the relative emphasis in the speech class on the *ends* and the *means* of persuasion a variable in the assessment of Sillars' assertion? Wherein lies the *business* of the speech teacher?

4. Review the relative importance to you, as a speech student, of "speech content" and "speech delivery." Do you recognize differing styles of delivery for differing forms of speaking, i.e., persuasion, debate, discussion? Explain. What to you is the functional relevance of your study of other disciplines to your study of speech? Do you achieve satisfactory "separation of powers"?

5. If it occurs to you that Sillars supplies more description of problems than prescription of solutions, list those aspects of your experience in speech classes which fit Sillars' description of weaknesses and prescribe solutions for them.

15

Liberalism, Conservatism, and the
Teacher of Speech

Thomas R. Nilsen

In a recent issue of *The Southern Speech Journal* Malcolm O. Sillars sets out in brief the tenets of liberalism and conservatism and then proceeds to show how teachers of speech under the influence of liberalism reveal certain "crucial weaknesses" in practicing their profession.[1] Sillars has done a very real service in discussing the possible relationships between these social philosophies and the practices of our profession. Much more of such discussion is needed, and much give-and-take will be necessary to clarify various views. But though we thus laud the intent of Sillars' article and feel it serves a valuable purpose, we also believe there is much in it that may be misleading.

We are fully aware of the difficulty of discussing liberalism and conservatism in our time. These terms have come to mean things so different and so similar that outside of a well-defined context they have all but lost their substantive meaning. But this makes it the more important that different views and interpretations be presented and compared to avoid oversimplification and the everpresent tendency we all have of seeing what we want to see in philosophy as in all else. We shall try to show that Sillars has presented views of liberalism and conservatism that are arbitrary and that his view of the relationships of the liberal philosophy to the stated weaknesses of our profession is untenable.

One must, of course, agree with Sillars that American society is a product of the liberal-democratic tradition. It is less easy to agree that his brief characterizations of the basic constituents of the liberal and conservative philosophies are accurate or that they prove an adequate basis for the kinds of conclusions he draws. One cannot but feel that Sillars has chosen a naive view of liberalism and a sophisticated view of conservatism and contrasted them, with

Thomas R. Nilsen is Associate Professor of Speech, University of Washington.
Reprinted by permission from *Western Speech*, 22(1958), 30–36.
[1] Malcolm O. Sillars, "The New Conservatism and the Teacher of Speech," *The Southern Speech Journal* (1956), 237–243.

the happy result that liberalism so viewed can bear the onus for certain short-comings in the teaching of speech and that conservatism can serve as the inspiration for their correction. Given his assumptions, he may be right. But the assumptions themselves are questionable, as well as the consistency with which they are developed.

The main problem in reading Sillars' article stems from a difficulty in keeping the concepts of liberalism and conservatism in perspective throughout the argument. For instance, as he describes liberalism and conservatism, he speaks of them as if they were two streams of thought within our culture. We infer that this is what he intends since, although he apparently recognizes the split that took place in liberalism (in this country at least) as the once liberating principle of laissez-faire became dogma and movements of reform and social planning arose, he does not label these divergent movements as conservatism and liberalism, respectively. Rather he leaves these two trends in the one large category of liberalism, which is, of course, historically justifiable if one takes a broad enough view. But having placed or kept these "liberalisms" together, which include all but the fringes of American thought, whence comes the philosophy of conservatism? Obviously it comes from the present philosophers of conservatism, who in effect are presenting what they feel *ought* to be the conservative doctrine. Of course there are historical roots. The present expounders of conservatism draw heavily on John Adams and James Madison for the American foundations and on Burke and Metternich for European. Respectable sources these are, although even their philosophic heirs do not take them straight. Having the experience, often sad, of western culture to draw on in general and the American experience in particular, these new conservatives are attempting to set up what they feel would be a social philosophy cleansed of past errors. That some of this new conservatism, thinking especially of Russell Kirk, would be old conservatism dressed up philosophically there can be little doubt. Where others are concerned, particularly Clinton Rossiter, the new conservatism could just as well be called a new liberalism. As Rossiter says in presenting a conservative theory for American democracy, "The first step toward an alert and responsible conservatism is for several million more old-fashioned liberals to wake up some morning and admit that they have been conservative all their lives."[2]

The point is, of course, that there has not been in our society a body of conservative doctrine of the kind Sillars describes. There have been individual expressions of it or parts of it, but it has been so submerged in or overshadowed by what Rossiter calls American Conservatism (with a capital C) that one can speak of it only as what might have been or ought to be. Liberalism there has been, both of the simple-minded variety Sillars describes and the more moderate, more substantial kinds, although there is as much confusion about what it really involves as there is about conservatism. At the extremes, both are recognizable, as reaction on the one hand and progressivism

[2]Clinton Rossiter, *Conservatism in America* (New York, 1955), p. 246.

or radicalism on the other. Near the middle, liberalism and conservatism blend so imperceptibly into one another that which is called *which* depends more on temperament and perspective than on basic differences in beliefs. Yet in his article Sillars contrasts liberalism and conservatism in such a way as to imply that he is contrasting the essence of the two main existing currents of thought in our society as apparently incompatible rather than interacting currents of thought. He does not take time to put the philosophies into anything like adequate perspective. This may serve his purpose but not the understanding of his readers.

The main contrast between liberalism and conservatism for Sillars stems from their respective conceptions of the goodness of man. This is historically sound, up to a point. But the contrasts used in the article are so oversimplified that they are distorting. And further, by implication the virtues ascribed to the conservative are apparently wholly lacking in the liberal. It takes an exceptional liberal or conservative not to describe the opposing view in such a way as to justify his criticism of it, and nothing is easier. So here we have an extreme of liberalism as it has been, contrasted with the center of conservatism as it ought to be. Small wonder we need a dose of the latter to modify the former. But we do not think that this approach helps us to understand the place of liberalism and conservatism in our society or their relationships to speech as a social process.

The constituents of liberalism and conservatism have been so inextricably intermingled in our society that to separate them is exceedingly difficult if not impossible. What is liberal in one context may not be so in another. What is a liberating principle in one period may become restrictive dogma in the next. And, too, what we see is a matter of how we look at it. It is not uncommon to look upon the American Revolution as a liberal revolt. Russell Kirk sees it differently and points out that ". . . the American Revolution substantially, had been a conservative reaction, in the English political tradition, against royal innovation."[3]

If we look for the essentials of conservatism and liberalism as they have been evident in our society, would we not find such trends as the following, with the degree of contrast varying from person to person and with even occasional reversals? Conservatism tending toward resistance to social change, tending to find in the *status quo* what ought to be, and liberalism being more hospitable to social change, seeking to alter the *status quo* when it became restrictive of opportunity? Conservatism seeing liberty in terms of economic freedom and property rights, and liberalism seeing liberty in terms of civil rights and economic opportunity widely based? Conservatism looking with suspicion on attempts at social planning, and liberalism seeking to apply human intelligence to the direction of social change? Conservatism tending to judge social institutions in terms of absolutes, and liberalism in terms of people? Conservatism being more conscious of the possibilities for evil in man,

[3]Russell Kirk, *The Conservative Mind* (Chicago, 1953), p. 6.

liberalism of the good? Both believing in democracy but seeing somewhat different values in it: liberalism seeing the possibilities, conservatism the necessities? "Man's capacity for justice," Reinhold Niebuhr is quoted as saying, "makes democracy possible; his inclination to injustice makes democracy necessary."[4]

What becomes apparent upon closer viewing is the necessity for both. Conservatism without liberalism becomes increasingly resistant to change and rigidified in absolutes. Liberalism without conservatism loosens the cement of social tradition and tends toward undue relativity of values. Since human beings are finite and fallible, their salvation lies in the vector of forces that keeps them orbiting around the vital center. Does this require a new conservatism or a new liberalism or both? Where would we put the man whom Viereck quotes Goethe as describing (in 1830) as the genuine liberal"?

> The genuine liberal tries to achieve as much good as he can with the available means to which he is limited; but he would not use fire and sword to annihilate the often inevitable wrongs. Making progress at a judicious pace, he strives to remove society's deficiencies gradually without at the same time destroying an equal amount of good by violent measures. In this imperfect world he contents himself with what is good until time and circumstances favor his attaining something better.[5]

With an altered perspective let us look at the weaknesses that Sillars finds in our profession. A passing reference should be made to the introductory statements of his second section. Freedom of speech is indeed basic to the liberal philosophy. But is it less basic to the conservative philosophy, at least to the new conservatism? We are confident that the new conservatives would ill appreciate any such implication. Furthermore, free speech is basic to democracy; it is hardly just a lubricant. Can democracy exist, or even begin, without it? And persuasion, at least in its conventional meaning, is perhaps not quite synonymous with free speech.

But be these details as they may, Sillars finds that as teachers of speech our crucial weaknesses are these: "(1) We tend to oversimplify the problems of man; (2) we overuse prescription in the solution of problems; and (3) we emphasize techniques far beyond their value." However, if the speech teacher is guilty of these, it is less because he is liberal than simply because he is naive. I wonder if Sillars has polled teachers of speech about their views in order to discover whether those who hold themselves to be liberal or conservative are the more prone to the weaknesses he describes? Does Sillars suppose that the liberals among us are more likely to oversimplify problems, neglect rigor of thought, be prescriptive about solutions than the conservatives?

---

[4]Lawrence Sears, "Liberals and Conservatives," *The Antioch Review*, XIII (September 1953), 369.

[5]Peter Viereck, *Conservatism Revisited* (New York, 1949), p. xv.

Of course, he might say with Rossiter that many of these liberals ought to wake up to the fact that they have been conservatives all along. Or he might reply that this is not a fair question since we are all liberals in the sense of being products of the liberal tradition. But if this is the case, might we not as well say that we ought to develop a new liberalism? Or does a sensible liberal automatically become a conservative, new, that is? Might it also not be true that we as teachers are guilty of the three weaknesses because we are conservative, thinking of conservatism as we have known it?

Specifically on oversimplification, are there really teachers of speech who tell their students that for every problem there must be *a* solution? Are there teachers who do not teach their students to weigh competing arguments? Are there teachers who are unaware of the elementary fact that problems are complex and that there may be several solutions to a problem? If so, they should be relieved of their positions on the grounds of incompetence. We doubt whether it would help them to become more conservative.

In touching on the burden of proof problem, it seems that Sillars has, knowingly or unknowingly, taken a uniquely liberal position. Conservatism, at least as we have known it, has traditionally felt that the *status quo* is the God-given order of things and has rarely felt the necessity of intellectually justifying it. It has been forced to justify this, to be sure, and has proposed such things as Social Darwinism. But was this because of a sincere conviction that the *status quo* needed philosophic defense, or was it to meet the telling intellectual and moral attacks of those who would upset the tidy arrangement of things as they are, in this "right" order of things? To suppose that the *status quo* needs to assume the burden of proof seems certainly to reflect the kind of application of free intelligence to social problems and hospitality to what is different, which has been characteristic of the liberal approach.

With what Sillars says about the need for recognition of "unpleasant but realistic positions" in class discussions of social problems, about the dangers of the demagogue on TV, about the need for a broad background in liberal arts as a basis for understanding an audience, one only can wholeheartedly agree. Where we may have erred in these things, it is probably more the absence of an adequate background in the liberal arts than the presence of the liberal faith that has been at the root of the difficulty. That early liberalism believed too wishfully in the power of truth to win out in the market place may be true, but the belief was based on the assumption that opposing views would find expression in public debate so that men could weigh and decide. How else, indeed, can social and political truths be found? It is the elimination of the function of debate, of the confrontation of opinion, in modern mass communication that is our danger; and of this Jefferson would hardly have approved. Our problem is that of restoring the early and basic liberal framework wherein there was such confrontation of opinion in the market place. As Walter Lippmann has expressed it, ". . . experience tells us that it is only when freedom of opinion becomes the compulsion to debate that the seed which our fathers planted has produced its fruit."

As to the problem of prescriptive analysis in discussion, plugging in a formula to get a solution, de-emphasizing conflict, presuming to find *the* truth with techniques of discussion, all that can fairly be said is that whoever taught these teachers of speech were remiss in their duties and the schools were gravely at fault for letting them graduate without studying some history. Again, we would question their competence in speech but would have great difficulty in seeing either liberalism or conservatism as providing the philosophic assumptions underlying such practices.

The imputed naiveté of the liberal in supposing that he can know the truth, or find it through method, as opposed to the conservative's insight into man's limitations is interesting in the light of our history. That Americans have been overly sanguine in their belief in their capacity to solve their own and even the world's problems no one can deny. Even many of the religious fundamentalists, with their conviction of man's depravity, felt at the turn of the century that their generation would see the conversion of the world and the millennium ushered in. This has been a besetting sin in our society. We fail, however, to find a conservatism that has been preaching a more sober doctrine. That we have had such a conservatism is a pleasant afterthought that has evolved out of the efforts to construct a conservative apologetics. As a matter of fact, that segment of our society that we have traditionally called conservative has been particularly guilty of assuming that it had possession of absolute truth. Laissez-faire economics has been elevated to dogma; the law of supply and demand, equated with natural law; and property rights have been called Divine. Are these not assumptions of knowledge of truth? On the other hand, it has been liberalism that has been willing to define social problems in terms of human needs rather than absolutes.

There seems to be a constant tendency in Sillars' article to consider all lack of realism or practical common sense as characteristically liberal, and the presence of these qualities as characteristically conservative. We have the disturbing feeling of having almost been duped by being asked by definition to include what is sensible and sane as conservatism and then asked to judge the teaching of speech in the light of such conservatism, or the resulting liberalism, as the case may be. Almost everyone in our society, liberals and conservatives alike, could without a doubt use a little more good sense. We question that its absence is unique to either type.

Presumably, according to Sillars, liberalism has been more prescriptive than conservatism. With the traditional concept of conservatism in mind one is tempted to ask whether the application of a demonstrably effective pattern of thought; i.e., reflective thinking, is more prescriptive than the failure to apply it, or the "you can't change human nature" approach which absolves one of the arduous task of trying to solve the problem, a not atypical conservative approach to social ills. Or is it prescriptive to use just the method of reflective thought, and non-prescriptive to use many methods? We wish Sillars had shared with us some of the many paths to the solutions of problems to which he alluded. It would be illuminating for those of us who do not know of any way except the application of free human intelligence in a disciplined, reflective way.

Sillars seems to identify the more extreme of the group dynamics enthusiasts with liberalism. "The dissenter," he says, "is not only in the minority; he is also maladjusted. Where is the liberal's love of liberty in such a construct?"[6] May we pose a question: Historically, as we have known them, who has been more hospitable to the dissenter, the liberal or the conservative? One further question: Is it also the fault of the liberal spirit that some teachers of speech have assumed ". . . that in some mysterious way students can master the 'content' of their speeches through the media of speech classes and speech activities" and that they ". . . imply that we can take the place of the historian, the political scientist, the economist, or the theologian?"[7] If speech teachers have assumed or implied this, they have been provincial, ignorant, and egotistical. To impute this to liberalism is simply absurd.

We feel that in looking for the ghost of liberalism in the extremes of group dynamics, in so-called prescriptive oversimplification, in emphasis on technique, in narrow and provincial viewpoints, Sillars' enthusiasm for the conservative analysis has over-extended itself to the point where it has all but lost its significance. We certainly would agree with Sillars that there are weaknesses in our field and that they probably stem largely from inadequate grounding in the liberal arts. But we cannot agree that the liberal faith has nurtured these ills or stood in the way of our search for truth. That liberalism has had its weaknesses no student of it will deny. That it has been overly optimistic about man's possibilities may be true, even though liberalism's faith in man has been an essential ingredient in what progress humanity has made. But the ready finding in liberalism of the basis for so many ills—real or supposed—in speech pedagogy suggests rather mounting the conservative bandwagon than an application to the problems of speech teaching of the cautious but rigorous and disciplined thought that Sillars calls upon our profession to apply.

[6]Sillars, op. cit., 242.
[7]Ibid., 243.

16

A Reply to Mr. Nilsen

Malcolm O. Sillars

Mr. Nilsen's reply to my exploratory article, "Liberalism, Conservatism, and the Teacher of Speech," is appreciated. I know that he is not one "to kick the old hound for failing to whelp." In fact, Nilsen has criticized well; so well that I am tempted to go through his text inserting annotated "amens." There are, however, some problems of language and belief which might be explored briefly.

The basic difficulty between Nilsen's and my thinking is in my oversimplification of the meanings of liberalism and the New Conservatism. As an excuse—a good conservative should not give excuses, I know, but should accept his sin for what it is—let me note that I was forced to define liberalism and the New Conservatism in two and one-half pages if I were to pose my hypothesis in one article. I meant to imply that we are all liberals, that conservatism is not really functional in our society. Bricker, Morse, Eisenhower, Truman, Jenner, Williams, Nilsen, and Sillars are all liberals in the sense in which I defined liberalism. Thus, by my definition, all the criticisms which compare liberal and conservative "traditions" (examples: polling liberal and conservative members of the profession or my alleged failure to see good in liberalism and support for and resistance to social change) have no real bearing on my position. The most potent criticism is of my "arbitrary" definition of liberalism. Liberalism and conservatism are such bankrupt terms that I may have been remiss in using them. What, then, shall we call these? American Optimism or naiveté for liberalism? Realism for conservatism? These terms may satisfy those with an affection for the term liberalism, but none of them does a better job of explaining that American society has emphasized, with little opposition, a set of premises which we developed, warped, utilized (choose the word you wish) until we became one-sided in our politics and pedagogy. My main point was made in the conclusion, "The New Conservatism forms a locus for criticism." It is nothing more than this. To make it a battle of

Reprinted by permission from *Western Speech*, 22(1958), 36–38.

truth against evil would be to accept the nomenclature of those whom I have chosen to call liberal. As for the New Conservatism, call it the New Liberalism if you like. It only raises some questions which we need to answer.

A second point of confusion was on my statement that the liberal is devoted to free speech. I did not mean to imply that the New Conservative is not or should not also be so devoted. I only wished to note that the conservative analysis should remind us that there are other forms of policy resolution even in a democratic society. As Lawrence Sears points out in the article quoted by Nilsen, the liberal tends to put faith in persuasion while the conservative tends to emphasize power. Put it hypothetically, the job I have applied for at the University of Washington should be offered to me because my letters have been brilliant. I have impressed the department head with my intelligence and ability, but I am two thousand miles away and Nilsen is there. He has power; I have none. Perhaps, I may get the offer, but factors other than persuasion will figure in the decision.

Almost every negative reaction to the article (and there have been many) has been on my definitions of liberalism and conservatism. Most have agreed with me on the weaknesses in our field. Nilsen, however, seems to imply that these are not serious problems. "Are there teachers who are unaware of the elementary fact that problems are complex and that there may be several solutions to a problem?" Yes, Mr. Nilsen, I am afraid there are. Even more, there are many teachers who fail to inform their students of the unpleasant job of telling audiences to choose the solution with the "fewest hazards." Too many teachers see argument in terms of good against evil. There are teachers who "plug in" formulas. There are teachers who de-emphasize conflict. Many of us who work in intercollegiate forensics have been disturbed for years by the emphasis put on cooperation in competitive discussion rather than on analysis. In short, I am surprised that Nilsen saw fit to de-emphasize the reality of these problems. I can understand, without sharing, his characterization of my associating liberalism with them as "absurd"; but I do not understand the underplay he gives these weaknesses.

To say that those who feel this way are "provincial, ignorant, and egotistical"; that the schools which trained them were "remiss in their duties," and that these people should be "relieved of their positions on grounds of incompetence" is to beg the question. In the original article I said, "We are not all guilty on all counts, but we are all, in one way or another, guilty at least in part." One important idea of the New Conservatism is the mixture of good and evil in all things. So by the same logic by which I do not wish to exterminate free speech because it has evils, I do not wish to exterminate speech teachers who disagree with me. I want to persuade them. We have come full circle. My critic wants to use the conservative tool of power to cure evils, and I want to use persuasion, the liberal tool. And this substantiates Nilsen's main contention: liberalism and conservatism are very dangerous terms to consider carelessly.

Questions for Analysis

1. Explain your reaction to Nilsen's allegation: "Yet in his article Sillars contrasts liberalism and conservatism in such a way as to imply that he is contrasting the essence of the two main existing currents of thought in our society as apparently incompatible rather than interacting currents of thought." In your conclusion what is the relevance of the political terms to the debate? Do they or do they not obscure the discussion of the profession of teaching speech? Could it be otherwise? Explain.

2. Choose an issue currently disputed by liberals and conservatives. Apply in topical terms the liberal-conservative distinctions Nilsen propounds in his series of questions. Does your application prove these distinctions valid? Explain. How does the extent of validity matter to the study of public speaking?

3. With reference to Reynolds' prognosis in "Public Speaking and the Mass Media," how real to you are the "dangers of the demagogue on TV"? Describe, for example, the significant distinctions between the rhetorical situations of Lincoln-Douglas and Kennedy-Nixon, or of William Jennings Bryan and Ronald Reagan. Which situation, if either, is more susceptible to the arts of demagoguery? How can "confrontation of opinion in the marketplace" be restored today?

4. How would you describe the relative tolerance of dissent by liberals and conservatives? To what degree has the uncivil disobedience become a factor in rhetorical situations today? Why might campaigners easily prefer the mass media to the stage? Is the study of "dissent" legitimate in the speech curriculum? Is it to be a study of ideology or of technique? Explain.

5. How is the relevance of the Sillars-Nilsen debate to the profession of speech teaching clearer to you after reading Sillars' "Reply"? Discuss the proposition that semantic liabilities can inhibit definitive debate. Cite instances of contemporary public debate in which rhetorical shadows may have overcast philosophical substances. Do you finally stand an advocate of "power" or of "persuasion" in your attitude toward reform?

17

The Responsibility of Speech
Departments in Time of Revolt

Ted J. McLaughlin

Speech departments today have an unusual opportunity to exercise direction and leadership in campus controversy. For speech professors this is a time to test theories of speech communication as a means of social co-operation and social control. If we forsake the challenge, we cannot expect others to respect our discipline. Faculty and administrative groups entrust to us the development of organized knowledge, critical insights, and personal proficiency in the useful art of oral communication. We violate their con-fidence unless what we profess is related to reality.

Speech professors can learn from the shadowed past. Our ancient disci-pline has moved in fitful ways across the centuries, sometimes distinguished in its contributions to the individual and to society, sometimes all but ex-tinguished as a recognized field of study and uncertain of its proper role in the education of the citizen. In our own country, "college students [in the first century of American history] were required to speak in Latin, not only in their formal speech appearances, but in their conversation as well. Scho-lastic debates were couched in the Roman tongue and carried on in the stilted manner of formal logic."[1] Formal speech instruction reflected, without serious questioning, the form and substance of the classical education which the tem-per of the age demanded. Not until the latter half of the eighteenth century did the social and collegiate environment permit "the transfer from the Latin to the English medium of communication and the inauguration of training in forensic debate. . . ."[2] In the nineteenth and early twentieth centuries training in elocutionary gymnastics nearly overwhelmed any progress toward realistic

Ted J. McLaughlin is Professor of Speech, University of Wisconsin–Milwaukee.
Reprinted by permission from *Speech Teacher*, 16(1967), 51-55.
[1]Ota Thomas, "The Teaching of Rhetoric in the United States during the Classical Period of Education," in *A History and Criticism of American Public Address*, ed. W. N. Brigance (New York: McGraw-Hill Book Co., Inc., 1943), I, p. 193.
[2]Thomas, p. 104.

speech education. The emergence of contemporary departments of speech has returned us to a concern for the world of real people and real problems. In common with our colleagues in the natural and social sciences, we have undertaken empirical research on the nature of the speech process in human communication, and we have assimilated the research findings of other disciplines into an impressive battery of academic courses. Speech departments have become safely scientific and properly scholastic. But we have paid a price.

Today, as throughout history, communities of scholars carry on their work in the midst of defiant and rebellious students. Social historians, including Professor W. J. Cowley of Stanford University, remind us that "student unrest is as old as higher education."[3] Professors of the past and of the present have responded with alarm, or embarrassment, or sympathy. Relatively few have joined in active protests. Almost none accept any responsibility for guiding or controlling campus agitation. Although "the college or university is at once a refuge from the world and a preparation for it . . . ,"[4] professors tend to see their own scholarly activity as a *refuge from the campus*. Perhaps they have always feared being charged with "fostering blasphemy, heresy, irreligion, or communism." As Kittell says, such charges "have plagued higher education since the first universities were founded in Germany and Italy some eight or nine hundred years ago."[5] As members of a humanistic discipline in the great liberal arts tradition, speech professors know today (as their historical precursors knew) the danger of creating an antagonism of the supporting community against the academic community. They prefer to be safe rather than sorry. And so, speech departments today tend to maintain an official silence about controversy whether on or off the campus. Instead of allowing their worried concern to become concerned responsibility, they develop safe theories of speech communication and offer safe courses in discussion, debate, public address, persuasion, and parliamentary practice.

Return now to the not so recent past which we might prefer to forget. The elocutionary movement which flourished in private schools of expression during the nineteenth century and persisted into our own century was led by educators who sought to prove that the rhetorical "art must rest upon a science."[6] In their zeal to be "scientific," they trained students in elaborate systems of vocal and gestural expression which largely ignored many aspects of speech communication. As a result of these excesses, the academic study of rhetoric was turned over to collegiate departments of English composition and literature. The lesson of this long period of dehumanized speech education is clear: unless it involves the total human enterprise, speech research and in-

[3]Quoted in *The Milwaukee Journal*, editorial, December 12, 1965.

[4]Allan H. Kittell, "Subversion, Progress, and Higher Education," *AAUP Bulletin*, LI (September 1965), 361.

[5]Kittell, 361.

[6]Mary Margaret Robb, "The Elocutionary Movement and its Chief Figures," in *A History of Speech Education in America*, ed. Karl R. Wallace (New York: Appleton-Century-Crofts, Inc., 1954), p. 199.

struction become unreal academic exercises, full of sight and sound, signifying little or nothing.

Just as the fortunes of speech education rose and fell in past centuries, so college students changed for better or worse. Less than a decade ago the typical campus was peopled with a feckless student body about whom the chief adverse criticism was apathy. In keeping with the overall atmosphere of tranquility, academic departments bestirred themselves only rarely from a lethargy of respectability. In his book *America Challenged*, published in 1960, Justice William O. Douglas charged that:

> Institutions of higher learning have reached the lowest common denominator of acceptable viewpoints on social and political issues. . . . we have often withdrawn to non-controversial positions where a narrow segment of life can be taught without danger of criticism. . . . none can accuse us of trafficking in ideas that are dangerous.[7]

But Douglas' accusation was generally unheeded. "Why go looking for trouble?" "We have enough to do keeping with the explosion of knowledge, parking, sex problems, and increasing enrollments." These are the pat answers to the critics of the campus.

Yesterday's critics are lost in today's confusion. Yesterday's spiritless generation has become today's public, worried about the full-scale revolt on our suddenly articulate campuses. What began as social concern about issues of war and civil rights has become vocal protest against what appears "to many students as a tyrannical 'Establishment.' "[8] Mario Savio, the philosophy student who led the revolt on the Berkeley campus of the University of California, recalls that "the focus of our attention shifted from deep concern with the victimization of others to outrage at the injustices done to ourselves. These injustices we came to perceive more and more clearly with each new attack upon us by the university bureaucracy as we sought to secure our own rights to political advocacy."[9] Justified or not, Savio's appraisal of the origins of the Free Speech Movement on campuses across the nation cannot be disregarded. For the new breed of campus protestors are rebels *with* a cause. They object to the conventionality of the established academic pattern. They charge that "American universities . . . have been systematically dehumanized."[10] Most of all, they are demanding the right to examine all issues that concern them and the means to discuss those issues.

Implicit in the continuing and spreading campus revolt is Franklyn S. Haiman's understatement that "freedom of speech is itself today a contro-

[7]William O. Douglas, *America Challenged* (New York: Avon Book, 1960), p. 24.

[8]Max Ways, "On the Campus: A Troubled Reflection of the U.S.," *Fortune* LXXII (September 1965), 204.

[9]Mario Savio, introduction in *Berkeley: The New Student Revolt*, auth. Hal Draper (New York, 1965), p. 6.

[10]Paul Krebs, quoted in New York Times News Service dispatch, *The Milwaukee Journal*, December 12, 1965.

versial question."[11] The adoption of the First Amendment to the United States Constitution did not resolve this basic controversy. Indeed, the First Amendment merely acknowledged and stated the issue which is central to the revolt on our campuses. Strangely, administrators and faculty members who are dedicated to the principle and practice of "academic freedom" for themselves have been slow to state and uphold the same freedom for students. Only recently has a special committee of the American Association of University Professors affirmed that "free inquiry and free expression are essential attributes of the community of scholars. . . . Students and student organizations should be free to examine and to discuss all questions of interest to them, and to express opinions publicly or privately."[12] The AAUP committee adds the hope that students will demonstrate maturity and responsibility as they exercise their freedom to inquire and to speak.

The challenge of the free speech controversy is not merely in the province of a formal statement on academic freedom. The challenge of campus controversy is addressed ultimately to the institution itself and to its academic departments and individual faculty members. Because protest is rhetoric in action, the primary challenge is to departments of speech in particular.

To be concerned is relatively easy; to embark on a program of concerned responsibility is difficult. Crisis often begets extremism. As institutions move to meet the challenge of coping with campus revolt, they tend to act or to react in sympathy with one of two extreme positions. At one pole is the new academic piety which absolves individual and departmental responsibility by providing forums to "foster the search for truths."[13] "We have done all that we can or should do," say the apologists for this approach, "if we make available classrooms and extra-curricular time and facilities for the expression of opinions." The forum is conceived as an escape valve for emotional dissent or as a vehicle to reconcile conflict. At the other pole is the new academic activism which places professors, individually or in concert, at the helm of campus agitation. Thus the professor or school of business administration faculty may assume active charge of a campus movement to defend or to promote "free enterprise" in the economic life of the nation. Or the professor or department of philosophy faculty may promote agitation for liberalized sex practices. Neither extreme position accepts the challenge and the opportunity of campus revolt. Neither passive permission nor active advocacy alone is the proper role of the academic community. Neither course commits faculty knowledge and integrity to the concerned study and practice of responsible free speech. Neither approach heeds Chancellor Adolfson's warning that "academic freedom is not a blank check. The fact is, that upon all members of the

[11]Franklyn S. Haiman, *Freedom of Speech: Issues and Cases* (New York: Random House, 1965), p. xiv.

[12]Committee S, "Statement on the Academic Freedom of Students," *AAUP Bulletin*, LI (December 1965), 447, 448.

[13]L. H. Adolfson, "A Message from the Chancellor," *The University of Wisconsin Center System Report*, II (December, 1965), 4.

university community there must be self-imposed *restraints* as well as asserted and recognized *rights*, if the university is to maintain its independent position in society."[14]

I have argued that departments of speech more than any other academic group face the primary challenge of the revolt on our campuses. No other group is more aware of the function of speech as a means of social control. No other group is more qualified in the education of students to discuss, to argue, to advocate, and to decide issues. No other group believes more firmly in the value of controversy. No other group is more committed to the philosophy stated by Dean McBurney: "We need differing points of view, and we need articulate spokesmen for these points of view."[15] Our urgent task now is to implement our commitment and knowledge both within and outside the formal academic program of instruction. We need to apply the concerted group efforts of speech departments in order to demonstrate that we are willing and able to accept our responsibility. We must be specific. The objectives and methods of a comprehensive departmental program will vary from campus to campus, of course. The following suggestions may offer a starting point:

1. *Departments of speech should assume curricular responsibility for instruction in the issues and responsibilities of free speech.* As Haiman says, "teachers of speech ought to play a leading role in the scholarly study of problems of freedom of speech and in communicating an understanding of such problems to our students."[16] Preferably in complete courses, at least in course units, more speech departments should offer formal instruction in this important area.

2. *Departments of speech are obligated to emphasize that free speech involves an ethical problem.* "It is time that teachers of communication confronted it squarely,"[17] Karl R. Wallace warns us. We cannot be content simply when our students communicate more effectively. They must recognize also that the right to speak carries with it an ethical responsibility: to communicate with consideration for the rights of others.

3. *Departments of speech should strive to train students to recognize and to use free speech as a tool of social control and co-operation.* "Such training . . . must be systematic rather than being left to the accidents of trial-and-error and of casual conditioning."[18] And such training ought to be co-

[14]Adolfson, 4.

[15]James H. McBurney, "The Plight of the Conservative in Public Discussion," *Quarterly Journal of Speech*, XXXVI (April, 1950), 164.

[16]Haiman, p. ix.

[17]Karl R. Wallace, "An Ethical Basis of Communication," *Speech Teacher*, IV (January 1955), 1.

[18]Karl R. Wallace, "Education and Speech Education Tomorrow," *Quarterly Journal of Speech*, XXXVI (April 1950), 179.

ordinated for maximum effectiveness. Instead of offering our safe courses as
isolated bits and pieces, we could better meet the challenge of the campus revolt through an integrated use of these speech courses.

Some speech theorists postulate a continuum for the processes of oral
decision-making. Careful planning could demonstrate the so-called communication continuum. Students could complete an intensive study of a current
campus issue such as free speech in the following sequence:

> a. *discussion*—investigation and preliminary identification
>   of crucial issues and problems in free speech;
> b. *debate*—systematic clash on specific, agreed upon points
>   of difference concerning free speech;
> c. *persuasion* or *public speaking*—individual advocacy of
>   proposals or goals for the practice of free speech;
> d. *parliamentary practice*—group deliberation or trial of
>   free speech issues leading to acceptance through ma-
>   jority expression.

Such a curricular program could do much to demonstrate values and limitations of free speech. But the role of the speech department is not complete
with its formal instruction.

4. *Departments of speech should actively solicit and assume a
major institutional responsibility for providing avenues and objective guidance
for episodes of campus agitation.* The institution as a whole may subscribe to
a philosophical statement concerning "Freedom of Thought and Expression,"
such as the one affirmed by the faculty and administration of Wisconsin State
University—La Crosse.

> . . . it is the task of the institution to make people safe for
> ideas, not to make ideas safe for people. Beyond formal
> class lectures and discussion the institution should provide
> opportunity for the presentation of diverse views in order
> to stimulate thought and discussion. . . . Thus the institu-
> tion seeks to increase student exposure to the ever-expand-
> ing world of ideas. In a democratic society we can do no
> less. No one shall be compelled to attend or listen. All must
> be free to hear.[19]

But without competent guidance campus controversy is likely to be empty
bombast, or slanted doctrine, or to be dominated by immature or crafty partisans, or subverted by the control of outside groups. "The answer [lies] in
keeping student activities in the open and providing opportunity for discussion
that is fully informative and objective, irrespective of how controversial it
may be."[20]

---

[19]Wisconsin State University—La Crosse, *General Catalog 1964-66* (July 1964), 38.
[20]Algo D. Henderson, *Policies and Practices in Higher Education* (New York: Harper
& Row, 1960), p. 208.

How can we accomplish this program? Those of us in departments of speech can commit our professional theories and skills to the real test outside our classrooms. We can demonstrate publicly our belief as a profession in the social utility of free speech. We can sponsor directed and balanced forums for informed student opinion. We can provide expert faculty and qualified student moderators for campus meetings dedicated to protest. We can offer sound advice about the techniques of oral decision-making in the academic community. We can support the appearance on campus of controversial speakers on both sides of significant public issues. We can do all of this, and more.

The rhetoric of revolt is our concern, and we should be involved.

Questions for Analysis

1. How have speech departments failed to test "theories of speech communication as a means of social cooperation and social control"? Why is this a propitious time for departments to begin such testing? Cite from personal experience instances in which "social cooperation" and "social control" might have been appropriate. Work out a functional understanding of each term.

2. Do you think the constitutional intention of "free speech" has been misconstrued on campuses today? Explain. What has made the term controversial? Does the exchange between Sillars and Nilsen enlighten your answer? In particular, is Sillars' suggested dichotomy between "power" and "persuasion" operative in the controversy?

3. How do you rate "the forum" as a token of institutional responsibility for student unrest? Give evidence to support your answer. How would you improve "the forum" approach? Do you consider institutional "advocacy" more to the point? Explain.

4. Substitute in the outline for the "communication continuum" a campus issue other than free speech. Add specific but hypothetical details, perhaps in the form of a "news story," for a continuum study as it might have been in your speech class: issues and problems identified after investigation, findings of debate, points of speaker advocacy, and results of discussion.

5. Suggest curricular or extracurricular expansions or innovations by which the speech department on your campus might implement both McLaughlin's recommendations and the Wisconsin State University-La Crosse statement, "Freedom of Thought and Expression." The recommendations and statement are also subject to your evaluation.

Freedom to Speak, Freedom to Listen

Lyndon B. Johnson

Americans of every viewpoint must be deeply concerned over the intolerance which prevented Presidential candidate George Wallace from speaking in Minneapolis last night. Freedom to speak, freedom to listen, the full and open right to communicate and reason together are essential to our system of government and our fulfillment as individuals. However ardently we may disagree with what a man says, we must stand with Voltaire in our defense of his right to say what he will. It is from our diversity, our tolerance of diversity, our reasoning together from the many different convictions we hold that the chief strength of our people derives. The conduct of a handful who interfere with the rights of others to speak is the antithesis of what we began 192 years ago today.

Every American should again resolve on this fourth day of July, 1968 that he will hear every point of view, that he will test all against his experience and his reason, that he will afford to everyone—and see that others do—the right to express their point of view, that he will lend all his energies to decide for himself what is best for his country. Having done these things we must within the framework of order under law and by the ballot through which American citizens direct their destiny, we must with tolerance and understanding, gently and humanely but clearly and firmly, steer the nation on that course which will fulfill its promise. While truth is free for all to see, we need never fear any ideology or candidacy.

On July 3, 1968, in the face of what *The New York Times* the next day described as "riotous heckling," George C. Wallace, presidential candidate of the American Independence party, was "forced to withdraw from a campaign platform" in Minneapolis. This statement by President Johnson was released in San Antonio, Texas, on July 4. In his own statement on the incident, as reported in a UPI dispatch on July 4, Mr. Wallace said the demonstrators were only "a small group of anarchists," led by college professors, and that "a good crease in the skull would stop this."

Reprinted by permission from the White House press release, July 4, 1968.

Credo for Responsible Communication in a Free Society

Speech Association of America

Recognizing the essential place of enlightened communication in a democratic society, members of the Speech Association of America endorse the following statement of principles:

We accept the responsibility of teaching by precept and example, in community as well as classroom; of developing in our students a respect for precision and accuracy in communication and for reasoning based upon valid evidence and a judicious discrimination among values.

We urge teachers to encourage students to accept the role of articulate and well-informed citizens.

We respect the rights of others when expressing contrary beliefs, and we are dedicated to a frank exchange of opinion, limited only by legal restrictions as interpreted by our courts.

We condemn intimidation which attempts to restrict the processes of free expression, whether by powerful minorities or ruthless majorities.

We dedicate ourselves fully to these principles, confident in the belief that reason will prevail in a free market place of ideas.

Adopted, August 20, 1963

Resolved: That this Association expresses its determined support for the constitutional right of peaceful protest, whether verbal or nonverbal, whether carefully reasoned or heatedly emotional, as long as it does not interfere with the free speech rights of others who may disagree;

These statements were adopted, on the dates indicated, by the Legislative Assembly and the Administrative Council of the Speech Association of America.
Reprinted by permission from the minutes of the Associaton.

That we criticize as misguided those who believe that the justice of their cause confers license physically and coercively to interfere with the speech and activities of others of a different persuasion.

Adopted, December 28, 1967

Questions for Analysis

1. Of what particular significance for "freedom to speak" is "freedom to listen"? What other suggestions of the rights of all listeners, not only of those in the immediate audience situation, do the articles in this section contain? Can all of these rights be legislated? Explain. Would you suggest "training" for listeners as we have it for speakers? If so, summarize briefly "the proper education of listeners."

2. With specific reference to activities on your campus today define "the rights of others" in the expression of "contrary beliefs." Are these rights uniformly respected? Support your answer with evidence.

3. Is it fair to say that articles in this section of the book serve to warn us that "reason will prevail in a free market place of ideas" *only* if purveyors of both the "market place" and the "ideas" are subject to vigilant public scrutiny? Explain. How much, if at all, are we to be disturbed by the current condition of public persuasion? How may you and your fellow students show your concern for the future of public persuasion?

20

Rights and Freedoms of Students

*American Association
of University Professors, et al.*

Preamble

Academic institutions exist for the transmission of knowledge, the pursuit of truth, the development of students, and the general well-being of society. Free inquiry and free expression are indispensable to the attainment of these goals. As members of the academic community, students should be encouraged to develop the capacity for critical judgment and to engage in a sustained and independent search for truth. Institutional procedures for achieving these purposes may vary from campus to campus, but the minimal standards of academic freedom of students outlined below are essential to any community of scholars.

Freedom to teach and freedom to learn are inseparable facets of academic freedom. The freedom to learn depends upon appropriate opportunities and conditions in the classroom, on the campus, and in the larger community. Students should exercise their freedom with responsibility.

The responsibility to secure and to respect general conditions conducive to the freedom to learn is shared by all members of the academic community. Each college and university has a duty to develop policies and procedures which provide and safeguard this freedom. Such policies and procedures should

In June, 1967, a joint committee, comprised of representatives from the American Association of University Professors, U. S. National Student Association, Association of American Colleges, National Association of Student Personnel Administrators, and National Association of Women Deans and Counselors, met in Washington, D. C., and drafted the Joint Statement on Rights and Freedoms of Students. By June, 1968, the statement had been endorsed by each of its five national sponsors, and by American Association of Higher Education, Jesuit Education Association, American College Personnel Association, Executive Committee—College and University Department—National Catholic Education Association, and Commission on Student Personnel—American Association of Junior Colleges.

Reprinted by permission, and omitting only sections not directly related to freedom of speech and assembly, from "Joint Statement on Rights and Freedoms of Students," *AAUP Bulletin*, June, 1968, pp. 258–261.

be developed at each institution within the framework of general standards and with the broadest possible participation of the members of the academic community. The purpose of this statement is to enumerate the essential provisions for student freedom to learn.

. . . .

II. In the Classroom

The professor in the classroom and in conference should encourage free discussion, inquiry, and expression. Student performance should be evaluated solely on an academic basis, not on opinions or conduct in matters unrelated to academic standards.

A. Protection of freedom of expression

Students should be free to take reasoned exception to the data or views offered in any course of study and to reserve judgment about matters of opinion, but they are responsible for learning the content of any course of study for which they are enrolled.

B. Protection against improper academic evaluation

Students should have protection through orderly procedures against prejudiced or capricious academic evaluation. At the same time, they are responsible for maintaining standards of academic performance established for each course in which they are enrolled.

C. Protection against improper disclosure

Information about student views, beliefs, and political associations which professors acquire in the course of their work as instructors, advisors, and counselors should be considered confidential. Protection against improper disclosure is a serious professional obligation. Judgments of ability and character may be provided under appropriate circumstances, normally with the knowledge or consent of the student.

. . . .

IV. Student Affairs

In student affairs, certain standards must be maintained if the freedom of students is to be preserved.

A. Freedom of association

Students bring to the campus a variety of interests previously acquired and develop many new interests as members of the academic community. They should be free to organize and join associations to promote their common interests.

1. The membership, policies, and actions of a student organization usually will be determined by vote of only those persons who hold bona fide membership in the college or university community.

2. Affiliation with an extramural organization should not of itself disqualify a student organization from institutional recognition.

3. If campus advisers are required, each organization should be free to choose its own adviser, and institutional recognition should not be withheld or withdrawn solely because of the inability of a student organization to secure an adviser. Campus advisers may advise organizations in the exercise of responsibility, but they should not have the authority to control the policy of such organizations.

4. Student organizations may be required to submit a statement of purpose, criteria for membership, rules of procedures, and a current list of officers. They should not be required to submit a membership list as a condition of institutional recognition.

5. Campus organizations, including those affiliated with an extramural organization, should be open to all students without respect to race, creed, or national origin, except for religious qualifications which may be required by organizations whose aims are primarily sectarian.

B. Freedom of inquiry and expression

1. Students and student organizations should be free to examine and discuss all questions of interest to them, and to express opinions publicly and privately. They should always be free to support causes by orderly means which do not disrupt the regular and essential operation of the institution. At the same time, it should be made clear to the academic and the larger community that in their public expressions or demonstrations students or student organizations speak only for themselves.

2. Students should be allowed to invite and to hear any person of their own choosing. Those routine procedures required by an institution before a guest speaker is invited to appear on campus should be designed only to insure that there is orderly scheduling of facilities and adequate preparation for the event, and that the occasion is conducted in a manner appropriate to an academic community. The institutional control of campus facilities should not be used as a device of censorship. It should be made clear to the academic and larger community that sponsorship of guest speakers does not necessarily imply ap-

proval or endorsement of the views expressed, either by the sponsoring group
or the institution.

C. Student participation in institutional government

As constituents of the academic community, students should be free, individually and collectively, to express their views on issues of institutional policy
and on matters of general interest to the student body. The student body have
clearly defined means to participate in the formulation and application of institutional policy affecting academic and student affairs. The role of the student
government and both its general and specific responsibilities should be made
explicit, and the actions of the student government within the areas of its
jurisdiction should be reviewed only through orderly and prescribed procedures.

. . . .

V. Off-Campus Freedom of Students

A. Exercise of rights of citizenship

College and university students are both citizens and members of the
academic community. As citizens, students should employ the same freedom of
speech, peaceful assembly, and right of petition that other citizens enjoy and,
as members of the academic community, they are subject to the obligations
which accrue to them by virtue of this membership. Faculty members and
administrative officials should insure that institutional powers are not employed to inhibit such intellectual and personal development of students as is
often promoted by their exercise of the rights of citizenship both on and off
campus.

B. Institutional authority and civil penalties

Activities of students may upon occasion result in violation of law. In such
cases, institutional officials should be prepared to apprise students of sources
of legal counsel and may offer other assistance. Students who violate the law
may incur penalties prescribed by civil authorities, but institutional authority
should never be used merely to duplicate the function of general laws. Only
where the institution's interests as an academic community are distinct and
clearly involved should the special authority of the institution be asserted. The
student who incidentally violates institutional regulations in the course of his
off-campus activity, such as those relating to class attendance, should be subject
to no greater penalty than would normally be imposed. Institutional action
should be independent of community pressure.

. . . .

Questions for Analysis

1. How are "free inquiry and free expression . . . indispensable to the attainment" of the goals of academic institutions? How can academic institutions ensure "the broadest possible participation of the members of the academic community" in the development of policies and practices?

2. What does it mean "to take reasoned exception to the data or views offered in any course of study"? Does this freedom extend to "approaches" to study as well as to "data and views"? Explain. How is this freedom relevant to Sillars' and Nilsen's discussion of speech teaching?

3. What "common interests" promoted by students organizing and joining "associations" are most controversial today? How is promotion of these interests raising new questions about "rights and freedoms of students"? Do you think the concept "common interests" has a different meaning for students today than it did for students twenty years ago? How so? Is it better?

4. Define "the regular and essential operation of the institution." How might "institutional control of campus facilities . . . be used as a device of censorship"?

5. Do you think your "rights and freedoms" of speech and assembly are stated adequately in this selection? Discuss.

Part II

Questions for Discussions

1. Do we need a code of ethical persuasion?
2. How can we expand free inquiry and free expression on the campus?
3. How moral is the teaching of persuasion?
4. The relevance of the speech curriculum: whose responsibility?
5. How relevant is intercollegiate debate today?

Topics for Speeches

1. The ethics of ethos
2. The fine art of the diatribe
3. A five-minute speech will solve it all
4. "Snake oil" and the mass media
5. Ethos: your prejudices and my principles
6. A consumer's guide to liberals and conservatives
7. Validity is not enough
8. Demagogues and sitting ducks
9. How to spot "sponsor's logic"
10. Freedom to speak—but who listens?

III

THEORIES AND TECHNIQUES OF LISTENING AND SPEAKING

Introduction

"None of the things which are done with intelligence are done without the aid of speech." Isocrates made this observation in Athens about 400 B.C., and it applies with even greater force in our own democratic society. Indeed, as Harold Laski put it, "the art of public discussion . . . is central to the achievement of the democratic purpose." Speechmaking got started, then, because it was recognized as a powerful social force; by means of it man could interpret, control, modify, or adapt to his environment. In part the very potency of speech doubtless led the Greeks to want to systematize its practice. This they did most notably in Aristotle's *Rhetoric,* for more than two thousand years a major source book on the instrumental art of acquiring and organizing learning in order to communicate it clearly and persuasively in thoughtful and ethical oral discourse. The subject matter of rhetoric (or speech-communication) used in this sense, therefore, is the management of the spoken, symbolic interaction that links speakers and listeners together; in short, it is concerned with theories and techniques of listening and speaking.

For the reader who is concurrently studying a standard speech textbook, Part III will require little or no rationale; he will see it as useful supplementation. The reader who comes to this volume in any other way, however, is entitled to a special note. We include this part because, as was suggested in the preface, an inescapable relationship exists among formal and psychological theories and techniques of listening and speaking and the end-products of those behaviors, i.e., the public discussion of the social and political discontents of our times.

In compiling this part we assume, first, that it is useful to show something of the derivational process by which listening and speaking techniques are related to theories, and the development of them through both humanistic and scientific approaches. Second, it is intended to provide a body of principles about listening and speaking for study and for practical application. Third, it includes materials that will show operationally how some people use these principles in developing their own rhetorical techniques.

As with most other forms of human behavior, we learn about speech-communication first of all by *observation,* by studying successful speakers to see what they do. Based upon what we see, we next engage in *speculation,* in attempts to develop plausible theories to explain the phenomena we have observed. The humanistic scholar at this point may move directly, and through

221

essentially critical and philosophical methods, to a consideration of techniques, and to judgments about the social impact and worth of specific acts of communication. The scientific scholar, on the other hand, moves from speculation to rigorous *experimentation,* as he seeks to validate or reject in controlled situations those behavioral hypotheses generated by his speculation. In the end, both approaches lead to the development and *application* of techniques or relatively established and universally received principles. These principles and techniques may be perpetuated in "axiomatic truths" (i.e., to get an audience's attention, speakers must start with something that makes a difference to the audience), or in pithier "maxims" (i.e., stand up, speak up, shut up). When we put a comprehensive collection of these principles and techniques together in a systematic way, we have a compendium of rhetorical theory, or even a textbook on public speaking.

Since the last century B.C. compendiums of rhetorical theory and techniques have traditionally been systematized by establishing four categories or "parts of rhetoric."[1] For pedagogical purposes and for analytical criticism these parts may be treated as related but separate entities. Operationally, however, the elements tend to overlap and interlock. This will be apparent as we list and describe them, and it may be better illustrated by adding appropriate quotations.

The study of listening and speaking properly begins with what the ancients called *invention,* or the discovery of ideas. The essential worth of what a speaker says is determined by the reasoning and evidence that go into it; thus invention is the development of facts, opinions, and arguments through research and contemplation. It includes logical and psychological procedures for selecting and synthesizing those materials most appropriate to the rhetorical problem at hand. The classicist described this total process as the development of proofs— logical *(logos),* emotional *(pathos),* and ethical *(ethos).* In modern terms we might call it problem-solving or critical thinking. But whatever the label, the heart of invention is Reason and Evidence.

> We use Reason, then, to solve our problems, to satisfy our desires, to lift ourselves upward toward higher values of life. We use Reason only as a means of satisfying human needs and wants. In persuasion, therefore, we use Reason to show others how to get what they want, how to reach a goal, how to lift themselves toward an ideal. Hence the maxim that those who persuade must rest Reason and Evidence on deep-seated wants and cultural patterns.
> —*William Norwood Brigance*

> Any educated man or woman should know what is evidence, should know when a thing is proved and when it is not

[1]The historic fact is that there were originally five parts, but *Memoria* was dropped as a separate category a long time ago, although the treatment of memorized speeches has usually been retained as part of delivery.

proved . . . should know how many interpretations the same
rival propositions would fairly bear, and what weight is to
be attached to rival authorities. —*Viscount Morley*

The second part of rhetorical theory is *disposition,* or the organization
and arrangement of the logical, emotional, and ethical proofs. More than merely a matter of outlining techniques, disposition involves the whole concept of
giving form and structure to ideas. Its theories are those of orderly thinking,
and its goal is learning how to see things whole, as well as in parts. In instrumental terms, of course, the structuring of discourse must be guided by
adaptation to the intended listeners, since the aim of the discourse is to get the
desired response from a particular audience. No matter how finely we may
subdivide the process of disposition, its hallmark is Order.

> Every speech ought to be put together like a living creature,
> with a body of its own, so as to be neither without head, nor
> without feet, but to have both a middle and extremities, de-
> scribed proportionately to each other and to the whole.
> —*Plato*

Following the discovery and ordering of ideas, they must be given concrete expression in language, and this is the component of *style* in rhetorical
theory and practice. We live in a world so wrapped in words that we often give
no thought at all to our choice of language. If we do think about it, we may
conclude that words are but symbols and that substance is more important than
symbol. This is true; but once developed, good ideas deserve good words and
good arrangement into sentences and other larger language structures. However detailed may be the rationale, the keys to appropriate style are Clarity and
Vitality.

> Logicians may reason about abstractions, but the great
> masses of men must have images. —*Thomas Babington
> Macaulay*
>
> Give me the right word and the right accent, and I will
> move the world. —*Joseph Conrad*
>
> Style, in its finest sense, is the last acquirement of the edu-
> cated mind. —*Albert North Whitehead*

Finally in the body of rhetorical theory comes *delivery,* the last step in a
speaker's "making a speech" to listeners. Not an end in itself, but a means to
an end, the concept includes a speaker's mental attitude as reflected in his poise
on the platform, his total bodily action and specific gestures, and his vocal
utterance. Though true eloquence "lies in the thought, not the throat," in
Woodrow Wilson's phrase, ancient and modern theory alike support the conclusion that a poor manner lessens the impact of good matter. Thus the characteristic of delivery, in any circumstance, is Appropriate Action.

> We are fortunate if the judge catches the fire of our passion;
> he will not be melted by our yawning. Actors add charm to
> our greatest poets when heard far more than when read;
> they even get a hearing for worthless authors who are de-
> nied a place in libraries. If delivery can count for so much
> in fictitious themes, I dare affirm that even a mediocre
> speech will be more effective, if delivered well, than the
> best speech, if poorly delivered. Demosthenes gave the palm
> to delivery as first in importance in speaking, and then
> added that it was the second, and also third. . . . Words
> count for much in themselves; when voice and gesture and
> motion add their force, something like perfection comes
> from these combined qualities. —*Quintilian*

In the choice of selections from contemporary writers on listening and
speaking we have deliberately picked materials that deal with both theory and
technique. We have also selected materials that encompass the totality of rhetorical theory: invention, disposition, style, and delivery. Finally, we have
included materials that comprehend, wherever possible, the findings of both
humanistic and scientific scholars. Here, as in Part II, the reader will profit
most by first examining broad and research-based surveys, then more particularized and personalized materials.

Speaking, as we have said earlier, is for listening. Our first article is thus
appropriately addressed to the listening process. Ralph G. Nichols summarizes
what research reveals and then describes practical ways of bringing our listening performance closer to our listening capacity.

Although we frequently encounter more discrete lists of the ends of speech-
communication, basically they reduce to informative and persuasive speaking.
What we have learned about rhetorical theory from quantitative research, and
especially from experimental studies of communicative behavior, is emphasized
in two articles dealing with informing and persuading. Each carries an extensive bibliography for the reader who may wish to examine reports of the
original investigations. Charles R. Petrie, Jr. deals with speaking to inform;
J. Jeffery Auer with speaking to persuade.

Reasons, facts, and opinions, we said, lie at the heart of invention. Together they make up the substance of rhetoric, and techniques for discovering
them are crucial for speakers. "Good reasons" is the focus of an article by
Karl R. Wallace; Henry Lee Ewbank and J. Jeffery Auer have written about
evidence.

In an article that centers upon the public speaking of John F. Kennedy,
James G. Powell analyzes Kennedy's delivery skills, and presents by implication general principles for application by others.

Truly distinguished public speakers in our times have been rare, indeed.
Even more exceptional are distinguished public speakers who are insightful
and honest enough to be able to write intelligently about their own motivations,

standards, and techniques as speakers. Among this very select few are Norman Thomas, Gerald Kennedy, and Alben Barkley.

Norman Thomas (1884–1968) was ordained as a minister, but devoted his life to social reform as a political campaigner ("for almost every conceivable public office from alderman of New York to President of the United States," he said), author, editor, and lecturer. In 1953 he was persuaded to write "Random Reflections on Public Speaking" for the *Quarterly Journal of Speech* (40 [1954], 141–51), and when he was past seventy he expanded it into *Mr. Chairman, Ladies and Gentlemen . . .* (1955), from which volume we have taken a chapter.

Gerald Kennedy, formerly a parish minister and a professor of homiletics, is now bishop of the Los Angeles Area of the Methodist Church. As a preacher he is in constant demand throughout the country; as a writer he has contributed a monthly column to *Pulpit Magazine,* and published more than twenty books, including *For Preachers and Other Sinners* (1964), and *While I'm on My Feet* (1963). From the latter volume comes Bishop Kennedy's article on preaching.

Alben Barkley (1877–1956) served as thirty-fifth Vice President of the United States, after a career as lawyer, judge, congressman, senator, and party leader for nearly three decades. In all of that time he was an effective public speaker, a vigorous campaigner, and a delightful raconteur. In 1952 he made what was one of the greatest of all political convention speeches. In our final article William J. Buchanan recounts Barkley's advice on public speaking.

21

Do We Know How to Listen? Practical Helps in a Modern Age

Ralph G. Nichols

In 1940 Dr. Harry Goldstein completed a very important research project at Columbia University. It was underwritten by one of our educational foundations, was very carefully drawn, and two very important observations emerged from it. One, he discovered that it is perfectly possible for us to listen to speech at a rate more than three times that at which we normally hear it, without significant loss of comprehension of what we hear. Two, he suggested that America may have overlooked a very important element in her educational system, that of teaching youngsters how to listen.

Shortly after that Richard Hubbell, an important figure in the television industry, produced a new book. In it, he declared without equivocation that 98 per cent of all a man learns in his lifetime he learns through his eyes or through his ears. His book tended to throw a spotlight upon a long-neglected organ we own, our ears.

Together, the declarations of Goldstein and Hubbell put into perspective the highly significant studies of Paul Rankin, of Ohio State University. Rankin was determined to find out what proportion of our waking day we spend in verbal communication. He kept careful log on 65 white-collar folk, much like you and me, at 15-minute intervals for two months on end. Here is what he found: Seven out of every ten minutes that you and I are conscious, alive and awake we are communicating verbally in one of its forms; and our communication time is devoted 9 per cent to writing, 16 per cent to reading, 30 per cent to speaking, and 45 per cent to listening.

Our Upside-Down Schools

Quantitatively speaking, America has built her school system upside down.

Ralph G. Nichols is Chairman of the Department of Rhetoric, University of Minnesota, St. Paul.
Reprinted by permission from *Speech Teacher*, 10 (1961) : 118–24.

Throughout the twelve years a youngster normally spends in school, some teacher is continually trying to teach him how to write a sentence, in the hope that sometime he will be able to write a full paragraph, and then a complete report. Countless tax dollars and teacher hours of energy go into improving the least used channel of communication.

For some reason inexplicable to me, we usually chop off all reading improvement training at the end of the eighth grade, and from that time on the reading done is of an extensive, voluntary and general character. Then we decry, sometimes, the fact that America is a nation of sixth-grade reading ability. We should not be shocked at that fact, in view of the maximum training received. However, a lot of tax dollars are devoted to improving this second least-used channel of communication.

Then we come to something important—speech itself. Thirty per cent of our communication time is devoted to it; yet speech training in America is largely an extracurricular activity. In a typical school you will find an all-school play once or twice a year. There may be a debating team with a couple of lawyer's sons on it. There may be an orator, along with an extempore speaker, and that is about the size of it. You will find it very difficult to discover a single high school in America where even one semester of speech training is required of the youngsters going through. Actually, much of the speech taught in America today is provided by Dale Carnegie and his cohorts in night classes at a cost of about $125 per student for enrollment. Too expensive, and too late in life, to do many of us much good!

Then we come to listening. Forty-five per cent of our communication time is spent in it. In 1948, when I first became concerned about this field, you could hardly find anyone really concerned about refining his listening ability. I asked my University for a sabbatical leave that year, and spent twelve months doing research related to the characteristics of good and bad listeners. First, I learned that nobody knew much about effective listening. Only three researches which you could call experimental and scientific had been published in 1948 in the field of listening comprehension. By comparison, over 3,000 scientific studies had been published in the parallel learning medium, that of reading comprehension.

Ten Years Make a Difference

Between 1950 and 1960 a very dramatic page had been turned. Many of our leading universities are now teaching listening, under that label. Today these schools are not only teaching listening—they are doing, at long last, graduate-level research in the field. Today, also, scores of businesses and industries have instituted their own listening training programs for selected management personnel. Three departments of the Federal Government and a number of units of our military service have followed suit.

Very important to the growing interest in listening training in the public schools has been the steady support given by the National Council of Teachers of English and the Speech Association of America. Under their guidance and help new "language arts guides" are being widely adopted. Typically, these guides give equal emphasis to the four communication skills of reading, writing, speaking, and listening.

Two Central Questions

In view of this rather sudden surge of interest in effective listening, I should like to raise two questions, and very closely pursue answers to them.

Question number one: Is efficient listening a problem? For insight on this issue, let us revert to the classroom for a moment, for the first person to produce important evidence on it was H. E. Jones, a professor at Columbia University. One year he was in charge of the beginning psychology classes there, and frequently lectured to a population of some 476 freshmen.

It seemed to him, when he gave comprehension tests over his lecture content, that the students were not getting very much of what he was trying to say. He hit upon a very novel idea for an experiment. He talked 50 of his colleagues on the faculty at Columbia into co-operating with him. Each professor agreed to prepare and deliver to Jones' students a ten-minute lecture from his own subject matter area. Each one submitted his lecture excerpt to Jones ahead of time, and Jones painstakingly built an objective test over the contents. Half of the questions in each quiz demanded a recalling of facts, and the other half required the understanding of a principle or two imbedded in the lecture excerpt.

Efficiency Level—25 Per Cent

Professor Number 1 came in, gave his little ten-minute lecture, disappeared, and the group was questioned on its content. Number 2 followed. At the end of the fiftieth presentation and the fiftieth quiz, Jones scored the papers and found that freshmen were able to respond correctly to about half the items in each test. Then came the shock. Two months later he reassembled the 476 freshmen and gave them the battery of tests a second time. This time they were able to respond correctly to only 25 per cent of the items in the quizzes. Jones was forced to conclude, reluctantly, that without direct training, university freshmen appear to operate at a 25 per cent level of efficiency when they listen.

I could not believe it could be that bad. I decided to repeat the experiment at the University of Minnesota, and did so. I did not let two months go by before the retest, for I was pretty certain that the curve of forgetting takes a downward swoop long before two months have passed. Yet I got exactly the same statistics: fifty per cent response in the immediate test situation; 25 per cent after two weeks had passed.

Several other universities have run off essentially the same experiment, and all tend to report approximately the same statistics. I think it is accurate and conservative to say that we operate at almost precisely a 25 per cent level of efficiency when listening to a ten-minute talk.

What Can Be Done?

Let us turn to a second major question: Is there anything that can be done about the problem? After all, if you and I listen badly, only 25 per cent efficiently, and can do nothing about it, the future holds a pretty dismal outlook. Fortunately, if we want to become better listeners, or to make our students or employees better listeners, it is a goal perfectly possible to attain.

A few years ago we screened out the 100 worst listeners and the 100 top best listeners we could identify in the freshman population on my campus. Standardized listening tests and lecture-comprehension tests were used, and we soon had two widely contrasting groups. These poor suffering 200 freshmen were then subjected to about 20 different kinds of objective tests and measures.

We got scores on their reading, writing, speaking, listening; mechanical aptitude, mathematics aptitude, science aptitude, six different types of personality inventories; each one filled out a lengthy questionnaire, and I had a long personal interview with each of the 200.

Ten Guides to Effective Listening

At the end of nine months of rather close and inductive study of these 200 freshmen, it seemed to us that ten factors emerged, clearly differentiating good and bad listeners. We reported in a number of articles what we called "the ten worst listening habits of the American people." In recent years the elimination of these bad habits, and the replacement of them with their counterpart skills, seems to have become the central concern of most listening training programs. Thus, we have ten significant guides to effective listening.

1. Find areas of interest

All studies point to the advantage in being interested in the topic under discussion. Bad listeners usually declare the subject dry after the first few sentences. Once this decision is made, it serves to rationalize any and all inattention.

Good listeners follow different tactics. True, their first thought may be that the subject sounds dry. But a second one immediately follows, based on the realization that to get up and leave might prove a bit awkward.

The final reflection is that, being trapped anyhow, perhaps it might be well to learn if anything is being said that can be put to use.

The key to the whole matter of interest in a topic is the word use. Whenever we wish to listen efficiently, we ought to say to ourselves: "What's he saying that I can use? What worthwhile ideas has he? Is he reporting any workable procedures? Anything that I can cash in, or with which I can make myself happier?" Such questions lead us to screen what we are hearing in a continual effort to sort out the elements of personal value. G. K. Chesterton spoke wisely indeed when he said, "There is no such thing as an uninteresting subject; there are only uninterested people."

2. Judge content, not delivery

Many listeners alibi inattention to a speaker by thinking to themselves: "Who could listen to such a character? What an awful voice! Will he ever stop reading from his notes?"

The good listener reacts differently. He may well look at the speaker and think, "This man is inept. Seems like almost anyone ought to be able to talk better than that." But from this initial similarity he moves on to a different conclusion, thinking "But wait a minute . . . I'm not interested in his personality or delivery. I want to find out what he knows. Does this man know some things that I need to know?"

Essentially we "listen with our own experience." Is the conveyer to be held responsible because we are poorly equipped to decode his message? We cannot understand everything we hear, but one sure way to raise the level of our understanding is to assume the responsibility which is inherently ours.

3. Hold your fire

Overstimulation is almost as bad as understimulation, and the two together constitute the twin evils of inefficient listening. The overstimulated listener gets too excited, or excited too soon, by the speaker. Some of us are greatly addicted to this weakness. For us, a speaker can seldom talk for more than a few minutes without touching upon a pet bias or conviction. Occasionally we are roused in support of the speaker's point; usually it is the reverse. In either case overstimulation reflects the desire of the listener to enter, somehow, immediately into the argument.

The aroused person usually becomes preoccupied by trying to do three things simultaneously: calculate what hurt is being done to his own pet ideas; plot an embarrassing question to ask the speaker; enjoy mentally all the discomfiture visualized for the speaker once the devastating reply to him is launched. With these things going on, subsequent passages go unheard.

We must learn not to get too excited about a speaker's point until we are certain we thoroughly understand it. The secret is contained in the principle that we must always withhold evaluation until our comprehension is complete.

4. Listen for ideas

Good listeners focus on central ideas; they tend to recognize the characteristic language in which central ideas are usually stated, and they are able to discriminate between fact and principle, idea and example, evidence and argument. Poor listeners are inclined to listen for the facts in every presentation.

To understand the fault, let us assume that a man is giving us instructions made up of facts A to Z. The man begins to talk. We hear fact A and think: "We've got to remember it!" So we begin a memory exercise by repeating "Fact A, fact A, fact A. . . ."

Meanwhile, the fellow is telling us fact B. Now we have two facts to memorize. We're so busy doing it that we miss fact C completely. And so it goes up to fact Z. We catch a few facts, garble several others and completely miss the rest.

It is a significant fact that only about 25 per cent of persons listening to a formal talk are able to grasp the speaker's central idea. To develop this skill requires an ability to recognize conventional organizational patterns, transitional language, and the speaker's use of recapitulation. Fortunately, all of these items can be readily mastered with a bit of effort.

5. Be flexible

Our research has shown that our 100 worst listeners thought that note-taking and outlining were synonyms. They believed there was but one way to take notes—by making an outline.

Actually, no damage would be done if all talks followed some definite plan of organization. Unfortunately, less than half of even formal speeches are carefully organized. There are few things more frustrating than to try to outline an unoutlinable speech.

Note-taking may help or may become a distraction. Some persons try to take down everything in shorthand; the vast majority of us are far too voluminous even in longhand. While studies are not too clear on the point, there is some evidence to indicate that the volume of notes taken and their value to the taker are inversely related. In any case, the real issue is one of interpretation. Few of us have memories good enough to remember even the salient points we hear. If we can obtain brief, meaningful records of them for later review, we definitely improve our ability to learn and to remember.

The 100 best listeners had apparently learned early in life that if they wanted to be efficient note-takers they had to have more than one system of taking notes. They equipped themselves with four or five systems, and learned to adjust their system to the organizational pattern, or the absence of one, in each talk they heard. If we want to be good listeners, we must be flexible and adaptable notetakers.

6. Work at listening

One of the most striking characteristics of poor listeners is their disinclination to spend any energy in a listening situation. College students, by their own testimony, frequently enter classes all worn out physically; assume postures which only seem to give attention to the speaker; and then proceed to catch up on needed rest or to reflect upon purely personal matters. This faking of attention is one of the worst habits afflicting us as a people.

Listening is hard work. It is characterized by faster heart action, quicker circulation of the blood, a small rise in bodily temperature. The overrelaxed listener is merely appearing to tune in, and then feeling conscience-free to pursue any of a thousand mental tangents.

For selfish reasons alone one of the best investments we can make is to give each speaker our conscious attention. We ought to establish eye contact and maintain it; to indicate by posture and facial expression that the occasion and the speaker's efforts are a matter of real concern to us. When we do these things we help the speaker to express himself more clearly, and we in turn profit by better understanding of the improved communication we have helped him to achieve. None of this necessarily implies acceptance of his point of view or favorable action upon his appeals. It is, rather, an expression of interest.

7. Resist distractions

The good listeners tend to adjust quickly to any kind of abnormal situation; poor listeners tend to tolerate bad conditions and, in some instances, even to create distractions themselves.

We live in a noisy age. We are distracted not only by what we hear, but by what we see. Poor listeners tend to be readily influenced by all manner of distractions, even in an intimate face-to-face situation.

A good listener instinctively fights distraction. Sometimes the fight is easily won—by closing a door, shutting off the radio, moving closer to the person talking, or asking him to speak louder. If the distractions cannot be met that easily, then it becomes a matter of concentration.

8. Exercise your mind

Poor listeners are inexperienced in hearing difficult, expository material. Good listeners apparently develop an appetite for hearing a variety of presentations difficult enough to challenge their mental capacities.

Perhaps the one word that best describes the bad listener is "inexperienced." Although he spends 45 per cent of his communication day listening to something, he is inexperienced in hearing anything tough, technical, or expository. He has for years painstakingly sought light, recreational material. The problem he creates is deeply significant, because such a person is a poor producer in factory, office, or classroom.

Inexperience is not easily or quickly overcome. However, knowledge of our own weakness may lead us to repair it. We need never become too old to meet new challenges.

9. Keep your mind open

Parallel to the blind spots which afflict human beings are certain psychological deaf spots which impair our ability to perceive and understand. These deaf spots are the dwelling place of our most cherished notions, convictions, and complexes. Often, when a speaker invades one of these areas with a word or phrase, we turn our mind to retraveling familiar mental pathways crisscrossing our invaded area of sensitivity.

It is hard to believe in moments of cold detachment that just a word or phrase can cause such emotional eruption. Yet with poor listeners it is frequently the case, and even with very good listeners it is occasionally the case. When such emotional deafness transpires, communicative efficiency drops rapidly to zero.

Among the words known thus to serve as red flags to some listeners are: mother-in-law, landlord, redneck, sharecropper, sissy, pervert, automation, clerk, income tax, hack, dumb farmer, pink, "Greetings," antivivisectionist, evolution, square, punk, welsher.

Effective listeners try to identify and to rationalize the words or phrases most upsetting emotionally. Often the emotional impact of such words can be decreased through a free and open discussion of them with friends or associates.

10. Capitalize on thought speed

Most persons talk at a speed of about 125 words per minute. There is good evidence that if thought were measured in words per minute, most of us could think easily at about four times that rate. It is difficult—almost painful—to try to slow down our thinking speed. Thus we normally have about 400 words of thinking time to spare during every minute a person talks to us.

What do we do with our excess thinking time while someone is speaking? If we are poor listeners, we soon become impatient with the slow progress the speaker seems to be making, so our thoughts turn to something else for a moment, then dart back to the speaker. These brief side excursions of thought continue until our mind tarries too long on some enticing but irrelevant subject. Then, when our thoughts return to the person talking, we find he's far ahead of us. Now it's harder to follow him and increasingly easy to take off on side excursions. Finally we give up; the person is still talking, but our mind is in another world.

The good listener uses his thought speed to advantage; he constantly applies his spare thinking time to what is being said. It is not difficult once one has a definite pattern of thought to follow. To develop such a pattern we should:

    A. Try to anticipate what a person is going to talk about. On the basis of what he's already said, ask yourself: "What's he trying to get at? What point is he going to make?"

    B. Mentally summarize what the person has been saying. What point has he made already, if any?

    C. Weigh the speaker's evidence by mentally questioning it. As he presents facts, illustrative stories, and statistics, continually ask yourself: "Are they accurate? Do they come from an unprejudiced source? Am I getting the full picture, or is he telling me only what will prove his point?"

    D. Listen between the lines. The speaker doesn't always put everything that's important into words. The changing tones and volume of his voice may have a meaning. So may his facial expressions, the gestures he makes with his hands, the movement of his body.

Not capitalizing on thought speed is our greatest single handicap. The differential between thought speed and speech speed breeds false feelings of security and mental tangents. Yet, through listening training, this same differential can be readily converted into our greatest single asset.

Questions for Analysis

1. Describe the speech training in your high school. How was listening stressed? Record the forms of listening you do on a given day. How much consistency of demand on the listener do you find in these forms? How does your "way" of listening change from form to form? Do you think Nichols' findings would be different if other forms of listening were tested? Explain. Discuss the difficulties of "listening" as a subject in the curriculum.

2. Do you agree with Chesterton: "There is no such thing as an uninteresting subject; there are only uninterested people"? Are there variables other than "subject" and "people" to consider? Explain. For what percentage of your listening do you have to "work at" your attentiveness? How important is "delivery" to you in these instances? Cite examples of delivery that genuinely *handicapped* your listening. Cite occasions when you were negatively "overstimulated" and preoccupied with your reactions. How do these two sets of instances correlate? Draw conclusions about the comparative influence of message and delivery on your *inefficient* listening. How might you improve your efficiency in such circumstances?

3. Is there an "academic attitude" in your listening that causes you "to listen for the facts in every presentation" and to "begin a memory exercise" at the outset of the speech? Explain. Why might it be said, "working too hard at listening is worse

than not working at it at all"? How is this related to note-taking? Illustrate the inadequacy of exclusive dependence on "outlining" as a form for taking notes. What training might facilitate your recognition of "the characteristic language in which the central ideas are usually stated"? Why must listeners be particularly "flexible" in response to the rhetoric of our times?

4. What importance do you ascribe to the listening "environment"? Cite examples of its influence on your listening and on that of others. What "mind exercises" do you suggest for improving listening efficiency? How important is the exercise of memory alone? How many expressions of audience interest affect the speaker? Is it fair to say "a good speaker will be a good listener"? Explain.

5. How is the fact of "psychological deaf spots" especially relevant to public speaking today? Add to the list of "red flag" words. What training would minimize the negative impact of these words? How may speaker purposes in using such words vary? What are the difficulties of developing Nichols' "definite pattern of thought to follow"? Define the "false feelings of security and mental tangents" to which he alludes. What could a speaker do about "the differential between thought speed and speech speed"? Study the text of a given speech, locate those parts that might stimulate "side excursions", and discuss the common features of those parts. How might both speakers and listeners capitalize on those features?

22

Informative Speaking: A Summary and Bibliography of Related Research

Charles R. Petrie, Jr.

Informative speaking, particularly as contrasted with persuasive address, has been such a neglected field for research that it seems worthwhile to formulate a basis for further investigation through a summary of previous studies. Not only has the number of experiments specifically designed to determine the nature of effective instructional speech been very small, but also the attempts to draw conclusions from studies in related areas have been based upon unexamined and doubtful assumptions. For example, since most studies of verbal learning have dealt with relatively short messages or with written rather than spoken content, generalizations about long informative speeches are dubious. Similarly, expository principles extrapolated from investigations of persuasive speaking may not be applicable to informative speaking.

The specific purposes of this bibliography and summary of research are to reveal the paucity of research in this area, to show some of the inconsistencies in the results of the available studies, to stimulate interest in informative speaking as an area for experimentation, and to create a background for the formulation of further investigations.

Limitations upon the present study are these: (1) The bibliography is not definitive; the objective is to include items which constitute a representative sample of the research which has been completed. (2) No attempt is made to resolve contradictory findings by assessing the quality of the experiments. The investigations undoubtedly vary in experimental rigor, but evaluation is a difficult, partly subjective process which the writer chooses to exclude from his study. (3) In summarizing and comparing the research reports some over-simplification is unavoidable.

The findings are summarized under four headings: "The Message," "The Speaker," "The Listener," and "The Environment."

Charles R. Petrie, Jr. is Chairman of the Department of Speech Communication, State University of New York, Buffalo.
Reprinted by permission from *Speech Monographs*, 30(1963) : 79–91.

The Message

The characteristics of the message which affect listening comprehension,[1] though many and varied, may be grouped under five headings.

Meaningfulness

According to demonstrations in both the classroom and the laboratory, meaningful messages[2] are learned more easily and retained better than are presentations with less meaning (1, 2).

Style and difficulty

Many investigators in this area have compared aural and visual comprehension of the same message. The level of difficulty in most instances has been measured in the written message on the assumption that the degrees of listenability are the same as the degrees of readability. The conclusions from such studies are few and tentative.

1. What rhetoricians have called an "oral" style appears to be approximately the same as the written style termed "easy" or "readable" by the inventors of readability indices. Such an "oral" or "readable" style is thought to be marked by the use of imagery, nuance words, concrete and specific words, personal pronouns, apostrophe, figurative speech, personification, illustrations, rhetorical questions, comparison and contrast, and other stylistic devices designed to personalize the composition and to make it more interesting and instantly intelligible (6, 8, 9, 10, 11, 17, 18, 19, 21).

2. Although common sense and some experimentation support the assumption that difficult messages are comprehended more easily when read than when heard (7, 13, 16), not all investigators agree. In some studies, difficult materials were comprehended as well or better when heard as when read (4, 5, 12, 14).

3. The conflicting results of the studies cited above suggest that readability indices are at best only rough indicators of listenability. Thus, although some investigators found that readability indices predicted the difficulty of oral messages fairly accurately, others found such indices to be unreliable (3, 8, 12, 14, 15, 18, 20). Furthermore, whether message "clarity" can be judged by rhetorical standards is questionable. Nebergall (19), for example, was unable to ascertain any relationship among the speaker's intended meaning, clarity as defined by rhetorical critics, and the amount comprehended by the listeners.

---

[1] Since the effectiveness of an informative speech is measured in terms of the degree to which the subject matter is comprehended, research in informative speaking is also research in listening comprehension.

[2] The term message is used here to refer to the verbal content of the speech. The message carried by gestures, verbal tones, etc. will be considered under "The Speaker."

Thus, the assumption that listenability can be predicted accurately from the written message prior to transmission probably is not justified. Although a message may be potentially "listenable," distortions caused by the speaker, noise in the channel, and other communicative factors may result in losses in listenability. In other words, what the receiver decodes may differ markedly from the original message.

Verbal emphasis

In general, experimentation has indicated that proactive emphasis (such as "now get this") and repetition serve to increase the comprehension of an oral message (22, 23, 24, 25, 26, 27). This result holds even though the audience dislikes the repetition (23).

Development of main ideas

Several studies suggest that generalizations or major ideas are better comprehended and retained than are details or specifics and that the better developed the generalizations are, the better they will be retained (23, 25, 28, 29, 30, 31). The rhetorical principle that a speech should be built around a few well-developed main ideas, thus, is partially supported.

Organization

Although the amount of research dealing directly with the organization of informative speeches has been slight, the fact that many experimental studies demonstrate the general superiority of organized learning over that which is poorly organized (29, 36, 37, 39, 42, 43, 44, 45, 46, 47) suggests that the better the organization of an informative speech the more will be comprehended and retained. On the other hand, studies of the effect of the "order of presentation" of the main ideas of persuasive messages on both comprehension and attitude change have been inconclusive (32, 33, 35, 38, 39, 40, 41, 49, 50). Moreover, although some studies of other aspects of the structure of the persuasive materials have indicated that well-structured messages improve comprehension (34, 48, 52), other investigations have found that structure does not affect significantly the amount comprehended and retained (4, 5, 51). The use of transitions, however, may increase comprehension (31, 51). In short, experimental evidence is inconclusive about the role of speech structure in informative speaking.

The Speaker

Speaker credibility

Although a considerable amount of experimental evidence indicates that source credibility influences opinion change (40, 55), there is little experimental support for the assumption that source credibility or source sincerity influences the amount of information learned and retained from an informative speech. Although Kelman and Hovland (40) report that high school students were able to recall persuasive material more readily when it was presented by a "neutral" source rather than by one which was "negative" or "positive," most investigators report that source credibility, source sincerity, and the audience's like or dislike for the speaker have no effect upon the listener's comprehension of the message (40, 53, 54, 56, 57, 58).

Delivery

The importance of effective delivery as a constituent of speech effectiveness seldom is debated, but experimental studies of the influence of various aspects of delivery on comprehension have had inconclusive results.

1. Although Weissman (86) and Knower, Phillips, and Koeppel (78) report that good speakers are able to produce significantly greater immediate recall than are poor speakers, other investigators report only slight differences in the amount recalled from the presentations of superior and untrained speakers (4, 5, 54, 56, 76). Beighley concludes, ". . . the influence of delivery in increasing an audience's comprehension may have been somewhat overrated" (4).

2. Experimental evidence is unclear about the effect of "formal" and "conversational" modes of delivery upon the amount comprehended (63, 64, 65).

3. Moderately poor vocal quality, poor pitch patterns, nonfluency, and even stuttering, according to four experiments, do not interfere significantly with comprehension (60, 62, 77, 85).

4. Perhaps the aspect of delivery which has been the most frequently and intensely studied is rate. Although several studies indicate that comprehension declines slightly when the rate is either very slow or very rapid and that a rate of 125–150 words per minute is optimal (12, 20, 23, 70, 73, 74), recent investigations using an automatic time-frequency compression-expansion device to shorten syllable duration show that in connected speech the rate can be increased to around 280 words per minute with little loss in comprehension (66, 67, 68, 69). Moreover, Diehl, White, and Burk (61) report that increasing the rate from 126 to 172 words per minute by reducing the length of pauses "does not interfere with listener comprehension and does not affect listeners' ratings, of the quality of a speaker's delivery."

5. Among the most successful means of emphasizing important points, according to Jersild (26), are pausing before a statement, raising the voice, gesturing, and banging the table. In this experiment, speaking slowly had a negative effect on comprehension. Ehrensberger (24) agrees that pauses and gestures are effective means of emphasis, but differs from Jersild in that he found that a slower rate was helpful and that raising the voice had a negative effect on comprehension.

6. Most investigators report that the speaker's visible action somehow increases the listener's comprehension of the speech (21, 24, 26, 65, 72, 79, 80). In fact, in one experiment even listeners who could not see the communicator learned more from a speaker who used gestures than from one who did not (72). Other findings, however, are contradictory: whereas some investigators suggest that seeing the speaker improves comprehension, particularly under adverse noise conditions, because of lip-reading (82, 83), others report that the presence of the speaker does not appear to enhance comprehension (23, 59, 71, 75). The use of visual aids, according to two studies, increases the amount which listeners recall (78, 84).

7. Poor eye contact with the audience may adversely influence comprehension. Knower, Phillips, and Koeppel (78) report an experiment in which good speakers were able to produce a greater amount of recall than were good readers and in which notes if used "well" did not appear to affect comprehension. Moore (81) found that students who were unaware that they were to be tested comprehended less from a speaker who spoke from notes than from one who spoke without notes. However, if the listeners knew that they were to be tested, the use of notes did not interfere with comprehension.

The Listener

In the final analysis the effectiveness of informative speaking must be measured in terms of how well the listener understands the speech. Consequently, the degree of comprehension depends in part upon such listener characteristics as the ability to hear the signals and knowledge of the code in which the message is sent. Many investigators, hypothesizing that individuals differ in their "ability" to comprehend aurally, have attempted to identify the characteristics, abilities, or skills which determine listening ability—i.e., the ability to comprehend aurally.[3]

Sex

Most, but not all, investigators report that males comprehend slightly more from lectures than do females (13, 58, 87, 88, 89, 90, 91, 92, 93, 94, 95), but such differences probably are a result of some aspect of the testing situation rather than of intrinsic sex differences (91).

Hearing acuity and auditory discrimination

Certainly an individual must be able to hear speech before he can comprehend it, and experimental evidence is overwhelming that children must have normal hearing acuity and auditory discrimination ability if they are to learn

[3]Since the concern here is not with whether a definable "listening ability" exists, the term listening ability is used as meaning "the amount comprehended from an oral message."

to speak, listen, and read well (88, 97). If the adult hearing acuity is within the broad range of normalcy, however, the degree of acuity and the extent of the ability to discriminate among speech sounds probably do not influence significantly the individual's ability to learn from informative speeches (28, 95, 96). Apparently, persons who have poor auditory discrimination or who are hard of hearing compensate successfully for these difficulties.

Personality attributes

Correlations between listening ability and various measures of personality traits, according to Nichols (95) and Haberland (98) are near zero. Prince (99), however, reports that good listeners tend to display "objective" tendencies but that poor listeners show "egocentric" characteristics. Similarly, whereas poor listeners tend to overestimate their listening ability, competent ones either underestimate or correctly judge themselves (22, 95). In general, though, experimenters have found no definite relationships between the ability to comprehend aurally and personality characteristics.

Intelligence

Any mental activity depends, at least in part, on the individual's intelligence, and thus it appears that a close relationship should exist between verbal intelligence and listening comprehension. However, correlations between measures of intelligence and listening ability, depending on the tests used and the subjects tested (20, 28, 70, 72, 78, 94, 95, 98, 100, 101, 102, 103, 104, 105, 107, 108, 109, 110, 111, 112, 113, 114, 115), range widely from .05 to .78 with the average correlation at about .46 (105). Peripheral to these results is the finding that the more intelligent persons appear to comprehend better what they read than what they hear (12, 16, 106). Intelligence probably is a constituent of aural comprehension, but the correlation is too low for it to serve as an accurate predictor of listening ability.

Scholastic achievement

Correlations between measures of listening ability and cumulative grade point averages for high school and college students are positive but moderate (.24 to .71) (28, 98, 102, 115), and relationships between measures of listening ability and high school rank are similar (91, 102). Since listening and reading have about the same correlations with grade point average, some investigators suggest that scholastic achievement depends as much upon aural comprehension as upon reading skill (28, 102).

Verbal ability

Listening ability is related to verbal ability in approximately the same way as to intelligence (28, 92, 94, 95, 98, 103, 111). Children with higher listening than reading scores however, have higher "nonlanguage" than "language" IQ scores (92).

Vocabulary

Experimental evidence suggests that vocabulary, although not in itself a determining factor of listening ability, probably is one of several significant constituents (28, 31, 90, 98, 99, 102, 105, 116, 117, 118).

Listening experience

According to Nichols (95), those who score well on listening comprehension tests engage more often in difficult listening tasks than do those who score poorly. Heye (119), on the other hand, found only a slight difference between the listening test scores of those who reported much time spent listening and those who said they spent but little.

Note-taking

Note-taking seems to have no significant influence on listening comprehension and retention (120, 121). A possible explanation is that listeners take poor notes and thus do not benefit fully from the activity (91, 93, 95).

Motivation

The importance of motivation to learning is so well established that it seems certain that motivation bears an essential relationship to aural comprehension (95, 128). Possibly because motivation defies accurate measurement, experimental knowledge of its effects on listening comprehension is limited.

1. *Interest.* Interest in the subject matter of a lecture, as expressed prior to listening, has not been found to be significantly related to comprehension (20, 22, 72, 90, 127, 129). Although several studies indicate that the arousal of interest during the speech (as measured during or after the speech) influences positively the amount recalled (23, 40, 56, 132), others report little relationship between aroused interest and comprehension (31, 87). Similarly, experimentation has not supported consistently the theory that comprehension will be improved by the inclusion of "human interest" factors in the speech (3, 11, 25, 124). These conflicting findings may have resulted from the introduction into the experimental situation of motivational factors other than those being studied. For example, Moore (81), Prince (99), and Knower et al. (78), found that if the subjects knew that they were to be tested after listening to a lecture, their comprehension scores tended to be higher than when they were not so motivated. The knowledge that tests are coming apparently creates an ego involvement and a preparatory learning-set which are stronger motivating forces than the interest intrinsic to the subject matter.

2. *Emotional appeals and attitudes.* The listener's "emotional" reaction toward the subject matter may affect the set to learn or attend and thus
either promote or hinder effective listening. Experimental evidence, however,
is contradictory. Although in several studies messages in harmony with the
listener's frame of reference, personal values, or predisposition toward the
subject were better recalled than were messages in conflict with his attitudes
(53, 123, 125, 126), in other investigations the listener's predisposition did
not influence the amount recalled (27, 122, 130). Moreover, Hovland, Janis,
and Kelley (40) suggest that the direction of the listener's predisposition toward the subject matter may exert less influence upon comprehension than the
intensity of the predisposition. Listeners with strong feelings about a topic,
they speculate, may be more inclined than neutrals to pay close attention, to
rehearse the messages afterward, and thus to remember effectively. In their
own studies of "fear-arousing appeals," Hovland, Janis, and Kelley found no
evidence to suggest that a strong appeal produces inattentiveness or distraction
which interferes with the amount comprehended or retained. Matthews (130)
also found that "loaded words" neither help nor hinder the comprehension of
a persuasive speech.

3. *Set.* C. T. Brown (22) reports that when a prefatory comment is
used to engender an anticipatory set, listeners score significantly better on
comprehension tests than when such comments are omitted. This finding
seems consistent with Ehrensberger's (24) report that proactive emphasis
(such as "now get this") facilitates comprehension. The promise of monetary
rewards, according to a study by Mullin (131), creates a set to listen which
produces significant increases in retention on both immediate and delayed
recall tests.

Although common sense and studies in learning suggest the probable
importance of motivation as a factor in communicating information, experimental findings regarding the effect of motivation upon exposition are inconclusive. Motivation in the form of anticipatory sets, artificial or extrinsic
motivations, and interest aroused during the speech appear to facilitate comprehension, but expressed or intrinsic interest in the subject of the lecture seems
to have little effect upon comprehension. Furthermore, some factors thought
to interfere with effective comprehension (such as emotionally laden words and
ideas or strong attitudes or predispositions toward the subject matter or the
speaker) may have a less inhibiting effect than has been presumed. In short,
we have much to learn about the role of motivation in informative speaking.

Organizational ability

Several investigators have suggested that the ability to reorganize, follow,
and grasp the main points and the organizational plan of an oral discourse may
influence the amount comprehended (93, 95, 102). Subjects trained in organizational skills, according to Postman (134), learn and retain visual material
better than do those not so trained, and two experimenters report moderate

positive correlations between a test of organizational skill and various tests of listening comprehension (52, 133). Thompson (52) found that subjects who scored higher on a test of organizational skill consistently obtained higher scores on both immediate retention and delayed recall tests.

The Environment

Common sense, observation, and rhetorical theory suggest that the immediate physical environment may influence the effectiveness of an informative speech. "Good" listeners told Nichols (95) that they did not allow environmental factors to interfere with their listening, whereas "poor" listeners told him that adverse conditions were a hindrance. He also found some evidence to suggest that room ventilation and temperature affect the amount comprehended but that distance from the speaker has but little effect. Several investigators found that the placement of the listener in the room and the density of the audience do not significantly influence comprehension (92, 135, 136). (Thomas and Ralph 136, it should be noted, were concerned only with attitude change, and Furbay 135, although he studied comprehension, used persuasive materials.) Irvin (93) reports that time of day does not affect the amount comprehended. Thus, the limited experimental evidence available suggests that the physical environment may not significantly influence listening comprehension.

Conclusion

Reading experimental literature about informative speaking is disappointing and sometimes frustrating. Such studies are so limited in number and the results are so inconclusive and inconsistent that few, if any, conclusions can be drawn. Moreover, since much of the research has serious theoretical and/or methodological weaknesses, many of the generalizations which appear to be valid must be advanced only with reservations. Likewise, as stated in the beginning, conclusions based upon experimental studies of informative and persuasive writings, of persuasive speaking, of verbal learning, and of other related areas rest upon analogies which in turn depend upon unexamined assumptions.

Such reservations, of course, do not mean that we know nothing about informative speaking. Our literature is rich in observational and speculative investigations of instructional speaking, and experimental research has provided the basis for some tentative hypotheses. But, surely, informative speaking deserves a greater amount of study than it has received. Many aspects have not yet been studied experimentally, and those which have been examined require additional investigation.

As students of rhetoric, we should attempt to test more thoroughly the principles upon which we base our teaching of informative speaking.

Bibliography

The Message

Meaningfulness

1. Cofer, C. N. (Ed.). *Verbal Learning and Verbal Behavior*. New York: McGraw-Hill, 1961.
2. Hovland, C. I. "Human Learning and Retention." Ch. XVII in S. S. Stevens (Ed.), *Handbook of Experimental Psychology*. New York: Wiley, 1951.

Style and difficulty

3. Allen, W. H. "Readability of Instructional Film Commentary." *JAP* 35 (1952): 164–8.
4. Beighley, K. C. "An Experimental Study of the Effect of Four Speech Variables on Listener Comprehension." *SM* 19 (1952): 249–58.
5. ———. "An Experimental Study of the Effect of Three Speech Variables on Listener Comprehension." *SM* 21 (1954): 248–53.
6. Borchers, Gladys. "An Approach to the Problem of Oral Style." *QJS* 22 (1936): 114–7.
7. Carver, M. E. "Listening Versus Reading." Ch. IX in Hadley Cantril and G. W. Allport, *The Psychology of Radio*. New York: Harper & Row, 1935.
8. Chall, J. S., and H. E. Dial. "Predicting Listener Understanding and Interest in Newscasts." *ERB* 27 (1948): 141–53, 168.
9. Dale, Edgar, and J. S. Chall. "A Formula for Predicting Readability." *ERB* 27 (1948): 11–20.
10. Flesch, Rudolf. "Marks of Readable Style." *Contributions to Education*, No. 897. New York: Teachers College, Columbia University, 1943.
11. ———. "A New Readability Yardstick." *JAP* 32 (1948): 221–33.
12. Goldstein, Henry. "Reading and Listening Comprehension at Various Controlled Rates." *Contribution to Education*, No. 821. New York: Teachers College, Columbia University, 1940.
13. Hampleman, R. S. "Comparison of Listening and Reading Comprehension Ability of Fourth and Sixth Grade Pupils." *EE* 35 (1958): 49–53.
14. Harwood, K. A. "Listenability and Readability." *SM* 22 (1955): 49–53.
15. Jones, E. C. "An Inquiry Into the Value of Applying a Readability Formula to Radio News." Unpubl. thesis, Syracuse, 1951; abstract in *SM* 19 (1952): 172–3.
16. Larsen, R. P. and D. D. Feder. "Common and Differential Factors in Reading and Hearing Comprehension." *JEP* 31 (1940): 241–52.
17. Lorge, Irving. "Predicting Reading Difficulty of Selections for Children." *EER* 16 (1939): 229–33.

18. Manion, O. G. "An Application of Readability Formulas to Oral Communication." Unpubl. diss., Michigan, 1953; abstract in *SM* 21(1954):151.
19. Nebergall, R. E. "An Experimental Investigation of Rhetorical Clarity." *SM* 25(1958):243–54.
20. Nelson, H. E. "The Effect of Variation of Rate on the Recall by Radio Listeners of 'Straight' Newscasts." *SM* 15(1948):173–80.
21. Thomas, G. L. "Effect of Oral Style on Intelligibility of Speech." *SM* 23(1956): 46–54.

Verbal emphasis

22. Brown, C. T. "Studies in Listening Comprehension." *SM* 26(1959):288–94.
23. Cantril, Hadley, and G. W. Allport. *The Psychology of Radio.* New York: Harper & Row, 1935.
24. Ehrensberger, Ray. "An Experimental Study of the Relative Effectiveness of Certain Forms of Emphasis in Public Speaking." *SM* 12(1945):94–111.
25. Harrell, T. W., D. E. Brown, and Wilbur Schramm. "Memory in Radio News Listening." *JAP* 33(1949):265–74.
26. Jersild, A. T. "Modes of Emphasis in Public Speaking." *JAP* 12(1928):611–20.
27. Pence, O. L. "Emotionally Loaded Argument: Its Effectiveness in Stimulating Recall." *QJS* 40(1954):272–6.

Main ideas
(See also: 23, 25)

28. Blewett, T. T. "An Experiment in the Measurement of Listening at the College Level." *JER* 44(1951):575–85.
29. English, H. B., E. L. Welborn, and C. D. Killian. "Studies in Substance Memorization." *JGP* 11(1934):233–60.
30. Spache, G. D. "The Construction and Validation of a Work-Type Auditory Comprehension Test." *JEPM* 10(1950):249–53.
31. Trenaman, Joseph. "Understanding Radio Talks." *QJS* 38(1951):173–8.

Organization
(See also: 4, 5, 29, 31)

32. Adams, H. F. "The Effect of Climax and Anti-Climax Order of Presentation on Memory." *JAP* 4(1920):330–8.
33. Cromwell, Harvey. "The Relative Effect on Audience Attitude of the First Versus the Second Argumentative Speech of a Series." *SM* 17(1950):105–22.
34. Darnell, D. K. "The Relation Between Sentence Order and the Comprehension of Written English." Mimeographed abstract of the speech "Toward a Theory of Organizations" delivered at the Central States Speech Association Convention, Chicago, April 9, 1960.
35. Gilkinson, Howard, S. F. Paulson, and D. E. Sikkink. "Effects of Order and Authority in an Argumentative Speech." *QJS* 40(1954):183–92.
36. Goyer, R. S. "A Study of Individual Differences in Ability and Achievement of College Students in the Organization of Ideas." Unpubl. diss., Ohio State, 1955; abstract in *SM* 23(1956):89–90.

37. Guilford, J. P. "The Role of Form in Learning." *JExP* 10(1927):415–23.
38. Gulley, H. E., and D. K. Berlo. "Effects of Intercellular and Intracellular Speech Structure on Attitude Change and Learning." *SM* 23(1956):288–97.
38. Hovland, C. I. (Ed.). *The Order of Presentation in Persuasion.* New Haven, Conn.: Yale University Press, 1957.
40. ———, I. L. Janis, and H. H. Kelley. *Communication and Persuasion.* New Haven, Conn.: Yale University Press, 1953.
41. Jersild, A. T. "Primacy, Recency, Frequency, and Vividness." *JExP* 12(1929): 58–70.
42. Katona, George. *Organizing and Memorizing: Studies in the Psychology of Learning and Teaching.* New York: Columbia University Press, 1940.
43. Key, C. B. "Recall as a Function of Perceived Relations." *AP* 13,lxxxiii(1926): 1–106.
44. Laird, D. A., H. H. Remmers, and L. J. Peterson. "An Experimental Study of the Influences of Organization of Material for Memorizing upon Its Retention." *JExP* 6(1923):69–81.
45. Paul, I. H. "Studies in Remembering." *PI* 1,ii(1959):1–153.
46. Reed, H. B. "Meaning as a Factor in Learning" *JEP* 29(1938):419–30.
47. ———. "Repetition and Association in Learning." *PS* 31(1924):147–55.
48. Smith, R. G. "An Experimental Study of Effects of Speech Organization upon Attitudes of College Students." *SM* 18(1951):292–301.
49. Sponberg, Harold. "A Study of the Relative Effectiveness of Climax and Anti-Climax Order in Argumentative Speech." SM 13(1946):35–44.
50. Tannenbaum, P. H. "Effect of Serial Position on Recall of Radio News Stories." *JQ* 31(1954):319–23.
51. Thistlethwaite, D. L., H. J. deHaan, and J. M. Kamenetzky. "The Effects of 'Directive' and "Nondirective' Communication Procedures on Attitudes." *JASP* 51(1955):107–13.
52. Thompson, E. C. "An Experimental Investigation of the Relative Effectiveness of Organizational Structure in Oral Communication." Unpubl. diss., Minnesota, 1959; abstract in *SM* 27(1960):94–5.

The Speaker

Credibility
(See also: 40)

53. Gilkinson, Howard, S. F. Paulson, and D. E. Sikkink. "Conditions Affecting the Communication of Controversial Statements in Connected Discourse: Forms of Presentation and the Political Frame of Reference of the Listener." *SM* 20(1953):253–60.
54. Haiman, F. S. "An Experiment in Informative Speaking." *QJS* 34(1948):355–60.
55. ———. "An Experimental Study of the Effects of Ethos in Public Speaking." *SM* 16(1949):190–202.

56. Highlander, J. P. "Audience Analyzer Measurements and Informational Effects of Speaker Variables in Radio Talks." Unpubl. diss., Wisconsin, 1953; abstract in *SM* 21(1954) :188–9.
57. Hildreth, R. A. "An Experimental Study of Audiences' Ability to Distinguish Between Sincere and Insincere Speeches." Unpubl. diss., Southern California, 1953; abstract in *SM* 21(1954) :146–7.
58. Paulson, S. F. "The Effects of the Prestige of the Speaker and Acknowledgment of Opposing Arguments on Audience Retention and Shift of Opinion." *SM* 21(1954) :267–71.

Delivery
(See also: 4, 5, 12, 20, 21, 23, 24, 26, 54, 56)

59. Anderson, J. C. "The Relative Effectiveness of Personal and Recorded Presentations of Persuasive Speeches." Unpubl. thesis, Oklahoma, 1950; abstract in *SM* 18(1951) :200.
60. Diehl, C. F., and E. T. McDonald. "Effect of Voice Quality on Communication." *JSHD* 21(1956) :233–7.
61. ———, R. C. White, and K. W. Burk. "Rate and Communication." *SM* 26 (1959) :229–32.
62. ———, R. C. White, and P. H. Satz. "Pitch Change and Comprehension." *SM* 28(1961) :65–8.
63. Dietrich, J. E. "The Relative Effectiveness of Two Modes of Radio Delivery in Influencing Attitudes." *SM* 13(1946) :58–65.
64. Ewbank, H. L. "Exploratory Studies in Radio Techniques," in *Education on the Air, Third Yearbook of the Institute for Education by Radio*. Columbus, Ohio: Ohio State University, 1932, 231–9.
65. ———. "Studies in the Techniques of Radio Speech." *QJS* 18(1932) :560–71.
66. Fairbanks, Grant, Newman Guttman, and M. S. Miron. "Effects of Time Compression upon the Comprehension of Connected Speech." *JSHD* 22(1957) :9–10.
67. ———, ———, and ———. "Auditory Comprehension of Repeated High-Speed Messages." *JSHD* 22(1957) :20–2.
68. ———, ———, and ———. "Auditory Comprehension in Relation to Listening Rate and Selective Verbal Redundancy." *JSHD* 22(1957) :23–32.
69. ———, and Frank Kodman. "Word Intelligibility as a Function of Time Compression." *JASA* 29(1957) :636–41.
70. Fergen, G. K. "Listening Comprehension at Controlled Rates for Children in Grades IV, V, and VI." Unpubl. diss., Missouri, 1954; abstract in *DA* 15(1955) : 89.
71. Gaskill, H. V. "Research Studies Made at Iowa State College," in *Education on the Air, Fourth Yearbook of the Institute for Education by Radio*, Columbus, Ohio, Ohio State University, 1933, pp. 322–6.
72. Gauger, P. W. "The Effect of Gesture and the Presence or Absence of the Speaker on the Listening Comprehension of Eleventh and Twelfth Grade High School Pupils." Unpubl. diss., Wisconsin, 1951; abstract in *SM* 19(1952) :116–7.

73. Goodman-Malamuth, Leo, II. "An Experimental Study of the Effects of Speaking Rate upon Listenability." Unpubl. diss., Southern California, 1956; abstract in *SM* 24(1957) :89–90.
74. Harwood, K. A. "Listenability and Rate of Presentation." *SM* 22(1955) :57–9.
75. Heron, W. T., and E. W. Ziebarth. "A Preliminary Experimental Comparison of Radio and Classroom Lectures." *SM* 13(1946) :54–7.
76. Jones, H. E. "Experimental Studies of College Training: The Effect of Examination on Permanence of Learning." *AP* 10,lxviii(1923) :1–70.
77. Klinger, H. N. "The Effects of Stuttering on Audience Listening Comprehension." Unpubl. diss., New York, 1959; abstract in *SM* 37(1960) :247.
78. Knower, F. H., David Phillips, and F. Koeppel. "Studies in Listening to Informative Speaking." *JASP* 40(1945) :82–8.
79. Kramar, Edward J. J., and Thomas R. Lewis. "Comparison of Visual and Nonvisual Listening." *JC* (1951) :16–20.
80. Loder, J. E. "A Study of Aural Learning With and Without the Speaker Present." *JEE* 6(1937) :46–60.
81. Moore, H. T. "The Attention Value of Lecturing Without Notes." *JEP* 10 (1919) :467–9.
82. O'Neill, J. J. "Contributions of the Visual Components of Oral Symbols to the Speech Comprehension of Listeners with Normal Hearing." Unpubl. diss., Ohio State, 1951; abstract in *SM* 19(1952) :119–20.
83. Sumby, W. H., and Irwin Pollack. "Visual Contribution to Speech Intelligibility in Noise." *JASA* 26(1954) :212–5.
84. Ulrich, J. H. "An Experimental Study of the Acquisition of Information from Three Types of Recorded Television Presentations." *SM* 24(1957) :39–45.
85. Utzinger, V. A. "An Experimental Study of the Effects of Verbal Fluency upon the Listener." Unpubl. diss., Southern California, 1952; abstract in *SM* 20 (1953) :161.
86. Weissman, S. M. "The Effect of Quality of Speech on the Listening Comprehension of Male College Students." Unpubl. Seminar Report No. 3036, School of Education, College of the City of New York, 1940.

The Listener

Sex
(See also: 13, 58)

87. Brandon, J. R. "An Experimental Television Study: The Relative Effectiveness of Presenting Factual Information by the Lecture, Interview, and Discussion Methods." *SM* 23(1956) :272–83.
88. Brown, D. P. "Auding as the Primary Language Ability." Unpubl. diss., Stanford, 1954; abstract in *DA* 14(1954) :2281–2.
89. Caffrey, J. G. "Auding Ability as a Function of Certain Psychometric Variables." Unpubl. diss., California, 1953.
90. ——, "Auding Ability at the Secondary Level," *Education* 75(1955) :303–10.
91. Green, M. E. "An Exploratory Investigation of Listening Ability and Certain

Factors Accompanying Listening in Selected Groups of College Students in the University of Tennessee at Knoxville." Unpubl. thesis, Tennessee, 1958.

92. Hall, R. O. "An Exploratory Study of Listening of Fifth Grade Pupils." Unpubl. diss., Southern California, 1954.

93. Irvin, C. E. "An Analysis of Certain Aspects of a Listening Training Program Conducted among College Freshmen at Michigan State College." Unpubl. diss., Michigan State, 1952; abstract in *SM* 20(1953):122–3.

94. Kramar, E. J. J. "The Relationships of the Wechsler-Bellvue and A. C. E. Intelligence Tests with Performance Scores in Speaking and the Brown-Carlsen Listening Comprehension Test." Unpubl. diss., Florida State, 1955; abstract in *SM* 23(1956):93–4.

95. Nichols, R. G. "Factors Accounting for Differences in Comprehension of Materials Presented Orally in the Classroom." Unpubl. diss., Iowa, 1948; abstract in *SM* 16(1949):350–1.

Hearing acuity and auditory discrimination
(See also: 28, 88, 95)

96. Ainsworth, Stanley, and Charles High. "Auditory Functions and Abilities in Good and Poor Listeners." *JC* 4(1954):84–6.

97. Rossignol, L. J. "The Relationships among Hearing Acuity, Speech Production, and Reading Performance in Grades 1A, 1B, and 2A," in *Contribution to Education*, No. 936. New York: Teachers College, Columbia University, 1948.

Personality attributes
(See also: 22, 95)

98. Haberland, J. A. "A Comparison of Listening Tests with Standardized Tests." *JER* 52(1959):299–302.

99. Prince, B. L. "A Study of Classroom Listening Effectiveness in Basic Communication and Its Relationship to Certain Other Factors." Unpubl. thesis, Denver, 1948; abstract in *SM* 16(1949):352.

Intelligence
(See also: 12, 16, 20, 28, 70, 72, 78, 94, 95, 98)

100. Biggs, B. P. "Construction, Validation, and Evaluation of a Diagnostic Test of Listening Effectiveness." SM 23(1956):9–13.

101. Brewster, L. W. "An Exploratory Study of Some Aspects of Critical Listening among College Freshmen." Unpubl. diss., Iowa, 1956; abstract in *SM* 24 (1957):86–7.

102. Brown, J. I., and G. R. Carlsen. *Brown-Carlsen Listening Comprehension Test, Manual of Directions.* Yonkers-on-Hudson, New York: World Book Co., 1955.

103. Crook, F. E. "Interrelationships among a Group of Language Arts Tests." *JER* 51(1957):305–11.

104. Dow, C. W. "The Development of Listening Comprehension Tests for Michigan State College Freshmen." Unpubl. diss., Michigan State, 1952; abstract in *SM* 20(1953):120.

105. Erickson, Allen G. "Can Listening Efficiency Be Improved?" *JC* 4(1954) :128–32.
106. Greene, E. B. "The Relative Effectiveness of Lecture and Individual Reading as Methods of College Teaching." *GPM* 4(1928) :457–563.
107. Heilman, A. W. "An Investigation in Measuring and Improving the Listening Ability of College Freshmen." *SM* 18(1951) :302–8.
108. Hollow, Sister M. K. "Listening Comprehension at the Intermediate-Grade Level." *ESJ* 56(1955) :158–61.
109. Johnson, K. O. "A Study of the Effect of an Experimental Course on Listening Comprehension." Unpubl. thesis, Minnesota, 1948; abstract in *SM* 16(1949) : 351.
110. ——. "The Effect of Classroom Training upon Listening Comprehension." *JC* 1(1951) :57–62.
111. Krueger, D. H. "A Study of the Results of Teaching Factors of Listening Comprehension to College Freshmen in the Basic Communications II Course." Unpubl. thesis, Whittier, 1950.
112. Pratt, L. E. "Experimental Evaluation of a Program for the Improvement of Listening." *ESJ* 56(1956) :315–20.
113. Rankin, P. T. "The Measurement of the Ability to Understand Spoken Language." Unpubl. diss., Michigan, 1926; abstract in *DA* 12(1952) :847–8.
114. Stark, Joel. "An Investigation of the Relationship of the Vocal and Communicative Aspects of Speech Competency with Listening Comprehension." Unpubl. diss., New York U., 1956; abstract in *SM* 24(1957) :98–9.
115. Still, D. S. "The Relationship between Listening Ability and High School Grades." Unpubl. diss., Pittsburgh, 1955; abstract in *DA* 15(1955) :1761–2.

Scholastic achievement
(See: 28, 91, 98, 102, 115)

Verbal Ability
(See: 28, 92, 94, 95, 98, 103, 111)

Vocabulary
(See also: 28, 31, 90, 98, 99, 102, 105)

116. Anderson, I. H., and Grant Fairbanks. "Common and Differential Factors in Reading Vocabulary and Hearing Vocabulary." *JER* 30(1937) :317–24.
117. Corey, S. M. "Learning from Lectures vs. Learning from Readings." *JEP* 25 (1934) :459–70.
118. Park, Joe. "Vocabulary and Comprehension Difficulties of Sound Motion Pictures." *SchR* 53(1945) :154–61.

Listening from experience
(See also: 95)

119. Heye, H. "A Study of the Effectiveness of Selected Auditory Presentations at the Adult Age Level." Unpubl. diss., Iowa, 1941; abstract in *State U. of Iowa Doc. Diss. Abstr. Ref.*, 4(1944) :82–5.

Note-taking ability
(See also: 91, 93, 95)

120. Crawford, C. C. "Some Experimental Studies of the Results of College Note-Taking." *JER* 12(1925) :379–86.
121. McClendon, P. I. "An Experimental Study of the Relationship Between the Note-Taking Practices and Listening Comprehension of College Freshmen During Expository Lectures." *SM* 25(1958) :222–8.

Motivation
(See also: 3, 11, 20, 22, 23, 24, 25, 27, 31, 40, 53, 56, 72, 78, 81, 87, 90, 95, 99)

122. Berlo, D. K., and H. E. Gulley. "Some Determinants of the Effect of Oral Communication in Producing Attitude Change and Learning." *SM* 24(1957) :10–20.
123. Carlton, R. L. "An Experimental Investigation of the Relationship Between Personal Value and Word Intelligibility." Unpubl. diss., Ohio State, 1953; abstract in *SM* 21(1954) :142–3.
124. Cartier, F. A. "Listenability and 'Human Interest.' " *SM* 22(1955) :53–7.
125. Conboy, W. A. "A Study of the Retention of Speech Content as Measured by Immediate and Delayed Recall." Unpubl. diss., Northwestern, 1954; abstract in *SM* 22(1955) :143.
126. Edwards, A. L. "Political Frames of Reference as a Factor Influencing Recognition." *JASP* 36(1941) :34–50.
127. Heath, M. A. "A Study in Listening: The Relationships Between Interest, Educability and Score on an Objective Examination Over the Factual Content of an Informative Speech." Unpubl. thesis, Florida State, 1951; abstract in *SM* 19 1952) :159–60.
128. Irvin, Charles, E. "Motivation in Listening Training." *JC* 4(1954) :42–4.
129. Karraker, M. E. "An Evaluation of the Influence of Interest and 'Set' on Listening Effectiveness in the Basic Communication Class." Unpubl. diss., Denver, 1951; abstract in *SM* 19(1952) :117–8.
130. Matthews, Jack. "The Effect of Loaded Language on Audience Comprehension of Speeches." *SM* 14(1947) :176–86.
131. Mullin, D. W. "An Experimental Study of Retention in Educational Television." *SM* 24(1957) :31–8.
132. Vernon, P. E. "The Intelligibility of Broadcast Talks." *BBC Quarterly*, 5(1950-51) :211–2.

Organizational ability
(See also: 52, 93, 95, 102)

133. Petrie, C. R. "An Experimental Evaluation of Two Methods for Improving Listening Comprehension Abilities." Unpubl. diss., Purdue, 1961; abstract in *SM* 29(1962) :94.
134. Postman, Leo. "Learned Principles of Organization in Memory." *PM* 68, ccclxxiv(1954) :1–24.

The Environment

(See also: 92, 93, 95)

135. Furbay, A. L. "A Descriptive Study of the Influence of the Physical Arrangement of the Audience upon Response to a Speech." Unpubl. diss., Wayne State, 1959; abstract in *SM* 27(1960) :84.
136. Thomas, G. L., and D. C. Ralph. "A Study of the Effect of Audience Proximity on Persuasion." *SM* 26(1959) :300–7.

Questions for Analysis

1. What makes "clarity" an especially difficult consideration in rhetorical criticism? What variables should be remembered when *reading* a speech manuscript for "clarity"? How may the speaker compensate with style for the "tough" content of an informative speech? Why do you think "order of presentation" matters less to listeners to informative speeches than does the "highlighting" of main ideas? What priorities does this suggest when you prepare informative speeches?

2. How may listener "opinion change" and "learning" matter differently to different speakers? Which studies indicate that delivery of an informative speech may have little influence on listener comprehension? How do you account for this? For speakers more concerned about "opinion change" than "learning", which aspects of delivery may be worth cultivating? Judge the importance to *you* of delivery of informative speeches.

3. Are you surprised by Petrie's findings of the significance in comprehension of listener intelligence, scholastic achievement, and verbal ability? Are these findings consistent with your observations? Explain. What characteristics of communication today might explain the greater importance of motivation to learning than to aural comprehension? Distinguish *direction* of disposition from *intensity* of disposition. How may a speaker profit by understanding these terms?

4. What is most likely to be responsible for the "arousal" of interest during an informative speech? Distinguish "extrinsic" from "intrinsic" motivation. How do they differ in different rhetorical situations? Why should one be more important than the other? How can the informative speaker capitalize on that importance? Why should "emotional words" or "strong attitudes" interfere little with the comprehension of an informative speech?

5. On the basis of Petrie's findings list *only* those considerations of preparation and delivery that may be of significant value to the informative speaker. Add to the list *only* those listener characteristics that may be significant. What does your list suggest about how much an informative speaker may expand listener comprehension? Is this conclusion consistent with your experience as a listener? Explain. How *could* informative speakers you have heard have increased your comprehension?

23

The Persuasive Speaker and His Audience

J. Jeffery Auer

The chief sources for our understanding of man's persuasive behavior are the traditional concepts of rhetorical theory as modified by the contemporary contributions of the behavioral sciences. What follows is not a complete manual of rhetorical practice, but is a summary of eight sequential concerns for those who would persuade. These concerns reflect some of the contributions of modern psychological concepts to classical rhetorical theory. Please note that each of the eight headings begins with a transitive verb: this is to emphasize that *action* of some kind is indispensable in every aspect of persuasive speechmaking. In addition, the middle four headings are really *functional* psychological factors: attention, interest, motivation, learning, and remembering. They are placed in the middle of the series in order to emphasize how they pervade the total process of communicating with an audience.

Analyzing Audience, Occasion, and Purpose

It is fashionable among modern rhetoricians—and psychologically sound —to describe public speaking as audience-centered rather than speaker-centered. The oratory of personal display is out of style, and never was in good taste. No matter how important the speaker's message, or how strongly he feels about it, the speaker must deal with the complex of beliefs and attitudes of his listeners. The key understanding to this complex is a careful analysis of the audience. Though it may be impossible to study a prospective audience at first-hand, an analysis of similar and familiar groups will be helpful: it is possible

J. Jeffery Auer is Chairman of the Department of Speech and Theatre, Indiana University.

Adapted from Jon Eisenson, J. Jeffery Auer, and John V. Irwin, *The Psychology of Communication* (New York, Copyright 1963 by Meredith Publishing Co.), pp. 286–309. Reprinted by permission from Appleton-Century-Crofts.

to make fairly safe generalizations, for example, about the attitudes of members of service clubs, labor unions, or college student-bodies, wherever they are. National or local public opinion polls can also provide useful information. The only alternative to advance analysis is to make impromptu adaptations when actually facing the audience, but this choice is a poor one, even for experienced speakers.

The occasion for the speech needs also to be understood. The concerned speaker will want to know what brings the audience together, what expectations it has both for his speech and the whole meeting. The speaker should notice the apparent spirit of the assembling audience, the organizational rituals, and other elements of "preliminary tuning" that may affect the tone of the occasion.

If the speech is to be audience-centered, then an analysis of both the listeners and the occasion for their meeting will help the speaker in determining his specific purpose, as well as the means he uses to achieve it.

Acquiring Prestige

A speaker's prestige, referred to in traditional rhetoric as *ethos*, or ethical appeal, determines his status with his audience. The first kind of status is ascribed—what the speaker is thought to be. This is determined by the business, professional, or social position he holds, and by his reputation, especially as an authority on his subject. Advance publicity for the meeting usually stresses this aspect of status and the chairman's introduction underscores it, sometimes ad nauseam. Experiments using speakers otherwise unknown to their audiences consistently show that appropriate introduction ascribing high status "credentials" will significantly increase favorable attitudes resulting from the speech. In their investigation of the effect of an audience's prior judgments of a speaker's ethos upon its acceptance of his point of view, Berlo and Gulley (1957) submit that the significant correlations between these two factors are explained by the Osgood and Tannenbaum "congruity principle," namely, that attitude changes always go in directions that will increase their harmony with existing listener frames of reference or sets of expectations.

A second kind of status is not given but earned—what the speaker proves himself to be. Since relatively few speakers possess, in advance, highly ascribed status, it is significant to report research on how speakers can earn status. Clark (1951) found that general audiences, ranking fourteen qualities of speakers and speaking, listed "sincerity" and "poise" as the first and second most essential. This judgment endorses speaker behavior that appears to be honest, purposeful, confident, and considerate.

A speaker's ethos may also be established by his manner: Bettinghaus (1961) found that effectiveness of delivery significantly correlated with credibility and thus with persuasiveness; and Harms (1961), using essentially "content-free" speech cues, found that high-status speakers (well-educated and in prestige occupations) not only can be distinguished from middle and low-status speakers by "the way they talked" but that high-status speakers are consistently rated as most credible. Credibility was greater for straightforward argumentative speeches, however, than for those using special techniques (such as deliberate attempts to manifest high integrity) in a series of political talks experimentally evaluated by Ludlum (1958). Part of this straightforward approach is using sound evidence to support a proposition rather than depending upon assertion and generalization. Cathcart (1955) discovered a significantly greater shift of opinion for speeches built on evidence. Enlarging upon them by citing or qualifying their sources does not, however, necessarily make them more credible.

Two special facets of credibility are fairness and trustworthiness. When there is reason to be suspicious of a speaker's motives, Hovland and Mandell (1952) found that audiences conclude that a speaker does "a very poor job" of giving the facts and that he presents them in a way that is "too one-sided." But, when the audience believes that the speaker has nothing to gain personally by having his proposition accepted, the same speech is rated "a very good job" and "fair and honest." Hovland and others in another study (1949, pp. 201–27) found that, when the weight of evidence supports the main thesis, it is more persuasive to introduce the arguments of those who oppose it, rather than to present only materials supporting the thesis, "at least for the better educated men and for those who are already opposed to the stand." For listeners less educated but favorably disposed, the reverse is true. When the speaker at least acknowledges the opposition arguments, he thus induces a feeling in his listeners that he is being fair. "Better educated" in this study means graduation from high school and accurately describes about half of the subjects. In Paulson's study (1954), which tests the same variable, all of the subjects are college students, and for them the introduction of opposing arguments is not more persuasive, though it improves retention. Paulson speculates that perhaps very sophisticated audiences feel that merely acknowledging, but not developing, opposing arguments is not so fair as it seems to less critical audiences.

In sum, experimentation supports the conclusion that even the speaker who lacks ascribed status has it within his power to earn status with his hearers by giving evidence of his sincerity, poise, credibility, fairness, and trustworthiness.

Focusing Attention

William James said that "what holds attention determines action," and James Winans added that "the key word (in public speaking) is Attention." These two statements point out the inevitable first step in addressing any audience, whether it seeks information or hopes for conversion. Without gaining his hearers' attention, nothing that a speaker says will make any difference, unless he enjoys talking to himself.

If a speaker comes to an audience with high ascribed status, if he has already earned status with a specific audience, or, if for other reasons his listeners are interested and friendly, he need make no special effort to gain attention. He can count on his prestige to work for him.

If, on the other hand, an audience is apathetic or skeptical about either the speaker or his subject, it must be roused or even jolted to attention. In his book on influencing human behavior, Overstreet (1925, pp. 110–124) described five of the available methods of "crossing the interest deadline," and we enumerate them here: "Start with situation. . . . Start with something that makes a difference. . . . Begin with an effect needing a cause . . . or begin with a cause implying an effect. . . . [Begin with] the shock technique. . . . Present a conflict. . . ."

When a speaker faces a hostile or critical audience, he must utilize all possible resources for gaining attention. Observations of effective speakers reveal that in this predicament, they most often work to find some common ground of agreement with the audience and then focus attention upon it. This platform of agreement with his hearers, upon which the speaker hopes to stand, may be built on common interests or associations: no matter how else they may be unlike, they all come from the same community, fought in the same war, belong to the same party, and so on. Common ground may also be sought in areas of belief or attitude: regardless of other differences, for example, the speaker and his audience believe in the same "way of life," worship the same God, revere the same flag, and share the same praiseworthy desire to solve their problems rationally and with justice for all. Like other persuasive methods, this one can be employed ethically and sincerely.

The common-ground technique is evidently effective. Schachter (1951) concluded that a speaker cannot win a hearing from his audience if he deviates too far from the group norm; and Ewing (1942) discovered that a speaker's acceptance is increased when, at the beginning of his speech, he asserts that his views correspond with those held by his hearers, even if he really advocates a proposition contrary to their initial opinions. In a similar study, Weiss (1957) demonstrated that a speaker discussing a controversial issue influences an audience more easily when he also expresses opinions that are in accord with those of his listeners. Should the speaker, by means of suggestion, persuade his hearers that the majority opinion is different than it appears to be, Marple (1933) reported, they will tend to shift their attitudes toward the alleged majority position.

On the basis of many experiments one can assume fairly that all audiences are susceptible to the influence of five *unlearned attention values: change, intensity, striking quality, repetition,* and *definiteness of form*. We conclude this discussion by briefly suggesting some ways by which speakers may apply these attention values to implement four significant principles.

1. To hold attention the content of a speech must be impressive. What the speaker says should have definiteness of form, that is, present clearly an easily

grasped pattern of information or course of action; if it is also novel, has a striking quality, it will gain attention on that basis alone; and if it is presented with enough repetition to be sure that every listener understands it, the communication will have maximum potency.

2. To hold attention the organization of a speech must be clear. A well-organized speech personifies definiteness of form, ordering information or arguments in a chronological, topical, logical, or some other pattern. Transitions between units of a speech are important; the form in which they are stated should change from time to time. Not all parts of a speech carry the same load of significance; in itself this may provide intensity. Intensification of a vital part may also be achieved by repetition.

3. To hold attention the style of a speech must be varied. A change in word stimuli will add variety, and speakers need to be wary, in any event, of using stock phrases to the point of redundancy. Putting ideas into words·offers many opportunities for striking quality, creating graphic images, novel expressions, and so on. At the same time the value of definiteness of form may be required in order to achieve precision and clarity.

4. To hold attention, the delivery of a speech must be compelling. A monotonous voice and a static body seldom gain audience attention, but a change in stimulus, and especially a variety of change, invariably will. Many distracting stimuli may operate in a lecture hall, and unless the speaker uses intensity to strengthen his own, they may be lost. His actions must be appropriate and coordinated, however, or they will lack definiteness of form and have reduced impact.

Maintaining Interest

"Thanks, anyway, but I'm just not interested," is a terminating statement that sends salesmen away from doors frustrated. Just as effectively as these words, vacant stares on the faces of a classroom audience, or bored expressions from a church congregation, can fill a speaker with despair. He, too, is a salesman of sorts, peddling his wares of facts and opinions, arguments and propositions. Though they may give him their momentary attention, they will not buy unless he can interest his prospective purchasers.

Exactly what will command the interest of an individual at any specific moment is hard to determine, but there is little question about the importance of interest itself in public address. The very act of listening depends upon the listener's interest in what is being said. In a pioneer study Nichols (1948) identified fourteen factors that influence listening comprehension significantly. Three of these are: "real *interest* in the subject discussed," "ability to see *significance* in the subject discussed," and "*curiosity* about the subject discussed." If not synonyms, interest, significance, and curiosity are at least closely related terms.

Karraker's later study (1951) of the influence of interest on listening effectiveness led to the generalization that familiarity with a subject creates interest in it. Edwards (1941) found that experiences in accord with existing frames of reference ("desires, attitudes, wishes, values, etc.") tend to be learned and remembered better than those in conflict. While he does not use the term "interest" in his description, it is clearly implied as an omnibus factor. In a follow-up study Gilkinson, et al. (1953) found the same tendency. When Thompson (1953) studied the factors considered by students in evaluating public discussions he found that "interestingness contributes the most to the student's over-all evaluation," even more than organization and material. Finally, we report studies by Kretsinger (1952) and Lyle (1953), which indicate that the degree of a listener's interest in a speech can be measured by electromagnetic movement meter recordings of gross bodily movements. When interest in the communication increases, as measured by subject-rating scales, gross bodily movements decrease; as interest decreases, bodily movements increase. While these experiments leave certain applicational values unexplored, they establish that listener interest, like other response behaviors, involves overt muscular activity.

Behavioral scientists generally agree upon eight common *natural factors of interest* relevant in persuasive speaking.

1. *Animation* is, of course, important in speech delivery; modulations of pitch, variations in rate and loudness, and shifts in vocal quality, all adapted to the ideas presented, and vitality of gesture and physical expression, suiting the action to the word, will not only reinforce what the speaker says but also provide a visible index of how he feels about what he says. When the speech is well-paced, straight exposition is enlivened with narrative illustrations, supporting material is varied, and so on. Under such circumstances animation aids content as well as delivery.

2. *Vitalness* is not inherent in every speech topic, even though the speaker may be totally concerned with it. William James said we attend to what interests us, not that we attend to what interests the other fellow. The speaker, whether hoping to inform or persuade his hearers, must find in them the sources for giving vitalness to his topic: the speaker must make clear the relation of their desires and needs to his subject if he is to maintain their interest.

3. *Familiarity* is an interest factor employed by speakers to provide a common point of reference for their listeners. When Joseph Jastrow said that man is more analogical than logical, he pointed the way to an effective rhetorical principle: a new and strange idea is less forbidding if it is compared with a similar one within the common experience of the audience.

4. *Novelty* is familiarity's counterpart, and equally important in

maintaining interest because too much reliance upon one stimulus may wear out its effectiveness. Listeners want enough novelty to offset monotony, just as they want enough familiarity to maintain stability. In supporting his arguments, for example, the speaker can employ unusual illustrations of familiar principles, and novel ways of phrasing traditional ideas.

5. *Conflict*, portrayed in narrative form or in straight exposition, tends to hold audience interest. It makes it easier for the listener to project himself, though vicariously, into the speaker's topic. The portrayal of conflicting forces—medical research against disease, tolerance against bigotry, democracy against totalitarianism—helps reduce complex problems to manageable proportions for the listener who is less well prepared to understand them than is the speaker. Speakers must use restraint in the portrayal of conflict, however, lest they oversimplify problems into sometimes unrealistic "either-or" patterns.

6. *Suspense*, when built by the speaker into long narrative explanations, or even short illustrations, is an adaptation to a public speech of the dramatic "chase technique" where the "good guys" pursue the "bad guys." Even when the listener knows who will win in the end, his interest is maintained by the tantalizing notion that "this one may be different," or by curiosity about how the conquest will be achieved. Active verbs and figurative language are stylistic aids in building suspense.

7. *Concreteness* in presenting ideas to an audience is like reducing a complex equation to a simple one. It holds the listener's interest because it makes it easier for him to understand; and it applies the principle of "mental economy" by giving him understanding with less effort than would be required by abstractions. Conceptually, concreteness is achieved by reducing an expansive idea into several smaller ones; stylistically, by substituting "picture words" and examples for vague terms.

8. *Humor* best maintains interest in the speaker's ideas if it is articulated with them. Thus the witty comparison, the incongruous application, or the clever turn of phrase that seems to grow out of a substantive idea is more effective than the isolated and often extraneous joke (Grimes, 1955). Even when a funny story is intended to illustrate a speaker's idea, his audience too often remembers the joke but not its point.

Providing Motivation

George Washington once said, "The people must feel before they will see." For that insight into human nature, he might be given a "first" in psychology as well as war and peace. Modern psychologists are probably more in agreement on the dominant strength of affective behavior, and its origins in powerful motivations, than on any other point (Jones, 1953–1961). They agree that men are most likely to behave in response to their own motivations, not to others' reasons.

When this concept of motivation is applied to communication it becomes the basis for persuasion. *Thus persuasion in public address is defined as the process of securing acceptance of an idea, or an action, by connecting it favorably with the listener's attitudes, beliefs, and desires.* This definition, which does not preclude the use of evidence and reasoning, acknowledges that we must persuade those whom logic alone cannot command. In reference to our definition let us also point out that the listener himself actually provides the motivations; the persuader's function is to channel them into support for his proposition.

As we have done with other elements in the speaker-audience relationship, we will summarize a sample of recent research that bears upon motivation. We should, however, make clear our understanding of how logic and reasoning are related to persuasion; for it is often assumed that the two are incompatible and that a speaker must depend either upon rational or emotional appeals. One may deal with this erroneous assumption in two ways.

In the first place, one of the elemental desires of humans is to be rational. Indeed, some persons become quite emotional if they are publicly accused of being irrational. Because men want to be rational, they seek to rationalize and find socially acceptable reasons for behavior that will satisfy their basic drives. As William Jennings Bryan observed, "it is a poor mind that can't fix up good reasons for doing what it wants to do!" We think it is a mark of the progress of civilization that men do prefer to believe, and to have their friends and associates assume, that they always behave on the basis of sound reasoning. Brigance constructed a theory (1931) about the genetic development of persuasion that puts the matter this way: primitive man relied first upon *authority*, then upon *experience*, as determinants of his behavior; only the man of an advanced culture, alert and intellectually aggressive, shows behavior that is also shaped by *reason*. Not only is this development apparent in the history of the race, it is also observable in the life of an individual: as a child, he behaves in response to authority; later he incorporates experience; and still later he puts reason into his patterns of action. In sum, we believe that a persuader who includes rational arguments in his speech is tapping an important motivation in his listener.

In the second place, no speech, we believe, depends solely either upon logical or upon emotional appeals. This conclusion is buttressed by our examination of the very experiments designed to test the separate effects of the two. In many studies the speech variable described as "logical" appears to be a persuasive speech, but with a minimum of connotative language that necessarily creates visual images or carries emotional overtones. Yet even the remaining argumentative discourse of, say, the formal debater, still asks support

for propositions on the grounds that they are practical, desirable, and benefi-
cial. The mere addition to such a speech, on the other hand, of "loaded language" does not eliminate the partitioning and ordering of arguments, which
are parts of the logical structures of any discourse.

In short, while decisions based upon the consideration of evidence and
argument are likely, we believe, to be better than those made under the spell
of overwhelming emotion, we maintain that emotional appeals may properly
be—and inevitably are—used to reinforce evidence and argument. This conclusion is the burden of pertinent research studies. They only substantiate the
axiomatic statement made years ago by Harry A. Overstreet (1925, p. 48)
that "no appeal to a reason that is not also an appeal to a want is ever effective." Indeed, many of us have a great want for others to appeal to our reason.

We turn now to brief summaries of representative investigations of motivation. Collins (1924) reported on the interaction of logical and emotional
appeals in four persuasive speeches. The most effective was the speech containing logical arguments, each followed by a short motive appeal. Less effective
were speeches developed by an extended logical appeal, or an extended logical
appeal followed by an extended emotional appeal. In an elaborate experiment,
which compared the effects of logical and emotional appeals as well as their
presentation orally, and in writing, Knower (1935) found "logical and persuasive speeches" are equally effective, and oral presentations produce consistently greater attitude shifts than written ones.

In studies by Menefee and Grannenberg (1940) and Millson (1932), it
was concluded that a predominantly emotional approach is more effective.
Some questions are implicitly raised about these findings, however, by an experiment designed to discover whether listeners are able to distinguish between
intellectual and emotional appeals in speeches they hear. Ruechelle (1958) reported that audiences could not dichotomize or classify, in speeches they hear,
persuasive materials as emotional or intellectual in content. Further, these
listeners made evaluations based mainly on general impressions, less on content, and still less on delivery.

In terms of the effect of emotive materials on listener comprehension and
recall, Matthews (1947) found that paired speeches containing "loaded" and
"unloaded" language are equally effective in promoting retention. Pence
(1954) discovered that emotionally loaded argument stimulates recall; he did
not compare, however, its effects with that of nonemotional argument.

We have already reported research upon certain other matters related
to motivation. In discussing interest, for example, we said that previous acquaintance with the subject of a speech apparently motivates greater interest
in it; we described the apparent effects of the prestige and ethical appeal in
establishing a speaker's influence upon his audience. In treating the stereotyped stimulus, we noted the listener's tendency to respond to it. Here we
cite one study of many to demonstrate the operation of this essentially non-
rational behavior. From an attitude test Hartmann (1936) found that his sub-

jects were generally favorable to such collectivist policies as public ownership of industry and national resources. But when these same policies were presented with stereotyped labels to indicate that they were socialistic or communistic, most of the subjects shifted to opposite positions.

A skillful persuader recognizes the potency of his listener's motivations when they can be linked to his speech purpose. How does he tap these resources? *First*, he considers whether he can show that the adoption of his proposal (or the acquisition of the information he offers) will satisfy fundamental wants, needs, or interests of his audience. If he identifies any such relationships, he includes in his speech repeated references to them. *Second*, he appraises the general beliefs of his listeners and their probable attitudes toward his proposition. In planning his speech, he attempts to integrate his thesis with the established beliefs of his listeners and devise ways to reinforce their favorable attitudes while breaking down hostile ones. *Third*, he inventories his stock of available evidence and argument. For his speech content he selects from it, on the basis of his analysis of their basic motivations, beliefs, and attitudes, material best suited to persuade his hearers. *Fourth*, he lists those emotionally loaded words and stereotypes to which his particular audience is likely to respond favorably, and those to which it will respond negatively. In phrasing his speech he makes free use of the first list when referring to his proposal or to those who already support it, and draws from the second list when talking about the opposition.

Perhaps only in a textbook on public speaking should one expect to find a detailed statement about ethical practices in employing motivational appeals. But it is pertinent here to note that most discussions of the ethics of persuasion are essentially elaborations of Aristotle's view that "sophistical dialectic, or sophistical speaking, is made so, not by the faculty, but by the moral purpose." One psychologist, Robert E. Merton (1948, p. 186) makes this distinction: "Appeals to sentiments within the context of relevant information and knowledge are basically different from appeals to sentiment which blur and obscure this knowledge." Appeals of the first type he approves, but not those of the second.

Assuring Learning and Remembering

Those who carefully prepare and deliver speeches naturally hope their listeners will comprehend and retain what they hear. Inexperienced speakers soon discover, however, that facts and opinions will not "speak for themselves." What they wish an audience to understand and recall must be presented in such a way as to make these processes as congenial as possible. Herbert Spencer (1907, p. 273) described the problem in terms of "mental economy" for the listener: "To so present ideas that they may be apprehended with the *least possible mental effort*, is the desideratum. . . ." His assumption that the listener has a limited amount of perceptive capacity available at any given moment is supported by the observations of Hyman and Sheatsley (1947) on selectivity in learning.

The numerous studies cited thus far report substantial shifts in audience opinion after the hearing of persuasive speeches. In each instance some degree of comprehension (learning) must precede each change. Remembering, when measured in these studies, continues for as much as nine weeks, but regression toward the original position is almost always discernible. In one study, however, Hovland, et al. (1949, pp. 182–200), discovered that "changes in opinion of a general rather than specific nature may show increasing effects [i.e., even greater strength] with the lapse of time."

After reviewing a number of studies on opinion change, Hovland, Janis, and Kelley (1953, p. 92) concluded that "attention, comprehension, and acceptance probably determine, to a very large extent, the degree of persistence of the opinion changes induced by a communication." Each of the basic, functional psychological factors in communication is, we claim, important in learning and remembering. Unless a listener's attention is focused, he can not perceive; if his interest lags, he will not be alert; and, without being motivated, he may not care. Beyond focusing attention, maintaining interest, and providing motivation, what can a speaker do to help his hearers comprehend and retain what he says?

To begin with, the speaker can study the conditions for optimum effectiveness in listening. At least for the presentation of informational materials, as in a college lecture, Brown (1959) found the listener's "anticipatory set" correlates closely to his comprehension. In his investigation Brown prefaced his experimental speeches with brief remarks to indicate the general nature and significance of their content, and thus shaped audience expectations. Significantly, these preliminary orientations aided good as well as poor listeners.

In a more comprehensive study of factors in listening, Nichols (1948) tested the comprehension of student subjects after hearing lectures in such fields as literature, economics, and biology. On the average they comprehended only 68 per cent of the materials on which they were tested. After studying correlations of effectiveness in comprehending with thirty-three possibly influential factors, Nichols established fourteen significantly positive ones. Among them are some over which a speaker can have no control, such as the hearer's intelligence, vocabulary, and physical fatigue. Also significant, however, are five factors of which a speaker can take advantage by deliberately adapting, organizing, emphasizing, and delivering his materials: ability to make inferences, ability to structuralize a speech (that is, to see the organizational plan and the connection of the main points), ability to listen for main ideas as opposed to specific facts, ability to see significance in the subject discussed, and audibility of the speaker.

Some specific techniques for making the adjustments called for by Nichols' findings are suggested by what we know about the importance, in the learning process, of selectivity, categorizing, suggestion, and impressiveness. By categorizing different objects, persons, and qualities discriminably, a speaker can, for example, assist his listeners in distinguishing main ideas. The formulation of generalizations helps the listener to cluster pertinent bits of evidence. The use of positive suggestion guides the listener in drawing correct inferences and understanding their significance. Various means of gaining impressiveness may emphasize the total plan of organization in a speech as well as units within it. Among these reinforcement techniques are repetition of key ideas, placement to reveal the primacy or recency of significant material, and variation of vocal and physical actions to reflect the speaker's judgment of the relative importance of what he is saying.

Constructing the Speech

Here we report on research studies relating to the speaker's threefold task after he has selected both the general subject and specific purpose of his communication—namely, how he can develop the substance, structure and style of his speech.

The public speaker who turns to psychological research for advice on kinds and quantities of substantive material to use in addressing information-seeking or conversional audiences will be disappointed. This is a matter that must largely be determined by coordinating a knowledge of the general psychology of public address with an analysis of the specific audience. We have already commented, for example, on the studies of logical versus emotional speech content: assuming that the two can be discriminated, both seem to be of about equal value. During World War II government agencies found it desirable to obtain some form of quantitative measurement of enemy broadcasts, and methodologies for content analysis of many forms of communication were subsequently developed (Berelson, 1954). These analyses, however, are largely concerned with categorizing and determining the frequency of various themes or lines of argument as they appear in propaganda materials. While the same techniques were applied to discover various rhetorical practices of individual speakers (Chester, 1949; Miller and Villarreal, 1945), the studies proved to be descriptive only and do not suggest principles to be applied generally.

Other specialized quantitative measuring techniques, such as the type-token ratio analyses ("types" are different words and "tokens" are the total number of words in a given communication) also provided descriptive studies of language usage (Fairbanks, 1944; Lerea, 1956), but are not of present value for public speakers. One of the few experimental studies dealing with varieties of proof materials was done by Grasham (1951). In speaking primarily to inform, he found, quotations or assertions are more effective means of support than specific instances. In speaking to persuade, supporting quotations are most effective, assertions less so, and analogies relatively ineffective. A study by Lull (1940) tested the effectiveness of humor in persuasive speeches; he found humorous and non-humorous speeches on the same topic about equal in interestingness and convincingness. Further research of this nature, and experimenting with a range of proof materials, may be fruitful in deriving principles applicable to development of speech content.

The first question concerning the structure of a speech is whether a formal overall organization is essential for retention or persuasion, and if so, what kind. Using relatively short speeches on current social and political topics, and varying the "normal" order by transposing introductions, conclusions, transitions, and the sequence of main arguments, Smith (1951), and Beighley (1952, 1954) found little difference in effects upon audiences. Gulley and Berlo (1956) organized similar speeches into climax, anticlimax, and pyramidal sequences of arguments according to their assertion-strength, both in the overall structure and within separate units of the speech, and found no statistically significant advantage for any one pattern. Only in a study by Thistlethwaite, et al. (1955) is a well-organized speech found to be more effective than a poorly organized one. In this study however, the speaker's explicit drawing or not drawing of a conclusion from the argument of the speech is also measured and to the substantial advantage of the former, even in cases of poorly organized speeches. The explicit statement of a speech goal may thus be more significant than how it is reached.

One of the investigators, Raymond G. Smith (1958, pp. 106–7), makes this summary comment on studies that experiment with speech structure: "Evidence has been gradually accumulating to indicate that speech organization, so far as its effect on the audience is concerned, is unimportant for many if not all speeches, both for amount of information remembered and persuasive effect." He speculates, however, that the importance of organization undoubtedly varies with the length and difficulty of the speech: "Audiences will be unable to remember the main ideas of long speeches unless the organization and transitions are clear. Likewise, unless such relationships are clear, difficult material will not be grasped."

From these and other investigations of effective speechmaking, distinctions can be made between well and poorly organized speeches. The overall criteria are suggested by these questions: Does the introduction orient the listener toward the subject, both in terms of its general nature and its relationship to listener needs and desires? Does the body of the speech consist of identifiable, separate but coherent, arguments for the speaker's proposition; are there clear topic sentences for each one, and transitions that show relationships among them? Does the conclusion summarize the arguments that support the proposition and motivate listeners to want to accept it as a means of satisfying their needs and desires? Detailed criteria applicable to the organization of supporting arguments involve other factors such as primacy vs. recency and climax vs. anti-climax.

A so-called "Law of Primacy" in the placement of materials in persuasive communications was first stated by Lund (1925), and this position of importance was verified in a later study by Jersild (1928). Using a wider range of subject matter and more sophisticated techniques of control and measurement, however, subsequent investigators, Berlo and Gulley (1957), Ehrensberger (1945), and Tannenbaum (1954) support a "Law of Recency" for the most effective placement of important materials. A fair comment is that the conclusion of a speech appears to be the position of the greatest potency for retention, but that either the conclusion or the introduction is superior to the middle.

Rhetoricians have long classified major argumentative units of a speech as strong, average, or weak in inducing belief-strength, but they have differed about whether arguments are most effectively presented in climax (from weakest to strongest) or anticlimax (from strongest to weakest) order. This aspect of speech structure has been studied both for its significance in retention and in attitude change. Sponberg (1946) found that an anticlimax order induced greater retention. In his test speeches, however, Sponberg progressively allotted more time for the presentation of weak, average, and strong arguments; he thereby introduced a variable of mass that may have been more influential than the variable of position. Later studies report no significant differences between climax and anticlimax order: Berlo and Gulley (1957), Gilkinson, et al. (1954), and Thistlethwaite, et al. (1956).

When considered in terms of effect upon attitude change, the accumulated evidence from the studies just cited, and from a study by Gulley and Berlo (1956), indicates that, while climax order appears to shift more opinions than anticlimax, this order is not significantly advantageous. As with the primacy-recency factor, no firm value can at present be ascribed to either principle of order; each has its merits. A decision on which one to use is thus best made on other grounds, such as the familiarity or complexity of the materials presented. In public address situations in which two or more speakers present opposite points of view, as in a debate or a symposium, two studies by Cromwell (1950–54) demonstrated that climax order (i.e., weaker speeches, in argument strength and organization, first; stronger speeches, second) has more effect upon initial attitude shift and upon persistence of that shift.

A substantially different aspect of structure was studied by Cohen (1957), who found that speech material is more effectively arranged when appeals to and arousal of audience needs are made first, and then followed by propositions alleged to satisfy those needs, rather than in the opposite sequence. When a single speaker has two sets of conclusions to present, one consonant with the desires and motives of his audience, and the other in conflict, McGuire (1957) concluded that greater opinion change was induced by presenting the more desirable propositions first. Both of these studies may be interpreted as supporting the significance of the primacy position and the anticlimax order, at least in the sense that in each case the most effective speeches present first what seems to be most necessary or desirable from the view of the audience.

The speaker's third task in constructing his communication is to choose the specific language forms to express the substance. While the importance of style in speechmaking has been stressed by the rhetoricians for over two thousand years, substantial objective studies of it have been undertaken only within the past few decades. As Cherry (1957, p. 108) noted, style is now "describable partly in statistical terms, by the comparative extent, richness, or poverty of vocabulary, by the syllabic length of words, the relative frequencies of sentences of different lengths, and by different grammatical structures." A good portion even of this research has been based upon analyses of written style in order to develop predictive formulas of "readability," such as those of Rudolf Flesch.

In developing approaches to the study of speech style, such as Ewbank's (1931), researchers assume that significant differences exist between spoken and written styles and that the principles governing the effectiveness of one do not necessarily apply to the other. Some studies, such as the early one by Borchers (1936), have thus concentrated on quantifying those differences. Studies of speech intelligibility received an impetus from the conditions of modern warfare, and the collection made under Army auspices and edited by Black (1946) has encouraged subsequent researchers. Primarily, however, these investigations have centered on such matters as the relation to intelligibility of loudness, pitch, articulation, and phonetic factors.

The single major study of the effect of specific word choice upon intelligibility in public address was made by Thomas (1956). Two speeches parallel in subject, substance, and structure were constructed for an experiment involving 2000 student subjects. One contained a maximum, the other a minimum, of those types of words, phrases, syntactical structures, and special language forms and usages characteristic of oral style. The major finding was that the use of certain elements of oral style definitely increased by about 10 per cent the amount of information imparted. This potency of oral over non-oral style was significant whether the listeners heard one or the other of two speakers involved, whether they heard a live speaker or a tape recording, and whether or not they were motivated to listen by being told they were participating in an experiment and would be tested after hearing the speech.

The eight specific types of oral style found in Thomas' study (1956) to contribute to intelligibility and listener comprehension were: specific words, colorful words, informality and simplicity of vocabulary, figurative language, personalization, informality of syntax, questions, and direct quotations. While these findings constitute specific direction for public speakers, additional research is needed, particularly to discover whether the same stylistic elements that appear to influence listener comprehension are equally efficient in changing listener attitudes.

Our previous discussions of functional psychological factors yield additional conclusions applicable to style. Recalling that listeners cannot give continuous attention, the speaker must, in style as in everything else, employ the attention values of change, intensity, striking quality, repetition, and definiteness of form. Indeed, when these values are compared with those oral stylistic devices recommended by Thomas, a reasonable causal relationship is apparent. Of these values it is likely that change is the most significant. Common in our own experiences, and in research literature, are these principles about language usage by the persuasive speaker: (a) language that requires the least effort to comprehend is best understood, (b) a speaker's words are always interpreted in the light of the listener's own experiences, (c) meanings are attached more easily to concrete and specific word symbols than to general and abstract ones.

Delivering the Speech

The culmination of the speaker's behavior is the oral delivery of his speech to an audience. Quantitative studies of delivery appeared fairly early in the literature on speech behavior, perhaps because of the, now fortunately past, high emphasis upon the "elocutionary" aspects of speaking. The more significant spur to quantitative studies is probably the voice scientist's laboratory equipment which permits more precise measurement of various vocal attributes than was once possible for other factors in the total speech process. Here we select a small sample from that literature in order to illuminate important topics.

Investigators are in substantial agreement that vocal skill (ability to be heard and understood) is positively related to the listener's comprehension, as is illustrated by Beighley's (1952) report. To be sure, most studies have measured gross impressions rather than the specific effects of variation in pitch, force, rate, and quality. Of these four, the effect of variable rate is most often investigated. Goldstein (1940) experimented with variations in reading aloud from 100 to 328 words per minute and found a consistent but not statistically conclusive decline in listener comprehension as the rate was increased, and Harwood (1955) reached a similiar conclusion. The same results were found in a study by Nelson (1948), but he also discovered that when subjects report their interest in the communications they hear, a rate between 175 and 200 words per minute is most satisfactory. In a study of modes of emphasis Jersild (1928) found a negative effect of slow speech on retention, but Ehrensberger (1945) discovered a positive one; both agree that a pause before a word or phrase to be emphasized significantly aids retention. In a later investigation Diehl, et al. (1955) altered recorded speech by reducing pauses in such a way as to vary the rate between 126 and 172 words per minute. It was found that such alterations do not interfere with listener comprehension nor do they significantly change listener ratings of the quality of the speaker's delivery.

A substantial number of studies which consider delivery factors other than voice, such as gestures and facial expressions, compare identical communications by live speakers, by recorded speakers, and in printed form, and establish the superiority of the live speaker in changing listener attitudes (Knower,

1936; Utterback and Harding, 1955; Wilke, 1934). The chief difference between live and recorded speeches, of course, is that visible as well as audible cues are given to the listener.

Although the differences between the live speaker and the recorded speech in affecting attitudes ranged, in the investigations just cited, as high as 20 per cent in favor of the former, the only study of the specific influence of gestures upon listener comprehension (Gauger, 1952) showed higher mean scores for those who saw and heard the speaker, but not statistically significant ones. The same measured advantage for a speech delivered with gestures and an identical speech without gestures was found in this investigation. In regard to the specific impact of facial expressions intended to express various emotional attitudes of the speaker, we know only that Dusenbury and Knower (1938) found listeners able to discriminate among as many as eleven different ones. No one has yet established, however, a correlation between the ability to make this correct identification of facial expressions of speakers and changes in listener attitudes because of such identification.

One investigation appears to contradict the conclusions concerning the significance of bodily action in public speaking. In his survey of general audiences, Clark (1951) found that only 27 per cent regarded "gesture," 46 per cent "co-ordinated bodily movement," and 54 per cent "animation" as essential to good speaking. While these findings seem to depreciate the positive effects of a speaker's action, they must be considered in the light of the conclusion of Monroe, et al. (1936) that listeners tend to respond and to evaluate speakers in terms of overall impressions rather than upon discrete elements in the speaking process.

Clark's audiences, it must be noted, reported only what they thought influenced them, not necessarily what did influence them. On this point such studies as Bettinghaus' (1961) are pertinent. In his investigation of listener shifts of attitudes toward congruous positions for various elements, including the speaker, his delivery, and his speech topic, he found that audiences do tend to balance their perceptions and, specifically, that hearers make their attitudes toward delivery congruous with their attitudes toward the speaker. The components of delivery rated in this study were: pitch, loudness, resonance, rate pronunciation, articulation, and vocal variety. In these terms, Bettinghaus concluded, "effective" delivery produced a more favorable shift of attitude toward the speaker than "ineffective" delivery. Dietrich's (1946) study of two different types of vocal delivery compared attitude shifts resulting from "dynamic" (rapid, dramatic, enthusiastic, and formal) with "conversational" (relaxed, quiet, and informal) to the significant advantage of the latter, both in the immediate situation and on a post-test two weeks later.

Any conclusion about the role of delivery in public address must incorporate the findings of this sampling of a large number of studies indicating that even though listeners may not always be able to identify the separate elements of delivery, their reactions to effective use of voice and bodily action are measurable in terms of comprehension and attitude changes. These findings support the rhetorician's axiom that a good speech, well-delivered, is more influential than the same speech poorly delivered.

A final comment should be made on listener reactions to one further variable in delivery: reading a speech from a manuscript versus speaking extemporaneously with no more than reference notes. The earliest objective study of this factor was by Moore (1919) who read and delivered extemporaneously the same materials to college classes and reported that the extempore method resulted in a 36 per cent greater retention. As Young (1958, p. 306) concludes from other studies "audiences, except highly specialized ones, react more sympathetically and with more attention to papers read informally or to speeches delivered freely than to more formal presentations." Because variety has an almost constantly positive effect upon listener reactions, the reading aloud from a manuscript, which is almost inherently more static, is understandably less effective than lively, direct, and extemporaneous delivery. The nature of the content of the speech is, of course, an important variable: the more highly technical it is, the less it lends itself to free extemporization. In any case, if a speaker recites long quotations or involved statistical data from memory, the listener may be less inclined to assume his accuracy than if he reads such material from a manuscript or a note card. Indeed, the speaker's ethos may be strengthened by this apparent concern for precision.

Bibliography

1. Beighley, K. C. "An Experimental Study of the Effect of Four Speech Variables on Listener Comprehension." *SM* 19(1952) :249–58.
2. ———. "An Experimental Study of the Effect of Three Speech Variables on Listener Comprehension." *SM* 21(1954) :248–53.
3. Berelson, B. "Content Analysis." In Lindzey, G. (Ed.) *Handbook of Social Psychology*. Reading, Mass.: Addison-Wesley, 1954, I, 488–522.
4. Berlo, D. K. & H. E. Gulley. "Some Determinants of the Effect of Oral Communication in Producing Attitude Change and Learning." *SM* 24(1957) :10–20.
5. Bettinghaus, E. P. "The Operation of Congruity in an Oral Communication Situation." *SM* 28(1961) :131–42.
6. Black, J. W. "Studies in Speech Intelligibility: A Program of War-Time Research." *SM* 12(1946) :1–68.
7. Borchers, G. L. "An Approach to the Problem of Oral Style." *QJS* 22(1936) : 114–17.
8. Brigance, W. N. "A Genetic Approach to Persuasion." *QJS* 17(1931) :329–39.
9. Brown, C. T. "An Experimental Diagnosis of Thinking on Controversial Issues." *SM* 17(1950) :370–77.

10. Cathcart, R. S. "An Experimental Study of the Relative Effectiveness of Four Methods of Presenting Evidence." *SM* 22(1955) :227–33.

11. Cherry, C. *On Human Communication.* New York: Technology Press of Massachusetts Institute of Technology; Wiley, 1957.

12. Chester, G. "What Constitutes Irresponsibility on the Air?—A Case Study." *POQ* 13(1949) :73–82.

13. Clark, W. K. "A Survey of Certain Audience Attitudes toward Commonly Taught Standards of Public Speaking." *SM* 18(1951) :62–9.

14. Cohen, A. R. "Need for Cognition and Order of Communication as Determinants of Opinion Change." In Hovland, C. I. (Ed.), *The Order of Presentation in Persuasion.* New Haven: Yale University Press, 1957, pp. 79–97.

15. Collins, G. R. "The Relative Effectiveness of the Condensed and Extended Emotional Appeal." *QJS* 10(1924) :221–30.

16. Cromwell, H. "The Relative Effect on Audience Attitude of the First Versus the Second Argumentative Speech of a Series." *SM* 17(1950) :105–22.

17. ———. "The Persistency of the Effect on Audience Attitude of the First Versus the Second Argumentative Speech of a Series." *SM* 21(1954) :280–4.

18. Diehl, C. F., White, R. C., & Burk, K. W. "Rate and Communication." *SM* 26(1959) :229–32.

19. Dietrich, J. E. "The Relative Effectiveness of Two Modes of Radio Delivery in Influencing Attitudes." *SM* 13(1946) :58–66.

20. Dusenbury, D., & Knower, F. H. "Experimental Studies of the Symbolism of Action and Voice—I. A Study of the Specificity of Meaning in Facial Expression." *QJS* 24(1936) :424–36.

21. Edwards, A. L. "Political Frames of Reference as a Factor Influencing Recognition." *JASP* 36(1941) :34–50.

22. Ehrensberger, R. "The Relative Effectiveness of Certain Forms of Emphasis in Public Speaking." *SM* 12(1945) :94–111.

23. Ewbank, H. L. "Four Approaches to the Study of Speech Style." *QJS* 17(1931) : 458–65.

24. Ewing, T. N. "A Study of Certain Factors Involved in Changes of Opinion." *JSP* 16(1942) :63–88.

25. Fairbanks, H. "Studies on Language Behavior: II. The Quantitative Differentiation of Samples of Spoken Language." *PM* 56(1944) :17–38.

26. Gauger, P. W. "The Effect of Gesture and the Presence or Absence of the Speaker on Listening Comprehension of Eleventh and Twelfth Grade High School Pupils." *SM* 19(1952) :116–7 (Abstract).

27. Gilkinson, H., Paulson, S. F., & Sikkink, D. E. "Conditions Affecting the Communication of Controversial Statements in Connected Discourse: Forms of Presentation and the Political Frame of Reference of the Listener." *SM* 20(1953) : 253–60.

28. ———. "Effects of Order and Authority in an Argumentative Speech." *QJS* 40(1954) :183–92.

29. Goldstein, H. *Reading and Listening Comprehension at Various Controlled Rates.* New York: Teachers College, Columbia University, 1940.

30. Grasham, J. A. "An Experimental Study to Determine the Relative Effectiveness of Various 'Forms of Support.' " *SM* 18(1952) :122–3 (Abstract).

31. Grimes, W. H. "The Mirth Experience in Public Address." *SM* 22(1955) :243–55.
32. Gulley, H. E. & Berlo, D. K. "Effect of Intercellular and Intracellular Speech Structure on Attitude Change and Learning." *SM* 23(1956) :288–97.
33. Harms, L. S. "Listener Judgments of Status Cues in Speech." *QJS* 48(1961) : 164–8.
34. Hartman, G. W. "The Contradictions between the Feeling-Tone of Political Party Names and Public Response to Their Platforms." *JSP* 7(1936) :366–55.
35. Harwood, K. "Listenability and Rate of Presentation." *SM* 22(1955) :57–9.
36. Hovland, C. I., Lumsdaine, A. A., & Sheffield, F. D. *Experiments on Mass Communication.* Princeton: Princeton University Press, 1949.
37. ———, & Mandell, W. "An Experimental Comparison of Conclusion-Drawing by the Communicator and by the Audience." *JASP* 47(1952) :581–8.
38. ———, Janis, I. L., & Kelley, H. H. *Communication and Persuasion.* New Haven: Yale University Press, 1953.
39. Hyman, H. H., & Sheatsley, P. B. "Some Reasons Why Information Campaigns Fail." *POQ* 11(1947) :412–23.
40. Jersild, A. T. "Modes of Emphasis in Public Speaking." *JAP* 12(1928) :611–20.
41. Jones, M. R. (Ed.) *Nebraska Symposium on Motivation.* Lincoln: University of Nebraska Press, 1953–61.
42. Karraker, M. E. "An Evaluation of the Influence of Interest and 'Set' on Listening Effectiveness in the Basic Communication Class." *SM* 19(1952) :117–8 (Abstract).
43. Knower, F. H. "A Study of the Effect of Oral Argument on Changes of Attitude." *JSP* 6(1935) :315–47.
44. ———. "A Study of the Effect of Printed Argument on Change of Attitude." *JASP* 30(1936) :522–32.
45. Kretsinger, E. A. "An Experimental Study of Gross Bodily Movement as an Index to Audience Interest." *SM* 19(1952) :244–8.
46. Lerea, L. "A Preliminary Study of the Verbal Behavior of Speech Fright." *SM* 23(1956) :229–33.
47. Ludlum, T. S. "Effects of Certain Techniques of Credibility upon Audience Attitude." *SM* 25(1958) :278–84.
48. Lull, P. E. "The Effectiveness of Humor in Persuasive Speeches." *SM* 7(1940) : 26–40.
49. Lund, F. H. "The Psychology of Belief." *JASP* 20(1925) :63–112, 174–224.
50. Lyle, H. M. "An Experimental Study of Certain Aspects of the Electromagnetic Movement Meter as a Criterion to Audience Attention." *SM* 20(1953) :126 (Abstract).
51. McGuire, W. J. "Order of Presentation in 'Conditioning' Persuasiveness." In Hovland, C. I. (Ed.), *The Order of Presentation in Persuasion.* New Haven: Yale University Press, 1957, pp. 98–114.
52. Marple, C. H. "The Comparative Suggestibility of Three Age Levels to the Suggestion of Group versus Expert Opinion." *JSP* 4(1933) :176–86.
53. Matthews, J. "The Effect of Loaded Language on Audience Comprehension of Speeches." *SM* 14(1947) :176–86.
54. Menefee, S. C., & Granneberg, A. G. "Propaganda and Opinions on Foreign Policy." *JSP* 11(1940) :393–404.

55. Merton, R. E. *Mass Persuasion*. New York: Harper & Row, 1946.
56. Miller, N. E., & Villarreal, J. J. "The Use of Clichés by Four Contemporary Speakers." *QJS* 31(1945) :151–5.
57. Millson, W. A. D. "Problems in Measuring Audience Reactions." *QJS* 18(1932) : 621–37.
58. Monroe, A. H., Remmers, H. H., & Venemann-Lyle, E. "Measuring the Effectiveness of Public Speech in a Beginning Course." *Purdue University Studies in Higher Education*, No. 29, 1936.
59. Moore, H. T. "The Attention Value of Lecturing without Notes." *JEP* 10(1919) : 467–9.
60. Nelson, H. E. "The Effect of Variation of Rate on the Recall by Radio Listeners of 'Straight' Newscasts." *SM* 15(1948) :173–80.
61. Nichols, R. G. "Factors in Listening Comprehension." *SM* 15(1948) :154–63.
62. Overstreet, H. A. *Influencing Human Behavior*. New York: Norton, 1925.
63. Paulson, S. F. "The Effects of the Prestige of the Speaker and Acknowledgment of Opposing Arguments on Audience Retention and Shift of Opinion." *SM* 21(1954) :267–71.
64. Pence, O. L. "Emotionally Loaded Argument: Its Effectiveness in Stimulating Recall." *QJS* 40(1954) :272–6.
65. Ruechelle, R. C. "An Experimental Study of Audience Recognition of Emotional and Intellectual Appeals in Persuasion." *SM* 25(1958) :49–58.
66. Schachter, S. "Deviation, Rejection and Communication." *JASP* 46(1951) : 190–207.
67. Smith, R. G. "An Experimental Study of the Effect of Speech Organization upon Attitudes of College Students." *SM* 18(1951) :292–301.
68. ———. *Principles of Public Speaking*. New York: Ronald, 1958.
69. Spencer, H. "The Philosophy of the Style." In Cooper, L. (Ed.), *Theories of Style*. New York: Macmillan, 1907, pp. 270–311.
70. Sponberg, H. "The Relative Effectiveness of Climax and Anti-Climax Order in an Argumentative Speech." *SM* 13(1946) :35–44.
71. Tannenbaum, P. H. "Effect of Serial Position on Recall of Radio News Stories." *JQ* 31(1954) :319–23.
72. Thistlethwaite, D. L., deHaan, H., & Kamentzky, J. "The Effects of 'Directive' and 'Non-Directive' Communication Procedures on Attitudes." *JASP* 51(1955) : 3–12.
73. ———, Kamentzky, J., & Schmidt, H. "Factors Influencing Attitude Change through Refutative Communications." *SM* 23(1956) :14–25.
74. Thomas, G. L. "Oral Style and Intelligibility." *SM* 23(1956) :46–54.
75. Thompson, W. N. "A Study of the Factors Considered by Students in Evaluating Public Discussion." *SM* 20(1953) :268–72.
76. Utterback, W. E., & Harding, H. F. "Some Factors Conditioning Response to Argument." *SM* 22(1955) :303–8.
77. Weiss, W. "Opinion Congruence with a Negative Source on One Issue as a Factor Influencing Agreement on Another Issue." *JASP* 54(1957) :180–6.
78. Wilke, W. H. "An Experimental Comparison of the Speech, the Radio, and the Printed Page as Propaganda Devices." *AP* 25(1934) :No. 169.
79. Young, K. *Social Psychology*. 3rd ed.; New York: Appleton-Century-Crofts, 1958.

Questions for Analysis

1. How does this statement prescribe the task of the persuasive speaker: "Attitude changes always go in directions that will increase their harmony with existing listener frames of reference or sets of expectations"? Describe effects you have observed of advance publicity on the prestige of a speaker. Characterize generally the optimal introduction for a persuasive speaker. Why do you think "credibility was greater for straight-forward argumentative speeches"?

2. Identify three situations in which modern persuasive speakers face relatively hostile audiences. How does each speaker stay near the group norm and assert correspondence of views? How does he assure the audience that it has some familiarity with his subject? What does it mean to animate content as well as delivery? Apply this observation: "Listeners want enough novelty to offset monotony, just as they want enough familiarity to maintain stability." Illustrate the portrayal of conflict in both narrative and expository modes. What does the persuasive speaker intend to achieve by portraying conflict?

3. What is the importance to an understanding of ethical persuasion of Auer's reminder that "we must persuade those whom logic alone cannot command"? Of what special pertinence is this concept today? Illustrate the truth that the listener "provides the motivations" and that the persuader "channels them into support for his proposition." Why should the persuasive speaker know how emotional appeals *reinforce* evidence and argument? From your observations of contemporary persuasion cite examples of emotional appeals both "properly" and "improperly" used. How were "motivational resources" tapped in your examples? Prove this: "Appeals to sentiments within the context of relevant information and knowledge are basically different from appeals to sentiment which blur and obscure this knowledge."

4. What does it mean to the persuasive speaker that "the listener has a limited amount of perceptive capacity available at any given moment"? How does the speaker use this assumption? Why is it difficult to assess the role of *substance* in persuasive speaking? Suggest why primacy-recency and climax-anti-climax alone appear to be important to *structure* in persuasive speaking. Why should *style* matter more to persuasive speaking than to informative speaking? How might you test this proposition? Refer to the "types of oral style" designated by Thomas.

5. What does this statement mean to the persuasive speaker's consideration of *delivery:* "Listeners tend to respond and to evaluate speakers in terms of over-all impressions rather than upon discrete elements in the speaking process"? How is the finding that "conversational" delivery shifts more attitudes than "dynamic" delivery related to congruity of attitude toward delivery and attitude toward speaker? Does this mean a speaker favored by his audience may safely deliver his speech indifferently? Explain. On the basis of your reading thus far in this section estimate the relative significance of delivery, message, and prestige.

24

The Substance of Rhetoric: Good Reasons

Karl R. Wallace

Rhetorical theorists have always recognized that speeches have content and substance, and that the content of a particular speech is derived from the setting and occasion. Yet unlike classical rhetoricians who presented systems of invention, modern writers who offer theories of rhetoric are unclear and uncertain what to say about the materials of discourse. They will include in their theories statements about methods, principles, techniques, and styles of discourse; that is, they talk of the forms and the handling of ideas and are mostly silent about the substance of utterance. Perhaps they are silent for three main reasons. Under the influence of structural linguistics, rhetoricians may uncritically believe that language is like the symbols of music and mathematics—empty and devoid of substantial meanings. Or they may overlook the full implication of Donald Bryant's reference to rhetoric as an art of adjusting ideas to people and people to ideas.[1] The notion of adjustment—and for that matter, adaptation—directs attention chiefly to acts of manipulation and treatment. It is easy to forget that one cannot engage in manipulation without manipulating something, and that speakers and audiences stand on common ground only through commonalities of meaning and partial identities of experience. If this simple fact is acknowledged, there always bobs up that old, bothersome question: With what ideas, with what materials do speakers adjust and adapt to their hearers? Finally, for the last century or so students of rhetoric seem to have been trapped into accepting a sort of scientific realism, or perhaps I might better say, a naive realism. The argument runs something

Karl R. Wallace is Professor of Speech, University of Massachusetts.

Reprinted by permission from *Quarterly Journal of Speech*, 49 (1963), 239-49.

[1] The point of view is fully expressed in Donald C. Bryant "Rhetoric; Its Functions and Its Scope," *QJS, XXXIX* (December, 1953) 401-424.

like this: Since man derives his substantial information and knowledge through his sensory apparatus and since the natural sciences have successfully claimed for themselves both the acquisition and interpretation of sensory materials, discourse is left with nothing to say about the real world that does not properly belong to the sciences. Furthermore, since the behavioral sciences and the disciplines of philosophy and ethics have asserted property rights over the study of human experience and conduct, rhetoric has nothing to say about the behavior of speakers and listeners that these sciences cannot say with greater reliability and authority. Ergo, the substance of discourse comes from finding the right scientific and historical facts and of consulting the right authority. To me this is very much like saying that rhetoric is nothing more than the art of framing information and of translating it into intelligible terms for the popular audience.

1.

My position is this. First, rhetorical theory must deal with the substance of discourse as well as with structure and style. Second, the basic materials of discourse are (1) ethical and moral values and (2) information relevant to these. Third, ethics deals with the theory of goods and values, and from ethics rhetoric can make adaptations that will result in a modern system of topics.

In developing these ideas we must try at the outset to indicate what we mean by *substance*. The concept has carried many meanings, but the ones that are relevant here may be suggested by calling attention to certain words as correlatives. On one side are *substance, matter, material, content,* and *subject matter*. On the other are *form, structure, order, arrangement, organization, shape,* and *figure*. The words on each side reveal overlapping meanings. This fact must be recognized, of course. But what is important is that the terms on one side are not fully intelligible in the absence of the terms on the other. The notion of form is useless without the notions of matter and material; the notions of order and arrangement are senseless without the notions of matter and substance—of something to be ordered and arranged. In every case we recognize the relationship of figure and shape to that which is figured and shaped, the relationship of form to that which is formed—to that which is material and substantial. In the same sets of words there is also lurking the idea of substratum—of that which stands under, of support. In this sense, form is inconceivable without something as its basis. One does not arrange and order bricks, or think of arranging or ordering them, without having bricks or the ideas thereof. One does not build a house without a foundation, nor an oration without spoken or written words and the meanings they carry.

In what sense, then, do we understand substance? An attempt to meet this question requires us to regard an utterance, a linguistic event, a speech, as an object. There are natural objects. These exist, or come into being, without the agency of man. They are the things of land and sea, vegetable and mineral. We say, depending upon our point of view, that natural objects are made by God, by Nature, or by some mysterious force. There are artificial objects, and these are said, in our language, to be man-made. Among these are language itself and whatever one makes with language—novels, poems, commands, instructions, laws, speeches, et cetera. If speeches are objects, rhetoric is related to speeches as theory is related to behavior. Since a theorist tries to explain the particular group of objects, events, and behaviors in which he is interested, a rhetorician endeavors to explain what speeches are, and this task involves his setting forth what speeches are about and how they come about. If speeches exhibit substance and materials—and it is nonsense to say they do not—the rhetorician must, among other things, characterize the substance of speeches, the materials of which they are made. Theories of rhetoric in the classical tradition, as we know, almost always said a good deal about the substance and materials of speeches. Under the heads Invention and Topics, they described the general material of speeches and their chief kinds, together with lines of argument that often recurred. Except for Kenneth Burke, the principal writers on modern rhetorical theory—e.g. I. A. Richards—neglect substance and concentrate on processes, methods, techniques, and effects. Most of our textbooks pay little attention to what speeches are about; rather, their point of view is pedagogical. They concentrate on how to make a speech and deliver it. I do not think this condition of affairs could long endure if rhetoric were to rediscover and reassert its concern with subject matter.

Rhetoric, then, ought to deal with the substance, the substratum or foundations of speeches. What is this stuff? In answer to this question, I shall offer three propositions. First, the underlying materials of speeches, and indeed of most human talk and discussions are assertions and statements that concern human behavior and conduct. They are prompted by situations and contexts that present us with choices and that require us to respond with appropriate decisions and actions. Second, such statements are usually called judgments and appraisals. They reflect human interests and values, and the nature of value-judgments and the ways of justifying them are the special, technical, and expert concern of ethics. Third, the appearance and use of value-judgments in practical discourse are the proper, although not the sole, concern of the theory and practice of rhetoric.

Probably most thoughtful persons will at once agree that the foundation materials of speeches are statements that are evoked by the need to make choices in order that we may act or get ready to act or to appraise our acts after their doing. Furthermore, choosing itself is a substantive act and the statement of a choice is a substantive statement. Rhetoricians will recall that the time-honored classifications of speeches are based upon the typical choice-situations that audiences confront. The deliberative or political kind of speech helps an audience decide what it ought to do, and the materials most often appearing are those that bear on the particular audience's ends and purposes and the means to those ends. More specifically, so Aristotle thought, these things give rise to considerations of what is good and evil and what is useful, and these again with respect to the problems of war and peace, of national defense, of taxation (or support of the state in relation to the citizen's purse), of the standard of living (or the welfare of the citizen), and of the making of laws and the good that laws can do. The forensic or legal speech helps a jury to decide upon the manner of treating a person who is accused of breaking the moral codes enshrined in law. What is justice in the case at hand? Is the man guilty or innocent? And if guilty, how should he be treated? The epideictic speech helps an audience to assess the ethics and morality of a person's actions. Whether the decision is to praise or blame him will depend upon whether his acts are judged virtuous, noble, right, and good. Evidently, then, large numbers of speeches employ statements whose content is ethical or moral, or they use language in a setting and in ways that logically imply ethical and moral ideas.

Still it may be asked whether there are not speeches in situations that have nothing to do with ethics and morality. What about discourse that is called informative, expository, or scientific?

We consider this question by pointing out that we often label a speech informative when in its proper context it is persuasive. Thomas Huxley's famous lecture, "On a Piece of Chalk," consists predominantly of factual sentences, yet to its English audiences in the 1870's it functioned as a plea for evolution. Much discourse and discussion that is thought of as didactic is probably persuasive in effect if not in intent. The character and bias of the state and nation function to select what is taught in the public schools. The teacher-learner relationship is accordingly less neutral and colorless than we think. Moreover, many teachers employ a method of learning that encourages students to think for themselves, to weigh and consider, to be intelligently appreciative and critical, to select and reject ideas and information that function indirectly, if not directly, to build attitudes and determine preferences. Furthermore, much newspaper discourse is in response to the widespread belief that knowledge is a good thing, and that certain kinds of materials and events are interesting, useful, and satisfying to readers, and other kinds are not. In brief, it would appear that expository speaking and writing recognizes choices and values that differ from those of persuasive discourse principally in that they are more remote and less apparent. So in saying that the materials and the substrata of speeches come about in response to contexts that present alternative possibilities, I want to include what is ordinarily thought of as informative utterance. First, much exposition is functionally persuasive, whether in intent or effect. This fact we have just remarked upon. Second, scientific discourse in itself cannot be utterly devoid of value. It owes its being to two assumptions: (1) knowledge in itself is a good thing, and (2) the information transmitted is accurate, reliable, valid, and true. Furthermore, scientific reporting of observations and experiments—and the criticism thereof—involves what a scientist did and did not do, how he did it and did not do it, and why he did it in one way rather than another. The scientist cannot escape choices whether he is addressing other scientists or a popular audience. His decisions are anchored in contexts governed by rules, conventions, and practices, whether they be those of the scientist or those of the non-scientist public.

2.

Although the basic substance of speeches comprises statements that are made when human beings must make choices, the consideration of such statements in their special and technical character is the proper concern of ethics. To support this assertion I must indicate what students of ethics today seem to be focusing on.[2] Despite differences in their special points of view and in the treatment of their material, they see the human being as he uses his reason in practical situations that involve choices and decision. Practical reason is revealed in judgments that guide man's conduct, i.e., judgments that are statements having to do with action, motives, feelings, emotions, attitudes, and values. They are responses to one of two fundamental kinds of questions: What shall I do or believe? What ought I to do?[3] Both Toulmin and Baier talk in terms that are familiar to every historian and theorist of rhetoric.[4] Practical reason, for example, appears in three types of behavior: deliberation, justification, and explanation. Deliberation uses reason prior to the act. Justification and explanation use reason after the act. When we justify, we praise or blame; we use terms like right and wrong, good and bad; in general we *appraise*. When we explain, we show what moved the agent and use terms untinctured by praise or censure. Because these three types of rational behavior are carried on almost exclusively in symbolic and linguistic terms, some writers tend to

[2]My chief informants have been Richard B. Brandt, *Ethical Theory: The Problems of Normative and Critical Ethics* (Englewood Cliffs, N. J., 1959) ; Kurt Baier, *The Moral Point of View: A Rational Basis of Ethics* (Ithaca, N. Y., 1958) ; Paul Edwards, *The Logic of Moral Discourse* (Glencoe, Ill., 1955) ; P. H. Nowell-Smith, *Ethics* (Baltimore, Md., 1954, [Penguin Books]) ; Philip Blair Rice, *On the Knowledge of Good and Evil* (New York, 1955) ; Charles L. Stevenson, *Ethics and Language* (New Haven, 1944) ; and Stephen Edelston Toulmin, *An Examination of the Place of Reason in Ethics* (Cambridge, Eng., 1961).

[3]Baier, p. 46.

[4]For example, see Baier, pp. 148–156.

treat ethics as consisting of statements, of kinds of statements, and of the content of statements. Of proper concern are statements in whose predicates are the words, *is a desirable thing, is morally obligatory, is morally admirable or reprehensible, is a good thing, is praiseworthy,* and the like.[5] Included, furthermore, are all statements that imply, though they do not specify, such evaluative words. Edwards achieves considerable simplicity when, following Broad and Findlay, as he says, he presents his theory in terms of two classes of judgments.[6] The first is the value-judgment or moral judgment in which key predicate words are *good, desirable, worthwhile,* and their equivalents. The second is the *judgment of obligation,* as signalled by words like *ought, oblige,* and *duty.* We may say, then, that students of ethics are concerned with choice situations that are always signalled by the question, "What ought I to do?" They are concerned, also, with the rational and reasonable responses that human beings make to the question, i.e., with the judgments that we use in making choices and in justifying them.

Since judgments either state values directly or imply them indirectly, ethics as a study examines all values that influence action and are imbedded in judgments. It attempts to explain value-terms and how they are used, to classify them, and to find values that apply widely to our actions. Those of greatest generality are called standards or criteria of conduct. Some of them are compressed in concepts with which all of us are familiar: good and evil, pleasant-unpleasant, duty, obligation, self-interest, altruism, truth-telling, promise-keeping, honesty, fairness, courage, law-observance, utility, right and wrong, and the like. They appear typically in general statements called rules of conduct, regulations, laws, codes, principles, and moral maxims. With such values in mind, ethics also asks and tries to answer questions like these: Why these values rather than some other ones? And are the methods employed to identify them valid and trustworthy? In a word, modern ethics undertakes to present a theory of values which includes an account of how value-judgments are justified.

It would seem apparent, accordingly, that ethics as a study derives its materials in large measure from men's linguistic behavior when they must choose among alternatives. Their behavior constitutes judgments, and these appear in their reasonings when they deliberate, explain, and justify their choices. It is possible to observe such behavior systematically, to analyze it and theorize about it, and this ethics does. It is also possible to observe such behavior, to note what judgments all men, or most men, or wise men, or the wisest of men in practice accept or reject, and to perceive which of these recur in the materials and premises of men's reasonings. This is what classical rhetorical theory did, and this is what modern rhetorical theory should do. If the modern

---

[5]See Brandt, pp. 2–4.
[6]Edwards, p. 141.

rhetorical theorist feels that he cannot in his textbook present a workable account of the material basis of speeches, perhaps much as Aristotle did in his
Rhetoric, at least he can assert that rhetoric is related to ethics as theory is to
practice. He can point out that the science of ethics deals with moral principles
and standards of conduct as they are abstracted from practice, and that the
art of rhetoric encounters moral principles in particular situations, in specific
cases in which man in his social and political roles must make up his mind
and act in concert, or be ready to act in concert.

If the materials of rhetorical discourse are fundamentally the same as the
materials of ethics, it should be possible to derive a scheme of rhetorical topics
from the study of ethics. Indeed, this can be done. I shall present now a brief
outline of topoi. In doing so I am not suggesting that it is a perfect product
and ready for incorporation into a textbook on public speaking. I aim only to
point the way to a practical instrument.

First I shall sketch the general categories of values that help us to decide
whether our decisions and actions are good or bad, right or wrong. There appear to be three, all-embracing classes—the desirable, the obligatory, and the
admirable or praiseworthy, and their opposites.[7]

Whether or not something is desirable depends upon one's motives, goals,
or ends—upon that for the sake of which we act. We act to reduce certain
painful or unpleasant tensions. We rid ourselves of disease and illness to restore health; we banish hunger by seeking and eating food. On the other hand,
some tensions produce pleasure, the chief among these being activity associated
with sexual behavior, comparative activity in both work and play, and aesthetic
excitement. Pleasurable tensions are involved, too, in activity that is venture-
some and that involves learning and knowing. We desire things, also, that are
in our own interests. Among interests, some are primarily self-centered, such
as property and security (although both of these directly depend on social
institutions and practices). Some interests are directly social—those for the
sake of the general welfare. Other interests are professional, vocational, and
recreational in nature. Desirable, furthermore, is personal and group achievement and its attendant pleasure and exhilaration. We derive satisfaction in
making and creating something. We take pleasure and pride in achieving the
"right" self-image. With this image is associated status—the respect and defer-
ence of others to us, and the power and ability to do what we wish. Desirable,
moreover, is freedom of choice and action; undesirable are arbitrary restraints.
A much-prized good is being loved and liked by others. Finally, there is an overriding, hedonistic desire, that of seeking anything that gives us pleasure and
of avoiding acts and states of being that are painful or unpleasant. These, then,
are things generally regarded as desirable and good. They are reflected directly

[7]In developing general categories of values, I have been most helped by Brandt.

or indirectly in the statements through which we make choices and explain or defend them.

Things that are morally obligatory and acts that are praiseworthy seem to acquire their meaning and force in the sort of regard that others have for us. The self-image is built up through the approvals and disapprovals of others, and thus we learn what is "right" and "wrong." Our integrity, our respect for ourselves, is a function of social rewards and sanctions. On the other hand, acts that are desirable and conduct that is goal-directed and that is said to be motivated, all seem to be built around, and come to focus on, the individual organism. The distinction between the desirable and the obligatory appears to be imbedded in our language. It is acceptable to say that playing golf is a good thing to do, but it is odd to say that playing golf is a right thing to do, or that golf playing is a matter of duty.

Within the class of things obligatory are duties. These are acts specified by one's position or role in a group or in a social institution. With respect to the family, a father has duties. With respect to his profession, a physician, a lawyer, a teacher has duties. With respect to the state, a governor has duties, and so does the citizen. There are obligatory actions so deeply woven into the social fabric that, once learned, they are rarely examined. They are truth-telling, promise-keeping, the paying of debts, and obeying the law. Finally, there are the *mores* of the group, as revealed in codes, customs, commandments, and moral maxims, and enforced by unwritten, social sanctions.

The last class of goods and values is that of the praiseworthy-blameworthy, the admirable-reprehensible. These value-terms are meant to refer to character traits, to behavior classes that have become stable, to what in the older literature of ethics were usually called *virtues*. Among these is conscientiousness, a term that refers not to some mystical, innate sense of the good, but to a concern for living up to one's own self-image and for fulfilling one's obligations. There are, too, the familiar virtue names—kindness, fairness, courage, veracity, honesty, prudence, persistence, tolerance, reliability, and good will (i.e., concern for the welfare of others). Although space does not permit the elaboration of these behavior traits, two or three observations should be made. Some writers call these traits *extrinsic* goods, or instrumental goods, because possession of them leads to the acquisition of other goods and ends. Honesty, for example, leads more often to desirable ends and less often to punishments than stealing and cheating. Although these terms may enter into all kinds of value-judgments, their long usage and genetic development suggest that they typically apply to behavior that is completed and past. Hence, to some writers they are technical terms of appraisal, and we use them most appropriately when we size up conduct that has become history. Yet terms of appraisal often appear in deliberative or policy contexts with persuasive intent. As Aristotle once observed, to praise a man is to hold him up for the imitation of others.

3.

This sketch of value categories has been presented entirely from the point of view of ethics. The categories represent a sort of *topoi* of values. Doubtless it is evident that rhetorical topics can be derived from them. One has only to recall the ordinary ways of analyzing a problem—the Dewey steps in problem-solving, for example, and the surveys for a proposition of fact and a proposition of policy—to perceive that they refer to situations in the present and the past and point to the possible future in terms that are ethical and moral. Such schemata of analytical thought originally had their basis in the logic of choice, decision, and conduct. Their long use and ready application have turned them into formulae whose derivation has been forgotten.

In presenting *topoi* of ethical values, I am not forgetting that the system must also include political values. Although this is not the place to spell out the significant differences between politics and ethics, we do well to remember that politics can be properly included within the scope of ethics, for the art of government is the art of adjusting the desires and values of the individual to the desires and values of others. Accordingly, rhetorical topics derived from ethics will point to political topics in the ways that genus relates to species, in those ways that the general idea suggests the specific idea. So some ethical premises will in use be indistinguishable from political premises. Take, for example, Kant's famous categorical imperative: Do only that thing which you would will all others to do. It appears to apply to political conduct as well as to individual conduct.

Nevertheless, some rhetorical topics will be characteristically political. We all know where to look for them. Government may be viewed as the formal instrument whereby individuals accept a system of law for the benefit of themselves and of each other. Hence from the point of view of politics there is always the triadic relationship of parties: the individual, the political group in which the individual plays the role and goes under the name of *citizen,* and the governor or ruler. With this relationship in mind, one can at once locate the foci of political explanations and arguments. These will center on such concepts as the powers, obligations, and duties of both the ruler and the citizen. These in turn derive much of their meaning from the concepts of liberty, freedom, and justice, and from our ideas about rights, both individual rights and civil rights. From these spring the standards, rules, and maxims of political conduct. Some political theorists, for example, believe that Roman law settled our custom of defining "private affairs in terms of rights, and public affairs in terms of power and responsibilities."[8] Political rules become the substantial bases and premises of appraisals and judgments. They also dictate the method and tone of rational criticism. These, perhaps, are our special heritage from the Greeks.[9] Possibly the deep-rooted, long-unquestioned habit of waving aside the "constitutionality" of debate propositions has led debaters to ignore the real sources of arguments that are simultaneously material, moving, and interesting.

To see that a *topoi* of values would indeed be possible we need only to glance swiftly at the debater's issues and sources of argument. The debater refers to "evils" and "difficulties" that give rise to "problems." These terms, I suggest, can refer only to situations, persons, groups, or institutions that have experienced unpleasant tensions of one kind or another. They are frustrated because they haven't secured their desires, their goals, their pleasures, and their interests. Somebody is threatening their freedom, their status, or their power. Somebody is accused of breaking the law, and his character and that of witnesses and of the trial system itself are put to the test. Self-interest, vested interest, or the entrenched power of some group or institution is interfering with the general welfare.

Once the debater has located the evils of the situation, he defines the problem. His explanation of it cannot avoid value-judgments and even his facts that support explanation function in a context of values. If the question be medical care for the aged, the description of the present state of medical care may well support different interpretations of the problem and point to different decisions.

Such, then, are the kinds of materials which, assembled and analyzed, provide the basis of decision. The decision itself—the solution of the problem —emerges either as a proposition in which the words *should* or *ought* appear, or as a proposition in which value-terms are expressed or clearly implied—e.g., the party is innocent (or guilty), the state has an obligation to provide employment opportunities for everyone, this person or this institution is responsible for doing so-and-so. It is well to remark that the *ought* in a proposition of policy means more than a vague pointing to the future. It is a decision in response to the question, What ought we to believe or do? And this question is always, so Baier asserts, an ethical or moral one.[10] Moreover, an *ought* proposition carries a meaning of obligation about it, such that if one accepts the proposition one feels bound to do what is specified or implied.[11] With either individuals or institutions in mind, one can ask sensible questions: Are obligations to be found in the context of the problem? Who is obligated to whom? What is the nature of the obligation? Furthermore, an *ought* seems

[8]D. G. Hitchner and W. H. Harbold, *Modern Government: A Survey of Political Science* (New York, 1962), p. 175.

[9]*Ibid.*, p. 174.

[10]Baier, p. 86.

always to imply that the decision is the best thing to do; it suggests that the speaker has compared all relevant alternatives.[12]

Perhaps enough has been said to show that many rhetorical *topoi* may be readily derived from ethical and moral materials. Indeed, I believe that topics and lines of argument *inevitably*, in the nature of things, lead the investigator to ethical and moral considerations, guide him to decisions and propositions that are ethical and moral, and furnish him with most of the explanation and arguments that support his decision and in whose terms he will recommend it to the consideration of an audience. If modern rhetoricians will face the fact that language symbols are not empty symbols, like those of symbolic logic and mathematics, that the language of practical discourse bears meanings that testify to man's attempt to identify and solve problems of action and conduct, modern rhetoric will formulate a theory of invention and will present a plan of *topoi* in the language of ethics and morals.

4.

If rhetoricians would see the materials of speeches in this light, they would do well, I believe, to take a special term from the field of ethics and employ it, perhaps with minor adjustments. The term is *good reason*, or in the plural form, *good reasons*. What are these? A good reason is a statement offered in support of an *ought* proposition or of a value-judgment. Good reasons are a number of statements, consistent with each other, in support of an *ought* proposition or of a value-judgment. Some examples may prove illuminating.

> The Federal government ought to provide for the medical
> care of the aged. (Or, more technically: It is desirable that
> the Federal government. . . .)
>> It will contribute to the security of the aged.
>> It will be in the welfare of everybody.
>> It is in the interest of equity.
>>> The aged spend a disproportionate amount of their in-
>>> come on medical care.
>>>> Their bill for drugs is twice that of persons in age
>>>> brackets below 60.
>>> The government has an obligation to finance medical
>>> care for the aged.
>
> X should not have copied from Y's paper.
>> It was an act of cheating
>> Cheating is wrong.

11Brandt, esp. pp. 353–354.
12*Ibid.*

Jones made a good speech.
It conformed to most of the principles and
rules of speechmaking.
Its consequences will be good.

This man ought not be elected sheriff.
He is not qualified to hold the office.
He cannot be depended on.

These illustrations serve to point out what good reasons are and what they support. If the rhetorician were to adopt the term, good reasons, he would have a technical label that refers to all the materials of argument and explanation.

There are advantages to the use of the term, good reasons. Both rhetorician and teacher would be ever reminding the speaker, as well as themselves, that the substance of rhetorical proof has to do with values and value-judgments, i.e., with what is held to be good. One can scarcely declare that something is desirable without showing its relevance to values. It may be desirable, for example, to adjust the balance of power between management and labor, on the ground that justice has become too partisan, that basic rights are not being respected, and the like. Moreover, the word *reason* indicates that the process of proof is a rational one and can be used to cover such traditional forms of reasoning as deduction and induction, the syllogism, generalization, analogy, causation, and correlation. Furthermore, the term *good reason* implies the indissoluble relationship between content and form, and keeps attention on what form is saying. If we could become accustomed to the concept, good reasons, we might cease worrying over our failure to find perfect syllogisms in the arguments of everyday life; rather, we would recognize, as the examination of practical reason seems to indicate, that reasons which govern practice are quite different from the syllogism as usually presented. I think that most ethicists would agree that the measurement of validity in practical discourse quite commonly resides in the general principle and its applicability. Brandt has this to say on the point: "Any particular ethical statement that is valid *can be supported by a valid general principle* . . ."[13] X should not have copied from Y's paper, for in doing so he cheated, and cheating is wrong. In this case, clearly there are facts that could or could not be established. Clearly, the general principle, "cheating is wrong," is relevant and functions as a warrant. The principle is applicable, or is applicable as qualified, if particular circumstances call for qualification. The principle itself is valid to the extent that it corresponds with the beliefs and conduct of the group which gives it sanction. Such statements, Edwards observes, are objective in the sense that they are independent of the speaker's subjective attitudes. It is true, of course, that the speaker's attitude may prompt his giving a general principle as a rea-

[13]*Ibid.*, p. 20.

son; nevertheless, the general principle can be tested for its truth-value quite apart from his attitude.[14] What a good reason is is to some extent fixed by human nature and to a very large extent by generally accepted principles and practices which make social life, as we understand it, possible. In a word, the concept of good reasons embraces both the substance and the processes of practical reason. One could do worse than characterize rhetoric as the art of finding and effectively presenting good reasons.

If rhetoricians could accept good reasons as the substance of discourse, we would immediately secure additional advantages. Any distinctions that modern rhetoric may be trying to maintain between logical, ethical, and emotional modes of proof would immediately become unreal and useless, except for purposes of historical criticism. For the practitioner, both communicator and respondent, the correct questions would always be: What is my choice? What are the supporting and explanatory statements? What information is trustworthy? It would be absurd to ask: Is my choice a logical one? Shall I support my position by logical, ethical, or emotional means? For the theorist, analyst, and critic of discourse, the disappearance of those weasel concepts, logical proof and emotional proof, would permit a description of the materials of practical discourse in terms of two broad categories: materials deriving from the specific occasion, and judgments. Furthermore, perhaps practitioners would get into the habit of applying first and foremost to any instance of communication, the searching queries: Who or what is the responsible agent? What person or agent is taking the responsibility, or should take it? If the proposition be supported by reasons that immediately or ultimately relate to value-statements whose content reflects the desirable, the obligatory, and the admirable, then for whom is the message desirable and admirable? Upon whom do the obligations and duties rest? Discourse to which such questions are habitually applied cannot long remain abstract, distant, colorless, and unreal. Rather, it could well become personal and direct. The speech-making of the Greeks, who understood ethos, was eminently personal.

5.

It seems probable that if students of rhetoric looked to the substance as well as to the forms of practical discourse, they would discover a set of statements or value-axioms that would constitute a modern system of invention. The axioms would consist of those political and ethical values that apply to public discussion. Derived in theory from politics and ethics and in practice from the rules and conventions that speakers appeal to explicity and implicity when they explain, advocate, deliberate upon, and justify, their choices, the

[14]Edwards, pp. 148, 157.

axioms would serve as a base for finding good reasons and thus for providing fundamental materials in any given case of rhetorical discourse. Eubanks and Baker have recently reminded rhetoricians of Arstotle's position that "If rhetoric has any sort of *special* subject matter province, that substance is constituted in the popular and probable value axioms related to the civil decision making of a free society."[15] The hypothesis should be put to the test.

Questions for Analysis

1. How do you describe the theoretical basis for a belief that rhetoric today has no true substance, that popular attitudes and values are beyond the persuasive means of the rhetoric of our times? To what popular influences do you attribute the currency of such a belief? What that you have learned about ethos aids your understanding of this belief? How does Wallace attempt to prove that speeches *are* objects, and that rhetoric, therefore, provides materials of which speeches are built, just as theory provides materials for behavior?

2. Cite some examples of contemporary rhetorical "choices." What purposes do your chosen "choices" serve: action, preparation for action, or appraisal of action? Are your "choices" political, legal, or epideictic? What ethical and moral considerations do statements of your "choices" imply? Demonstrate how even an informative speech may be "functionally persuasive, whether in intent or effect."

3. How are "evaluative words" important determinants in the ethical processes of deliberation, justification, and explanation? Do you agree that these "words" sincerely reflect "judgments"? Explain. How would you characterize the regard for language in the rhetoric of our times? Cite instances in which you think "evaluative words" have been improperly employed for the sake of persuasion. How does this suggest to you a fusion of ethical and rhetorical concerns? Are Wallace's three "general categories of values" sufficient for study of the rhetoric of our times? Choose several propositions currently debated and consider arguments for and against each one as it may be considered pleasure ("desirable"), duty ("obligatory"), or virtue ("admirable").

4. How do the arguments for and against propositions you chose "point to political topics"? On the basis of current debate do you think, as Wallace suggests, that rhetorical statements of policy are themselves "materials" that affect the method and tone of debate? Explain. Prove by examples that public debaters define and explain their positions by "value-judgments" and suggest solutions by "value-terms."

5. Isolate one of the proposals currently debated and demonstrate, in application to it, these advantages of "good reason(s)" as the substance of rhetorical proof: a. The debate becomes relevant to values; b. The debate becomes rational and can

---

[15]Ralph T. Eubanks and Virgil L. Baker, "Toward an Axiology of Rhetoric," *QJS*, XLVII (April, 1962), 162.

be conducted by traditional forms of reasoning; c. The debaters consider content and form as one; d. The debaters become objective and need not distinguish between logical, ethical, and emotional appeals; e. The topic derives from the specific occasion and consists of general value-judgments; g. The topic becomes personal and direct, a matter of responsibilities and obligations.

25

The Materials of Reasoning: Evidence

Henry Lee Ewbank
J. Jeffery Auer

Evidence is the body of facts and opinions bearing on the problem under consideration. *Reasoning* is the process of drawing conclusions from *evidence*. When an individual uses *reasoning* to get others to accept his conclusions we have *argument*. To put it another way, *evidence* refers to the materials of *reasoning; argument*, to the purpose of *reasoning*. In this essay we consider the materials of reasoning, or evidence. We write in the conviction, as Jefferson put it, that "in a republican nation, whose citizens are to be led by reason and persuasion, and not by force, the art of reasoning becomes of first importance."[1]

All evidence should be ultimately based upon facts. It may come from two sources, observations of facts and opinions about the meaning of facts. Therefore we must consider both (1) *evidence of fact*, and (2) *evidence of opinion*. Some confusion between these two often arises because, in one circumstance, a piece of evidence may be evidence of fact, but in another it may be evidence of opinion. Or the same circumstance may lead one man to a statement of fact, another to a statement of opinion reflecting his interpretation of that circumstance. Consider this example: during an air attack on London, early in World War II, a bomb destroyed an apartment house located some distance from any military target. Here is what four observers said:

> 1st observer: "There isn't a wall of that apartment building left standing." Evidence of fact.

> 2nd observer: "There isn't a depot, a power center, or a soldier within five miles of that apartment building." Evidence of fact.

Henry Lee Ewbank was Professor of Speech, The University of Wisconsin.

Adapted from Henry Lee Ewbank and J. Jeffery Auer, *Discussion and Debate*, 2nd ed., (New York, Copyright 1951 by Appleton-Century-Crofts, Inc.), pp. 104–36. Reprinted by permission.

[1]Jefferson to David Harding, April 20, 1824, in Adrienne Koch and William Peden, eds., *The Life and Writing of Thomas Jefferson* (New York, Random House, 1944), p. 173.

3rd observer:	"The destruction of this apartment build-ing proves that the Nazis are deliberately bombing civilian areas." Evidence of opinion.
4th observer:	"This kind of thing ought to persuade America to get into the war on our side." Evidence of opinion.

Or, to take another example, a scientist in his laboratory may repeat an experiment many times. After each test he records a statement of fact describing the result. When he has satisfied himself that the result is always the same, he may publish his conclusion in what he regards as another statement of fact. But some of those who read his statement may not be convinced of its validity; for them the scientist's statement is one of opinion, not fact. Thus ". . . whether a statement is regarded as a fact or as an opinion is a matter of degree dependent on how convincing is the proof or disproof of the statement. It is also clear that what is an opinion for one individual may be a fact for another, depending on the amount of information available to each individual."[2]

In the first example, the evidence of all four observers was first-hand; it was their personal observation or their personal opinion. This is not true of all evidence: we often accept facts observed and reported by others, and the opinions of someone else. A senator in debating a bill may rely upon the facts reported by a dozen witnesses in open hearings; a student in a discussion may supplement his own judgment with the opinions of others, laymen or experts. The senator may never have been in China and the student may never have seen a federal housing project, yet each one is equipped by the evidence of others to speak on his problem. In dealing with (1) *evidence of fact,* therefore, we must recognize (a) facts of personal observation, and (b) facts observed by others. In discussing (2) *evidence of opinion,* we must consider (a) personal opinions, (b) lay opinions, and (c) expert opinions.

Each of these varieties of evidence will frequently be found in exploring a problem; we need, then, to be able to recognize them and to be familiar with ways of testing each type of evidence for validity.

I. Evidence of Fact

Discussions are often opened with the statement, "Now here are the facts of the situation. . . ." If these are honestly conceived and presented they are limited to statements which accurately report, describe, or classify, on the basis of personal observation or authentic testimony of others, some event, circumstance, or phenomenon that has happened or is happening. Their existence is not a matter of opinion; the statements are based upon more than assertion.

[2]C. I. Hovland, A. H. Lumsdaine, and F. D. Sheffield, *Experiments in Mass Communication* (Princeton, N. J., Princeton University Press, 1949), p. 265.

"It's outrageous," cried the lawyer, "they can't put you in jail for walking on the grass in the city park!" "Maybe not," replied the client, "but here I am." Evidence of fact is the best answer to assertion.

An objective description, then, independent of judgment or interpretation, constitutes an observed fact. If we say that food prices are too high we are stating a conclusion or an opinion. But if a housewife compares her weekly food bills for the past year and reports that local meat prices have risen 17 per cent, canned goods 11 per cent, and fresh produce 15 per cent, she is stating a fact of her own observation, and it may be verified by anyone who examines the same evidence. The speaker who says, "It is a *fact* that women are more attractive in the West than in the Northeast," mislabels his statement. The Census Bureau reported that only 17 of every 100 women were single in the West, whereas 25 out of 100 were single in the Northeast. These were facts, established by careful observation; the statement of the speaker was only an opinion which purported to explain the facts. We must learn how to establish the validity of factual evidence lest we be misled by our own investigations or by those of others.

A. Facts of personal observation

It is axiomatic that if one is to think straight he must be able to see straight. Although our senses are sometimes deceived, if they are exercised properly our observations are likely to be accurate. How can we be sure that we will see and see correctly? Much that we will say about the observations of others applies equally to our own; but three special considerations are appropriate here.

1. *To observe accurately we must have a definite purpose.* Just as the first step in the scientific method is recognizing the existence of a properly located, defined, and limited problem, so in observation the first step is to know what we are looking for. We need to narrow our attention area so we can recognize the facts we want when we find them; the umpire, referee, and head linesman at a football game each has his own area of concentration.

2. *To observe accurately we must have an honest attitude toward the problem.* While investigating a problem for relevant facts we need to free ourselves as far as we can from prejudice and preconceived notions. Facts favorable and unfavorable should receive an equal reception. The investigator whose pre-judgments distort his perception is not trying to solve a problem, he is rationalizing his point of view.

3. *To observe accurately we must record rather than remember.* At best, memory is unreliable; it tends to screen out the commonplace and the uncomfortable facts so that we recall best those that are colorful and pleasant. The written reports of Robert Kennedy, Arthur Schlesinger, Jr., and Theo-

dore Sorenson often disagree on specific facts concerning events that took place when all three were present. A written record, made at the time of our observation, is not infallible, but it is more reliable than our recollection.

We have no wish to discourage reliance upon facts of personal observation; the world would be far poorer without Franklin's autobiography, John Quincy Adams' diary, or Churchill's memoirs. Indeed, we generally find reports of first-hand observations more interesting than second-hand summaries. We get close attention when recounting what we have witnessed or experienced.

B. Facts observed by others

None of us was present at the battle of Gettysburg; what we know about it must be based upon evidence gathered and reported by others. Few of us have seen an atomic chain reaction, interviewed Ho Chi Minh, or investigated living conditions among Southern sharecroppers, but we have read and heard the testimony of those who have done these things. Thus in speechmaking we frequently must rely for evidence upon the observations of others. But we should not accept without qualification the statement that "this is a fact because Mr. Jones, an eminent authority in his field, says it is." Mr. Jones, too, has his limitations as a witness.

In the first place, any testimony by a witness involves three elements: *observation*, *memory*, and *narration*. We have already suggested that accurate observation is not common: twenty people reporting what they thought they saw in a traffic accident, or in a touchdown play on the gridiron, are likely to disagree on major items as well as upon minor details. In one classic example, 20,000 people testified as to the physical characteristics of a man they saw commit a crime; on the average they overestimated his height by five inches, his age by eight years, and in 83 per cent of the cases gave the wrong color for his hair.[3] Similarly, the average individual is relatively unreliable in recalling what took place one, two, or five years ago. Who followed you in the diploma line at your high school graduation? Can you name the author of the textbook used in your freshman composition course? In the element of narration we often find even greater inadequacies. "I know just what happened but I can't describe it" is a common phrase; our powers of narration are not always equal to describing what we see. Limitations such as these exist quite apart from deliberate dishonesty or incompetency. Taken together, they demonstrate the need for critical evaluation of all testimonial evidence.

Traditionally the evaluation of "fact" witnesses has followed the patterns set in law courts.[4] In general, the legal standard includes these considerations:

[3]Freling Foster, "Keeping Up with the World," *Collier's*, Vol. 106 (August 17, 1940), p. 6.

[4]See G. P. Baker, *The Principles of Argumentation* (Boston, Ginn & Co., 1895), pp. 230–37; J. M. O'Neill, C. Laycock, and R. L. Scales, *Argumentation and Debate* (New York, The Macmillan Co., 1917), pp. 107–12.

1. *A reliable witness must be in a position to observe clearly.* Accurate observation may depend upon being near enough to the scene to view it clearly, being in time to see an event take place, having enough light to see it, or being close enough to hear.

2. *A reliable witness must be physically able to observe accurately.* A reliable observer must have the sensory qualifications necessary to observe the fact in question. A deaf witness cannot testify as to what was said unless he qualifies as a lip reader; a blind person may give valid descriptions only of objects he can feel or hear.

3. *A reliable witness must be able intellectually to understand and report what he sees.* Inasmuch as accurate observation may involve understanding a witness must have powers of discrimination; he must also be able to report what he has observed in clear, unambiguous language.

4. *A reliable witness must be able morally to report only what he sees.* It may be impossible to secure otherwise competent witnesses who have no personal interest in the facts under discussion, but precautions should be taken to discover whether the moral character of a witness is such that he may be presumed not to falsify deliberately.

C. Testing facts

So far we have been concerned with checks upon the reliability of our personal observations and those reported by others. The following questions test the validity of the asserted facts.

1. *Is the asserted fact clearly accessible to observation?* The accuracy of an alleged fact cannot be established if the witness was not in a position to observe it clearly. In an early law case Abraham Lincoln is said to have examined a witness who testified that the light of the moon had enabled him to identify a man running away from the scene of a murder. When Lincoln produced an almanac which showed that there was no moonlight on the night in question the asserted fact was disproved. Many people who could not possibly be in a position to observe the facts like to speak with assurance; the necessity of testing military "scuttlebutt" and civilian rumors in wartime is equally important in everyday discussion.

2. *Is the reporting of the asserted fact complete?* If evidence is to be meaningful it must include every relevant aspect of the asserted fact and the circumstances in which it was observed. In the early days of "extra-sensory perception" experiments some people accused Dr. J. B. Rhine of reporting only high scores and omitting low ones, but a review of the original data showed

that all scores were properly accounted for in the final report. A team of debaters who broke even in six tournament debates, however, triumphantly reported to the press that they had won three debates, period. To use the courtroom phrase, this assertion may have been "the truth" but not "the whole truth."

3. *Can the asserted fact be checked by other observers?* The famous accounts of "sea serpents" inevitably are traced back to only one alleged observer; this is their weakness. The best scientific tradition, of course, calls for multiple verification: if *X* plus *Y* gives *Z* result for one observer, it should yield the same results for others. When an investigator is told that *"everybody* knows this is a fact" he should ask whether *anybody* else knows it. Even when an alleged fact has been observed by a number of witnesses, it is wise to inquire whether they all agree on essential points. This is why lawyers may introduce apparently repetitious testimony by a succession of witnesses; juries are more likely to accept a fact if a number of people give consistent testimony concerning it. If different observers disagree, the investigator must "check and double check" by testing the alleged fact in other ways.

4. *Is the asserted fact consistent within itself?* Asserted facts must not be self-contradictory; they must have "internal consistency" in that their several aspects are compatible with each other. If a speaker argues that federal welfare programs should be expanded, he cannot consistently also call for decreased federal taxes; if he submits percentage figures they cannot total more than 100 per cent; if he contends that two groups fail to cooperate on a voluntary basis, it will seem inconsistent to argue that they can work together in an organic union.

5. *Is the asserted fact consistent with known facts?* Asserted facts must also have "external consistency"; they must agree with other definitely established facts. If it is true that all textbooks are dull we should beware the instructor who promises a sprightly one. In some cases, to be sure, valid facts cannot pass this test: most rivers in the United States do run from north to south, but the Red River in North Dakota happens to be an exception. Consistency with known facts, however, usually suggests the probable truth of the newly asserted fact.

6. *Is the asserted fact probably true?* This is not the ultimate test of an asserted fact, but it is the broadest. It might be called the "common sense test." If a police captain is found to have a bank account of $300,000, does it make sense to accept his statement that he saved it from his $10,000 a year salary? Knowing what we do about the laws of physics, is it likely that a perpetual motion machine has been invented? Is it probable that the United States might be importing wheat, or Venezuela, tin? An asserted fact is not necessari-

ly invalidated if it cannot pass the probability test; it once seemed improbable that a plane could exceed 400 m.p.h., or that the atom could be split. But if an alleged fact seems improbable, the investigator should be slow to accept it.

These tests are not designed to make the reader suspicious of all evidence, but to encourage a healthy skepticism until the asserted facts have been adequately tested.

II. Evidence of Opinion

We are eternally confronted with other people's opinions: "The Secretary of State believes. . . ." "Hanson Baldwin, the New York *Times* military expert, says. . . ." "The men who know tobacco best say. . . ." If these opinions are honestly arrived at and fairly presented they are statements made by persons who are alleged to have special qualifications for expressing pertinent judgments or beliefs. While opinions may be based upon facts, they should be distinguished from facts per se.

As with evidence of fact, we may cite the opinions of other laymen, or quote the opinions of experts. In the latter case, evidence of opinion comes from the judgments or beliefs of someone who has relatively complete knowledge of the facts, an authority in his field. We therefore frequently refer to an expert's opinion as "argument from authority," and in this essay we use *authority* as synonymous with *expert*. Let us consider an example of each type of evidence of opinion.

1. In preparing to speak on the desirability of having your town own and operate the light and power company you may examine a financial statement of the present private utility, investigate the probable purchase price and maintenance cost, and study present utility rates. Upon the basis of the facts you may conclude that public ownership of these utilities would result in very small savings to the consumer-taxpayer. In the final speech you properly express your belief: "After a thorough study of the financial aspects of municipal ownership it is my honest opinion . . . ." (Personal opinion.)

2. If you take part in a panel discussion about increasing federal power projects, opinions about the values of the TVA will almost certainly be expressed. Though you may never have visited in TVA territory, you may cite the observations of a friend whose judgment you respect: "Of course, I've never seen the TVA development, but a friend of mine who has tells me. . . ." (Lay opinion.)

3. On another occasion you take part in a group discussion on the powers of the Federal Bureau of Investigation. You may have no direct knowledge of that agency's relation to espionage activities, but you have recently read an article by someone who does. "Just a few days ago," you may say, "I read an article in *This Week* magazine by J. Edgar Hoover, who has been director of the FBI since 1924. On this point he says. . . ." (Expert opinion.)

In our treatment of evidence of opinion we will describe and evaluate (a) opinions we hold personally, (b) those of other laymen, and (c) opinions of experts.

A. Personal opinions

Plutarch long ago observed that "to err in opinion, though it be not the part of wise men, is at least human." Those who take part in public discussion must learn how to formulate their own opinions wisely and express them concisely. Much has been written about this subject in such books as *How to Think Straight, Thinking to Some Purpose, Language in Action,* and *The Art of Straight Thinking.* The three points which follow summarize some general principles.

1. *A sound personal opinion is based upon a clear understanding of the problem.* Unless we make a comprehensive analysis of questions on which we express opinions we risk "talking off the top of our heads." The first requisite, therefore, is a distinct and orderly picture of the problem.

2. *A sound personal opinion is based upon a systematic study of available evidence.* In Sir James Barrie's *Auld Licht Idylls,* Bowie Haggart says, "I am of the opeenion that the works of Burns is of an immoral tendency. I have not read them myself, but such is my opeenion." Predetermined notions, stereotypes, traditions, and guesses seldom lead to valid opinions. The only adequate basis for sound judgment was phrased long ago by Isaac Watts: "Let the degrees of your assent to every proposition bear an exact proportion to the different degrees of evidence."

3. *A sound personal opinion is based upon careful testing wherever possible.* One cannot always subject his judgments to a pragmatic test, but they are better when he can. Next best, often, is to see how our opinions square with those of others who are well informed on the problem.

B. Lay opinions

A layman is one who is not an expert on the problem about which he speaks; he lacks the professional training, the experience, or the reputation necessary to speak with authority. As Abraham Lincoln once wrote to a man asking for a testimonial on his soap: "Some specimens of your Soap have been used at our house and Mrs. L. declares it is a superior article. She at the same time protests that I have never given sufficient attention to the 'soap question' to be a competent judge." The layman may, however, be in a position to observe facts not accessible to us; at such time, and when expert testimony is not available, he may provide our best evidence. Until better is found it must carry some weight.

The public opinion survey, such as the Gallup Poll or the Harris Survey, is one of the most common devices for gathering lay opinions. While some politicians may throw doubt on their accuracy in predicting what people will do in an election, such surveys are the best methods available for obtaining cross-sections of public opinion on current issues.

Special considerations in evaluating individual lay opinions parallel those suggested for checking your judgments: they should be based upon (a) a clear understanding of the problem, (b) a systematic investigation of available evidence, and (c) careful testing wherever possible.

C. Expert opinions

Nicholas Murray Butler was perhaps the first to refer to the expert as "one who knows more and more about less and less." Others have attacked experts, especially academicians in government service, as theorists, suggesting that "what we need are practical men." Yet, as Kurt Lewin once remarked, there is nothing so practical as a good theory. The expert, or authority, is a man qualified to give an opinion upon a problem by reason of his special competence. We recognize, for example, Amy Vanderbilt as an authority on etiquette, Webster on definitions, U Thant on the United Nations, and the chairman of the Federal Communications Commission on radio. We should also recognize, however, that the use of authority is not of itself an argument or a method of reasoning. Expert opinion is evidence; like all other evidence, it furnishes only the material of reasoning.

It has sometimes been the fashion to look with disdain upon the speaker who cites authorities to support his own views. In his *Notebooks* Leonardo da Vinci complained that "Whoever in discussion adduces authority uses not intellect but memory." And today we often hear the college debater assert that "Quotations don't prove anything!" He is very wrong; a quotation from an authority does prove something; at the least it proves that the expert has an opinion. These criticisms of the use of expert testimony are really leveled against excessive reliance upon authorities, and against so-called authorities who really possess no special qualifications for judgment. With such criticism we are in agreement; we believe that those who attempt to solve problems must select expert testimony with care. In the fabric of proof authoritative opinion should be skillfully interwoven with substantial evidence of fact.

We have already said that the fact witness must be in a position to know the facts, and physically, intellectually, and morally qualified to testify. This is also true of those offering expert opinion. In addition there are special tests which should be applied.

D. Testing opinions

The following tests are concerned chiefly with the authority himself, rather than with the opinions he expresses, since his opinions will be acceptable as valid evidence only if he is respected. No matter how reliable or competent he may be, his opinions will carry little weight if his hearers do not regard him as an authority.

1. *Is the reference to authority specific?* How frequently we hear these vague references, "according to an eminent authority," "most economists agree . . .," or "one expert in the field says. . . ." We read in a newspaper that "a source close to the President," "a high government official," or "a usually reliable source" said so-and-so. Whether the authority referred to is eminent, expert, or usually reliable cannot be determined unless the reference is specific: who is he? under what circumstances did he testify? This does not mean that we expect a speaker laboriously to cite date, volume, and page for every statement attributed to someone else, but it does mean that some degree of specificity is essential. A lawyer may express a different view on the powers of the Supreme Court before he is appointed to the bench; an ex-Secretary of State may speak more freely on some issues than when he held office. We need to know the exact degree of expertness of any alleged authority. And if we are to check a speaker's references we must know his sources.

2. *Is the authority generally qualified to testify?* We cannot accept the testimony of a color blind person concerning the color of a traffic light at the scene of an accident, nor should we put much faith in the opinions of anyone whose powers of observation, memory, or narration are questionable. If, because of his religious or political views, or the nature of his private or public life, a man's character is suspect, his testimony must also be looked upon with suspicion. Even though an individual may be in an unusual position to know the facts he must be generally qualified—physically, mentally, morally, and even psychologically—if he is to be regarded as an authority.

3. *Is the authority in a position to know or interpret the facts?* A common failing is to regard an authority in one field as an expert in others, even where he has little knowledge or experience. Thus a physicist may be quoted on foreign policy, a banker on domestic relations, or a college president on economics. Now it is conceivable that some physicists, bankers, and college presidents may be qualified in these other fields, but unless we can show this to be true, we should not presume it. We should learn the opinions of men who have established their competency in the field in question. A fairly safe generalization, though not without its exceptions, is that a specialist is more likely to know the facts in his field and to interpret them better than the non-specialist. As Plato wrote in *Protagoras,* "even though a man may be a good flute player, this is no reason to consider him an authority on politics."

4. *Is the authority aware of the significance of his testimony?* An expert may sometimes casually hazard a prediction, make a guess, or play with an hypothesis, but to take any of these as deliberate testimony on the facts in

his field would be unfair to him and to the audience. "Off the record" remarks are seldom proper evidence. We should also be cautious about taking too literally statements made "in the heat of the moment" and which the maker would no doubt admit were exaggerated. Wendell Willkie's famous confession of the extravagances of his "campaign oratory" is a case in point. The rule of reason must be applied in weighing all testimonial evidence.

5. *Is the authority reluctant to testify?* If an individual's testimony seems against his own best interests or desires, his evidence may be regarded as exceptionally valuable. The Republican who endorses a Democratic measure, the labor leader who admits the virtue of a particular company union, the textbook writer who praises the work of a competitor, fall into this category. Such apparently reluctant testimony must always be examined carefully, however, for the lion may have an ulterior motive in professing friendship for the lamb.

6. *Is the authority free from hidden bias?* It would be unreasonable to expect a truly unbiased judgment from an expert in a given field; his very judgment is a bias, though it may have been arrived at by the most careful and scholarly methods. As Oscar Wilde once said, "One can give a really unbiased opinion only about things that do not interest one, which is no doubt the reason an unbiased opinion is always valueless." But we are asking here whether the alleged expert has a hidden bias, a special interest which he carefully conceals. Several years ago a prominent economist wrote a series of articles for a popular weekly magazine in which he subtly praised a particular industrial corporation. When the praise seemed inordinate, the editor investigated his writer and then publicly apologized because he had learned that the economist was on the corporation's payroll. The objection in such cases is not that the authority is really an advocate, but that he pretends an objectivity he does not have.

7. *Is the authority supported by factual evidence?* Too frequently we hear speeches where reference to authority constitutes all of the evidence. There are situations, such as a layman gathering information on technical medical questions, where all valid evidence must come from specialists. But in general it should be regarded as a dubious practice to rely only upon any one type of evidence. So-called authorities, for example, can be found to "prove" that the world is flat, that capitalism is dead, or that an apple a day keeps the doctor away. "Mark you this, Bassanio. The devil can cite Scripture for his purpose." Recognizing that on some questions evidence other than that of authorities may not be available, we should nevertheless accept with caution any reasoning based solely upon opinions.

8. *Is undue reliance placed upon a single authority?* No matter how competent a man may be, we should be reluctant to accept his word alone if other experts are available. On some personal problems only the person involved

may be qualified to speak as an authority, but when we confront a serious problem we prefer a consultation of experts and their combined judgment. Suppose,
for example, that Louis Agassiz, the great Harvard scientist, were the only authority cited on the validity of Darwin's *Origin of the Species*. Expert though he
was, Agassiz labeled Darwinism "a scientific mistake, untrue in its fact, un-
scientific in its method, and mischievous in its tendency."[5] Rather than relying
solely upon Beard, Commager, Nevins, or Schlesinger on a point of historical
controversy we should check the opinions of them all. It may be remarked, in
this connection, that not every opinion which achieves the distinction of print
thereby acquires value: many foolish as well as wise ideas have been published
in large type and fine bindings. A critical mind, combined with a fine sense of
discrimination is the best equipment for exploring evidence.

9. *Is the reference to an authority who will be accepted?* This final
test is quite different in character from those already suggested: here we ask,
"no matter how competent this man may be, will this particular audience accept
him as an authority?" There are some matters upon which the president of the
National Association of Manufacturers is the best authority available, but it is
unlikely that his testimony on wages and hours would impress a labor union
meeting. Men like Walter Reuther, George Wallace, Rap Brown or Max Raffer-
ty have special competencies, but prejudices against them are so strong among
some groups that they must be used as authorities with great care. In general
it is good practice to cite authorities who are not extreme in their views. We
agree with Thomas Huxley that "it is the customary fate of new truths to begin
as heresies and to end as superstitions," yet we would beware of insisting on
quoting the supposed heretic when authorities with more prestige are available.

III. Special Ways of Presenting Evidence

Two special ways of presenting evidence are so frequently employed that
they deserve attention here. These are (1) *the citation of statistics*, and (2)
the citation of examples.

These special methods of presentation may be used for evidence of fact or
for evidence of opinion. If, for instance, we have made a personal survey of
unemployment in Ohio we may present the observed facts *statistically* in order
to conserve time or space. Or, we may wish to pick out one specific city from
all those surveyed and present its problems in detail as a typical *example*. We
might also present evidence of opinion by these methods. The results of a
questionnaire asking opinions on unemployment sent to 150 leading economists
might be summarized in *statistics;* we might single out Professor Slichter's
reply, after determining that it was typical, and cite it as a single *example*.

We often use these special methods to condense a large body of material

---

[5]"Professor Agassiz on the Origin of Species," *American Journal of Science and Arts*,
Vol. 80 (November, 1860), p. 154.

so that it may be presented in a brief period. This is particularly true when a few comparative figures may quickly demonstrate the result of investigating a thousand cases. We may also use these devices to make our material more vivid or graphic for the listener. "One out of every ten workers in Rocktown is unemployed" is more graphic than "6,714 workers in Rocktown are unemployed." A case history of Joe Brown may make the unemployment problem much more vivid than enumerating a series of conclusions based upon studying hundreds of cases.

In the following pages we will discuss statistics and examples as methods of presentation and suggest ways of testing their value as evidence.

A. Citation of statistics

One of the most common conversational clichés is the phrase "Statistics prove. . . ." Thus the fans of the American and National baseball leagues carry on their ceaseless arguments by citing statistics or numerical records which are presumed to prove their respective points. Many persons are inclined to mistrust statistically expressed information: "Figures don't lie, but liars figure," they say, with the air of enunciating a profound truth. Nevertheless, statistics may serve as an effective and reliable method of presentation. "On a nation-wide average basis," says a speaker, "consumer living costs have risen 19 per cent since 1957; 11 per cent since 1964; and 5 per cent since 1967." This means that he has taken certain numerical records of facts and placed them in a position of relationship. As a device for presenting evidence, then, statistics offer a method of judging phenomena collectively on the basis of enumeration of single instances. Statistics themselves are reports, numerically expressed, of observed facts.

One of the most common uses of statistics is in presenting evidence gathered by the questionnaire or sampling technique. Originally this procedure was used mainly for commercial purposes. A door-to-door canvass in a selected town furnished examples for a generalization as to how many people used Ivory soap, owned a vacuum cleaner, or planned to buy an electric dishwasher. With the development of commercial radio, sponsors were vitally interested in knowing the size of their listening audiences. Again the sampling technique was used: perhaps a thousand people in St. Louis were chosen at random from the phone book, called, and asked what radio program they were listening to. These folks were regarded as typical of the whole listening public in St. Louis and generalizations were made as to the total number of listeners for a given broadcast. The most recent application of this technique has been the public opinion poll; it attempts to discover mass opinion on specific legislative proposals, governmental policies, and other current problems. In planning discussion meetings this same technique is often useful: a survey of those who usually attend may guide leaders in the selection of topics, a questionnaire may reveal the general character of the forum constituency or be an index to the reactions at a specific meeting.

The most obvious advantage of using statistics is that we may present a descriptive survey of a body of data that would otherwise be difficult or impossible to comprehend. They also enable us to compute averages which are helpful in predicting future phenomena in the same class; this is the purpose of the life insurance actuarial table. Finally, by using statistics we can present large quantities of data more graphically so that relationships and trends become more apparent.

Before using statistics to present evidence we should subject them to certain reasonable tests.

B. Tests of statistics

1. *Are the units compared actually comparable?* It may be said that nation X has twice the naval strength of nation Y, but if the units compared are variable the statistics are unreliable. In one case only fighting ships may be counted; in the other, tankers, mine-sweepers, and repair vessels may be included. The definition of units is always basic: what is a crime, a student, a highway, a Protestant, an amateur athlete, an unemployable, or a drunkard?

Care must also be taken to see that the unit has not been changed in the course of investigation. We would have to remember, for example, in surveying the prevalence of crime from 1900–1950, that some actions not considered criminal in 1900 are so classed in 1950. After 1934 it became a criminal offense to fail to register securities offered for sale in interstate commerce; in 1947 it became a crime for an employer to make a gift to a bargaining representative of his employees. These extensions of the term *crime* must be considered in weighing the data collected.

If it is said that divorces in the United States have increased rapidly since 1900 because in that year there were 9.32 divorces *per 1000 population* and in 1960 there were 26.8 divorces *per 100 marriages,* any conclusion is ambiguous. Divorces per 1000 population or divorces per 100 marriages must be calculated for each of the years to establish a valid statistical comparison. In other cases, the same test should be applied: in comparing child labor in several states we would have to know that the term is used in the same way in each state. The student who added beans and corn and got succotash had the right answer.

2. *Are the statistics really an index to what we want to know?* We must guard against being trapped by statistics which seem relevant but are not. The hourly wage rates for carpenters in Lewisburg may have little connection with the standard of living in Lewisburg. The number of persons attending a Democratic rally in Yanktown bears little direct relation to the probable success of the Democratic ticket in the next election. Such figures may serve as a

partial basis for constructing hypothetical judgments, but they are far from conclusive. Similarly, statistical evidence may be limited in value if it is premised upon an implied analogy between the situation covered by the statistics and the situation we are investigating.

       3. *Are the statistics presented in their most significant form?* When statistics are presented in gross numbers or *totals,* they are often apt to be misleading; *percentages* or *rates* may present a truer picture. If, for example, we say that there were 385,000 divorces in the United States in 1950 and 494,000 in 1966 we cannot conclude on this basis alone that the divorce rate has increased; while the total number increased, so did the total population. On the other hand, if we examine statistics in terms of percentage of population, we would find that there were exactly 2.6 divorces per 1000 people in both years, and conclude that the divorce rate had not actually increased. Here percentages are more meaningful than gross numbers. If, finally, we present statistics in terms of the number of divorces per 100 marriages we would find the figure at 24 in 1950, and 28 in 1966, and conclude that the divorces-per-marriages rate had gone up. In this case, statistical rates or ratios are also more meaningful than gross numbers.

      Americans seem to like figures, but we frequently err by failing to use them in their most significant form. In 1940 the Republicans took consolation in the fact that Wendell Willkie polled more votes than any previous Republican candidate, but the fact was that on at least three previous occasions a losing candidate had received a greater *proportion* of the total vote. After the same election the Democrats boasted that Franklin Roosevelt received more votes than any previous candidate for the presidency, but the *distribution* of this support gave him fewer electoral college votes than in two previous elections.

      Another factor in presenting statistics in their most significant form is the choice between *average, median,* and *mode,* three terms which are frequently confused. Ordinarily we think of *average* as meaning "typical" or "medium," but this is often misleading. If a dozen dub golfers were joined by Arnold Palmer or Jack Nicklaus their average score would be lowered considerably, but the dubs would still be dubs. In a mathematical sense *average* means the total of a number of individual items divided by the number of items; thus one extreme item, such as Palmer's score, may change the average figure a great deal and give a distorted picture of the whole group. The *median,* on the other hand, is that figure which stands in the middle of a series. If grades in the speech class are 34, 41, 48, 53, 55, 75, 81, 86, 95, 95, and 98, then the middle figure of 75 is the median grade. The average is 69+. What we often refer to when we speak of "average income," "average man," and so on, is the *mode,* or the measure which occurs with greatest frequency. Using the same set of class grades, we say that the central tendency, or modal grade is 95.

      The concept of the "average man" as really a "statistical man" was illustrated in the survey of its male readers taken by *Time* magazine twenty years ago.[6] On the basis of questionnaires returned by 3,041 men it was found that the "average *Time* reading male" had an income of $7,600, held $20,158 worth of stocks and bonds, carried $30.50 in his pocket, shot a 95 in golf, entertained eleven guests a week at a cost of $1,000 per year, had 34,859 miles on his car, carried 6.0 keys of which 1.1 he never used, owned 31 ties, and used 82.6 strokes in shaving. But this average or typical man had no flesh and blood counterpart in real life![7]

4. *Do the statistics cover a sufficient number of cases?* The law of statistical regularity indicates that a fairly large number of items selected at random from a very large group of similar items is almost certain to have the characteristics of the larger group, and that the items represent the whole group. The danger in presenting statistical data on this premise is that we may overlook the necessity for a large number of items. The golfer who scored a hole in one his first time on the course, and then swore off the game, makes a pretty story about how every time he played he scored a hole in one. But the man who plays regularly knows better. To be statistically reliable, data must be gathered in large numbers if random selection is used: a survey of 300 out of the 1,000 graduates of Home High School, might be an adequate basis for a conclusion that 50 per cent of the graduates went on to college. However, if a scientific sampling is employed, with known factors of difference among cases properly weighted, a smaller number of samples may be statistically reliable: some polling agencies, for example, use as few as 3,000 carefully selected interviews as a basis for determining national opinion on current issues.

5. *Do the statistics cover a sufficient period of time?* As with the last test, our concern here is with an adequate sample, a period of time that is fair and not exceptional. In the month of September in a given year the average temperature in Chicago might be 76.3 degrees, but this investigation would hardly justify a general rule. If a September survey for thirty years showed 65.2 degrees as the average temperature in that month for that whole period, however, a general conclusion would seem valid. Similarly, we might question the validity of the average monthly sale of automobiles if the data were based upon June figures, or the average number of out-of-town visitors to New York City if the data were collected during the World's Fair. In situations where it is highly probable that the operating causes are constant, however, statistics based upon short periods of observation may be acceptable. The batting averages of American League champions from 1916–1966, for example, may be fairly calculated on the basis of any five-year period, or the average cost of living for this year may be accurately estimated by checking figures for the second Tuesday of each month.

---

[6]"Your Time Exposure," Research Report No. 1019, Time, Inc., January, 1949.

[7]See also Darrell Huff, "How to Lie with Statistics," *Harper's*, Vol. 201 (August, 1950), pp. 97–101.

The importance of these two tests of sufficiency in number of cases and period of time, may be illustrated by imagining a series of ten individual items ranged along a scale of continuous variation.

Grades	10	20	30	40	50	60	70	80	90	100
Students	A	B	C	D	E	F	G	H	I	J

Let them be the grades of ten students on an examination. If we select at random students *A, B, C,* and *F* as bases for a statistical picture of the whole group we would find that the average grade appeared to be 30. An equally misleading result would appear if we chose students *D, E,* and *J,* or *G, H,* and *I.* It is clear that we must have a sufficient number of cases of *representative character.* If we were to use the same illustration, but substituting "Years" for "Grades" and "National Income" for "Students," we would find that a wide range would again be necessary to derive valid statistical data, in this case to insure a *representative period of time.*

6. *How strongly were the gatherers of the statistics interested in the outcome?* In examining any type of evidence we must be alert to any apparent bias, error, or misinterpretation resulting from the special interests of the person gathering the data. People often, intentionally or unintentionally, find what they are looking for; this seems to be especially true of statistical data. For this reason, professional research agencies are often employed to collect and interpret data. If we are considering the cost of living as a factor in possible wage raises, for example, we might find five different estimates made by the Bureau of Labor Statistics, the AFL-CIO, the Republican National Committee, the National Association of Manufacturers, and a presidential fact-finding committee. In each instance, the gatherers of the statistics might conceivably have a strong interest in the outcome of the investigation, and their findings should be judged accordingly. The best procedure, in such a case, is to examine the data of as many different agencies as possible; this advice is applicable, of course, to the evaluation of all types of evidence.

C. Citation of examples

To guard against the specious use of examples in presenting evidence requires careful analysis and testing; the device of citing examples is frequently misused. To cite a single example means to select one fact or opinion as typical of a whole class of ostensibly similar instances and to draw from it a conclusion concerning the whole class. After reading one short story by Somerset Maugham, we pass judgment on all of his writing; our neighbor denounces frozen foods in general because one package of beans failed to please; the drivers of Texas are condemned because one reckless Texan was met on the high-way. In each of these cases a single example is used unwisely to judge an entire class.

In sound reasoning, of course, an isolated example should rarely be relied upon. Rather, a large group of typical examples should be selected from the whole class and a conclusion based upon them. This judgment we call a *generalization,* a general conclusion based upon a limited number of facts or opinions. If we want to draw a reasonable conclusion about Maugham's ability as a writer, we must observe a large number of samples. We will probably discover some stories that are excellent, others that are fair, and a few quite undistinguished. On the basis of these examples, the only reasonable *generalization* would be that Maugham is very much like other writers: some of his work is better than the rest.

It may seem that the categories of statistics and examples overlap in terms of the methods of selecting them and the purposes for which they are used. There is an essential difference, however, in that examples are more vivid and concrete; they are usually more interesting to the listener, and might well be described as animated, personalized, or vivified statistics.

D. Tests of examples

1. *Have the examples been chosen to support a preconceived conclusion?* There is a proper place for advocacy, but even there we want to feel that examples have been selected honestly: in investigating a problem, of course, we should examine as many examples as possible. Sometimes a newspaper editorial, or a book, reads as though the writer had been told, "Here is our policy; now dig up some examples to support it!" This is typical for any-one who feels obliged to support any kind of party line. Examples handpicked to support a predetermined point of view should have difficulty passing the tests which follow.

2. *Are the examples fair representatives of their class?* It may be difficult to determine how representative a single example may be, but it is seldom impossible to discover other examples of the same class so that a valid collective judgment can be expressed. It would be manifestly unfair to judge a whole race of people by an unfortunate acquaintance with one representative, the entire Congress by an experience with one senator, or a newspaper by a single editorial. The way to avoid this error is to study many examples chosen from the same class so that we may be sure those presented as evidence are representative.

3. *Are there contrary examples which have not been considered?* Closely allied with the preceding test is this one which asks whether there are any known exceptions to "the general rule" which appears to govern a whole

class of examples. Contrary examples do not necessarily invalidate the rest of the evidence, but they should be recorded and accounted for in the conclusion. Suppose that we poll half the seniors at Hapgood College to find what they expect to be earning five years after graduation. These might be the results:

1 person	$3,000
8 persons	8,000
9 persons	9,000
6 persons	10,000
1 person	20,000

From these twenty-five examples we might conclude that "as a general rule Hapgood College graduates expect to be earning $8–10,000 five years after graduation." This conclusion agrees with the evidence, but it would have greater validity if it included the two extremely contrary examples, the men expecting to earn $3,000 and $20,000. These unusual cases help define the extent to which the general rule may be considered valid.

4. *Do the examples represent a large enough portion of their class to justify a generalization?* There can be, of course, no absolute measure of "enough" in applying this test; the answer depends largely upon the phenomena being studied. In certain areas of physics or chemistry a very few examples may be sufficient evidence to permit a valid generalization: if several properly conducted experiments show that when M is added to N the result is O there is little value in endless repetition of the test. But in other areas, where belief, opinion, prejudice, personal likes and dislikes are concerned, a much larger collection of examples is necessary to justify a generalization. We should not be satisfied with two or three answers to the question "What do the American people think of socialized medicine?" or "Should the student council raise the activity fee?" A good general rule is that "the greater the possible variations in answer to our question, the wider must be the field of observation, in order to justify a generalization."[8]

5. *Are the facts concerning the examples verifiable?* One obvious test of an example is to examine its factual basis or the authority behind it. If we generalize that not one in ten Whitetown voters would support Senator Blank for reelection we have proved nothing about his chances unless we know whether he carried Whitetown six years ago. Opposition to him may have been even greater in the last election. Sometimes, of course, the factual bases of a generalization cannot be investigated: it took ten years before Hermann Rauschning's example of Hitler's views were verified. But whenever possible

8J. M. O'Neill, C. Laycock, and R. L. Scales, *Argumentation and Debate* (New York, The Macmillan Co., 1917), p. 162.

an example or a generalization should be tested not only as to the facts under-lying it but also as to its real significance for the problem being investigated.

6. *Is there other evidence to support probable validity of the gener-alization?* This test should be applied to any evidence, no matter how it is presented. If we cite Winston Churchill's 1940 proposal for a union of England and France as typical of British opinion at that time we may put too much reliance on a single example. Before we are satisfied we should look for other observed facts or authoritative opinions which might support the generaliza-tion. A high probability of validity is established if a varied body of evidence supports a single example or a generalization; but if it stands unsupported by other evidence it should be regarded as of at least doubtful value.

IV. Suggestions for Gathering Evidence

In concluding our discussion of evidence three admonitions may be ap-propriate.

Gather enough evidence

There is no definite answer to the obvious question, "How much evidence do I need?" But it is fair to observe that very few participants in public speak-ing suffer from having too much. Seldom will every piece of evidence gathered be immediately useful but, because every audience situation is different, the more evidence a speaker has gathered the better he can adapt his argument to any specific group.

Seek a variety of evidence

A judicious combination of facts and opinions is usually superior to sole reliance upon either one. Whenever possible, factual evidence should come from personal observation, and evidence of opinion from the most competent authorities available. And it is wise to consider the possible efficiency and inter-est value of using statistics and examples as ways of presenting evidence.

Document evidence carefully

Knowing the evidence includes knowing and judging the source of the evidence. Without a proper knowledge of the source it is difficult to evaluate a fact or an opinion. Accurate and complete documentation of each piece of evidence as it is gathered may save many hours of later research and avoid possible embarrassment.

The *World Almanac* has long been recognized as an authoritative refer-ence volume. The late Robert Hunt Lyman, who edited it for many years, used to say "The surer I am of a 'fact,' the more pains I take to verify it."[9] We can think of no better advice.

Questions for Analysis

1. Why are *reasoning* and *argument* necessary sequels to *evidence?* What considerations may bear on a speaker's decision to emphasize either fact or opinion in presentation of evidence? How might a given rhetorical situation influence these considerations? How may assertion, although not evidence, figure in the presentation of evidence? What added responsibilities does its use entail? Choose a topic for which either statistics or examples might be the best evidence. Illustrate by comparison the advantages of each form of presentation. How will speaker purpose influence the selection of either form?

2. Why are principles for observing facts correctly similar to those for listening correctly? What precautions do these similarities suggest to the speaker preparing a presentation of facts? How should the use of "facts of personal observation" differ from the use of "facts observed by others"? Illustrate how you might test an asserted fact for: a. completeness, b. internal consistency, c. external consistency, d. probable truth.

3. What have studies of listener response to informative and persuasive speaking proved to the value of "argument from authority"? (See Petrie; Auer) How does such argument affect the speaker's "credibility"? (See Andersen and Clevenger) What are the liabilities of the use of lay opinion, particularly of opinion polls? What reservations might discerning listeners have about the validity even of expert opinion? Illustrate how you might test an authority for each of the following contingencies: a. character and competence, b. awareness of testimony's significance, c. ulterior motives or special interests, d. acceptability to listeners.

4. Select a specific and current campus social issue and consider what type of evidence would likely be most effective in speaking on it before: a. a cross-section student audience, b. members of a student social action group, c. the board of trustees. How might the alleged "generation gap" influence the choice of types and amounts of evidence used in communication between the generations? What kinds of evidence do you suppose are most acceptable personally to an activist who uses "agitative rhetoric" when he makes speeches? Explain.

5. Review Griffin's article in Part I and assess the kinds of evidence employed by "New Left" speakers. Look ahead in Part IV and read the Asinof study of Dick Gregory and the Williams study of the Klansmen. How to they compare in the kinds of evidence they use? By reading only the excerpts from their speeches, and noting their use of evidence, what can you generalize about the nature of their audiences?

9"Bookmarks," *Saturday Review of Literature,* Vol. 31 (October 23, 1948), p. 22.

26

Reactions to John F. Kennedy's Delivery Skills During the 1960 Campaign

James G. Powell

In retrospect, the urbanity of our late President seemed as much a part of his total platform performance as the epigrammatic phrase and the flash of wit. The ease and assurance, indeed the brilliance of a Kennedy press conference, remain an inseparable part of our memory of the man. Fortunately or unfortunately, this concept, reflecting equal portions of rightful sentiment and historical accuracy, overlooks some of the awkwardness of the speaking of the pre-presidential years. For when Kennedy began his 1960 campaign, his voice was taut and tense, his delivery rapid and rushed, and, says Theodore H. White, he was not totally certain just "what was quite the proper manner and posture of a man who seeks the presidency."[1] It was to be this campaign, then, which would provide the testing ground for Kennedy as an orator. That he succeeded is self-evident, journalists and professional speech critics concur, but the success was not achieved without some struggle.

In the early weeks of the campaign, Kennedy had not learned to project his voice properly, and an ominous hoarseness crept into his voice from sustained speaking which Marquis Childs believed "would even have put a strain on the vocal cords and lungs of a carnival barker."[2] In short, said Richard L. Strout, he "was having voice trouble even with amplifiers."[3] The problem lay in the fact that Kennedy (self-admittedly) had been speaking from his throat; he had been taking lessons in diaphragmatic breathing from a voice coach even prior to Labor Day.[4] And because he abused his throat early in the campaign, or as one journalist said, "He tends to rise up to a high monotone at a cruising

James G. Powell is Associate Professor of Speech, California State College at Long Beach.

Reprinted by permission from *Western Speech*, 32(1968), 59–68.

[1]Theodore H. White, *The Making of the President*, 1960 (New York, 1961), p. 255.

[2]Marquis Childs, St. Louis *Post-Dispatch*, September 11, 1960, p. 10; also, *Time*, September 19, 1960, p. 23.

[3]Richard L. Strout, *Christian Science Monitor*, September 22, 1960, p. 18.

[4]New York *Times*, August 22, 1960, p. 13.

altitude too thin for his voice,"[5] on flights between speeches he would frequently rest his voice and communicate by writing notes.[6] Professor Orville Hitchcock noted this misuse of the larynx during the Senator's acceptance speech at the Democratic Convention. "Kennedy's New England speech does not bother me any more than Roosevelt's 'cultivated' accent did. I am bothered, however, by the way he uses his voice, especially when talking loudly as he is required to do for larger audiences. I gather that what he does is to strain his throat muscles—to try to control his projection through the use of the muscles of his neck."[7]

Even more critical was a British correspondent who stated flatly that the "metallic tenseness" of the voice—"high, rapid, and devoid of natural rhythm"—resulted in his rarely establishing any intimate relationship with his audience.[8] Despite this, Kennedy was capable of a rich, resonant voice; yet with his habitual pitch higher than his optimum pitch, more often than not he was flat, nasal, and harsh. Further, observed Gilbert Schaye, he had a lateral lisp similar to that of Roosevelt; for example, "s" and "z" sounds came out "sh" and "zh." Words such as "per cent," "question," "cause," and "us" became "pesshent," "queshion," "cawzh," "and "ush." Additionally, Kennedy dropped the endings of many of his words or substituted other endings. Words such as "vigor," "more," "world," "just," "aware," and "Cuba" were pronounced as "viga," "moah," "wirl," "jes," "awaya," and "Cubar." A flat nasal "a" sound was alternated with a broad one, Schaye observed, so that "last" and "Castro" became "lasht' and "Cahshtro." Moreover, Schaye went even further and speculated that the slimness of Kennedy's margin of victory in the presidential election might have been caused by poor pronunciation and delivery which made it difficult for people to understand him. "To many midwesterners and southerners, Mr. Kennedy must have sounded like a foreigner."[9]

Although Kennedy's voice and pronunciation drew negative comments, his rate of speaking was meeting with mixed reactions. With his head tilted back, the Senator rattled off lines at a ferocious pace; the New York *Times* noted that he had been clocked at 240 words per minute, approximately 100 words a minute faster than normal speaking rates. The result, said the *Times*, is a "high, passionate ring" which became "hypnotically sing-song" as he sped along, and was difficult to follow because of the rhythm.[10] In sum, said *Newsweek*, his timing was deplorable. "He doesn't try for applause and scarcely acknowledges it. Instead, he plunges into his speech with almost messianic fervor, delivers his message and ends with an abruptness that often seems anticlimactic. Yet his speech packs a wallop, not because of what he says, but

[5]Saul Pett, Milwaukee *Journal*, October 2, 1960, Part I, p. 6.
[6]*Ibid.*, p. 6.
[7]Orville Hitchcock, Department of Speech, State University of Iowa, in answer to a questionnaire sent by this writer.
[8]"The Next President," *The Economist*, September 17, 1960, p. 1078.
[9]Gilbert Schaye, quoted in the Milwaukee *Journal*, March 13, 1961, p. 1.
[10]New York *Times*, September 25, 1960, p. 59.

simply because he is there."[11] On the other hand, Professor Hitchcock was not at all concerned about Kennedy speaking too fast—if anything, the rate of speed was in the Senator's favor.

> He seems to me to talk fast but not too fast. As Ralph Nichols has pointed out, most speakers talk too slowly. I never daydream when Kennedy is talking, because he keeps ideas popping at me. This is partly because he has very little padding in content and partly because of his rate. He uses his voice with energy and enthusiasm, which I like in a speaker. He has variety of a sort, but does not use his voice to full effectiveness to convey meaning. What I mean is that he seldom uses the pause, for example, to create an effect. He tends to plunge ahead, like a college debater, to cram as many ideas and facts into his time as he can. He doesn't have the niceties of timing that F. D. R. had.[12]

Here, Hitchcock pinpoints Kennedy's real delivery problem during much of the campaign (above and beyond the early voice factor): it wasn't the speed of speaking as much as it was a lack of pause and emphasis. This failure to pause immediately, to give his audience a deserved opportunity to react, resulted in a smothering of his own audience response. The belated pause, then, was less than effective, as if it were a sudden recognition on his own part that he had scored a point.[13] A second failing was Kennedy's inability (or refusal) to highlight his important points with any emphasis. Words and phrases were not something to "play with," and this attitude resulted in too many points receiving too equal treatment.

But as the campaign progressed there were to be some notable improvements in delivery; for instance, my notes of the speech of October 31, 1960, at Madison, Wisconsin, read, "Kennedy has moments of real fire . . . shows indignation over what the United States is *not* doing."

Professor Glen Mills of Northwestern University reported during the same period that Kennedy was becoming less strident and was bringing his speaking rate under better control.[14] Further, noted a Milwaukee *Journal* correspondent, the Senator now paused for applause and seemed to have learned much about gauging the mood of the crowds: "He tailors his basic speech, his emphasis and even his tone of voice to fit them. . . . He is a more forceful speaker now, too, in both what he says and how he says it. The level of his voice rises and falls more

---

[11]*Newsweek*, October 10, 1960, p. 26.

[12]Hitchcock questionaire reply.

[13]During the primary campaigning it was noted that pauses which might have lent clarity and significance in one position frequently appeared at points where they served only to confuse the thought. (See Harry P. Kerr, "John F. Kennedy: Shamrock and Shillelagh." *Presidential Campaign, 1960: A Symposium,* mimeographed paper edited by Paul H. Boase for the Subcommittee on Contemporary Public Address of the Speech Association of America, Oberlin College, February, 1961, pp. 33–34.)

[14]Professor Glen Mills, School of Speech, Northwestern University, in answer to questionnaire sent by this writer.

than it ever did, as he emphasizes his points."[15] Others shared the same opinion: Douglas Cater, writing in the *Reporter*, stated that Kennedy "has come a long way"; and, though he "still hammers a particular point with monotonous consistency," with the help of coaches "he is beginning to master the art of projecting his voice so that it has lost some of its shrill, grating quality."[16] Moreover, Professor Frederick Haberman of the University of Wisconsin cited the improved articulation:

> When he began he had a mushy "s" and he also had an obscure "l" sound. He would say "miyyon" instead of million. Both the mushy "s" and the sloppy "l" sound are carry-overs of careless speech that probably began in his youth. He has been able to remedy both of these defects, however, in the last three months, and it is rare that they are now noticeable.[17]

If Kennedy's use of his voice was something less than an asset, his physical presence on the speaking platform was, by-and-large, in his favor. After first-hand observation, Haberman noted the "appeal about him" and how "he gave an impression of caring mightily—not simply about himself—but about an idea that was external to him."[18] And my notes throughout the campaign underline this same infectious energy: physically, he looked, acted, and talked in a vigorous way. Indeed, so much so that during the televised speeches of October 31 and November 4, 1960, Kennedy's characteristic jabbing of the lectern with his index finger came over the microphone as a heavy "thump-thump." But on other occasions, said *Time* magazine, there was less confidence, especially when he was waiting his turn to speak on the stump: "He fidgets with his coat buttons, smooths his hair and swings his right foot restlessly. A gesture of extreme agitation: a desperate fingering of his necktie, reserved for the approach of Indians bearing war bonnets, nuns, or other disconcerting greeters. He obviously has a New England reticence about himself, is unwilling to surrender some recess of his privacy."[19]

As he spoke, Kennedy used but two gestures—movements which *Newsweek* tagged the "chop" and the "swoop". The common chop was a short downward right jab with finger extended: whereas the rarer swoop resulted in bringing the right hand from behind, arcing it over in a flat trajectory, and pointing his finger at the platform in front of him. The chop was used for underlining points, but the swoop was reserved for major emphasis, as, for instance, when he would say, "I think we can win this election right he-ah."[20]

[15]Ira Kapanstein, the Milwaukee *Journal*, October 18, 1960, p. 12.

[16]Douglas Cater, "En Route with the Candidates," *The Reporter*, October 27, 1960, pp. 19, 20.

[17]Professor Frederick W. Haberman, Department of Speech, University of Wisconsin, in a lecture to the "Freshman Forum," Bascom Hall, University of Wisconsin, November 8, 1960.

[18]Haberman lecture.

[19]*Time*, October 3, 1960, p. 17.

[20]*Newsweek*, October 10, 1960, p. 24.

Hitchcock also noted the lack of variety in gesturing, but felt that the chopping gesture was a good one which served to emphasize:

> He doesn't "dramatize" gestures—use them for effect as such. He seems to speak with his whole body. That is, I have an impression that all of his muscles are working, that he is putting himself into it. There is nothing "lethargic" about his speaking. Max Eastman, you will remember, pointed out that lethargy was one of the great faults of modern oratory. Kennedy displays a sort of "personal energy" in his speechmaking that I like. But it must be admitted that he wears you down a bit. Also, he doesn't seem to use his delivery to "work on you" in any specific way— to compel your attention toward this particular point by slowing down, or by saying it quietly, or by making a dramatic gesture. Too much of this is a fault, of course, but I don't think Kennedy has enough of it.[21]

There were moments when Kennedy exhibited some nervous shifting of weight, for instance, the televised Philadelphia speech of October 31, 1960, but the gestures, platform vigor, and thrust-out jaw tended to project what Professor Wil Linkugel labeled "a certain cockiness."[22] In fuller detail, Professor Haberman's notes of October 23, 1960, describe Kennedy's performance at a partisan rally.

> He is keeping his transitions clear . . . uses his right hand exclusively up to this point. Has looked to his right only, never to his left. Cocks his head slightly to the left. Uses index finger and saws the air. Voice strong. Tenor pitch has solid undergirding . . . one section not too clear. Intense movement of ideas. Rapid delivery. Still hasn't looked to his left. Almost never uses left hand. Almost never uses both hands in conjunction. Barely pauses. No variety in gesture. Arresting quality in voice; has a ring to it. Rhythm seems to be stronger here than on TV. . . . Gesture operates in a short circle. Extends arm quite far from body. Almost never pauses for applause. Seems not to know when to build to a climax. When he does turn to the left he has to turn the whole body, not just his head. . . . Almost never uses his notes. This is a well worn speech. Never stumbles. Very fluent.[23]

During a speech Kennedy smiled very little, if at all, usually looking quite serious; in fact, my notes reveal that he even looked a little angry at times during the televised speech of October 31, 1960. Not really contradictory was

[21]Hitchcock's questionnaire reply.

[22]Professor Wil Linkugel, Department of Speech, University of Kansas, in answer to questionnaire sent by this writer.

[23]Notes taken by Professor Haberman during the Kennedy speech at the University of Wisconsin fieldhouse, October 23, 1960.

Professor Mills' observation of the same broadcast, "at least since last summer his smile has been cultivated noticeably."[24] Nor was there a division of opinion over Kennedy's eye-contact, which usually was quite good. For example, during the nationally televised speech of September 20, 1960, he glanced from his text to his immediate audience and occasionally looked directly into the cameras even though reading. Again, during the Houston speech of September 12, 1960, in which he adhered completely to the prepared script, he still directed his gaze from his text to the churchmen and then back to the text again. This establishment of "excellent eye contact" during the speech of acceptance at the Democratic Convention was one of several factors praised by Hitchcock. "He holds you with his eyes, but he doesn't stare you down. His eyes seem to reflect sincerity and drive."[25]

Several writers have commented on Kennedy's stubborn resistance to the traditional political niceties. Douglas Cater has summed up this attitude: "In his every gesture there is understatement, almost an indifference to the customary wiles of the politician. He never pays the usually fawning lip service to local leaders and localities. There are no applause triggers in his speeches. He delivers them with a tenseness and at a clip that all but ignore the crowd's right to respond. He ends so abruptly that frequently he has returned to his seat before anyone is aware he is finished."[26] *Time* magazine, in an early campaign issue, said essentially the same in even fuller detail:

> Kennedy on the speaker's rostrum is tense and brief. Although his speech writers work hard at their craft, Kennedy makes so many cuts and interpolations that advance copies of his text are almost useless. Says Arthur Schlesinger, Jr.: "The difference between Stevenson and Kennedy is that Adlai puts subordinate clauses in all the speeches you write and Jack takes them out." Frequently, sensing the mood of his audience, Kennedy discards his prepared text altogether and speaks fluently off the cuff (both Nixon and Kennedy are at their best in ad-lib situations). His speeches are breathlessly brief: never more than five minutes in daytime appearances, with an outside limit of 20 minutes in an evening speech. Oftentimes people who have waited long wish there were more. Kennedy seems almost apologetic about keeping his audiences too long; he plunges directly to the issue at hand, with only the barest amenities for the local celebrities, and races quickly through to the end, discarding the oratorical filigree as he goes.[27]

Remarks like these serve to identify a rare commodity; the campaigner of

[24]Mills' questionnaire reply.
[25]Hitchcock's questionnaire reply.
[26]Cater, p. 19.
[27]*Time*, October 3, 1960, p. 17.

the "no-nonsense-let's-get-to-the-point" school. But such observations need some qualifications. Admittedly, Kennedy did plunge into speeches with little in the way of introductory palaver, but he was not as insensitive to audience needs as some journalists would have us believe. Cases in point are the speech of acceptance at the Democratic Convention and the election eve final from Faneuil Hall, both of which were filled with adaptive remarks containing references to the occasion and the surroundings. Several other examined speeches contained lengthy introductions; and if there were any consistency, it lay in the fact that there was no stock Kennedy introduction. He might at times enlist attention; he might seek audience good will; but rarely were both within the same speech. The same can be said about the conclusions. They varied from an abrupt "thank you" to a lengthy quotation or to a call for action or both. For instance in Washington, D. C., on September 20, 1960, facing both a nationwide audience and an immediate group of Democrats, Kennedy said simply, "Governors and Senators, fellow Democrats, ladies and gentlemen," and he was then into his first topic. Contrast that with the televised Chicago rally speech of November 4, 1960, which contained lengthy extemporized remarks providing his partisan audience the opportunity to respond on key.

Reporters traveling with Kennedy on his early September campaign swing noted a curious unevenness in performance, an ebb and flow that seemed to depend on the warmth of the reception.[28] One writer said—"If he doesn't think they're likely to be for him he's likely to be dead serious." and he cited Kennedy's appearance before the business editors on October 12, 1960, which featured an address and a question-and-answer session which lasted an hour and a half; yet neither he nor his hosts so much as cracked a smile.[29] Notwithstanding, by the end of the campaign, Kennedy had learned a technique which Nixon had long since mastered—the "Yes" and "No" technique which summons the audience to respond. Whereas Nixon used "applause points," Kennedy did it with laughter. It was especially apparent in his comparison of the GOP with circus elephants and in his listing of past Republican leaders ("where do they get these candidates?"), and it prompted Theodore H. White to say that Kennedy had become as able as Nixon in milking his punch lines.[30] This quality had not been achieved without a struggle, though; Kennedy's advisers had long wanted him to loosen up and laugh a little, to open a talk with a droll story or a light gag to soften up his audiences.[31] But it was not until later in the campaign that his oratory became less frenetic, and even spiced now and then with humor and a sense of kinship with his audiences. As Marquis Childs remarked at the time: "Much of the tension seems to have gone."[32]

Kennedy also displayed sensitivity of another sort in his ability to "play

28Newsweek, September 19, 1960, p. 38.
29James McCartney, Chicago Daily News, October 15, 1960, p. 3.
30White, pp. 328–9.
31McCartney, p. 3.
32Marquis Childs, St. Louis Post-Dispatch, November 1, 1960, p. 1C.

to the cameras" during his nationally televised speeches. While he was never as consistently competent as Nixon in adapting to the demands of the television cameras, still, there were no crude transitions in switching from one camera to another, and eye-contact was largely good. Of the two contestants, however, Kennedy showed the greater disparity in performance between his televised addresses and his rally speeches. One journalist summed it up accurately following the televised speech of October 31, 1960: "The Senator again showed that he speaks more impressively at the street corner rallies, and in private talks to a few people, than he does in a major set speech on television."[33]

A journalistic source, Beverly Smith, Jr., reported a high level of moving eloquence during a rally speech late at night in Portland, Maine, on September 2, 1960. "He held an outdoor audience of thousands in the palm of his hand. Teen-agers ceased from squealing, and veteran reporters, under the spell, forgot to take notes. The speech, broadcast only locally, and too late for most of the morning papers, got little national attention. Yet to me it seemed his best. Later, when I studied the speech in transcript, I found it not notably better than some of his hurried, rapid-fire efforts. But for some unknown reason, that night, he was in the vein, speaking with a power comparable to that of great orators of the past."[34]

Ernest K. Lindley, apparently, had not heard that speech, at least his following comments reflected somewhat less enthusiasm:

> Kennedy leaves me with the impression that he does not enjoy public speaking or perhaps even crowds. Despite all his experience, he is not a very good speaker. He tends to talk too fast and without suitable pauses or other forms of emphasis. When he reads from a manuscript, he often gets only part value from his better lines. Most of his short, ad-libbed speeches sound like a phonograph record being played too fast and skipping a groove now and then as he jumps from one theme to another. He often scants the preliminary amenities or expresses his appreciation to introducer and audience with such reserve as to sound unappreciative. The warmth of his face seems to offset his lack of palaver. One hears many comments on his "sincerity." Indeed, some appear to find his directness refreshing in contrast with more familiar styles.[35]

But Smith, previously cited, presented a more flattering picture. And his reaction was characteristic of most journalists who, while finding flaws with Kennedy the orator, were at the same time impressed by Kennedy the campaigner:

> As for the boredom factor, there was another reason for its

[33]*Christian Science Monitor*, November 1, 1960, p. 1.

[34]Beverly Smith, Jr., "Campaigning with Kennedy," *The Saturday Evening Post*, October 29, 1960, p. 80.

[35]Ernest K. Lindley, *Newsweek*, September 26, 1960, p. 56.

absence in traveling with Kennedy. His every speech—and
I listened to more than 150 of them—was different from the
others. Of course, there were favorite themes, recurrent in
many of his talks. Even then, the approach, the words, the
emphasis varied—and above all his style and manner. His
platform performance was as unpredictable as Babe Ruth
at bat. . . .

So with Kennedy. Sometimes, carried away by the tide
of his own swift thoughts, he would talk so fast—that is
his frequent oratorical fault—that even I, right up front and
familiar with his enunciation and thinking, could scarcely
follow him. As for the great majority of listeners, his meaning sped right past them. When they applauded him, it was
not because they understood what he was saying, but because they liked him and felt he was trying hard to communicate important ideas in which he sincerely believed.
You may remember how the crowds used to cheer Babe
Ruth even when he struck out—they could see he was putting his heart into those swings.[36]

Others impressed by Kennedy's campaigning included Professor Haberman, who said he "gave the impression of a man with a message, striking a
kind of evangelistic note";[37] columnist Roscoe Drummond, who felt Kennedy
conveyed "an impression of intensity and grasp of his subject matter which tends
to overcome his relative youthfulness";[38] and *Time* magazine, which found
the Senator's manner "alert, incisive, speaking in short, tense sentences in a
chowderish New England accent that he somehow makes attractive (even
when he pronounces Cincinnati as "Since-in-notty" while in Cincinnati)."
Further, said the same publication, he was like Ike in that he "projected a kind
of conviction and vigor when talking of commonplace things in a commonplace
way."[39] Slightly less impressed was the *Manchester Guardian Weekly* which
held that Kennedy's performance, at least on the television screen, looked amateurish in comparison to Nixon. However, the British weekly did feel there was
"something engaging about his tousled earnestness and the seriousness of his
Massachusetts drawl," although they questioned whether the American people
"want a President who only looks engaging."[40]

But despite these limitations, Kennedy was communicating. With his chin
stuck out in an FDR-stance he conveyed conviction to his audience in delivering
a crowd-pleasing brand of oratory which W. H. Lawrence characterized as falling "about midway between Truman's 'give-'em hell' techniques and Stevenson's
flights of oratorical fancy."[41] It is a simple fact that Kennedy's vigorous advo-

[36]Smith, p. 80.
[37]Haberman lecture.
[38]Roscoe Drummond, *Christian Science Monitor*, September 24, 1960, p. 13.
[39]*Time*, November 7, 1960, p. 27.
[40]*Manchester Guardian Weekly*, October 27, 1960, p. 1.
[41]W. H. Lawrence, New York *Times*, September 11, 1960, p. 68.

cacy of change, delivered in his earnest way, came through to audiences and served to complement his theme of urgency—"Let's get this country moving!"

Questions for Analysis

1. What does Kennedy's purported uncertainty about "the proper manner and posture of a man who seeks the presidency" suggest to you of the popular expectations for the campaign speaker today? How was this uncertainty confirmed by Kennedy's earliest voice problems? What other delivery problems might reveal uncertainty? How important is an appearance of "certainty" or "confidence" to the campaign speaker's ethos? What does the speculation that Kennedy's pronunciation cost him votes reveal about campaign audiences?

2. What advantages of a fast rate of delivery does Nichols point out in his study of listening? How may rate of delivery affect timing? What is the particular importance in campaign speaking of regular pause and emphasis? What does Kennedy's disregard for emphasis suggest of his attitude toward campaign speaking? How common is this attitude among public speakers today?

3. Were the uncertainty and impatience of Kennedy's vocal delivery sustained in his physical presence? Explain. What is listener reaction when a speaker conveys an "impression of caring"? Discuss the relative merits of "variety" and "intensity" gesturing. How may gesturing influence listener comprehension? How may eye-contact?

4. How was "Kennedy's stubborn resistance to the traditional political niceties" consistent with the dominant aspects of his delivery? Characterize the appearance of Kennedy's attitude toward audiences. Name public speakers today who seem to share Kennedy's attitude. How does this attitude relate to ethos? What might it mean to candidates of the future to speak more impressively at "street corner rallies, and in private talks" than "in a major set speech on television"? Review the introduction to Part II, and the Reynolds article on public address and the mass media, as you contemplate the last question.

5. What do the mixed reactions to Kennedy's delivery skills suggest as problems in evaluating delivery? Are these problems reflected in references to delivery earlier in this book? How might the effects of delivery in campaign speaking be isolated from those of message? Do you think the American people "want a President who only looks engaging"? What kind, rhetorically speaking, did they get in the election of 1968? How does this study suggest that "listeners tend to respond and to evaluate speakers in terms of over-all impressions rather than upon discrete elements in the speaking process"?

27

Mr. Chairman, Ladies and Gentlemen

Norman Thomas

In our western civilization, ever since the times of Cicero and Quintilian, speakers have been showered with advice. The number of textbooks on public speaking here in America grows year by year, and those which I have submitted to cursory examination are good. Dale Carnegie, his assistants and imitators, do a very lively business in training men to sell themselves and their products, if not their ideas. All sorts of organizations, women's clubs, labor unions, and what-have-you, sponsor classes or training groups in public speaking. Some colleges make a course in public speaking compulsory. The mediocre quality of American speaking is not due to educational indifference to the subject.

My impression, unsupported by proper scientific inquiry, is that there has been a definite and marked improvement in quality of teaching in the field of public speech since my youth. At any rate, such formal instruction as I had in high school and college and until I got to Union Theological Seminary was superficial, routine, and of no great value. On the other hand, I was much helped by the old-fashioned requirement in grade school that occasionally each of us should say our piece at the Friday speakin'. That usually consisted in reciting what was, or was alleged to be, poetry. The work in high school in Marion, Ohio, in one of the literary societies into which we were all divided was better. I gained a great deal in Princeton from practice in debating and in the general exercises of Whig Hall. That institution, in my day, had passed its pristine glory, and had not yet been reorganized along the present lines. Nevertheless, for those of us who cared, it was a useful training school of a sort that perhaps was more valuable than any single course in public speaking under modern conditions. Union Seminary offered good training in homiletics.

In this little book of mingled reflections and reminiscences, I repeat that I

Norman Thomas, public speaker and author, was six times candidate for the Presidency on the Socialist Party ticket.

Reprinted by permission from *Mr. Chairman, Ladies and Gentlemen . . . Reflections on Public Speaking.* (New York, Hermitage House, 1955). "The Speaker," pp. 49–68.

have no intention of competing with existing textbooks or adding to their number. I merely venture on some counsel derived from personal experience.

I begin with what ought to be obvious assertions. The speaker should be a man of character. He should know his subject. He should study the most effective presentation of it. He should learn the arts of the orator, but never stoop to use them like a sophist or a demagogue simply for his own profit or power. If he wants to know the arts of the orator in the classic sense even today he can scarcely do better than to study, let us say, Cicero's *De Oratore*. But reading it will no more make him a Cicero than taking singing lessons will make him a Caruso.

One thing the orator must have in common with the work-a-day professional speaker or the citizen functioning in his community. Whoever you are you must begin by having something to say that to you at least is worth saying. Presumably no one would want the labor of speaking without a desire to communicate something which was of some importance to the audience and the occasion. But having something worth saying is more than having an impulse to speak. An urge, great or small, to exhibitionism by no means brings with it an idea worth expounding. (The exhibitionist urge led delegates to demand roll call votes at the Democratic Convention in 1952 so that the folk back home over television could see and hear them in action.) Stage fright, or fear of it, deters many a potential speaker. But not every one suffers from stage fright. Indeed a good many of us manage to acquire an opposite disease: a rush of words—not ideas—to the mouth when confronted by an audience. We have all suffered under the resultant speeches.

Then there is the plight of professional speakers, preachers, office holders, *et al.*, who often have to speak when they have nothing new or fresh to say. And the result is a bad speech no matter how glib the speaker.

Gov. Thomas E. Dewey of New York is an able man, an experienced, and, on occasion, an effective and forthright speaker. In his presidential campaign in 1948 he was so sure of winning that he apparently decided not to commit himself closely by careful discussion of issues. Deliberately, in speech after speech he mouthed safe Republican generalities. Every morning, some of us thought, he asked himself: "Which pair of platitudes shall I wear today?" There is small doubt that this policy not only deprived his speaking of any claim to excellence, but also was a factor in his surprising defeat.

The thing that you, the prospective speaker, may want to say need not, of course, be of world shaking importance or of startling originality. It should always be something that you sincerely believe is pertinent to the occasion and worth sharing with your fellows. The suspicion in which oratory is held is due to the fact that eloquence or mere facility in speech is so usually on hire; that it so often serves the speaker's desire for gain or fame rather than his love of truth or justice.

You can have something to say and yet make a very poor speech. It's very rarely that an idea takes such possession of you that it inspires its own perfect or even reasonably effective expression. A good speech requires work, and work along two lines: first, in the logical and appropriate development of your ideas or your theme; and, second, in its presentation. You must think through your subject. If it is in any way controversial you must in your own mind raise every conceivable objection to it. It may be neither necessary nor appropriate to answer all these objections in your speech, but you must have them in mind as you prepare your presentation. I think that I have failed in a debate unless I had thought of more objections to my cause than my opponent has raised.

In every speech in behalf of a theory, a cause, a party, or line of action, it is even more important for a speaker than for an audience continually to bear in mind the two test questions: Is that so? and, So what? Instruction in good speaking should begin with instruction in straight thinking.

Not only the logical skeleton of your speech requires work, but also the rhetorical flesh which clothes it. Good speaking requires a mastery over a large vocabulary. Basic English has its uses but no oration can be made in it. Wise exhortations to clarity and simplicity of speech warn us against undue use of technical terms, words unknown to the general audience, and heavily polysyllabic discourse. But simplicity and clarity depend upon the choice of the right word, and that right word is very rarely outside the comprehension of your audience. It's up to you as a speaker to find and use it.

Too many speakers fall into a kind of platform gobbledygook, a use of cliches, and pompous but colorless words which make their style comparable to that of so many of our bureaucrats. Yes, and of professors who write in the field of the (so-called) social sciences. (On the average, the English in the same field do a better job of expressing themselves—at least in writing.)

The late George Orwell gives us a fine example of how important style and choice of words is to a subject. He writes:

> I am going to translate a passage of good English into modern English of the worst sort. Here is a well-known verse from "Ecclesiastes":
> "I returned and saw under the sun, that the race is not to the swift, nor the battle to the strong, neither yet bread to the wise, nor yet riches to men of understanding, nor yet favor to men of skill; but time and chance happeneth to them all."
> Here it is in modern English:
> "Objective consideration of contemporary phenomena compels the conclusion that success or failure in competitive activities exhibits no tendency to be commensurate with innate capacity, but that a considerable element of the unpredictable must inevitably be taken into account."*

Alas, too many speakers habitually employ the latter style.

*A Collection of Essays by George Orwell (Anchor Books).

Whether or not a speaker reads his principal speeches, it will help him, especially in his earlier years, to write out occasional speeches. A little later I shall deal with important differences between writing and speaking. A good essay is not necessarily a good speech and most assuredly an effective speech is rarely a good essay. Nevertheless, in my experience it pays the speaker to write out occasional speeches in more than outline. In general, practice in writing—not necessarily speech writing—helps a speaker's style. It teaches him a logical handling of his subject, enlarges his vocabulary, and gives him a chance to experiment in the order of words and the cadence of sentences.

It is commonplace to observe that speeches are enriched by illustrations, quotations, wit and humor. The accumulation of such material stimulates observation; it requires reading which, as Francis Bacon tells us, "maketh the full man."

Looking back on my own experience, I think I should have been wise to do what comes hard to me: Keep a systematic card catalog in which to enter striking quotations and illustrative material. I'm not sure that I could have found time to do a good job. As it was I collected material rather spasmodically for particular articles, books or speeches.

I never excelled in the use of quotations or stories. I shared the general handicap of speakers in our day; less than the orator of old can we count on an effective use of allusions. Popular culture, such as it is, is diffuse. In sum total, an audience knows a lot of things. But there are very few books that almost everybody reads or historic facts that they remember or literary allusions—even to the Bible or Shakespeare—which they recognize. I speak from bitter experience. An allusion is very widely understood in America only if it is to a popular character in the so-called and mis-called comics or perhaps to a current popular song. I once ventured a reference to Lot's wife before what I was told was a picked group of young people who had grown up in the church. As I remember it, no one, in answer to my question, knew what I was talking about.

A public opinion poll showed that only 21 per cent of the public have an approximate idea what the Bill of Rights is. The most one can expect from an allusion to Hamilton, Jefferson, Webster, Calhoun, Henry George, Adam Smith, Karl Marx is identification of them as somehow good or bad—in Marx's case mostly very bad.

As for illustrations and quotations, like other good things, they can be badly used or overused. We all know the speaker whose funny stories we remember but not what they were supposed to prove. You have made a poor speech when the listener can only remember or praise you for its quotations from other men. More than once I have listened to a sermon or a speech and felt as if I were looking at a drab cloth on which were loosely stitched patches of purple and gold. Whereas a good speech should have reminded me of a well woven tapestry. Too many quotations and illustrations are disastrous. They may make a speech mildly pleasing to the audience; they do not carry conviction. A man with something to say doesn't say it out of Bartlett's *Familiar Quotations*, still less out of *Joe Miller's Joke Book*. It is one of the virtues of Alben Barkley as a speaker that usually he is able to employ one of his fund of Kentucky stories to make a point and not just to get a laugh.

You will learn to manage both the logical structure of your speech and your use of illustrations and quotations better if you will literally live with any important speech that you are about to make. I know no other way to make a first rate speech, especially if the subject is of first rate importance. One speaks best on a general theme in line with one's major interest. In a true sense, the preparation for some of the great speeches of history was the life work of the speaker, his absorbing preoccupation. Is there not a story to the effect that Daniel Webster told a questioner that his reply to Hayne, delivered in a Senate debate, had been twenty years in the making?

I early discovered that the best way to prepare a speech is to get firmly in mind your major theme and then live with it, carry it around with you. Fortunately, we are so made that we can stow an important matter in the back of our minds, attend to necessary business, and then find that the mind has been working on our theme without our conscious attention. How else explain the fact of the sudden intrusion on your conscious attention of a phrase, an illustration, a solution of some problem of order or argument which had bothered you? Repeatedly, I have been happily surprised at the way some valuable hint or illustration would leap at me from the newspaper or from some happening as I went about my business. Looking back on the years I think that I have composed more of my speeches walking around, going to bed, getting up, or sometimes by flashes in the night, than at my desk.

I hasten to add that I lay no claim to the inspiration of genius in these flashes. For a great many years, I was almost obsessed with the notion that to advance my cause I had to speak whenever possible. Doubtless I sacrificed to some extent quality for quantity. In any case, I was carrying a load of work that made my method of composing speeches a necessity. I had no time to seek perfection in an artist's seclusion.

I have heard the theory that a truly great oration has rules for its composition almost comparable to the rules for writing a sonnet or a symphony. The comparison seems to me somewhat extreme. But an oration or even an effective speech requires a logical order. It should have a certain unity; the speaker shouldn't roam over the earth as if he were killing time in a filibuster nor drag in to every speech his pet creedal formulations on the road to secular or otherwordly salvation. A speech should have a beginning, a logical development, a climax or at the least a dignified end. My own sins, as my wife and other friendly critics often reminded me, were to try to make too many points in one speech and to have too many climaxes or postscripts to the climax. I personally have worried more over the proper beginnings, especially since I often was in the position of one who must get his audience's attention promptly or not at all. There isn't one formula—too much depends on the audience, the occasion, the subject. As I grew more accustomed to speaking in all sorts of places, I came more and more to depend upon some event, some remark of a preceding speaker, or, for example,—on a street corner—a reference to something before my listeners' eyes and ears, to get me started.

It was, of course, important to relate my beginnings to my theme. I have known speakers whose method reminded me of the English author, who, having been told that his novel was passable but its beginning too dull, returned it with the opening: " 'Bloody hell,' said the countess as she stumbled into the room." This time the ms. was returned because it could not sustain the expectation awakened by the opening sentence.

So far we have discussed the preparation of a speech. What about its delivery? I scarcely agree with the oft quoted but anonymous orator who said that the first, second, and third points of a good speech were delivery. But proper delivery is much neglected among us. My own first commandment would read: Speak to the audience as if you not only believed what you are saying is true but that it is important, that you are vitally interested in it and therefore think that it ought to interest your listeners.*

I am continually surprised by the number of speakers who act as if they were bored almost to tears by their own remarks. At the opposite pole are those who feign a false, synthetic enthusiasm like the reader of commercials on radio or, heaven help us, like most adult speakers to an audience of children. Both errors argue a lack of sincere interest on the speaker's part in his own theme, or in his audience, or both.

Many of the difficulties a man has in effective speaking would be solved or on their way to solution if he would learn to show a personal interest in his subject. He might forget himself in that interest, and find it easier to talk out loud. There are few persons who, in conversation, can't talk audibly and with a certain animation on a matter which interests them. It is easy to carry that interest over to a platform. The speaker's enthusiasm for his subject or the points he wants to make is likely to be contagious. It begets interest in the audience which in turn stimulates the speaker.

The kind of interest which I bespeak and a completely natural willingness to show it cannot successfully be simulated. It has to be real. It has little to do with the elocutionary ardors still somewhat in vogue in my boyhood. As late as my years in Union Seminary, I remember the rather cruel mirth with which we greeted a young man's efforts to simulate in a classroom what he thought was Patrick Henry's style and his revolutionary fervor. He succeeded only in making his eloquence seem ridiculous.

Nowadays simulated enthusiasm is primarily the mark of the readers or singers of commercials. They at least can be heard in tones more or less agreeable. But no one seriously believes that their hearts are in their extravagant praise of Coca-Cola, cars, coffee or cigarettes.

For years, I listened when possible to an excellent morning news summary

*It is better, however, to tell funny stories dead pan than to laugh at your own jokes.

over the radio. It was long sponsored by one coffee company. Then there was a switch to another house selling tea and coffee. Later I listened without conviction to the pleasant voice of the same newscaster as he read or recited the same extravagant praise of his new sponsor's coffee as formerly of the old. No one is the worse for it—unless, perhaps, public confidence in the spoken word is unconsciously lowered.

The announcer who deals in commercials has to build up a capacity to feign enthusiasm. I shall never forget the courteous program director of an Illinois station who was called upon in a political campaign to substitute, literally at the last moment, for my designated interrogator. (The latter, a professor in the University of Illinois, was called off at the last moment by the almost tearful pleas of the head of his department to consider the interests of the University. Academic freedom can be curbed by other than direct commands.) The radio announcer read admirably the interviewer's part of the script, but with such complete inattention to content that at one point he ignored the break and brightly declaimed his intention to speak at a socialist meeting to be held that night in Chicago. I had to interject, "I thought I was going to do that"—not only to keep the record straight but to save the announcer from a possible fate worse than death at the hands of his employers.

When the tricks and insincerities of commercials and the manners of successful announcers are transferred to the political platform or the pulpit, you have at best empty elocution, a spurious eloquence, at worst, blatant demagoguery and hypocrisy. That there is so much of this sort of thing goes far to explain the extent of popular cynicism. The hungry sheep who look up and are not fed know it.

I have written a bit scornfully of oratory as taught by teachers of elocution in my boyhood. But at least they did teach men and women to speak audibly. In this mechanized age speakers, not only beginners but the more experienced, are so sure of a loudspeaker's aid that they don't trouble themselves to project their voices, to speak distinctly, to avoid a slurring of syllables and a dropping of the voice at the end of every sentence. When I remember the awful task of trying to make oneself heard in the recesses of the old Madison Square Garden before electronic public address systems were invented I bless the loudspeaker. When I remember the encouragement it gives to slovenly speech, its frequent echoes, and the mechanical quality it too often imparts to the human voice, I am inclined to curse it. I never use it in a hall if I can help it. Some halls are so large and some address systems so well engineered that the loudspeaker is welcome. What is bad is too great dependence on it.

On a recent alumni day in Princeton, I dropped in to listen to one of the time honored inter-class debates in Whig Hall. The room was not large, the audience much smaller than at that debate in my day; the speakers, I think, more sophisticated and better coached than I and my youthful fellows. But not one of these moderns was easily and distinctly heard. They were obvious children of a mechanical age, sure of going out to a world of that democratic leveller, the microphone of a public address system, an instrument designed to raise or reduce all speech to a common denominator of audible sound. In quality, that denominator is usually very low.

My own convictions on this subject were strengthened by an unsolicited letter from Robert D. Howard of the Astor Hotel. He had answered my inquiry about the number of affairs in the hotel at which there was public speaking. A few days later he felt moved, to my delight, to write me as follows:

"Believe it or not, it has become the custom for a group as small as 50 persons to demand amplification and one of our greatest difficulties is to try to keep unaccustomed speakers from freezing through the microphone.

"It takes the sound engineer a few minutes to make his adjustments after the remarks are made by the Speaker.

"Unfortunately, however, if after opening the tones do not appear to be sufficiently loud, a great many speakers raise their tones to unusual proportions and they don't give the operator a chance to level the tones mechanically.

"There are a few 'musts' that should be stressed such as hanging on to the instrument, turning the head and therefore directing the voice too far to one side or the other and the slowed-up start of the speech in order to afford the necessary adjustment timing."

There is no excuse for this sort of indifference to the effective use of the voice. We white Americans from whatever region we come are not notable for the music of our speaking voices. Our Negro fellow citizens are more likely to be natural possessors of resonant voices. But most of them, like the whites, are careless about enunciation and pronunciation. All of us are prone to drop our voices at the end of sentences, and, so far as I can judge from current crops of young speakers, our numerous courses and classes in public speaking do nothing or nothing effective about it. Nature gives us our voices but most of us could improve them. Enunciation and pronunciation can be learned and the least pleasant qualities of voice somewhat corrected. Some colleges try to do that for their students. In the process one can and should learn how to breathe and how to support the voice from the diaphragm. It is not necessary even for political campaigners to speak themselves hoarse unless they are afflicted with colds.

More than any systematic instruction in speech, a comparatively few lessons in singing in my youth have helped me through the years to support the rigors of much speaking on New York street corners. They even helped me cope with stage fright in my younger days. It didn't tie my vocal cords up in knots.

In developing an effective use of the voice in public speech, the practice of reading aloud is helpful. It's better if you can get a small audience, say the children in your family. Your desire to hold their interest may unconsciously teach you something about the art of putting appropriate feeling and expression into the stories you read them. To read poetry out loud is also invaluable in helping one to acquire a feeling for rhythm and cadence and to convey that feeling in one's voice.

In learning to improve your use of voice and your manner of speech one of the greatest aids did not come into existence until after I was well launched as a speaker. I refer to disk or tape recordings. (The old wax cylinders served a singer like Caruso fairly well but as records of speeches all that I have ever heard were very unsatisfactory.) In the early days recordings of speeches were rather expensive and I was singularly slow in recognizing their value. Hence it was fairly late in my career that I first heard myself over the radio by a recording. As almost everyone is now aware, our voices reach our own ears by other channels than the ears of our auditors. They sound better to us than to listeners. I was not only surprised but disappointed by my own voice when I first heard this recording. I had heard it away from home. When I got home, with carefully assumed nonchalance, I asked my wife if she had heard the speech over the radio. "Yes," she said. "Was it a good record?" I asked. "Oh, yes," she replied, "it sounded just like you." I never told her what a blow that was. As time went on I think I was helped by often listening to a recording, but I should have begun sooner.

The speaker should be concerned not only about his voice and its effective use, but about his action—including gestures—when he is on the platform. A speaker can stand motionless, read a good speech with deadpan face and no gestures and in the process convey information. But he can scarcely move an audience more than would a motionless actor on the stage.

In the whole business of expressing emotion and conveying ideas by bodily action the actor on the stage has a great advantage over the speaker. He has one special and definite role to consider, study and express. He can work out in advance his motions and gestures. He is acting in an intimate group and his actions are appropriate to his part in the group. He never has a monologue comparable in length to a speaker's address. To be sure, he, no less than the speaker, must be aware of the audience with which he is communicating, but in his case through the medium of his role in a play which makes far easier the whole problem of appropriate action.

Moreover, the speaker is compelled to relate his action while speaking to such important externals as the size and shape of his platform: lectern, pulpit, soap box, podium, rear end of truck or train. Usually he must also consider the necessity of keeping contact with a microphone for a loudspeaker, if not for radio or recording device. Finally my experience suggests, rather tentatively, that different types of audiences in different nations or in different regions of the same nation have quite different standards for evaluating a speaker's gestures and action during an address. It is certain that everywhere the degree and kind of action should vary with subject and occasion.

The one thing that can definitely be asserted is that a speaker penalizes himself if he cannot use bodily action as well as variations in voice to convey his message. That is one reason why I have found it so unsatisfactory to be merely a disembodied voice in a radio studio.

Rules for gesturing and other action beyond the most obvious and elemental, are hard to frame and difficult to apply. In this field, the man determines the style in the light of his own feeling for his subject, the audience and the occasion. The old-fashioned elocutionary efforts of which I saw something in my youth went out of favor because gestures as well as vocal inflections seemed artificial, imposed on the speech rather than truly expressive of it.

Only a few years ago I saw an able college speaker in a national contest lose first place which otherwise would have been his because a select audience, asked to vote as judges, didn't like his self-consciously studied gestures. I asked his college coach why he hadn't trained so promising a speaker out of such elocution-school gestures. "Don't think we haven't tried," he replied. "But he was too well taught elocution in his high school."

That, nowadays, is an unusual fault. Most of our speakers, professional as well as amateur, suffer because they obviously are afraid to use action and so stand glued to a desk, if not a manuscript, and move arms and hands very awkwardly if at all.

My sympathy with such speakers is great. In my student days and for a long time thereafter, I was plagued before and during a speech by my hands. They were always in my way. What should I do with them? I welcomed the kind of pulpit or speaker's stand which hid my knees and much of my body. Now for a great many years I have preferred room for action. To my surprise I lived to see a day when a woman, obviously not too happy about the content of a certain speech, told me months later that she remembered me and the speech, "for your expressive use of your hands."

What made the change I can't tell. Except this: with experience I became far less conscious of my own feelings, more aware of my audience, and being freer from inhibitions, unconsciously more inclined to action. Moreover, I had acquired close contact with people who used their hands far more in ordinary conversation than those with whom I grew up! Even today I become embarrassed as a schoolboy on being asked by a news photographer, eager for an "action picture," to "make like you're speaking." I literally don't know just how I gesture when speaking, and I always become very self-conscious at the photographer's demand. (Incidentally, a large proportion of the pictures showing, allegedly, persons performing some interesting act are phony; they are staged before or after the real event.)

Such authorities as the eminent classical scholar Dr. Gilbert Highet of Columbia and Dr. Houston Peterson of Rutgers, in discussing Cicero with Lyman Bryson in the program, *Invitation to Learning*, pictured an orator who planned everything—presumably including gestures. "Cicero," according to Dr. Highet, "composed a speech months before the occasion, learned it all by heart like an opera singer learning a difficult piece and then improvised freely on it." He added that "all good orators, like Churchill or Lincoln, at their best, had a kind of instinctive rhythmic pattern" but "the old maestro himself [Cicero] knew the pattern and it wasn't instinctive with him. It was just as careful as a composer's work with rhythms and balances."

Something like Cicero's method, the learned professors seemed to agree, was a necessary condition for the preparation and delivery of great oratory. Cicero, in Dr. Highet's opinion, was the greatest orator who ever lived, to which judgment Dr. Peterson added that he was the greatest theoretician on oratory.

I am too poor a Latinist to pass on Cicero's pre-eminence. I should go a long way in agreeing with the professors that Cicero's method was the proper method for the preparation and delivery of an oration worthy of comparison with other works of art. I accept the general judgment of authorities on the low estate of most modern speech—at least in English. But I decidedly disagree with Dr. Highet's assertion that Adlai Stevenson's campaign speeches in 1952 were not really speeches but mere "collections of points." Even more do I disagree with Dr. Highet in his extreme disparagement of the effectiveness of speech which does not conform to oratorical models or which can hardly qualify as a work of art. When I saw, at a later time, Dr. Peterson's choice of speeches for inclusion in his newly published *Treasury of the World's Great Speeches,* I doubted his agreement with his colleague. Many of the speeches he chose were great, not by reason of perfection as works of art but by reason of the importance of the man, the subject, the occasion, and hence their effect on history. By this test, a great many speeches were more important than any of Cicero's.

The primary business of most public speech is communication. Few public speakers can work on their necessary speeches months in advance or learn them by heart. Cicero was in his day a man of affairs but he never campaigned for the presidency. (Maybe he would have insisted on reforming our present procedures in the interest of fewer speeches and better.) There are occasions in which the most effective speech is not after the manner either of Lincoln's Gettysburg Address, or Webster's dedication of Bunker Hill monument. Nevertheless, there are few speeches, even those which are primarily informative, which cannot profitably be improved in preparation and delivery. A good speaker must marry his delivery to his argument far better than most of us do. He must avoid alike the monotony of sustained vehemence or under emphasis.

All of this is a kind of preface to our tackling the problem of the reading of written speeches which is so widespread a practice among us. Few of us have the photographic memory or the time which might enable us to memorize our written speeches. More than that would be necessary for the most effective effort. There are not many occasions when awareness of a specific audience will not suggest to a speaker what he could not wholly anticipate. He should, therefore, ideally not only be able to memorize a set speech but improvise on it easily.

If we cannot satisfactorily memorize, should we read our speeches? Perhaps, if we will learn to read well and be able to improvise occasionally even with a written manuscript to follow. There are occasions when it is almost necessary to read a speech. For example, speeches, as in a radio studio, where timing is all important and every second counts in putting over your message.

Speeches which must convey accurately facts, figures, or formulations of a program better be read unless one has a remarkable memory and confidence in it. It is, also, I think, better to read speeches on ceremonial occasions when dignity and beauty of language are peculiarly important—always providing, that is, that one cannot or will not memorize one's oration.

No speaker needs to read as badly as most speakers do. A manuscript need not put a man in a straitjacket or serve as a kind of wall between him and his audience. But it always has that tendency. The all-important feeling of communication between speaker and audience is of necessity somewhat impaired if the speaker must look chiefly at his manuscript.

The speaker must always be aware of his audience—that is, of his particular audience—all the more so if he is repeating a much used lecture or speech. He must come to each audience with some anticipatory notion of its probable makeup, attitude, and interest. He should look at his audience; only so can he judge the effect of his speech. He should be prepared to change pace; to indulge in humor—even the wisecrack; to introduce the unexpected, but not the irrelevant. It is not only legitimate but sometimes necessary for a speaker to rephrase and repeat an important fact or opinion until he feels that the audience understands.

It cannot be too strongly insisted that the written and spoken word, while they have much in common, are by no means the same. The speaker is concerned with the particular group before him; he is not speaking to a scattered group of readers or to posterity. Sometimes he can communicate more effectively by repetition, intonation, gesture, unfinished sentence. I wince at stenographic reports of my speeches even when they have gone over well enough to receive much applause. But I am convinced that I would have made a mistake to have read a smoother speech. The answer may be harder work on a speech but not a reading of a written production.

One of the penalties of the method I describe is that, probably more than if I had written out my speech, I think after it's over of a point I might have made or a phrase I might have used. But such regretful reflections are keenest when the occasion was a debate or discussion which couldn't have been entirely written out in advance, and I can remember suffering from this occupational disease of speakers, this belated access of wisdom, even on occasions—as on radio—when I had read my speech. Few things hurt a speaker worse than the bright idea that came too late.

In college I always tried to memorize a major speech—even in debate. But I have a poor photographic memory; as I grew busier I lacked time to memorize, and my attempts to recite my own speeches, like pieces in school, seemed to cut me off from my audience. Hence I adopted the plan of writing out important speeches, but memorizing only the outline, trusting that my effort in writing would improve the quality of the speech. I soon found that I was trying so hard to recall what I had thought were felicitous phrasings that I turned my eyes inward instead of looking at my audience. Hence while

I have done much writing, it has not been the writing of speeches. As time went on, I discovered that it took an audience to make me think of many of the phrases, especially the wisecracks which proved effective. I can't think of quips cold-bloodedly when looking only at my pen or typewriter. (But once made, I can and do remember and repeat them before different audiences, until I almost gag at their repetition.)

In an earlier chapter I have said that during political campaigns I wrote out rather fully a few basic speeches or summaries of speeches. Unless I had occasion to use one of these over the radio from a studio I never read or recited it as written. But I had one or another of these summaries in mind as the foundation or skeleton of each particular speech. I also used them as summaries to the press. I followed a similar plan in shaping up speeches for a lecture tour. I never exactly repeated myself. For speeches not of the campaign variety where I was less concerned for publicity I wrote less and depended more simply on outlines. But it must be remembered that at the same time I was doing much writing on my general themes for articles, pamphlets, and books. I do not urge my own particular practice upon other speakers. I merely insist that good speaking requires thought and effort.

A man may lack the great artistry of a Cicero (or in our day of a Churchill at his best) and yet become an effective speaker. But only if he has something to say, in which he is deeply, sincerely interested, the presentation of which he will carefully work out and then go before an audience thinking more of it and his message than of himself.

Questions for Analysis

1. What are "the arts of the orator" a speaker today might use "like a sophist or a demagogue simply for his own profit or power"? How have listeners become susceptible to these "arts"? Do you believe, "The hungry sheep who look up and are not fed know it"? Explain.

2. Describe occasions on which you have thought "that eloquence or mere facility in speech is so usually on hire; that it so often serves the speaker's desire for gain or fame rather than his love of truth or justice." Illustrate what Thomas means by "exhibitionism," "platform gobbledygook," and "a drab cloth on which were loosely stitched patches of purple and gold."

3. How does Thomas suggest various ways in which you might "literally live with any important speech you are about to make"? What is the significance of "a reference to something before my listeners' eyes and ears, to get me started"? How may a speaker prepare himself to "come to each audience with some anticipatory notion of its probable makeup, attitude, and interest"?

4. Describe what to you seem to be Thomas' attitudes toward "classical form" in delivery and message. What does his statement "A good speaker must marry his delivery to his argument" mean? How can a speaker sometimes "communicate more effectively by repetition, intonation, gesture, unfinished sentences"? Why are there "not many occasions when awareness of a specific audience will not suggest to a speaker what he could not wholly anticipate"?

5. Characterize Thomas' attitude toward audiences. How does he prepare to persuade? What do "the two test questions: Is that so? and, So what?" appear to mean to him? How does a speaker truly consider his listeners "hungry sheep"? What does it mean for a speaker to "go before an audience thinking more of it and his message than of himself"? How can you, as a listener, tell when a speaker is fulfilling Thomas' high expectations for all speakers? Do you often find such a speaker?

28

While I'm on My Feet

Gerald Kennedy

I entered the Methodist ministry to preach. From the time when I was sixteen years old and made a speech (really a kind of sermon) in the student body assembly of my high school, I understood Paul's proclamation: "For if I preach the gospel, that gives me no ground for boasting. For necessity is laid upon me. Woe to me if I do not preach the gospel!" (I Cor. 9:16) It is my conviction that anything less than this is not enough to be considered a call to preach. I meet too many young ministers who say in effect, "Well, I do not mind preaching. As a matter of fact, I rather enjoy it." This is not to say that such young men will not perform a valuable service for the church. But they will never be men with prophetic authority and pentecostal fire.

As a college student and then as a seminary student, I preached twice a week. Harry Emerson Fosdick was reported to have said that no man could prepare more than one sermon a week which would be worth hearing. I agree with him, and unless a man can be set free to do nothing but preach, one sermon a week is enough. So in those good old days, I leaned heavily on other men's sermons. Right from the beginning I admired simple language, clear outline, and a message relevant to my daily life.

I began using my notes but always I knew it would be better preaching if there were no notes. So, because preaching was my main ambition, I resolved to learn how to do it with freedom. From my seminary days onward, nothing went into my pulpit with me except my preparation and hard work. I have so few virtues that I mention (perhaps boast is the proper word) one quality which gives me great satisfaction. So far as I can recall, I have never stood in my pulpit without having prepared for the event to the very best of my ability. This is not to say that every sermon has seemed satisfactory to me. None of them have. But it has never been necessary to apologize to God or man because I let other things crowd into my time for preparation. I have

Gerald Kennedy is Bishop of the Los Angeles Area, Methodist Church.

Reprinted by permission from *While I'm on My Feet* by Gerald Kennedy. Copyright, 1963 by Abingdon Press. "Preaching," pp. 135–140.

neglected other matters connected with my work, but it never seemed permissible to give my congregation less than my best.

This was due largely to an ironbound schedule which became almost as much a part of me as breathing. I outlined my sermon on Wednesday morning and then talked it through Thursday, Friday, and Saturday mornings. Sunday morning I rarely got involved in other activities, although I broadcast over the radio before my service for several years. Sunday morning was my last chance to meditate on the sermon, although sometimes I am afraid it was merely worrying about it. But I could never be at ease if anything interfered with this schedule, and even when I was traveling, it was kept faithfully. Sometimes it meant getting up pretty early in the morning, but nothing went well unless I followed the routine.

I do not know what conscious aim other preachers have when they preach. For me it was to proclaim a conviction about God's nature, God's will, God's resources, God's promises. It was to bear a testimony to the truth of Christ and to help people see themselves as the objects of God's love revealed in Jesus. It was to create a faith that the gospel is the answer to all human questions and the solution to all human problems. It was to prophesy against evil and heal the brokenhearted. I would sometimes become so frustrated with my inadequacies that it seemed only a stupid egotist or a blind fool could continue as a preacher. But I have never been able to escape the conviction that preaching is nothing less than God in Christ using a poor, unworthy man to proclaim his Word.

It is the terrible vision of God and the horrible knowledge of one's own pettiness and sin that constitute the preacher's dilemma. One of my colleagues in the Council of Bishops once said that a preacher's wife has the impossible task of living with him all week and of regarding him as the voice of God on Sunday. For this and other reasons all preachers' wives are assured of heaven, for they have suffered enough hell on earth. But as long as the preacher himself does not succumb to pride, his situation is not to be envied either. Why should a congregation gather week after week to hear me? Do they not know how limited is my knowledge and how small is my virtue? I suppose this is the reason that the half hour from ten-thirty to eleven on Sunday mornings has always been agony of mind and spirit. Will anyone come today? Is my word worth even a moron's consideration? I tell you the man who is never nervous before he preaches and never suffers the despair of the damned when he finishes is either an angel or a fool.

Yet I would be less than candid not to confess that when the hour has struck and the text is announced, I come closest to understanding the psalmist's word about man: "Yet thou . . . dost crown him with glory and honor" (Ps. 8:5). For of all the privileges bestowed upon any of his creatures, to proclaim the unsearchable riches of Christ is surely the highest. Of all the tasks that men are given to do, preaching seems to me to be the greatest. You may recall that in Moby Dick Herman Melville speaks of the pulpit as the place where the storm is first described and where the fair breeze is first invoked. "Yes," he writes, "the world's a ship on its passage out, and not a voyage complete; and the pulpit is its prow."

While my present job does not involve preaching to a continuing congregation—which is a great personal loss—still I do as much or more preaching than when I was in the pastorate. And I have learned more about preachers than I knew then, for they have talked to me and so have their laymen. While I still have a very limited opportunity to hear other men preach, for what it is worth they seem to me to fail mostly at three points.

First, too many of us do not work on our preaching hard enough or long enough. The more gifted a man is, the more he is tempted to neglect his preparation. You listen to a man and he brings out an interesting point here or there, but there is no sense of solid structure. He makes too much of one point and too little of another. He milks an illustration dry, and what would have been effective if kept short and sharp loses its cutting edge and gets wearisome. Such a man circles back to something already dealt with and there is no sense of the inevitable, forward march of the thought.

Secondly, too many preachers fail to organize their material so that it is at once plain and clear. The people leave with a vague sense of something religious having been said, but the points which give a subject directness are either hopelessly smudged and muddled or they were never there in the first place. I have lectured on this, written about it, and discussed it at every opportunity, but it has done little good. So many preachers will not believe that their first responsibility is to be understood. I still have church members come up after the sermon and say, with a kind of wonderment, "I understood you." To organize your material does not take special gifts and it does not demand any great intelligence. But it does demand the assumption that an involved and obscure style is not so much a sign of profundity of thought as of confusion of mind.

Thirdly, the sermon falls flat when the preacher has no sense of the dramatic. This is the place where one is tempted to say, "If he has it, fine; if he lacks it, nothing much can be done about it." The man who is not easily bored will probably never sense when he is boring others. The man who does not feel chills run up his spine when the right word is spoken or when an incident is observed that makes truth leap up and march may be an acceptable lecturer or writer. But he will never preach. Emily Dickinson said, "If I read a book and it makes my whole body so cold no fire can ever warm me, I know that is poetry. If I feel physically as if the top of my head were taken off, I know that is poetry. These are the only ways I know it. Is there any other way?" And, brethren, this is the only way you can know you have been listening to a real sermon. Truth is personal and truth is glimpsed in the midst of conflict. Great teachers can help a man understand that somewhat, but not much.

Of one thing I feel very sure. If the idea does not hit me with an excitement I cannot contain, it is not the Holy Spirit speaking. Furthermore, it can never be made exciting to my hearers, no matter how many cheap tricks and melodramatic tactics are employed. The drama has to be intrinsic, and discerning people will spot the pretender immediately. As a matter of fact, sincerity itself is dramatic. Timing is very important, and I have heard some fine illustrations fall flat as a statistical report because the preacher had no sense of when and how much. I have an increasing belief that the heart of drama is concreteness. Abstract preaching is always poor preaching.

Speaking with neither manuscript nor notes doubles the pleasure of the preacher and increases it tenfold for the congregation. When I read some fellow's article in a ministerial magazine arguing for the reading of sermons, I wonder if he has ever talked with his laymen. He may convince a few scholarly brothers who would rather be caught undressed than split an infinitive, but I never met a layman who would agree with him. Even an elementary understanding of communication will dispose of his arguments. I tried in vain to open an important pulpit for a sermon-reader, and the committee would not even take the time to go and hear him preach. A man may stubbornly hold to his custom of reading his sermons, but let him never deceive himself to the extent of believing that the people like it.

Anything that is done effectively and well always seems easy. This is true of all artists and craftsmen who know their jobs. Whenever I see a championship golf match on TV, it looks so smooth and simple that I wonder why we duffers make such a mess of it. A gushing woman came up after a sermon I preached on the "Lurline" en route to Honolulu and said, "My father preached just like you. He just stood up and talked." I wanted to say to her, "Lady, if that is true, he wasn't worth hearing." For to be free of manuscript will not lessen the work or demand less time for preparation. It may increase the work and it will certainly increase the strain of delivering a series of sermons if you have more than one a day. But it is worth it.

Every now and then somebody comes along to predict the end of preaching. True, we never have enough good preachers to go around. Many a thoughtful Protestant layman leaves the church feeling empty and frustrated, wondering if he would have been better off to read a book or listen to the radio. But the Reformation was born of great preaching, and every important rebirth of faith has been associated with the rediscovery of the centrality of preaching. For the spoken word is still the most powerful instrument for shaping society and affecting human lives. The church needs all sorts and conditions of men to do its work. But it will die without preachers, and a democracy cannot exist without free and flaming pulpits.

I have been preacher and teacher. Preaching is better. I have been preacher and writer. Preaching is better. I have been preacher and administrator. Preaching is better. When about once in a year I have a free Sunday, eleven o'clock finds me restless, nervous, and unhappy. I try to remind myself that a man needs a change of pace—to say nothing of his congregation. But there is a kind of panic takes over as I think what life would be without preaching. My friend W. E. Sangster of England wrote in the preface of his last book, shortly before he died: "I am a traveling preacher unable, by reason of sickness, either to travel or preach." I knew those were the saddest words any preacher could write.

Questions for Analysis

1. How does Kennedy testify to his singular devotion to preaching? Why would he agree that "no man could prepare more than one sermon a week which would be worth hearing"? How might contemporary rhetoric, that of campaigns and campuses, for example, be improved if all public speakers agreed to abide by Fosdick's proposition? How many of them can say, "I have never stood in my pulpit without having prepared for the event to the very best of my ability"? What does it mean to a speaker's concept of his work to be "nervous before he preaches" and to suffer "the despair of the damned when he finishes"?

2. Add to Kennedy's description of speeches inadequately prepared. What is the "sense of solid structure" to which he refers? How does a well-prepared speech ensure a "sense of the inevitable, forward march of thought"? How is this "march of thought" related to organization? What may account for a speaker's failure to distinguish between "profundity of thought" and "confusion of mind"?

3. How does a speaker develop a "sense of the dramatic"? How does he learn "when the right word is spoken or when an incident is observed that makes truth leap up"? How, for example, did John F. Kennedy learn the importance of timing? Describe the "Cheap tricks and melodramatic tactics" by which speakers may attempt to induce excited response.

4. How is Kennedy's belief, "Abstract preaching is always poor preaching," consistent with findings about effective style in informative and persuasive speaking? Illustrate with two contrasting introductions a concrete and an abstract approach to an issue of our times.

5. How may concreteness of style serve to increase the probability that "the spoken word is still the most powerful instrument for shaping society and affecting human lives"? What in the rhetoric of our times suggests the validity of this assertion? How is our democracy in a sense now enduring its "free and flaming pulpits"?

29

The Veep's "Kentucky Windage"

William J. Buchanan

The late Vice President Alben Barkley once told me a fascinating little story. Over the years I've come to recognize it as the best advice I ever had.

I was a senior at the University of Louisville that February in 1949, and failing miserably in a public-speaking course. When I learned that the newly elected Vice President would address the annual Jefferson-Jackson Day Democratic gathering on the 26th, I badgered my father, a longtime friend of Barkley's, into getting me an invitation. Here, I realized, was an opportunity to study one of the great speakers of all time.

The ballroom of Louisville's Seelbach Hotel was packed that evening with proud Kentuckians come to hear their state's honored son. They were not disappointed. In fine form, Barkley delivered a rousing speech, full of humorous barbs chastising all Republicans to the glory of all Democrats. He closed to a standing ovation. As the band struck up, a stranger tapped my shoulder. "The Vice President would like to see you," he said.

Barkley shook my hand and asked about my father. Then, admitting curiosity, he questioned my intense note-taking during his talk. "Are you," he asked somewhat wryly, "planning to go into politics?"

His good humor disarmed me. Compulsively, I started pouring out my troubles to the Vice President of the United States. I'd come tonight, I told him, to study his speaking style. I confessed my failing grade at the university, named the good speakers I'd tried to copy, allowed as how it was all probably useless.

Barkley stared at me in amusement, and I became acutely aware of what I was doing—rambling on to the Vice President. I tried to mumble an apology, but he smiled and said, "Son, that was a pretty good speech right there. All you need is a little Kentucky Windage.

William J. Buchanan is a Lieutenant Colonel, United States Air Force.

Reprinted with permission from the June 1968 *Reader's Digest*, pp. 130–32. Copyright 1968 by The Reader's Digest Assn., Inc.

"When I was about your age," the Vice President went on, "a friend of mine down in Paducah asked me to go skeet shooting with him. I'd never shot skeet, but I was pretty good with a shotgun, so I obliged. On the first round I powdered 21 of 25 clay birds. 'Good shooting!' my friend said. 'But there are a few things you should watch.' He then showed me the 'proper' stance, how to sight with both eyes open, and a whole slew of other things absolutely guaranteed to improve my style.

"Well, my friend was an expert, so I practiced his way. Only problem was, as my style improved my score went down. One afternoon, after I succeeded in breaking only eight birds, I asked a young lady watching from the sidelines how my form looked.

" 'Your form's fine, Alben,' she said. 'But aren't you supposed to break *all* those little black things?' Typical female reply, I thought. But her words bothered me; I found myself repeating them over and over. Was I really trying to 'break all those little black things?' Or was I more concerned with trying to imitate a prima ballerina?"

He paused and chuckled softly. "Well, I realized right then that I'd never be much of a ballerina. I could hardly wait for the next round. I discarded all the fancy frills and went back and used my best Kentucky Windage.* I beat my friend that round—and he never outshot me again."

Barkley leaned forward in his chair, and looked directly at me. "What had I done wrong?" He paused to let the question soak in. "I had ignored my natural abilities, traded a way that worked well for me for one that didn't because I was overly impressed with my friend's criticism.

"Now don't mistake me. Expert advice can be a blessing. But only when it's used to sharpen your own instincts and talents—never as a substitute for them."

The Vice President held out his hand and said, "Next time you get up to speak, remember, use a little Kentucky Windage."

On my way to class next morning I threw away my carefully prepared notes with the marginal references to "pause briefly" and "emphasize here." I knew that never again would I try to imitate someone else's formula for success. When my turn at the lectern came I made my point as simply as I could and sat down. The startled professor nodded his approval. I finished that semester in the top quarter of the class.

Over the years I've repeated Barkley's story many times. In one way or another I find that it applies to nearly everyone who seeks my advice—whether it's a young officer worried about his first staff briefing or my own son trying to decide how to perform a junior rodeo event. I first give what guidance I can. Then I tell them about my chat with Vice President Barkley, advise them to use a little Kentucky Windage and go right ahead.

*The term is derived from Kentucky frontiersmen's unique long-rifle shooting style: instead of relying solely on gunsights, they estimated wind conditions and offset aim accordingly. Among Kentucky hill people today, the expression means using one's own personal estimate and judgment in a situation as well as, and sometimes in spite of, precedent.

Questions for Analysis

1. How does Barkley demonstrate a cultivated audience awareness? How is audience awareness related to the point of his anecdote?

2. What distinguished Buchanan's effective "rambling on" from his ineffective efforts in class? How may "classroom consciousness" adversely affect delivery? List features of highly stylized delivery.

3. How does Barkley's prescription of "Kentucky Windage" conform to requirements for speaker "credibility"? What is the optimal relationship of "substance" to "form," of "message" to "delivery"?

Part III

Questions for Discussions

1. Can listening find a place in the curriculum?
2. Audience adaptation: the fine art of ambiguity?
3. How can we reform the informer? the persuader?
4. How important is delivery on the platform? on television? in the classroom?
5. Opinions and polls: a study in circular response?

Topics for Speeches

1. The case against platform gobbledygook
2. The freedom of the flaming pulpit
3. Is that so? So what?
4. Mass media and the need to make a face
5. How to succeed on the platform without even trying
6. Listeners as hungry sheep
7. Give me a *better* reason
8. The lost art of oratory
9. Let talk of images and kings
10. Red flag words, yours and mine

IV

CASE STUDIES IN CONTEMPORARY RHETORIC

Introduction

In the introduction to Part III of this volume we suggested that observation, speculation, and experimentation all play a part in generating theories and techniques of listening and speaking. In the logical progression of things, after the practitioners and theorists come the critics, those who provide—as your dictionary might put it—reasoned opinions, expressed as appreciations of art or technique, or as judgment of truth or social value. In fact, there are different kinds of critics, each with his own special point of focus. These are suggested by hyphenated labels: *scholar-critics* ("what happened?"), *peer-critics* ("how was it done?"), and *citizen-critics* ("is it significant?").[1] Both as producers and consumers of speech communication we have an interest in evaluations made from each of these points of view. Because this is so, Part IV consists of a series of studies, by competent critics, of specific instances of contemporary speechmaking.

Viewed as a group, although individually they may emphasize different purposes, these studies serve three ends:

1. *To report,* to tell what happened. In this respect the collection supplements Part I, exemplifying a variety of listener attitudes and anxieties and the ways in which different speakers relate to them.

2. *To theorize,* to formulate generalizations about communication. In this sense the studies provide examples of speaker concepts and concerns discussed in Part II, and of theories and techniques presented in Part III.

3. *To evaluate,* to judge social impact and worth. In this regard the studies offer comprehensive judgments on specific efforts at public persuasion, and relate audience, occasion, and purpose to the behavior of the speaker.

These three ends of speech criticism are reflected in the twelve studies that follow. While they are representative in many respects, none of them deals with communication in committees or conferences, with international diplomacy or cross-cultural settings, or with communication through radio or television. Rather, in each case the study focuses on one or more speakers dealing

---

[1]See J. Jeffery Auer. *Brigance's Speech Communication,* 3rd ed. (New York, Appleton-Century-Crofts, 1967), pp. 201–209.

with public issues of our own times in face-to-face contact with groups of listeners.

One of the ways of grouping studies of this kind is according to the posture of the speaker as spokesman, whether for himself, with others involved in a social or political movement, or as part of an institution. For convenience we have sequenced our collection in this way.

Although Adlai Stevenson was a child of the Fifties, serving in that decade as Governor of Illinois, and Democratic presidential nominee in 1952 and 1956, his life and public service extended into the decade of the Sixties. Thus he falls within our categorical definition of "contemporary." Richard Murphy's study is a general appraisal of Stevenson as a speaker, and especially as a political campaigner. Maxine Schnitzer Ferris treats another kind of campaigner in her comprehensive study of Roy Wilkins, longtime leader of the National Association for the Advancement of Colored People.

The next grouping is also one of studies dealing with individual speakers, but focusing upon a particular aspect in each case. Robert N. Hall discusses the way Lyndon B. Johnson's speeches are prepared, and also reveals how the Johnson methods changed as did his attitude toward public speaking when he moved from Senate majority leader to Vice President and then to President of the United States. In her study of Stokely Carmichael's emergence as a spokesman for Black Power, Pat Jefferson traces the development of his seemingly incompatible images. Ronald Reagan's rise to political prominence is traced by Kurt W. Ritter back to a single, oft-repeated speech, built from a special kind of "public relations rhetoric." The unique role of Dick Gregory in the Black Power movement is portrayed in a first-hand report by Eliot Asinof.

While all speakers engage in solo performances, many are really speaking in concert with others who are committed to the same social or political movement. Thus, in the next group of three studies, Donald E. Williams surveys the Ku Klux Klan spokesmen and their arguments in a concerted campaign early in the Sixties. Barnet Baskerville singles out Frederick Schwarz, Billy James Hargis, and Carl McIntire in his study of the radical right. In a third study of a movement Donald H. Smith describes the long fight for human rights by American Negroes and includes brief sketches of contemporary leaders of the black revolt: A. Phillip Randolph, Roy Wilkins, James Farmer, John Lewis, Martin Luther King, Jr., Malcolm "X", and Stokely Carmichael.

Sometimes public speakers do not officially represent an organized movement, but do talk within an institutional context and thus indirectly speak also for their business or professional associates. We include two studies of such institutional persuasion. Randall M. Fisher concludes that public presentations by businessmen are often over-reactions to criticism of business as an institution, rather than positive arguments. A second study with an institutional focus is Howard H. Martin's report of protests against the Vietnam war organized by concerned students and faculty on a single university campus.

If political parody is a form of humor, then we have in this collection of studies one note of fun. William Safire has abstracted from his recent collection of political argot[2] an "all-purpose speech" that permits candidates to take "firm stands on all sides of every issue." For those who lived through the 1968 primary and presidential campaigns, this piece may seem more grotesque than humorous. Fittingly enough, our contemporary studies conclude with William H. Honan's article, published the day before Richard Nixon's inaugural in January, 1969, reporting on the speech-writing team that had worked for Nixon through the 1968 campaign and that would begin the new administration with him.

Even the imposition of limitations described earlier did not make easy the choice of studies for inclusion in this volume. And the task was made more difficult by deciding to have no more than one study of any one speaker. Thus there is a substantial body of studies that "might have been." From this number, and for those who would like to read additional studies of the rhetoric of the Sixties, we list here a selected bibliography.

Anatol, Karl W. and John R. Bittner. "Kennedy on King: The Rhetoric of Control." *TS* 16(No. 3, 1968) : 31–4.

Andrews, James R. "Confrontation at Columbia: A Case Study in Coercive Rhetoric." *QJS* 55(1969) :9–16.

Bormann, Earnest. "The Southern Senators' Filibuster on Civil Rights," *SSJ* 27(1961) :183–94.

Bostrum, Robert N. " 'I Give You a Man'—Kennedy's Speech for Adlai Stevenson." *SM* 35(1968) :129–36.

Butterfield, Roger. "Ghost Writers" [Presidential]. *Life* (July 5, 1968) :62–4.

Cornwell, Elmer E., Jr. "Johnson's Press Relations Style." *JQ* 43(1966) :3–9.

Fisher, Randall M. "Modern Business Speaking: A Rhetoric of 'Conventional Wisdom'." *SSJ* 30(1965) :327–34.

Golden, James L. "John F. Kennedy and the 'Ghosts'." *QJS* 52(1966) :348–57.

Gregg, Richard B. and A. Jackson McCormack. "Whitey Goes to the Ghetto: A Personal Chronicle of a Communication Experience with Black Youths." *TS* 16(No. 3, 1968) :25–30.

Jefferson, Pat. "The Magnificent Barbarian at Nashville" [Stokely Carmichael]. *SSJ* 33(1968) :77–87.

Jefferson, Pat. " 'Stokely's Cool': Style." *TS* 16(No. 3, 1968) :19–24.

Logue, Cal M. "The Political Rhetoric of Ralph McGill." *SM* 35(1968) :122–8.

Makay, J. J. "George C. Wallace: Southern Spokesman with a Northern Audience." *CSSJ* 19(1968) :202–8.

Naughton, James M. "The Contrasting Life and/or Campaign Styles of Nelson (Zap) Rockefeller and Richard (Cool) Nixon." *NYTM* (July 28, 1968) :7,44ff.

Rae, Douglas W. and Peter A. Lupsha. "The Politics of Theatre: Reagan at Yale." *NR* (February 3, 1968) :11–2.

Rein, Irving J. *The Relevant Rhetoric: Case Studies in Public Speaking* [including

2*The New Language of Politics: An Anecdotal Dictionary of Catchwords, Slogans and Political Usage* (New York, Random House, 1968).

Malcolm X, Lyndon Johnson, Eugene McCarthy, and Richard Nixon]. New York: The Free Press, 1969.

Ricks, Christopher. "The Literary Style of L.B.J." *Esquire* (November, 1966): 117, 162–4.

Scott, Robert L. "A Rhetoric of Facts: Arthur Larson's Stance as a Persuader." *SM* 35(1968):109–21.

Scott, Robert L. and Wayne Brockriede. *The Rhetoric of Black Power.* New York: Harper & Row, 1969.

Smith, Donald H. "Martin Luther King, Jr.: In the Beginning at Montgomery." *SSJ* 34(1968):8–16.

Smith, Donald H. "The Rhetoric of Riots," in Carl E. Larson and Frank E. X. Dance, eds. *Perspectives on Communication.* Milwaukee: Speech Communication Center, University of Wisconsin–Milwaukee, 1968, pp. 90–7.

Thurber, John H. and John L. Petelle. "The Negro Pulpit and Civil Rights." *CSSJ* 19(1968): 273–8.

Viorst, Milton. "Honk, Honk, the Marigold" [Everett McKinley Dirksen]. *Esquire* (October, 1966):116–9, 181–5.

Windes, Russel, Jr., and James L. Robinson. "Public Address in the Career of Adlai E. Stevenson." *QJS* 51(1956):225–33.

Wrage, Ernest J. "The Little World of Barry Goldwater." *WS* 27(1963):207–15.

Although speech scholars have felt comfortable with adaptations of the historical-critical method in studying the history of public address,[3] they often seem somewhat unsure about the study of contemporary rhetoric. In part this is because of the hazards of studying anything contemporary: Can we get enough facts to judge now? Can we judge objectively events of which we are a part? Will our present judgments hold up in the light of later evidence, such as publication of the diaries and memoirs of today's principals? But these are the same concerns inevitably felt by Walter Lippmann, James Reston, and Eric Sevareid, who must not only report but judge today's events for tomorrow's newspaper, or tonight's news broadcast. And if we agree that the function of rhetoric is to give form to contemporary economic, social and political problems, and to establish alternative solutions, then identifying persuasive appeals and examining causative factors which influence men is the rhetorician's business as it is the journalist's.

Though the art of evaluating contemporary rhetoric may be inadequately developed, it needs to be more widely practiced. Each day it becomes increasingly urgent that we study and understand the logical and psychological forces that set off reactions and motivate decisions in the House and the Senate, the convention of the Congress on Racial Equality (CORE), the campus chapter of Young Americans for Freedom (YAF), and on the political platforms and

[3]In addition to the files of *QJS* and *SM*, see these collections: William Norwood Brigance, ed. *A History and Criticism of American Public Address*, 2 vols. (New York, McGraw-Hill, 1943), and Vol. 3, Marie K. Hochmuth, ed. (New York, Longmans, Green, 1955); J. Jeffery Auer, ed. *Antislavery and Disunion, 1858–1861: Studies in the Rhetoric of Compromise and Conflict* (New York, Harper & Row, 1963).

ghetto street corners. For those who would like to undertake such studies we have compiled a selected bibliography on methods and approaches.

Auer, J. Jeffery. *An Introduction to Research in Speech*. New York: Harper & Row, 1959, pp. 118–46.

Boorstin, Daniel J. *The Image: A Guide to Pseudo-Events in America*. New York: Harper & Row, 1961, 3–6, 7–44.

Brigance, W. Norwood. "What Is a Successful Speech?" *QJS* 11 (1925) :372–7.

Cathcart, Robert. *Post-Communication: Critical Analysis and Evaluation*. Indianapolis: Bobbs-Merrill, 1966.

Clevenger, Theodore, Jr. *Audience Analysis*. Indianapolis: Bobbs-Merrill, 1966.

Croft, Albert J. "The Functions of Rhetorical Criticism." *QJS* 42 (1956) :283–91.

Griffin, Leland M. "The Rhetoric of Historical Movements." *QJS* 38 (1952) :184–8.

Hillbruner, Anthony. *Critical Dimensions: The Art of Public Address Criticism*. New York: Random House, 1966.

Hofstadter, Richard. *The Paranoid Style in American Politics and Other Essays*. New York, Random House, 1965, p. vii–xiv, 3–40.

Lomas, Charles W. *The Agitator in American Society*. Englewood Cliffs, N. J.: Prentice-Hall, 1968, pp. 1–24.

Nichols, Marie Hochmuth. "Ghost Writing: Implications for Public Address," in *Rhetoric and Criticism*. Baton Rouge, 1963, pp. 35–47.

Nilsen, Thomas R. *Essays on Rhetorical Criticism*. New York: Random House, 1968.

Prosser, Michael. "Selected Sources on Contemporary Communication and Politics, 1948–1968." *TS* 16 (No. 4, 1968) :95–118.

Prosser, Michael. "Selected Sources on Modern Communication, Human Rights and Social Protest." *TS* 16 (No. 3, 1968) :55–8.

Scott, Robert K. and Donald K. Smith. "The Rhetoric of Confrontation." *QJS* 55 (1969) :1–8.

Thompson, Wayne N. "Contemporary Public Address: A Problem in Criticism." *QJS* 40 (1954) :24–30.

Wrage, Ernest J. "Public Address: A Study in Social and Intellectual History." *QJS* 33 (1947) :451–7.

30

Adlai E. Stevenson

Richard Murphy

Part I. Stevenson as Spokesman

One of the phenomena of a free society is the spokesman, the man who, with something to say, and some skill and persistence in saying it, achieves an influence and prominence quite beyond any office he may hold. The prime example in this decade is Adlai Stevenson. Although he held elective office for only four years, and during the past eight no public office at all, he has a national, and at times, a world audience.

In considering Stevenson as spokesman, we need larger objectives than are found on a critic's sheet for a beginning course in public speaking. He has explained his purpose. Since 1952, he has been "titular head" of a party, but with "no party office, no staff, no funds," no direct way of shaping his party's policy, and with "no devices such as the British have developed . . . to communicate directly and responsibly with the leaders of the party in power." Yet, the party's candidate for President "is generally deemed the leading spokesman of his party."[1] Stevenson determined to accept full responsibility as spokesman.

He speaks at college commencements and convocations, at forums, and interviews; he tours the world to collect his details. (This month he is in Latin America.) He has advocated many causes unpopular at the time, but which have since gained in support: presidential and federal leadership rather than force in the Supreme Court decision on integration of schools; revision of the draft; stopping atomic tests; adjudication of Formosa; co-existence with Russia; support of summit conferences.

Richard Murphy is Professor of Speech, University of Illinois.

Reprinted by permission from *Today's Speech*, 8(February 1960):3–5, and 8(April 1960):12–14.

[1]Adlai E. Stevenson, *What I Think* (New York: Harper & Brothers, 1956), pp. ix–x. Italics supplied.

In his role as spokesman, Stevenson has gone beyond partisan politics. Here are two examples. He broke a silence of four months, in 1955, to talk over the radio on Matsu and Quemoy, when it looked as though we were at the brink of war with China. In advocating relinquishing the border islands, and turning Formosa over to the United Nations for settlement,[2] he opposed not only the Republican administration policy, but that of Democratic Senator George, then chairman of the Senate Foreign Relations Committee. A period of thoughtful discussion followed his speech. People began looking at maps and speculating about what Chiang was doing on those border islands. At a time when Senator McCarthy was at the height of his power, and it seemed he might prevail, Stevenson spoke to the country. He had often challenged Senator McCarthy, but this time, in a desperate attempt to unite Democratic-Republican bipartisan values, he put the responsibility on McCarthy's party:[3]

> Twenty years of bipartisan policy, highly intelligent and highly successful, have been called "Twenty Years of Treason"—under the auspices of the Republican National Committee.

Within a few days, Vice President Nixon talked to the nation in direct reply to Stevenson, and agreed that communism should not be fought in this country by anti-democratic and irresponsible methods. The President, in his press conference, in reply to a question about the Stevenson speech, said that Mr. Nixon and not Senator McCarthy represented his views. That same week, Senator Flanders rebuked Senator McCarthy on the floor of the Senate.[4] The party began to take some responsibility for one of its members, there was a resolution of censure in the Senate, and the end of a man and a period came rather quickly.

The importance of Stevenson's role as spokesman is attested by the number of studies of him made by graduate students. Among Stevenson's contributions to life and letters is his service in supplying rhetorical specimens. Last year four M.A. theses and a Ph.D. dissertation were done on him. *Speech Monographs* lists fourteen theses and dissertations in the last four years. This figure does not include the current crop. The subject has been very cooperative, has supplied texts and information and personal interviews, but has balked at such tasks as describing his typical written and typical spoken style. His courtesy to scholars goes beyond the call of a man not on duty. As evidence of essential thoughtfulness and stylistic care, here is a note in reply to a critic who sent him an article:

> Last night I read your piece about my speeches in *The Quarterly Journal of Speech* . . . and I have been unbal-

[2]*Ibid.*, pp. 215–224. The speech was given by radio from Chicago, April 11, 1955.
[3]*Ibid.*, p. 64. The speech was given at Miami Beach, March 7, 1954.
[4]This sequence of events is reported in one issue of *Time* (March 22, 1954), pp. 22, 28.

anced ever since! That you could have found so much of merit and retained it so well fills me with a craftsman's envy, a politician's confidence and a human being's profound gratitude.

Cordially yours,
Adlai E. Stevenson

Mr. Stevenson is very much aware of criticism of his speaking, we are told by two professors who interviewed him, and gives intense "self-evaluation after every speech." He reports: "I am always depressed."[5] But there are lighter touches in the criticisms, which might give him some amusement and ease his post-prandial depression. One M.A. candidate tried to apply to Stevenson's speeches I. A. Richards' formula for metaphor, and decided the theory couldn't be applied to anybody's metaphors.[6] A Ph.D. candidate made a study of 27 metropolitan newspapers to see how they covered the speeches of Mr. Eisenhower and Mr. Stevenson in 1952. One of the findings was that 20 of the 27 supported Mr. Eisenhower, that "bias appeared in the tenor of follow-up stories," and that "fuller treatment of audience reactions was given to Eisenhower speeches than to those of Stevenson."[7] This ought to be reassuring evidence to a man who made a rather well known speech, in 1952, "On the One Party Press."[8] Another Ph.D. candidate found his subject fond of *bon mots*, and noted that in Stevenson they "are artistic, for they are based on partial maxims or disjointed enthymemes."[9] Another Ph.D.-er, comparing the winner and the loser, found Stevenson's pessimism "established . . . (him) as a more conservative person than Eisenhower, although still a liberal in the school of Burke. . . ."[10] An ambitious Ph.D. candidate,[11] class of possible 1960, is making a linguistic study of selected written and oral passages by Stevenson, including correlations of actor, actor-verb, adverb, and adverb-verb archetypes. So the studies go.

[5]Russel Windes, Jr., and James A. Robinson, "Public Address in the Career of Adlai Stevenson," *The Quarterly Journal of Speech*, XLII (October, 1956), 230.

[6]Fanny Jane Blankenship, "I. A. Richards' Theory of Metaphor Applied to Selected Speeches of Adlai E. Stevenson." M.A. thesis, University of Illinois, 1957.

[7]Georgia B. Bowman, "A Study of the Reporting by Twenty-Seven Metropolitan Newspapers of Selected Speeches of Adlai Stevenson and Dwight Eisenhower in the 1952 Presidential Campaign." Unpublished Ph.D. dissertation, State University of Iowa, 1956. Abstracted in *Speech Monographs*, XXIV (June, 1957), 101–102.

[8]Portland, Oregon, September 8, 1952. *Major Campaign Speeches of Adlai E. Stevenson, 1952* (New York, Random House, 1953), pp. 78–82.

[9]Raymond Yeager, "A Rhetorical Analysis of the 1952 Presidential Campaign Speeches of Adlai Ewing Stevenson." Unpublished Ph.D. dissertation, Ohio State University, 1956. Abstracted in *Speech Monographs*, XXIV (June, 1957), 114–115.

[10]Malcolm O. Sillars, "An Analysis of Invention in the 1952 Presidential Campaign Addresses of Dwight D. Eisenhower and Adlai E. Stevenson." Unpublished Ph.D. dissertation, State University of Iowa, 1955. Abstracted in *Speech Monographs*, XXIII (June, 1956), 111–112.

[11]Fanny Jane Blankenship, Mount Holyoke College, "A Linguistic Study of Stevenson's Spoken and Written Style."

Before the graduate students are finished, Stevenson will be studied within an inch of his rhetorical life. We know he feels uncomfortable without a prepared speech to work from, that instead of relying on a few set speeches with some local variations, he tries to do a specific speech for each occasion. We know he is his own best speech writer, and if time will permit, he works over his text up to the last moment. An instance of the detail in which he has been observed is the study by Ralph Richardson,[12] of a speech made at the Hollywood Bowl in 1954. Stevenson is traced from the time he left Denver, through his weary attempts until 4:30 a.m. to get his speech finished despite callers, and through the actual delivery. Reproduced are pages of the original handwritten manuscript, the final typescript with pencilled annotations, and the taped recording version. There were eighty-two instances of overt audience response, and the eye-contact was checked at seventy-five per cent.

Since 1952, Stevenson has developed remarkably as a speaker. I remember a speech early in his campaign for governor in 1948, when he appeared with Senator Paul Douglas. Stevenson was rather apologetic, somewhat uncertain. It was Douglas who took the house.

During his term as governor, Stevenson was not considered an orator, although he had some mastery of exposition, as his radio reports to the people showed. The time for greatness came at the 1952 convention, when, in welcoming the delegates to Chicago and to Illinois, he went beyond the occasion, and issued a call to public duty, for which he himself was drafted. During his development as a speaker Stevenson had his moods of seriousness and jest. At one time, it appeared his sense of humor might diminish his stature as a statesman; he was too fond of gags. Today he is criticized for being pessimistic. You who saw him on Edward R. Murrow's Small World Program this year will understand Douglass Cater's phrase, Stevenson's "evangelism of quiet desperation."[13]

How can his substance and style be quickly described? Consistently, he has weight of idea. Consistently, he adapts his materials to a fast moving world. In the crisis of Suez, in 1956, he quickly prepared a telecast answer[14] to the President the day following his address. In fifteen minutes he reviewed policy in the Middle East, showed how failures could have been averted, and attacked the administration on various counts—all in fifteen minutes, and about the Middle East, a region his audience probably thought was somewhere around Buffalo, where he gave the telecast. When Theodore Roosevelt was trying to get Taft elected in 1908, he told him "he must treat the political audience as one coming, not to see an etching, but a poster. He must, therefore, have streaks of blue, yellow, and red to catch the eye, and eliminate all fine lines

[12]Ralph Richardson, "Adlai E. Stevenson, Hollywood Bowl, October 6, 1954," *Western Speech*, XIX (May, 1955), 137–174.

[13]Douglass Cater, "What Makes Humphrey Run," *The Reporter*, XX (March 5, 1959), 16.

[14]Telecast at Buffalo, November 1, 1956. Adlai E. Stevenson, *The New America* (New York: Harper & Brothers, 1957), pp. 34–8.

and soft colours."[15] Mr. Stevenson presents etchings rather than billboards.

Mr. Stevenson's style is rich in figurative language. What a shame he was not available to rhetoricians of the nineteenth century, when figures and tropes were studied. "No gains without pains"[16]—that is genus *antimetabole,* specie *annomination,* words of similar sound but dissimilar meaning. Sometimes his figures are apt, even brutal: "The Vice-President has put away his switchblade and now assumes the aspect of an Eagle Scout."[17] Sometimes they are a little mixed: "We should not put too many of our eggs in the atomic and hydrogen basket."[18] Sometimes they are a little tired—"reality" is always "stark." Sometimes his best figures get lost in run-on sentences.

Mr. Stevenson's style is essentially egotistic. In his acceptance speech of 1952, he made 67 references to himself in a short speech. This indicates no lack of humility, but rather a practice of setting his speeches where he, rather than the audience, is on a subject. Of course, he rigorously builds his ethical proof, snatches at every possible connection with his audience, but his speeches are at times essayish in that they grow from his rather than the audience's mood. But he can appeal to community interests in his peroration, in combination of democratic and religious faith.

Mr. Stevenson likes to quote from the Bible, and Emerson and Channing —Unitarian standbys he has known since his days in Sunday school. His recall is stocked with handy literary allusions and anecdotes which he draws upon particularly in times of strong feeling. There is the little Lincoln story, of the boy who stubbed his toe, and who said it hurt too much to laugh, and he was too big to cry—used as the final lines in his concession of 1952. In the 1956 concession—now a speech form he was becoming accustomed to—there were two allusions not identified in the dispatches until the following day. One was a quotation from "A Christmas Letter" by Fra Giovanni, written in 1513 A.D., "there is radiance and glory in the darkness, could we but see, and to see, we have only to look." The other quotation was "a merry heart doeth good like a medicine, but a broken spirit drieth the bones." The process of memoriter, of filing away passages to be used in emergency, is a classical procedure. His sister[19] tells the story that back in 1952 Stevenson was listening to a radio news commentator criticizing him for making jokes in his speeches. He then quoted the line, "a merry heart," and speculated on its source. He started with Shakespeare, and found it in Proverbs 17:22. Four years later, the quotation was there for use as he painfully wrote his speech in the Blackstone Hotel. Mr. Stevenson's allusions have made even newsmen bibliographers. There was the Christmas card of 1955 with the Confederate soldier's prayer. The trouble Mr.

[15]*The Letters of Archie Butt,* ed. Lawrence F. Abbott (New York, Doubleday, Page & Company, 1924), pp. 143-4.

[16]Acceptance speech, July 26, 1952. *Major Campaign Speeches of Adlai E. Stevenson, 1952* (New York: Random House, 1953), p. 10.

[17]Minneapolis, November 5, 1956. *The New America,* p. 39.

[18]Speech at Chicago, October 15, 1956. *Ibid.,* p. 45.

[19]Elizabeth Stevenson Ives, *My Brother Adlai* (New York: William Morrow & Company, 1956), p. 169.

Stevenson took to get his quotation straight that time has been variously reported.[20]

As to Stevenson's delivery, there is general agreement. At his worst, he is a bit jumpy, nervous, and arouses empathic responses of tension. Not always can one sit back and enjoy his flow of language; you must lean forward to help. At his best, his periods are delivered in a poetic as well as rhetorical mode. Often as I listen to him, I find myself muttering directions about conversational quality as I would in a classroom: "Express the full meaning of your words as you utter them; strive for a lively sense of communication; let yourself respond fully to your meaning and your communication." Mr. Stevenson never had any formal training in speaking. His voice, which in the early days of his first strenuous campaign was of concern to his managers, holds up remarkably well. Not having had a public speaking course in college is something like not having a college degree; you may not have missed much, but you will always suspect you did. Some teachers of speech argue that if Stevenson had had academic work in persuasion and communication, the course of history would have been changed. Who knows? But Mr. Stevenson's relations with his audience is the subject of the second article.

Part II. Stevenson and His Audience

Adlai Stevenson spoke to his first national audience on the hustings of 1952, when he ran for President. On his second attempt, in 1956, he again appeared as candidate, soliciting the support of the millions, and again was quantitatively rejected. But Stevenson's public is something more than a quadrennial electorate. Through his lectures and writings he has been in rapport with a vast audience which regards him not merely as a candidate for something, but as a spokesman on public affairs. Since 1952, five volumes of his speeches have been published, and a sixth[1] has been announced. His reports on affairs here and abroad have been syndicated by newspapers, issued by picture magazines—*Look* in America and *Picture Post* in Britain—and published by such erudite journals as *Centennial Review of Arts and Sciences* and *Foreign Affairs*. A study of Stevenson's relations with his audience is a tantalizing affair and involves many speculations. But since it concerns what is supposed to be fundamental in democracy—but is actually a rarity—a spokesman's attempts to reason ideas and values with his audience, it is worth attempting.

It is the vogue nowadays to speak learnedly of myths, and myth patterns,

[20]Stevenson saw "A Soldier's Prayer" in *Think on These Things* by John Ellis Large, Rector, Church of the Heavenly Rest, New York City. Details of Stevenson's attempt to identify the prayer are given in the church's publication, *Disciple*, VI (February 26, 1956), p. 4. See also *Time* (January 2, 1956), p. 13; (February 20), p. 10.

[1]*Putting First Things First* (announced for publication in March by Random House).

of folkloristic images, and to study speakers, as one savant has done, in terms of "mythological status in public life." What is the Stevenson image? In making the refraction, more of the American public than of Stevenson may be revealed.

One thinks first of the egg. "Via oviciptum dura est," said Stevenson in his first Godkin lecture at Harvard in 1954, "The way of the egghead is hard."[2] He is an egghead, and candles AA fresh, jumbo. There have been other eggheads, of course. Thomas Jefferson was one, and being an Anglo-Saxon scholar, would have known that egg is from the old English, *heafod*. But men of intelligence and learning were held in some esteem in the eighteenth century. Theodore Roosevelt was an egghead, until his later years when hatred of Wilson consumed him; but he was so busy busting broncs and trusts, and shooting lions, the public was not so aware that he wrote a five-foot shelf of books and was president of the American Historical Society. Woodrow Wilson was an egghead, and paid for it with his life. But Stevenson even looks like an egghead. He appeals to the intellectuals. Will someone versed in images then explain why, according to the sample of social science professors reported by Lazarsfeld and Thielens in *The Academic Mind*,[3] the professors voted 68 per cent for Truman, but only 59 per cent for Stevenson? Or why in samples from Catholic colleges the drop from Truman was 67 per cent to 47 per cent, and in teachers colleges, from 60 per cent to 49 per cent?

He is an earnest student, reads reports instead of relying on briefing, travels widely, but not in processional, and makes his own observations.

He is not popular, it is said. "I don't know why it is," says the voter who votes for him, "but he is not popular"—27,000,000 votes in 1952, 3,000,000 more than the successful Mr. Truman got the election before, but he is not popular. He came within 10 per cent of equaling the most publicized, the most mass-communicated candidate in American political history, but he is not popular. To some degree he does lack the common touch. I have seen him on the campaign train, tolerating the handshaking and the picture-taking with local politicians between whistle-stops, but obviously eager to get back to his MS. He confessed to Eleanor Roosevelt that he is not so much at home in talking to people as she is. She advised him to get a small automobile and travel leisurely in various sections of the country, talking with people, always accompanied by someone of the region as interlocutor, "until you can feel what they are feeling."[4] This advice, she sadly notes, was not followed. The truth is, I think, that Stevenson meets people well enough when they have something to say, but he does not enjoy sheer chit-chat and backslapping, especially when there are speeches to be prepared.

[2] Adlai E. Stevenson, *Call to Greatness* (New York: Harper & Brothers, 1954), p. xi.

[3] Paul F. Lazarsfeld and Wagner Thielens, Jr., *The Academic Mind* (Glencoe, Illinois: The Free Press, 1958), p. 28.

[4] Eleanor Roosevelt, "On My Own," *The Saturday Evening Post*, CCXXX (March 8, 1958), 33.

He is a clever man, with a razor wit, a sense of comedy in Meredith definition, able to laugh at himself and at the people and ideas he loves. "I am accused of talking over people's heads," he says as he stands on a high platform. "This time I must admit it is true." In his not recorded but much circulated—in various mimeographed versions—Gridiron speech of 1952,[5] he laughed at the "Good old Ad-lie" greetings he had received, and advised the newsmen, if they had an unusual name, either to change it or accept usage without complaint.

He knows much of the world, has traveled in it since childhood, and is regarded highly abroad. He is an internationalist from the heart of isolationism, midwest America.

He is an apprehensive man, hoping for the best, fearing the worst, anticipating rebuttal in his positive statements,[6] dispensing good cheer before, during and after his Jeremiads. He is said to be a rather indecisive man, a cross between a precinct committeeman and a college professor, not quite knowing whether this day he should run for President or have his shoes resoled.

This, then, is the Stevenson image which has been rejected for what we are told is the father image. Clearly he is not the father, he is not even the son, although he may somewhat resemble the holy[7] . . . but let us not press this; Stevenson is a Unitarian.

The image of Stevenson cannot be communicated in a word. It is not the same for all people. He is too complex an individual to be so projected. Therein lies one of his difficulties, or one of his strengths.

But enough of images. Let us look at some of the facts. In the matter of Mr. Stevenson's "indecisiveness," what is the situation? In 1952, he simply did not want to run for President. He was in his first term as governor of Illinois, and was running for reelection. He had committed himself; he had a program to carry on. His reluctance to be drafted came not from coyness but a determination to do what he thought was his duty. In 1953 he began his campaign for 1956, and there was no doubt about it. He entered the primaries and toured the nation. He worked intensively, not in lining up delegates, but in preparing himself for the job. The story of his seminars, his files of materials, his consultations with experts in the problem fields, has been told by Professor Windes in the February *Quarterly Journal of Speech*.[8] As the campaign for 1960 got under way in late 1959, Mr. Stevenson avoided involvement; he does not care to be a perennial office seeker. Consistent with his

---

[5]Gridiron Club Dinner, Washington, D. C., December 13, 1952. By tradition these speeches are not reported, but I have seen two mimeographed versions of Stevenson's speech.

[6]Noel F. Busch, *Adlai E. Stevenson of Illinois* (New York: Farrar, Straus and Young, 1952), p. 143. See the veto of the [loyalty oaths] Broyles Bills—"I know full well that this veto will be distorted and misunderstood."

[7]See the cover of *Newsweek* (January 11, 1960), and the title, "The Lively Ghost: Adlai Stevenson."

[8]Russell Windes, Jr., "Adlai E. Stevenson's Speech Staff in the 1956 Campaign," *QJS*, XLVI (February, 1960), 32–43.

policy of being informed, he went to Latin America—which he considers an increasing problem area for the United States—and left Kennedy, Humphrey, Symington, Johnson, et al., to make their kickoffs. But there is no doubt he is on call if needed.

There is the question of why Stevenson did less well in 1956 than in 1952, losing by 9,000,000 votes rather than the former 6,000,000. Many studies have been made of his rhetoric to explain this relapse. Professor Beattie[9] ran a Flesch Readability Formula test on Stevenson's 1956 speeches and found them 5.8 points higher than the 1952 speeches in *mean reading ease,* but the *human interest* score 4.7 points lower. The general impression is that Stevenson's speaking was less effective in 1956 than in 1952.

There are more obvious, if not more satisfactory explanations of the 1952-56 comparisons. In '52 Stevenson was unknown, but drafted. He had a freshness, a novelty, a wit, an unstudied enthusiasm. His campaign was run by amateurs. In 1956 he had pondered and studied his role, and was in the hands of the old pros. He was worn down by the primary fights in the states. He made in nine months 300 speeches and travelled 15,000 miles. With his desire to avoid repetition, he slaved at new speeches, and in his desire to be obliging, he spent his energies on little, local groups, and had to face the larger groups or the television audience in a state of fatigue. These elements might explain the difference.

But there is an even more obvious explanation; he was running against Mr. Eisenhower, whose magic for being associated with all that is good, and disassociated from anything troublesome, had been demonstrated for four years. Two of Stevenson's major issues blew up like the trick cigars he sometimes refers to. One, the appeal for stopping nuclear tests, was promptly endorsed by Russia, and that was the end of that—the kiss of death. The other issue, getting rid of the draft, was developed, and then came Suez and the explosions in the Middle East. After Stevenson's amateurish tinkering with a world in eruption, it was rather comforting to know that we already had in the White House the world's greatest living military authority, who was willing to stay on.

Every man has his idea of what gets votes. One advertising man[10] claims that if Stevenson had had that million and a half dollars for those twenty-second spot announcements his opponent had in 1952, he would have been elected. What the influence of speaking may be in a campaign, we simply do not know. Much of our rhetorical study is based on a static concept that if, in some way, one can well select, arrange and deliver his materials he will succeed. But the world, and especially these days, is a dynamic, changing scene, and despite our progress, people have not entirely overcome their immutability

[9]William E. Beattie, "A Readability-Listenability Analysis of Selected Campaign Speeches of Adlai E. Stevenson in the 1952 and 1956 Presidential Campaigns," *Central States Speech Journal*, X (Spring, 1959), 16–18.

[10]Martin Mayer, *Madison Avenue, U.S.A.* (New York: Harper & Brothers, 1958), p. 307.

to new ideas. Then there are the vagaries of existence; one little sputnik in the sky can ruin the best Ciceronian *inventio, dispositio* and *elocutio*. Evidently candidates regard speeches as important, else they would not half-kill themselves making them. But it is one of the ironies of the Stevenson campaigns that while he sweated over his manuscripts, polished his metaphors, and spoke in some doubt of his final effort, his opponent in deep conviction read from the papers before him, or gaily extemporized without the slightest sensitivity to syntax.

So far as Stevenson's popular appeal goes, he has been dogged by ill luck. He was hardly settled in the Governor's Mansion when his wife asked for separation, and then received an uncontested divorce. There was no scandal involved. As Kenneth S. Davis puts it in his biography of Stevenson, *A Prophet in His Own Country*,[11] Mrs. Stevenson preferred her world of poetry and fine arts to politics. But in these neo-Victorian days when the consort must be seen from the bubbletop to assure the populace that God's in His Heaven, all's right with the world, absence of a wife is a handicap. Stevenson's sister, schooled in the ways of politics from being the wife of a man in the diplomatic service, appeared as hostess, and waved from cavalcades and the vestibule of trains. But it was Albert without Victoria.

In the 1952 campaign, as the final train made its way through the East, there was a riot at Manard prison, and the Governor had to interrupt the finale to go back to Illinois to settle the difficulty, leaving Senator Fulbright to carry on for him.

There was the horse meat scandal in his last year as governor, and of all years, the campaign year 1952. A superintendent of foods and dairies, appointed by the governor, had taken a bribe of $3,500[12] from a packer who found it more profitable to grind up horses than cows for hamburgers. The public servant was indicted, and the packer was tried and convicted in short order. It wasn't much of a scandal, as political scandals go in Illinois, and the governor was not directly involved, but it was an unsavory sort of thing. One still hears the old jibe, "How do you want your hamburger done, win, place, or show?"

Then there was the Alger Hiss affair. Mr. Stevenson was in various branches of government service, including AAA and the State Department, at the time Mr. Hiss was also employed. They had had some official associations, but no personal ones. When Hiss was tried, Stevenson was asked for an opinion on his character, and he gave a deposition[13] from Springfield—he did not attend the New York trial—that so far as he was aware Mr. Hiss's reputation for integrity, loyalty and veracity had been "good." Mr. Hiss's reputation was

---

[11]Kenneth S. Davis, *A Prophet in His Own Country* (New York: Doubleday & Company, Inc., 1957), pp. 311–317.

[12]See John Bartlow Martin, *Adlai Stevenson* (New York: Harper & Brothers, 1952), pp. 134–136.

[13]See Busch, pp. 175–184.

excellent; had it not been, there would not have been so much sensation about the charges of perjury. For that mild and honest statement, Stevenson was brutally attacked, and in various forms of innuendo, linked with Hiss. You may recall Senator McCarthy's epanorthosis, "Did I say Alger, . . . I meant Adlai."

How much of the charges of subversion and communism rubbed off on this man, who never had any communist connections, is a matter of speculation. But in those days of semantic terrorism, when the whispered mention of subversive, fellow-traveler, pink, caused people to crawl under the bed, Stevenson's record of travel in Russia, of entertaining Russian diplomats here, his policy of co-existence with Russia, his veto, as governor, of the loyalty oath for teachers—these were suspicious actions.

What Mr. Stevenson's devotees lack in number, they make up in intensity. Were candidates determined by applause meters, Stevenson could be elected. Even his opponents are only mildly opposed; he has stirred up no violent personal opposition. The American public is accustomed to pre-cooked, pre-digested, handily packaged foods. Do they want political ideas served in the same fashion? Mr. Stevenson is not the great generalizer; he does not speak in clichés. As a thoughtful man, he has no packaged solutions.

As Robert Lasch, of the *St. Louis Post-Dispatch*, wrote following the 1956 campaign, "It is fashionable to say that . . . (Stevenson) cannot project himself to large audiences. But nobody can establish communication when one end of the line is cut off."[14] Or to use an old figure of Plutarch's,[15] with slight modernization, the audience has some obligation to adapt also, even as one who is to receive a ball from a pitcher does not cup his hands rigidly, in fixed position, but is prepared to adjust to the projection, and asks only that it be in reachable vicinity of the base.

Questions for Analysis

1. Define by examples "spokesmen" in public life today. How would you describe their appeal, the "listener anxieties and attitudes" rendering them acceptable? What made Stevenson both behind and ahead of his time? How different might his reception be today? Why?

2. Choose an issue of the day and apply Stevensonian "substance and style" in writing a speech about the issue. Compare your speech to those actually being made. How would your speech "sell"? What specific alterations must you make to conform

[14]Robert Lasch, "Stevenson," *QJS*, XLIII (February, 1957), 36.
[15]Plutarch, Moralia. "On Listening to Lectures."

your speech to the standards of your "competitors"? Do you have a sense of the odds against Stevenson's success? Explain.

3. Murphy says a study of Stevenson's audience relations "concerns what is supposed to be a fundamental in democracy—but is actually a rarity—a spokesman's attempt to reason ideas and values with his audience. . . ." What that you read in previous sections of this book prepared you to accept this statement? How do you regard the statement as commentary on public speaking and listening today? Which facets of Stevenson's "image" would most affect his *ethos* now?

4. How do you react to Murphy's assertion that today "immutability to new ideas" and the fact of "one little sputnik" make adherence to traditional concepts and techniques of persuasion a capricious virtue at best? If those "twenty-second spot announcements" truly make the difference, why *do* candidates "half-kill themselves" making speeches? Try to list and to evaluate the variety and degree of public demands on candidates today. Consider responses to these demands as they affect the listener, the speaker, and the mass media. What compromises are inevitable?

5. Consider Stevenson a possible candidate for *you*. How, if at all, would you ask him to change? How, if at all, would he ask you to change? Would *you* be content with a "spokesman"? How have "spokesmen" fared in the dissenting movements of today? How might they fare tomorrow?

31

The Speaking of Roy Wilkins

Maxine Schnitzer Ferris

Roy Wilkins, the Executive Secretary of the National Association for the Advancement of Colored People, sees himself as "an incurable optimist,"[1] one who believes that "it's really thrilling and exciting to be a Negro in the 1960's."[2] For him contemporary Negro life is an adventure. This spirit is reflected in his public utterances.

The grandson of a Mississippi slave, Wilkins speaks for the almost 400,000 members of the NAACP. As one of the Negro's most able and articulate spokesmen, he has testified before Congressional committees, conferred with the President, appeared on television and radio, and written extensively for both Negro and general publications. Roy Wilkins—he has no middle name—has been a blunt oral advocate for his race since 1920 when a mass lynching in Duluth, Minnesota, so aroused him that he entered a university oratorical contest and won first prize with his strong anti-lynching speech.

Wilkins was born in 1901 in St. Louis. His father, a Methodist minister, had left Mississippi because of "an irrepressible resentment at the treatment of Negroes."[3] Although a college graduate, Pastor Wilkins was at times forced to earn a living by tending a brick kiln. When his wife died in 1904 and he was unable to keep his family together, the three children were sent to St. Paul to live with relatives. There Roy Wilkins grew up in a poor but racially mixed community and attended unsegregated schools. Perhaps it was during these formative years that he developed his appreciation for equality.

In 1923 Wilkins received his B.A. degree from the University of Minnesota with a major in sociology and course work in journalism. During his college years he supported himself by working as a red cap, a dining-car waiter, and a clean-up man in the South St. Paul stock-yards. At the same time he was the night editor of the university newspaper, editor of a Negro weekly, and an officer of the local NAACP chapter.

Maxine Schnitzer Ferris is Lecturer in Speech, Michigan State University.
Reprinted by permission from *Central States Speech Journal*, 16 (1965) :91–8.
[1] *Time*, August 30, 1963, p. 14.
[2] *Current Biography*, January, 1964, p. 45.
[3] Langston Hughes, *Fight for Freedom* (New York, 1962), p. 169.

After graduation Wilkins accepted a position with the Kansas City *Call,* a leading Negro weekly, and for the first time faced widespread segregation. "Kansas City ate my heart out," he recalls. "It was a Jim Crow town through and through."[4]

In 1931 he left the *Call* to join the staff of the NAACP. One of his first assignments for the organization was to investigate charges of discrimination and unjust treatment of Negro workers on a federally financed flood control project in Mississippi. Wilkins and an associate were able to substantiate the charges, and their report led to Congressional action to improve the situation.

Roy Wilkins became editor of *The Crisis,* the official magazine of the NAACP, in 1934, a position which he held until 1949. During this period, he was an active speaker and writer on the Association's behalf. He served as a consultant to the War Department during World War II, worked as a negotiator in several labor disputes involving Negro workers, and was an advisor to the American delegation at the United Nations conference in San Francisco in 1945. On April 11, 1955, he was unanimously selected to fill the post he now holds.

A modest man, Wilkins is content to leave his own publicity to the public relations department of the organization which he serves. "Stressing himself as a personality does not seem to concern him at all."[5] A slender, stoop-shouldered, dignified-appearing man, Wilkins regularly puts in a fourteen-hour day. Dedicated to his mission, he has been described as "a rebel whose anger burns fiercely."[6] Zealous though he is, he seems to maintain an ability to analyze rationally even the most emotional of problems.

Wilkins is respected by most of the Negroes he represents and in 1959 made a strong impression on thousands of television viewers when he replied to newscaster Chet Huntley's charge that "The NAACP may have outlived itself."[7] One viewer's response is indicative of sentiment at the time: "Roy Wilkins was the best advertisement the NAACP has had for a long time."[8]

Although he is frequently called upon to address national and regional meetings of both Negroes and whites, few speeches have been published in newspapers and magazines. The eighteen speeches that form the basis of this analysis were published or duplicated by the National Association for the Advancement of Colored People. Four[9] appeared in *The Crisis;* five[10] were

---

[4]*Current Biography,* January, 1964, p. 43.

[5]Hughes, p. 169.

[6]*Time,* August 30, 1963, p. 14.

[7]Chet Huntley Telecast, February 1, 1959.

[8]Hughes, p. 268.

[9]"Undergirding the Democratic Ideal," *Crisis, LVIII* (December 1951), 647–651; "Desegregation and Racial Tensions," *Crisis, LXIII* (December 1956), 197–201, 254–255; "Dixie Challenge to Democracy," *Crisis, LXV* (October 1958), 471–477; "Barriers Broken, Pathways Cleared," *Crisis,* LXVI (August–September 1959), 394–399, 450.

[10]*Integration Crisis in the South* (New York, 1957) ; *Deep South Crisis* (New York, 1957) ; *Mr. Wilkins Replies* (New York, 1959) ; *Humiliation Stalks Them* (New York, 1963) ; "The Enemies of Mankind," *Vital Speeches at the Freedom House Annual Award Dinner* (New York, 1963), pp. 14–19.

published as pamphlets; and nine[11] were prepared as press releases. Twelve of the speeches were selected by Wilkins' administrative assistant as "representative" of the kind of speaking done by the Executive Secretary. Included in the eighteen are speeches presented to NAACP groups, addresses given before student audiences of predominantly Negro colleges, remarks before professional organizations, and comments made on special occasions. The earliest speech studied was delivered in 1951; the most recent was given on January 29, 1964. Possibly the pamphlet and magazine texts were slightly modified for publication, and the speaker in actually presenting the speech may have deviated from the text released to the press; information could not be obtained to clarify these points.

Materials of Speaking

Wilkins makes use of the three kinds of proof identified by classical rhetoricians, his heaviest concentration being upon the logical. His personal proofs are derived, for the most part, from sources external to the speech text. Emotional proofs are used sparingly and with subtlety. Even though the heart may be touched, the basic appeal is to the head. Wilkins tends to be informative and convincing but not necessarily motivating.

Most persons seem to respond favorably to Wilkins as a person. Members of an audience are aware of facts that contribute to his credibility as a speaker; he is well known, the head of a sizeable national organization, a person with whom the President of the United States confers. Moreover, his extensive work experiences, professional training, demonstrated competence, firsthand observations of racial strife, and life in an integrated neighborhood identify him as a concerned and knowledgeable advocate. His calm, reasonable, refined manner inspires confidence. Some, however, look upon his age, poor health, and calm exterior as signs of weakness and, consequently, find him lacking as a speaker. Identifying with the emotional, the militant, is not Wilkins' aim; the opinions of this group, therefore, do not seriously mar his *ethos* for most listeners.

In his speeches, as well, Roy Wilkins puts forth a positive image. His addresses demonstrate no strong feelings against white people and clearly reveal his disassociation with all "hate groups." He employs little name-calling and few personal attacks; invective is missing. The speaker emerges as a "fair" man. Not only does the Executive Secretary refrain from attacking others, but he identifies himself and his position with persons who are generally respected —men such as Justice John Marshall Harlan, Abraham Lincoln, John F. Kennedy, and Booker T. Washington.

[11]"Address of March 16, 1961"; "Address of November 6, 1961"; "Address of June 10, 1962"; Address of April 9, 1963"; "Address of June 15, 1963"; "Address of November 8, 1963"; Address of November 18, 1963"; "Address of November 26, 1963"; "Address of December 2, 1963"; "Address of January 29, 1964."

A stylistic device also contributes to his ethical proof. The first person plural is a trademark of Wilkins' workmanship as a speaker. The extensive use of "we," "us," and "our," especially noticeable in speeches before predominantly Negro groups, suggests a desire on the part of the speaker to identify with his listeners and point up the need for joint effort in solving problems. He rarely uses the first person singular and second person; he does not see himself apart from the Negro race, nor does he see the Civil Rights struggle as a job belonging to others.

Although Wilkins' discourses are concrete, factual, statistical, they also have an emotional quality about them. The nature of the Negro's crusade, his quest for freedom and equality, and his struggle against overwhelming odds have emotional overtones—at least for most people. Then too, some of the occasions are emotional in themselves: the funeral of the murdered Medgar Evers, the memorial service for the slain American President, the 50th anniversary of the NAACP.

Moreover, emotion is potential in several lines of thought put forth by Wilkins; his expressed pride in the achievements of his organization, his optimism that progress *will* be made in race relations, his earnest plea for cooperation by *both* races. His frequent references to religion, expressed concern for the well-being of the *entire* country, and emphasis on the threat of Communism are topics that may prompt feelings of patriotism, love of God, and desire for peace and security. His description of Negro injustices, enumerations of denied rights, and discussion of preferential treatment appeal to feelings of remorse, revulsion, guilt, sacrifice, desire for fair-play, and determination.

Wilkins often focuses upon incidents that strike close to home, incidents with which his listeners are almost compelled to identify. For example, in testimony given before the Senate Commerce Committee on July 22, 1963, he said:

> For millions of Americans this is vacation time. Swarms of families load their automobiles and trek across the country. I invite the members of this committee to imagine themselves darker in color and to plan an auto trip from Norfolk, Va., to the Gulf Coast of Mississippi, say, to Biloxi. Or one from Terre Haute, Ind., to Charleston, S.C., or from Jacksonville, Fla., to Tyler, Texas.
>
> How far do you drive each day? Where, and under what conditions can you and your family eat? Where can they use a rest room? Can you stop driving after a reasonable day behind the wheel, or must you drive until you reach a city where relatives or friends will accommodate you and yours for the night? Will your children be denied a soft drink or an ice cream cone because they are not white?

In the same address he raised another series of provocative rhetorical questions:

Why does Congress balk at legislation for the welfare of
its nearly 20,000,000 loyal Negro citizens? . . . Are cows,
hogs and sheep more valuable than human beings? Is their
rest, water, and feeding a proper subject for Congressional
legislative action, but the rest and feeding of Negro
Americans in hotels, restaurants and other public places an
improper subject for Congressional action?

Close connection exists between Wilkins' emotional proof and his word
choice and composition. References to justice, dignity, destiny, equality,
morality, truth, honor, and integrity—verities which most people value—are
included in all of his discourses. Similarly, his choice of vivid action verbs
not only adds clarity and interestingness to his message but also arouses connotative images. Wilkins' emotional proof is suggestive and implicative; it
appears throughout a speech, not just in the introduction or conclusion; it
does not offend.

Wilkins, as was stated earlier, places the weight of his rhetorical proof
on the logical. "His mind," says *Time,* "drives toward specific detail rather
than fuzzy generalization."[12] His speeches are well supported with factual information. Materials derived from the *Statistical Abstract,* the *Congressional
Quarterly,* and the book, *Southern Schools,* are used most frequently. Reference is also made to items appearing in *Harpers, Newsweek, Look, Fortune,
Ebony,* and *The New York Times* and other newspapers. Each speech contains
specific instances illustrating the racial progress or the lack of it in areas
related to the particular audience being addressed. Wilkins seems equally
adept in discussing the lack of school integration in Little Rock, the sit-ins in
St. Louis, or selective buying in Chicago. He gives evidence of up-to-the-minute
information concerning all aspects of the racial issue.

Although on occasions he inserts a detailed illustration or two, such examples are not usually part of his invention. He seldom makes use of hypothetical illustrations or personal experiences. One historical illustration, however, that is included in several speeches concerns Booker T. Washington who,
when told to dust a room at Hampton Institute, dusted the room three times
to be certain that not a speck of dust would be found. Wilkins relates this incident to several college audiences and encourages them to strive for similar
excellence.

Because rejection of the "separate but equal" principle is basic to Wilkins'
point of view, he frequently discusses the case of Plessy v. Ferguson and the
more recent Brown v. the Board of Education. Other court cases are cited
with regularity, too—perhaps because so much of the NAACP's attack has
focused upon court action. In addition Wilkins makes reference to the Declaration of Independence, the Emancipation Proclamation, and current legislative
proposals. He defines, explains, and gives opinions relating to such documents.

The Executive Secretary reasons extensively on the basis of causation,

12*Time,* August 30, 1963, p. 14.

concluding that desegregation in the schools is at the heart of the racial question. Once this ill is eradicated, he believes that other goals can be achieved. He generalizes on the basis of instances he cites and builds a strong argument that significant inequalities are meted out to the Negro. He analyzes the world situation and sees signs that indicate the broader ramifications of the race problem. Wilkins is especially creative, however, in reasoning from analogy. He sets forth at least one analogy in every speech and draws comparisons that serve both a stylistic and inventional purpose. Evidence and reasoning appear to meet accepted tests.

Wilkins has a basic message, one that appears with some modification in all of his addresses. The planks of his argument can be phrased as follows: (1) although progress is being made, the Negro continues to receive unfair treatment in education, industry, politics, law, travel, and housing; (2) the problem goes beyond the question of Negro and white and is related to our constitutional system; (3) no single solution to the problem will suffice, and, therefore, many approaches must be undertaken; (4) Negroes and whites must work cooperatively to correct the situation; (5) the NAACP has no connection with the Communists and is the only organization that can handle the long sustained fight; and (6) the time to act is now.

Organization

Organization is not one of the Executive Secretary's rhetorical strengths. Although most of his speeches have a discernible introduction, body, and conclusion, the internal organization is often loose. He at times seems to ramble. His speeches move from the specific to the general. Proof is offered, and then the conclusion is drawn or, in many instances, left at the level of implication. Main heads are poorly worded and few internal "sign posts" are included to indicate that point "1," "2," or "3" is being discussed. The inclusion of transitional summaries, however, tends to lead the listener into an awareness that a new point is being considered.

The basic partition of speeches is problem-solution. Subordinate divisions fall into topical, time, space, and journalistic sequences. Wilkins' organization—or the lack of it—suggests little or no effort to outline the speech prior to its wording in manuscript form. Speeches before the National Bar Association, the American Association of Advertising Agencies, and the Southern Police Institute are tighter in structure than those for NAACP audiences. Both of the eulogies studied—one written for the Kennedy Memorial service in New York and the other delivered at the Medgar Evers funeral in Jackson, Mississippi—are well unified in theme but loose in structure.

Wilkins has a standard pattern for his introductions. He expresses appreciation for the speaking opportunity, refers to any previous association with the group, relates to the particular locale or occasion, and launches into the development of his argument. His introductions are straightforward and to the point, largely expository in form. They are not, however, highly imaginative.

In beginning the two eulogies, he utilized description and poetry as introductory materials.

The conclusions of most of Wilkins' addresses are generalized appeals for action—*now!* Both Negro and white citizens are called upon to face up to their responsibilities and devise creative methods of eradicating the inequalities that continue to exist. Wilkins leaves the impression that change will come and that the Negro's position will be righted. At times he elaborates upon specific targets of the NAACP. On other occasions he relates his closing remarks to scripture, a Lincoln quotation, or a phrase from the Declaration of Independence; the eulogies are concluded with poetry. No ending can be classified as an extended emotional appeal. Generally the conclusions are quite brief—three or four paragraphs. In speeches before college students, they are longer and the proposal for action more detailed. The endings usually contain language refinement for emphasis and clarity.

Language and Composition

Style is a strong point in Roy Wilkins' rhetorical workmanship. He puts his journalistic training and experience to good use and is lucid, appropriate, and interesting. Sentences vary in length, but the majority are terse and periodic. The speaker does not belabor points or become tedious and wordy. The who, what, where, when, why, and how of his line of thought can be discerned easily.

Extensive use is made of series construction, parallelism, alliteration, and repetition. Wilkins condemns the "stand patism of the past," is distressed by the "crippled chances . . . of Negro children," and speaks of eliminating "inequalities and indignities based upon irrelevancies." "We ask," "we cannot," "we must," are sentence beginnings that frequently introduce a three, five, or six item series. At times contrast is combined with series construction and parallelism. At a college commencement in Wilberforce, Ohio, in 1962, he observed:

> Where once we were defenseless, we now have political,
> economic and social weapons. We have education in greater
> and greater measure. And we have the law. Where once we
> were inarticulate, we now speak, not in supplication, but in
> the dignity and confidence born of the struggle against
> degradation and persecution.

Rhetorical questions are frequently introduced, and imagery is made meaningful through the use of descriptive adjectives, action verbs, turned phrases, and figures of speech. He borrows the phrase "rendezvous with destiny" and amplifies the theme in terms of "the call of destiny" and "destiny at a crossroads." He speaks of the "tyranny of the unfettered state" and warns that "it is long past time to begin." Wilkins' word choices and combinations do not call attention to themselves; rather, they seem to give impact and focus to the message he is trying to communicate.

Wilkins shows artistry and originality in the comparisons he makes. All of the speeches studied reveal a flair for this compositional technique. The speaker showed an impatience for "snail-like tokenism in industry" and pointed out that "we are not talking about carrots and cockleburrs but are talking about public education." "If this be speed," he commented, "then the hippopotamus is a greyhound." In support of the public accommodations section of the Civil Rights Bill he observed, "The players in this drama of frustration and indignity are not commas or semi-colons in a legislative thesis. They are PEOPLE, human beings, citizens of the United States of America."

Wilkins makes excellent use of satire, irony, and innuendo. Numerous words in each speech are enclosed in quotation marks or printed in *italics,* suggesting a stipulated meaning. For instance in a November, 1963, speech after making reference to the four children killed in a Birmingham church, he remarked:

> Yet we don't need "haste." We must be "reasonable." We must observe the amenities of Senate and House protocol. We must remember holiday recesses. We must examine the periods and commas and paragraphs and sections. We must ponder on feasibility. We must calculate how much restraint the murderers will tolerate and impose not a whit more.

Profanity does not appear in any of the speeches. Language is adjusted to the group being addressed. Wilkins' preference seems to be for simple and concrete words; however, in his addresses before professional groups, vocabulary of greater complexity is used. Humor appears in many of the speeches, and on one occasion, a speech before an NAACP group, the slang expressions "hog wild" and "pig crazy" are used.

Delivery

Wilkins' delivery, like his style, is simple and unaffected. Some have charged that he lacks vigor and dynamic communicativeness, but most concede that he is sincere and speaks what he feels rather than what is expected of him. Wilkins often carries notes with him to the platform but seems to use them very little. He does not move about on the platform but stands slightly hunched over the podium. He makes a few gestures with his hands but has very little facial expression.

His listeners recall a voice that is pleasant, but not especially deep or resonant. His pitch lacks variety and at times sounds high; his voice seems slightly strained. Nevertheless, he sounds literate, cultured, and refined. Few articulatory deviations mar his speech although on occasion final consonants are sluffed. His seems to be standard American speech. Wilkins gains emphasis and climax through inflection and innuendo rather than through an increase in volume. He frequently emphasizes the last word of a sentence by giving it a rising inflection. He does not sound "preachie"; nor does he possess a ministerial cadence. However, at times he sounds non-fluent. He speaks slowly and deliberately; frequent pauses are inserted.

Roy Wilkins is no spellbinder. As one student listener put it, "He makes no verbal exclamations; one is moved to thought rather than action."[13] Another listener commented, "He seems to lack the capacity to take charge of an audience. He doesn't get all fired-up."[14]

Conclusions and Evaluations

What can be said of the speaking of Roy Wilkins? Several conclusions seem valid. He is a speaker who regularly addresses large groups of people, both Negro and white, in all parts of the country. Although a basic theme undergirds all of his remarks, he seems to adapt his emphasis and arguments to the group being addressed. He likewise adapts his materials and language for different audiences, a practice that is considered desirable in a speaker.

He is content oriented, other aspects of his rhetorical workmanship complementing his ideas rather than competing with them for attention. He offers adequate proof in support of his arguments and blends ethical, emotional, and logical proofs to build a strong case for his position. He places his greatest emphasis on logical materials, but his strong personal proof is an additional asset on the platform. His reasoning, like his evidence, is varied and meets accepted tests.

Because of the basic unity of his ideas, he is able, in part, to compensate for a lack of tight organization in the developmental portion of his speeches; however, he may on occasion lose his listeners because of a rambling loose style. His introductions and conclusions, although perhaps lacking in creative development, are appropriate for his message and are in harmony with the over-all impression he creates.

Wilkins seems aware that certain occasions demand a more elevated style than others, and he adjusts accordingly. Generally, however, he is simple and direct. His use of language and stylistic embellishment is well controlled; he never plays with words for the sake of ornamentation, nor creates the impression of being radical or irresponsible. Clarity, interestingness, and good taste are keystones of his language usage.

His delivery is probably insufficiently forceful. His pitch is rather high; he lacks variety and at times faulty breathing distorts thought units. He has good articulation and few, if any, of the peculiarities of pronunciation sometimes identified with his race. Nothing in his voice or bodily action calls atten-

[13]Interview with a Negro college student at Bowling Green State University, March, 1964. The student is a member of the National Association for the Advancement of Colored People and has spent several summers in Association work with Wilkins. She is a speech minor and has heard Wilkins speak on numerous occasions.

[14]Interview with a Negro professor at Bowling Green State University, March, 1964. The professor holds a doctorate in sociology and has heard Wilkins and other Negro spokesmen repeatedly during the past ten years.

tion to itself. He is more communicative when making impromptu remarks than when presenting prepared statements. In the latter situation he at times seems "readie." His delivery, like his message, is moderate and reasonable—simple and unassuming.

Roy Wilkins' speaking, like his basic position on the Civil Rights issue, offers a rational and moral approach. It makes him an effective spokesman for the Negro revolt. Never ostentatious or militant, always well-grounded in fact and flexible in method, Roy Wilkins speaks with authority. An example of subdued eloquence, he is an advocate who in practice as well as preachment demonstrates calm reasonableness, an attribute necessary in today's struggle for racial equality.

Questions for Analysis

1. What purpose does biographical information serve in this study in particular and in case studies of public speakers generally? Is such information appreciably more or less important for studying social action speakers than for studying purely political speakers; for "spokesmen" than for "partisan advocates"? Explain. List a few contemporary speakers, the understanding of whom seems to you to depend significantly on biographical information. Do these speakers fit a category? How does Wilkins' background lend itself to consideration of Wilkins as "spokesman" in the sense of the term developed by Murphy?

2. Describe the consistency of "image" which Wilkins the man sustains in his speeches. Is there a premium on such consistency in public speaking today? Explain. How does the calculated use of "agitative" rhetoric affect this consistency? Does the use of the mass media increase the temptation to be "all things to all people"?

3. Characterize Wilkins' rhetorical reliance on: a. audience identification, b. emotional appeal, c. logical proof, d. illustrative proof, e. causative proof.

4. Choose a topic for a civil rights speech. Consider three different audiences to which Wilkins might give the speech. Organize the speech as Wilkins might, but choose alternative instances of "proof-conclusion" and "problem-solution" to use for different audiences. Outline several possible conclusions. Now select one audience and write the speech. Depend on as many of Wilkins' stylistic devices as possible. Describe what you learned about "audience adaptability" for Wilkins.

5. Draw conclusions about Wilkins' conception of his "role" as a spokesman for civil rights. Speculate about his relative effectiveness, about the value of his "role" to the movement. Would Wilkins be appealing to "power-vulnerables"? How might he be received on your campus? Is his form of persuasion "appropriate" today? Do you agree with Ferris (she wrote in 1964–65) that being "never ostentatious or militant" is a necessary attribute in "today's struggle for racial equality"? Do you observe these attributes in contemporary speechmaking on racial issues?

32

Lyndon Johnson's Speech Preparation

Robert N. Hall

Probably no politician in American history attached so little importance to public speaking as did Lyndon Baines Johnson before his advent to the presidency. He did not find public speaking a challenge; he preferred to communicate with individuals rather than with an audience. On at least two occasions during his tenure as leader of the Democratic majority in the Senate, he relegated public speaking to a minor position in the over-all picture of practical politics. On one of these occasions he asserted that little could be accomplished by polemics[1] and on the other he said: "I proceed on the rule that you don't have to explain something you don't say."[2] To some extent, such an attitude prevented the public from knowing Johnson the man, Johnson the politician, Johnson the statesman, or Johnson the president, even though he had spent over twenty-five years as a public servant before assuming the presidency. Few people could recall any significant words which Johnson had uttered in the course of his public life, and as a result few people felt that they knew him intimately as they felt they knew Franklin D. Roosevelt or John F. Kennedy. Indeed, millions of Americans hardly recognized the name of Lyndon Johnson, when on that fateful day in November, 1963, he became president. In part, this lack of knowledge about the man stemmed from his failure to build a national following as other politicians have done; and, in part, it was a result of his attitude toward public speaking.

Another factor which prevented Johnson from being widely known was that historians and biographers had not written about him, a paradoxical situation considering the prominent role he played in national politics during the

Robert N. Hall is Associate Executive Secretary, Speech Association of America.
Reprinted by permission from *Quarterly Journal of Speech*, 51(1965) : 168–76.
[1]Douglas Cater, "Lyndon Johnson, Rising Democratic Star," *The Reporter*, VIII (January 20, 1953) , 34–36.
[2]"General Manager," *Time*, LXI (June 22, 1953), 21.

decades preceding his advent to the presidency.[3] His speeches and papers were never investigated and probably will not be until he leaves the White House.[4] No one attempted to present his political, economic, or social philosophy.[5] Until all of these areas about Johnson are investigated and reported in detail to the public, he probably will remain somewhat of a political enigma. It is not my purpose here, however, to cast light on the real President Johnson; but rather, it is my purpose to discuss how he prepared the texts of his speeches. This investigation is concerned with his speech preparation while he was in the Senate, during his vice-presidential years, and during the early period of his presidency.

Political speeches are not written, they are rewritten, not chiefly by the speaker but by his aides. The preparation of political speeches varies among politicians and their speech writers. Naturally there are a few politicians who write their own speeches or at least try to, but the pressures of campaigning or the burdens of political office usually prevent their utilizing a personal approach to any great event.

There are, however, three main ways in which a politician can prepare his speeches. John Franklin Carter, who worked on the speeches of Presidents Roosevelt and Truman and of former New York Governor Thomas E. Dewey, classified the methods of governmental speech preparation as judicial, executive, and legislative.[6] To illustrate the judicial system, Carter described the preparation of Roosevelt's speeches:

> He prepared a speech as though he were correcting the architect's blueprints for a cottage at Hyde Park. The task of assembling the material and putting it into draft form was farmed out to subordinates. . . . Then F.D.R. would take it under advisement and retire to his study with a stenographer and, usually, one of his confidants, like Judge Rosenman or Harry Hopkins, to put it into his own language. He never seemed hurried or harried.[7]

Carter used President Truman to illustrate what he called the executive approach:

[3]Although historians and scholars have still not written about Johnson, the professional biographers, including William S. White, have deluged the market with "campaign" biographies. At this writing ten books about the exemplary and humanitarian life of President Johnson were on the book stands, and there are more to come. For an evaluation of three of these volumes see my review in *QJS*, L (December 1964), 463–464.

[4]As late as June, 1964, only one graduate thesis in any field had been written about Johnson. The one study was my unpublished diss., "A Rhetorical Analysis of Selected Speeches of Senator Lyndon B. Johnson, 1955–1961" (University of Michigan, 1963).

[5]The only material that reveals much about Johnson's philosophy of political life is: Lyndon B. Johnson, "My Political Philosophy," *Texas Quarterly*, I, No. 4 (Winter 1958), 17–22. This article has recently been published in numerous popular periodicals, as well as in Booth Monney, *The Lyndon Johnson Story*, rev. ed. (New York, 1964).

[6]John Franklin Carter, *Power and Persuasion* (New York, 1960), p. 25.

[7]*Ibid.*, pp. 25–26.

> In preparing his speeches, Truman used the assembly-line technique. The various government departments provided the raw material. The night shift put it into draft form. Clark Clifford and Matt Connelly edited it. The President looked it over, often discussing it with his wife, made a few changes, and then delivered it. The whole process was crisp and authoritative.[8]

Carter presented Dewey as a proponent of the legislative pattern. Of the former New York governor, Carter said:

> Governor Dewey's method of speech preparation is legislative. That is to say, it is deliberative and involves a committee of advisors, with himself as chairman, sitting almost continuously until the final draft is approved. This is the most exhausting method of speech-writing known to man— I have seen a Dewey speech go through as many as eight drafts—but the result is something that approaches the smooth perfection of a Bach concerto.[9]

Johnson does not easily fit into any one of these classifications, chiefly because during his early years in public life he was not concerned with the fastidious refinements of speech. He had none of the eloquence of a Roosevelt or a Kennedy, he had no time for eloquence; he was too much of a feudal baron to delegate complete authority to his speech writers as Truman did; and he rarely took the time to be legislative in his preparation of a speech. Occasionally he utilized characteristics of all three; occasionally he was solely executive in his approach. Much depended on time, setting, and purpose. As Johnson said: "I do not have any particular rules for producing a speech but tailor the procedure according to circumstances."[10]

Johnson, as senator, like most government officials, relied heavily on manuscript speaking. According to congressional assistants who often do much of the administrative speech work, this official reliance on prepared scripts is a result of two factors: first, since members of the press want to assure accuracy in quoting a speaker while still meeting copy deadlines, they desire copies of the speeches before they are delivered; and second, since the Senate became a world forum after World War II, each senator has to be very careful of what he says.[11] Although cautiousness is important for all government officials, it is especially important for high-ranking personnel who can have their remarks erroneously interpreted as official government policy. During the Eisenhower administration when the Democrats controlled both Houses of Congress, John-

---

[8]*Ibid.*, p. 26.

[9]*Ibid.*, p. 27.

[10]Personal letter from the Vice-President, Washington, D. C., August 4, 1962.

[11]Personal interview with Jerry C. O'Callaghan, administrative assistant to the late Senator Joseph C. O'Mahoney and executive secretary to former Senator J. J. Hickey, both of Wyoming, February 24, 1961.

son's position as Senate majority leader virtually made him second in importance to the president. Obviously, Johnson needed to be careful of how he phrased his political pronouncements and, therefore, he relied heavily on manuscript speaking.

The amount of care given to the preparation of one of Senator Johnson's manuscripts usually was determined by the occasion of the speech and the amount of time available for work on it. He had a staff that ranged in size from twenty to eighty people. From this group of assistants he selected the people who would help him in preparing a speech. If the speech was not considered a major address, the assistants did most of the work, with Johnson having the final say, often making language changes that gave the final draft his personal stamp. In most instances when Johnson used a manuscript, he put his trust in George Reedy, a former newspaperman, former staff director of the Senate Democratic Policy Committee, and now press secretary to the president, to see that the speech was correct in content and organization. It was Reedy's job to see that the staff assistants did whatever research was needed and then prepared the draft or drafts of the speech. The final draft was then presented to Reedy who either approved or rejected it. If he approved of the work he gave the speech to Johnson for final revision and approval.[12] As with many public figures, Johnson sometimes sought help from sources other than his staff. He admitted: "I receive help and editorial assistance both from my staff and from people of my acquaintance who are skilled in this field."[13] The procedure depended on the circumstances surrounding the purpose, occasion, and significance of the speech.

One example of a speech, classified by Johnson as a minor speech, which he gave during his Senate tenure was "Among the Stars," presented to a student-faculty convocation at St. Louis University in St. Louis, Missouri, on December 7, 1959. The speech was the first of a series of talks given in Missouri, Kansas, and Iowa during a three-day period. It was classified as minor because Johnson's purpose in making the trip was to assess the state of the nation and the Republican abandonment of the Midwest.[14] Everywhere he went he met and talked with Democratic state party leaders.[15] With his attention focused on political matters, formal speaking took its usual minor position. One may grasp the method of Johnson's preparation by briefly looking at the organization of this speech. In the introduction he presented his thesis by saying:

> Let me say, the future is not a prediction. It is not a promise.
> The future is a journey—not a goal. And we need to talk
> about the trip—not the destination. For of this one thing I

[12]Personal interview with Ralph Huitt, Professor of Political Science, University of Wisconsin, Madison, Wisconsin, February 10, 1961. Professor Huitt served as a staff assistant to Senator Johnson in 1953–1954, and as a speech writer during the 1960 presidential campaign.

[13]Letter from the Vice-President.

[14]William M. Blair, *New York Times*, December 8, 1959, p. 54.

[15]*St. Louis Post-Dispatch*, December 7, 1959, p. 1.

> am sure: no other generation has ever had the promise of
> so thrilling a journey as the journey awaiting you.[16]

A metaphorical approach is apparent. But in the body of the speech instead of talking about a journey, the Senator talked about communism, leadership, federal aid to education, and a number of other public issues. Since he used the journey theme for his title and thesis but not for the body of the speech, and since he failed to show the relationship between the journey and his various other ideas, the speech lacked unity. Likewise, he failed to make a concrete connection between his ideas about leadership and the theme of communism which he introduced. Thus, the absence of a coherent pattern is apparent throughout "Among the Stars." This type of disruptive unity was typical of Johnson's speeches when he was not really concerned about his immediate audience.[17]

The lack of unity in "Among the Stars" may indicate that Johnson gave little care to revision of some of his addresses. He seemed more concerned with presenting raw ideas than with presenting ideas in a unified and organized manner. As he said:

> I am constantly on the alert in talking to my friends and
> people with whom I am associated for ideas. If the ideas
> are practical and strike me as worthy of being put into
> effect, I try to place them into speech form so they may be
> explained to the public as one step in the process of making
> them effective.[18]

If Johnson and his staff thought a given speech was good enough to satisfy the requirements of a particular audience, the speech very likely stood without further revision. No attempt was made to polish the speech. Thus, many of his speeches were wanting in continuity, unity, and coherence. A lack of unity often meant that the speeches were filled with undeveloped ideas.

Obviously, Johnson's preparation for major addresses was more involved than that for minor addresses. When a speech was classified as a major one, a conference might be held between Johnson and key members of his staff or with people of his acquaintance. Those who were not members of his staff who helped him were referred to as his "brain trust." The trust included Dean Acheson, Truman's secretary of state; Thomas Corcoran and Benjamin Cohen, members of Roosevelt's brain trust; James H. Rowe, Jr., a Roosevelt administrative aide; Anna M. Rosenberg, an industrial consultant; Clark Clifford, a Truman special counsel; and Abe Fortas, a liberal lawyer.[19] During a confer-

[16]"Among the Stars," Text of the speech from the Office of the Democratic Leader, Washington, D. C., June 27, 1960.

[17]For a more thorough and comprehensive study of Johnson's speeches, see my unpubl. diss., "A Rhetorical Analysis of Selected Speeches of Senator Lyndon B. Johnson, 1955–1961."

[18]Letter from the Vice-President.

[19]"Building a 'White House' on Capitol Hill," *U.S. News & World Report,* XLVI (February 13, 1959), 64–65.

ence Johnson explained the general ideas that he wanted covered in a speech. The people assembled would then present information and methods for developing the topic. From the information initially presented a first draft of the speech was prepared by one or more of Johnson's staff. The draft was then submitted to Reedy or to Walter Jenkins, one of Johnson's personal assistants. On a number of occasions a speech went through five or more drafts before it reached Johnson for final approval. In some instances, if the Senator felt the speech did not express exactly what he wanted to say, he attempted to rewrite the speech himself.[20] His main objective, as noted earlier, was the explanation of ideas; therefore, the conferences and revisions were meant to clarify the thoughts which he wanted to express.

One major speech, the first address in his campaign for the vice-presidency, was delivered to the American Political Science Association on September 9, 1960, in New York City. Johnson had a great deal of respect for the political scientists for three reasons: first, the president of the association was a native Texan and a good friend of his; second, several members of the audience had worked with him in the Senate; and third, most of his audience knew a great deal about his selected topic, "Divided Government and Stalemate." As a result, he gave adequate time to preparing the speech, and it turned out to be one of the finest he made during the campaign. After a lengthy introduction, he stated his thesis:

> If I may, I would like to talk with you specifically of a con-
> dition in our American government which I believe deserves
> far more serious attention than it is receiving.
> I refer to the condition of divided government.[21]

Using the inductive method, he presented a series of particulars leading to a general conclusion. He began by contending that divided government had worked by accident and then said that although divided government had worked, it was not normal. Furthermore, he averred that divided government was a nonsensical doctrine that had not been envisioned by the founding fathers. Another contention was that divided government led to stagnation and stalemate. The idea of a checkmated government brought him to his contention that since the Democrats would continue to control Congress after the 1960 election, divided government would continue if the executive branch was again won by the Republican party. Johnson reached the conclusion, as determined by the particulars, that two parties with divided purposes could not constitute a majority government and, therefore, the solution to the problem was the election of a Democratic congress and a Democratic president.[22] By con-

    [20]Professor Huitt noted this procedure in the author's interview with him. It was also covered in an article that dealt with Johnson's speechmaking techniques, "Democrat Tries for Lead in Space Statesmanship," *Business Week* (January 18, 1958), pp. 29–30.
    [21]"Divided Government and Stalemate," Text of the speech from the office of the Vice-President, Washington, D. C., September 21, 1962.
    [22]*Ibid.*

certed preparation, the speech as presented in its final form was a coherent and unified study of the problems surrounding a government whose legislative branch was controlled by the Democratic party and whose executive branch was controlled by the Republican party. Thus it is apparent by the examples of "Among the Stars" and "Divided Government and Stalemate" that when Johnson was concerned with the effect of his communication, he was capable of presenting a well-prepared speech.

When preparing speeches for a national campaign as he did in the fall of 1960, Johnson combined the techniques used for major and minor addresses. While making his bid for the vice-presidency, Johnson campaigned in all parts of the country. He opened the contest in Boston on September 8 and ended it in Austin, Texas, on November 7. Between these two speaking engagements, he traveled from New York to Los Angeles, and from Chicago to Miami. The most important part of his campaign endeavors, however, occurred in mid-October when he made a five-day, 3800-mile, fifty-seven speech, whistle-stop tour of the South.[23] When Johnson left Washington on his swing through eight Southern states in late October, he left part of his staff in Washington, D.C., to serve as an information center. Professor Ralph Huitt of the political science department of the University of Wisconsin was one of those who remained in the capital. Huitt's job was to assist in writing speeches, averaging about two pages in length. These speeches were wired to Reedy, who was on the campaign train with Johnson. The content of these speeches constituted about 300-to-400-word replies to charges made by Richard Nixon, Henry Cabot Lodge, and other Republican campaigners. Since Johnson felt platform speeches should not be read, he did not deliver these short talks, but he did use them to supply himself with information that could be incorporated into purely extemporaneous speeches delivered from the rear platform of the train. Like any other campaigner for public office, Johnson had a store of speeches that he used. Adding whatever was necessary from the material supplied by Huitt, Johnson drew on his stock speeches and altered them to suit whatever audience he faced.[24] Johnson took this approach to his campaign speeches because he felt that if he did not have to spend time reading speeches in preparation for delivery, he could spend more time "politicking."

It is clear that as a senator, Lyndon Baines Johnson granted speechmaking a minor role in his total picture of politics: (1) he noted that you do not have to explain something you do not say; therefore, he took few pains to develop the techniques of the accomplished speaker, techniques of style, rhythm, ornamentation, organization, and delivery; (2) he relied rather heavily on ghost writers who were generally members of his large staff to supply the initial

---

[23]"Y'all Come Aboard," *New Republic*, CXLIII (October 24, 1960), 4.

[24]All of the information about this portion of the 1960 campaign was supplied by Professor Huitt in the interview of February 10, 1961. Huitt served in the capacity of speech writer from September to November. He also traveled with Johnson during part of the campaign.

manuscript; (3) he left many of the decisions about the content and style of the speeches to George Reedy of the Senate Democratic Policy Committee; and (4) he divided the speeches into major and minor categories based on his own evaluation of the importance of the audience. The minor addresses received less attention than the major ones; the responsibility for the minor ones was left to his staff while the responsibility for the major addresses rested with Johnson and the noted leaders and authorities whose advice he sought.

The methods Johnson used in preparing speeches when he became vice-president were the techniques developed for the major addresses given during his senate tenure. He relied on conferences, nongovernment personnel, and other authorities to help formulate and organize the ideas to be presented in the speeches. He thus spent more time on their preparation and took greater care to secure a higher degree of eloquence. As a senator, except when he was campaigning, Johnson made few speeches to the general public; he chose instead to concentrate on the business of the Senate and the government. But since the vice-president's ceremonial duties call for much speechmaking, and since the person holding that office automatically falls heir to those duties, it was only natural that as vice-president, Johnson gave greater attention to the role of speech as an important means of communication. His speech writers remained basically the same but they concentrated more on the mechanics of the speech text and they also had available to them writers in the White House and other branches of the executive department. As a result, Johnson's speeches were better organized, were more stylistically refined, and were better adapted to the audience. During the three years spent as vice-president, Johnson and his staff of writers seemed to concentrate more on explaining, clarifying, and applying the ideas to the specific audience involved than they had previously done. Most of the speeches took on the aura of major addresses. Furthermore, the new approach to style made the speeches much better than most of those delivered earlier in his career.

As vice-president, Johnson placed more emphasis on speechmaking as an art than he had previously done. This tendency was primarily the result of two factors: (1) the office itself compelled him to devote more time to public speaking because it was so much a part of the office; and (2) both he and his staff had more time to spend on organization and style. In addition, once he began speaking more, he had to explain what he was saying and this led to greater attention to both substance and method. The speeches, as is customary in government circles, often were reviewed by the White House, the State Department, or other executive agencies. The effect of this new emphasis on speechmaking made Johnson more eloquent than he was in the Senate.

When Johnson became president, he inherited Kennedy's speech writers and at first, at least, the preparation of his speeches changed and new tendencies began to develop. President Johnson's first speech, a speech to a joint session of Congress, was prepared by Theodore Sorenson, President Kennedy's speech writer. Other drafts were prepared by John Kenneth Galbraith and Horace Busby, but Johnson selected Sorenson's for presentation.[25] This decision marked a new approach for Johnson: it was the first time he gave a speech which was prepared by someone outside his personal staff and by someone who had never been part of his brain trust. Usually his speeches were at least reviewed by Reedy or other members of his personal staff, but such was not the case this time. Johnson, as usual, made some changes in language and sentence structure. Sorenson, however, was the real architect of the speech. The result was "an address that surprised even his [Johnson's] admirers with its force, its eloquence, its quiet mood of confidence."[26] The second major address of Johnson's administration, the Thanksgiving Day message, was prepared by Horace Busby, a veteran Johnson speech writer.[27] The result was a speech that was neither eloquent nor forceful. The speech was primarily the product of one man and was a demonstration of the writer's ability rather than of Johnson's ability. The Busby speech was more typically Johnsonian than was the Sorenson speech.[28]

The December address to the United Nations was prepared by Dean Acheson; the speech was reviewed by a host of people, however, before it was delivered in New York City. Changes were recommended by key State Department personnel, by Senator J. W. Fulbright of Arkansas, Senator Eugene McCarthy of Minnesota, Representatives Jack Brooks and Homer Thornberry of Texas, Clark Clifford, and Thomas Mann. The President invited them all to dinner, and when they had finished dinner he passed out copies of the Acheson draft of the speech and asked them for their comments and suggestions. Some of the recommendations were substantive and others were merely grammatical, but Johnson was utilizing a new concept in his speech preparation.[29] From the single ghost-writer approach of the first two major addresses of his administration, Johnson shifted to a ghost-written speech which was then reviewed and changed by a new brain trust. Some changes were also made by the President himself. The method of preparing the speech had some resemblance to the conference method used for his major senatorial addresses; however, the conference personnel were entirely new. Although this speech also lacked the eloquence of his first address as president, it still ranked above the Thanksgiving Day message.

The preparation of the State of the Union message went through the same system of analysis as did the message to the United Nations. Sorenson and McGeorge Bundy began the speech and then Johnson reviewed it with Senator Mike Mansfield and other Democratic leaders of Congress, with Cabinet members, and with business and labor leaders.[30] After several days of review, a final draft was prepared for delivery on January 7, 1964. With the bulk of the

25Rowland Evans and Robert Novak, *St. Louis Post-Dispatch*, January 2, 1964, p. 1B.
26Tom Wicker, *New York Times*, November 28, 1963, p. 1.
27Evans and Novak, *loc. cit.*
28James Reston, *New York Times*, January 8, 1964, p. 34.
29Evans and Novak, *loc. cit.*
30Nan Robertson, *New York Times*, January 7, 1964, p. 14.

speech written by Sorenson and Bundy, Johnson again presented a speech that was stylistically eloquent.

To facilitate reading of speeches, Johnson had them prepared on a type-writer with extra large print. This type of printing which, for ease in reading, he utilized as a senator, he is still using today. He has copies stenciled for distribution to the press, for inclusion in his files, and for mailing to persons who might be interested in a given speech or its topic.[31]

During the first few months of his presidency, Johnson seemed to have no definite pattern for speech preparation. He fluctuated from one writer to several writers and again to one writer and a conference. But with the departure, in late January, of Sorenson, Johnson began to rely heavily on one man: Horace Busby, who is now recognized as the real ghost writer of the Johnson administration.[32] One fact, however, must not be overlooked; although Johnson uses a ghost writer, his own personal touch is always evident in his speeches.

One may conclude that certain changes occurred in the preparation of Johnson's speeches during the last twenty-five years: (1) As he advanced up the political ladder his attitude toward speaking changed. As a senator, Johnson saw little value in developing artistic speech techniques. Speeches were sometimes mediocre simply because they were not well prepared. He placed almost all other aspects of his political career ahead of his speeches. When he became vice-president, however, the duties of the office brought about a new respect for the art of speechmaking. During the three vice-presidential years both he and his staff worked to improve his image as a speaker. The presidency brought the change full circle. Whereas Senator Johnson was indifferent to speechmaking, President Johnson is concerned with his public image as a speaker. (2) The responsibility for the preparation of his speeches has shifted from unknown employees to well-known government and national leaders. Senator Johnson delegated his speech preparation to members of his large staff, with George Reedy serving as the final review before Johnson delivered the finished product. President Johnson, at least early in his administration, depended on such noted government men as Theodore Sorenson, Dean Acheson, McGeorge Bundy, and others to write his speeches. Reedy and the presidential staff were no longer an important part of the preparation. The more significant Johnson's statements became, the more emphasis he placed on their careful preparation. Such emphasis meant a need for the best speech architects he could secure, and this has resulted in a diminished reliance on his close coterie of employees. (3) As he paid more attention to preparation he became more eloquent. To be sure, the degree of eloquence depended on who did the ghostwriting, but on the whole the presidential speeches are superior to the senatorial addresses. Better preparation has resulted in better organization,

[31]Interview with Huitt.
[32]"When Johnson Plans a Speech," *U.S. News & World Report*, LVI (February 3, 1964), 33.

greater unity, and a clearer sense of purpose. The result of the new emphasis on preparation has been an improved image of Johnson as a speaker. A good public image has led to a greater approval of the man and his policies. (4) The one tendency that has been consistent throughout Johnson's career is his reliance on manuscript speaking. As a senator, as vice-president, and in the early period of his presidency, Johnson almost always used a manuscript. A campaign generally resulted in the extensive use of extemporaneous delivery, but even in a campaign, as with the address to the American Political Science Association, if the speech was a major address, he read it. (5) From the division of speeches into major and minor categories as was done during his senatorial career, only the major category survived through the vice-presidential years and into the presidency. This change is not so much a result of deliberate decision by Johnson, although his changed attitude toward speechmaking helped, as it is a result of the nature of the office. A senator is a minor figure when compared to a president. Senators often give speeches that are never reported; rarely, however, are the words of an American president not recorded and transmitted for all the world to hear. Therefore, no speech can truly be thought of as minor. (6) From the apparent confusion of the early days of the administration, Horace Busby now has emerged as the real ghost writer. He is expected to be as influential in this field as was Theodore Sorenson during the Kennedy years.

There is still much to be learned about the preparation of a Johnson speech. One thing is clear: no matter who writes the speeches the end product is likely to be strictly Johnsonian. The achievement of a distinctive flavor is the result of Johnson's effort to get his habits of language and of structure integrated into the work of the ghost writer. Without such integration there would be no Johnsonian style as we know it today.

Questions for Analysis

1. Delineate both the advantages and the disadvantages of speech preparation "by committee." How do the three methods (judicial, executive, legislative) classified by Carter compare? Did it matter, apparently, that a Dewey speech approached "the smooth perfection of a Bach concerto"? What considerations must a politician weigh when deciding the time to spend preparing speeches? How do Stevenson and Johnson apparently differ in their decisions? Is the rule that "you don't have to explain something you don't say" a phenomenon of our time? Explain.

2. What were Johnson's criteria for distinguishing a "major" from a "minor" speech? How might the distinction affect both the preparation and the content of a speech? How do the mass media today bear upon the impact even of a "minor"

speech? Does the procedure of distinguishing "major" from "minor" speeches raise both ethical and practical questions? Explain.

3. How may "applying the ideas to the specific audience involved" complicate the process of political speech preparation? How many different "appeals" can you develop for a given topical theme? How might your choice of consultants reflect this diversity? Why is one "real ghost writer" so important? Describe the probability among various audiences that the calculated "appeal" will be detected.

4. Obtain copies of several of Johnson's early speeches as President. Compare them for "eloquence." Do the comparisons suggest the obvious influence of different consultants? How do topic and audience contribute to "eloquence"? Imagine yourself present at the meeting for preparation of the United Nations address. Describe the contributions made to the speech by those Hall names as consultants. Do the consultants appear to play specific "roles" in the preparation? Contrast the "roles" of Acheson, Fulbright, Clifford, and Johnson.

5. On the basis of what you have read, how do you think Johnson rated the "aspects of his political career" at various times during that career? How significantly did his personal attention to speech preparation change? Do you find evidence that his attention to it continued to change after 1965? Use his Howard University speech (June, 1965) as a standard by which to judge subsequent efforts. What do these comparisons suggest about the emergence of a "Johnsonian" style?

33

The Schizoid Image of Stokely Carmichael

Pat Jefferson

Stokely Carmichael, the twenty-four-year-old Negro leader of the Student Nonviolent Coordinating Committee, became known nationally during the James Meredith March in June, 1966, when he skyrocketed to fame with his cry for black power. Because in this country a psychological restriction existed prohibiting the "use of the word 'power' in conjunction with the word 'black,' "[1] newsmen seized upon the term and gave it their definition. Carmichael believed reporters distorted the slogan by quoting him out of context and identifying black power with violence. He became antagonistic; when asked to explain his own philosophy already badly misinterpreted by the press, he reacted defensively and refused to clarify the term.[2] The rhetoric surrounding black power grew more extreme and, in accordance with Edwin Black's belief that rhetoric influences the actions of the speaker,[3] Carmichael's public image became identified with his language.

When SNCC elected Carmichael its executive chairman, the event characterized the complexity of the organization in all of its moodiness, brilliance, and contradictions. Prior to the election, SNCC battled against charisma and the cult of the personality.[4] Then the staff elevated to the highest position of leadership their most flamboyant member—Stokely Carmichael, the rebel

Pat Jefferson is a Teaching Associate in Speech, Indiana University.

Adapted from "The Rhetoric of the 'Magnificent Barbarian,' Stokely Carmichael," unpublished Master's thesis, Indiana University, 1967. Published by permission.

[1] Paul Good, "A White Look at Black Power," *The Nation*, August 8, 1966, 112.

[2] Interview with Pat Weatherly, SNCC staff, Selma, Alabama, March 17, 1967.

[3] Edwin Black, "The Practice of Rhetorical Criticism," *Rhetorical Criticism: A Study in Method* (New York: The Macmillan Company, 1965), 35. Black criticizes the neo-Aristotelian critics because they do not account for the influence of the discourse on its author: the future commitments it makes for him; the choices it closes to him; the public image it portrays to which he must adjust.

[4] Gene Roberts, "The Story of Snick: From 'Freedom High' to 'Black Power,' " *The New York Times Magazine*, September 25, 1966, p. 124.

whom Bernard Lee described as "all image and charisma."[5] Although he was infamous at twenty-six and the target of much invective, few press releases looked beyond his rhetoric for insight into the real nature of the black power firebrand. Perhaps the most illuminating description came from Lerone Bennett, Jr., who wrote: ". . . Carmichael walks like Sidney Poitier, talks like Harry Belafonte and thinks like the post-Muslim Malcolm X."[6] His closest friends, however, concurred in describing him as "charming." In private life his personal magnetism hypnotized women. Aware of his effect on the ladies, SNCC officials publicized his eligibility and, consequently, the unmarried Stokely Carmichael helped recruit females to the organization. His charm proved financially rewarding, for when contributions declined, wealthy white women who knew him before his elevation to leadership continued to send donations.[7] Pat Weatherly, a SNCC staff member, speculated that his success with women stemmed from the gentle and kind manner with which he treated them, but added his obvious physical sex appeal was no hindrance. A real "man's man" as well, Carmichael's male associates labeled him "dangerous," "electrifying," and a real "jive-muther," and even attested to his innate kindness. Refuting the accusation that Carmichael hated whites, H. Rap Brown quietly replied, "He's the last man in the world to hate."[8] Liked and respected among his friends, Carmichael created vastly different images among various segments of society.

When Daniel Boorstin hypothesized that the "hero" of American society had been replaced by the "celebrity," he hinted that the United States had seen the last of her great men—not because men and women were no longer made of that "sterner stuff," but because prevailing social phenomenon prevented the hero's emergence. The democratic system fostered a mistrust of the leader, because it rested on the premise that common people should rule themselves. The social sciences minimized the magnificence of a hero by teaching that he was a mere occurrence habitual in any society. Such an attitude rendered its believers more sophisticated and less given to worshipful respect of any man's essential greatness. Scientific and critical histories and biographies replaced the eulogistic works of yesteryear and objectively exposed the defects and weaknesses in would-be heroes. Karl Marx and his economic determinism pictured man as a parsimonious creature governed by his own monetary achievements. Thus, when Charles A. Beard wrote *An Economic Interpretation of the Constitution,* he even battered the armor of our Founding Fathers by enumerating the financial rewards they accumulated after the passage of the Constitution. Sociological and psychological influences finally chipped away the

[5]"Marching Where?" *The Reporter,* July 14, 1966, p. 16.

[6]Lerone Bennett, Jr., "Stokely Carmichael: Architect of Black Power," *Ebony,* September, 1966, p. 26.

[7]Interview with Pat Weatherly.

[8]Interview with H. Rap Brown, SNCC executive chairman, Selma, Alabama, March 18, 1967. At the time of the interview, Brown was the Alabama field secretary.

remaining mold of the American hero. Men no longer ruled their destinies but became the victims of emotional and environmental factors in their lives. With the aid of the press, Boorstin concluded, the hero evaporated into the celebrity. From the "big man" who "created himself" and was distinguished by his achievements, evolved the "big name" produced by the "media" and famous for his image or trademark.[9]

Boorstin, however, did not discuss an environment devoid of the social phenomenon and technological advances that hindered the making of a hero. If the presence of these factors prevented the development of idolatry, conceivably their absence would allow its existence. Under such isolated conditions, therefore, a hero could be born. Lowndes County, Alabama, with its culture-starved inhabitants, provided conditions favorable to the birth of a hero.

Although twelve thousand Negroes populated the Black Belt county and outnumbered the whites four to one, political and economic control rested with the blue-eyed monsters. Until August, 1965, for example, not a single Negro registered to vote. Subdued by educated Negroes and whites, the poor blacks knew nothing of the democracy founded on human equality that made others suspicious of individual heroic greatness. With ninety percent of the land owned by eighty-nine white families,[10] the poor blacks were mere chattel on a planter's estate, sweating in the cotton fields and earning three dollars for a ten hour day.[11] Economically and mentally impoverished, their median family income was $935.00 annually while eighty percent of the county's total population remained functionally illiterate.[12] Financially unable to purchase adequate transportation, the black man's mobility slowed to a halting pace. Geographically confined, some Negroes were born, reared, and died in Lowndes, never once leaving the county. Few knew that their state capital was only an hour's drive north.[13] Isolated from the nation and ostracized by the white community, these people learned no new trends in political thought. Social sciences did not add to their sophistication; they did not read Karl Marx, Charles A. Beard, or scientific histories; and psychological influences had no relevance in their lives. Childlike in his intellectual naivete, the poor black man remained untouched by the social phenomenon that toppled white America's hero from his throne.

Carmichael came to Lowndes County as a representative of the Student Nonviolent Coordinating Committee. Like all SNCC workers, he brought knowledge, skills, and ideas—but not domination. SNCC's policy focused on helping to build local leadership. As a fieldworker, he lived with the people,

[9]Daniel J. Boorstin, "From Hero to Celebrity: The Human Pseudo-Event," *The Image: A Guide to Pseudo-Events in America* (New York: Harper & Row, 1964), 45–61.

[10]Andrew Kopkind, "The Lair of the Black Panther," *The New Republic*, August 13, 1966, pp. 10–13.

[11]Good, *The Nation*, p. 113.

[12]Kopkind, *The New Republic*, p. 10.

[13]Personal observations and interviews with people in Lowndes County, Alabama, March 17–18, 1967.

shared their food, and slept in their shacks. Similar to the circuit riders and other itinerant clergymen, Carmichael spread the word: that neither poverty nor lack of education disqualified an individual from exercising his political rights and participating in government. He preached from the bible he called Black Power, which served as a rallying cry for hundreds of poor blacks who dared to register to vote and run for office.[14] In Lowndes County, poor Alabamans needed such a slogan where the price of acceptance often was loss of job, eviction, and eventual starvation.[15]

To them, Carmichael represented a new American Negro—not a "Tom" (a black man who nods and subserviently does the bidding of his white master), but a proud man who out-stared the "Miss Ann's" and the "Mr. Charlie's" (white women and men) with unflinching directness. A Negro journalist noted that Carmichael had a "cool, outwardly imperturbable" look that gave onlookers the impression "he would stroll through Dixie in broad daylight using the Confederate flag for a handkerchief."[16] Lowndes County black folk took vicarious pleasure in such an image and delighted when "their boy, Stokely" gave the white folk "hell." When Carmichael boldly challenged the supremacy of white men, he performed an heroic act and won the respect of the people. After he became executive chairman, he left Lowndes County and began traveling extensively. Although geographically separated, a closeness still existed between Carmichael and his people. In anticipation of the second anniversary of the Lowndes County Freedom Organization, with shining eyes Mrs. Jackson, a local resident, expressed her hope that "Stokely" would return for the celebration. His people idolized him.[17] Then, consistent with Boorstin's theory, the mass media created a new "celebrity." Almost overnight, Stokely Carmichael became a national "big name." Few Americans heard of his achievements in Lowndes County, but all knew his trademark, Black Power.

Carmichael, the celebrity, also starred in pseudo-events[18] around the country. One such occurrence climaxed on April 8, 1967, in Nashville, Tennessee, and supported the sociologists who concluded that television broadcasting conformed to the viewers' expectations.[19] The Nashville citizenry associated Carmichael's name with riots, and as early as March 25 announced its displeas-

---

[14]"The Story of SNCC," a brochure published by the Student Nonviolent Coordinating Committee.

[15]The landowners in Lowndes County evicted those tenants that voted in the 1966 November elections. The Student Nonviolent Coordinating Committee set up tents until the displaced persons could find new homes. "Tent City" remained in existence through March, 1967.

[16]Gordon Parks, "Whip of Black Power," *Life*, May 19, 1967, p. 78.

[17]Personal observations and interviews with people in Lowndes.

[18]Daniel Boorstin defined the pseudo-event as a happening that possessed three characteristics: it is not spontaneous but arises through planning or incitement; it is planted primarily for the purpose of being reported; and it has a sense of ambiguity and the question "What does it mean?" has a new dimension. See *The Image*, p. 11.

[19]Boorstin, "From News Gathering to News Making: A Flood of Pseudo-Events," *The Image*, p. 28.

ure with Vanderbilt University for inviting him to speak at Impact '67, a symposium examining the individual and his future in American society. The front page editorial of the *Nashville Banner* succinctly stated this position in the headline: "Hate Spieling Carmichael Unwelcome in the City."[20] In the interim —between the appearance of the headline and the Impact symposium—the Tennessee State Legislature, the American Legion Post 5, Nashville's largest radio station, WLAC, and the *Nashville Banner* denounced Carmichael, requested Chancellor Alexander Heard to withdraw Vanderbilt's invitation, and warned him that Carmichael's speech would incite a riot. Vanderbilt officials, however, met the challenge. Chancellor Heard reaffirmed the right of free speech and complimented Impact for organizing a "Stimulating program of diverse speakers."[21] Over four thousand people, predominantly white, filled the Memorial Gymnasium at Vanderbilt University. Students crowded the aisles and lined the walls anticipating the arrival of the controversial speaker. Police patrolled the area, plainclothesmen scattered throughout the audience to discourage anticipated riots, and national television networks stood by for immediate news coverage if disturbances occurred. Carmichael, however, adapted well to the situation and delivered a scholarly talk on black power. Impressed, most auditors concluded that he "appeared in sharp contrast to what they expected."[22] A listening banker "didn't realize Carmichael could conduct himself in such a manner."[23] and Frank A. Rose, President of the University of Alabama and the following speaker, deleted the portion of his prepared address attacking Carmichael for his "passionate intensity," because the speech was not as militant as he had anticipated.[24] Carmichael thus left a favorable impression on the Impact audience. The American public, however, associated the Negro celebrity with black power, incitement to riot, and violence. When his speech failed to conform to this preconceived stereotype, the national television networks did not televise the event. Four hours after Carmichael delivered his speech, however, riots broke out in the Negro section of Nashville. The networks featured on-the-spot reporting, emphasized that Stokely Carmichael had been in the city, and flashed the story from coast to coast. The telecast conformed to the viewers' expectations and the negative image of the advocate of black power remained fixed in the public's mind.

A lunacy of language, characterized by distortion, hyperbole, bitter in-

[20]Stokely Carmichael, tape recording of a speech delivered at Impact '67, Vanderbilt University, Nashville, Tennessee, April 8, 1967.

[21]"Local Leaders Should Support Unrestricted Campus Debate," *The Vanderbilt Hustler*, April 7, 1967.

[22]John Haile, "Confederate Flag Display Greets Stokely Talk," *The Nashville Tennessean*, April 9, 1967.

[23]Personal observations and interviews with people in Nashville, Tennessee, April 8, 1967. Also see Pat Jefferson, "The Magnificent Barbarian at Nashville," *Southern Speech Journal*, 33 (1967), 77–87.

[24]Brad Edgerton, "Rose Emphasized Dialogue, Deletes Carmichael Attack," *The Vanderbilt Hustler*, April 11, 1967.

vective, and unnecessary accusations, clouded events concerning Carmichael. At the center of this fanaticism was a belief in the existence of a systematic plot formed to pollute a way of life. Richard Hofstadter labeled this exaggerated passion for abusive verbal expression the "paranoid style." It did not refer to the validity of arguments—just the manner in which these ideas were expressed and believed.[25] Two days after Carmichael's speech at Vanderbilt, a searing front-page editorial appeared in the *Nashville Banner* which exemplified the paranoid style and its preoccupation with thoughts of a conspiracy. "This violence occurred precisely as planned," insisted the editor, "and concerning it the public had been amply warned." With "infamy" as Carmichael's "stock in trade," he exhorted "violence" toward the country he adopted for purposes of "arson." The *Banner* then reminded its readers that Memorial Gymnasium was dedicated "to the memory of Vanderbilt men who died in their country's service in World War II." Contrary to the building's original "patriotic" purpose, "Comes then, by invitation, this enemy of America and Americanism whose ideological pitch it is to walk on these graves, to smear every man—regardless of color—now in uniform; to insult the nation which has given him sanctuary, solicit total defiance of 'Kill and Burn' . . . —the malevolence of a mind berserk with its own consuming hate." The editorial climaxed its attack by noting Carmichael's sinister plot against the United States: "If there is a degree of public insanity that conditions some minds to filth, or gets its kick out of subversion by exhibitionist, itinerant firebrands, soiling and vandalizing this nation's temple, with kindred designs upon its soul, let it be said that majority America—young and old, and irrespective of race—shuns this contagion."[26]

While Nashville residents believed that they were the victims of Carmichael's devised deviltry, SNCC diametrically opposed this view. Likewise indulging in the rhetoric of monomania, the organization attacked the press for failing to report the calculated frame-up of the police, maintaining that black students were the unsuspecting prey of a "police set-up," formulated weeks before when Vanderbilt first announced that Carmichael would be a guest speaker. According to an immediate release that SNCC mailed to supporters, the police department ordered special "riot equipment," prepared themselves for battle, and went on "riot alert." The release stated that "Stokely Carmichael went to Nashville, spoke to several student groups there, and then left for a speaking engagement in another city—with no trouble breaking out. But—the white powers-that-be in Nashville could not let their prediction fail to materialize. After all," insisted SNCC, "they had prepared for a so-called riot and had told everyone that there would be such a riot. So they quickly went into action to create a situation which they knew would force the black students and citizens of Nashville to act and to defend themselves. Then, they

25Richard Hofstadter, "The Paranoid Style in American Politics," *The Paranoid Style in American Politics and Other Essays* (New York: Alfred A. Knopf, 1965), 5.
26"What Price Folly? An Editorial," *Nashville Banner*, April 10, 1967.

could call it a 'riot' and put their gestapo-like tactics into action."[27] The Nash-ville drama ended the way it began—in a violent display of bitter language. Blacks and whites expressed their views in a distorted, paranoiac manner, hindering the discovery of truth rather than assisting it. Consequently, while Carmichael starred in the pseudo-event, the director of the action remained anonymous.

According to Hofstadter, American minority groups have preferred the paranoid style. They have interpreted history as a major conspiracy directed against themselves while their enemy controlled an effective source of power which he utilized against the minority group to keep them in a subservient state. Although the paranoid style used distorted language, paranoid speaking began with defensible arguments and was characterized by an all-inclusive theory, consistently organized, that explained reality.[28] Carmichael's speech-making and the ideas he espoused conformed to this format. He believed that throughout history the Negro had been victimized and exploited by the white man. In America, the white man deliberately rewrote the history of his country to exclude the black man. Carmichael reiterated the need for Negroes to re-claim their history and identity from the "cultural terrorism and degradation of self-justifying white guilt." The corruptness of the society led to distortion of news reporting—a media controlled by white power. Individual reporters and commentators, "conditioned by the enveloping racism of the society," were "incapable even of objective observation and reporting of racial incidents, much less the analysis of ideas."[29] The white press not only badly misinter-preted black power, but it distorted the objectives of the entire civil rights movement as well. Carmichael's philosophical concepts appeared infallibly rational. He defined the concepts and included an explanation of man's total existence in one over-reaching, consistent theory. While he began with certain tenable judgments, he used exaggerated language to convey his ideas. This choice of words contributed to white America's image of the black power leader—an outspoken articulator emitting treasonous phrases in the name of civil liberties.

A hero to poor blacks and a controversial celebrity to others, Carmichael's reputation had an unusual effect on his ethical appeal. He excited contrasting opinions in two different audiences. While the name Stokely Carmichael sparked fear and hatred in the white community, it injected courage and pride in op-pressed blacks. His reputation illustrated the polarities of ethos, hindering his persuasibility to whites, but enhancing his effectiveness to Negroes. When he spoke before a white group, he spent the first portion of his address minimizing the unfavorable impressions held by his auditors. At Vanderbilt University, for example, he achieved his goal largely through humor. Carmichael seized upon

[27]"Black Students in Nashville Victims of Police Set-Up," an immediate release of the Student Nonviolent Coordinating Committee, April 10, 1967, author anon.
[28]Hofstadter, *Paranoid Style*, pp. 36–37.
[29]Carmichael, "Impact Speech."

the audience's respect for the concept of free speech and complimented them on their courage to fight for this principle. Then he launched a humorous attack on Nashville's anti-Carmichael newspaper. Announcing that he would read from the "modern day theatre of the absurd—the *Nashville Banner*," he urged the "honkies of the *Banner*" to write "comic strip" on the front cover and suggested they leave the gymnasium, because his lecture was on an "in-tel-lec-tual level."[30] The white audience then rose for the first of three standing ovations. Consequently, before he began reading his prepared manuscript, he succeeded in strengthening his ethos. By the time he completed the speech, his auditors moved from a position of tolerance and curiosity to a favorable inclination toward the man. If his concept of black power did not gain acceptance, Carmichael did. His outstanding personality and personal magnetism contributed greatly to his effectiveness as a speaker. Thus while his prior reputation was an initial disadvantage, he skillfully enhanced his ethos as he spoke—developing it into his greatest single source of persuasion.

Carmichael adapted to audiences by relating his remarks to their set of values.[31] At Nashville, he realized Vanderbilt students supported the right of free speech and made reference to the concept immediately. Before a white audience, however, alignment with their value system for the most part ended with his opening remarks. Carmichael, believing that his role in the white community was to relate the mood of the black,[32] bluntly told his auditors his conception of the Negro's innermost thoughts. Since Carmichael blamed the white man for the Negro's degradation, few whites accepted his black power philosophy *in toto*, because to support it meant finding themselves guilty. Some facets of the program gained at least a sympathetic ear, however. On certain subpoints, Carmichael appealed to the white man's sense of fair play and justice. When he questioned the validity of nonviolent schools in the racist South, for example, he asked, "Can they conduct it [a nonviolent school] among the white people in Granada where six-foot-tall men kick little black children?"[33] Such pathos would naturally evoke a compassionate response from the audience.

When he spoke to an audience of blacks, he appealed to their basic needs. Black power became the answer to better living conditions, economic security, and an improved psychology. Carmichael gave the black man a new sense of dignity. Dispelling the stereotype of the lazy Negro, he repetitively insisted, "We are the hardest working people in this country. . . . It is we who dig the ditches. It is we who are the maids. It is we who pick the cotton. It is we who pick the fruit, and they let the Mexicans come in with us." Interrupted by zealous applause, Carmichael concluded, "That's right. Yes, sir. It is we who are

[30]*Ibid.*

[31]Bernard Weintraub, "The Brilliancy of Black," *Esquire*, January, 1967, p. 132.

[32]Interview with Rap Brown.

[33]Stokely Carmichael, Text of a speech delivered at the University of California at Berkeley and published in *Aframerican Report*, p. 16.

the porters. It is we who are the elevator boys. It is we who are the garbage collectors, and it is we who are the unemployed." He upgraded the status of their menial jobs even further when he maintained that if hard work led to success, as this country promised, the black man would own the United States "lock, stock, and barrel."

Black power was also a call for the Negro intellectual to come home. Carmichael appealed to the intellectual's sense of duty and reminded his auditors that individualism was a luxury they could no longer afford. Group standards had to be raised before equality would be reached. "You have a duty and a responsibility to come back to the black ghettoes and help your people," insisted Carmichael.

He employed the device of common ground when he attempted to minimize the strife in Negro communities. He spoke of gang shootings, killings, and other forms of violence that existed in the black ghettoes and emphasized, "We ought to teach each other to love each other."[34] An intelligent and educated man, Carmichael used the plain clothes device when talking to black audiences. At Tennessee State University in Nashville, for example, he shed his suit coat shortly after he began speaking and remarked, "I try to keep it on but it never works. I guess I'm just a field nigger."[35] Perhaps the most effective emotional device used was a form of exact repetition or slogan. Carmichael told his auditors that the war in Vietnam would end only when young men who were made to fight said, "Hell no. We ain't going."[36] Crowds modified this phrase and often chanted "Hell no. Won't go" in thunderous unison while waiting for him to begin his address. During the speech, cries of "black power" rang through the air. Such uniformity of response created common unity in the audience and thus led to greater uniformity of response concerning the issues Carmichael discussed.

Difficult to assess, the Carmichael image typified the complexity of his character. Finding him irresistible, women viewed him as the Casanova of the civil rights movement and vied for his attentions. The poor black people of Lowndes County worshipped him, and took on a new sense of dignity at the mention of his name. With the aid of the press, he moved rapidly from hero to a controversial celebrity. The white community condemned his licentious vapourings and attacked his concept of black power. Lost in the paranoid style, Carmichael became identified with the rhetoric of lunacy, solidifying his negative image even more. When he ascended a rostrum and stood before an audience, however, the magnetism and charm described by his friends captivated his auditors. So overpowering was his personality that even white audiences, apparently forgetting the newspaper attacks, rose to thunderous ovations. Relatively few Americans, however, heard Carmichael speak in person. Denied the

34Stokely Carmichael, tape recording of a speech delivered at Reverend Clegg's Church, 7621 Linwood, Detroit, Michigan, 1966.

35Doug Looney, "Stokely Pushes Negro Takeover," *Nashville Banner*, April 8, 1967.

36Carmichael, "Berkeley Speech," p. 12.

impact of his charisma that charmed even the most hostile, they formulated their impressions from the mass media, and the Carmichael image reflected the violence of his language. Trapped in the extremism of his own rhetoric, the black power leader adjusted his image to his language causing even greater militancy in SNCC's policies, so that two years after the first press attacks, the organization advocated overt violence for the first time "with GUNS and STRATEGY . . . the word is MAXIMUM RETALIATION TO THEM with MINIMUM LOSSES TO US!"[37]

Questions for Analysis

1. How did Carmichael manage to achieve a reputation which, Jefferson says, "illustrated the polarities of ethos"? How is the consistency of "image" in the man and in his speeches different for Carmichael than for Wilkins? By what overt means did Carmichael attempt to "bridge" his images for white audiences, especially in Nashville? It is proper to say of Carmichael "that rhetoric influences the actions of the speaker. . . ."? How did the mass media share in the influence of rhetoric on Carmichael's actions?

2. How does this study suggest the particular importance of biographical information to full consideration of Carmichael? Why does Jefferson say, "From the 'big man' who 'created himself' and was distinguished by his achievements evolved the 'big name' produced by the 'media' and famous for his image or trademark"? What does this suggest about the difficulties of advocacy in rhetorical movements today? How do you account for these difficulties? Do you agree, as Jefferson suggests, that Carmichael in Lowndes County was a "hero" as Carmichael in the culture at large simply could not be? Explain. Do any contemporary spokesmen approach "heroic" proportions? What seems to make them or break them?

3. Discuss the currency of "the paranoid" style in public speaking. How does the style rely in differing degrees on logos, ethos, and pathos? How does it depend on implicating the audience in responsibility for the paranoia? What peculiar problems does this pose for the speaker? How does Carmichael attempt to implicate his audiences? How well does he succeed? How well do other spokesmen on the campus lecture circuit?

4. Discuss "paranoid" approaches to other social and campus problems. Choose one such problem and write a "paranoid" speech. Keep this statement in mind: "Although the paranoid style used distorted language, paranoid speaking began with defensible arguments and was characterized by an all-inclusive theory, consistently organized, that explained reality." After you understand Carmichael's Vander-

[37]"What You Can Do!" an immediate release of the Student Nonviolent Coordinating Committee, February, 1968.

bilt speech in terms of this statement, develop your speech in a manner parallel to Carmichael's.

5. Review the articles by Simons and Burgess in Part I. How do you think Carmichael conceives of his "role" in the civil rights movement? How does his conception compare with that of Wilkins in ethics and in effectiveness? Can the two concepts "coexist"? How does this study confirm the problem, noted by Burgess, of interpreting the rhetoric of Black Power? Do you think Carmichael's rhetoric and the responses it stimulates can be transcended and constructive institutional responses engendered? Explain. Remembering that Jefferson wrote in 1967, how would you update and modify her conclusions about the role of Carmichael today?

34

Ronald Reagan and "The Speech": The Rhetoric of Public Relations Politics

Kurt W. Ritter

On Tuesday evening, October 27, 1964, less than a week before the presidential election, actor Ronald Reagan, co-chairman of the California Citizens for Goldwater-Miller Committee, delivered a thirty-minute Republican appeal on a nationwide television broadcast.[1] Reagan called for a defense of "the freedoms intended for us by the Founding Fathers," and urged a rejection of government by a "little intellectual elite in a far-distant capital."[2] According to Stephen Shadegg, Senator Barry Goldwater's long-time campaign manager, "thousands of Republicans . . . classified this as the most effective program of the Goldwater campaign." Republican committees in most states rebroadcast the speech under local sponsorship during the next week, and the Republican National Committee quickly published the text in a special pamphlet.[3] Reagan's address brought an estimated $750,000 in campaign contributions, of which $100,000 came in even after Goldwater had lost.[4] William F. Buckley, Jr.'s conservative *National Review* described it as "probably the most successful single political broadcast since Mr. Nixon's Checkers speech" in 1952.[5] With this speech, Reagan rose out of a disastrous Republican defeat to establish him-

Kurt W. Ritter is a National Defense Education Act Fellow, Speech and American Studies, Indiana University.

Reprinted by permission from *Western Speech*, 32(1968) :50–58.

[1]Los Angeles *Times*, October 27, 1964, part IV, p. 11, and November 2, 1964, part I, p. 31; Louisville *Courier-Journal*, January 9, 1966, p. A-3.

[2]Ronald Reagan, "A Time for Choosing," p. 1, mimeographed copies distributed by Friends of Ronald Reagan, Southern California office of Spencer-Roberts and Haffner, 1300 W. Olympic Blvd., Suite 300, Los Angeles, Calif., hereafter cited as Reagan, "A Time."

[3]Stephen Shadegg, *What Happened to Goldwater?* (New York, 1965), p. 252.

[4]*Time*, LXXXVI (July 30, 1965), 14; Walter Pincus, "The Fight Over Money," *Atlantic Monthly*, CCXVII (April 1966), 73.

[5]*National Review*, XVII (December 1, 1964), 1039.

self as a potential candidate for Governor of California, and the "hottest new product on the Republican horizon."[6]

Early in 1965, a group of conservative southern California businessmen,[7] impressed by Reagan's Goldwater address, urged the actor to run for governor and engaged the public relations firm of Spencer-Roberts and Haffner to manage his campaign.[8] On March 27, 1965, Reagan "made it abundantly clear" that he would run for governor if he was convinced that all major factions of California's Republican Party supported him. Under the guidance of his public relations firm, Reagan immediately launched a state-wide "survey," ostensibly to determine whether he commanded public support. He opened his unannounced campaign for governor with an expansion of his Goldwater television address, which Reagan called simply "The Speech," delivered at the annual convention of the conservative California Republican Assembly in San Diego. The convention "went wild" over the movie and television personality, contributing a standing ovation before and after his forty-five-minute speech.[9] During the remaining nine months of 1965 his public relations firm scheduled 150 more speaking engagements. Reagan traveled 10,000 miles to deliver his speech throughout California and across the nation before officially announcing his candidacy for the Republican gubernatorial nomination on January 4, 1966.[10] The thirty-minute announcement address, a retooled version of "The Speech," was carried on fifteen television stations throughout the state.[11]

Through his sudden rise from a recent Republican convert[12] who had never held a public office to an important political figure, Reagan provides a contemporary case study in the rhetoric of public relations politics. Although public relations firms have been active in California politics since 1930, Reagan's lack of reputation as a political leader placed an extra burden of persuasion on Spencer-Roberts and Haffner and increased the significance of his nine-

[6]Stewart Alsop, "The Good Guy," Saturday Evening Post, CCXXXVIII (November 20, 1965), 18.

[7]Henry Salvatori, a Los Angeles banker; Holmes Tuttle, an auto distributor; and A. C. (Cy) Rubel of the Union Oil Company of California headed this group. See Richard Oulahan and William Lambert, "The Real Ronald Reagan Stands Up," Life, LX (January 21, 1966), 82; James Phelan, "Can Reagan Win California?" Saturday Evening Post, CCXXXIX (June 4, 1966), 91; and New York Times, June 6, 1965, p. L-54.

[8]The firm's past political clients include liberal Republican Senator Thomas H. Kuchel of California; the John Birch Society's national public relations director, John Roussellot, in his successful 1960 campaign for Congress; New York Governor Nelson A. Rockefeller in his unsuccessful 1964 California presidential primary election battle against Senator Barry Goldwater of Arizona.

[9]Los Angeles Times, March 28, 1965, sec. A, p. B.

[10]Louisville Courier-Journal, January 9, 1966, p. A-3; Time, LXXXVII (January 14, 1966), 28.

[11]Los Angeles Times, January 5, 1966, part I, p. 3.

[12]Reagan (born February 6, 1911) was a Democrat and avid New Dealer; he organized the Labor League of Hollywood Voters to support President Truman in 1948 and campaigned for the liberal Helen Gahagan Douglas against Richard Nixon in their 1950 senatorial race in California. He did not change his voting registration to Republican until 1962.

month unannounced campaign.[13] This study focuses on Reagan's speaking as an unannounced candidate from March, 1965, to January, 1966, and suggests a rhetorical strategy of "The Speech."

Reagan started to form his speech in 1954, ten years before his Goldwater address. In conjunction with his duties as host of the television program *G. E. Theatre*, he contributed to General Electric's public relations program by speaking to hundreds of "routine weekly luncheon clubs," state Chamber of Commerce banquets, and national business conventions. Reagan became an increasingly popular "nonpartisan" speaker during his eight-year association with General Electric; when *G. E. Theatre* was canceled in 1962, he had speaking tours booked as far ahead as 1966. This speech, entitled "Encroaching Government Controls," warned of Communist subversion in the United States and decried the "swiftly rising tide of collectivism" in America. As Reagan spoke in the Republican campaigns of 1962 and 1964, his speech "underwent a kind of evolution," and the attack on big government became his major theme.[14]

In various versions of "The Speech," Reagan spelled out the dangers of "a Big Brother or paternalistic government."[15] He attacked the "planners" who have uprooted "our limited government" philosophy and the economists "who breathe too deeply of the mists off the Potomac." The actor-politician often asserted a simple, all-or-nothing relationship between freedom and private property: "You can't be a little bit Socialist and you can't be partly free." Freedom, Reagan claimed, comes only under a system of capitalism. He warned that the farm subsidy program, the National Labor Relations Board, and the Area Redevelopment Administration erode our freedoms, while federal aid to education and Medicare present a harmful centralization of America's traditionally local institutions. Reagan condemned rising taxes and the growing federal budget; with a vivid analogy, he dismissed the Democratic administration's tax cuts as "bookkeeping tricks that would jail a private citizen." Appealing to an audience unfamiliar with Keynesian economic theory, Reagan insisted that "to pretend" taxes can be reduced without a cut in government

[13]Robert C. Jeffrey most recently touched upon the influence of public relations firms on political rhetoric in his paper, "The Congressional Primary: An Exercise in Deception," read at the 1966 Convention of the Central States Speech Association, Chicago, April 16, 1966. The most thorough study of public relations firms in California politics is Robert J. Pitchell, "The Influence of Professional Campaign Management Firms in Partisan Elections in California," *Western Political Quarterly*, XI (June 1958), 278–300. Stanley Kelley, Jr., *Professional Public Relations and Political Power* (Baltimore, 1956), provides the best treatment of public relations in our national politics and its implications to American government.

[14]Ronald Reagan with Richard G. Hubler, *Where's the Rest of Me?* (New York, 1965), pp. 266–267, 297, 273; hereafter cited as Reagan, *Where*. For a text of the General Electric speech see Ronald Reagan, "Encroaching Control: Keep Government Poor and Remain Free," *Vital Speeches of the Day*, XXVII (September 1, 1961), 677–681.

[15]Ronald Reagan, *A Plan for Action: An Address by Ronald Reagan, January 4, 1966*, p. 10, distributed by Friends of Ronald Reagan, Northern California office of Spencer-Roberts and Haffner, 47 Kearny St., Suite 800, San Francisco, Calif., hereafter cited as Reagan, *A Plan*. A comparison of this pamphlet with a tape recording of Reagan's announcement address verified it as an accurate transcript.

spending "is to perpetrate a fraud upon the people." He admonished economists for paying only "lip service" to the "ancient truths" while they advocated "managed money" and "planning in the market place." Throughout his attack on big government, Reagan did not categorically oppose aid to education and adequate medical care for all citizens. Instead, he asserted that these "problems would all be solved if the Federal Government would return to the states and communities some of the sources of taxation the Federal Government has usurped for itself." Reagan concluded with a sober warning that freedom might be lost "in our lifetime," with its failure being recorded in "a book not yet written: *The Rise and Fall of the United States of America*." Amid an appeal for Republican unity and Democratic converts, he proclaimed: "You and I have reached our moment of truth, our rendezvous with destiny. You and you alone must make the decision as to whether freedom will perish from the earth."[16]

From March through December, 1965, the various versions of Reagan's speech followed the same general theme. Specific examples often changed from speech to speech, but Reagan did not find such rewriting difficult, since he could "reach out blindfolded and grab a hundred examples of overgrown government."[17] The actor-politician admitted that while his lyrics changed, the tune remained the same. When accused of having only one speech, however, Reagan replied, a little angrily, that he varied his speeches from day to day, "taking an introduction from one, the middle from another and the conclusion from a third."[18] Running through all the speeches was a series of commonplace jokes and "big government" jabs that balanced Reagan's grim economic warnings and unfailingly drew laughter and newspaper attention. "Government," he explained, "is like a baby. It's an alimentary canal with an appetite at one end and no sense of responsibility at the other." "The *status quo*" he defined as "Latin for the mess we're in."[19]

In Reagan's unannounced campaign, "The Speech" served a two-fold rhetorical strategy: the identification of the actor with diverse political factions, and the manipulation of his reputation to present the "reasonable picture of a candidate" that his public relations firm desired.[20] By adapting "The Speech" to his different audiences, Reagan attempted to retain the confidence

[16]Ronald Reagan, "California Republican Assembly Address," San Diego, Calif., March 27, 1965, hereafter cited as Reagan, "C.R.A. Address"; all quotations from this address are from a tape recording in the possession of the author. Ronald Reagan, "A Moment of Truth: Our Rendezvous with Destiny," *Vital Speeches of the Day*, XXXI (September 1, 1965), 681–686, hereafter cited as Reagan, "Moment." This speech was delivered at a testimonial dinner for U.S. Rep. John M. Ashbrook in Granville, Ohio, June 8, 1965, and was published in pamphlet form under the title *The Granville Rally*, distributed by Friends of Ronald Reagan, Southern California office.

[17]Reagan, *Where*, p. 270.

[18]San Francisco *Chronicle*, September 25, 1965, p. 6; San Jose (Calif.) *News*, December 21, 1965, p. 3.

[19]Reagan, "Moment," pp. 685, 682; Reagan, "C.R.A. Address."

[20]William E. Roberts of Spencer-Roberts and Haffner quoted in *Newsweek*, LXV (June 7, 1965), 19.

of the Republican right wing, while publicly modifying his recent position as a political conservative. The televised and published speeches addressed to the general public did not dwell on the Communist menace to America, but rather on Reagan's eagerness to solve the problems of age, health, poverty, and housing "without compulsion and without fiscal irresponsibility."[21] By emphasizing a positive program in his announcement address, Reagan appeared "no more far-out than a Rotarian," and moved closer to what his public relations firm called "Nixon types" and Rockefeller supporters.[22]

In contrast to his publicized speeches, Reagan's unpublished talks to conservative groups stressed the dangers of Communistic collectivism and the "yeast-like growth" of government.[23] The California Republican Assembly, which favors repeal of the income tax and wants a "complete investigation" of the United Nations,[24] heard Reagan warn that our nation is engaged in a contest, "a war between philosophies: Communism versus Capitalism," which will determine whether the "nation and way of life" our forefathers created can endure. In the face of the "all embraced, all blood-soaked reality of the Communist program," he argued, "we must do everything we can to strengthen capitalism" and "repudiate everything that weakens it." The right-wing version of "The Speech" differed from the moderate version by explicitly citing Communism as an exterior enemy to whose philosophy our nation might unwittingly succumb through "voluntary slavery" to a "controlled economy" and a "proliferation of bureaucratic agencies."[25] By carrying on Barry Goldwater's rhetoric of limited government, [26] Reagan inherited the Goldwater supporters and financial contributors. The right-wing version reflected the political reality expressed by one John Birch Society section leader, that "a lot of conservatives aren't going to contribute if they don't have someone of Barry Goldwater's philosophy."[27] Whenever newspaper reporters asked Reagan about the Birch Society, he read his "500-word statement" denouncing the Society's president, Robert Welch, but "The Speech" did not mention extremism or the Birch Society.[28]

In appealing to Democrats, Reagan often referred to his own switch to the Republican Party in a search for the old Democratic "principles of Jef-

[21]Reagan, "Moment," p. 685.
[22]*Newsweek*, LXVII (January 17, 1966), 32; Fred J. Haffner of Spencer-Roberts and Haffner quoted in the New York *Times*, June 6, 1965, p. L–54.
[23]Reagan, "C.R.A. Address."
[24]Los Angeles *Times*, March 29, 1965, part I, pp. 3, 24.
[25]Reagan, "C.R.A. Address."
[26]John Hammerback, "The Rhetorical Effectiveness of Barry Goldwater From 1960–1963," unpublished M.A. Thesis, University of Oklahoma, 1965, pp. 45, 48–52. The right-wing version of Reagan's speech reflects a point of view strikingly similar to "The Little World of Barry Goldwater," described by Ernest J. Wrage in *Western Speech*, XXVII (Fall 1963), 207–215.
[27]San Jose *News*, December 21, 1965, p. 44Z.
[28]San Francisco *Examiner*, October 2, 1965, p. 5; *Christian Science Monitor*, Western Edition, January 6, 1966, p. 3.

ferson, Jackson and Cleveland."[29] He attempted to win a hearing from liberals by stressing that he attacked neither their sincerity nor their humanitarian motives, but only their measures. He shrewdly called out to the voter bloc "that crosses party lines" and to the "unsung heroes" who "pay their bills, contribute to their church and their charity and their community." Reagan's rhetoric was geared to picture him as the leader of these "forgotten Americans" who "believe in God as the Creator of all our rights and freedoms" and are "disturbed because their children can't ask His blessing on a lunch in the school cafeteria."[30]

The second objective of Spencer-Roberts and Haffner's rhetorical strategy was to make Reagan appear as "a sensible, reasonable guy" who "had the intellectual capacity" to be a state governor. This public relations firm hoped to "prove, symbolically" that Reagan was "a good administrator."[31] By speaking from three-by-five cards, rather than from a manuscript or a memorized text, Reagan gave the impression of a well-informed "citizen politician," not of an actor reading his lines.[32] Reagan's well-publicized claim that he "has always written his own speeches and done his own research work" helped counteract the charge that he knew only what his public relations firm told him.[33] The actor-politician gained academic respectability from frequent references to Professor Alexander Frazer Tyler, Lord Atkin, Alexis de Tocqueville, Thomas Wolfe, and of course, Abraham Lincoln.[34] More important to Reagan's speaker credibility were "the facts." He lamented that it required 520 pages to list all the executive agencies of the federal government. A federal ruling on cabbage, Reagan pointed out, took 29,911 words, while the Declaration of Independence used only 300. One federal questionnaire, he testified, "was 428 pages long, weighed ten pounds, and each page was twenty-four inches long." Interspersed with such statistics, Reagan offered unrelated and unsupported generalizations: Federal loans to college students have "an extremely high rate of default"; and the United States is taxing a "higher percentage from the free, productive economy than any society has ever taken without ruin."[35]

Reagan carefully denied ever attending "dramatic school," but often mentioned his college degree in economics.[36] Such appeals to personal authority

[29]Reagan, "Moment," p. 685; Reagan, "A Time," p. 1; Reagan, *A Plan*, p. 18.

[30]Reagan, "Moment," pp. 683, 685; Reagan, "C.R.A. Address"; Ronald Reagan, "The Republican Party and the Conservative Movement," *National Review*, XVII (December 1, 1964), 1055.

[31]William E. Roberts quoted in *Newsweek*, LXV (June 7, 1965), 19.

[32]A teleprompter was used in the announcement speech. San Francisco *Examiner*, January 9, 1966, sec. II, p. 2; Louisville *Courier-Journal*, January 9, 1966, p. A–3; Reagan, *A Plan*, p. 20.

[33]Correspondence from William E. Roberts, January 12, 1966; Los Angeles *Times*, October 26, 1965, part II, p. 4.

[34]Reagan, "C.R.A. Address"; Reagan, "Moment," pp. 682, 685-686.

[35]Reagan, "Moment," pp. 682–683; Reagan, "C.R.A. Address"; Reagan, "A Time," p. 1.

[36]Reagan, *A Plan*, p. 21; Reagan, "C.R.A. Address"; San Francisco *Examiner*, October 21, 1965, p. 6.

presumably lent weight to his economic analysis. Reagan has stated, however, that he chose economics and sociology as his major subjects "because they afforded him more free time for the things he liked better—dramatics, football and student politics."[37]

In addition to presenting Reagan as a plausible gubernatorial candidate, "The Speech" provided his campaign with a fighting spirit. California political management firms consider this spirit vital in appealing to an American audience that enjoys a contest.[38] Here Reagan's acting career, which he minimized in his addresses, played a significant but silent role. The dark-haired, six-foot one-inch smiling politician projected a crusading image by attacking "encroaching government" and defending individual rights against "federal control." Reagan's audiences knew him as the handsome host and actor in the television series, *Death Valley Days;* when he spoke, he carried this rugged western image with him. Before Reagan arrived at a rally, the public address system would blare out the Notre Dame fight song, subtly reminding the waiting crowd of Reagan's aggressive acting roles, including his movie portrayal of the Notre Dame football hero, George Gipp.[39]

Spencer-Roberts and Haffner manipulated Reagan's personal appeal by using "The Speech" to create the impression of Ronald Reagan as a national Republican spokesman. Although Reagan was preparing for a California state office, he spoke on national issues. The actor-politician admitted that "by deliberate intent" California was only mentioned incidentally during his unannounced campaign. Less than a tenth of Reagan's opening speech to the California Republican Assembly dealt with state issues. Reagan indicated he would discuss California "if and when" he became a candidate;[40] yet, much of his announcement address was devoted to topics "beyond the scope of purely state issues." By transferring his attack from federal bureaucracy to the "dangerously top-heavy" executive branch of California's state government, Reagan placed California issues within the ideological framework of "The Speech."[41] California Democratic leaders, who had ignored Reagan's earlier speaking on national issues, promptly charged that he was "simply wrong" on state issues.[42]

Since "The Speech" did not center on California topics, Reagan could deliver it across the nation. In June, 1965, he spoke at a series of Ohio Republican rallies, which concluded with a Cincinnati banquet that placed him on a

[37]"Ronald Reagan," *Current Biography: Who's News and Why, 1949*, ed. Anna Rothe (New York, 1950), p. 503.

[38]Pitchell, "Campaign Management Firms in California," p. 288.

[39]"GOP 'Fight Song' Cheers Ex-Film Gridder Reagan," San Jose *News*, December 21, 1965, p. 3; Reagan, *Where*, pp. 90–95.

[40]San Jose *News*, December 21, 1965, p. 3.

[41]Reagan, *A Plan*, pp. 13, 10–12, 18–20.

[42]Rebuttals to Reagan's comments on national issues were published only after he announced his candidacy; see Oulahan, "The Real Ronald Reagan Stands Up," pp. 72, 74. Los Angeles *Times*, January 5, 1966, part I, p. 3; San Francisco *Examiner*, January 4, 1966, p. 8.

state-wide program with nine major Republican leaders, including former President Eisenhower, former Vice President Nixon, and California's Senator Murphy. Reagan and Murphy "drew the lion's share of the applause."[43] In October, 1965, Reagan attracted the attention of the national news media by taking up a year-old invitation to speak in New England, where he addressed the National Federation of Republican Women in Boston and the "right-wing" Connecticut Republican Citizens Committee in New Haven.[44] The strategy of "The Speech" was so effective that before Reagan declared himself a candidate, he was ahead of California's Democratic Governor Edmund G. (Pat) Brown in public opinion polls and had received nearly $140,000 in campaign contributions.[45] Ironically, Reagan managed to condemn such "false-image making" while announcing his candidacy from "a homey setting" in a Hollywood movie studio.[46]

Ronald Reagan's all-purpose speech and unannounced campaign suggest that in today's public relations politics a state candidate's pre-campaign oratory can effectively promote a planned rhetorical strategy of identifying the candidate with diverse political factions and manipulating his image. With this strategy, the state candidate can create a national reputation as a political spokesman, take advantage of national news media, and later discuss the specific state campaign issues in terms of his national posture.

Questions for Analysis

1. Describe the key rhetorical precepts of "public relations politics." How did Stevenson and Carmichael in various ways violate them? What made Reagan such an appropriate vehicle for "public relations politics"? How has the public been rendered susceptible to that approach? Why is biographical information not of particular importance to full consideration of Reagan?

2. How is Reagan's appeal also "paranoid"? How does he soften the impact of "paranoia" on his audiences? Why would audiences be more receptive to Reagan's appeal than to Carmichael's? How does Reagan as a "celebrity" differ from Carmichael as a "celebrity"? Describe the attitude of the mass media toward each. What does this suggest to you of the relative rhetorical risks the two could take?

[43]Cincinnati *Enquirer*, June 10, 1965, p. 1; New York *Times*, June 10, 1965, p. L–21.

[44]San Francisco *Examiner*, October 6, 1965, p. 38; *Newsweek*, LXVI (October 11, 1965), 42.

[45]These polls, of course, were taken too far in advance of the November 1966 election to be a necessarily valid prediction of the final result. *Time*, LXXXVI (November 5, 1965), 38; Louisville *Courier-Journal*, January 9, 1966, p. A–3.

[46]Reagan, *A Plan*, p. 21; Los Angeles *Times*, January 6, 1966, part I, p. 3; San Francisco *Examiner*, January 9, sec. II, p. 2.

3. How did Reagan adjust "The Speech" to identify with "diverse political factions"? Summarize, for example, the adjustments he might make in discussing taxes or foreign policy with the general public, with conservatives, and with Democrats. What does this practice of adjustment suggest to you of the "public relations" politician's concept of persuasion? What must be his assumptions about his audience? How do his assumptions compare with Stevenson's? Refer to Braden's article in Part II to discuss the ethics of speaker assumptions.

4. How did Reagan's use of each of the following contribute to his "credibility": delivery? testimonial? personal authority? subliminal effects? How did his use of these rhetorical devices add up to the impression that "any good man can play the political game"? Why is this impression especially appealing to audiences today? How do other public speakers promote the same impression? Does Ritter's study suggest that the impression is false? Explain.

5. How do both the message and the delivery of "public relations" rhetoric "prove, symbolically" the speaker's capacity to do the job for which he is being "sold"? Refer to Nichols' article in Part III. To which of the ten listener weaknesses does this "symbolic" approach cater? Review the dominant tenets for speech preparation of Norman Thomas, Gerald Kennedy, and Alben Barkley. How does the "public relations" approach violate them? Formulate an exchange between Thomas and a public relations representative attempting to "sell" Thomas on the "public relations" style.

35

Dick Gregory Is Not So Funny Now

Eliot Asinof

The scene is the Massachusetts Institute of Technology—the spacious Kresge Auditorium packed with students waiting for the guest lecturer. He is not a leading world scientist or engineer, nor is his subject matter of any technological concern. He is Dick Gregory, the ubiquitous Negro comedian, author, actor, Presidential candidate (without a party) and crusader for human rights who—to emphasize his commitment—has virtually given up profitable night-club engagements to tour college campuses.

Since Gregory has been tied up in traffic driving down from Portsmouth, N.H., where he lectured earlier in the day, the audience grows good-humoredly restless, tossing paper airplanes with a technical artistry befitting M.I.T. In time, there is a rhythmic clapping and foot stamping in the classic undergraduate appeal for action.

"What brings you here?" I ask a few students seated around me.

"Well, I hear he's very funny," replies a very serious-looking boy with horn-rimmed glasses. There are more young men wearing glasses than not. A small percentage are long-haired, and it is difficult to find one with a necktie and a jacket. It is almost impossible to find a Negro.

"I got interested in Gregory because of his fast. That's what impressed me," says another.

"I'm just curious to see what he's like, and what he has to say. I mean, you just *know* he's going to be different."

Finally, an hour late, Gregory strides on stage to an extremely warm greeting. He is wearing blue coveralls—with uncut hair and a six-week-old beard—and he is far leaner than I remember him, especially around the face, after his recent 40-day fast.[1] He stands there for a long moment in the anticipa-

Eliot Asinof is the author of five books—fiction and non-fiction—short stories and magazine articles, and a screenwriter.

Excerpted from *The New York Times Magazine* (March 17, 1968) : 37–45. © Copyright by the New York Times Company. Reprinted by permission.

[1]Since his M.I.T. appearance, Gregory has begun a new 40-day fast, to coincide with Lent, as a protest against the war in Vietnam.

tory silence, looking them over. Finally, he walks to the front of the huge stage and takes an even closer look. "Why, you're *normal*. You're just a bunch of cats like anywhere else. . . . Man, it's M.I.T. and I expected *robots!*"

They roar with laughter and he is off and running. Like Bob Hope at a Vietnam airbase, he unravels a string of local jokes, taking off on the formidable-looking pipe organ that lines the wall. "Ain't that a computer? One of them mad machines you put the questions in, like: 'Is there a God?' and it goes *whirr* and *whickitcha-whickitcha* [his whole body shakes and he rolls his eyes, miming a computer in action], and finally comes out with a slip of paper with the answer: 'There is *now!*'?"

An old joke, but there is more big laughter.

He barrels into the political world now, a string of *ad hominem* gags aimed at L.B.J. "You know, right this minute, the Prez is telling the nation what the scene is all about. Can't you just see him? I mean, that beautiful face of his, all dripping with barbecue sauce. You look at that man with your Bible turned to the Ten Commandments and you just *know* he's violated every damn one of them!"

And just to be fair, he takes a few shots at Ronald Reagan. He says, "Reagan is 'nigger' spelled backwards. Imagine, we got a backwards nigger running California."

He jokes about his fast, describing how he weighed 158 at Thanksgiving when he began and dropped to 103 at New Year's. "You should see the mail I got: 'Dear Mr. Gregory. This is to inform you that yesterday I had the following for dinner: [pause for laughter] fried chicken with gravy, mashed potatoes, black-eyed peas. . . .' How do you like that? Nigger hate mail!" See? He is fair. He even jokes about his own people.

Then, suddenly, after 45 minutes of this, he stops—to begin his lecture, he tells his listeners. He regards them all again, his entire style changing like an actor playing a whole new role. Even before he says a word, the audience senses the difference. He stands a little taller; frown lines crease his forehead; hands clench the sides of the podium. He leans closer to the mike and he spits out his opener like venom: "In case you don't know it, America is the No. 1 racist country in the world!"

They take this mouthful and audibly gulp it down, for now he is going to rub their white faces in the muck of American hypocrisy. They visibly brace themselves. This is what many of them have come to hear.

"Brother, I'm gonna tell you straight and true, this nation is insane!" He begins to blast away at them in a totally new tone of voice, generating an emotion light-years away from comedy. "This nation is insane because it has been swallowed up by lies. We have been lied to so often, there are no more lies left. It's not just the white man, it's the black man who is racist too. Hell, he's got to be racist!

"I don't believe in racism, but I sure do understand it. I'm here to tell you, we're not in a battle between black and white; the real battle is between right and wrong. I want to be your friend, brothers, not your *black* friend. You dig? But there ain't gonna be *any* friendships until we clear away the mess.

"Now dig, brothers: White man holds a nice cool glass of water. Black man is dying of thirst, wants to share it. White man says, 'Get your own water.' Black man says, 'How can I? You got the glass.' White man rattles the ice cubes in the black man's face and says, 'Nigger, that's the trouble with you; you ain't got the education to make your own glass.' For hundreds of years, the white man has been doling out water in eyedroppers, but now the black man is fighting for his share of the drink, and he's gonna get it or break the damn glass trying!"

The audience applauds for 10 solid seconds. Gregory extends his arm and points his finger at the center of them all. "Now, dig: Negro soldier is ordered to Vietnam to chase the V.C. through the jungle to kill him. Yet it's a damn crime in the U.S.A. for that same Negro to chase a K.K.K. through the swamp when the K.K.K. bombs his home or his church! I say that's insane!"

For the next five minutes, he punches away at the structure of race relations, his voice slowly escalating in power as he challenges them. "The white man says the nigger smells. That's like Hitler visiting the concentration camps saying how the Jews smelled. I say, it wasn't the Jews he was smelling; it was Nazism. I say, it's not the greasy, dirty, filthy niggers that's smelling; it's democracy! In Los Angeles, they've got 34 garbage trucks hauling off the garbage, 27 of them in that sweet-smelling Beverly Hills and only seven in all of Watts. No wonder the niggers stink. I say, if you don't share your garbage trucks with us, one day we're gonna share our garbage with you!"

The audience cracks up with laughter. A joke in the midst of his fury! Then, just as suddenly, he blasts them again. "It's not just poverty, brothers, it's insult. If some Nazi killed my daddy in 1943, that same Nazi can come here and live where my daddy never could and I can't now. Insult! You dig? Charles Drew was a Negro you never heard of, but he helped invent blood plasma. Yet Charles Drew died in the waiting room of an Atlanta hospital from lack of blood, just sitting there waiting to be treated. Insult!

"The system has herded the black man into the ghettoes but refuses to take the consequences. It's like a man lying wounded in the street and you tell him to stop bleeding! That man is bleeding for a reason. You can't *order* a baby to stop crying; you got to change the diaper. That is nature. The ghetto is crying, brother, and that, too, is nature. That was nature working in Watts and Detroit and Newark. And don't tell me those riots didn't accomplish anything. They blew up Chicago a while back because the kids couldn't play with water in the streets. Since that riot, you can't walk in that section without stepping into a swimming pool!"

They laugh, acknowledging the sarcasm while braving themselves for the next sortie. There is something marvelously subtle about the way he builds up to these little climaxes, altering the very style of his speech and the tone of his voice to suggest the coming of a joke. If he is raging—which he definitely is—it is not without a well-formed plan, enhancing his appeal with these nuances so that he never gets too far away from his comedic image. He is delivering the message, yes, but in a way that makes it memorable.

"I tell you again, this country is insane. If you dump a pile of greasy, oily rags into a hot closet and let them set, you're gonna get spontaneous combustion and the house will burst into flames. That's nature again. I'll tell you something else: That's Black Power.

"When we were trying to integrate the schools of Mississippi, we took those cute little 5-year-old kids by the hand and walked them to the clean white schoolhouse, just like the U.S. Supreme Court said we could. And there they were, waiting for us, the sheriff and all them cracker K.K.K.'s and they cut us down with bats and bricks and stomped on us. I looked up into the barrel of that sheriff's shotgun, and not 10 feet from me I saw the little 5-year-old girl with her head busted open by a brick. Brothers, you ain't never seen nothing in your life until you see a 5-year-old kid get hit by a brick. You think a black man who lives through that is going to stay nonviolent?"

He stops, choked by his own emotion. The audience is silent, waiting for the extension of his rage, even hungering for it. Caught up by his delivery, they will willingly share his torment.

"Nonviolence is not an obligation, brothers. It's a *favor*. The Negro has been getting lynched and beaten and ghettoed and cheated and lied to, and still this country says he should be nonviolent. I'm nonviolent, but I'll be damned if I'll preach it to a man whose 5-year-old kid got her head busted open by a brick! I'd take back that favor. The white man has got to learn that. He'd damn well better learn it, because unless he does, the black man is going to burn him down, house by house, city by city!"

He stands there with his bearded face thrust forward, his large eyes bulging out of their sockets and his fists clenched tightly by his sides. Beside me, a girl is containing her need to sob, but tears are racing down her face. The boy with her is literally shaking in his seat. I close my eyes to judge the full extent of the silence, wondering if I can pick up a single sound. There is not a one. A thousand kids in one room and not a murmur, not even a rustle of clothes. Gregory stops to take a drink of water, knowing he has grabbed them all.

He smiles, just enough to tip them off. "You kids . . . you're groovy. You're the new niggers. I was in Colorado, and this cop is pushing around a bunch of demonstrators for peace, and you know what he said? 'They're acting like niggers so we treat 'em like niggers!' "

They laugh, loving this new identity, enjoying his enjoyment of them. His eyes have lost their anger. He rests his hands on the podium, fingering the note cards he has brought with him, and his voice becomes soft and pleasant, like a friendly professor winding up a lecture. "I don't have any answers. This is an insane country and you kids are going to have a rough time handling it.

We're told this is a great democracy, but nobody believes that any more, so America goes around the world trying to ram it down everybody's throat. Well, that's why I fast. That's why I wear these work clothes and don't shave no more. And I'm not going to, either, not until L.B.J. makes peace."

He says this in very low key, but the message is so clear it rips right through the room. A swelling sound of applause rises from them all, no shouting, just hand-clapping, as though this were a statement of tremendous importance to be treated with maximum dignity.

He smiles, almost paternally now. He lets them know this is to be his conclusion, merely by bringing those note cards together and nodding his head at them. "You kids are the hope of this country. It's all yours. My mammy used to say, 'Learn to live, not just make a living. Otherwise, you might die rich without ever having really lived.' You dig? . . . Well, God bless you all."

He bows humbly and they rise to their feet in a standing ovation, all of them, applauding and cheering, and many of them crying. It's late, closing in on 11 P.M. They have been in this hall for more than three hours, but only a few of them leave. They want to ask questions, to hear more, to laugh and cry with him.

One girl stands up and boldly challenges him: "You say you're nonviolent, Mr. Gregory, but you keep threatening to burn my house down."

"Sure, I'm nonviolent," he replies. "I'd just make sure you weren't home."

Another contentious student tries a different tack: "Mr. Gregory, do you really expect us white people to appreciate your problems when you threaten us this way?"

He shrugs. "I don't give the least damn *what* you appreciate. Do *you* really believe us black people ought to wait for your appreciation? Brother, I'm *telling* you what's happening."

"No wonder there's violence against you," the youth adds.

"I know," Gregory smiles. "We niggers are always moaning about that. We say, 'If only Whitey was nonviolent. . . .' "

And so it goes, for another hour, and the last thing he tells them is that they alone have the power to change it all if they want to badly enough. "You kids could work wonders. Ten thousand of you marching together could take over any town in America!"

The audience breaks up finally, and I turn to the group around me for their reactions.

"Oh, he's funny, all right . . . but crazy, too."

"Crazy? How so?" I ask.

"Well, that romantic nonsense about 10,000 of us marching to victory. I think he really means it!"

It was, in effect, the essence of the man, this call to the streets, a people's army against oppression with Gregory himself at the head of it, storming the bastions of privilege with a list of grievances written on the back of an old envelope.

Questions for Analysis

1. Review Gittelson's comments on Gregory among campus lecturers. Why in contrast to others is he apparently "the darling of the college lecture circuit"? How is his ethos particularly favorable in light of the variety of student motivations? Why is it significant to the campus lecturer when he causes a comment such as: "I'm just curious to see what he's like, and what he has to say. I mean, you just *know* he's going to be different"? Estimate the risk of "novelty" run by campus lecturers of serious intent.

2. How does Gregory's introductory use of humor compare with that of Carmichael in his Vanderbilt speech? What purpose for Gregory does nearly an hour of topical humor serve? Explain the implication that Gregory is *using* his image, not *transcending* it. How is Reagan different in this respect? Do the approaches of both men appear to temper an otherwise "paranoid" style? Explain. Describe Gregory's transition from humor to seriousness in terms of devices for effective delivery.

3. Refer to Auer's article on persuasive speaking for description of these "unlearned attention values: change, intensity, striking quality, repetition, and definiteness of form." Cite examples of each in Gregory's speech. How does Asinof's depiction of sequential listener reactions suggest their effectiveness? What may the persuasive speaker learn from this observation: "If he is raging—which he definitely is—it is not without a well-formed plan, enhancing his appeal with these nuances so that he never gets too far away from his comedic image"?

4. Refer to Auer's article again for description of these "natural factors of interest": animation, vitalness, familiarity, novelty, conflict, suspense, concreteness, and humor. What use does Gregory make of each one? How do you consider this commentary on his audience's interest: "The audience is silent, waiting for the extension of his rage, even hungering for it. Caught up by his delivery, they will willingly share his torment"? What distinguishes this behavior from responses to Stevenson? to Wilkins? to Carmichael? Describe the means by which some speaker elicited a response from you similar to that of Gregory's audience. Why is Asinof's "depth" study of a single appearance more appropriate to Gregory than a "survey" study, such as Ferris did on Wilkins?

5. Describe in rhetorical terms the apparent effectiveness of Gregory's conclusion. How does he induce his listeners to enjoy "his enjoyment of them," and yet to respond with "just handclapping, as though this were a statement of tremendous importance to be treated with maximum dignity"? Does the conclusion give the speech a cumulative effect? Explain. What is the nature of Gregory's final "appeal"? How does it suggest the contribution Gregory intends to make to the rhetoric of our times?

36

Protest Under the Cross: The Ku Klux Klan Presents Its Case to the Public, 1960

Donald E. Williams

Bleak Stone Mountain near Atlanta, Georgia, is a mecca for loyal members of the Ku Klux Klan; it was here that the old Klan of Reconstruction days was revived in 1915 and started on the road to its ignominious downfall of the late 1920's. A new spurt of life for the Klan was proclaimed at Stone Mountain in the fall of 1956, after the implications of the 1954 Supreme Court decision against enforced segregation of races in public schools had become apparent. At the biggest Klan rally since World War I, a Klan leader, in denying that the "new Klan" had any connection with the original one, promised that it would stay within the laws—"laws that are just," he added.[1]

The year 1960 was a particularly opportune time for the Klan to present its best case to the public because this was the year of the first presidential contest since the practical meaning of the momentous 1954 decision of the Supreme Court had been fully comprehended; social and political developments had made supremacy of the white race, an idea always central to Klan philosophy, assume even more importance. Initiating a great program of persuasion, the Klan, on March 1, announced plans for a recruiting drive for 10,000,000 members in 30 states.[2] Its determination in purpose was evident when burning crosses, the eerie, unmistakable Klan trademark, appeared around 10 o'clock, Saturday evening, March 26, in far-flung places across the South.[3]

This impressive, co-ordinated effort, however, belied the extensive splintering within the Klan movement. The Klan concept of 1960 was plural in nature;

Donald E. Williams is Associate Professor of Speech and Coordinator of the Rhetoric and Public Address Program at the University of Florida.
Reprinted by permission from *Southern Speech Journal*, 27 (1961) : 43–55.
[1]New York *Times*, October 1, 1956.
[2]*Ibid.*, March 1, 1960.
[3]*Ibid.*, March 27, 1960.

rivalry among some of the groups was often bitter as Klankraft was perpetuated through such groups as the Gulf Ku Klux Klan, the Dixie Klan, the 1866 Klan, the Southern Knights of the Klan, the Christian Knights, the United States Knights, and the Federated Knights. At a Stone Mountain rally, a Klan official reported that twenty-seven different Klan groups were represented.[4]

But the general public was not cognizant of all these different organizational titles. For all intent and purpose, "the Klan" was *the Klan;* in the South, the Klanland of today, a Kluxer was a Kluxer, regardless of whether there was any centralized authority in the Klan realm.[5] Unity in concept and in function, in effect, was provided by similar symbols, practices, and purposes. One Klan speaker, in calling for greater cohesiveness among Klan groups, explained: "Every Klan group has practically the same obligation."[6] Any study of the Klan, therefore, must deal with the consolidated image of the Klan held by the public, not with the image of any one or any group of the Klan factions.

This image was not a favorable one. Throughout the South, the Klan was suspect. The Augusta, Georgia, *Herald* put it bluntly:

> Georgia has been disgraced too often in the past by night-riding cowards who viciously take the law into their own hands. Thus any revival of such activities by the Klan, or any facsimile thereof, should be promptly and positively suppressed.[7]

Claiming that the Klan's plan was to resort to mob rule, the Texarkana, Arkansas, *Gazette* charged: "The Ku Klux Klan should never be recognized as anything else but a mob."[8] The Palatka, Florida, *News* found the principal Klan symbol especially repugnant: "Every time human beings make a public spectacle of burning a cross we can't help but wonder if Christ remains nailed upon it."[9] In reply to the question, "How do you think your community, in general, looked upon the Klan in 1960," 90 per cent of the newspaper editors in southern states who participated in a public opinion survey indicated, "Negatively."[10]

Communities flatly indicated that the Klan was not welcome in their midst. "There is no excuse for the existence of the Klan today," contended the Plant City, Florida, *Courier*.[11] The Hampton, South Carolina, *Hampton County Guardian* clearly agreed with this:

[4]*Decatur-DeKalb News*, September 8, 1960.
[5]"What the 'Sit-Ins' Are Stirring Up," *United States News and World Report*, XLVIII (April 18, 1960), 54.
[6]Unless otherwise indicated, all quotations of Klan speakers presented herein were taken from the author's transcriptions and notes of speeches given at the public Klan meetings which he attended.
[7]Augusta *Herald*, October 19, 1960.
[8]Texarkana *Gazette*, November 7, 1960.
[9]Palatka *News*, October 28, 1960.
[10]Fifty-two representative editors from the states of Texas, Louisiana, Arkansas, Mississippi, Alabama, Georgia, Tennessee, Florida, South Carolina, and North Carolina participated in this poll, which was conducted by the author.
[11]Plant City *Courier*, June 2, 1960.

> Activity of the Ku Klux Klan in the Low Country is about as needed as coals in Newcastle. . . . It is to be hoped that Klan rallies receive no local sanction or that no man is so greedy as to seek to profit by renting meeting places to a faceless, nameless mob.[12]

In registering its disdain for the Klan, the Texarkana *Gazette* made economic considerations paramount:

> Why won't the Klan get off Texarkana's back? Here we are, trying our best to become a decent city, the kind of city that will attract new citizens, new business enterprises, new heavy industry—and just when we think that perhaps we are making a little progress, along comes the Ku Klux Klan and gets us branded anew all over the nation as a city afflicted by bigots inflamed with intolerance and ignorance.[13]

Even though the *Rebel*, an important Klan paper, announced that the Klan would "welcome all organizations which are helping to keep the beloved South white,"[14] many people in sympathy with the program of the White Citizens' Councils requested them to inform the country at large that the South was not a "segment of the United States filled with blind racial prejudice, teeming with . . . Ku Klux Klanners."[15] The Tampa, Florida, *Tribune* wanted it understood by all that "the Klansman's hood-muffled voice is not that of Tampa or Florida."[16] When the Jacksonville, Florida, *Chronicle* thought that some people might believe that it had "some affiliation with the Klan" because it covered some of its activities, it declared, "Nothing could be further from the truth."[17] As a matter of fact, not one of the southern editors responding to the questionnaire previously referred to indicated that he thought the Klan served a "worthwhile purpose" in 1960.[18]

Proffered Klan political support was also rebuffed. After a Florida Klan official had endorsed Governor Orval E. Faubus of Arkansas for President, the State Chairman of the States Rights Party, which was backing Faubus, said that the Klan endorsement came "as an unwelcome surprise" since this support "was neither solicited nor wanted."[19] The most stinging slap given to the Klan

---

[12]*Hampton County Guardian*, June 22, 1960.

[13]Texarkana *Gazette*, November 2, 1960.

[14]College Park, Georgia, *Rebel*, September 30, 1960.

[15]Sumter, South Carolina, *Item*, July 26, 1960. Also see Florence, South Carolina, *News*, October 19, 1960, and Blountstown, Florida, *Record*, September 15, 1960.

[16]Tampa *Tribune*, October 18, 1960.

[17]Jacksonville *Chronicle*, August 12, 1960.

[18]It should by no means be assumed that this anti-Klan sentiment correlated with racial integration sentiment. Some editors participating in the poll, while expressing disfavor for the Klan, made remarks similar to this one made by a Mississippi editor: "My answers do not in any sense mean that I am a 'moderate' or an integrationist. I am for segregation 100% and am a member of the Citizens' Council."

[19]Miami *News*, September 26, 1960.

was that of Vice President Richard M. Nixon when he told the nation in a televised speech, after the Klan had announced it would support him for the presidency, "I obviously repudiate the Klan."[20]

Thus, in executing its large-scale program of persuasion, the Klan faced a large-scale problem of ethos. Realizing this, a Public Relations Director for the organization said he planned "to change the image of the Klan." "People think we are hoodlums but we ain't," he told the public.[21]

But the public had to be convinced that the Klan was truly a respectable, significant organization. "No organization in the country has a clearer image than the Klan," observed the Columbus, Georgia, *Ledger-Enquirer*.[22] Much to the Klan's regret, it did not enjoy its prestige of the middle 1920's. At that time, the well-known Kansas editor, William Allen White, a leading opponent of the Klan, admitted that it was "one of the powerful, probably the most powerful, single minority solidarity in American politics."[23] Thirty-five years later, in 1960, the Greenville, South Carolina, *News* could say with confidence: "The fact is that there are not enough Klansmen in the whole United States to have any effect on the outcome of the presidential election."[24] And the Spartanburg, South Carolina, *Herald* could state: "Anyone who claims the South is being led, or influenced, by the Ku Klux Klan is either totally misinformed, or abjectly dishonest."[25]

The Klan, nevertheless, tried to enhance its ethos with the public by emphasizing how popular it was. While it claimed Governors and United States Senators as members,[26] its favorite ego-building technique was the announcing of inflated estimations of attendance at its public meetings. A speaker estimated the crowd at a Stone Mountain rally at 15,000; a generous newspaper estimate was 400.[27] An agent of the Klan announced to reporters that 3,000 Klansmen would attend a meeting at Danville, Virginia;[28] 350 attended this meeting, and this number dwindled to less than 100 before the program was over.[29] In Decatur, Georgia, a local Klan dignitary predicted that 20,000 would attend a rally on the courthouse lawn;[30] newspaper reporters placed the crowd at around 2,000.[31] Gross exaggerations like these made it difficult for the public to accept any claim to significance which the Klan made; instead, they made it all the easier to accept statements of public officials as to the strength of the Klan, such as the one made by Florida Governor LeRoy

[20]New York *Times*, October 14, 1960.
[21]Raleigh *Times*, November 25, 1960.
[22]Columbus *Ledger-Enquirer*, November 26, 1960.
[23]William Allen White, *Politics: The Citizens Business* (New York, 1924), 11–12.
[24]Greenville *News*, quoted in Columbia *Record*, October 24, 1960.
[25]Spartanburg *Herald*, October 26, 1960.
[26]Texarkana *Gazette*, November 1, 1960.
[27]*Decatur-DeKalb News*, September 8, 1960.
[28]Greensboro *News*, August 21, 1960.
[29]Richmond *News Leader*, September 5, 1960.
[30]Decatur *DeKalb New Era*, June 2, 1960.
[31]*Decatur-DeKalb News*, June 2, 1960.

Collins: "The whole concept of Klanism is a spurious one from a standpoint of . . . any specific influence. That I think is true in Florida, and I think it is true elsewhere."[32]

The Klan's effort to counteract this discouraging reception was evident in the speeches at the public meetings as it tried to present a favorable image. A Klan preacher insisted that the only real white men he had ever found were in the Klan.[33] Another speaker said that the Klan chose only patriotic white men devoted to the protection of their race:

> We do not seek the membership of the weak-kneed; if you don't believe in your country enough to preserve it, you got no business not only in the Klan but you got no business in this country. If you do not believe in your race enough to help preserve it, you are unworthy of being called a white man.

The same speaker completed his defense by contending that the leaders of the Klan were churchmen and that they reflected the high morals of the entire membership:

> You have heard about irreligiousness of the Klan and its being composed of hoodlums. . . . Maybe there have been some that entered the Klan that were unworthy; there have been. . . . But of the thirteen men who compose the governing body of our Klan, . . . eleven are bona fide members of the Gospel of Jesus Christ, many of them with more than thirty years in the ministry. That's the kind of Klan that we are trying to build.

These limited attempts to bolster group ethos suggested a consciously defensive organization striving to overcome an inferiority complex. Public opinion compelled the Klan to defend a character badly blotched with deeds and thoughts which most citizens branded repulsive. But to defend to the degree the situation demanded could have resulted in a negative reaction from Klan members, especially those of lukewarm enthusiasm; an inadequate defense, on the other hand, would have been unrealistic in terms of what successful persuasion called for. Content to picture themselves as the whitest of white men, with churchmen as their leaders, Klan speakers did little to bypass either horn of this dilemma; greatly selling defense short on a point where any underdevelopment was dangerous, they hindered more than they helped the Klan cause.

The Klan cause of 1960 was definitely the cause of racial segregation. A Klan paper's report of the inaugural address of a top officer was limited to one sentence: He "gave a forceful speech to keep the races separated and the

[32]Miami *Herald*, October 15, 1960.
[33]*Rebel*, October 28, 1960.

schools segregated."[34] All other considerations dear to the organization, i.e., the anti-Semitic, anti-foreigner, anti-Catholic themes, were secondary to this particular goal. The Klan's mission had its practical basis, as one Imperial Wizard, the highest Klan officer, told an audience: "We white people are the inheritors of this country. We do not intend to surrender it."[35] To the Klansman, the mission also had its Biblical basis; a second Imperial Wizard explained it in this way:

> We always look to God's Holy Word as revealed in the
> Bible for our belief in the supremacy of the white race. . . .
> We know that we are the direct creation of God himself as
> recorded in Genesis. No man has ever presumed, not the
> rankest integrationist has ever presumed to say that Adam
> wasn't a white man . . . that Abraham was not a white man;
> the rankest integrationist has never denied that the Christ
> . . . was anything but a white man. So we have a wonderful
> heritage to protect and preserve.

In the Klan speeches, there was an annoying sameness in the treatment of this central theme. A paper in sympathy with Klan principles thought it wise to make this statement in announcing a public meeting: "We can promise you something different in this meeting from what you have been hearing."[36]

Klan meeting audiences, therefore, heard "the problem" discussed at length, in a highly disjointed fashion. There was little agreement, however, as to what had brought about an awakened public interest in the Negro's civil rights. One speaker charged that Hollywood was making "a lot of race-mixing pictures" to promote integration, that "Judas Iscariot preachers" were advocating desegregation, that Sunday School teachers were teaching children that "there was no difference between a white rabbit and a brown rabbit and it followed from that there was no difference between white people and black people."[37] A speaker from Tennessee contended that the civil rights philosophy had gained ground because "the dollar sign is in the eyes of the people," i.e., they are attracted more to the liberalism which is concerned with government power projects, social security legislation, and price controls than they are attracted to the conservatism which holds that civil rights legislation for the Negro has gone too far. Still another speaker charged that the growth of Communism "in the last few years" in this country had influenced preachers to preach "that the Christian thing to do is to mix the blood of the races."

Whatever the operating causes were, declared the speakers at Klan meetings, a dismal picture had resulted. It was dismal economically speaking, said one speaker:

[34]*Ibid.*, September 30, 1960.
[35]Greenville *Piedmont*, August 2, 1960.
[36]Decatur *Suburban Sentinel*, November 23, 1960.
[37]Kannapolis, North Carolina, *Independent*, September 5, 1960; Durham *Herald*, September 4, 1960.

> F.E.P.C., that means guaranteeing the niggers a right to
> work in the same job and on the same job as you do or I do.
> In effect, if that nigger comes to get a job before you do and
> he is turned down and then you go to get a job, and they
> hire you, well, you know what will happen, they'll go to
> Washington, take it into court, fire you off your job and put
> the nigger to work. Now that's F.E.P.C. . . . That's not
> America. A man has a right to select who he wants to work
> for him, whether he's a Negro, white, or whatever national-
> ity he is.

But it was even more dismal socially speaking, warned another speaker:

> A man called me up from Athens, Georgia, and he says . . .
> "My daughter left Athens, she's had one year at the Uni-
> versity. She went to . . . North Carolina, got there and then
> came downstairs . . . a time of a student conference in
> North Carolina, just week before last. She came down, and
> there in the lobby, the girls, white girls, some of them were
> dancing in the arms of Negro boys. She ran on out and in
> the pool, she found there they were more than half naked
> . . . out there they were swimming in the lake with Negro
> boys." That's in North Carolina, and that was a girl from
> Athens, Georgia.

The revolting picture presented, the implied threats to economic security
and social status, and the instilled fear of people in influential places working
for the Negro, were enough to renew and to re-enforce many listener's feeling
of need for a well-directed program of action and retaliation. Yet, Klan members and most potential Klan members, seeing how boldly the Negro was assert-
ing himself all around them in matters involving individual rights, did not
need to be convinced that they faced a problem with serious ramifications. To
these people, who were the targets of the Klan's communication, the time to
elaborate on the problem, other than to revivify its effects once again, was past
—the problem was real and they were worried, concerned people. It was time
to consider solutions and to come to a decision, without further delay, as to
what could be set in motion so as to rectify the wrongs which they thought had
been done to them.

As for the solution, Klan speakers were certain as to what it was not. It
was not an extension of the concept of equality of men. One speaker went to the
Bible and to the history of Man to find his justification for ruling out this
solution:

> You hear lots today about all people being equal—well, the
> Bible doesn't say that. Thomas Jefferson said it . . . even
> though I'm a great admirer of his, I don't rank him with
> the Godhead. . . . Certainly, we do not deny that in the
> beginning, probably they all were, sixty centuries ago, all

> men started equal. But racial equality ended right there
> and then, because the white face forged ahead and has been
> ahead ever since and will stay ahead if we don't give our
> birthright away.

Neither was the solution the election of a particular party or a particular candidate over another. This became apparent to the Klan when both the Democratic and Republican Parties featured strong civil rights planks in their platforms. Both Senator John F. Kennedy and Vice President Nixon, therefore, were roundly castigated, often during the same Klan meeting. One speaker referred to Kennedy and asked:

> He's got Negroes all over the South working; in fact, he
> stated that he would integrate Negroes everywhere possible
> in his campaign for the presidency. Now how can our gov-
> ernors come out and support an integrationist, outright
> integrationist?

Another speaker later shouted:

> Anybody that'll vote the Democratic ticket . . . will become
> a traitor to the Southland and to the Constitution of the
> United States.

And yet another Klan speaker addressed his audience in this manner:

> Nixon is the first American that I ever heard of that went
> down into a nigger country and let them spit on him and
> didn't say anything about it. . . . And he even said that he's
> going to . . . call the troops out more than Eisenhower did
> in Little Rock.

With both major candidates and both major parties eliminated from further consideration as solutions, and with no serious thought given to form-ing a third party, especially after Governor Faubus' declination of a third party nomination, the person wanting to follow Klan policy was a man without a party. This was the way one Klan speaker put it: "The white people of Amer-ica have no one, actually, that they can honestly support in this great cam-paign."

Thus, with philosophical and political solutions both discarded, the solu-tion vacuum remained. Bizarre plans were plentiful. One speaker pleaded for 100 per cent support for a "fire-your-Negro-campaign," as he said, "If you have a nigger employed in your home or business, I call upon you as a loyal white man to fire him as soon as you can replace him with a white man."[38] More than one speaker seriously called for closing of the schools. One speaker indicated how gladly he would accept this solution:

[38]Richmond *News Leader*, September 5, 1960; Danville, Virginia, *Register*, September 4, 1960.

> I'd rather my children would play down in the pasture with
> the yearlings and the hogs; I'd rather they'd fail to get any
> education at all, I'd rather they'd be as ignorant as a bull
> or a mule, than for them to sit down in classrooms with
> Negroes. . . . One of the best things . . . would be tonight if
> every school in America could be torn down, and I'm not
> advocating violence—were to be torn down, and especially
> colleges and universities. . . . I tell you where your trouble
> is—it's in your schools, and in your colleges, in your
> churches, and not in your back alleys.

Other solutions were mentioned. One speaker suggested that the welfare
program for Negroes be terminated and that they be sent "up North where they
belong." A Georgia speaker advocated county redistricting: He recommended
that Georgia's 159 counties be reduced to 60 so that there would be at least
twice as many white voters as Negro voters in each county.[39]

The most striking thing about the entire discussion of solutions was the
prevalence of the idea that physical force could be used if necessary; while
there was no direct appeal to resort to violence, there was often strong intima-
tion that it could be relied upon if other measures failed. There were definite
overtones in a statement like this, for instance:

> Back in the early days of our country, there was a rebellion,
> and it was called Shay's Rebellion. It was a bunch of poor
> people, like us, that had to work for a living that got out
> and rebelled. Here's what Jefferson said about it. He said,
> "God forbid that we should ever be twenty years without
> such a rebellion. . . . What signify a few lives lost in a
> century or two? What country can preserve its liberty if
> the rulers are not warned from time to time that the people
> preserve the spirit of resistance? Let them take arms; the
> tree of liberty must be refreshed from time to time with the
> blood of tyrants." That's what Thomas Jefferson said—he
> was as much a Klan as anybody in the country—that's
> what we said, too.

Similarly, when a high Klan officer said, in referring to the Negroes' recent
attempts to use public beaches formerly reserved for white people, "The nigger
may swim in, but he will never know when he comes out,"[40] and when another
referred to the efficacy of the "Klan Bureau of Investigation,"[41] there was more
than a suggestion that these leaders approved of vigilante justice, if they were
in the positions to administer it.

Even though some Klan speakers cautioned against the use of force, such
as the speaker who said, "For God's sake don't go out there and take your gun

[39] Atlanta *Constitution*, December 1, 1960.
[40] *Rebel*, September 30, 1960.
[41] Tucker, Georgia, *Tribune*, June 2, 1960.

and kill a bunch of innocent niggers," there were others who openly sanctioned the use of force, such as the speaker who counseled his listeners:

> Any white man . . . in a restaurant when a nigger sits down next to him ought to stand right up and knock the nigger down to the floor; and I'll tell you one thing, a Klansman or any white person that wouldn't come to their aid and help and defend them, legally and in every way possible, isn't a white person. They ought to move to Africa and live with niggers, if that's the way they feel.

The same speaker made no apology for not specifically explaining how the Klan as a group would accomplish its ends:

> You don't know how many we are, you don't know how strong we are, or how we are going to go about accomplishing the aims that we intend to do, but I'll tell you right now, we are not going to allow any niggers to destroy our schools, churches, homes, or we're not going to let them sit down next to us in restaurants.

More often than not, therefore, the threat and the justification of force were always in the background; Klansmen themselves said that the purpose of staging organized Klan street-walkings was to show the strength of the organization.[42] "THERE WILL BE PROTECTION IN ATLANTA should a crisis arise!," exclaimed the *Rebel*, after a Klan demonstration in downtown Atlanta.[43]

Even though the Klan surely recognized that the situation called for discussion of courses of action, Klan speakers failed to explain and defend in a rational way a single, direct answer to the troublesome problem that they developed in detail. A thoughtful person arriving at a Klan meeting wondering what exactly he could do, without resorting to violence, to help effect a more desirable situation, was probably in an even more bewildered state when the meeting ended. Frustrated all the more by the unsolved problem which he knew he and his fellows faced and which had again been ramified, he had listened to different speakers cursorily discuss different solutions; regardless of how much he had hoped for a reasonable, down-to-earth consideration of the practicality of some one solution, he had heard nothing of the kind. More than that, since the Klan offered no solution to satisfy an already suspicious public that it was clearly *not* contemplating use of force, its critics could now be certain that their derogatory opinion was warranted. Klan speakers, in a rambling fashion, may have intensified the awareness of a problem among supporters and doubters alike, because their emphasis was here; but speaking as leaders of an "action organization" at the opportune time to explore solutions judiciously and to weigh various recommendations carefully in terms of their promises and

[42]Savannah *News*, November 24, 1960.
[43]*Rebel*, December 12, 1960.

consequences, they made little contribution in the respect of connecting a specific solution with a felt need. In the larger view, rather than allaying unrest and confusion in the alarmed South, Klan speakers only aggravated the situation.

Certain conclusions can be drawn from this study of the Ku Klux Klan's attempt to present its best case to the public. Protesting under its blazing crosses on hilltops, in pastures, at motor speedways, and in vacant lots alongside highways, the Klan in 1960 offered no inviting program of constructive action. Weakened from within and without, it ground out the story that had been told many times o'er, not precisely sure as to what or whom its enemies were, but flailing about, striking at many. All the familiar Klan paraphernalia and customs were present—the crosses, the Confederate flag by the United States flag, the high peaked hats, the white clusters of garbed Klansmen and Klanswomen, the lusty singing of the hymn, "The Old Rugged Cross," the swishing satin robes in brilliant hues of red, blue, black, green, and gold worn by the Wizards, Cyclopses, Dragons, Kluds, Night Hawks, and Titans—but these had little distinctly 1960 about them. There were some visible signs of 1960, to be sure—the "No Integration" banners on car windows, the "Vote White—Vote Faubus" signs, a new theme song: "Send Them Back to Africa, Every One." But the speeches, the core of the Klan's persuasive effort, were not shaped according to what 1960 demanded if they were to do their share in halting the continuing demise of the Klan, thereby removing the organization from what one of its members called its Gethsemane.

According to one student of the South, Rembert W. Patrick, that will never be possible:

> The world is in ferment, and a majority of the peoples of the world belong to the colored races. As a world power, and for the sake of her very life, the United States cannot agree to any system which makes any part of her colored population second class citizens. Thus any victory which the segregationists may win will be temporary. . . . For too long the Negro has been held in the caste system. That system cannot endure with a majority of the nation and of the world in opposition to it.[44]

As 1960 closed, nevertheless, the Klan gave no suggestion that it would change in purpose or in method. For the most part, the Klan is impervious to criticism, whatever its nature. It states its attitude toward its critics:

> Opposition to the Klan emanates from sources which do not, or will not learn, and evil groups whom we restrain by reflecting the light of truth, where cunning prevails. If no evil intention existed there would be no criticism of the Klan.[45]

[44]Rembert W. Patrick, *Race Relations in the South* (Tallahassee, 1958), 21.
[45]Printed card, "The Ku Klux Klan" (Atlanta?, n.d.), in author's possession.

Exonerating itself in this way, the Klan renewed its determination in purpose as it faced the future. "We shall never surrender," cried a speaker at a Klan meeting, "We have just started to fight. . . . We must be willing to pay the price whatever the extremes to turn back black tyranny."[46]

The Klan is determined, whatever its self-styled methods are, to be eternal. "When the last shot is fired and the smoke has cleared away, we will stand victorious over the forces of Satan," prophesized a Klan preacher.[47] Whether it is eternal or not, its counterparts, with different trappings and titles, will be; protected by a government under law in their right to express their convictions, they will use this right to attempt to deny the rights of others. In trials such as these, the spirit of our republic must find its breath and vigor.

Questions for Analysis

1. How does the public image of a minority organization compound the difficulty of attempts to present its "case"? Compare the image of the Klan in 1960 with those of minority groups presenting cases today. How do changing social and political conditions "date" the rhetoric of minority organizations? Demonstrate this with examples of "dated" rhetoric in the civil rights-Black Power, student protest, and New Left movements. How did reactions to the Klan in 1960 suggest distinctions between *rhetorical* and *ideological* support for the organization? Are these distinctions true for support of minority movements today? Explain and refer to Haiman's article on "the rhetoric of the streets."

2. Did Klan speakers in 1960 develop a "paranoid style" distinctly different from that of Carmichael? of Reagan? of Gregory? Explain. What persuasive approach might reward "a consciously defensive organization striving to overcome an inferiority complex"? How would you manage public relations for the Klan?

3. Illustrate the dependence of Klan speakers on pathos, on rendering audiences suggestible to a message. To which "motivational resources" did Klan speakers appeal to justify their rhetorical positions? Characterize the "annoying sameness" Williams notes in treatment of central Klan themes, religious, economic, and social. Try to reproduce this "sameness" in a paragraph or two of political treatment of a Klan theme.

4. How did the Klan's attempt "to consider conclusions and to come to a decision" substantiate Griffin's "New Left" study assessment of the challenge faced by *anti* movements practicing "the rhetoric of rejection"? What is the problem of persuasion in a "solution vacuum"? Describe the Klan's rhetorical *cul-de-sac*. Are other minority organizations today in similar straits?

[46]Atlanta *Constitution*, December 1, 1960.
[47]Vicksburg *Post*, August 5, 1960.

5. With reference to the three statements of freedom of speech in Part II consider Williams' concluding statements. Why might public interest be served by adoption of a code for ethical persuasion? Why might such a code require the presentation of rhetorical alternatives? How might the Klan have shaped speeches "according to what 1960 demanded"? How might other minority groups shape speeches to the demands of our times?

37

The Cross and the Flag: Evangelists of
the Far Right

Barnet Baskerville

My original assignment was to analyze the methods of discourse of
the principal spokesmen of the American radical right. It became immediately
apparent that this was far too ambitious a project for the space allowed. The
tremendous number and variety of right-wing organizations makes any comprehensive analysis a formidable, indeed an utterly impossible, undertaking. A
study financed by the Fund for the Republic and published in 1960 by the
University of Illinois Graduate School of Library Science estimates that there
were at that time approximately 1,000 voluntary organizations in the United
States which might be called rightist, and which regularly publish or distribute
great quantities of rightwing literature.[1] A complete list of the weeklies, month-
lies, newsletters, pamphlets, syndicated columns, newspapers, brochures, tape-
recordings and films carrying the rightist message would fill many pages. The
organizations range from flagrantly fascist groups like William Pelley's Silver
Shirts, George Rockwell's American Nazi Party, and the activist Minutemen, to
the allegedly educational study groups of Dr. Frederick Schwarz. They include
the John Birch Society; the Citizen's Councils; the National Educational Program with headquarters at Harding College in Searcy, Arkansas (source of the
film "Communism on the Map"); and the various Christian Crusades of
Gerald L. K. Smith, Verne Kaub, Billy James Hargis, and Carl McIntire. The
rightist faith is propagated on radio and television by such able spokesmen as
Fulton Lewis, Jr., Dan Smoot, and Clarence Manion, and in newspaper columns
by George Sokolsky, Westbrook Pegler, and many others.

Accurate estimates of the numerical strength of the right wing and of its
actual influence are difficult to come by. The response to Schwarz's anti-com-

Barnet Baskerville is Chairman of the Department of Speech, University of Washington.
This paper was presented at the Speech Association of America convention, December
1962, as part of a program on "The Rhetoric of Contemporary Politics." Reprinted by permission from *Western Speech*, 27 (1963) : 197–206.
[1]Ralph E. Ellsworth and Sarah M. Harris, *The American Right Wing*, p. 3.

munist schools has evidently been phenomenal, and he seems to have at his disposal an almost unlimited supply of funds. His three-hour television extravaganza from Hollywood in October, 1961, "Hollywood's Answer to Communism," which was carried to an audience of 7,000,000 over a 35-station network at an estimated cost of $50,000 was paid for by Richfield Oil and the Schick Safety Razor Company. Carl McIntire's daily broadcast is carried on 485 radio stations. Billy James Hargis, whose daily broadcast is heard "in nearly every state in the union," and who claims a mailing list of 300,000 for his weekly newsletter, told a newsman in Chicago that his operating budget for 1960 was $1,000,000 and that it costs $75,000 a month "just to open our doors down in Tulsa." According to Hargis, when his Christian Crusade joined with the John Birch Society in support of General Walker, 140,000 telegrams poured into Washington.[2] Peter Edson, a Scripps-Howard columnist, notes that 50 right-wing organizations maintain national headquarters or active lobbying offices in Washington, D. C. And Professor Alan Westin of Columbia estimates on the basis of corporation reports of donations that the business community contributed $10,000,000 dollars to the radical right in 1961.[3]

While the amazing *number* of far right organizations and spokesmen makes an analysis of the movement difficult, the problem of definition is even more perplexing. How far is far? How radical is radical? Although we can probably agree on the Nazis, the John Birchers, and the Minutemen, how about Fred Schwarz? Is he a member of the radical right? He indignantly denies the allegation. How about William Buckley? How about Senator Eastland? And how about the heads of large corporations who neither give speeches nor write pamphlets, but who generously finance those who do?

The effort is sometimes made to distinguish between the "respectable" and the "radical" right, to create a continuum ranging from responsible, philosophic conservatives to militant extremists and crackpots. Such a categorization would place among the "respectables" men like Senators Goldwater and Tower, and intellectuals such as Buckley and Kirk, while the "radicals" might range from Schwarz near the center to Robert Welch or Gerald Smith out at right end. I shall not presume to separate rightists into respectables and radicals, nor shall I assume that a rightist is a rightist, and that all are essentially the same. Obviously there are differences between a Goldwater and a Pelley, a Buckley

[2] John Kay Adams, "Saving America, Inc.," *Nation*, September 30, 1961, pp. 192, 194.

[3] Fred J. Cook, "The Ultras," *Nation*, June 30, 1962, p. 571. The past year has brought some evidence of an apparent decline in influence. The radical right was not notably successful in the 1962 elections, even in California, presumably a stronghold. Fred Schwarz's New York City crusade in August, 1962, lost $75,000; his Omaha School of Anti-Communism was a great disappointment; and his Northern Ohio School in Cleveland was a colossal flop, drawing fewer than fifty persons to the opening meeting. Hargis's World Fair Christian Crusade Congress in Seattle was, despite its pretentious title, a pitiful thing. At the two sessions I attended I was one of a half-dozen men in a total audience of thirty or forty, the great majority of whom were elderly ladies with Bibles in their hands. Hargis has described 1962 as a poor year, with total receipts dropping to only $760,000. Whether all this represents the beginning of a trend, or is merely a temporary setback, remains to be seen.

and a Pegler. Nevertheless, it should be observed that in many basic articles of faith the radicals and the respectables are in agreement. They agree that America is in imminent danger of being betrayed by a monstrous Communist conspiracy, and that the internal threat is more dangerous than the external. They agree in regarding most of the reforms that have taken place since the 1930's as "socialism" or "leading to socialism." They tend to identify New Dealers, liberals, and all non-rightists with socialists, and socialists with Communists—don't forget that the Soviet Union is a union of *Socialist* republics. They are opposed to one-worldism, and all manifestations thereof—the United Nations, the World Council of Churches, foreign aid, UNICEF. They are convinced that you can't do business with Communism or any of its representatives, that co-existence is unthinkable, and that negotiation is treasonable.

Moreover, it should be noted that the radical and respectable rightists need one another. Radical spokesmen, irresponsible as they often are, are valuable allies whom the respectables are reluctant to alienate. Despite repeated efforts of newsmen to get Goldwater, Tower, and Co. to repudiate the Birch Society and its ilk, they steadfastly refuse to do so. And without the tacit support of the respectables, without the substantial support of respectable money, the radical movements could not continue to exist.

Since the enforced brevity of this report necessitates severe limitations, I have chosen to concentrate upon three far-right evangelists: Dr. Frederick Schwarz, Dr. Billy James Hargis, and Dr. Carl McIntire. Hargis and McIntire are blood-redemption Christian clergymen who combine fundamentalist religion with anti-communism; Schwarz, though not a clergyman, has served as a Baptist lay-preacher and uses evangelistic techniques in his Christian Anti-Communism Crusade. These three doctors—one of medicine, two of divinity—are sure they know what ails society and how it can be cured.

Schwarz

Of the three, Schwarz, the Australian physician, is probably the best known. His Christian Anti-Communism Crusade is described as a non-profit, tax-exempt educational organization devoted to the battle against Communism, and to the propagation of the Christian faith. Schwarz uses his Crusade to generate fervor for his Anti-Communism Schools. He has been invited to speak on college campuses and before state legislatures, at military establishments like the Glenview Naval Air Station, defense industries like the Boeing Aircraft Company, and before a variety of business, religious and patriotic groups.

Schwarz is a remarkably persuasive speaker. Facile, fluent, adaptable, he is able to address a college audience in a disarmingly reasonable, good-humored, professorial manner, or to bring a mass audience to its feet with such a blood-tingling exhortation as this: "Christians, to arms! The enemy is at the gate. Buckle on the armor of the Christian and go forth to battle. With education, evangelism and dedication let us smite the Communist foe and if necessary give up our lives in this noble Cause!"[4] Despite such rousing (if unspecific) calls to action, Dr. Schwarz insists that he has no program. The need of the hour is for *information*. If Americans understand Communism they will know how to combat it. Schwarz's mission is to provide knowledge. If his auditors go forth from his Crusades and Schools to join the Birch Society or the Minutemen, that is their business, not his. His is an educator, an awakener.

Hargis

Another crusader is Dr. Billy James Hargis of Tulsa, Oklahoma, whose Christian Crusade is billed as "America's largest anti-Communist movement dedicated to the survival of the Church and freedom."

Hargis, a rotund, handsome young man of 38, devotes his daily broadcasts to what the announcer describes in the sign-off as the "fight of the century to preserve the testimony of the Gospel and free America from the Communist encroachment." Although insisting that his message is not political but religious, he vigorously urges election of conservative candidates, repudiation of social-service legislation, repeal of the income tax, withdrawal from the United Nations, and cessation of all negotiations with Russia. He blasts away at Khrushchev, liberals, professors, the N.A.A.C.P. and the National Council of Churches, and excoriates the administration for its softness toward Cuba and its hardness toward Governor Barnett and General Walker.

Like Schwarz, Hargis also conducts various schools and conferences throughout the nation, featuring such speakers as Westbrook Pegler, Bracken Lee, John Rousselot, ex-Communists Bella Dodd, Barbara Hartle, and Benjamin Gitlow. In February, 1963, he began a coast to coast speaking tour with General Edwin A. Walker—"Operation Midnight Ride"—to alert the nation to the Communist menace. This summer Dr. Hargis opened his Anti-Communist Youth University at Pike's Peak, Colorado, devoted to producing every two weeks during June and July a graduating class of trained Communist fighters.

Hargis's aim, explicitly stated in his voluminous literature, is "to safeguard and preserve the conservative Christian ideals upon which America was founded . . . and to oppose . . . any person or organization whose words or actions endorse . . . the philosophies of leftists, socialists or communists, intentionally or otherwise . . . and to defend the Gospel of Jesus Christ." In recent months Hargis has taken the line that liberals are even more dangerous than Communists, since they have the same goals, and are more numerous and more effectively financed. His State of the Union Address of August 4, 1962, contained this remarkable statement: "Our threat is not so much from the outside as it is from the inside, and our greatest threat is not internal communism. Strange words from a professional Anti-Communist Crusader! I am convinced

[4]*Ibid.*, p. 573.

after fifteen years in this fight to save our country by awakening our people, that the greatest threat to freedom, New Testament Christianity, and Constitutional Government is the powerfully entrenched Liberal Establishment." Hargis's fellow midnight rider, General Walker, declared in Greenville, South Carolina, on March 12, 1963, that "No man can be a Communist, a Socialist, or a Kennedy liberal, and follow the teachings of Christ."

McIntire

Our third anti-communist evangelist is Dr. Carl McIntire of Collingswood, New Jersey, founder of the Twentieth Century Reformation Hour. Dr. McIntire has apparently drifted into the anti-communist crusade a little at a time, one thing having led to another. Active in the fundamentalist-modernist battle of the late 1920's, he was ordained a Presbyterian minister but was ejected from that church in 1936 for causing dissension and strife. He straightway founded a new denomination, the Bible Presbyterian Church; a new national fundamentalist organization, the American Council of Christian Churches; and subsequently an International Council of Churches. McIntire has for years charged the main line National Council of Churches with religious apostasy, later adding the charge of Communism. In 1961 McIntire's group called for a Congressional investigation of Communist penetration of the National Council, and demanded withdrawal of the United States from the United Nations. In recent years he has taken up other right-wing causes in which his interests are involved. For example, since the tax-exempt status of certain independent church groups has been called into question by the Internal Revenue Department, he has become an active crusader for repeal of the income tax.

The man has an amazing verbal facility. His 30-minute program is all talk —most of it extemporaneous. There are no hymns, soloists, or organ music. Except for an occasional heartfelt "amen" from his otherwise silent partner Amen Charlie, it is all Carl McIntire. He beseeches the Almighty to insure contributions sufficient to provide 600 radio stations. He reads with enthusiastic approval—or with venomous sarcasm—editorials, news items, and letters. He pounces on each item with the exuberance of discovery, sharing with his listeners the excitement of uncovering a dark conspiracy, of "watching this thing unfold." His touchstone is always the infallible Bible. "We're approaching this problem of Communism," he says, "from the moral standpoint." "Send us your gifts," he pleaded in a recent broadcast, "and we'll come talking like this right out of our heart with the facts in one hand, with the Bible in the other, and with the Holy Spirit guiding us as we speak."

Political Evangelism

To refer to these men as political evangelists is not to employ a mere figure of speech. They are revivalists in a most literal sense; they are seeking to bring about a great awakening. But it is revivalism with a difference. And it is this new modulation of old themes, this adaptation of familiar revivalistic means to serve new ends, that makes these attempts at a mid-Twentieth Century Great Awakening such a fascinating study.

While evangelists of old preached the gospel (the "good news") of Christ's saving grace, the new gospel emphasizes the very worst of *bad* news. The Church of Christ, this nation, the world, are in imminent danger of destruction by a godless Communist conspiracy. Unless we awaken to the danger, unless this conspiracy is exposed and destroyed, churches will be pulled down, money and lands confiscated, people tortured and driven into slave labor camps. There is no need to preach in the manner of a Jonathan Edwards of the horrors of a hell awaiting us on the other side, for the triumph of Communism would create an equally horrendous hell right here on this earth.

Revivalists have always understood the tremendous tactical advantage in having a specific enemy. Dwight Moody fought the devil; Billy Sunday was most effective when attacking booze. Schwarz, Hargis, and McIntire battle Communists and liberals with the same zest. In our day the devil has become an unreal Halloween-type spectre; sin and booze have for some become downright attractive; but Communism is a real and present danger: Communists are tangible embodiments of evil. In the new theology, Khrushchev has replaced the devil as the explanation for the world's afflictions. In fact, as both Hargis and McIntire assert, Khrushchev *is* the devil. "You can't negotiate with the Devil," says Hargis. "Khrushchev is the devil personified."

This identification of the enemy and all his assistants with Satan himself makes possible a neat alignment of good versus evil, Christ versus antichrist, which admits of no middle ground. "Since Communism is founded on atheism," says Dr. Schwarz, "it is the enemy of all religious groups professing some belief in a Supreme Being." "And now," says the announcer's familiar introduction, "speaking *for* Christ, and *against* Communism, Dr. Billy James Hargis." On the one side, it seems, is the American Way of Life, which is Christ's way and which embraces free-enterprise capitalism (called "Christian economics"), conservatism, nationalism, and militant anti-communism. On the other is all that is not the American way of life so defined. Such a simple dichotomy makes evaluation of individuals, organizations, and policies an easy matter. Evangelist Billy Sunday put the matter succinctly many years ago: "I'm in favor of everything the devil is against, and I am against everything the devil is in favor of. . . . If you know which side the devil is on, put me down on the other side every time."[5]

It was also Billy Sunday who, in his post-World War I fight against radicals, social gospelers, and the League of Nations, discovered the efficacy of linking patriotism and fundamentalist religion. "I think that Christianity and Patriotism are synonymous terms," he said, "and hell and traitors are synonymous."[6]

---

[5]William T. Ellis, *"Billy" Sunday: The Man and His Message* (L. T. Myers, 1914), p. 186.

[6]William G. McLoughlin, Jr., *Modern Revivalism* (New York, 1959), p. 444.

And Gerald L. K. Smith, whose journal *The Cross and the Flag* still makes its way through the mails in plain brown wrapper, once advised: "Religion and patriotism, keep going on that. It's the only way you can get them 'het up'."[7] Billy Hargis offers to his followers for $6.50 a color photograph of himself posed before a painting of Jesus Christ. Hargis holds in his hand a parchment copy of the Constitution; to one side is an American flag, to the other a Crusader in armor. If people are to fight Communism, explains Dr. Fred Schwarz, they must have a powerful reason. The man whose message will be heard "tunes in to their religious aspirations, their national aspirations. . . ."

A traditional weapon in the arsenal of the evangelist is the apposite Biblical quotation. The Doctors Hargis and McIntire know their Bible, and find it an indispensable aid in their anti-communist crusades. They discover in the holy scriptures warnings against the United Nations, the New Deal, medicare, the income tax, Khrushchev, social security, and the World Council of Churches. "I just love to take the Bible in my hand," says McIntire, "and explain these great truths that have been here all the time." Samples of these great truths, together with the contemporary applications made by these interpreters of scripture, are as follows:

1. "Behold ye trust in lying words that cannot profit."— We're believing in lying words of the Communists when they speak of co-existence. It's morally wrong to believe your enemy is not your enemy. Christ said: "He that is not with me is against me." Communists are against us. (McIntire)
2. "Blessed is the man that walkest not in the counsel of the ungodly."—The United Nations is anti-God, anti-Christ, anti-Holy Spirit. As a Christian I have no choice but to oppose the U.N. Participation in the U.N. is a sin. (Hargis)
3. "The poor you shall always have with you."—All these international do-gooders that think by legislation and foreign aid they're gonna do away with poverty, they just don't know what they're talking about. You can't do away with poverty. Jesus said so. (Hargis)

After the medicare bill failed to pass, President Kennedy called it a defeat for every American family, and mentioned especially young people from 35 to 40 whose parents might soon be needing medical aid. Dr. McIntire immediately accused the President of subverting the Ten Commandments. In McIntire's view the Commandment "Honor thy father and thy mother," gives to children the responsibility for the care of their parents; Kennedy wants to relieve them of this responsibility by giving it to the government—a sacrilege. On the same broadcast McIntire invoked another Commandment, "Thou shalt not steal," to attack the whole institution of taxation, which in his view is often just plain

---

[7]Quoted in Arthur M. Schlesinger, Jr., *The Politics of Upheaval* (Boston, 1960), p. 627.

robbery. He says, in effect, when you take money out of one man's pocket to put it into the pocket of someone else, that's *stealing!* All these socialistic schemes are stealing.

Present always in the exhortations of these right-wing evangelists is a note of terrible urgency. "Repent at once," pleaded the revivalist of old, "tomorrow may be too late!" "Pledge your support today," urges Dr. Hargis. "Don't wait till tomorrow. Tomorrow may never come. . . ." "The hour is late," says the announcer in sepulchral tones at the close of each Hargis broadcast, "Communism is a threat to your church, your home, your very life." No one, apparently, really understands the magnitude of the danger but this handful of courageous professional anti-communists. The President, Congress, the Supreme Court, the press—all are asleep, or are actually conniving with the enemy. Dr. Schwarz predicts surrender of the United States by 1973 unless . . . unless. "Oh," an old lady said to me in agonized impatience at a Hargis meeting, "Oh, if people would only wake up!"

And to what must they wake up? Why, to the need for *action,* for vigorous, sacrificial action. What action? Fighting Communism. But since the external Communist threat is negligible and the number of Party members within our borders is admittedly small, this becomes a fight also against those who are allegedly advancing the Communist cause, namely: liberals, modernists, New Dealers, and the like. And how is the fight carried on—with what weapons and tactics? Principally by forming more schools and study groups, by contributing more money for more radio stations and more anti-communist literature so that more people may be alerted to the deadly menace of Communism—so that they may be persuaded to form other study groups and buy more literature.

What can you do? asks Hargis. Accept the challenge, send your gifts. Christian Crusade needs $100,000 now. Give us 600 stations, pleads McIntire, so people can hear editorial opinion grounded on a standard of morality which we call the word of God. Even Dr. Schwarz, who denies that he has any specific program, called at the Glenview Naval Base for a "positive program of effective action." But the positive program is apparently to buy literature, tapes, and films, and to "study, study, study." Faith without works is dead, said Schwarz. But the *works* of which he spoke seem to be more schools and study groups for the further propagation of the *faith.*

Despite perfervid cries for action, there is really no program of action. It is as if these evangelists, committed in the religious realm to a doctrine of salvation by grace through faith, were unconsciously taking the same approach in their anti-communist crusades.[8] People must be made to understand, they must *believe* in the menace of Communism, in the enormity of its crimes; they must learn that not to hate the enemy and all who, intentionally or unknowingly, aid him, is a sin. And then, when a sufficient number of people have been

[8]This idea was first suggested to me by Robert T. Reilly, "Schwarz Was Here," *America,* March 24, 1962, pp. 820–821.

educated and aroused—then somehow, through some mysterious working of Grace, salvation will be bestowed and America will be saved from the forces of antichrist. It would be preposterous to pretend that such a doctrine had been consciously worked out by these evangelists of the far right. But to one who has subjected himself to hundreds of hours of listening to their utterances, this seems the most accurate analysis of their actual practice.

Although they repeatedly employ the *imagery* of warfare, there is surprisingly little talk among the evangelists of actual international armed conflict or seldom any suggestion that nuclear holocaust might result from the doctrines they preach. Nevertheless, to one who cannot accept the doctrine of national salvation through grace, their policies seem to leave no other alternative. For if all negotiations, all discussions, all attempts to find a way to live on the same planet with Communist nations are treasonous and sinful, then the only alternatives are surrender or war. Since the rightists reject surrender, only one avenue remains.

I offer as an appropriate conclusion to this examination of these allegedly *Christian* crusades, an observation from a recent issue of the *Christian Century*: "If we Americans know as little about communism as Dr. Schwarz thinks we do, our case is bad. But if we know so little about Christianity as to accept the Schwarz approach as 'Christian,' our case is tragic."[9]

Questions for Analysis

1. What is the relevance to the rhetoric of our times of efforts "to create a continuum ranging from responsible, philosophic conservatives to militant extremists and crackpots"? How do the questions "How far is far?" "How radical is radical?" apply to other contemporary spokesmen and organizations? What does public fascination with such questions and continuums suggest of the power of rhetorical distinctions today? Refer to Burgess' article on the Black Power movement for discussion of the dangers of rhetorical over-reaction. How does the Far Right pose these dangers?

2. What by way of a common concept of the role of "spokesman" emerges from Baskerville's brief identifications of Schwarz, Hargis, and McIntire? In his article on listening Nichols cites examples of "red flag" words to which listeners respond most subjectively. What are the attracting and repelling "red flag" words of the Far Right? How does reliance on such words suggest necessary revisions of Murphy's term "spokesman" for Adlai Stevenson when the term is applied also Schwarz, Hargis, and McIntire?

3. How is "the tremendous tactical advantage in having a specific enemy" re-

[9]George G. Hill, "Christian Crusade?" *Christian Century*, July 11, 1962, p. 864.

lated to your understanding of ethos? How did Reagan exploit this advantage? How did Carmichael? How does this rhetorical attitude preclude any possibility that "good reason(s)", defined by Wallace in Part III, may become the substance of contemporary rhetoric? How are the meanings of "evaluative words" by which Wallace linked ethical and rhetorical concerns abused by the "specific enemy" tactic of the Far Right? Illustrate the use of this tactic by each of these movements: Black Power, anti-war, student protest. Illustrate for each that "such a simple dichotomy makes evaluation of individuals, organizations, and policies an easy manner."

4. Study Baskerville's examples of the Far Right's use of Biblical quotations in general and the Ten Commandments in particular. Demonstrate that opponents of the Far Right might use the very same examples in a similar rhetorical manner but for opposite purposes. Relate this to considerations of the "morality of rhetoric" discussed in Part II by Kruger, Ehninger, and Braden.

5. How does the Far Right share the problems of the Klan's "solution vacuum"? What are the dangers of effective persuasive appeal without proposals for solution? What do these dangers add to the responsibilities of the agitative speaker in our times? What part may "rhetoric unrestrained" play in the future of this country's social problems?

38

Social Protest and the Oratory of Human Rights

Donald H. Smith

We can take pride in the knowledge that throughout the history of mankind great orators have, in times of need, stepped forward to help man see his direction, to lead man toward fulfillment of his destiny. Great men speaking on the great themes of liberty, justice, and egalitarianism have inspired mankind to loftier ideals and nobler deeds than man's collective nature might have sought, left to its own inclination.

Yet these exhorters of justice, liberty, independence and freedom did not all have the same referents for these worthy concepts. Many did and do believe, in the Orwellian sense, that some men or groups of men are more equal than others; some more deserving of justice than others. Apparently Demosthenes and Pericles saw no moral inconsistency in advocating democracy for Athenians while at the same time Athenians held other people as captive slaves. Churchill, who would fight on the seas and oceans, on the beaches and in the hills to save English freedom, fought just as vigorously to maintain English colonialism and oppression in India. Churchill looked upon Gandhi as an enemy of the British Empire, and he rebuked the British Government for daring to deal with Gandhi as an equal.

In our own country, the facts are no less revealing of the dichotomy between pronouncements which cry liberty for all and actions which secure liberty only for some. A classic case in point is the Virginian, Patrick Henry, who preferred death to the denial of liberty yet held many slaves.

The oratory of President Woodrow Wilson presents another example of this schism between the humane word and the inhumane deed; the noble generalization and the ignoble specific. Speaking before a joint session of

Donald H. Smith is Professor of Speech and Education, University of Pittsburgh.

Taken from an address to the annual convention of the Speech Association of the Eastern States, April 6, 1967. Reprinted by permission from *Today's Speech*, 15 (September, 1967) : 2–8.

Congress, in January 1918, Wilson delivered his "Fourteen Points Address," described by Robert T. Oliver and Eugene White as "pleas for international understanding . . . unmatched for their eloquence and idealism." In this address the President asked for tolerance, freedom, and the redress of grievances of the Russians, French, Belgians, Turks, Poles, and others

Yet even as Wilson spoke and as Negro troops were dying in the "war to end all wars," Negroes in America were the victims of untold savagery and barbarism. In 1916 and 1917, ninety-two lynchings of Negroes went on record. Wilson had won many Negro voters in 1912 by declaring, "I want to assure them that should I become President of the United States they may count upon me for absolute fair dealing, for everything by which I could assist in advancing the interests of their race in the United States." Not only did Wilson fail to respond to the lynchings and other brutalities perpetrated upon Negroes, but by his own executive order he assisted in relegating the Negro to second-class status by segregating the eating and rest-room facilities of most Negro Federal employees. A group of Negroes who went to the White House to protest the executive order were summarily dismissed because the President found the language of one, Monroe Trotter, to be "insulting."

Even the man whose deeds record him as the Great Emancipator is found wanting in the area of human rights when his speeches are scrutinized. For example, in a Senatorial campaign speech delivered in Chicago in July, 1858, the same speech in which he said "Let us unite as one people throughout this land, until we shall once more stand up declaring that all men are created equal," Lincoln also asserted "God made us separate, we can leave one another alone and do one another much good thereby."

After he became President, Mr. Lincoln, in August 1862, assembled at the White House a group of prominent free Negroes whom he urged to accept and support colonization for the Negro. The President argued: "Your race suffers greatly, many of them by living among us, while ours suffers from your presence. In a word, we suffer on each side. If this is admitted, it affords a reason why we should be separated."

Thus, incongruously, as the pages of history tell of the great men who have championed the causes of the downtrodden, a reassessment of their words and deeds leads us time and again to the conclusion that when such men as the founding fathers spoke of "inalienable rights" and of "all men created equal" they spoke of only some men: white men. One wonders how these men called great shall fare when a larger hand writes a final history. But that is a matter for the historians, the philosophers and the religionists. My purpose, at this time, is but to point out why it has been and is necessary for black people to speak for themselves and to protest over and over against the immoral philosophies and practices which have kept them psychologically enchained though physically emancipated. Further, it is my purpose to comment briefly on the oratorical efforts of a few black voices of protest.

The Negro revolt which had its official beginning with the Martin Luther

King-led Montgomery bus boycott of 1955–1956 and which climaxed in Washington in 1963 has been fomenting for almost three hundred and fifty years. Even before the first slave ships reached America's shores, some jumped overboard, committing suicide, rather than be slaves. Once they reached America, many slaves continued to plot surreptitiously for their freedom. In spite of systematic efforts to isolate slaves from others who spoke their African tribal dialects, in spite of the deliberate breaking up of family groups, in spite of laws which forbade the teaching of reading to slaves, slaves did learn to communicate through linguistic and non-linguistic means. They learned that spirituals and work songs were a safe medium for communicating escape plans and thoughts of protest. Many a night the plantations rang of such lyrical messages as "Steal Away . . . Steal Away to Jesus (translate "Jesus": North), I Ain't Got Long to Stay Here," or "Soon I Will Be Done Wid De Troubles of De World." Other escape signals would be conveyed by "Children Go Where I Send Thee" or "Follow the Drinking Gourd." The slaves even had ways of protesting intolerable conditions right in front of their masters, through songs such as this one which mocks the un-Christian behavior of church-going slave owners: "I Got Shoes, You Got Shoes . . . gonna walk all over God's Heaven," and then the telling line "Everybody talkin' 'bout Heaven ain't goin' there."

Before the American Revolution, slaves in Massachusetts had petitioned their owners for freedom, and after the war Negroes asked state and federal governments to discontinue slave trade and to begin emancipation procedures. Among the black abolitionists who spoke out fervently were Prince Hall, Benjamin Banneker, Absolom Jones and Richard Allen, all of whom had strongly repudiated the practice of slavery before 1800.

By 1830 fifty black abolitionist groups were functioning in such Eastern cities as New Haven, Boston, New York and Philadelphia. These groups included as agents and spokesmen Frederick Douglass, Soujourner Truth, Charles Lennox Redmond, Samuel Ringgold Ward, Williams Wells Brown and Sarah Parker Redmond. Many of the black abolitionists spoke out against slavery in England, Scotland, France, and Germany, as well as in America.

Certainly the most famous of the black abolitionists was the majestic Frederick Douglass, the fugitive slave who joined Phillips and Garrison on the lecture platform and whose own newspaper *The North Star* strongly denounced slavery. A brilliant orator, Douglass vigorously attacked social injustices. Speaking in England against slavery and its masters, Douglass clearly enunciated his feelings:

> I would have condemnation blaze down upon him [the slaveholder] in every direction, till stunned and overwhelmed with shame and confusion, he is compelled to let go the grasp he holds upon the persons of his victims, and restore them to their long-lost rights.

In a speech in 1879, he warned former slaveholders that it would be a mistake for them to govern their future relationships with the Negro "upon presumption that the Negro's cowardice or forebearance has no limit." Forespeaking events to come, Douglass affirmed: "The fever of freedom is already in the Negro's blood."

An aggressive crusader against the Fugitive Slave Law of 1793, much of his energies and purse, before 1865, were devoted to helping Negroes escape bondage via the Underground Railroad. A social and political activist, Douglass advocated political suffrage as the key to Negro advancement, but if need be then bullets might have to be used. "Ballots or Bullets" was his cry.

The most famous Negro spokesman prior to Martin Luther King was certainly Booker T. Washington.

Washington, a former slave, through his own ingenuity and perseverance not only succeeded in acquiring an education for himself and in building Tuskegee, brick by brick, but also in becoming the most revered and respected Negro in America, during the latter quarter of the nineteenth century and the beginning of the twentieth century. So powerful was Booker T., that Presidents Roosevelt and Taft entrusted to him the distribution of Negro patronage. Just a word from him could determine the fate of a Negro college's application to a philanthropic fund.

Principal Washington achieved his position of influence and prestige through his masterfully planned, skillfully executed program of self-uplift for the Negroes and conciliation for the white power structure, North and South.

The apex of Booker T. Washington's career came when the Board of Directors of the Atlanta Exposition invited him to be one of the speakers for the opening of the exposition. On September 18, 1895, Washington stood before the throng, which included the South's most distinguished whites and members of his own race, and enunciated what has come to be known as the "Atlanta Compromise." Imagistically brilliant and forceful in delivery, Washington gave his personal sanction to second-class status for the Negro. He assured his audience: "In all things that are purely social we can be as separate as the fingers, yet one as the hand in all things essential to mutual progress." Denouncing any attempt by Negroes to secure equal treatment as "extremest folly," Washington advised the Negro to gain privileges by struggle and sacrifice rather than by "artificial forcing."

By the time Booker T. finished speaking, many in the audience had tears in their eyes, especially the Negroes. Clark Howell, successor to Henry Grady, told Washington the speech had signalled "the beginning of a moral revolution in America."

Later Washington became the center of severe criticism from Negro intellectuals for his pronouncements that bright September day. His name would become almost synonymous with that of Miss Stowe's "Uncle Tom." But Washington, believing his course was wise and the only course possible at the time, remained stoic.

August Meier's excellent research suggests that Washington did believe in integration, and in fact, secretly gave huge sums of money for legal attacks on segregation, but on the surface used ambiguous language to convince white people of his "sincere" belief in accommodation.

Prior to the era of the modern black revolt, there were, in addition to the spokesmen mentioned, numerous other Negro voices who joined in a resounding chorus of social protest: names like Ida B. Wells, newspaper editor and spokesman; Marcus Garvey, the Jamaican who proposed to lead Negroes home to Africa; and Walter White, long-time Executive Secretary of the N.A.A.C.P. One of that group, A. Phillip Randolph, deserves special attention.

Randolph is president of the Brotherhood of Sleeping Car Porters which he founded in 1925, president of the Negro American Labor Council, and a vice-president of the AFL-CIO. In 1941, Randolph organized a March on Washington to protest discrimination in defense plant hirings, but the march never had to take place. Its threat was sufficient for President Roosevelt to sign an executive order abolishing discriminatory hiring practices and creating the President's Fair Employment Practices Committee. It was A. Phillip Randolph's earlier plan which served as impetus for the 1963 March on Washington. A man of learning, possessed of keen mind and powerful oratory, Randolph's entire adult career has been spent in decrying injustices to the Negro and other laborers. The septuagenarian Randolph, like many other civil rights spokesmen, sees a strong relationship between the current Negro revolt and a world-wide revolt of colored people against oppression. Addressing the United Automobile Workers' Social Justice Award Banquet in 1964, Randolph explained this relationship:

> The world of colored people is in flames. The Civil Rights
> Revolution now shaking the United States is a phase of the
> flames of the revolutions of human rights and nationalism
> sweeping across the world.

Most recently, Randolph has proposed a massive multimillion dollar program of federal assistance to the sick ghettoes of America, which threaten increasingly with each new summer to explode into a black-white bloodbath.

As convenor of the committee which planned the March on Washington, Randolph assembled all of the important Negro leader-spokesmen except two, the late Malcolm "X" and the not yet risen star Stokely Carmichael. Those who did join Randolph as co-chairman were the key Negro spokesmen of the second half of the twentieth century: Roy Wilkins of the N.A.A.C.P., James Farmer of C.O.R.E., John Lewis of S.N.C.C., Whitney Young, Jr., of the National Urban League, and Martin Luther King, Jr., of the Southern Christian Leadership Conference.

Roy Wilkins, Executive Director of the National Association for the Advancement of Colored People, represents the oldest of the American civil rights organizations. The tactics of the N.A.A.C.P. have generally centered around legal attacks on segregation. N.A.A.C.P. lawyers were responsible for such victories as the abolishment of the Oklahoma Grandfather clause and the Supreme Court Decision of 1954. Because its achievements are not heralded by fanfare, the N.A.A.C.P. is looked upon by most Negroes as a conservative group. In some cities, this charge is no doubt true; in others it is not. As in the case of most civil rights organizations, the personality and oratory of the N.A.A.C.P.'s chief spokesman conforms to the organization's style of operation. Thus Wilkins, a journalist by training, behaves like a lawyer: thoughtful, calculating, calm, logical and generally unemotional. With a delivery ranging from dull to mildly inspiring, Wilkins, with a minimum of embellishment, speaks directly to the issues of segregation, education, housing and employment, and he does not hesitate to call the names of politicians who impede Negro progress.

Wilkins, speaking in Jackson, Mississippi in 1962, attacked verbally a Mississippi Senator, a Congressman, and the state's Governor, and he pledged support for student James Meredith and praised the federal government for sending troops to Oxford. A paragraph near the end of the speech is typical of Wilkins and typical of the N.A.A.C.P.:

> We of the NAACP, far from being trouble-makers, are in reality the kind of Americans who founded America. These are the ones who campaigned against injustice and tyranny, who fought for freedom, who wrote the immortal Declaration of Independence and later the Bill of Rights and the rest of our Constitution.
>
> We intend to continue our crusade for freedom, to back up James Meredith with the kind of courage he, himself, has displayed. We intend to support all the other Merediths in Mississippi and elsewhere who seek equality of opportunity in accordance with the laws and the Constitution.

James Farmer, formerly Executive Director of the Congress of Racial Equality, is one of America's finest orators. He has no peer in his ability to respond to difficult and loaded questions with a convincing combination of logic and emotion. On television programs such as "Meet the Press," "Face the Nation," and William Buckley's "Firing Line," Farmer has demonstrated his mastery of repartee and his great skill in calling forth appropriate commonplaces. Farmer is a college graduate and a graduate of divinity school, though never ordained. Possessed of a keen intellect and a powerful baritone voice, Farmer has been one of the most dynamic of the civil rights spokesmen. Like his organization, Farmer is militant and direct-action oriented. He has had many encounters with law officials because of his civil disobedience activities, and he has also several times narrowly escaped death at the hands of Klansmen and their sympathizers. Typical of Farmer's oratory and his social insights is this excerpt from a talk he gave at Colorado State University in 1965:

People ask me why the senseless futile riots of last summer. in that long hot summer. The answer is simple, crystal clear: the unemployed youth who rioted, 16–21, were empty-pocketed, far too hot to be up in the stinking flats, running from rats and chasing cockroaches. They toil in the streets, building up in frustration and anger, feeling they have been expelled from society; feeling as Richard Wright put it in one of his characters from *Native Son*, Bigger Thomas, "Sometimes I feel I'm on the outside of the world looking in through a knothole in the fence." And that I think was the feeling of most of these youngsters, hot—their frustrations joining hands and congealing into a hard mass of counter-hate, they struck out blindly, futilely, senselessly.

It could have been prevented, the tragedy of last summer which damaged all of us, damaged the cause of civil rights, and many people were injured. Some were killed. It could have been prevented if our cities of the North had shown foresight and imagination.

CORE held a meeting with Mayor Wagner last April before the long hot summer, and he said to me what about the long hot summer you've been talking about? I told him that it could be prevented, but I told him I thought there would be a long hot summer because the frustration was so clear that you could see it. It was like a billboard in Times Square. And as the kids got out of school when high school was over they'd be walking the streets mad. I told him I thought it could be prevented if the city did one thing: If it would set up work brigades of unemployed youth from the ghetto. Set the machinery in motion and have it ready to roll as soon as school was out. Put the kids to work. The Mayor said he would take it under advisement. He took it under advisement and no move was made until the riots were over.

As Farmer so clearly explained it, those are the ingredients of a riot, which burst into life because men who have the capacity to remove the sick causes will not listen. And so the black orator goes on, beseeching and screeching but not reaching.

On the first of February in 1960, four young Negro college boys, students at North Carolina A&T College seated themselves at the lunch counter of a Woolworth's ten-cent store and attempted to secure food. At was the usual custom, they were told that they could not be served. Sitting and eating was for whites only. But these young men were caught up in the Zeitgeist and, like Mrs. Rosa Parks whose refusal to give up a seat on a Montgomery bus ignited the contemporary black revolt, their determination to sit-in until served sparked the tremendous Negro student revolt of the 1960's. Students, black and white, North and South, directed and participated in the greatest wave of sit-ins, stand-ins, pray-ins, and wade-ins this nation has ever witnessed. Once the group became formally organized with the assistance of Martin Luther King, Jr., they named themselves the Student Nonviolent Coordinating Committee, better known as S.N.C.C. (Snick). The man who emerged as chairman and spokesman of the group was John Lewis, then a divinity student at Vanderbilt, later expelled for his civil rights activities.

As in the case of many civil rights leaders, the moment of Lewis' oratorical zenith came at the Washington March, and Lewis made the most of it. Typifying the youthful fervor and the impatience of the student movement, Lewis delivered an oration that the New York Herald Tribune described as "a Fire-eating speech that slashed away at the Kennedy administration in merciless fashion." Reminding the crowd that "the party of Kennedy is the party of Eastland," and that "the party of Javits is the party of Goldwater," Lewis beseeched the mass, "where is our party?" In strident, emotional outpourings, he exhorted the crowd to "March through the streets of the South, through the streets of Jackson [Mississippi], through the streets of Danville [Virginia], through the streets of Cambridge [Maryland], and through the streets of Birmingham," and then remembering the teachings of Jesus, Gandhi, and King, Lewis added, "but we will march with the spirit of non-violence, with the spirit of love which we have shown here today." Few speakers so charged the audience, and so moved them to shouts and applause as did John Lewis of Snick. Lewis articulates poorly and frequently delivers too rapidly, but before an audience friendly to his point of view he is electrifying. Within the last year, in a coup that ousted white participants from Snick, Stokely Carmichael took the leadership from Lewis.

The most renowned of the human rights orators in America is the Reverend Martin Luther King, Jr. Dr. King, the fourth generation in a line of Baptist preachers, is president of the Southern Christian Leadership Conference. He was born in Atlanta and has spent most of his life in the South. His career as a civil rights spokesman began with his leadership of the Montgomery bus boycott in 1955–56 and reached its peak in 1963 as he led the March on Washington and delivered its most eloquent address.

Some distinguishing characteristics of his oral discourse are worth examination. First, Dr. King's prose is clear, appropriate, highly stylized, and frequently ornate. Typically, his rhetoric is characterized by striking images, including metaphors, figurative analogies, and Hegelian contrasts; by sententious sayings; by single word modifiers; by repetition; and by variety in sentence structure.

Second, Dr. King is skilled in adapting his style to the needs of the audience and occasion, and in making word choices which contribute to optimum communicator-audience identification and message reception. In his oral persuasion he is one of the few speakers in America, today, who can so adjust linguistic style and themes that audiences of all levels of education, and of diverse castes and religious beliefs, can relate to him.

Third, King uses an admixture of ethical and logical proofs, psychological techniques, and motive appeals to persuade his receivers. In developing his ethical proofs King establishes that he is a scholar, selfless, a man of probity and good will, and an expert on civil rights affairs. His logical forms consist of enthymemes, and arguments from analogy, authority, example, and statistics. His psychological techniques take the form of suggestion, togetherness and bandwagon, repetition, and various elements of communicator-audience identification. The motives to which he has appeals are religion, patriotism, freedom, morality, anger, economic well-being, power, sympathy, preservation of the human race and personal comfort. Characteristically, these proofs, techniques, and appeals are used conjointly and in multiplicate forms.

Fourth, in the case of oral persuasion one of the hallmarks of the King performance is powerful delivery. King's presentation is characterized by a slow, deliberate beginning, by a series of ascending minor climaxes in the body, and by a highly emotional peroration. The force of the delivery is carried mainly by the vocal mechanisms with little assistance from facial or bodily gestures.

Undoubtedly, Martin Luther King, Jr. is *sui generis*. No other Negro has ever so captivated the conscience of Negro and white Americans and of peoples around the world as has the Reverend Dr. King.

In unifying a majority of America's Negroes into a force of direct social action, Dr. King has made a phenomenal achievement. The Negro, historically beset with disfranchisement and its engineered reinforcement, wracked by self-abnegation and hostility toward whites and other Negroes, and frustrated in his attempts to have his grievances redressed, has found in King a longed-for Messiah. When King tells the Negro people they are worthy, that they are no longer afraid, that they must stand up for justice, the people believe him, and the prophecy is fulfilled.

This brief excerpt from an address King gave in 1956 to the N.A.A.C.P. Convention in San Francisco demonstrates how he has attempted to plant the seeds of the self-fulfilling prophecy:

> The Negro's re-evaluation of himself has made him determined to stand up and struggle until the walls of injustice have crumbled. There is a brand new Negro in the South with a new sense of dignity.

As a result of his artistic efforts of social reform, Dr. King has helped the American Negro to gain a higher personal image of himself, and he has inspired the Negro to take non-violent direct-action in behalf of his own social well-being. Moreover, he has given the Negro, through non-violent crusades, a wholesome channel for the ventilation of suppressed rage. Further, King has rallied to the Negro cause white people of good will and moral conscience.

Finally, King has forced the American Church to re-evaluate its earthly mission, and in so doing has been heralded by the nation's religious leaders as America's moral conscience, a man who has given new meaning to the American pulpit.

Two more spokesmen will receive brief attention. These are, of course, Malcolm "X" and Stokely Carmichael, the spokesmen who have most frightened and antagonized white people.

Malcolm was a highly intelligent, dynamic spokesman and leader, capable of starting a riot—which he never did, and capable of aborting one—which he did on several occasions. Best known for his work with the Black Muslims, Malcolm was a sought-after speaker, particularly on the campuses of the great universities, Harvard, Berkeley, Chicago, and others.

In his autobiography Malcolm admits to having lived a life of degradation, committing all manner of criminal acts, short of murder. It was during a long prison sentence that he was converted from his life of crime to the teachings of Elijah Muhammad, leader of the Black Muslims.

Basically, the Muslims advocate black unity and black pride, abstinence from crime and vice, black economic power through the development and utilization of black businesses, respect for black women, isolation from and hostility toward white people, and adherence to the teachings of Elijah Muhammad and the Muslim faith. The Muslims do not subscribe to non-violence and they will return violence if attacked. Malcolm X stated on national television in 1963 that Martin Luther King is a dupe of white people. As Malcolm expressed it:

> *White* people follow King. *White* people pay King.
> *White* people subsidize King. *White* people support King.
> . . . King is the best weapon that the white man, who wants
> to brutalize Negroes, has ever gotten in this country, be-
> cause he is getting up a situation, where, when the white
> man wants to attack Negroes, they can't defend themselves
> because King has put this foolish philosophy out—you're
> not supposed to defend yourself.

A basic assumption of Black Muslin teaching is that white men are inherently evil and will soon be destroyed by Allah. Therefore, the black man, who is one of God's chosen people, can save himself by moving away from the doomed white man. In his earlier speeches Malcolm played many variations on the theme of evil white blue-eyed devils and the necessity for black separatism. Toward the end of his life, however, Malcolm had broken with the Muslims and had formed his own black nationalist group. Further, he had made a lengthy trip throughout the Arab world, climaxed with a pilgrimage to Mecca. As a result of these experiences, Malcolm began to accept the possibility that some white people are worthwhile, and philosophically, he moved a good deal closer toward Martin Luther King's beloved society. In fact, for a brief period, he joined King in the Selma march.

Malcolm died violently at the moment when he showed his greatest promise. A pity twice over—a pity that he never lived in the kind of world where his brilliant mind could develop unfettered by racism and bigotry, and a pity that he was assassinated as he was on the threshhold of self-renewal and community reconciliation.

Last spring and summer, in Lowndes County, Alabama, and in Grenada, Mississippi, another protest voice spoke out stridently, but clearly, and the cry of "Black Power" was heard all over Alabama, Georgia, and Mississippi. And the chant was picked up in Chicago, San Francisco, Detroit, New York, Philadelphia, Atlanta and Washington, D. C. "Black Power," cried the young man from Trinidad, a graduate of the Bronx High School of Science and a graduate of Howard University and Parchman Farm.

Stokely Carmichael, the twenty-six year old head of Snick, has ridden the crest of Black Power to a position of fear and prominence. He is feared by white people because he is radical and fearless. Like Malcolm, he speaks the idiom of urban Negro ghettoes and the dialect of the rural dispossessed. And like Malcolm, he is bold and audacious. Speaking at Berkeley and the University of Chicago and in the streets of Atlanta, Harlem and Watts, Stokely urges Negroes to form political and economic power blocks, buying and voting in ways that will help them to bargain for some of America's affluence.

Mr. Carmichael condemns the war in Viet Nam and describes Negro soldiers as mercenaries who fight to secure for Vietnamese, rights they do not themselves enjoy. Stokely advocates that young Negroes refuse to go to Southeast Asia; that instead, they fight racism and bigotry right here in America. Stokely realizes that he is courting heresy, but he is willing to pay the price. In a sense he is saying what Henry said: "Give me liberty or give me death." Just as Henry saw no in-between, Stokely cannot abide some liberty and some freedom; he must have it all, now.

I cannot predict how many more long hot summers we can endure, before New York and Miami and Oakland and Chicago and all the rest explode and the tanks and the teargas and the machine guns destroy America. But I can say to you that teachers of speech have a special obligation to teach our students the true meaning of democracy and liberty and justice. As long as we delude ourselves that Lincoln and Jefferson and Wilson and Patrick Henry were speaking for the dignity and rights of all men, so much longer do we bury our heads in the sand, hoping the thing will go away, which it will not. You must tell your students the truth so that together we can save our nation by making it the democracy it was intended to be.

In closing I would like to repeat the words of a white Southerner who won the Nobel Prize. William Faulkner, speaking in 1955 to the Southern Historical Association warned us:

> Soon now all of us—not just Southerners nor even just Americans but all people who are still free and want to remain so—are going to have to make a choice. We will

have to choose not between color nor race nor religion nor between East and West either, but simply between being slaves and being free. And we will have to choose completely and for good; the time is already past now when we can choose a little of each, a little of both. We can choose a state of slavedom, and if we are powerful enough to be among the top two or three or ten, we can have a certain amount of license—until someone more powerful rises and has us machine-gunned against a cellar wall. But we cannot choose freedom established on a hierarchy of degrees of freedom, on a caste system of inequality like military rank. We must be free not because we claim freedom but because we practice it. Our freedom must be buttressed by a homogeny equally and unchallengeably free no matter what color they are, so that all the other inimical forces everywhere—systems political or religious or racial or national—will not just respect us because we practice freedom, they will fear us because we do.

Questions for Analysis

1. How does Smith's historical description of the oratory of human rights suggest we consider "rhetoric of accommodation" a legitimate "subject" for the study of persuasive means? Describe the apparent evolution of this rhetoric, for example, from Booker T. Washington through Randolph to King, and from Lincoln through Wilson to John F. Kennedy. How did the rhetorical expression of "accommodation" change radically with the beginning of "the era of the modern black revolt"?

2. Relate to the concept "accommodation" the significance of Smith's term "referents" for rhetorical concepts. With the articles by Simons and Burgess in Part I in mind, compare the referents for "peaceful persuasion" with those for "coercive persuasion," and the referents for "Freedom Now" with those for "Black Power." How have the referents also changed for the concept "accommodation" in the current rhetoric about peace, student rights, and civil disorders? Compare what it meant to "accommodate" each of these protests in 1964 with what it means to "accommodate" them now.

3. Study the extended excerpts from speeches by Farmer and by Lewis. What is "peaceful" about Farmer's appeal? What is "coercive" about Lewis' appeal? What is the relative "psychological proximity" to white listeners of each? Would you say Farmer's speech was "logically correct" but "rhetorically inadequate"? Explain. How does each appeal to different "motivational resources"? What would you judge to be the comparative impact of each?

4. Which characteristics of King's "oral discourse" seem to you to distinguish

him particularly among public speakers of our times? Compare him with Stevenson. Of what special significance was King's talent for so adjusting "linguistic style and theme" that "audiences of all levels of education, and of diverse castes and religious beliefs" could "relate to him"? What does it mean that King's "proofs, techniques, and appeals" were "used conjointly and in multiplicate forms"? Illustrate. How had changing notions about "the rhetoric of accommodation" begun to affect King's ethos at the time of his death? How had he attempted to adjust his rhetorical position?

    5. How did Malcolm X and Carmichael specifically repudiate "the rhetoric of accommodation"? What dimension did they add to consideration of the impact-potential of the rhetoric of our times? Were they substantially different in their use of the "specific enemy" tactic? in their respect for "evaluative words"? Explain. How has Carmichael subsequently changed in these respects? How might the rhetoric of Malcolm X and Carmichael be employed by the teacher of speech interested in elucidating "the rhetoric of accommodation"? Do you think the time will come when they are charged with "accommodation"?

39

A Rhetoric of Over-Reaction

Randall M. Fisher

With the possible exception of those seeking political office, no other group in the nation is more fully engaged in efforts to inform and persuade the electorate than the American business community.[1] Because businessmen make themselves heard in almost every public debate of consequence, the speeches of businessmen deserve the attention of students of rhetoric and public address.

While the persuasive efforts of the country's businessmen are broadly diversified in content and method, those varied efforts have often had a common motivating factor: the critics of business. The nearly common motivator has, in turn, produced a nearly common response. This essay will consider that response. As business speakers have reacted to their critics, they have, in many instances, created a rhetoric of over-reaction.

Business Description of Criticism

For years the businessman has pictured himself as the object of unremitting, unjust, and vicious damnation. An officer of the American Banking Association complained in 1950 because businessmen had been labelled "the worst kind of reactionaries, spending their time trying to turn back the clock to the time of feudalism and serfdom."[2] In 1956, the president of du Pont expressed chagrin at having been called a "monopolist by marriage."[3] In 1961, the executive vice president of the Michigan Chamber of Commerce insisted,

Randall M. Fisher is Associate Professor in Speech, Vanderbilt University.

Reprinted by permission from *Central States Speech Journal*, 17(1966) : 251–256.

[1]The volume of the business persuasive effort is discussed in Randall M. Fisher, "Modern Business Speaking: A Rhetoric of Conventional Wisdom," *Southern Speech Journal*, XXX (Summer, 1965), 326–327.

[2]William E. Knox, "Where in the World Are We Going?" *Vital Speeches*, September 1, 1950, p. 679.

[3]Crawford H. Greenewalt, "Key to Progress—the Uncommon Man," address before the Bureau of Advertising, American Newspaper Publishers Association, New York, April 26, 1956 (Wilmington, Del.: E. I. du Pont de Nemours and Company), p. 5.

"Picturing businessmen as sinister characters has become a studied technique."[4] In 1964, the new president of the Chamber of Commerce of the United States lamented, "I'm getting a little tired of business being a whipping boy for critics who make no contribution to America's greatness anything like that of the men who create jobs."[5] "There is seldom a meeting of a business association," a Sears Roebuck executive observed, "where the problem of public attitudes toward business does not occupy an important place on the agenda."[6] No other single topic so occupies the business speaker as his apparent concern with the "barrage of abuse and misrepresentation . . . so violent and so continuous that the historians may wonder how free enterprise survived at all."[7] The following example, drawn from the narration for a Chamber of Commerce slide presentation, illustrates the completeness of articulated business frustration:

> Here's an ambitious and capable young fellow. He's an accountant and, as you see, is employed by the Smith and Brown Accounting Firm. Now should this young man apply himself, improve his skill, work hard and make a better wage, he will be admired by one and all and praised for his initiative and determination. But look here . . . the young man has accumulated a good name and a few dollars and set himself up in a business of his own. Now . . . if through the same application of skill and hard work, he manages to operate his business at a profit, is he admired? Is he praised? Well, yes he is, by those who understand our profit system. But in some circles . . . he is called a "profiteer," motivated by an evil lust for money, and always at the public expense. Furthermore, should his business grow in its service to more and more people, and should he expand and, finally, incorporate, in order to provide better service —his company's profit, a sure sign of responsiveness to public wants, is looked upon as an admission of guilt.[8]

Criticism, especially in published sources, prompts the businessman's response. He expresses the conviction that unfavorable comment is but rarely tempered or balanced by accounts of the accomplishments of the executive. The modern manager has discovered to his sorrow that he is not the hero that the captain of industry of an earlier day was. The contemporary entrepreneur has learned that Charles E. Wilson received ten times more press notices as a

[4]Harry R. Hall, "The Need for Politically Sophisticated Managers," *Vital Speeches*, November 1, 1961, p. 52.

[5]"New Business Spokesman Urges Positive Approach," *Nation's Business*, May, 1964, p. 42.

[6]James C. Worthy, *Big Business and Free Men* (New York, 1959), p. 8.

[7]Clarence B. Randall, *A Creed for Free Enterprise* (Boston, 1952), pp. 78–79.

[8]"Who Profits from Profits?" (A slide presentation, Washington, D. C., *circa* 1960), p. 2.

cabinet officer than he did as a General Motors executive.[9] The public, an oil company public relations director wrote, has worshipped "slaughterers like Genghis Khan or Napoleon," but has relegated the "economic adventurers and engineers who through their imagination, audacity, and persistence have actually made life better for the common man" to the role of the clown.[10]

As businessmen respond to critics few slights are overlooked. One businessman noted that in 1960 the federal government gave Harvard $18 million in grants, apportioning but $25 thousand to the School of Business. Because "even the divinity school got more than that,"[11] the slight was taken personally.

From the mid-1930's to the present businessmen have consistently noted the supposed enemies and would-be destroyers of the business system. The foe has been identified as "a formidable array of writers, teachers, and politicians";[12] or as "government officials, administrators, academicians, particularly social scientists and 'cause' preachers."[13] One speaker argued that advertising men have been made to suffer "by college professors, by the eggheads, by novelists, by the Federal Trade Commission—and even by their wives."[14] Saboteurs of American business ideals are found among the "crooks, racketeers, gangsters and hoodlums" who occupy union front offices,[15] and among college teachers who live in "selective ignorance" preferring "the security of book covers rather than the competitive authority of a life in the turbulence of the crowd."[16] Primarily, then, business oratory has located the enemy who needs to be met with counterattack in three main categories: politicians, both elective and appointive, who criticize business or promote governmental activity which is considered undesirable; labor leaders and organizers; and intellectuals, who may be teachers, writers, or advisers to politicians.

The business speaker's expressed resentment of critics is heightened by his own avowed certainty that America's salvation lies in careful protection and preservation of the business system as it exists. In 1920, newly elected President Warren G. Harding observed that "this is essentially a business country."[17] He was echoed in 1923 by Calvin Coolidge with, "The business of America is business."[18] In the 1930's, the Chamber of Commerce undertook a gigantic campaign to popularize the slogan, "What Helps Business Helps

[9]Mabel Newcomer, *The Big Business Executive* (New York, 1955), p. 7.

[10]Reynolds Girdler, "Businessman: Hero or Scapegoat?" *Saturday Review*, April 19, 1958, p. 51.

[11]Byron J. Nichols, "Education for Management Leadership," *Vital Speeches*, December 15, 1961, p. 155.

[12]W. Randolph Burgess, "How Much Government?" *ibid.*, August 15, 1950, p. 666.

[13]Carl A. Gray, "Take Off the Blinkers," *ibid.*, June 1, 1950, p. 509.

[14]William H. Burkhard, "Advertising as a Tool," *ibid.*, July 15, 1959, p. 604.

[15]Cola G. Parker, "Union Monopoly Powers," an address (New York: National Association of Manufacturers, 1957), p. 7.

[16]"Mammon's Untouchables," *Dun's Review*, January, 1965, p. 31.

[17]Cited by Richard Hofstadter, *Anti-intellectualism in American Life* (New York, 1963), p. 237.

[18]*Ibid.*

You."[19] The concept has remained an important part of the entrepreneur's oral image of himself to the present. Alfred P. Sloan, chairman of the board of General Motors, offered as indisputable fact in 1953 that "our country is predominantly a business society—as business goes so do we all."[20] Perhaps Sloan's statement came in part as support for another GM executive, Charles E. Wilson, who had told the Senate Armed Forces Committee just three days earlier that he "thought what was good for our country was good for General Motors and vice versa."[21] Wilson had merely observed that he could visualize no conflict of interest between his relationship to General Motors and decisions he might have to make as Secretary of Defense simply because the interests of the two institutions involved were identical. Neither Wilson nor a great many other businessmen could understand why the casual reply to a question created a journalistic storm. Businessmen had always asserted the truth of such a point of view and had evidently assumed everyone else agreed to it.

A mainstay of the American businessman's rhetorical self-evaluation is pride of accomplishment. Business has built America's homes and cities, provided it with transportation, contributed mightily to winning its wars, given it luxuries as well as necessities. Because business has done these things, its rhetoric insists, criticism of the mechanics of the system, criticism of the decisions of businessmen, criticism of a corporation's public relations efforts is criticism of the American standard of living, of the American way of life.

A Ford Motor Company spokesman replied in this vein to the suggestion that the automobile industry had unnecessarily imposed excessively luxurious automobile features on the helpless public:

> What all the criticism came down to was that a bunch of arrogant bastards sit out here in Detroit and if they should decide to put pyramids on tops of cars, the public would goddam well have to take it. The Ford Motor Company was especially sensitive because we spend a small fortune on consumer research—much more than on public relations.[22]

In other words, according to the speaker, Ford had been criticized for doing just what the public had wanted done. The company had provided good big cars.

Former U.S. Steel president and board chairman, Benjamin Fairless, complained that critics within government had treated his company the same way. They had censured the corporation for doing what had been asked of it, in this instance, boosting production. After World War II, Fairless claimed, the government

> denounced us because we could not produce instantly all

[19]Fred DeArmond, "The Creed of a Conservative," *The Freeman*, September, 1956, p. 49.

[20]Alfred P. Sloan, Jr., " 'Road to Serfdom' Has Been Blocked," *Vital Speeches*, March 1, 1953, p. 297.

[21]United States Congress, Senate, Committee on Armed Forces, *Nominations*, Hearings, 83rd Congress, 1st Session, January 15–16, 1953 (Washington, D. C., 1953), p. 26.

[22]Cited by Irwin Ross, *The Image Merchants* (Garden City, N. Y., 1959), p. 175.

> the steel that was needed to meet the pent-up demands of a
> world that had been starving for civilian goods for four
> long years. It urged us to expand our plants and facilities.
> And we did so.
>
> Today, this . . . is forgotten, but the Government con-
> tinues to attack us. It now appears that we are too big,
> and that we have been all the time.[23]

Apparently no one has doubted Fairless' sincerity. The criticism was beyond
his comprehension. Many attacks on business practices seem, somehow, more
than incomprehensible; they are inconceivable when one argues, as did advertising executive Ross Roy, "Business produces everything—all the necessities
and luxuries of life . . ."[24] John Chamberlain summarized the contemporary
business belief in his 1963 history of business, "The rich have got richer, the
poor have got richer, too—and as for the middle class, it bids fair to include
practically everybody."[25]

Criticism of businessmen and business practice may not be as all-en-
compassing or as severe or as unfounded as corporate speakers indicate; the
role of the business system within American economic and social structures
may not be exactly as management pictures it; but, nearly the whole of a massive business persuasive effort has nonetheless been influenced by business
reaction to criticism. Given their assumptions about the role of the business
system, businessmen have found it easy to look upon critics as enemies rather
than as advocates with arguments deserving of careful refutation. The principal loss has been to public debate processes. Reaction has, in many instances,
created a rhetoric of over-reaction.

Private Views and Public Statements

One phenomenon of over-reaction is the business speaker who may not
say in public what he really means. A variety of evidence suggests caution in
accepting the speeches of many businessmen at face value. As one writer asserted: "Considerable care must be exercised in separating what Businessmen
say they want from what they really want, and in determining what they want
most."[26] In 1956, *Time* claimed that

> though some businessmen still argue publicly that the
> Federal Government should stop regulating business, the

[23]United States Congress, House, Committee on the Judiciary, *Study of Monopoly
Power*, Part 4A, Hearings before Subcommittee on Study of Monopoly Power, 81st Congress, 2d Session, April 17–May 11, 1950 (Washington, D.C., 1950), p. 468.

[24]Ross Roy, "What Businessmen Can Do to Relieve the Tax Burden," *Vital Speeches*,
March 15, 1957, p. 341.

[25]John Chamberlain, *The Enterprising Americans: A Business History of the United
States* (New York, 1963), p. 244.

[26]Edmund K. Faltermayer, "What Business Wants From Lyndon Johnson," *Fortune*,
February, 1965, p. 122.

majority agree the Government intervention is preferable to the economy of the jungle.[27]

Business historian Arthur H. Cole wrote in 1959, "Acquiescing in governmental 'interference' has become a normal element in the role of the American entrepreneur."[28] These observations of business attitude toward government have much support as valid descriptions of the real feelings of a considerable segment of the business community, but those same descriptions are not reflected in the rhetoric of American business in its most widely disseminated forms. That rhetoric does not acquiesce in governmental interference. The "directives, rules, regulations, agencies, bureaus, departments and branches" of government are rarely categorized as good or bad in managerial accounts; they *all* have evil "octopus-like tentacles extending into every phase of business management."[29] For decades, "government controllism"[30] has been consistently, blanketly, and publicly resisted by the great body of corporate persuasion reaching the public.[31]

The difference between private views and public statements on such matters as the role of the federal government can be explained in part by the possibility that the businessman is not sure what he really stands for. As *Business Week* explained, on one side of his mind the businessman "believes in a pure form of free enterprise, in which 'each man should be free to go wherever his selfish instincts take him.' "[32] However,

> On the other side of his brain, the businessman despises unrestrained competition, free-floating prices, and the discipline of the market. . . . He regards economists who actually believe businessmen can or should passively submit to the "invisible hand" as naive.[33]

Another partial explanation for the apparent differences between private views and public arguments may lie in the fact that a few business organizations, corporations, and individuals tend to speak for the whole. "Whatever the diversity of belief among businessmen," Galbraith noted,

> it is almost certainly greater than among those who speak for businessmen. The individual businessman is also much more flexible in his views and much more pragmatic in his judgments than his spokesmen.[34]

[27]"The New Conservatism," *Time*, November 26, 1956, p. 99.

[28]Arthur H. Cole, *Business Enterprise in Its Social Setting* (Cambridge, Mass., 1959), p. 95.

[29]Harry R. Hall, "The Need for Politically Sophisticated Managers," *Vital Speeches*, November 1, 1961, p. 52.

[30]Arch N. Booth, "Making Self Government Work," *ibid.*, July 15, 1963, p. 606.

[31]Business attitudes toward government are discussed in Randall M. Fisher, "The Persuasive Efforts of American Businessmen at Mid-Century," unpubl. diss. (University of Missouri, 1964), pp. 197–221.

[32]"The Split in the Businessman's Mind," *Business Week*, June 6, 1964, p. 164.

[33]*Ibid.*

[34]John Kenneth Galbraith, "The Businessman as Philosopher," *Perspectives, USA*, XIII (1955), 58.

Business failure to record its flexible judgments in public speeches may have many causes, but one of the most important is revealed by those speeches themselves: some businessmen have, and others seem to have, a persecution complex that prevents them from viewing critics as honorable and worthy opponents. Instead, those who have differing opinions are enemies to be dealt with rather than reasoned with, as foes from whom the public must be protected. The result has often been a rhetoric of over-reaction, a rhetoric which interprets the slightest deviation from long-standing business argument as weakness in the face of the enemy, a rhetoric which repeats that traditional argument whether it is believed or not.

Rhetorical Results of Reaction

Over-reaction has other consequences, all damaging to public consideration of issues.

Over-reaction often leads to over-statement. A du Pont public relations director claimed that the anti-trust division of the Justice Department, the Securities Exchange Commission, the Federal Trade Commission, and high income taxes were all created for the single and express purpose of punishing business.[35]

Over-reaction often leads to uncertainty. Even businessmen themselves are occasionally confused by the speeches of their peers, as illustrated by the statement of Robert Schultz, director of statistical analysis for the Union Bag-Camp Paper Corporation:

> . . . one feels as if he is the only sane person in a lunatic asylum. . . . I attended a meeting on the business outlook where various leading industrialists discussed the prospects for their particular industries. Invariably, each man said in effect, "Things in my industry are pretty bad. Prices are low because there is too much capacity, and we need to get our prices up so that we can make more profits in order to pay for more capacity expansion." And as each industrialist concluded this preposterous threnody of circular illogic, he was warmly applauded by his listeners. . . .[36]

Reaction may lead to censorship. A *Saturday Review* writer claims that the "business elite in many communities has been gagged on important issues."[37]

Economist-journalist Hobart Rowen has argued that the "built-in prejudices" of businessmen prevented meaningful debate during the Kennedy

[35]Glenn Perry, "The Responsibility of the Businessman," a speech before the Greater New Brunswick, N. J., Chamber of Commerce, March 15, 1960 (Wilmington, Del.: E. I. du Pont de Nemours and Company), p. 3.

[36]Cited by John R. Bunting, "The Disturbing Economics of Affluence," *Dun's Review*, April, 1964, p. 41.

[37]Peter Bar, "Corporate Censorship," *Saturday Review*, June 13, 1964, p. 57.

administration on other than outmoded methods of dealing with unemployment and economic growth. Against the standard of inflexible business attitude, Rowen added, "Mr. Kennedy could never have achieved rapport with business unless he abdicated all responsibility and de-regulated everything."[38]

As banker John R. Bunting observed, "The businessman does not admit it openly, but he is aware of the broad changes that have taken place in the American economy."[39] Refusal to "admit . . . openly" and to bring to the American voters often expert views on important issues must hamper the public debate process, the tool of rational decision-making. Such refusal may have many causes but one is certainly the rhetorical view of many businessmen—a view which evaluates themselves as persecuted individuals and their corporations as vilified institutions. The businessman's view of his critics as ignorant, misled, or evil adversaries has colored and motivated the great outpouring of industrial persuasion of recent years. The businessman's frame of reference has too often replaced debate with oratorical warfare. The businessman's rhetoric is a rhetoric of over-reaction.

Questions for Analysis

1. Relate the following thesis from Wallace's study, in Part III, on the substance of rhetoric to the rhetoric of business: "evaluative words" associated with "desirability" may be attributed to "self-image." How does the "self-image" of business contrast rhetorically with its "public image"? Why is the "self-image" particularly vulnerable to assault by the rhetoric of our times? Characterize the rhetorical approach of business to defense of this "self-image."

2. What "evaluative words" are relevant to business images? How do these words become the actual substance of business rhetoric? How do they constitute "value-judgments" in the ethical process of justification? Is this an example of the fusion of rhetorical and ethical concerns necessary to Wallace's analysis of the substance of rhetoric? Explain.

3. How has business rhetorically justified its values as those of "the American way of life"? How does this justification impinge upon the motives of the critics of business? Is this a rhetorical tactic of today? What other rhetoric of our times is based on identification with "the American way of life"? May "the American way of life" be considered one of the "good reasons" Wallace claims as the substance of rhetoric? Explain.

4. How do you account for the discrepancy Fisher suggests between "private views and public statements" in the rhetoric of business? What does this suggest

[38]Hobart Rowen, *The Free Enterprisers: Kennedy, Johnson and the Business Establishment* (New York, 1964), p. 293.
[39]John R. Bunting, "What's Ahead for Business?" *Atlantic*, June, 1964, p. 75.

are the problems of rhetorical defense of image? In what other rhetorical positions today may such discrepancies exist? How consistent is the perpetuation of these discrepancies with the contemporary regard for "good reasons" as the substance of rhetoric? Do these discrepancies preclude any relevance for public debate on values? Explain.

5. What is your understanding of Fisher's distinction between "debate" and "oratorical warfare"? Cite other examples of "oratorical warfare" today. How might debate be improved by understanding and acceptance of Wallace's theory of "good reasons"? Make specific applications of this theory to the rhetoric of business. By what concessions might the businessman lend objectivity and the opportunity for direct and personal "public statements" to the debate?

40

The Rhetoric of Academic Protest

Howard H. Martin

The academic protest against United States policy in Viet Nam may not be over, but it has come far enough to permit speculation about the nature and effects of "the rhetoric of the faculty." In the year between March 14, 1965, when several faculty members of the University of Michigan announced their intention to call off their classes to protest American bombing raids on North Viet Nam, until March 25, 1966, when two professors of the University addressed a half-hearted group of prospective student demonstrators on the steps of the library, the faculty-led movement to force a change in national policy in southeast Asia seemed to have completed a cycle. The critical gestures of a few individuals had brought together like-minded people who forged a large and efficient organization that reached, finally, across the nation. The group had staged dozens of campus "teach-ins" following the initial one at Michigan. The protestors had sought to initiate conversations with Congressional and Administration leaders, and, failing that, had arranged for several national confrontations between the Administration policy-makers and faculty opponents. They had seen most of their efforts ignored or frustrated by Administration supporters. They had seen forces in Viet Nam multiplied many times. They had seen public opinion strongly crystallized against them, and, apparently convinced that change could not be achieved at present by any available means, had lapsed into silence.

The movement's progress provokes two questions: (1) To what extent was this protest a "rhetorical movement," one that relied on the effects of persuasive talk, and (2) how much of the success or failure of the movement can be laid to the rhetorical sophistication and skill of the faculty people who took part?

The first question—to what extent was this protest a rhetorical movement —is not as easy to answer as it might appear. Of course, the movement was characterized by a good deal of talk, both public and private, but one may ask

Howard H. Martin is Associate Professor of Speech, The University of Michigan. Reprinted by permission from *Central States Speech Journal*, 17(1966) :244–250.

whether this talk was conceived of as an instrument to change the opinions of those in a position to act. Did the faculty who engaged in talk believe that their talk could bring about changes in opinions or behavior? Or, was the talk only part of a grander gesture of opposition, a declaration that "We are not reconciled!"? Was the talk intended to be persuasive or coercive? Was it to be an argument or a threat? The answer lies in an examination of the progress of the movement.

Gathering the Like-Minded

Two kinds of events that occurred in February, 1965, on the Michigan campus precipitated the protest movement. One was the publication of several individual expressions of discontent. A professor of sociology wrote a letter to the *Michigan Daily*, the campus newspaper, criticizing American policies in Viet Nam. A professor of public health announced that he would not pay his income tax in protest over raids in the north. A student collected medical supplies for the wounded in South Viet Nam. The second type of event reflected a search for information. A Harvard historian was invited to campus to lecture on Viet Nam, and a few days later a political science professor discussed the circumstances that had brought the United States to its current status in Viet Nam. These events, largely rhetorical in character, produced a first major stage in the academic protest movement—*the gathering of the like-minded*.

As in most social movements, the gathering of the like-minded occurred partly by accident. At Michigan, leaders emerged from two departments, sociology and psychology. Fifteen of 22 spokesmen came from these two departments. Three other departments produced two each—physics, anthropology, and philosophy.[1] At other universities, leadership came from faculties of mathematics, chemistry, and other departments, which raises doubt that the protest had professional relevance for members of certain departments. When questioned about the absence of political scientists in the movement—a fact sometimes remarked—one of the leaders speculated, "Perhaps they felt—and they may have been right—that they had the ear of some Administration people in Washington, while some of us felt we did not." He pointed to their professional reliance upon negotiation and compromise: "They're accustomed to approaching problems cautiously, and going through channels."[2]

That most of the like-minded people who got together on March 14, 1965, to announce a moratorium on classes had been active in civil rights activities

---

[1]Thomas Conlon, head of the government's three-man "truth team" that visited several midwestern universities not including Michigan, blamed "extremist" professors from departments of psychology, the exact sciences, and literature. *The New York Times*, May 8, 1965.

[2]The fact that no members of the speech department were involved in the protest, which I gather was true of other campuses, may be taken—depending on one's view—as a shameful desertion of professional responsibility or as a laudable and predictable unwillingness to take part in poorly conceived rhetorical enterprises.

is significant. In fact, the thinking of these civil-rights oriented faculty may account for certain unrhetorical aspects of the Viet Nam protest. The civil rights tactics of public demonstration and acts of civil disobedience, appropriate where talk has not worked, seem to have been first considered the proper means of bringing about change in national policy in Viet Nam. The moratorium on classes was such a tactic. It was not adopted, of course; the group, under some pressure from the state legislature and faculty colleagues otherwise sympathetic with the protest, abandoned the moratorium in favor of an all-night teach-in, which had more obvious rhetorical intentions.

Besides the accidental gathering of like-minded people within departments and within buildings, others were brought into the movement by concerted effort. Letters of criticism published in the *Michigan Daily* alerted others to those who shared their views. By March 24, the day of the teach-in, the number of faculty sponsors had grown to at least the 108 whose names were listed in a full-page newspaper advertisement. Moreover, several faculty participants spoke to students in 35 fraternity and sorority houses to gain support for the teach-in.[3] At this stage, the movement was clearly rhetorical; it used talk aimed at bringing together the like-minded and reinforcing their shared convictions about United States Viet Nam policy. The teach-in itself seems to have been conceived of as an effort at reinforcing the opinions of those who might attend, and thereby extending the dimensions of dissent. One leader declared that its purpose was "to demonstrate the bankruptcy of Viet Nam policy," and little attention was paid to alternative views. The affair was punctuated at midnight by a "rally" at which two faculty orators sought to whip up enthusiasm for sharp criticism of government policies. In short, insofar as the faculty protest sought to build support among "believers" and to reinforce their convictions, the movement was clearly a rhetorical one.

Addressing the Power Agents

But what about the second major stage of the movement—*the address to the power agents?* The protestors seem to have made a series of successive assumptions about the dispositions of the power agents:[4] (1) The power agents agree with us and can be encouraged to act if they know our concern. (2) The power agents are on the fence and are looking for indications of public senti-

---

[3]Several leaders of the protest identified faculty participants as either "organizers" or "orators." The organizers, who spoke to many small groups to gain support, wrote letters to colleagues and the press, and helped plan the larger efforts, were continually identified with the movement. The orators, three or four professors sympathetic with the movement whose glamour and drawing power with students recommended them as rally keynoters, spoke once or twice and then went about their other business.

[4]Expediency led the protestors to address the second-string power agents—Congressmen and Administrative people—instead of the President, the Secretary of State, and their immediate advisors.

ment which, if strongly in favor of a certain policy, will convince the leaders and induce them to act. (3) The power agents disagree with us but can be converted if they see our protest as a significant threat to their tenure.

Operating on the first assumption shortly after the Michigan teach-in, a delegation of faculty members travelled to Washington to establish communication with Congressmen, Senators, and staff people in the Vice President's office. Although the group was well received and encountered little disagreement from legislators, the result of the excursion was general disappointment. One of the delegates said that the group felt it had friends among the "Kennedy people" in Washington who had not yet become alienated from the Johnson administration, and that these people would be amenable to talk. But the first assumption proved false; "friends" in Washington *were* willing to talk but were unwilling to act.

Congressmen put off the delegation with the excuses that they had other irons in the fire, that they could not afford a battle with the President on foreign policy, or that foreign policy was simply not Congress's business. Delegates came home from the Washington interviews with a sense of the impossibility of influencing foreign policy from the "inside," or rousing any Congressional action. A case in point: efforts to encourage the Senate to hold public hearings on Viet Nam at that time were unsuccessful. Private talk, it was generally agreed, could not work. Henceforth the group's energies were to be concentrated on widely publicized manifestations of dissent. This new tactic was based on the second and third assumptions above, that the power agents were either undecided or unsympathetic but would be induced to act favorably when they saw the strength of the opposition.

The first of these public manifestations of dissent was the national teach-in of May 15. Supporters hoped to bring about a public confrontation between the Administration and those who opposed its war policies. If the chance for a productive dialogue between the defenders and antagonists of Administration policy had passed, protestors hoped at least that the juxtaposition of the two views would publicly expose the dangers of Administration views. The people would be enabled to see the contradictions in national policy, and public opinion would be brought to bear on the policy-makers. However, the Administration recognized what the faculty people did not—that no serious disaffection from conduct of the Viet Nam war existed—and refused to expose their most prestigious defenders. Indeed, the indefiniteness of McGeorge Bundy's responses to invitations to defend Administration action, and his last-minute withdrawal from the debates—as much as his brusque dismissal of the academic protest—reflected the government's assurance of popular support and exposed the weakness of the academic protest. It is not at all clear that anything said at the national teach-in either converted Administration supporters or attracted substantial additional support from the like-minded.[5] A later debate

[5]Max Frankel expressed a similar opinion in *The New York Times*, May 17, 1965.

between Bundy and faculty critics on national television, June 21, fulfilled Bundy's promise to respond. But this was a more amiable exchange than might have occurred a month earlier, and the occasion was nowhere near as well-publicized or dramatic as the national teach-in.

Two other local events displayed the altered tactics of the faculty protestors. The first was a successful effort to have the Ann Arbor Democratic Club adopt a resolution condemning the conduct of the war in Viet Nam. All of the faculty leaders of the movement are members of the Democratic party, and the fact that most were active in local party councils may account for the accomplishment of this public expression of dissent.[6] The second local event designed as a public manifestation of dissent was the so-called International Conference on Alternative Perspectives on Viet Nam held in Ann Arbor on September 14–18, 1965. The presence of playwright Arthur Miller and of Emil Mazey, secretary-treasurer of the UAW, produced some national attention, but the greatest impact was local and seems to have been the reinforcement of the convictions of those already convinced.

Two subsequent events of national scope seem to have been almost wholly coercive in intent. These were the International Days of Protest held in mid-October of 1965, and again on March 25, 1966. The first event was marked in Ann Arbor by scheduled acts of civil disobedience: a number of students and junior faculty sat-in at the offices of the Selective Service Administration. Considerable national publicity attended these coercive acts and their consequences —the arrest of students, their conviction for trespassing, subsequent cancellation of student deferments, appeals, and in some cases, re-classification in the 2–S category. Nothing so rash was attempted on the recent days of protest, which passed without local disturbance. As a result, the activities could hardly be called a significant manifestation of dissent. Moreover, almost no faculty participated. Two young faculty members spoke to a student group before they moved to picket the draft board, but they faced a small and unresponsive crowd that seemed merely to be going through the motions.

In this stage of the movement—the address to the power agents—faculty activity seemed much less rhetorical than coercive. After having been rebuffed in their attempts to open discussions in Washington with Congressmen and Administration leaders, the faculty group seems to have shifted strategy. If talk cannot work, they reasoned, we must flex our muscles and display our strength in public manifestations of dissent. The national teach-in, the Bundy debate, the International Days of Protest all seem to have been designed more to threaten non-support than to encourage productive talk. Having relied upon rhetorical means to gather the like-minded, the faculty protest movement abandoned rhetorical means in addressing the power agents and relied instead upon other techniques to bring about coercion.

[6]The passage of the resolution was hardly an unqualified success; it alienated a substantial opposing minority and split the local Democratic party. Recent reconfirmation of that resolution in March, 1966, has deepened the schism.

How Successful?

How successful were these faculty efforts, and how much of the success or
failure of the movement can be laid to the rhetorical sophistication and skill
of the faculty people who took part? That was the second question proposed
for this discussion.

Because a proposal to conduct a student referendum in connection with
the fall student government elections was defeated, no dependable measure has
been made of the degree of student opposition to the war in Viet Nam before
and after the faculty efforts to stir the student conscience on the issue. My
impression is that never more than a minority, perhaps a substantial minority,
joined in opposition to national policy. And, because student opposition had
been organized before the faculty began to talk about Viet Nam, attributing
what opposition existed to faculty talk might be unjustified. Two factors may
have influenced the effectiveness of faculty rhetoric among students. The first
was the information situation. The little "hard" information available on
several crucial issues seemed confusing, contradictory, and indecisive. Did we
enjoy substantial popular support among the Vietnamese people? Were the
Viet Cong native dissenters, rebels, or hostile foreign invaders? Would our
withdrawal from Viet Nam mean Communist control of South Viet Nam?
Would the ascendancy of the Communists in Viet Nam inevitably lead to Communist—or Chinese Communist—domination of all southeast Asia? Because
evidence on these questions was contradictory and incapable of being tested
for reliability by listeners, conviction could be based on little more than the
ethos of the advocates. Because professors are presumed to enjoy fairly high
prestige with their students, their effectiveness as advocates might have been
greater on campus than off. Apparently, the faculty succeeded in rallying
like-minded students and teachers on the campus and in reinforcing their convictions, but it is not clear that they were strikingly successful in *converting*
large numbers of students to their cause.

The fact that United States policy in Viet Nam moved in a direction
opposite that advocated by faculty critics is one reason for considering the
movement a failure. When the academic protest began, 23,300 United States
troops were in Viet Nam. The troop build-up that began in early May, 1965,
had raised our troops to 80,000 by July, to 130,000 by September, to 165,000
by November, and to 220,000 by April, 1966.[7] That Congressmen were apathetic or otherwise unwilling to stir themselves to press for a re-examination of
the war was unfortunate, but was not due to the rhetorical ineptness of the
faculty critics. Moreover, that they faced canny and powerful opponents in the
Administration policy-makers is no criticism of the professors. But there may

[7]From figures in "Vietnam: A Debate," *Saturday Review*, December 18, 1965, p. 20.

have been some tactical defects in the rhetorical strategy of the academic protest movement. First, the protestors may have seriously misjudged the *ethos* of
the University in the area of foreign policy-making. Having seen the warm
reception Washington had given to economists, physicists, and other technical
specialists from academia, the Viet Nam protestors seem to have assumed their
views would be welcomed with the respect tendered those of Gardner Ackley,
John Galbraith, and Edward Teller. But Washington dismissed the professors
as uninformed, refused to recognize that they had any special competence to
speak on military and political commitments in southeast Asia.

With the general public, the *ethos* of the University seemed no higher.
And, rather than seeking to strengthen their prestige before recommending
unpopular proposals or modifying their aims to fit their prestige, the professors
proposed what seemed to most people an impossible reversal of policy in Viet
Nam. The polls seem to show that, while a great many people wished we were
not fighting in Viet Nam and would like to have seen the war brought to an
end, few indeed accepted the radical alternative—cessation of fighting and
withdrawal of United States troops—proposed by the academic protestors.

By failing either to recognize the disposition of listeners toward their
proposals or to adjust their recommendations to the inclinations of most of
their audience, the faculty protestors set themselves up for rejection.[8] One of
the leaders of the movement offered the opinion that Administration spokesmen
withdrew from discussions with faculty critics "because they were getting
clobbered right and left." Another interpretation is possible: when the Administration observed no general dissatisfaction with its war policy, it felt no need
to defend itself and was unwilling to dignify the critics by sending its "big
guns."

Not only did the protestors misjudge their *ethos* with the Washington
policy-makers and the general public, but they seemed on occasion bent on
undermining what prestige they might have enjoyed. Their language was often
the language of unabashed partisans. One campus orator, for example, spoke
at length about the seven "myths" on which Viet Nam policy was based in
highly provocative and depreciatory language, the language of the true believer
rather than that of the patient inquirer. Another was quoted in the *Daily* as
having used these words—and the report must have been substantially accurate
for no denials or retractions appeared—the United States government "is a
virulent military dictatorship, a self-perpetuating, unstoppable juggernaut

---

[8]The Quayle Poll, summarized by Stewart Alsop in "What the People Think," *Saturday
Evening Post*, October 23, 1965, p. 27, showed 77 per cent approving the President's conduct
of the war, 65 per cent declaring that the United States must stay in Viet Nam, only 14 per
cent favoring an end to bombings of the North, and 17 per cent favoring immediate withdrawal from the war; 59 per cent were willing to bomb Hanoi and take whatever steps
necessary to end the war. The Louis Harris Poll, reported by Richard Rovere in *The New
Yorker*, December 18, 1965, p. 191, showed 71 per cent affirming that we should "keep on
fighting until we can negotiate on our own terms." Only 4 per cent were for "unconditional
withdrawal," and 13 per cent were ready to "stop now and negotiate."

which dictates U.S. foreign policy."[9] Such extravagances were infrequent, but they were given widest publicity, no doubt with unfortunate results. By seeming to abandon the task of patient inquiry in order to assume the role of agitators, the University critics further weakened the prestige they may have enjoyed with students and the general public.

Maybe their modest prestige in the realm of foreign policy did not ultimately harm their cause. One of the leaders of the local movement said that he felt the teach-ins had paved the way for the Fulbright committee hearings, suggesting that the academic protest developed issues which—according to studies which have shown that listeners, after a few weeks, forget the high or low prestige of the original source—at last became dissociated from their advocates and were given consideration on their merits. One might then conclude that the faculty protest raised several pertinent questions—Can our conduct of the war be defended on moral grounds? Have we any legitimate national interests in Viet Nam? Is there any chance at all that we can achieve our objectives there?—questions that are being considered at this moment and are being considered at all because they were raised by academic critics. From that perspective, the movement might be judged a "success." On the other hand, since no change in our conduct of the war is imminent, indeed, even likely, such a conclusion is uneasy at best. One of the professors who led the Michigan movement confessed that he did not look for change unless some new internal crisis in Viet Nam such as the collapse of the Ky government might force a serious reappraisal of our position. Such a view implies that the "rhetoric of the faculty" has moved the Administration no closer to a reversal of national policy, and suggests that the matter is now beyond the reach of any rhetoric, however skilful.

Questions for Analysis

1. How would you characterize today the ethos of the academic community with the national government and with the general public? Cite significant changes in ethos with both since the Kennedy administration and the advent of student protest. Assess the present chances for significant impact by the rhetoric of academic protest. Explain why you think this rhetoric can "bring about changes in opinion or behavior," or is bound to be "only part of a grander gesture of opposition."

2. What was specifically rhetorical about "the gathering of the like-minded"? How was the persuasive intent similar to that early in the "New Left" movement? Is it fair to say that participants in the Michigan movement attempted for Viet Nam

[9] *Michigan Daily*, September 18, 1965.

rhetoric what participants of the "New Left" attempted for Cold War rhetoric? Explain.

3. How sharply was the parallel with the "New Left" movement sustained in the Michigan movement's "address to the power agents"? How valid is the faith reflected in this action about the capacity of rhetoric to direct change? Do you think government response to the protestors' actions justified a change from tactics essentially rhetorical to those essentially coercive? Explain. Compare your explanation with Haiman's defense of "the rhetoric of the streets." How by comparison to the "New Left" did the Michigan movement suffer for want of civil rights and peace movements with which to unite? Generalize about the importance of inter-movement support for individual protest movements.

4. Describe the importance of the "information situation" to campus protest movements today. What questions of possible consequences tantamount to those facing the Michigan faculty now confront advocates of institutional reform? How does the fact that available evidence is "contradictory and incapable of being tested for reliability by listeners" handicap student protests? How does the current ethos of student activists accentuate the handicap? Assuming these problems, why may protestors ultimately resort to "the language of unabashed partisans," "the language of the true believer rather than that of the patient inquirer"?

5. With reference to McLaughlin's article in Part II, what might be a speech department's contribution in a circumstance like the Michigan movement? How might "social cooperation" and "social control" have been appropriate? Was an operative guide to the extent of "free speech" necessary? Apply to the Michigan movement the outline for the "communication continuum" proposed by McLaughlin. Are you prepared now to define to your satisfaction the point, if you think it exists at all, at which peaceful persuasion legitimately gives way to coervice persuasion? Explain the influence of various articles throughout this book on your conclusion.

41

The All-Purpose Political Speech, 1968

William Safire

Political argot, in its refined form, permits some candidates to take firm stands on all sides of every issue. If he applies his skill, the man who deeply understands the language of politics can earn the supreme accolade: "Nobody can quarrel with that." Here is the unassailable, meaningful, knowledgeable speech of 1968, lavishly footnoted to show derivations.

My friends:

In this campaign, the burning questions and paramount issues cannot be straddled by me-tooers and yes-butters who would be all things to all men.[1]

We will talk sense to the American people in this grassroots crusade to throw the rascals out—the hacks, hangers-on, henchmen and hatchetmen, the wardheelers and wheelhorses, the gophers[2] and snollygosters[3] who feed at the public trough.

At the outset, let me make clear that I will not join a cabal of any stop movements, dump movements, power-grabs or whispering campaigns; at the same time, I will not be steamrollered, smoke-screened or subjected to gag rule by any bloc of sachems, satraps, high mucky mucks[4], solons or kingmakers

William Safire is author of *The New Language of Politics: An Anecdotal Dictionary of Catchwords, Slogans and Political Usage* (New York, Random House, 1968). In the Nixon Administration he is a member of the White House staff.

The New York Times Magazine, June 9, 1968, pp. 39, 42, 47, 49, 52. © 1968 by the New York Times Company. Reprinted by permission.

[1]*All things to all men:* now two-facedness, but originally the strategy of the Apostle Paul, quoted in the Bible as, "I am made all things to all men, that I might by all means save some."

[2]*Gopher:* a political volunteer willing to "go for" coffee and assume other menial tasks.

[3]*Snollygoster:* according to Harry Truman, who reactivated this Civil War epithet, "a man born out of wedlock."

[4]*High mucky mucks:* big shots; from Chinook Indian jargon, *hiu* (plenty) *muck-a-muck* (food); hence, one who has plenty to eat, a powerful chieftain. Powwows of political party elders also include "sachems" and "mugwumps," both American Indian words, though the latter has gained a pejorative connotation, as an insurgent who straddles a fence with "his mug on one side and his wump on the other."

power-brokering their handpicked dark horses[5] in smokefilled rooms, nor stampeded at a rigged convention by gallery-packing or a voice from the sewer.[6]

I am neither running like a dry creek nor running for the exercise; in this crunch, I am running scared, like a singed cat, despite my above-politics role as noncandidate.

Mine shall be a whirlwind[7], whistle-stopping[8], flat-out campaign; on the hustings I shall eschew the front porch; I am hell-bent for election and throw my hat in the ring to joyfully stump the rubber-chicken circuit.

Though I am a regular and against insurgents, I am for reform; while I would like to see a new face at the top of the ticket, I will not turn my back on an old pro willing to press the flesh and lay on the hands.

To the angry young men, I say: I was once a Young Turk[9] myself and reject the prophets of gloom and doom who make up the standpatters and mossbacks of the Old Guard. However, mavericks and mugwumps only splinter our power bases, and though I may decide to go fishing, I frown on going off the reservation and condemn those who take a walk.[16]

My front-running opponent is a lightweight, no heft at all, devoid of a *weltanschauung* and unfamiliar with *realpolitik*[11], a straw man and stalking horse for the fat cats and special interests.

He cannot see the wave of the future or feel the winds of change, which, like a cloud no bigger than a man's hand, will one day thunder on the left and

---

[5]*Dark horse:* a long-shot or compromise candidate; coined in a novel by Benjamin Disraeli in 1831. Probably first used politically sometime between the elections of James Polk in 1844 and Franklin Pierce in 1852. "We Polked You in 1844, We'll Pierce You in 1852" was Pierce's slogan, despite which he won. Other horseracing metaphors in politics include "bolt," "running mate" and "shoo-in."

[6]*Voice from the sewer:* the voice that began the chant, "We Want Roosevelt," when it appeared that F.D.R. was unwilling to run for a third term; later identified as a member of Chicago Mayor Kelley's staff at the 1940 Democrat convention, working at a microphone in a subterranean chamber. Now, any offstage voice that seeks to stampede.

[7]*Whirlwind campaign:* any mildly aggressive effort. Disaster metaphors abound in politics: support grows like a "prairie fire," leading to "avalanches" and "landslides"; politicians pray for "lightning to strike." Almost any natural catastrophe is synonymous with good news in politics.

[8]*Whistle-stopping:* a political term unintentionally coined in 1948 by Senator Robert A. Taft.

[9]*Young Turk:* insurgent or restive element; from the reformers who seized power in the Ottoman Empire in 1908 from the aging sultans. First used in U.S. to describe a group of Republican Senators who broke with the leadership in 1929 over tariff legislation.

[10]*Go fishing:* to refuse to support a candidate of one's party, but without supporting his opponent. *Off the reservation:* to temporarily stray—to support an opposing party's nominee with the intent of returning to the party after the election. *Take a walk:* an outright bolt, coined by Al Smith in 1936.

[11]*Weltanschauung:* German for "world view," something people like Joseph Alsop have. *Realpolitik,* pronounced re-AL-pol-i-TIK: often used in the U.S. to mean the realities of politics, or practical politics. In Europe, the German word means power politics, international diplomacy based on strength rather than appeals to world opinion. The use of foreign words in political discourse adds cachet and confusion to a speech.

pour a storm of criticism and hail of dead cats[12] on those who, like the floo-floo bird[13], cannot begin a meaningful dialogue with the charismatic movers and shakers[14] who have a rendezvous with destiny.

Though I never engage in personalities, my opponent is a captive candidate of a palace guard, surrounded by a kitchen cabinet or brain trust— including a rustling behind the jalousies[15]—who make up a government by crony[16], caucusing all too often to strike a blow for freedom.[17]

But my own political coloration is not that of a chameleon on plaid: I am against black power, white racism, red menaces, yellow perils and gray eminences. I turn away from the bleeding hearts[18], the Comsymps, the welfare staters, the fellow travelers; with equal vehemence, I reject the radical right, the lunatic fringe[19], the little old ladies in tennis shoes, the old fogies (who are not to be confused with our constructively conservative senior citizens). The middle-of-the-roaders are not dynamic enough for me; my own politics of hope can be found in the mainstream of the vital center, implacably opposed to consensus.

What is the thrust of my own position papers?

In foreign policy, where partisanship should end at the water's edge, I believe in containment and the domino theory, though I feel it is time to make an agonizing reappraisal of brinkmanship and entangling alliances.[20] The Foggy Bottom cookie-pushers, with their no-win policy, should unleash the shirt-sleeve diplomats unafraid of go-it-alone[21], eyeball-to-eyeball confrontations. Only by honoring our genuine commitments and developing situations

[12]*Hail of dead cats:* criticism accompanying the resignation of an unpopular public figure, coined in 1934 by the departing head of the National Recovery Administration, Gen. Hugh Johnson.

[13]*Floo-floo bird:* one which flies backward because it is more interested in where it has been that where it is going; a jocular symbol of reaction.

[14]*Movers and shakers:* influentials; coined by a 19th-century English poet, Arthur O'Shaughnessy, to mean artists and poets: "We are the music-makers,/ And we are the dreamers of dreams,/ . . . Yet we are the movers and shakers/ Of the world for ever, it seems." Now applied mainly to mucky mucks (see footnote 4), rarely to poets.

[15]*Rustling behind the jalousies:* unsolicited advice on political matters from the candidate's wife.

[16]*Government by crony:* the buddy system in national affairs; often attributed to F.D.R.'s Interior Secretary, Harold Ickes, but coined in 1946 by an anonymous "press gallery wit" quoted by columnist Arthur Krock; Mr. Krock now admits that the wit was himself.

[17]*Strike a blow for freedom:* to enjoy an alcoholic beverage in the privacy of a politician's office.

[18]*Bleeding hearts:* conservative's epithet for ultra-liberals, possibly derived from the semireligious "Order of the Bleeding Heart," founded in the Middle Ages to honor the Virgin Mary, whose "heart was pierced with many sorrows."

[19]*Lunatic fringe:* originally applied to leftists by Theodore Roosevelt in 1913, as "every reform movement has its lunatic fringe"; currently used to refer to extremists of the right.

[20]*Entangling alliances:* usually misattributed to George Washington; written by Thomas Jefferson.

[21]*Go-it-alone:* forthrightly independent or foolishly isolationist; a metaphor from the card game of four-handed euchre (not "cut-throat" euchre), in which the player doubles his point total if he takes in his tricks without the help of his partner.

of strength in our proper spheres of influence can we avoid becoming the policemen of the world.[22]

I don't want to see another Munich, but we must guard against another Sarajevo. We cannot implement a craven let-the-dust-settle policy when the exacerbating exigencies of overkill call for a bold strategy of watchful waiting.

My defense policy is equally in-depth:

Within given parameters, we must maximize our options to escalate the state of the art—especially the software—which will quantify a credible deterrent, restructure the infrastructure, crank in a fallback position, and make a quantum leap to a preemptive strike contingency. Any less viable scenario would be counterproductive.

As for fiscal integrity, I stand for a hold-the-line policy on inflation's cruel spiral, hard money but not tight money, trade-offs to redirect the gold flow, judicious pump-priming to overcome profitless prosperity, and an application of the new economics to get our affluent society out of any rolling readjustments, avoiding boom-and-bust cycles that could curl your hair.

For those of you who have never had it so good, I say don't let them take it away; for those of you who have had enough, I say let's get this country moving again.

On civil rights, I am against Jim Crow and against crime in the streets; I am for all deliberate speed[23], and I am for law and order and against police brutality during the long hot summer ahead.

I stand foursquare against the logrolling tactics of those who would dip into the pork barrel and pass the Christmas-tree bills[24], but hasten to assure the swing voters whose turnout in squeakers is crucial that my advice and consent[25] will never be given to shortchange this banner district.

In my dealings with the pundits of the fourth estate, I have not stooped to backgrounders, leaks, dope stories or trial balloons. Instead, I insist that what I say is not for attribution, preferring the plant to come from reliable sources or official circles, thereby avoiding the foot-in-mouth disease associated with the news-management bloopers of the opposition standard-bearer.

A few simple moral precepts have been my guidelines:

"You Scratch My Back, and I'll Scratch Yours"; "If You Can't Stand the

---

[22]*Policemen of the world:* coined in 1888 by Benjamin Harrison as, "We Americans have no commission from God to police the world."

[23]*With all deliberate speed:* a jarring juxtaposition of words going in different directions—verging on the oxymoronic; an old phrase from the English Chancery, first used in U.S. law by Supreme Court Justice Oliver Wendell Holmes in 1912 and applied in 1954 to school desegregation.

[24]*Christmas-tree bill:* legislation that contains a variety of pet projects attached as riders; not to be confused with *"put in a Christmas tree,"* a directive to include a note of idealism in a factual speech.

[25]*Advice and consent:* perhaps the oldest English political phrase still in active current use; best known for its use in Article II, section 2, of the U.S. Constitution, the phrase is traceable to Anglo-Saxon King Sigiraed's gift of land to Bishop Eardwolf in 759 A.D. "with the advice and consent of my principal men."

Heat, Get Out of the Kitchen"; "When the Water Reaches the Upper Deck, Follow the Rats."[26]

On that platform, which I call the Great New Just Fair Square Deal Frontier Society, I plump for vox populi's[27] mandate, consistent with my previous Sherman statements and my conviction that the office seeks the man.

Questions for Analysis

1. Of what value to the political campaigner is "an old pro willing to press the flesh and lay on the hands"? How has the "old pro" figured in protest movements? Summarize the influence of the "old pro" on the attempts at ethos of campaign and agitative speakers. Relate the "old pro" to "the rhetoric of accommodation."

2. Substantiate the contributions of "the floo-floo bird" to the rhetoric of our times. Select from Safire's speech samples of the popular rhetoric of "the floo-floo bird." Work the samples into an appeal bearing on a contemporary issue.

3. Apply the following statement in a rhetorical consideration of modern persuasion: "We cannot implement a craven let-the-dust-settle policy when the exacerbating exigencies of overkill call for a bold strategy of watchful waiting." Refer specifically to the issues of persuasive means discussed in Part II by Kruger, Ehninger, and Braden. How do the contradictions within the statement reflect various reactions to the rhetoric of our times?

4. Discuss the implications of this statement for political speaking today: "I insist that what I say is not for attribution, preferring the plant to come from reliable sources or official circles, thereby avoiding the foot-in-mouth disease associated with the news-management bloopers of the opposition standard-bearer." How has the substance of campaign oratory been made responsible to "news-management"? Refer to Reynolds on "Public Speaking and the Mass Media" and relate the mass media to the absurdity of "The All-Purpose Political Speech." What in particular has the William McChesney Martin anecdote to do with this?

5. Write "The All Purpose Anti-Establishment Speech."

[26]In order, these political proverbs are attributed to (1) Simon Cameron, Lincoln's first Secretary of War; (2) Harry Truman; (3) Claude Swanson, F.D.R.'s first Navy Secretary.
[27]*Vox populi:* the voice of the people, most effectively used as doggerel in the Harding-Cox race in 1920; "Cox or Harding, Harding or Cox/ You tell 'em, populi, you got the vox."

42

The Men Behind Nixon's Speeches

William H. Honan

From the men who scripted the plain, tough, cagey, and for the most part wingless words with which Richard Nixon won the last election and will now seek to unite and govern the nation, about the last thing one might expect would be a penchant for irreverence and self-satire.

But hark! Bill Safire, one sober-faced member of this youthful team of speechwriters, suddenly crinkles around the eyes with impish delight as he recounts what happened along the campaign trail in Virginia. It seems that one day back in September, as the Tricia was leaping Nixon and his entourage from one jet stop to another, the speechwriters happened to be seated in the rear of the plane with John Hart, the CBS News correspondent. Hart was genially chewing them out.

The punchlines that the candidate had been repeating at stop after stop, Hart said, were empty slogans calculated to inspire applause rather than thought. Then he concluded loftily: "You guys oughta remember that line from e. e. cummings—'dive for dreams, or a slogan may topple you.' " Having been reproached with a classic, the speechwriters drew long faces and appeared contrite.

A few days later Nixon was speaking in Williamsburg. At one point a grin sneaked across Safire's face—he had written the speech—and Hart was flabbergasted to hear Nixon declaim: "An American poet put it this way: 'dive for dreams, or a slogan may topple you.' We must turn away from the old slogans that trigger responses that are no longer responsive; we must dive for the dreams we can make come true. . . ."

Pat Buchanan, another young hand in the Nixon word-factory—all of

William H. Honan is a staff writer for the *New Yorker*; his articles have also appeared in *American Heritage*, *Esquire*, *New Republic*, *Quarterly Journal of Speech*, and *Speech Monographs*.

The New York Times Magazine, January 19, 1969, pp. 20–1, 63, 65–7, 73, 75. © 1969 by The New York Times Company. Reprinted by permission.

whose members will start sharing an office-complex in or near the White House
on Tuesday morning—tells a similar story from the campaign. One of those
punchlines to which Hart objected, and which Nixon repeated again and again
even after his brief flirtation with cummings's admonition, went something
like this: "No, my fellow citizens, we're *not* going to let them make a doormat
out of the American flag!" It was a pretty awful line, the speechwriters private
ly conceded, but it invariably brought forth tremendous applause. So Nixon
used it almost every day.

Soon the speechwriters could repress their embarrassment no longer and
this routine developed: Buchanan would come up to Ray Price, a third member
of the team, and say with mock-urgency, "Hey, Ray. They've done it again!"

"Done what?"

"In Tunis this time. They've just made another *doormat* out of an *American flag!*"

Price would reply, in a commanding tone, "I'll get right over there, Pat."

The gag went on so long, and seemed so hilarious at the time, that the
fun-loving Buchanan considered having a miniature American flag made up
to look like a doormat as an insiders' souvenir of the 1968 campaign. It was to
be the equivalent of the PT-boat tie pin worn by top staff veterans of the 1960
Kennedy campaign, but somehow the idea "wound up in the circular," as the
speechwriters say.

Such irreverence high up in the coming Administration exists, in part,
because wryness is a symptom soon displayed by men who put words into the
mouths of politicians and, more important, because the Nixon crew happens
to be remarkably young, saucy and, in surprising ways, unconventional.

The most accomplished writer in the group and the key man to watch is
Raymond K. Price Jr., who is 38, slightly built, fine-featured, a pipe puffer, a bit
of a mumbler, a Yale man, a Protestant of distant Welsh ancestry and former
editorial-page editor of the New York Herald Tribune. Price is a liberal, yet
anything but doctrinaire about it. Just before joining Nixon's staff nearly two
years ago he wrote a sort of valedictory essay for Mademoiselle summing up
his nine years of editorial writing in which he remarked that he felt "less and
less certain about more and more things" and would like to see "more people
with the courage of their own uncertainties—a bit less arrogance and more
intellectual humility."

Price is the only speechwriter who did not call Nixon; Nixon called him.
After The Trib folded Price turned down several gilt-edged job offers and
started work on a novel that was to "take a serious look at the city as a human
institution." Just then, Nixon, whom he did not know, invited him over for
lunch and offered him a job. It was Washington's Birthday, 1967. Price pondered the offer for a week and then, not without misgivings, one suspects, said
yes.

Since then he has written the majority of Nixon's set speeches, notably the first formal speech in the New Hampshire primary campaign calling for new leadership to provide "the lift of a driving dream"; the "bridges to human dignity" radio address proposing new ways to bring Negroes to the economic mainland; and other think pieces on "an expanded democracy" and the nature of the Presidency.

Besides speechwriting, Price is also an important adviser to the President-elect. It was he, for example, who persuaded Nixon to go to the United Nations last month. The idea for the visit originated with Richard Hudson, editor of the internationalist journal, War/Peace Report, who had become concerned that the poor communication between Lyndon Johnson and U Thant might carry over to the next Administration. Accordingly, Hudson, who is close to U Thant, offered the idea of the U.N. meeting to Price, who liked it and had it "memoed over" to Nixon. About ten days later the President-elect was on the 38th floor of the U.N. sipping champagne and nibbling frogs' legs with the Secretary General.

Patrick J. Buchanan, at 30, is the youngest of the four writers. Husky, ham-faced, rough-looking but with dancing Irish eyes and a bright, rapid-fire line of gab, Buchanan is a former editorial writer for the conservative St. Louis Globe-Democrat, a job he landed at the age of 23.

An Irish Catholic and a strong William F. Buckley conservative, he is skeptical of the capability of virtually all government programs to solve the domestic crisis, and this even includes the Computer Job Bank proposal that he helped originate. He likes to interrupt himself suddenly to ask, somewhat portentously, "But what *can* governments do?" or "It's that old problem: How can one know when one is entering a Dark Age?"

Buchanan comes on brash, but guilelessly, so one gets to like him for it. Back in December, 1965, he marched up to Nixon at a cocktail party in Belleville, Ill., near St. Louis, and said, "Sir, if you're going to run for President in 1968, I want to get aboard early." Nixon hedged, but a month later Buchanan wangled an interview with "The Boss" in New York. He held forth in Nixon's law office for a full three hours, got Nixon to agree to hire him, and then pressed him to cinch the deal on the spot by telephoning the publisher of The Globe-Democrat, the late Richard H. Amberg, to request that he be granted a leave of absence. Nixon obliged, with Buchanan standing at his elbow.

During the campaign Buchanan made a specialty of writing the daily, changeable-with-the-news openings of the basic stump speech. He also ghosted Nixon's syndicated newspaper column, "The Loyal Opposition," and was the author of the tough-sounding speech on "the explosion of crime in America," which Nixon released last May. Like Price, Buchanan also serves the President-elect as an adviser, and Nixon once told a writer for The Globe-Democrat that he regards Buchanan as "one of the most brilliant political analysts in the nation today. . . ." Partly, of course, that was to flatter The Globe-Democrat. But Nixon is obviously charmed by Buchanan's braininess, quick wit and smart way of delivering a "Yes, sir!" in the finest aide-de-camp tradition.

The "old man" among the speechwriters is William Safire, 39, a tall, dark, slouchy and deceptively dour-looking former public-relations man. A native New Yorker, he is Jewish and "leans liberal" in Republican circles.

He met Nixon in Moscow in 1959 after virtually stage-managing, without the knowledge of the then Vice President, the famous "kitchen debate" between Nixon and Nikita Khrushchev. Safire was working for Tex McCrary, the publicist, handling the account of All-States Properties, the construction company that built the "typical American house" at the American National Exhibition in Moscow. Nixon had flown to the Soviet capital to open the exhibition and Safire was watching when Khrushchev unexpectedly ripped into Nixon in front of Soviet TV cameras.

Safire recognized that Nixon, who had been caught off guard, would have to counterattack. So he plotted to have round two take place where it would do All-States Properties the most good. Accordingly, later in the day when Nixon and Khrushchev strolled together through the entrance of the model home— security by this time had completely broken down—Safire sent a crowd he had assembled outside spilling in through the exit, thus trapping the two world leaders inside, near the kitchen. Since a good audience was gathered, Nixon seized that moment to harangue the Soviet Premier about the American Way, the wonders of color TV, and all the rest.

At one point in the "debate" an Associated Press photographer who could not get close to the action tossed his camera to Safire over the heads of the astonished Soviet guards. Safire composed a shot of Nixon and Khrushchev and, in the background, Jinx Falkenberg, his boss's wife, and another client's washing machine. He waited for Nixon to pound his hands together, then popped the famous A.P. picture of the "kitchen debate."

The following year Safire joined the Nixon-Lodge volunteers as chief of special projects, and he has been working for Nixon (and Rockefeller and Javits) off and on ever since. Safire is also the author of three books. The current one, called "The New Language of Politics," is a somewhat Menckenesque, anecdotal dictionary of political catchwords and slogans—rhetorical gimmickry for which Safire has an unquenchable thirst. During the past campaign he was the author of Nixon's speech on the "new alignment." ("My point is this: The Republicans, the new liberals, the new South, the black militants are talking the same language.") He also wrote speeches on "the American spirit," labor, youth and, dutifully, maritime development.

William F. Gavin is 33, freckle-faced and very Irish-looking. Like Buchanan he is Irish Catholic and a conservative. He is, politically, the greenest of the group. Just a year ago Gavin was a high school English teacher in Abington, Pa. He had published a few Elizabethan sonnets in the English Journal and several satirical essays in the National Review, but the latter was as close as he had come to dirtying his hands in politics. Then, one day last May, he wrote a fan letter to Richard Nixon, urging him to run ("Run. You can win. Nothing can happen to you, politically speaking, that is worse than what *has* happened to you") and to campaign live on TV. ("It is the only way to convince people of the truth, that you are beyond rhetoric, that you can face reality.")

Nixon took the first tip but not the second and, perhaps compensating for what he recognized as good advice that he did not intend to follow, hired Gavin.

Assigned to write the least important of the campaign speeches—on the American Indian and conservation—Gavin performed these tasks with such zeal and contributed such ripe, juicy language that he was flown around on the Tricia with Nixon and is now being taken to Washington as a sort of poet-in-residence.

Besides the four writers,* the Nixon word shop will include several researchers and a managing editor, James Keogh, who also worked in the campaign. A compactly built, soft-spoken former executive editor of Time, Keogh, 52, is the author of "This is Nixon," a Time cover story he wrote in 1955 and later expanded to a book. His role will be chiefly administrative—attending to the "care and feeding" of the writers, scheduling, assigning, riding herd and copy-editing.

Nixon's dependence on his speechwriters is fairly typical of the practice followed by heads of state the world over, most of whom have neither the time nor the gift to write well. (Lincoln, who wrote his own memorable speeches, and Franklin D. Roosevelt, who had a stable of speechwriters but frequently outdid them in turning a glittering phrase, were rare exceptions to the rule.)

Nixon's speeches usually are born in conferences with his writers during which the President-elect outlines his ideas, suggests various sources of information and often cites one or two of his previous statements on a similar theme. The writer assigned then follows up Nixon's leads, tries a draft or two, kicks it around with Keogh and perhaps another writer, and then submits his work to Nixon, who may either discuss further revision with him verbally or write notes in the margins. Nixon has a habit of writing long notes across the top of a page, down the right side and all the way around. So, when a speechwriter aboard the Tricia was observed reading his manuscript and slowly

---

*During the campaign, there were several others—notably Bryce Harlow, who wrote the "security gap" speech, borrowing heavily from Kennedy's "missile gap" speech of August, 1958, and who will serve as the President-elect's assistant for Congressional liaison; also, Richard V. Allen, who wrote the "research gap" speech and will serve as an assistant to Henry A. Kissinger, Nixon's assistant for national security affairs.

rotating it clockwise, it was a sure bet his speech had just been bounced back from "The Boss."

During the hectic latter days of the campaign, of course, Nixon was not able to lavish nearly so much time as this on his speechwriters. At least once, for example, he took a speech written by a writer he had scarcely met—not a regular member of his staff—and recited it almost word for word. It was probably a mistake to do so since this was the much-criticized radio address on law and order, sometimes erroneously attributed to Buchanan, but actually the work of Jeffrey Hart, a young Dartmouth English professor, an associate editor of the National Review and a speechwriter for Ronald Reagan until after the 1968 Republican convention.

Nixon, or Keogh perhaps, would have been well advised to tone down some of Hart's more demagogic attacks against the courts and Attorney General Ramsey Clark: "Today, it is comparatively safe to break the law. Today, all across the land, guilty men walk free from hundreds of courtrooms. . . . Is it any wonder that criminals in America are not losing much sleep over the efforts of the Department of Justice?"

In another instance, however—the acceptance speech at the convention— Nixon wrote the text himself. He had idea conferences with several of his writers, and all of them submitted drafts or at least cheer lines—lines aimed at applause—some of which he used; but Nixon put it together and wrote it out —first in outline form on a legal-sized yellow tablet, and then draft after draft by dictaphone.

Rose Mary Woods, Nixon's personal secretary for many years, is the only person ever to type his reading copy of a speech. She types it in such a way as to reveal his rigorous demand for tight organization, starting almost every sentence as a new paragraph, indented five, ten or fifteen spaces, according to its position in the structure.

A good illustration of the kind of help Nixon received on the acceptance speech was the contribution made by Safire. At the time, Safire had just finished writing an entry for his anecdotal dictionary in which he identified and analyzed that rhetorical device in which a speaker begins each of a series of statements with "I see. . . ." "The 'I See' construction," Safire had written, is "a favorite of speechwriters outlining a vision of the future." He had dug up examples of such usage from the speeches of Robert G. Ingersoll and Franklin D. Roosevelt, and variations by Adlai E. Stevenson, John F. Kennedy ("I look forward to . . .") and Martin Luther King Jr. ("I have a dream . . .").

Safire sent a copy of this material to Nixon along with a memo suggesting that, since the "I see" construction is "tried and true" in ceremonial oratory, Nixon should use it in his acceptance speech. Safire appended a sample list of 10 "I see" sentences to show how it might be done.

When Nixon read the memo he crossed out what Safire had written after the 10 "I sees," and substituted eight of his own visions of the future (precisely as F.D.R. had once done with a similar draft by Judge Samuel I. Rosenman). The result was the beginning of the peroration of the acceptance speech:

"I see a day when Americans are once again proud of their flag. . . .

"I see a day when the President of the United States is respected and his office is honored. . . .

"I see a day when every child in this land, regardless of background. . . ."

The device went a long way to relieve the banality of what Nixon said he saw in the future, and also provided a rhetorical setting for the most effective moment of the speech, when he went on to recall his childhood yearnings:

"But this is only part of what I see in America. I see another child tonight. He hears the trains go by at night and he dreams of faraway places where he'd like to go. . . . He is helped on his journey through life. A father who had to go to work before he finished the sixth grade. . . . A gentle, Quaker mother, with a passionate concern for peace. . . . A courageous wife and loyal children who stood by him in victory and also defeat. . . . And tonight he stands before you nominated for President of the United States of America. You can *see* why I believe so deeply in the American dream. . . ." All that was pure Nixon.

One of the most interesting things about Nixon's speechwriters is the way they work together. "We try to take advantage of our differences," explains Price. "I can flag something that might be construed as a code word or phrase that liberals might have an anguished reaction to. Buchanan, who is a conservative, can do the same from his viewpoint."

For example, Nixon originally assigned Buchanan to write the radio talk that would be addressed to the black community. Buchanan sat up all night writing the speech in a hotel room in Cheyenne, Wyo., and came down the next morning looking wan and red-eyed but with a 23-page manuscript that he declared to be one of his best efforts. When Price read the speech, however, he must have winced. In one passage Buchanan had referred to the stability of the American dollar as the "linchpin" of the world monetary system. Later on Buchanan had denounced the guaranteed-annual-income plan, saying, "The American Negro will never find his place in the sun on a Federal plantation." Finally, Buchanan had declared in the middle of a long, complex sentence that "slums are . . . created by people." Taken out of context, Price believed, that last remark would have been as much a blooper as the notorious Spiro Agnewism: ". . . if you've seen one city slum you've seen them all."

In the editorial conference that followed, Buchanan's brainchild was spiked. He was particularly enamored of the "Federal plantation" line, and salvaged it for another speech. But the phrase never saw the light of day. Price's criticism of the speech won him the chance to take a crack at the assignment himself. It took him just a couple of days and one all-night stint to write what came to be known as the "bridges to human dignity" speech, probably the best of Nixon's entire campaign.

Buchanan had many chances to get even. One occurred during a discus-

sion with Nixon of a Price speech on Vietnam (which, as it turned out, was
never delivered either). A sentence declared that the B-52 bomber was an in-
appropriate weapon for hunting "a guerrilla with a knife." While that phrase
did not originate with Price, he liked it and defended it.

Buchanan argued that conservatives and war hawks would hit the ceiling
over the implication that B-52's had fought duels with knife-wielding guerrillas
when, in fact, the bombers had been used to attack suspected troop concentra-
tions, supply depots and so forth. Buchanan prevailed, and the entire sentence
was cut.

On some issues, of course, Price and Buchanan saw eye to eye, only to be
overruled by Nixon himself. One such case occurred in Buchanan's "explosion
of crime" speech. In the final draft Buchanan included a paragraph supporting
the then-pending gun-control bill. Price liked it. So did the others. Shortly before delivering the speech, however, Nixon chanced to have lunch with Senator
Roman L. Hruska of Nebraska, the leader of the opposition to the bill. The
paragraph on gun-control mysteriously vanished.

And on other issues, although Price and Buchanan disagreed with each
other, *both* seem to have gotten their way. Nixon's campaign speeches, accordingly, became a forum for a running debate between the two. One day, Buchanan would have Nixon say: "There is . . . [a] socially suicidal tendency—
on the part of many public men—to excuse crime and sympathize with criminals because of past grievances the criminal may have against society. . . ."
Another day, when Price had written the speech, Nixon would reply to Nixon:
"Finding that we do have shared grievances is the first step toward breaking
down those barriers that have set group against group, generation against
generation. . . ."

Stylistically, the most polished of Nixon's four speechwriters is Price, and
this fact usually makes his handiwork the most difficult to recognize. Indeed,
it is remarkable today to find a writer like Price—at a time when smartness
characterizes so much journalistic and political prose—whose work is distinguished chiefly by its lack of affectation, shrillness and rhetorical hokum.
What he writes is typically plain yet vivid, moderate in tone, perhaps a little
long-winded now and then, but more often quite graceful. Here, for instance,
is a passage from Nixon's radio talk on "an expanded democracy," which
Price wrote last June:

"One reason people are shouting so loudly today is that it's so far from
where they are to where the power is. If we fail to bring power closer—if we
persist in treating complex local needs from remote centers—we'll be repeating tomorrow mistakes that already have added dangerously to the frictions of
today." Vivid, moderate, and, in this case, graceful.

Beyond these qualities, however, Price's major stylistic asset is that whatever he sets his hand to seems to come off with a sort of high-minded, idealistic,

good-guy shine to it. His "bridges to human dignity" speech was an example: "We need new bridges between the developed and underdeveloped segments of our society—human bridges, economic bridges, bridges of understanding and help."

In fact, Price can even turn an essentially backlash sentiment into something admirable: "Beyond the disorders, there's another rebellion going on today. This other is a quiet revolution. It's a rebellion by the great, quiet majority—those who pay their taxes, go to their jobs, perform their civic duties, send their children to school or college. . . . In part, this quiet revolution is a protest against the violence and the excesses that have marked a time of tumultuous change, and also against the heavier and heavier demands of an age of impatience. . . . The people who make up this great, quiet majority want a voice in the shaping of their own future. They're not against change; what they want is to participate in the process of change, to help mold the future to their own designs rather than be swept along by impersonal forces. They too want a voice. In fact, if there is one thing common to all groups, all races, all ages, in America today, it is this deep, gut feeling that they want to be part of things, to have a say in things, to have a *voice*—and to have that voice heard."

Just as Price's polished style was appropriate for writing most of Nixon's reflective and statesmanlike radio addresses, Buchanan was better suited to batting out the more combative, daily stump speeches. In contrast to Price, Buchanan writes what one of his former colleagues describes as "bang-bang-socko stuff." His sentences are short and snappy. He likes a metaphor you can really taste or feel: Organized crime is the "tapeworm" of American society. Where Price is inclined to express himself in shades of gray, Buchanan paints in black and white: "Equally obvious . . ." is the way he will introduce Nixon's second point; what Nixon's opponents say may be dismissed as "nonsense."

In the closing weeks of the campaign, Buchanan had Nixon go after Humphrey as if with a heavy, blunt instrument: "Mr. Humphrey's political philosophy has failed him—and it has failed America. The United States cannot be led into the future by a candidate who turns his back on the present and lives in the past. His team has had its chance. We now ask for the chance to succeed where it has failed America."

Price, on the other hand, had Nixon kill with kindness: "Vice President Humphrey is a man I respect. He is a man of honor and a man of his convictions. And he honestly believes in the old ways. I believe in a new way."

Although the youngest and probably the least widely read of all Nixon's speechwriters, it is usually Buchanan who sprinkles his speeches with literary quotations and allusions. Every time during the campaign that Nixon started off a sentence with "As Chaucer put it . . ." or "In his poem, 'The Waste Land,' the late T. S. Eliot wrote . . . ," it was Buchanan ransacking his college notes. In the syndicated column he wrote for Nixon, Buchanan once tossed off a real classic in this genre: "In Arkansas, the Democratic party has dredged through the early novels of William Faulkner to come up with its Snopsian candidate, Jim Johnson. . . ."

Rough, tough and occasionally sophomoric though he may be, Buchanan also possesses unmistakable talent, as evidenced by his turning out of an occasional line with genius to it. There was the ring of Rooseveltian mastery, for example, in Buchanan's line, which Nixon used in September, calling Humphrey "a man lost in memories of days gone by."

The word factory's resident pro for zingers and snappers (as punchlines are known in the trade) is, of course, Safire. In his anecdotal dictionary Safire confesses his relish for all manner of high-blown rhetoric, whether the inverted parallelisms that Theodore Sorensen confected for John F. Kennedy, or the rollicking low comedy of Franklin D. Roosevelt's "Martin, Barton and Fish" speech, in which F.D.R. poked fun at his opponents by rhythmically linking their names with Wynken, Blynken and Nod. (Humphrey missed an opportunity to ridicule Nixon's right-wing speechwriters in the same way: Buchanan, Gavin and Hart.)

Being so disposed, Safire frequently locks horns with Price, for although the two are ideologically *simpático*, Price distrusts anything that smacks of sloganeering, whereas catchy language is, for Safire, food and drink. To take one illustration, when Safire read Price's "bridges to human dignity" opus he was strong in his praise for its lucidity, especially for the bridge image, but gagged when he came to the third bridge, which Price had spelled out as "the development of black entrepreneurship." Aside from the fact that "entrepreneurship" does not exactly fall trippingly from the tongue, Safire complained to Price that nobody would know what it meant.

"If we're talking about capitalism, let's call it capitalism," said Safire. Price thought that "black capitalism" sounded too self-consciously rhetorical. But rhetoric—good rhetoric—Safire came back, is the stuff of politics. At length, Price was won over, "black capitalism" went in, and overnight the expression became one of the catch phrases of the campaign.

Safire also liberally handed out his zingers and snappers to Buchanan, Gavin and Hart, among others. One was contributed to Buchanan's law-and-order statement that Nixon gave to the G.O.P. resolutions committee in July: "We cannot accept a wave of crime as the wave of the future." Safire was so tickled with the line that he revised it slightly and popped it into Jeffrey Hart's radio speech on crime: "Let us resolve that the wave of crime and violence will not be the wave of the future." The doormat line was also a Safire gem. Here are yet more samples of his fluorescent prose:

Clanging contrapuntal clauses: "Personal freedom will not insure that every man will get all he desires; it will insure that every man will get all he deserves. Those Americans who once had personal freedom and lost it, now want it back; those who never had it at all, want it now. In striving for a worthy goal—security—we have lost a worthy asset—individuality, the hallmark of personal freedom. In trying to provide for the material needs of all, we have stolen from the personal freedom of each. . . ."

Epigram: "Welfare is too important to be left to the Welfare Staters."

Stand back, everyone, that metaphor is sticking: "The American spirit demands an explosion of education into the mind of every child in every corner of this land. . . ."

Flossy peroration: "That next President will lead this nation in its reach for greatness only if he summons a new 'spirit of '76'—a spirit conceived in old glories, born to speak to its own time, destined to shape a glorious future!"

Safire is also as hung up on the word "watershed" as Price is on such words as "bridges," "input," "frictions" and "tumultuous"—more so, in fact. Safire has a long, almost mystical passage about "watershed" in his dictionary, and he squeezed it into practically every speech he wrote for Nixon: "In the watershed year of 1968 . . . ," "At watershed moments like these . . . ," "This watershed political year . . . ," etc. After a while, he began to make Nixon sound like a Chinese astrologer proclaiming 1968 the Year of the Watershed.

Gavin, the former high-school English teacher, is the staff poet. Not that he really writes poetry for Nixon; his specialty in the word-factory is the rich, velvety, rippling sort of stuff one used to hear on "March of Time." Gavin himself calls it "emotional writing."

A fair illustration comes from Gavin's conclusion for Nixon's campaign speech on conservation: "Americans, every one of us, must be able to look at all of America and say: This is my country, not only its material power but its natural glory. Not only the dynamic sound of its industries, but the silence of its great forests. Not only the march of technological progress, but a casual stroll along a beach at night. Not only the material benefits of today, but the deeper, richer gifts I can leave my children. . . ."

One can almost hear the violins.

The inaugural address Nixon will deliver tomorrow afternoon, like the acceptance speech, is, of course, an important personal statement. In this case, too, the President-elect might prefer to do the composition himself. Because of the heavy pre-inaugural demands on his time, however, the job of writing at least a first draft has fallen to his speechwriters, chiefly to Price.

Price will say very little about what he has been doing the past few weeks (he comes closer to having a "passion for anonymity" than any of his colleagues), except to acknowledge that he has been "dipping into" the Presidential inaugurals of the past and has come particularly to admire Lincoln's second, Franklin D. Roosevelt's first and Kennedy's. (Nixon himself is said to prefer Wilson's first.)

Price's friends declare that he has been toying with such phrases as "a country not at peace with itself" and "a depression of the spirit at a time of material abundance," although he disclaims them. In any case, with Price its principal draftsman, long, clear, highly honed sentences and plenty of fresh, good-guy verve are sure to work their way into the finished product.

Inaugural-watchers should also keep on the lookout for zingers and snappers of the sort that Safire will try to slip in, a little bang-bang-socko stuff from Buchanan, and perhaps a touch of Gavin, bard of Abington, Pa. Whether these rhetorical fingerprints are detectable in the inaugural or not, they will turn up sooner or later in the months ahead. And when they do, and the pundits are pointing to them as subtle indices of the Presidential mood or whim, wiser heads will know it isn't that at all. It is just a matter of who happened to have written the President's speech that day—Buchanan, Gavin, Safire or Price.

Questions for Analysis

1. Read Richard Nixon's inaugural address (in the *New York Times*, Jan. 21, 1969, or in *Vital Speeches* Feb. 1, 1969, pp. 226–8), and see if you can, using Honan's descriptions of their "rhetorical fingerprints," identify the "men behind Nixon's speeches." Did the inaugural address have echoes of any earlier campaign speeches? Were changes those of mood, style, or substance? Honan quotes William Safire's view that good rhetoric is the stuff of politics. Apply this test to Nixon's inaugural.

2. Consider the general nature of the inaugural address. Does it represent a distinctive and useful form of rhetoric? How would you assess its purpose and potential? Would you accept the judgment of one critic that despite "the inevitable straining for eloquence" most inaugurations have been "little noted nor long remembered"? One of Nixon's speechwriters, Honan reports, especially admires Lincoln's second inaugural address, Franklin D. Roosevelt's first, and Kennedy's. Does your knowledge of history tell you that these men had something in common? That they spoke in similar periods of national urgency? Or that presidents study precedents?

3. Review Murphy's article on Stevenson and Hall's on Johnson, and compare their methods of speech preparation with Nixon's. Could Murphy's description (Stevenson "sweated over his manuscripts, polished his metaphors," or "Stevenson is not the great generalizer; he does not speak in clichés") be applied to Nixon? Hall says of Johnson that as his speeches took on greater significance he placed more emphasis on careful preparation; and that as he prepared more carefully "he became more eloquent." Could the same be said of Nixon? As Hall and Honan report on them, does Johnson or Nixon appear to have best managed the "team effort" approach to speechwriting?

4. Consider the general nature of campaign speaking. Is the traditional long campaign, with its many speeches, anachronistic in the television age? Did Nixon act wisely in curtailing his 1960 activities (travelling over 65,000 miles, visiting 50

states, speaking in 188 cities) in 1968 to flying 44,000 miles, visiting 35 states, and speaking in 118 cities? How was the electorate served by the failure to repeat 1960 with televised debates between the candidates? What might be done in the future to improve political campaigning?

5. In his *Six Crises*, p. 422, Richard Nixon regretfully concluded that "I spent too much time in the last campaign (1960) on substance and too little time on appearance." Against that view is Eric Sevareid's dictum that "a man's own words are a man's own self." What do these two statements say about the role of "image" in contemporary speechmaking? What is the relationship of the ghostwriter, or the speechwriting team, to his principal's "image" and to the listener's perception? What ethical considerations do you find in this type of "collaboration"?

Part IV

Questions for Discussions

1. Can man live by images alone?
2. How can we raise the level of political campaigns?
3. Is there any common ground for "old pros" and "young turks"?
4. What has been the role of the agitator in American history?
5. Who has academic freedom now?

Topics for Speeches

1. The public speaker as hero
2. The public speaker as "spokesman"
3. Ghost writing as a profession
4. Red flag words: black and white, left and right
5. The cross as a rhetorical symbol
6. Black Power and the rhetoric of accommodation
7. Ethos in chaos: the search for leadership today
8. Your prejudice and your language
9. You get the argument; I'll get the facts
10. The self-image of conservatism

Index

The index does not reflect the total substantive content, or the names of all persons mentioned in the articles in this volume. It is limited to (1) authors of articles in the volume, (2) contemporary speakers discussed in one or more articles, (3) basic rhetorical concepts, and (4) essential elements in the communication process.